Teacher's Edition

FOUNDATIONS OF PERSONAL FINANCE

Sally R. Campbell
Winnetka, Illinois

Publisher

The Goodheart-Willcox Company, Inc.
Tinley Park, Illinois
www.g-w.com

Cover image: Gettyimages RF

CONTENTS

Foundations of Personal Finance

A teaching package to help students make important financial and economic decisions with assurance and competence.

Topics include

- the global economy
- decision making
- income and taxes
- financial institutions and services
- credit
- insurance
- saving, investing, and estate planning
- consumer rights and responsibilities
- shopping for food, clothing, housing, transportation, and electronics
- career planning and job skills

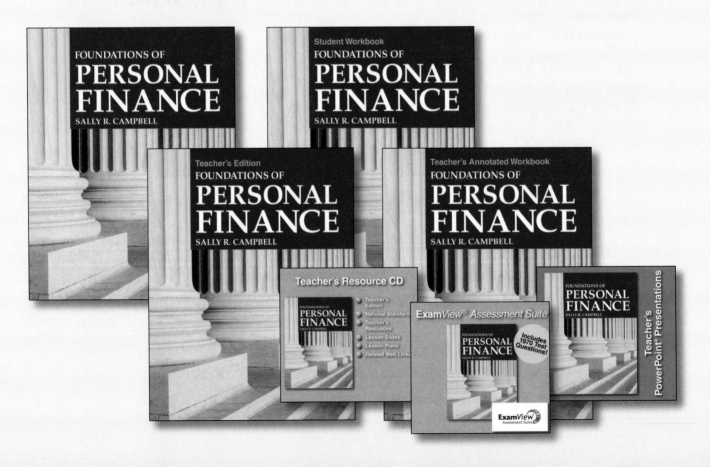

The Essential Program Components

A variety of support materials are available to help you teach *Foundations of Personal Finance*.

Student Text

Colorful design, easy-to-read typeface, and logical organization support reading comprehension and learning. (See pages 4–5 for a summary of text features.)

Teacher's Edition

The text provides a variety of teaching aids in the page margins to help you review and reinforce chapter content. Answer keys appear next to review questions.

Student Workbook

Includes a wide variety of activities to help students review and apply chapter concepts.

Teacher's Annotated Workbook

Presents answers to workbook activities right where you need them.

Teacher's Resource CD

Includes introductory activities, teaching strategies, reproducible masters, blackline transparencies, and tests for each chapter, all in PDF format. Also includes correlations to national standards, color lesson slides, a lesson planning feature for customizing daily lesson plans, and the *Teacher's Edition* of the text in PDF format.

Exam*View*® Assessment Suite

Contains all the test master questions in the *Teacher's Resources* plus 25 percent more. Lets you choose specific questions, add your own, and create different versions of a test.

Teacher's PowerPoint® Presentations

Includes colorful presentations for each chapter to reinforce key concepts and terms.

Introduction

Foundations of Personal Finance is a comprehensive text designed to help student make important financial and economic decisions with assurance and competence. The text helps students learn basic economic concepts related to their roles as consumers, producers, and citizens. They will learn how to shape their own financial lives, influence government and business economic policies, and participate fully in the economic system of the United States.

Strategies for Successful Teaching

You can make the *Foundations of Personal Finance* subject matter exciting and relevant for your students by using a variety of teaching strategies. Many suggestions for planning classroom activities are given in the various teaching supplements that accompany this text. As you plan your lessons, you might also want to keep the following points in mind.

Helping Your Students Develop Critical-Thinking Skills

As today's students leave their classrooms behind, they will face a world of complexity and change. They are likely to work in several career areas and hold many different jobs. Young people must develop a base of knowledge and be prepared to solve complex problems, make difficult decisions, and assess ethical implications. In other words, students must be able to use critical-thinking skills. These skills are often referred to as the higher-order thinking skills.

Critical thinking goes beyond memorizing or recalling information. It requires individuals to apply what they know about the subject matter. It also requires students to use their common sense and experience. It may even involve controversy.

Critical thinking also requires *creative thinking* to construct all the reasonable alternatives, consequences, influencing factors, and supporting arguments. Unusual ideas are valued and perspectives outside the obvious are sought.

Finally, the teaching of critical thinking does not require exotic and highly unusual classroom approaches. Complex thought processes can be incorporated in the most ordinary and basic activities, such as reading, writing, and listening, when activities are carefully planned and skillfully executed.

Debate is an excellent way to explore opposite sides of an issue. You may want to divide the class into two groups, each to take an opposing side of the issue. You can also ask students to work in smaller groups and explore opposing sides of different issues. Each group can select students from the group to present the points for their side.

Problem-Solving and Decision-Making Skills

An important aspect in the development of critical-thinking skills is learning how to solve problems and make decisions. Some very important decisions lie ahead for your students, particularly those related to their future education and career choices.

Simulation games and role-plays are activities that allow students to practice solving problems and making decisions under nonthreatening circumstances. In role-playing, students can examine others' feelings as well as their own. They can learn effective ways to react or cope when confronted with similar situations in real life.

Using Cooperative Learning

Because of the emphasis on teamwork in the workplace, the use of cooperative learning groups in your classroom will give students an opportunity to practice teamwork skills. During cooperative learning, students learn interpersonal and small-group skills that encourage them to function as part of a team. These skills include leadership, decision making, trust building, communication, and conflict management.

In cooperative learning groups, students learn to work together toward a group goal. Each member is dependent on others for the outcome. This interdependence is a basic component of any cooperative learning group. Students understand that one person cannot succeed unless everyone succeeds. The value of each group member is affirmed as learners work toward their goal.

The success of the group also depends on individual performance. Group members should be selected depending on the purpose of your grouping. As you differentiate your instruction, sometimes you may form groups based on interest. Other times, you may form diversified groups so a mix of abilities and talents are included. You might form groups with specific leveled learning tasks assigned to various groups. Within groups, individuals' roles can change so all students have opportunities to practice and develop different skills. In all situations, students can learn from working with one another.

As you monitor the effectiveness of group learning, you may need to intervene to provide task assistance or help with interpersonal or group skills. If you expect a group to carry out a particular skill on their own, you need to teach the skill to the large group first. Model the expected activity, assign various roles, and have students model the skills used in that role. Then, when you assign different tasks to groups, members will be able to move ahead on their own, utilizing the skills you taught.

Finally, you can evaluate each group's achievement of specific learning goals. Use rubrics to identify the extent to which the group reached the goal. In some scenarios, you may just give participation points to the group for completing their task. This is effective when you have differentiated the learning for the various groups and their tasks are not the same. In group settings, the learning that takes place is often in the discussion and processing of various ideas. In these cases, a summary of what students learned can be written in a journal or added to a portfolio.

Helping Students Recognize and Value Diversity

Your students will be entering a rapidly changing workplace—not only in matters pertaining to technology, but also in the diverse nature of its workforce. The majority of the new entrants to the workforce are women, minorities, and immigrants, all representing many different views and experiences. The workforce is aging, too, as the ranks of mature workers swell. Because of these trends, young workers must learn how to interact effectively with a variety of people who are considerably unlike them.

The appreciation and understanding of diversity is an ongoing process. The earlier and more frequently young people are exposed to diversity, the more quickly they can develop skills to bridge cultural differences. If your students are exposed to different cultures within your classroom, the process of understanding cultural differences can begin. This is the best preparation for success in a diverse society. In addition, teachers find the following strategies for teaching diversity helpful:

- Actively promote a spirit of openness, consideration, respect, and tolerance in the classroom.

- Use a variety of teaching styles and assessment strategies.

- Use cooperative learning activities whenever possible and make sure group roles are rotated so everyone has leadership opportunities.

- When grouping students, have each group's composition as diverse as possible with regard to gender, race, and nationality.

- Make sure one group's opinions do not dominate class discussions.

- If a student makes a sexist, racist, or similarly offensive comment, ask the student to rephrase the comment in a manner that will not offend other class members. Remind students that offensive statements and behavior are inappropriate in the classroom.

- If a difficult classroom situation arises involving a diversity issue, ask for a time-out and have everyone write down their thoughts and opinions about the incident. This helps to calm the situation and allows you time to plan a response.

- Arrange for guest speakers who represent diversity in gender, race, and ethnicity.

- Have students change seats occasionally throughout the course and introduce themselves to their new "neighbors" so they become acquainted with all their classmates.

- Several times during the course, ask students to make anonymous, written evaluations of the class. Have them report any problems that may not be obvious.

Differentiating Instruction for Students with Varying Needs

In addition to having specific learning needs related to their abilities, students come to you with various backgrounds, interests, and learning styles. Differentiating instruction can help all students attain learning goals. The strategies you use to differentiate instruction in your classroom will depend on the specific learning needs of the students.

Several strategies for differentiating instruction will be included throughout the *Teacher's Edition* and *Teacher's Resources*. They include suggestions for reteaching lessons for students who need more repetition; strategies to extend learning for students who need more application to real life; and strategies to enrich learning for students needing more challenge. Some strategies involve a variety of learning styles so all students have an opportunity to fully grasp and understand the concepts.

Assessment Techniques

Various assessments strategies are included throughout each chapter. Some can be used to measure student progress in understanding the concepts (*formative assessment*), while others can be used to measure the extent to which they have mastered the concepts (*summative assessment*).

Formative assessment takes place often and is ongoing throughout a course. The many comprehension strategies used throughout the text can be used as formative assessment techniques. They measure students' grasp of the concepts as well as their abilities to internalize the skills and apply them to new situations. Many formative assessments can be completed as groups, because the main focus is on the learning that is taking place. Students can assess their team members and use a rubric to self-assess their own learning. The *Teacher's Resources* can be used to identify formative assessments for key knowledge, understandings, and skills being learned.

Written tests in the *Teacher's Resource TRCD* and **Exam**View Assessment Suite* have traditionally been used to evaluate performance. This method of evaluation is good to use when assessing knowledge and comprehension.

Performance Assessment

When assigning students some of the projects from the text that you plan to use as either formative or summative assessment, a rubric can be helpful for measuring student achievement. A *rubric* consists of a set of criteria that includes specific descriptors or standards that can be used to arrive at performance scores for students. A point value is given for each set of descriptors, leading to a range of possible points to be assigned, usually from 1 to 5. The criteria can also be weighted. This method of assessment reduces the guesswork involved in grading, leading to fair and consistent scoring. The standards clearly indicate to students the various levels of mastery of a task. Students are even able to assess their own achievement based on the criteria.

When using rubrics, students should see the criteria at the beginning of the assignment. Then they can focus their effort on what needs to be done to reach a certain level of performance or quality of project. They have a clear understanding of your expectations of achievement.

Though you will want to design many of your own rubrics, several generic ones are included in the Introduction of the *Foundations of Personal Finance Teacher's Resource CD.* These are designed to assess the following:

- *Individual Participation*

- *Individual Reports*

- *Group Participation*

These rubrics allow you to assess a student's performance and arrive at a performance score. Students can see what levels they have surpassed and what levels they can still strive to reach.

Portfolios

Another type of performance assessment that is frequently used by teachers today is the portfolio. A *portfolio* consists of a selection of materials that students choose to document their performance over a period of time. Therefore, it is a good tool for gathering formative assessment data. Students select their best work samples to showcase their achievement. These items might provide evidence of employability skills as well as academic skills. Some of the items students might include in portfolios are

- work samples that show mastery of specific skills, including photographs, video recordings, and assessments

- writing samples that show communication skills

- a résumé

- letters of recommendation that document specific career-related skills

- certificates of completion

- awards and recognition

The portfolio is completed at the culmination of a course to provide evidence of learning, and therefore can be used as a summative assessment tool. As students choose items to include in the final portfolio, they should include items that specifically show how they met or answered the key questions for each chapter studied. A self-assessment summary report should be included that explains what has been accomplished, what has been learned, what strengths the student has gained, and any areas that need improvement.

Portfolios may be presented to the class by students, but they should remain the property of students when they leave the course. They may be used for interviews with potential employers.

Teaching the Learner with Special Needs

The students in your classroom will represent a wide range of ability levels and needs. Special needs students in your classes will require unique teaching strategies. This chart provides descriptions of several of the types of special needs students you may find in your classes, followed by some strategies and techniques to keep in mind as you work with these students. You will be asked to meet the needs of all your students in the same classroom setting. It is a challenge to adapt daily lessons to meet the demands of all your students.

	Learning Disabled*	Mentally Disabled*	Behaviorally Emotionally Disabled*
Description	Students with learning disabilities (LD) have neurological disorders that interfere with their ability to store, process, or produce information, creating a "gap" between ability and performance. These students are generally of average or above average intelligence. Examples of learning disabilities are distractibility, spatial problems, and reading comprehension problems.	The mentally disabled student has subaverage general intellectual functioning that exists with deficits in adaptive behavior. These students are slower than others their age in using memory effectively, associating and classifying information, reasoning, and making judgments.	These students exhibit undesirable behaviors or emotions that may, over time, adversely affect educational performance. Their inability to learn cannot be explained by intellectual, social, or health factors. They may be inattentive, withdrawn, timid, restless, defiant, impatient, unhappy, fearful, unreflective, lack initiative, have negative feelings and actions, and blame others.
Teaching Strategies	• Assist students in getting organized. • Give short oral directions. • Use drill exercises. • Give prompt cues during student performance. • Let students with poor writing skills use a computer. • Break assignments into small segments and assign only one segment at a time. • Demonstrate skills and have students model them. • Give prompt feedback. • Use continuous assessment to mark students' daily progress. • Prepare materials at varying levels of ability. • Shorten the number of items on exercises, tests, and quizzes. • Provide more hands-on activities.	• Use concrete examples to introduce concepts. • Make learning activities consistent. • Use repetition and drills spread over time. • Provide work folders for daily assignments. • Use behavior management techniques, such as behavior modification, in the area of adaptive behavior. • Encourage students to function independently. • Give students extra time to both ask and answer questions while giving hints to answers. • Avoid doing much walking around while talking to MD students as this is distracting for them. • Give simple directions and read them over with students. • Use objective test items and hands-on activities because students generally have poor writing skills and difficulty with sentence structure and spelling.	• Call students' names or ask them questions when you see their attention wandering. • Call on students randomly rather than in a predictable sequence. • Move around the room frequently. • Improve students' self-esteem by giving them tasks they can perform well, increasing the number of successful achievement experiences. • Decrease the length of time for each activity. • Use hands-on activities instead of using words and abstract symbols. • Decrease the size of the group so each student can actively participate. • Make verbal instructions clear, short, and to the point.

*We appreciate the assistance of Dr. Debra O. Parker, North Carolina Central University, with this section.

Academically Gifted	Limited English Proficiency	Physical Disabilities	
Academically gifted students are capable of high performance as a result of general intellectual ability, specific academic aptitude, and/or creative or productive thinking. Such students have a vast fund of general knowledge and high levels of vocabulary, memory, abstract word knowledge, and abstract reasoning.	These students have a limited proficiency in the English language. English is generally their second language. Such students may be academically quite capable, but they lack the language skills needed to reason and comprehend abstract concepts.	Includes individuals who are orthopedically impaired, visually impaired, speech impaired, deaf, hard-of-hearing, hearing impaired, and health impaired (cystic fibrosis, epilepsy). Strategies will depend on the specific disability.	Description
• Provide ample opportunities for creative behavior. • Make assignments that call for original work, independent learning, critical thinking, problem solving, and experimentation. • Show appreciation for creative efforts. • Respect unusual questions, ideas, and solutions these students provide. • Encourage students to test their ideas. • Provide opportunities and give credit for self-initiated learning. • Avoid overly detailed supervision and too much reliance on prescribed curricula. • Allow time for reflection. • Resist immediate and constant evaluation. This causes students to be afraid to use their creativity. • Avoid comparisons with other students, which applies subtle pressure to conform.	• Use a slow but natural rate of speech; speak clearly; use shorter sentences; repeat concepts in several ways. • Act out questions using gestures with hands, arms, and the whole body. Use demonstrations and pantomime. Ask questions that can be answered by a physical movement such as pointing, nodding, or manipulation of materials. • When possible, use pictures, photos, and charts. • Write key terms on the board. As they are used, point to them. • Corrections should be limited and appropriate. Do not correct grammar or usage errors in front of the class, causing embarrassment. • Give honest praise and positive feedback through your voice tones and visual articulation whenever possible. • Encourage students to use language to communicate, allowing them to use their native language to ask/answer questions when they are unable to do so in English. • Integrate students' cultural background into class discussions. • Use cooperative learning where students have opportunities to practice expressing ideas without risking language errors in front of the entire class.	• For visually and hearing-impaired students, seat them near the front of the classroom. Speak clearly and say out loud what you are writing on the board. • In lab settings, in order to reduce the risk of injury, ask students about any conditions that could affect their ability to learn or perform. • Rearrange lab equipment or the classroom and make modifications as needed to accommodate any special need. • Investigate assistive technology devices that can improve students' functional capabilities. • Discuss solutions or modifications with the student who has experience with overcoming his or her disability and may have suggestions you may not have considered. • Let the student know when classroom modifications are being made and allow him or her to test them out before class. • Ask advice from special education teachers, the school nurse, or physical therapist. • Plan field trips that can include all students.	Teaching Strategies

Incorporating Career and Technical Student Organizations

Career and Technical Student Organizations (CTSOs) offer a wide variety of activities that can be adapted to almost any school and classroom situation. A brief introduction to CTSOs follows. If you would like more details, visit their Web sites.

CTSOs Officially Recognized by the U.S. Department of Education		
Short Name	**Full Name**	**Web Site**
BPA	Business Professionals of America	www.bpa.org
DECA	DECA—An Association of Marketing Students	www.deca.org
FBLA/PBL	Future Business Leaders of America/Phi Beta Lambda	www.fbla-pbl.org
FCCLA	Family, Career and Community Leaders of America	www.fcclainc.org
FFA	National FFA Organization	www.ffa.org
HOSA	Health Occupations Students of America	www.hosa.org
SkillsUSA	Formerly VICA—Vocational Industrial Clubs of America	www.skillsusa.org
TSA	Technology Student Association	www.tsaweb.org

Purpose

The purpose of CTSOs is to help students acquire knowledge and skills in career and technical areas as well as leadership skills and experience. These organizations achieve these goals by enlisting teacher-advisors to organize and lead local chapters in their schools. Support for teacher-advisors and their chapters is often coordinated through each state's education department. The chapters elect officers and establish a program of work. The program of work can include a variety of activities, including community service, cocurricular projects, and competition preparation. Student achievement in specified areas is recognized with certificates and/or public acknowledgement through awards ceremonies.

Competitive Events

Competitive events are a main feature of most CTSOs. The CTSO develops events that enable students to showcase how well they have mastered the learning of specific content and the use of decision-making, problem-solving, and leadership skills. Each CTSO has its own list of competitive events and activities. Members develop career and leadership skills even though they may not participate in or win competitions.

Incorporating the Career Clusters

In the mid 1990s, a project called Building Linkages began development, led by the Office of Vocational and Adult Education (OVAE). Building Linkages was funded in partnership by the U.S. Departments of Labor and Education. The goal of the project was to create a reliable set of standards for the integration of academics with workplace skills. Another goal was to show how higher levels of skills and knowledge lead to higher positions. Eventually the organization of the project emerged as career clusters, and The States' Career Clusters Initiative was launched in 2001.

There are 16 career clusters, and among these are 81 different career pathways. Three levels of knowledge and skills exist in each cluster. The levels start with broad categories and move up to more specific categories. The *foundation* level applies to all levels of all careers. The *pathways* level lists the skills necessary for all careers in one cluster or employment area. The *specialty* level is the highest level of skill and knowledge within a given cluster. All levels create employability, academic, and technical skills.

The career clusters are introduced on page 8 of the student edition of *Foundations of Personal Finance* and are discussed in Chapter 21. In addition, each chapter features three occupations related to chapter content. These features will appear scattered throughout the text and appear with the associated career cluster icon. Typical job duties and working conditions are highlighted.

Integrating Academics

No matter what career path a student chooses, academic skills will be critical to his or her success. The following are core academic subjects in schools: English, reading, language arts, math, science, foreign languages, civics and government, economics, arts, history, and geography.

The *Foundations of Personal Finance* program supports student growth and achievement in key academic areas in several ways. The academic areas are highlighted where they are covered in the end-of-chapter sections *Academic Connections* and *Math Challenge*. Further connection to the academic areas of math, history, and science are provided in the "Linking to…" boxed features.

Reading, English, and Language Arts

The entire *Foundations of Personal Finance* student text is designed to encourage reading and understanding. Central ideas and objectives are listed at the start of each chapter to focus on the information to come. Each chapter begins with a *Reading for Meaning* activity to engage student interest. Key terms are shown in bold and highlighted in the text copy to draw attention to the reader. The *Teacher's Edition, Student Workbook,* and *Teacher's Resources* provide more activities designed to develop skills in English and language arts.

Teaching Reading Across the Curriculum

All teachers need to be teachers of reading. In all content areas, teachers need to teach students how to use reading as a tool to enhance their learning. The following strategies will help you teach reading skills that help students create meaning and understand what they read.

- Use prereading activities to help students prepare for learning. *Reading for Meaning* activities in each chapter of the text are designed to help students make the connection between what they already know and the new concepts to be learned. This connection is critical for students to be able to remember new information. Introductory activities for each chapter of the *Teacher's Edition* and *Teacher's Resources* can also be used as prereading activities.

- Use strategies that help students comprehend what they read. Examples of comprehension strategies include having students question what they read, think about the concepts, talk about content with a partner or in small groups, summarize ideas, and organize ideas graphically. Strategies that help develop comprehension are included in the student text and *Teacher's Edition*. The questions at the end of each section help students clarify their comprehension of key concepts. The various strategies for reteaching and reinforcing concepts in the *Teacher's Resources* are also designed to help students think about what they have read and gain understanding.

- Use strategies that help students incorporate the new knowledge they have acquired into their own system of thinking. Such internalization is needed in order for students to remember concepts and be able to apply them to daily living. Throughout the student text and *Teacher's Edition*, you will find questions that ask students to analyze concepts and apply information to their own lives or to a new situation. The *Case Study* scenarios in each chapter provide this opportunity. The various strategies listed under *Critical Thinking*, *Academic Connections*, *Math Challenge* ,and *Tech $mart* are designed to help students incorporate their new knowledge. Strategies such as journaling allow students a time to connect new concepts to their personal situations. The *Teacher's Resources* contain strategies for enriching and extending the text into real-life situations. As students extend and refine the new knowledge they have acquired, the learning takes on personal meaning.

It is important to model these three steps before, during, and after text reading. Explain to students why you are using various strategies. Continual practice of reading skills in all classes will help students develop these lifelong skills.

Math

Mathematics is a tool necessary for managing personal finances as well as achieving success in the workplace. Unfortunately, some students have not learned math basics. To strengthen these skills, *Math Challenge* activities are found at the end of each chapter, and "Linking to…Math" boxed features are found throughout the text. Various math activities also appear in the *Teacher's Edition, Student Workbook,* and *Teacher's Resources* as chapter content dictates.

Social Studies

Social Studies is an important part of explaining economics and finance. Psychology is especially helpful in understanding self and recognizing personal interests when choosing and preparing for a fulfilling lifestyle. A discussion of how laws and other government influences affect the family, work, and community is important as students learn to become responsible citizens. Appropriate activities are found at the end of each chapter under *Academic Connections* and throughout the text in "Linking to…History" boxed features. Additional activities appear in the *Teacher's Edition, Student Workbook,* and *Teacher's Resources*.

National Standards in K-12 Personal Finance Education

Foundations of Personal Finance is correlated with the national standards developed by the Jump$tart Coalition for Personal Financial Literacy. The goal of these standards is to ensure that high-school graduates have the knowledge necessary to become financially responsible adults. Standards are provided for three grades: 4th, 8th, and 12th. These levels indicate what students should know and be able to do by the end of the designated grade. Ideally, the knowledge and skills are obtained by students gradually over time. In the correlation table found on pages T16–T28, these grade levels have been indicated with the colors yellow, orange, and red.

The standards are meant to be an ideal for a personal finance course. All standards may not be appropriate for all classes. The correlation table provided will help you choose the standards and material that are applicable for your course.

National Standards for Family and Consumer Sciences Education with *Foundations of Personal Finance*

The National Standards for Family and Consumer Sciences address Consumer and Family Resources plus 15 other areas of study. Each area has a comprehensive standard describing the overall content, which is further detailed in several content standards. Each of these standards list several competency statements that describe the knowledge, skills, and practices expected of learners.

By studying *Foundations of Personal Finance,* students will be prepared to master the performance expectations for both personal finance education and the study of consumer and family resources. To help you see how this can be accomplished, a *Correlation of National Standards for Consumer and Family Resources with Foundations of Personal Finance* is included here on pages T29–T30, as well as in the *Teacher's Resources.* If you want to make sure you prepare students to meet the National Standards for Family and Consumer Sciences Education, this chart should be of interest to you.

Planning Your Program

Program planning guides suggest ways to schedule the chapters of *Foundations of Personal Finance* for different course calendars. Planning guides are suggested for trimester, semester, and full-year courses. Chapters are grouped according to the suggested depth of coverage and duration of instruction time.

Goodheart-Willcox Welcomes Your Comments

We welcome your comments or suggestions regarding *Foundations of Personal Finance* and its supplements. Please send any comments you may have to the editor by visiting our Web site at www.g-w.com or writing to

Editorial Department
Goodheart-Willcox Publisher
18604 West Creek Drive
Tinley Park, IL 60477-6243

Correlation of National Standards in K-12 Personal Finance Education* with *Foundations of Personal Finance*

This chart lists the performance expectations for the national standards developed by the Jump$tart Coalition for Personal Financial Literacy. It also identifies the chapters in *Foundations of Personal Finance* that relate to each performance expectation.

Performance expectations are included for 4th, 8th, and 12th grades. The expectations indicate the knowledge and skills students should demonstrate by the end of each grade. In the correlation table, 4th grade expectations are indicated in yellow, 8th grade in orange, and 12th grade in red.

National Standards in K-12 Personal Finance Education

Financial Responsibility and Decision Making

Comprehensive Standard
Apply reliable information and systematic decision making to personal financial decisions.

Content Standard 1: Take responsibility for personal financial decisions.

Performance Expectations	Chapter Location
List examples of financial decisions and their possible consequences.	5, 7
Identify ways to be a financially responsible youth.	5, 9
Identify ways to be a financially responsible young adult.	5, 9
Give examples of the benefits of financial responsibility and the costs of financial irresponsibility.	5, 9, 10, 11, 12
Explain how individuals demonstrate responsibility for financial well-being over a lifetime.	1, 5, 6, 7, 8, 9, 10, 11, 12, 13, 14, 15, 16, 17, 18, 19
Analyze how financial responsibility is different for individuals with and without dependents.	7, 10, 12
Given a scenario, discuss ethical considerations of various personal finance decisions.	5, 14, 22

Content Standard 2: Find and evaluate financial information from a variety of sources.

Give examples of situations in which financial information would lead to better decisions.	12, 13, 14
Identify sources of financial information.	12, 13, 14

(Continued)

*Third Edition, 2007. Developed by the Jump$tart Coalition for Personal Financial Literacy

Content Standard 2: Find and evaluate financial information from a variety of sources *(continued)*.

Performance Expectations	Chapter Location
Analyze and evaluate advertising claims.	14
Identify online and printed sources of product information and list the strengths and weaknesses of each.	14
Determine whether financial information is objective, accurate, and current.	14
Investigate current types of consumer fraud, including online scams.	14
Given a scenario, identify relevant financial information needed to make a decision.	5, 14
List factors to consider when selecting a financial planning/ counseling professional and legal/tax advisor.	6, 7, 12

Content Standard 3: Summarize major consumer protection laws.

Performance Expectations	Chapter Location
Compare product return policies at local retail stores.	13, 14, 20
Research the primary consumer protection agency in the state of residence.	9, 20
Give examples of unfair or deceptive business practices that consumer protection laws forbid.	14
Given a scenario, explain steps in resolving a consumer complaint.	14
Match consumer protection laws to descriptions of the issues that they address and the safeguards that they provide.	14
Research online and printed sources of up-to-date information about consumer rights.	14
Given a scenario, write a complaint letter that states the problem, asks for specific action, includes copies of related documents, and provides contact information.	14

Content Standard 4: Make financial decisions by systematically considering alternatives and consequences.

Performance Expectations	Chapter Location
Explain how limited personal financial resources affect the choices people make.	1, 5
Rank personal wants/needs in order of importance.	1, 5
Set measurable short-term financial goals.	5
Outline the steps in systematically evaluating alternatives and making a decision.	5
Apply systematic decision making to a short-term goal.	5
Set measurable short- and medium-term financial goals.	5
Prioritize personal financial goals.	5
Evaluate the results of a financial decision.	5
Use a financial or online calculator to determine the cost of achieving a medium-term goal.	—
Apply systematic decision making to a medium-term goal.	5
Set measurable short-, medium-, and long-term financial goals.	5
Use a financial or online calculator to determine the cost of achieving a long-term goal.	5, 12

(Continued)

Content Standard 4: Make financial decisions by systematically considering alternatives and consequences *(continued)*.

Performance Expectations	Chapter Location
Apply systematic decision making to a long-term goal.	5
Analyze how inflation affects financial decisions.	2, 7
Analyze how taxes affect financial decisions.	7
Give examples of how decisions made today can affect future opportunities.	3, 5, 18

Content Standard 5: Develop communication strategies for discussing financial issues.

Give examples of how members of previous generations spent money as children.	1, 11, 16
Analyze the values and attitudes of members of previous generations from their personal stories about money.	11
Explain how discussing important financial matters with household members can help reduce conflict.	6
Identify differences among peers' values and attitudes about money.	3, 5, 9
Explain the value of discussing individual and shared financial responsibilities with a roommate before moving in.	18
Discuss the pros and cons of sharing financial goals and personal finance information with a partner before combining households.	6, 18, 22
Give examples of contracts between individuals and between individuals and businesses, and identify each party's basic responsibilities.	2, 6, 9, 12, 13, 14, 17, 18, 19, 20, 21

Content Standard 6: Control personal information.

List types of personal information that should not be disclosed to others and the possible consequences of doing so.	14
List actions an individual can take to protect personal identity.	14
Describe problems that occur when one is the victim of identity theft	14
Identify ways that thieves can fraudulently obtain personal information.	14
List entities that have a right to obtain individual Social Security numbers.	14
Recommend actions a victim of identity theft should take to restore personal security.	14

Income and Careers

Comprehensive Standard
Use a career plan to develop personal income potential.

Content Standard 1: Explore career options.

Explain the difference between a career and a job and identify various jobs in the community.	21
Explain the difference between a career and a job and identify various jobs in the community.	21
Give an example of how an individual's interests, knowledge, and abilities can affect career and job choice.	21

(Continued)

Content Standard 1: Explore career options *(continued)*.

Performance Expectations	Chapter Location
Identify a topic of personal interest and research a career related to that topic of interest.	21
Examine a job related to a career of interest.	21
Give examples of entrepreneurs in the community.	1, 22
Give an example of how education and/or training can affect lifetime income.	21, 22
Identify online and printed sources of information about jobs, careers, and entrepreneurship.	21, 22
Compare personal skills and interests to various career options.	21, 22
Describe the educational/training requirements, income potential, and primary duties of at least two jobs of interest.	21, 22
Identify individuals who could provide a positive job reference.	22
Complete an age-appropriate, part-time job application, including references.	22
Describe the risks, costs, and rewards of starting a business.	22
Outline the main components of a business plan.	22
Analyze how economic, social-cultural, and political conditions can affect income and career potential.	1, 2, 3, 4, 21
Identify a career goal and develop a plan and timetable for achieving it, including educational/training requirements, costs, and possible debt.	21, 22

Content Standard 2: Identify sources of personal income.

Explain the difference between a wage and a salary.	7
Identify jobs children can do to earn money.	—
Give examples of sources of income other than a wage or salary.	7
Define gift, rent, interest, dividend, capital gain, tip, commission, and business profit income.	7
Explain the difference between earned and unearned income and give an example of each.	7
Give an example of a government transfer payment.	7
Describe how a local government assistance program can benefit people in the community.	7
Explain the effect of inflation on income.	2, 7
Use a financial or online calculator to determine the future income needed to maintain a current standard of living.	2, 3

Content Standard 3: Describe factors affecting take-home pay.

Define tax and explain the difference between sales and income taxes.	3, 7
Give an example of how government uses tax revenues.	7
Explain all items commonly withheld from gross pay.	7

(Continued)

Content Standard 3: Describe factors affecting take-home pay *(continued)*.

Performance Expectations	Chapter Location
Give examples of employee benefits and explain why they are forms of compensation.	7
Explain the difference between Social Security and Medicare programs.	7
Explain the effect on take-home pay of changing the allowances claimed on an "Employee's Withholding Allowance Certificate" (IRS form W-4).	7
Transfer information on "Wage and Tax Statement" (IRS form W-2) and "Interest Income" (IRS form 1099-INT) to "U.S. Individual Income Tax Return" (IRS form 1040) and comparable state income tax form.	7
Complete "Income Tax Return for Single and Joint Filers with No Dependents" (IRS form 1040EZ) and comparable state income tax form.	7
Examine the benefits of employer-sponsored savings plans and other options for shifting current income to the future.	7

Planning and Money Management

Comprehensive Standard
Organize and plan personal finances and use a budget to manage cash flow.

Content Standard 1: Develop a plan for spending and saving.

Give examples of household expense categories and sources of income.	5, 6
Describe how to allocate a weekly allowance among the financial goals of spending, saving, and sharing.	5, 6, 11
Prepare a personal spending diary.	6
Calculate the sales tax for a given purchase.	2, 3, 7, 14, 19
Discuss the components of a personal budget, including income, planned saving, taxes, and fixed and variable expenses.	5, 7, 11
Given a household case study, calculate percentages for major expense categories.	6
Explain how to use a budget to manage spending and achieve financial goals.	5, 6, 11, 12
Identify changes in personal spending behavior that contribute to wealth-building.	5, 6, 11, 12
Given a scenario, design a personal budget for a young person living alone.	5, 6, 11
Analyze how changes in circumstances can affect a personal budget.	5, 6

Content Standard 2: Develop a system for keeping and using financial records.

Prepare a personal property inventory, including locations and estimates of value.	6, 10, 16, 18
Set up a file system for household product information and warranties and financial documents such as receipts and account statements.	6, 13, 14
Develop a filing system for keeping financial records, both paper and electronic.	6, 8
Describe recordkeeping features that financial institutions provide for online account management.	8

(Continued)

Content Standard 3: Describe how to use different payment methods.

Performance Expectations	Chapter Location
Describe different types of local financial institutions and explain the differences between them.	8
Explain how checks and debit and credit cards work as payment methods.	8
Discuss the advantages and disadvantages of different payment methods, such as stored value cards, debit cards, and online payment systems.	8
Compare the features and costs of a checking account and a debit card offered by different local financial institutions.	8
Compare the costs of cashing third-party checks at various local financial institutions, including a check-cashing service.	8
Demonstrate skill in basic financial tasks, including scheduling bill payments, writing a check, reconciling a checking/debit account statement, and monitoring printed and/or online account statements for accuracy.	8

Content Standard 4: Apply consumer skills to purchase decisions.

Performance Expectations	Chapter Location
Compare prices for the same item at two different stores.	13
Apply systematic decision making to a personal age-appropriate purchase.	5, 6, 13
Explain how peer pressure can affect spending decisions.	13
Explain the relationship between spending practices and achieving financial goals.	5, 6, 9, 11, 12
Give examples of how external factors, such as marketing and advertising techniques, might influence spending decisions for different individuals.	14
Given an age-appropriate scenario, describe how to use systematic decision making to choose among courses of action that include a range of spending and non-spending alternatives.	5
Apply comparison shopping skills to purchasing decisions.	13
Given a personal finance scenario for a family of four, describe how to apply systematic decision making to choose among alternative consumer actions.	5
Compare the benefits and costs of owning a house versus renting housing.	18
Explain the elements of a standard apartment lease agreement.	18
Describe the effect of inflation on buying power.	2, 3, 6, 9, 11, 12

Content Standard 5: Consider charitable giving.

Performance Expectations	Chapter Location
Identify a private charitable organization and the people it serves.	6
Determine whether charitable giving fits one's budget and, if so, how much is appropriate.	6
Use online charity-rating organizations to compare information about specific charities, such as the percentage of money spent on programs versus salaries and fundraising.	6

(Continued)

Content Standard 6: Develop a personal financial plan.

Performance Expectations	Chapter Location
Give examples of household assets.	3, 6, 7, 12
Explain the difference, with examples, between assets and liabilities.	3, 6
Given a simplified case study, construct a net worth statement.	6
Discuss the factors that affect net worth.	6
Explain the difference, with examples, between cash inflows (including income) and cash outflows (including expense).	6
Explain the difference between a cash flow statement and a budget.	6
Given a simplified case study, construct a cash flow statement.	6
Develop, monitor, and modify a personal financial plan, including goals, net worth statement, cash flow statement, insurance plan, investing plan, and a budget.	6, 7, 10, 12

Content Standard 7: Examine the purpose and importance of a will.

Identify an item that a household member has inherited.	—
Research the age at which an individual can write a valid will in the state of residence.	12
Describe the main components of a simple will and research the typical cost of having one drafted.	12
Identify the individuals and/or charitable organizations that are potential beneficiaries of personal property.	12
Explain how the law in the state of residence specifies the disposition of an estate when there is no valid will.	12
Explain the purpose and importance of a "living will" (durable power of attorney for health care).	12

Credit and Debit

Comprehensive Standard
Maintain creditworthiness, borrow at favorable terms, and manage debt.

Content Standard 1: Identify the costs and benefits of various types of credit.

Explain the difference between buying with cash and buying with credit.	6, 9
Describe the advantages and disadvantages of using credit.	9
Explain why financial institutions lend money.	9
Identify credit purchases that adults commonly make.	9
Explain why using a credit card is a form of borrowing.	9
Explain how debit cards differ from credit cards.	8, 9
Explain how interest rate and loan length affect the cost of credit.	9

Content Standard 1: Identify the costs and benefits of various types of credit *(continued)*

Performance Expectations	Chapter Location
Using a financial or online calculator, determine the total cost of repaying a loan under various rates of interest and over different periods.	9
Give examples of "easy access" credit.	9
Given an "easy access" loan amount and a two-week borrowing fee, calculate the interest rate for the loan period and its annual equivalent.	9
Discuss potential consequences of using "easy access" credit.	9
Explain how students, homeowners, and business owners use debt as an "investment."	18
Explain the potential consequences of deferred payment of student loans.	9, 21
Compare the cost of borrowing $1,000 by means of different consumer credit options.	9
Define all required credit card disclosure terms and complete a typical credit card application.	9
Explain how credit card grace periods, methods of interest calculation, and fees affect borrowing costs.	9
Using a financial or online calculator, compare the total cost of reducing a $1,000 credit card balance to zero with minimum payments versus above-minimum payments.	9
Given a scenario, apply systematic decision making to identify the most cost-effective option for purchasing a car.	19
Identify various types of student loans and alternatives to loans as a means of paying for post-secondary education.	21
Identify various types of mortgage loans and mortgage lenders.	18

Content Standard 2: Explain the purpose of a credit record and identify borrowers' credit report rights.

Performance Expectations	Chapter Location
Describe the qualities that would be desirable in a person who borrows a favorite personal possession.	9
Give examples of reasonable conditions to set for the use of borrowed personal property.	9
Given a scenario, describe steps that a person could take to regain a lender's trust after losing or damaging borrowed personal property.	—
Explain why it is important to establish a positive credit history.	9
Explain the value of credit reports to borrowers and to lenders.	9
Describe the information in a credit report and how long it is retained.	9
Give examples of permissible uses of a credit report other than granting credit.	9
Describe the elements of a credit score.	9
Explain how a credit score affects creditworthiness and the cost of credit.	9

(Continued)

Content Standard 2: Explain the purpose of a credit record and identify borrowers' credit report rights *(continued)*.

Performance Expectations	Chapter Location
Explain the factors that improve a credit score.	9
Identify organizations that maintain consumer credit records.	9
Explain the rights that people have to examine their credit reports.	9
Analyze the information contained in a credit report, indicate the time that certain negative data can be retained, and describe how to dispute inaccurate entries.	9
Discuss ways that a negative credit report can affect a consumer's financial future.	9

Content Standard 3: Describe ways to avoid or correct credit problems.

List ways to avoid credit problems, including not overspending.	9
Give examples of legal and illegal debt collection practices.	9
Identify possible indicators of excessive debt.	9
Describe possible consequences of excessive debt.	9
List actions that a consumer could take to reduce or better manage excessive debt.	9
Evaluate various credit counseling services.	9
Describe the purpose of bankruptcy and its possible effects on assets, employability, and credit cost and availability.	9
Given a scenario, write a billing dispute letter that states the problem, asks for specific action, includes references to copies of related documents, and provides contact information.	9
Describe debtors' and creditors' rights related to wage garnishment and repossession when an overdue debt is not paid.	9

Content Standard 4: Summarize major consumer credit laws.

Give examples of protections derived from consumer credit laws.	9
Summarize consumer credit laws and the protections that they provide.	9
Research online and printed sources of up-to-date information about consumer credit rights.	9

Risk Management and Insurance

Comprehensive Standard
Use appropriate and cost-effective risk management strategies.

Content Standard 1: Identify common types of risks and basic risk management methods.

Give examples of risks that individuals and households face.	3, 6, 9, 10, 12
Given an age-appropriate activity such as riding a bicycle, analyze how to reduce and avoid different kinds of risk.	10

(Continued)

Content Standard 1: Identify common types of risks and basic risk management methods *(continued)*.	
Performance Expectations	**Chapter Location**
Discuss the relationship between risk and insurance.	10
Explain how insurance deductibles work.	10
Determine how to evaluate an extended warranty.	13
Give examples of how people manage risk through avoidance, reduction, retention, and transfer.	10, 11, 12
Explain how to self-insure and give examples of circumstances in which self-insurance is appropriate.	10
Recommend insurance for the types of risks that young adults might face.	10, 17, 18, 19

Content Standard 2: Explain the purpose and importance of property and liability insurance protection.	
List valuable items that households commonly own.	10
Describe how valuable items might be damaged or lost and ways to protect them.	10
Identify the types of insurance that might cover accidental damage to another person's property.	10
Give examples of the kinds of a typical auto insurance policy covers.	10
Give examples of the kinds of expenses that a typical renter's policy and a typical homeowner's policy cover.	10
Identify the factors that influence the cost of insurance for vehicles and housing.	10
Differentiate among the main types of auto insurance coverage.	10
List factors that can increase or reduce auto insurance premiums.	10
Determine the legal minimum amounts of auto insurance coverage required in one's state of residence and recommend optimal amounts.	10
Given a scenario, calculate the amount paid on an insurance claim after applying exclusions and deductibles.	10
Compare the costs of auto insurance for the same vehicle, given two different deductibles and two different liability coverage limits.	10
Explain the benefits of renter's insurance and compare policies from different companies.	10

Content Standard 3: Explain the purpose and importance of health, disability, and life insurance protection.	
Explain why people need health insurance.	10, 17
List the main threats to household income and assets.	6, 10, 17
Give examples of the kinds of expenses that health insurance can cover.	10, 17
Describe the purpose of disability insurance.	10
Explain the primary purpose of life insurance and the characteristics of people who need it most.	10

(Continued)

Content Standard 3: Explain the purpose and importance of health, disability, and life insurance protection *(continued)*.

Performance Expectations	Chapter Location
Analyze the conditions under which young adults need life, health, and disability insurance.	10
Identify government programs that provide financial assistance for income loss due to illness, disability, or premature death.	10
Compare sources of health and disability insurance coverage, including employee benefit plans.	10
Explain the purpose of long-term care insurance.	10

Saving and Investing

Comprehensive Standard
Implement a diversified investment strategy that is compatible with personal goals.

Content Standard 1: Discuss how saving contributes to financial well-being.

Describe the advantages and disadvantages of saving for a short-term goal.	5, 6, 11
Describe ways that people can cut expenses to save more of their incomes.	11
Give examples of how saving money can improve financial well-being.	11
Describe the advantages and disadvantages of saving for short- and medium-term goals.	5, 6, 11
Explain the value of an emergency fund.	11
Explain why saving is a prerequisite to investing.	11, 12
Describe the advantages and disadvantages of saving for short-, medium-, and long-term goals.	5, 6, 11
Identify and compare saving strategies, including "paying yourself first," using payroll deduction, and comparison shopping to spend less.	11
Develop a definition of wealth based on personal values, priorities, and goals.	3, 6

Content Standard 2: Explain how investing builds wealth and helps meet financial goals.

Give an example of an investment and explain how it can grow in value.	12
Apply systematic decision making to determine when to invest cash not needed for short-term spending or emergencies.	5, 6, 12
Define the time value of money and explain how small amounts of money invested regularly over time grow exponentially.	12
Use the Rule of 72 to estimate the time or interest rate needed to double an amount of money.	11
Calculate and compare simple interest and compound interest earnings and explain the benefits of a compound rate of return.	11

(Continued)

Content Standard 2: Explain how investing builds wealth and helps meet financial goals *(continued)*.

Performance Expectations	Chapter Location
Determine the average, median, or estimated costs of a four-year college education, a wedding, a new business startup, and the down payments on a new car and a house.	12
Devise a periodic investment plan for accumulating the money for a four-year college education, a wedding, a new business startup, and the down payments on a new car and a house.	12
Identify and compare strategies for investing, including participating in a company retirement plan.	11, 12
Describe the effect of inflation on investment growth.	11, 12
Given rate of return, and years, use a financial or online calculator to figure (a) the end value of an invested lump sum and (b) the lump sum needed to reach a specific investment goal.	12
Given rate of return, years, and frequency, use a financial or online calculator to figure (a) the end value of an invested periodic amount and (b) the periodic amount needed to reach a specific investment goal.	11, 12
Explain the relative importance of the following sources of income in retirement: Social Security, employer retirement plans, and personal investments.	6, 7, 12
Explain why games of chance are not good investments for building wealth.	12

Content Standard 3: Evaluate investment alternatives.

List the advantages of investing money with a financial institution.	8, 11
Give an example of an investment that allows relatively quick and easy access to funds.	11
Compare the main features of interest-earning accounts at local financial institutions.	11
Explain how stocks and bonds differ as investments. Explain how to match investments to financial goals.	12
Compare investing in individual stocks and bonds with investing in stock or bond mutual funds.	6, 12
Compare the investment potential of stocks, bonds, and real estate to collectibles and precious metals.	12
Explain how inflation affects investment returns.	11, 12
Explain how to match investments to financial goals.	12
Discuss common types of investment risk.	12
Compare the risks and returns of various investments.	12
Calculate investment growth given different amounts, times, rates of return, and frequency of compounding.	11, 12
Describe the benefits of a diversified investment portfolio.	12

(Continued)

Content Standard 3: Evaluate investment alternatives *(continued)*.

Performance Expectations	Chapter Location
Identify the appropriate types of investments to achieve the objectives of liquidity, income, and growth.	11, 12
Identify the appropriate types of investments for accumulating the money for a four-year college education, a wedding, a new business startup, the down payments on a new car and a house, and retirement.	12
Use systematic decision making to select an investment.	5, 11, 12

Content Standard 4: Describe how to buy and sell investments.

Compare the rates of return on basic savings accounts at different financial institutions.	11
Identify and describe various sources of investment information, including prospectuses, online resources, and financial publications.	12
Interpret the financial market quotations of a stock and a mutual fund.	12
Research and track a publicly traded stock and record daily market values between two specified dates.	12
Analyze how economic and business factors affect the market value of a stock.	12
Compare the investment objectives and historical rates of returns in two mutual fund prospectuses.	12
Compare the advantages and disadvantages of buying and selling investments through various channels, including financial advisors, investment clubs, and online brokers.	12
Describe the benefits of dollar-cost averaging and calculate the average cost per share of investments using this strategy.	12

Content Standard 5: Explain how taxes affect the rate of return on investments.

Identify the income tax-free earnings limit for an investor under the age of 18.	—
Identify the tax rate for dividends.	—
Compare the returns of taxable investments with those that are tax-exempt or tax-deferred.	12
Contrast the benefits of a traditional IRA versus a Roth IRA.	12
Describe the advantages provided by employer-sponsored retirement savings plans, including 401(k) and related plans.	12

Content Standard 6: Investigate how agencies that regulate financial markets protect investors.

Explain how deposit insurance protects investors.	8
Explain how federal and state regulators protect investors.	8

Correlation of National Standards for Family and Consumer Sciences Education with *Foundations of Personal Finance*

This chart lists the performance expectations for *Consumer and Family Resources*, one of the 16 areas of study within the National Standards for Family and Consumer Sciences Education. It also identifies the chapters in *Foundations of Personal Finance* that relate to each performance expectation.

Consumer and Family Resources

Comprehensive Standard
Evaluate management practices related to the human, economic, and environmental resources.

Content Standard: 2.1 Demonstrate management of individual and family resources such as food, clothing, shelter, health care, recreation, transportation, time, and human capital.

Performance Expectations	Chapter Location
2.1.1 Apply management and planning skills and processes to organize tasks and responsibilities.	5, 6, 7, 8, 9, 10, 11, 12, 13, 21
2.1.2. Analyze how individuals and families make choices to satisfy needs and wants.	1, 5, 6, 7, 8, 9, 10, 11, 12, 13, 14, 15, 16, 17, 18, 21
2.1.3 Analyze decisions about providing safe and nutritious food for individuals and families.	13, 15
2.1.4 Apply consumer skills to providing and maintaining clothing.	13, 16
2.1.5 Apply consumer skills to decisions about housing, utilities, and furnishings.	10, 18
2.1.6 Summarize information about procuring and maintaining health care to meet the needs of individuals and family members.	10, 17
2.1.7 Apply consumer skills to decisions about recreation.	17
2.1.8 Apply consumer skills to acquire and maintain transportation that meets the needs of individuals and family members.	10, 19

(Continued)

Content Standard: 2.2 Analyze the relationship of the environment to family and consumer resources.	
Performance Expectations	**Chapter Location**
2.2.1 Analyze individual and family responsibility in relation to the environmental trends and issues.	23
2.2.2 Summarize environmental trends and issues affecting families and future generations.	23
2.2.3 Demonstrate behaviors that conserve, reuse, and recycle resources to maintain the environment.	1, 23
2.2.4 Explain government regulations for conserving natural resources.	23
Content Standard: 2.3 Analyze policies that support consumer rights and responsibilities.	
2.3.1 Analyze state and federal policies and laws providing consumer protection.	2, 4, 7, 8, 9, 10, 12, 16, 17, 19
2.3.2 Analyze how policies become laws relating to consumer rights.	2, 9, 14, 16, 17
2.3.3 Analyze skills used in seeking information related to consumer rights.	3, 9, 13, 14
Content Standard: 2.4 Evaluate the effects of technology on individual and family resources.	
2.4.1 Summarize types of technology that affect family and consumer decision-making.	1, 8, 13, 20
2.4.2 Analyze how media and technological advances affect family and consumer decisions.	1, 8, 12, 13, 19, 20, 21
2.4.3 Assess the use of technology and its effect on quality of life.	1, 8, 12, 13, 20, 21
Content Standard: 2.5 Analyze relationships between the economic system and consumer actions.	
2.5.1 Analyze the use of resources in making choices that satisfy needs and wants of individuals and families.	1, 5, 6, 7, 8, 9, 10, 11, 12, 13, 14, 15, 16, 17, 18
2.5.2 Analyze individual and family roles in the economic system.	1, 3, 5, 6, 7, 8, 9, 10, 11, 12, 13, 14, 21
2.5.3 Analyze economic effects of laws and regulations that pertain to consumers and providers of services.	1, 2, 7, 8, 9, 10, 12, 19, 20
2.5.4 Analyze practices that allow families to maintain economic self-sufficiency.	5, 6, 7, 8, 9, 10, 11, 12, 13, 14, 15, 16, 17, 18, 19, 21, 22
Content Standard: 2.6 Demonstrate management of financial resources to meet the goals of individuals and families across the life span.	
2.6.1 Evaluate the need for personal and family financial planning.	3, 5, 6, 7, 8, 9, 10, 11, 12, 18
2.6.2 Apply management principles to individual and family financial practices.	5, 6, 7, 8, 9, 10, 11, 12, 14
2.6.3 Apply management principles to decisions about insurance for individuals and families.	3, 10
2.6.4 Evaluate personal and legal documents related to managing individual and family finances.	6, 7, 8, 9, 12, 17, 18, 19

Planning Your Program

Foundations of Personal Finance program planning guides are provided for the following course calendars:

- Trimester course, twelve weeks
- Semester course, eighteen weeks
- Full-year course (six grading periods, six weeks each)

- Full-year course (four grading periods, nine weeks each)

Chapters are grouped according to the suggested depth of coverage and duration of instruction time. Incorporate activities from the *Teacher's Edition*, *Teacher's Resources*, or *Student Workbook* to provide variety during extended class periods.

Trimester Course, Twelve Weeks	
Week	Chapter Numbers and Names
1	**Unit 2: Managing Your Finances** **Chapter 5** Making Smart Decisions **Chapter 6** Personal Finance: An Overview
2	**Chapter 7** Income and Taxes
3	**Chapter 8** Financial Institutions and Services
4	**Chapter 9** Credit
5	**Chapter 10** Insurance
6	**Chapter 11** Savings **Chapter 12** Investing and Estate Planning
7	**Unit 3: Managing Your Spending** **Chapter 13** Smart Shopping Basics **Chapter 14** Consumers in the Marketplace
8	**Chapter 15** Spending for Food **Chapter 16** Clothing
9	**Chapter 17** Health and Wellness
10	**Chapter 18** Housing
11	**Chapter 19** Transportation **Chapter 20** Electronics and Appliances
12	**Unit 4: Planning Your Future** **Chapter 21** Planning for Your Career **Chapter 22** Entering the Work World **Chapter 23** Your Role in the Environment

Semester Course, Eighteen Weeks	
Week	Chapter Numbers and Names
1	**Unit 1: The Economic System** **Chapter 1** What Is Economics? **Chapter 2** Government and the Economy
2	**Chapter 3** Consumers in the Economy: An Overview **Chapter 4** The Global Economy
3	**Unit 2: Managing Your Finances** **Chapter 5** Making Smart Decisions
4	**Chapter 6** Personal Finance: An Overview
5	**Chapter 7** Income and Taxes
6	**Chapter 8** Financial Institutions and Services
7	**Chapter 9** Credit
8	**Chapter 10** Insurance
9	**Chapter 11** Savings **Chapter 12** Investing and Estate Planning
10	**Unit 3: Managing Your Spending** **Chapter 13** Smart Shopping Basics **Chapter 14** Consumers in the Marketplace
11	**Chapter 15** Spending for Food
12	**Chapter 16** Clothing
13	**Chapter 17** Health and Wellness
14	**Chapter 18** Housing
15	**Chapter 19** Transportation
16	**Chapter 20** Electronics and Appliances
17	**Unit 4: Planning Your Future** **Chapter 21** Planning for Your Career **Chapter 22** Entering the Work World
18	**Chapter 23** Your Role in the Environment

(Continued)

Full-Year Course, Six Grading Periods, Six Weeks Each

First Grading Period

Unit 1: The Economic System

Chapter 1 What Is Economics?

Chapter 2 Government and the Economy

Chapter 3 Consumers in the Economy: An Overview

Chapter 4 The Global Economy

Second Grading Period

Unit 2: Managing Your Finances

Chapter 5 Making Smart Decisions

Chapter 6 Personal Finance: An Overview

Chapter 7 Income and Taxes

Chapter 8 Financial Institutions and Services

Third Grading Period

Unit 2 (continued)

Chapter 9 Credit

Chapter 10 Insurance

Chapter 11 Savings

Chapter 12 Investing and Estate Planning

Fourth Grading Period

Unit 3: Managing Your Spending

Chapter 13 Smart Shopping Basics

Chapter 14 Consumers in the Marketplace

Chapter 15 Spending for Food

Chapter 16 Clothing

Fifth Grading Period

Unit 3 (continued)

Chapter 17 Health and Wellness

Chapter 18 Housing

Chapter 19 Transportation

Chapter 20 Electronics and Appliances

Sixth Grading Period

Unit 4: Planning Your Future

Chapter 21 Planning for Your Career

Chapter 22 Entering the Work World

Chapter 23 Your Role in the Environment

Full-Year Course, Four Grading Periods, Nine Weeks Each

First Grading Period

Unit 1: The Economic System

Chapter 1 What Is Economics?

Chapter 2 Government and the Economy

Chapter 3 Consumers in the Economy: An Overview

Chapter 4 The Global Economy

Unit 2: Managing Your Finances

Chapter 5 Making Smart Decisions

Chapter 6 Personal Finance: An Overview

Second Grading Period

Unit 2 (continued)

Chapter 7 Income and Taxes

Chapter 8 Financial Institutions and Services

Chapter 9 Credit

Chapter 10 Insurance

Chapter 11 Savings

Chapter 12 Investing and Estate Planning

Third Grading Period

Unit 3: Managing Your Spending

Chapter 13 Smart Shopping Basics

Chapter 14 Consumers in the Marketplace

Chapter 15 Spending for Food

Chapter 16 Clothing

Chapter 17 Health and Wellness

Fourth Grading Period

Unit 3 (continued)

Chapter 18 Housing

Chapter 19 Transportation

Chapter 20 Electronics and Appliances

Unit 4: Planning Your Future

Chapter 21 Planning for Your Career

Chapter 22 Entering the Work World

Chapter 23 Your Role in the Environment

FOUNDATIONS OF
PERSONAL
FINANCE

8th Edition

Sally R. Campbell
Winnetka, Illinois

Publisher

The Goodheart-Willcox Company, Inc.
Tinley Park, Illinois
www.g-w.com

Library of Congress Catalog Card Number 2009039160

ISBN 978-1-60525-089-2

1 2 3 4 5 6 7 8 9 – 10 – 15 14 13 12 11 10 09

Library of Congress Cataloging-in-Publication Data

Cambell, Sally R.
   Foundations of personal finance / Sally R. Cambell. – 8th ed.
    p. cm.
   Rev. ed. of: The confident consumer. c2004.
   Includes index.
   ISBN 978-1-60525-089-2
   1. Finance, Personal. 2. Consumer education. I. Cambel, Sally R.
   Confident consumer. II. Title.
HG179.C32 2010
332.024--dc22
                    2009039160

Cover image: Gettyimages RF

Introduction

Foundations of Personal Finance serves as a guide to the U.S. economic system and an introduction to the global economy. It will help you understand the system and how it affects you as a consumer, producer, and citizen. It will also help you make the most of the future opportunities that come your way in the global economy.

The text outlines the key characteristics of the free market system and the challenges of globalization. It describes your financial activities as worker, consumer, manager, and shopper. Mastering these decision-making functions lays the foundation for personal financial competence through all the stages of your life.

To manage personal finances, you need to define the economic goals you want to achieve and the steps you can take to achieve them. *Foundations of Personal Finance* explains how to identify your most important needs and wants and how to manage your resources to reach your goals. It can help you make the best use of all your resources to raise your standard of living and create financial security in your future.

As you use this book, you will learn how to make financial decisions related to routine spending for food, clothing, and personal needs. You will learn where to find reliable information about consumer products and services, government policies, and economic conditions. You will find out what to consider when making big spending decisions for items such as cars, housing, and home furnishings. You will also learn what is important to know when you use credit, buy insurance, and invest your money. In addition, the text identifies the tools you can use to protect your consumer interests as you carry out your financial transactions in the marketplace.

You will find a section on planning your future. These chapters will describe the education and job training that will prepare you to take your place in the work world. Finally, you will look at your role as a citizen of the world and custodian of the environment.

Foundations of Personal Finance is straightforward and easy to read. Each chapter begins with learning objectives and new terms to understand. Each chapter ends with review questions, critical thinking questions, and activities to help you study effectively and organize what you learn. The case studies provided throughout the text will help you relate the material to lifelike situations. You will also find features on careers; real-life connections to the text content; and links to history, math, and science.

About the Author

Sally R. Campbell is currently a freelance writer and consultant in consumer economics. She develops educational materials, including teacher's guides, curriculum guides, textbooks, and student activity materials.

She was formerly the editor and assistant director of the Money Management Institute of Household International where she wrote educational materials related to money management, consumer information, and financial planning.

Sally has a master's degree in education from St. Louis University and has completed the Certified Financial Planning Professional Education Program of the College for Financial Planning. She taught consumer education in the St. Louis public schools.

Welcome to Foundations of Personal Finance

Foundations of Personal Finance is designed to help you succeed. Each of the following features will assist you in mastering the concepts presented in the textbook.

Reading for Meaning provides tips to improve reading comprehension and understanding. Review the tip before you read each chapter.

Key Terms appear in bold, highlighted type in the text where they are defined.

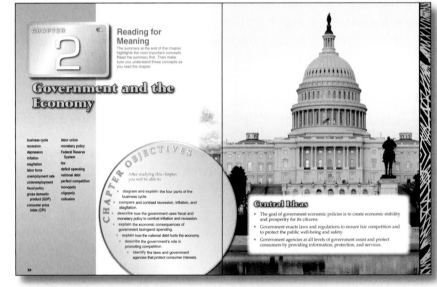

Chapter Objectives outline skills you will build while studying the chapter.

Central Ideas present the main concepts discussed in the chapter.

Real Life Connections features apply chapter concepts to real-life situations.

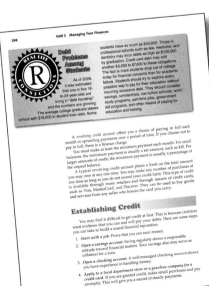

Linking to… features connect key topics to the academic areas of history, math, or science.

Economics in Action features discuss economic principles in evidence today.

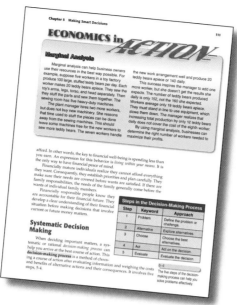

Case Studies bring financial concepts to life through realistic scenarios and follow-up questions.

Chapter Summary covers the main ideas of the chapter.

Review questions reinforce important concepts and help you recall, organize, and use the information presented in the text.

Critical Thinking activities expand chapter concepts and challenge you to use problem-solving skills. Thought-provoking questions motivate you to seek further information or exchange thoughts and opinions with classmates.

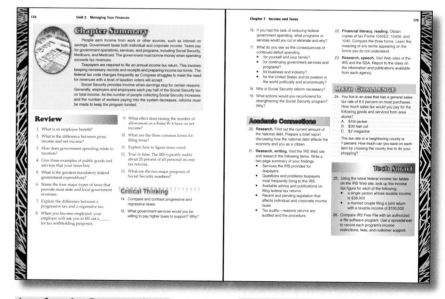

Academic Connections activities increase personal finance knowledge while developing academic skills. Academic areas include history, math, reading, research, science, social studies, speech, and writing. Activities may involve individual or team work.

Math Challenge helps you develop critical math skills related to personal finance.

Tech Smart encourages the exploration of financial concepts through high-tech means.

Student Organizations

You may be familiar with many student organizations at your school. Some exist specifically to help you and other young people learn the skills they will need in the work world. These organizations are known as Career and Technical Student Organizations (CTSOs). Joining one or more of these organizations can benefit you in many ways.

Reasons to Join

A CTSO related to your career interests can help you develop the skills you will need to succeed in your career. As part of an organization, you will have access to in-depth, profession-related knowledge. You will be working with peers who share similar values and goals. Staff, organization leaders, and teachers can provide you with valuable insights you will need on your career path. The friendships and networking connections you nurture now can also be beneficial throughout your career.

No matter what career you choose, a CTSO will help you acquire and develop abilities you will need for career success. Qualities such as leadership, cooperation, creativity, responsibility, and fairness will help you advance in any job. Skills in planning, communication, and teamwork will make you an essential employee.

Some CTSOs are directly involved in the subject of personal finance. They include FCCLA, DECA, FBLA, BPA, and SkillsUSA.

Family, Career and Community Leaders of America (FCCLA)

FCCLA is a student organization that promotes personal growth and leadership development through family and consumer sciences education. As the only in-school student organization with the family as its focus, FCCLA is an ideal companion to personal finance and other courses in your school's family and consumer sciences program.

Involvement in FCCLA offers the opportunity to

- participate in activities and events at local, state, and national levels

- develop leadership and teamwork skills

- help others through community service projects

- prepare for future roles in your family, career, and community

STAR Events—Students Taking Action with Recognition

Students compete in events that test their leadership and career preparation skills. Students participate in cooperative, individualized, and competitive events. Topics include career investigation, entrepreneurship, job interviewing, and life event planning.

For additional information, visit the organization's web site at www.fcclainc.org.

DECA

An Association of Marketing Students

DECA is an organization for students interested in marketing, management, finance, entrepreneurship, and business administration. DECA provides teachers with classroom activities related to developing career skills and business leadership traits. Community service is also emphasized. Competitive events allow students to demonstrate what they have learned and measure their progress.

More information can be found at www.deca.org.

Future Business Leaders of America (FBLA)

FBLA is an organization that helps students develop confidence as they prepare for business management careers. Students participate in activities and competitions that help them develop leadership skills and make connections in the business world.

Visit the Web site at www.fbla.org.

Business Professionals of America (BPA)

BPA focuses on developing skills that will aid those seeking careers in the professional business workforce. Problem-solving, leadership, technology, and citizenship are just some areas emphasized. The workplace Skills Assessment Program helps students measure their readiness for careers in office administration, business technology, and related areas.

The Web site can be found at www.bpa.org.

SkillsUSA

SkillsUSA is an organization of students preparing for careers in trade, technical, and health services. Students may compete in the SkillsUSA Championships at the local, state, and national levels. SkillsUSA emphasizes not only those qualities necessary to begin a successful career, but also the importance of lifelong education and training.

Check out the organization's Web site at www.skillsusa.org.

Explore Careers Through Foundations of Personal Finance

Your career decisions have a lasting impact on your personal and financial goals. *Foundations of Personal Finance* challenges you to plan for the future—and provides the information you need to make sound decisions.

Chapter 21, *Planning for Your Career,* explains how to develop a career plan based on your personal interests, aptitudes, abilities, values, and goals. You will learn about important resources for exploring careers, including the career clusters. The chapter also helps you determine the education and training needed to meet your career goals.

Chapter 22, *Entering the Work World,* discusses preparing résumés and cover letters and attending job interviews. You will also learn skills that lead to career success and explore entrepreneurship opportunities.

Look for the career clusters icons throughout the text to learn about occupations related to chapter content. The career clusters—16 general groupings of occupational and career areas—are a helpful resource for exploring careers. Each chapter features three occupations and highlights typical job duties and working conditions. More than 60 occupations are featured throughout the textbook.

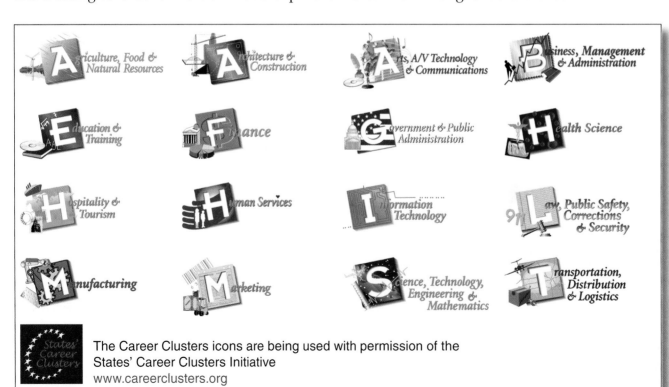

Agriculture, Food & Natural Resources

Architecture & Construction

Arts, A/V Technology & Communications

Business, Management & Administration

Education & Training

Finance

Government & Public Administration

Health Science

Hospitality & Tourism

Human Services

Information Technology

Law, Public Safety, Corrections & Security

Manufacturing

Marketing

Science, Technology, Engineering & Mathematics

Transportation, Distribution & Logistics

The Career Clusters icons are being used with permission of the States' Career Clusters Initiative
www.careerclusters.org

Featured Occupations

CONTENTS

Unit 3
Managing Your Spending 310

FEATURES

ECONOMICS in ACTION

REAL LIFE CONNECTIONS

Case Studies

Unit 1
The Economic System

In This Unit

You make many economic choices each day. When you spend money, you make economic choices. If you do without spending today to save for tomorrow, you make economic choices. How you spend your free time—working to earn money, studying to boost your grades, or just hanging out with friends—involves making economic choices. Over time, these choices will largely determine your overall quality of life. You can influence the economic choices of government by participating in the political system and making yourself heard. As you will see, the choices you make connect you to millions of other people in the U.S. and around the world.

CHAPTER

1

Reading for Meaning

Before reading the chapter, scan the vocabulary list for words you can define. Based on your definitions, predict the content of this chapter. Review your predictions after reading the material.

What Is Economics?

needs

wants

goods

services

economic system

traditional economy

market economy

free enterprise
  system

consumer

producer

marketplace

command economy

mixed economy

resources

scarcity

nonhuman resource

human resource

trade-off

opportunity cost

profit

innovation

technology

supply

demand

CHAPTER OBJECTIVES

After studying this chapter, you will be able to

- **distinguish** between needs and wants.
- **compare** different types of economic systems.
- **define** scarcity in terms of needs and wants.
- **analyze** a decision in terms of trade-offs and opportunity cost.
- **explain** the role of the profit motive in the economic system of the U.S.
- **evaluate** how competition among producers influences the price of goods in a market economy.
- **interpret** the relationship between supply and demand.

Central Ideas

- Economics is the study of how people use scarce resources to satisfy their unlimited needs and wants.

- In a free enterprise system, market forces allocate the resources.

You live in an economic world. Money changes hands every time you buy a snack, rent a movie, ride a bus, turn on a light, text a message, or see a doctor. Economic wheels turn to keep schools open, maintain streets and parks, and provide police and fire protection. Your home receives electricity, your television receives broadcasts, and your favorite stores are stocked with items you want to buy. Every day, you use and depend on items generated by the U.S. economy.

Did you ever wonder how all these events happen? You will learn in this chapter about the powerful forces that link you to the nation's goods and services. You will also learn how these forces work and the important role you play.

Economic Systems

In earliest times, families were relatively self-sufficient. The family was the basic economic unit. It provided members with food, shelter, protection, hides for wearing and staying warm, and other needs. **Needs** are items a person must have to survive. Needs differ from **wants**, which are items a person would like to have but that are not essential to life.

As families formed communities and moved away from an agricultural base, life became more complex. No longer were families so self-sufficient. They became consumers who looked beyond the family to meet many of their needs. They began to trade with one another. Artisans and tradesmen became expert in their work.

As individuals and communities provided specialized labor, a wider variety of goods and services flourished. **Goods** are physical items such as food and clothing, while **services** refer to work performed. Examples of services include work done by a carpenter, plumber, or accountant. The interdependence of providers and users of goods and services marked the beginning of an economic system. An **economic system** is the structure in which resources are turned into goods and services to address unlimited needs and wants.

Types of Economic Systems

Every nation has an economic system. Economists have defined four basic types—traditional, market, command, and mixed economies.

Traditional

The **traditional economy** is a system in which economic decisions are based on a society's values, culture, and customs. Today this type of economy exists mostly in underdeveloped countries or nations governed by strong cultural, religious, or tribal leadership.

In these areas, change comes slowly. People tend to stick with what they know and do as they have always done. For example, if you lived in a traditional economy and your parents raised sheep, chances are that you would too. You would likely grow your own food and make your own

1-1

In traditional economies, change comes slowly from generation to generation.

clothing. You would probably have little interest in doing something new or different from what your friends and family do, 1-1.

In recent years, some traditional economies have begun to develop a new approach to economics. They have come to recognize the advantages of technology and other advances in the modern world. There is a desire both to keep the old and to accept some of what is new.

Market

A **market economy** is a system in which privately owned businesses operate and compete for profits with limited government regulation or interference. It is also called a **free enterprise system** or *capitalism*.

In a market economy, consumers are important and businesses react to their demands. A **consumer** is a buyer and user of goods and services. A **producer** is an individual or business that provides the supply of goods and services to meet consumer demands. The activities and decisions of consumers determine in large part what goods and services businesses will produce and sell. A market economy offers many opportunities for businesses to grow and profit. It also offers hard-working individuals with education and training the incentives and opportunities to develop their talents and succeed in fields of their choice.

In economic terms, the **marketplace** or *market* is not a physical place like a mall or a grocery store. It is an arena in which consumers and

Discuss

What are some examples of the market economy responding to consumers and of the government responding to the people?

Reflect

How many different times have you acted as a consumer today? How many different producers' goods and services have you used?

Activity

In the library, obtain past and current computer magazines. Compare product design, features, accessories, and capabilities of past computer models with current models. Relate this to the development of other products and services.

Case Study: Living in a Market Economy

Anita and Juan Search for Housing

Anita and Juan are in their mid-twenties and plan to marry in six months. They decide to buy their first home in the city and move to the suburbs once they have school-age children. They see two new one-bedroom apartments in their price range, but prefer a higher-priced loft apartment. The loft is a little over their spending limit, but the high ceilings, wood floors, and interesting floor plans tempt them. The units also have new kitchens and laundry equipment. Their real estate agent says the loft should have an excellent resale value when they decide to sell and move in a few years.

Case Review

1. How are housing costs determined in a market economy? Why are they likely to be higher than in a command economy?
2. What would happen to housing costs in a market economy when the supply is severely limited? How would prices change when there are more sellers than buyers?
3. How do you see the supply and demand for housing in your area? Would you rather be a buyer or a seller?

Reflect

In what specific ways do you think your life would change in a command economy?

Resource

Market or Command?
Activity A, WB

Discuss

What are some advantages of the command economy approach to housing?

producers meet to exchange goods, services, and money. The term *market* may refer to all goods and services in an economy or to a limited number of goods in a selected segment. For example, there is a market for children's clothes, for luxury cars, and for electronics. There also is a global market that encompasses trade among all the nations of the world.

Command

A **command economy** is a system in which a central authority, usually the government, controls economic activities. A central authority decides how to allocate resources. It decides who will produce what. It decides what and how much to produce and sets the prices of goods and services.

In this type of system, the needs and wants of consumers are not generally a driving force in the decision-making process. Consumers do not have broad freedom of choice. They often cannot decide for themselves how to earn and spend income. A command economy often exists in socialist and communist forms of government.

Case Study: Living in a Command Economy

Mariya's and Sasha's Apartment

Mariya and Sasha plan to marry after they find a place to live. Now they each live in a small apartment with family members. Mariya works in a factory an hour away. Sasha works in the same factory and lives an hour away in another direction.

Every Sunday Mariya and Sasha go to a place where people gather to find living space. Hundreds of people carry handmade signs advertising living quarters to trade or living space wanted.

When housing agreements are made, the authorities must approve them. The parties involved must show their registration cards to prove they had permission to live in the country. In addition, the agreement cannot violate living space restrictions for different categories of people.

After several months of searching, Mariya and Sasha make an agreement with a man who plans to move from town to the country. He wants the U.S. equivalent of $300 for his one-room apartment. This is most of their savings, but Mariya and Sasha consider it a bargain. They do not see the apartment right away, but they know it is in a fairly new building not far from their workplace. More important, it will be theirs.

Case Review

1. How might a severe housing shortage affect you over the next 10 years?
2. Housing costs in command economies are controlled by the state and are very low compared to those in the United States. To what extent would you be willing to sacrifice privacy, quality, and availability of housing to cut housing costs by 70 to 80 percent?
3. Why is housing likely to be more limited in a command economy than in a market economy?

Mixed

Most economies are mixed. A **mixed economy** is a combination of the market and the command systems. For example, a mixed economy may function through a marketplace, although the government or central authority regulates the prices and supply of goods and services. Government may regulate certain industries such as utilities and airlines.

Discuss

How would the search for housing be likely to differ in a market economy? How do you explain the differences?

Although the U.S. economy is technically a mixed economy, in this textbook and elsewhere it is labeled a market economy. Compared with other mixed economies, the U.S. has minimal government involvement. The government's limited role in the U.S. economy is varied and important. That role will be covered in detail in the next chapter.

The Challenge of Scarcity

All economic systems attempt to resolve the problem of unlimited needs and wants and limited resources. Here the term **resources** refers to any input used to generate other goods or services. The challenge of stretching resources to cover needs and wants is called **scarcity**. Individuals, families, companies, and nations are all limited in the resources available to meet needs and wants. Deciding how to deal with scarcity is the basis for the study of economics.

Over your lifetime, your needs and wants will never end. There are many reasons for this. The most obvious is that you outgrow your current needs and wants and develop new ones. For example, as your feet grow bigger, you need larger shoes. Another reason is your needs and wants change as you grow mentally and emotionally. See 1-2.

Also, fulfilling one want often creates new ones. For example, if you buy a new music system, you will want music to play on it. You may want headphones and a shelf to hold your equipment. When your music system becomes outdated, you will want a new improved model.

Scarcity forces people, businesses, and governments to make choices in the use of resources and the needs to be met. There are two basic types of resources that are considered.

- **Nonhuman resources** are external resources, such as money, time, equipment, and possessions.

- **Human resources** are qualities and characteristics that people have within themselves.

Human resources include qualities that make workers more productive, such as good health, skills, knowledge, and education. *Entrepreneurship* is a type of human resource, too. It is a set of personal qualities that helps an individual create, operate, and assume the risk of new businesses.

Consumers have unlimited needs and wants for different goods and services. These include food, clothes, housing, medical care, cars, and spending money. Since resources are limited while wants are unlimited, it is necessary to choose which wants to satisfy.

For example, suppose you must choose between seeing a movie and going bowling because you do not have time for both. You may need to choose between a new pair of gym shoes and a pair of boots if you do not have money for both. Families may have to choose between buying a new car and taking a family vacation, or between buying a home and starting a business. Economic choices are endless.

Scarcity applies to government in the same way. The needs of citizens far exceed the resources of the government. That is why it is necessary to make choices. Local governments may need to choose between raising taxes and cutting services. The federal government makes the same types of choices.

Trade-Offs and Opportunity Cost

Making choices involves evaluating two or more options and selecting just one. Making choices entails trade-offs. A **trade-off** is the item given up in order to gain something else. For example, there is a trade-off when you spend $50 to buy a jacket. The trade-off is the other ways you could have spent the $50, including saving it for a future purchase.

Making a choice results in a trade-off, and a trade-off results in an *opportunity cost.* **Opportunity cost** is the value of the best option or alternative given up. If you turn down an after-school job because you have to be at soccer practice, there is an opportunity cost. The opportunity cost of playing soccer may be the amount you could have earned working. On the other hand, the opportunity cost of working instead of playing soccer could be the pleasure and enjoyment of playing a sport you love.

Opportunity cost can be measured in terms of dollars, time, enjoyment, or something else of value. The opportunity cost of a decision often varies from one person to the next. It depends on what the person who made the decision values.

For example, if spending time with your family is most important to you, missing family meals may be the opportunity cost of going to soccer practice. If getting good grades is most important to you, losing time to study may be the opportunity cost.

Opportunity cost applies to economic choices of families, businesses, and governments as well as individuals. Weighing opportunity cost is a valuable decision-making tool. You will read more about decision-making tools in Chapter 5.

1-2

Clothes can be both a need and a want.

Reflect

What are some of the most difficult trade-offs you've had to make?

Note

The concept of opportunity cost will be reinforced in Chapter 4, which discusses comparative advantage.

Discuss

Discuss a recent situation in which the local government had to deal with scarcity and choose one option over another.

Scarcity and Economic Systems

All societies are faced with scarcity and must make choices. The problem of scarcity applies to individuals, families, businesses, and organizations. Governments also make economic choices that affect everyone.

At the local level, governments make many choices in allocating limited resources. For example, a local government may need to choose between using funds to build a public swimming pool or to repave the streets.

The federal government makes the same types of choices. For example, the government may have to decide between investing in oil drilling and investing in new energy sources. Major political and economic decisions center on how to divide limited national resources given unlimited national

ECONOMICS in ACTION

More Tools to Evaluate Economic Choices

Marginalism is the added value versus the additional cost of one more unit or item. For example, suppose you buy two pairs of jeans at $65 and consider a third pair. Will the added pair bring as much satisfaction as the first two? As you buy more jeans, the per-unit price stays the same, but the "marginal" or extra value of one more pair decreases.

You can also approach economic choices through a *cost-benefit analysis*, which is similar to marginalism. The *cost-benefit principle* states that you should take an action or make a purchase only if the benefit is at least as great as the cost. For example, using the jeans example, suppose you see a casual jacket that complements the first two pairs of jeans. With the jacket and those jeans, you could coordinate several outfits. A third pair of jeans, on the other hand, would not benefit your wardrobe to the same degree as the jacket.

These principles apply to economic decisions of individual consumers, businesses, and governments. You'll read more about them in Chapter 5.

Discuss

Name a country whose religious leader makes decisions that affect the economy.

Vocabulary

Define *circular flow* and tell how it demonstrates the movement of goods, services, and money in a market economy. Within the circular flow, what goes to and comes from government?

needs. These needs may include crime control, health care, environmental protection, education, national defense, and aid to the poor and homeless.

The scarcity of resources leads to three problems for all societies:

- what and how much to produce
- how to allocate resources in producing goods and services
- how to divide the goods and services produced

The way a society solves these problems defines its economic system. If these decisions are made by the country's religious leader, the nation's economic system is probably a traditional economy. If a central planning authority decides, the economic system is probably a command economy. In the U.S. free enterprise system, these decisions are made primarily by market forces.

How the U.S. Economy Works

A circular flow of goods, services, and money takes place within the economy, as shown in the circular flow model in 1-3. The blue outer circle shows the flow of consumer goods and services from producers/sellers to consumers/workers. It also shows the flow of the resources (labor, land, capital, and entrepreneurship) from consumers/workers to producers/sellers.

The orange circle shows the flow of payments for goods and services from consumers/workers to producers/sellers. It also shows the flow of payment for resources from producers/sellers to consumers/workers.

This model is a good snapshot of how consumers and producers interact in the economy. However, it does not show the whole picture. For example, producers and sellers can also be consumers. Businesses buy the goods and services that other businesses produce. In the next chapter, you will see how the government fits into this picture.

You can gain a better understanding of how the U.S. economy works by studying the basic qualities of a market economy. These are discussed in the following sections.

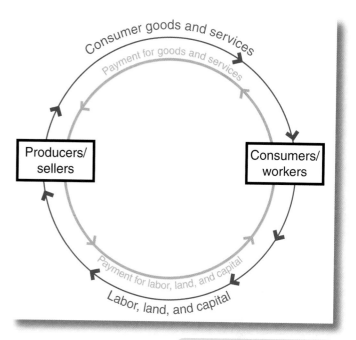

Four Qualities of a Market Economy

Four unique qualities—private ownership, profit, free choices, and competition—characterize a market economy. The dynamic combination of these qualities explains many aspects of the inner workings of the U.S. economy. A study of the law of supply and demand helps to complete the picture.

1-3

This chart shows the circular flow of goods, services, and money between producers/sellers and consumers/workers.

Private Ownership and Control of Productive Resources

Productive resources include the human and nonhuman resources used to produce goods and services. In the U.S. economic system, citizens and businesses own and decide how to use these resources. Businesses invest in the equipment, labor, and land needed to produce goods and services. They exercise the right to own private property. Individuals and businesses can buy and sell property; they can use it or give it away. This includes personal property such as clothes, cars, and electronics. It also includes real estate and business enterprises.

The Profit Motive

The promise of earning money inspires the worker, shop owner, manufacturer, and investor to engage in economic activity. For businesses and investors, **profit** is the total amount of money earned after expenses are subtracted from income. The profit motive drives businesses to produce goods and services to meet consumer demand.

For individuals, profit comes in the form of income. Individuals sell their productive resources, such as labor, ideas, land, and capital. In return, they receive income or a return on their investments. This is what brings people into the workforce and investors into the stock market.

If there were no opportunity to earn profits, the U.S. economy would falter. Individuals would be less motivated to work. Investors would not invest in businesses and provide the money needed to turn resources into goods and services. Businesses would not grow and try to increase sales. All businesses, from the corner grocery to a worldwide corporation,

Business Development Managers
Business development managers plan strategies to improve a company's performance and competitive position. They analyze, interpret, and evaluate various types of data in order to make sound business decisions.

1-4

All businesses, such as this neighborhood florist, must earn a profit in order to stay open.

Resource

Money Makers, Activity B, WB

Entrepreneurs

Entrepreneurs are people who organize, operate, and assume the risk for a business venture or enterprise. Successful entrepreneurs have business management skills, marketing knowledge, and an understanding of the demand for the product or service they provide.

depend on profits, 1-4. It is a positive number. The *profit motive*, or the desire for profit, drives both individuals and businesses to produce.

Free Economic Choice

In the United States and other market economies, consumers are free to make many choices. This is good news for you. Free choice opens the doors of opportunity in many areas. Both individuals and businesses have the right to freely decide how they will earn, spend, save, invest, and produce. You choose

- what you will buy
- where you will buy it
- how much you are willing to pay
- whether you will use cash or credit
- whether you will spend or save

Businesses respond to consumer choices by producing and selling the goods and services consumers want. In the economy, the combined choices of individual consumers make the greatest impact. Your decision to buy a new cell phone will not greatly impact the manufacturer's bottom line. However, if thousands of others buy it, the company will make money.

You are also free to choose how to earn your money. There is a vast menu of job possibilities in a free market economy. Your future income will depend on the career choices you make and the abilities and skills you develop. If you are willing to work hard and get the training and education required, you can succeed in a market economy. This is not always true in a command economy, where a central authority controls much of the opportunity.

A free market economy is also ideal for starting your own business. The path of the entrepreneur is not an easy path, but it is open to anyone with a sound idea and the willingness to take risks and work hard. Take a look at the stories of those who founded well-known corporations such as McDonald's, Microsoft, and Walmart. Almost all of them started with an idea that greatly appealed to consumers.

Competition

Economic competition occurs when two or more sellers offer similar goods and services for sale in the marketplace. Each seller tries to do a better job than the other in order to attract more customers, make more sales, and earn more profits. Businesses compete with each other in many ways. They compete in the areas of price, quality, features, service, and new products.

In a market economy, **innovation** is the engine that sparks growth and prosperity. Innovation is the process of creating something—new or improved products and new ways to do things and solve problems.

Research and development (R&D) is the key to realizing the potential of innovation. It is an investment in the future. In simple terms, the innovator comes up with a new idea, explores its practicality, and turns it into a new product or service. Businesses, universities, and government agencies all participate in research and development, both independently and in cooperation with each other.

The U.S. invests more money in research and development than any other country in the world. This is one reason America is among the most prosperous nations. The same is true of businesses. Those that invest the most in research and development tend to be the most competitive and successful.

Technological advances are a major force in the creation of new products and services. **Technology** is the application of scientific knowledge to practical uses and product development, 1-5. Computers, cell phones, and fuel-efficient cars are examples of technological advances.

The companies providing the best products and services at the lowest prices generally achieve the highest sales and profits. Ideally, this results in higher quality at lower prices for consumers. Competition encourages competence and efficiency in the production and sale of goods and services.

Electronic products are a good example. Consider the development of personal media players that started out as simple audio players. Today you can use these players to view videos, text, photos, and lyrics. You can listen to and record FM radio, store data, and tell time. You get voice recording and computer interface. All these functions are contained in a player about the size of a credit card. You are getting more for your money with each new innovation. Most of this innovation was driven by competition and the profit motive.

There is also competition in the job market. The highest incomes go to the educated, trained, and skilled workers who produce the goods and services in greatest demand. This demand increases the competition among workers. They try to update their skills and education in order to qualify for better jobs, so they can then earn higher incomes and better benefits. This, in turn, improves a company's ability to compete.

Laws of Supply and Demand

These key principles—private ownership, free choice, profit motive, and competition—come together to create a dynamic, ever-changing economy. Individuals and families are free to act in their own best economic interests in the marketplace. By doing this, they make the economy work better for everyone.

Remember the economic challenges common to all societies? In short, the challenges are: what and how much to produce, how, and for whom. The U.S. economic system addresses these questions largely by letting the forces of supply and demand operate in competitive markets. **Supply** is the

1-5
New technology is constantly being developed, tested, and marketed to consumers.

Discuss

How have you seen competition work in school and business?

Discuss

What forms of competition can you identify in local businesses?

Reflect

How do you think competition in the job market will affect you? What are some ways you can prepare to compete?

Reflect

What abilities and talents do you possess that work to your advantage in competitive situations?

Resource

Laws of Supply and Demand, color lesson slide, TR

Linking to... Math

Graph Reading

A candy company sells 5,000 candy bars a day when they are priced at $1 each. When the company raises the price to $1.25, it sells 4,500 a day at the higher price.

Draw a graph and plot the coordinates. Approximately how many candy bars would they sell per day if they were priced at $1.50 each?

Note

Answer for *Linking to Math* is 4,000.

Discuss

How have prices for the following items changed over the past five years: gasoline, health care, new cars, movies, computers, TVs? How do price changes relate to supply and demand?

Resource

Local Economy in Action, Activity C, WB

Discuss

What examples can you name in which consumer demand led the way to a new product or service?

Activity

List goods and services that are produced largely in answer to consumer demand. How can consumers make their demands felt in the marketplace?

amount of a product or service producers are willing to provide. **Demand** is the quantity of a product or service consumers are willing to buy. Both supply and demand are closely connected to price.

For example, suppose you own a gym shoe company. When you price them at $80 a pair, you sell 1,000 pairs. At $40 each, you sell 3,000 pairs.

When the chart's coordinates are plotted on a graph and connected, they form a line called the *demand curve*. Price and demand move in opposite directions, so the curve has a negative slope. This illustrates *the law of demand*—the higher the price of a good or service, the less of it consumers will demand.

As a producer, you want to sell your goods for the highest possible price. If you think you can get $80 for each pair of sneakers, you would want to produce more. If you think you can only get $20 a pair, you would want to produce less.

When the chart's coordinates are plotted on a graph and connected, they form a line called the *supply curve*. Price and supply tend to move in the same direction, so the curve has a positive slope. This illustrates the *law of supply*—the higher the price of a good or service, the higher the quantity supplied by producers.

Equilibrium

The laws of supply and demand work together. When demand and supply are relatively balanced, the market is said to be in *equilibrium*. Equilibrium is the approximate point at which the supply and demand curves intersect, 1-6. It is the price at which the quantity supplied equals the quantity demanded. This is when the market is operating at maximum efficiency.

Equilibrium is more of an idea than a reality. Markets are usually not in equilibrium. Changes in supply or demand trigger price adjustments. When a price for a product is set too high, products stack up on store shelves. When a price is set too low, there are shortages.

What conditions might cause price to increase? Prices rise when the demand for an item is greater than the supply, or when demand rises and supply remains the same. For instance, airline ticket prices are highest during peak travel times. Seasonal foods become more expensive when the season ends and they become less plentiful. Food prices also rise when crops are lost to severe weather.

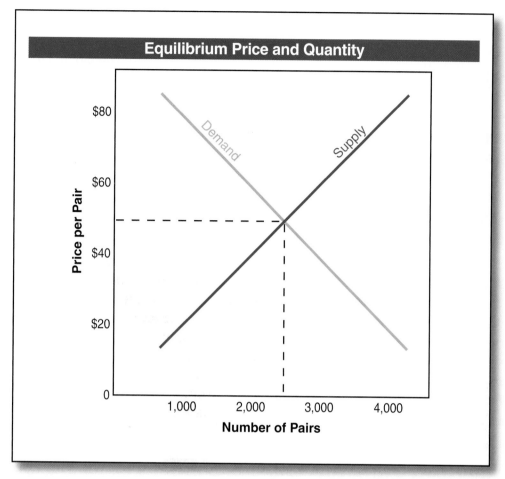

Equilibrium Price and Quantity

Demand

Supply

Price per Pair: $80, $60, $40, $20, 0

Number of Pairs: 1,000 2,000 3,000 4,000

What conditions might cause price to decrease? Prices fall when the supply for an item is greater than the demand, or when supply rises and demand remains the same. For instance, at the end of winter, the demand for coats and gloves drops. Stores drop prices and hold end-of-season clearance sales.

The Market's Answer to Scarcity

To a large extent, demand in the marketplace determines *what* and *how much is produced*. Demand is expressed by the spending choices of consumers, businesses, and governments. These choices, to a large degree, determine what and how much producers will bring to the marketplace. In many cases, consumer demand leads to new and improved products.

Businesses generally own and control productive resources. They determine the right mix of productive resources when they make products and deliver services to meet consumer demands. They determine *how to produce goods and services*.

The forces of supply and demand in the job market largely determine *how to divide the goods and services produced*. Those who can offer the skills, knowledge, materials, or capital needed for production receive income or profits. In job markets, those who have the qualifications to perform the work most in demand generally earn higher incomes and can buy more of the goods and services they need. This helps determine how production is divided.

Chapter Summary

You and other consumers carry out economic activities every day. These activities range from spending money to participating in the economic life of your community and government.

Needs and wants are unlimited, while the resources used to satisfy them are limited or scarce. Economists have defined four types of economic systems. Most economies, including that of the U.S., are mixed.

People, families, and governments make choices involving trade-offs and opportunity costs. These two concepts refer to what you give up when you choose one item over another.

In the economy of the U.S., the laws of supply and demand serve to answer the problem of scarcity. In the act of balancing supply and demand, the system determines what to produce, how, and for whom. Consumers play an important role in creating demand. Producers strive to meet demand and earn a profit doing it. The competition for profits in this system leads to the development of new and improved products.

Review

1. What are the four types of economic systems?

2. Why is the economic system of the U.S. a mixed economy?

3. Describe the concept of scarcity and how it applies to individuals, families, and government.

4. Why are human needs and wants unlimited?

5. What is the difference between human resources and nonhuman resources?

6. What three challenges caused by scarcity must all societies face?

7. What are the four basic concepts that drive the economy of the U.S.?

8. Why is innovation important in encouraging competition?

9. What is the relationship of trade-offs and opportunity cost?

10. Why would the U.S. economy falter if there was no opportunity to make a profit?

11. How do the laws of supply and demand relate to the prices of goods and services in the marketplace?

Critical Thinking

12. What can you gain by learning more about the economic system?

13. How do you and your family decide what needs and wants to satisfy? What trade-offs have you made in the marketplace? What were the opportunity costs of your trade-offs?

14. Suppose you started a service business such as babysitting or dog walking. Describe how you would assess the demand for your service.

Answers to Review

1. traditional, market, command, and mixed

2. It is based on a market economy with minimal government interference.

3. Wants and needs are unlimited while the resources to satisfy them are limited. This makes it necessary for individuals, families, and governments to make choices.

4. As people grow and move through life stages, their needs and wants change. Satisfying one need or want can create new needs and wants.

5. Human resources are qualities found within a person. Nonhuman resources are external resources such as time, money, equipment, or possessions.

6. what and how much to produce, how to allocate resources

15. Demonstrate the concept of scarcity in your own life. Make a list of items you want and need over the next five years of your life. What resources will you use to get what you want and need? Will you be able to satisfy all your wants? What compromises or trade-offs will you have to make? What will be some of the opportunity costs of your choices?

16. Interpret the following quote: "One person's wage increase is another person's price increase."

Academic Connections

17. **Social studies.** Invite an economist or another qualified authority to speak on the role of profits and competition in the U.S. economy.

18. **Reading, research.** Create a bulletin board of newspaper and magazine articles and advertisements illustrating different economic concepts in action.

19. **Research, writing, social studies.** Research a country that has a command economy to discover how industries develop and grow. Write a report of your findings.

20. **Writing.** Search the Internet for information on entrepreneurship at sites such as the U.S. Small Business Administration Teen Business Link (www.sba.gov/teens), National Foundation for Teaching Entrepreneurship (www.nfte.com), or Junior Achievement (http://studentcenter.ja.org). Gather information and write a "Do's and Don'ts" manual for a startup business.

Math Challenge

21. Justin graduates from high school in one month. He already has an offer for a full-time job that would pay $25,000 a year. He is also considering going to college for the next four years. Tuition is $8,000 a year. Room and board is $10,000 annually. If he works, he will not be able to make more than $3,000 a year doing part-time and summer work.
    A. What is the opportunity cost of attending college?
    B. What is the total cost of college?
    C. How many years would it take for college graduate Justin to catch up with the earnings of high school graduate Justin? On average, college graduates earn double what high school graduates earn.

Tech Smart

22. Use the Internet to research the economic system of each of the following countries. Write a report, including footnotes to the bibliography of your sources.
    - China
    - Cuba
    - Brazil
    - Congo

10. Profits provide the incentive to produce, work, and invest. It brings out the best efforts and performance from business and workers.

11. Price and supply tend to follow demand. When demand is greater than supply, prices go up; when supply is greater than demand, prices fall.

Answers to Math Challenge

21. A. Working for four years, Justin would earn $25,000 × 4 or $100,000. The opportunity cost of college would be $100,000 he could have earned if he had worked instead.
    B. A year of college would cost $18,000 – $3,000 for part-time work = $15,000 a year × 4 years = $60,000. The total cost is $60,000 plus the $100,000 he could have earned had he taken the job = $160,000.
    C. With a high school degree, Justin makes $25,000 annually. With a college degree, he would make $50,000 a year. $160,000 ÷ $25,000 = about 6 years.

in producing goods and services, and how to divide the goods and services produced

7. private ownership and control of productive resources, the profit motive, free economic choices, and competition

8. Innovation is the process of creating a new product or new ways to solve problems, and should result in higher quality. Businesses compete to produce the highest quality at the lowest prices to attract more customers.

9. A trade-off is an item that is given up in order to gain something else. Opportunity cost is the value of the best item or alternative given up.

Government and the Economy

Reading for Meaning

The summary at the end of the chapter highlights the most important concepts. Read the summary first. Then make sure you understand those concepts as you read the chapter.

business cycle

recession

depression

inflation

stagflation

labor force

unemployment rate

underemployment

fiscal policy

gross domestic product (GDP)

consumer price index (CPI)

labor union

monetary policy

Federal Reserve System

tax

deficit spending

national debt

perfect competition

monopoly

oligopoly

collusion

CHAPTER OBJECTIVES

After studying this chapter, you will be able to

- **diagram and explain** the four parts of the business cycle.

- **compare** and contrast recession, inflation, and stagflation.

- **describe** how the government uses fiscal and monetary policy to combat inflation and recession.

- **explain** the economic consequences of government taxingand spending.

- **explain** how the national debt hurts the economy.

- **describe** the government's role in promoting competition.

- **identify** the laws and government agencies that protect consumer interests.

Central Ideas

- The goal of government economic policies is to create economic stability and prosperity for its citizens.

- Government enacts laws and regulations to ensure fair competition and to protect the public well-being and safety.

- Government agencies at all levels of government assist and protect consumers by providing information, protection, and services.

The U.S. economic system is called a market or a free enterprise system. Compared with many other nations, the United States government plays a small role in the economy. However, the economy could not function without certain types of government participation.

For example, government provides the legal and institutional environment that permits and encourages economic activity. Government protects individual liberties and private property rights and enforces contractual agreements. It provides the political stability and the *rule of law* that are necessary for economic prosperity. This is what enables individuals and businesses to carry out productive economic activities.

Government plays these specific roles in the operation of our economy:

- It sets economic policies in an effort to create stability and prosperity.

- It makes tax and spending decisions in response to economic conditions.

- It controls the money supply.

- It regulates business and economic activity to ensure fair business practices and to protect public well-being and safety.

The following section explores these government functions in greater detail.

Economic Conditions Monitored by the Government

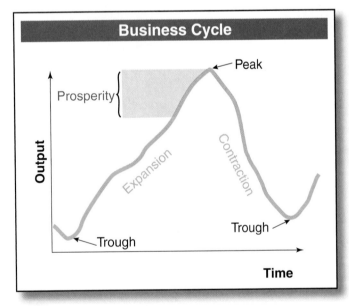

2-1

One business cycle consists of the time from one trough to the next.

The U.S. economy fluctuates between periods of economic growth and slowdown. This is true of economies in other industrialized nations as well. The term **business cycle** describes these ups and downs, 2-1. Some economists prefer the term *business fluctuations* because there are not predictable patterns to the ups and downs. The business cycle has four parts.

- *Contraction* is a period of slow or no growth.

- *Trough* occurs when a contraction stops.

- *Recovery* is the period when business activity begins to grow again.

- *Peak* is the height of recovery and lasts until growth begins to slow again. Then the cycle starts all over again.

Each period can last months or even years. For example, the longest economic expansion in modern U.S. history occurred during the 1990s and lasted 10 years. However, the average length of an expansion is about three years. Economists use measurements, or *indicators*, to figure out how the economy is doing and to try to predict its direction.

The following sections describe the most serious problems of a troubled economy.

Recession and Depression

When the business cycle starts a downward trend, people fear a **recession**, which is an extended period of slow or no economic growth. Technically a recession exists if negative growth lasts two quarters or more. (The business year is divided into four three-month quarters.) A recession is marked by

- high unemployment

- a decline in retail sales

- lowered average personal incomes

- decreases in consumer spending

- reduced spending by businesses on plants, equipment, and expansion

Overall economic activity declines. People lose their jobs and businesses fail. It may also be difficult to obtain a mortgage for a home, or to start a new business. When a recession goes on for several years, which is rare, the economy is said to be in a **depression**.

During the Great Depression of the 1930s, one out of four workers was unemployed. Pay cuts were common among those who had jobs. People lost their savings and investments. There was mass hunger, homelessness, and migrations of people across the country looking for work. It lasted for almost ten years. More recently, in 2008, the economy went into a recession and again many people lost their jobs and homes, businesses failed, and the value of savings and investments fell dramatically.

Inflation

Inflation is an overall increase in the price of goods and services. It threatens the nation's prosperity because it decreases the value of a dollar. Due to inflation, today's dollars buy less than last year's dollars.

For example, in 2006, a family that made an income of $65,000 could buy $65,000 worth of goods and services. However, in 2009, they would need $69,434 to buy the same goods and services. That extra $4,000 is the impact of inflation. The CPI Inflation Calculator at the Web site of the U.S. Department of Labor's Bureau of Labor Statistics calculates the cost of inflation. It is at http://data.bls.gov/cgi-bin/cpicalc.pl.

According to government data, the U.S. inflation rate is fairly low compared with the rates of other countries. For example, in 2008, the estimated rate of inflation in the U.S. was 4.2 percent. However, in India it was estimated at 7.8 percent. In Russia, it was about 14 percent, and in Iran it was 28 percent. Inflation is especially hard on individuals and families who live on fixed incomes. Income stays the same over the years, while costs climb. There are several types of inflation.

Discuss

What actions can the federal government take to stimulate the economy during a recession?

Reflect

How might inflation affect you and your family?

Enrich

Research the economic recession in 2008. Use the Internet to locate news articles from reputable sources. Create a timeline of events before, during, and after the recession.

Vocabulary

Compare and contrast *demand-pull inflation* and *cost-push inflation.*

Enrich

Use the Internet to research the episode of stagflation that took place in the 1970s.

Demand-Pull Inflation

This type of inflation occurs during the recovery and peak periods of the business cycle. When the economy is growing, consumers are more likely to be employed and have spending money. Spending increases at a faster rate than supply. Put another way, there are too many dollars chasing too few goods. According to the laws of supply and demand, as demand goes up, so do prices.

Cost-Push Inflation

This type of inflation is triggered by an increase in the price of a widely used good. For example, when the price of oil rises, consumers pay more for fuel to power their cars and heat their homes. Many other goods and services—from food and flowers to building materials and airfares—increase in price as well. This is because so many businesses require fuel to operate and bring goods to market. Petroleum is also an ingredient in many products, particularly plastic.

Stagflation

Stagflation describes a period of slow growth (economic stagnation) and high inflation. The best-known episode of stagflation took place during the 1970s. Oil producers raised oil prices that triggered inflation as the costs of many goods and services rose. This occurred at a time of slow growth and high unemployment.

Impact of Unemployment and Underemployment

A nation's prosperity and stability depend on full use of its productive resources, including the labor force. This is one of the goals government seeks to achieve through its economic policies. The **labor force** is composed of people, age 16 and over, who are employed or looking for and able to work.

The **unemployment rate** is the percentage of the labor force that is out of work and seeking employment. That percentage fluctuated between 4 percent and almost 10 percent over the past 30 years, 2-2. Unemployment figures are closely tied to business fluctuations. The highest unemployment rates occur during periods of contraction.

Unemployment hurts workers and their families. When the family breadwinner is unemployed, the entire family suffers. Some families must move because they lose their homes or cannot afford to make rent payments. Some people go into debt and lose health benefits that are usually provided through an employer. Unemployment is also associated with health problems such as stress-related illnesses, depression, and substance abuse. There are several types of unemployment that economists consider.

Government & Public Administration

Labor Economists
Labor economists study changes in the supply and demand for labor. They analyze reasons for unemployment, identify factors that influence the labor market, and collect data on wages. Labor economists usually work for the government.

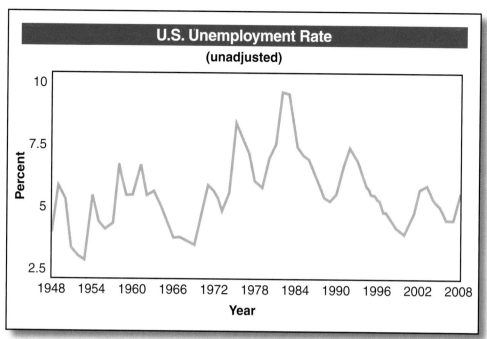

U.S. Unemployment Rate
(unadjusted)

Bureau of Labor Statistics

2-2

The U.S. Department of Labor keeps track of the civilian unemployment rate.

Frictional Unemployment

This is short-term unemployment that affects people who are between jobs. These are people who have moved or changed jobs or careers. They can often find employment by matching their qualifications to available jobs. Some workers will be temporarily unemployed even in a strong and growing economy.

Structural Unemployment

Structural unemployment tends to be long-term, difficult to correct, and the most damaging to both workers and the economy. It refers to unemployment among workers who drop out of the labor force or do not enter. There may be a mismatch between their skills and available jobs. Often the old jobs were moved to cheaper labor markets or eliminated by new technology.

Cyclical Unemployment

Cyclical unemployment is tied to the business cycle. It occurs when the economy slows or is in a recession. Workers are laid off. When the economy moves into the recovery phase, workers are rehired.

Seasonal Unemployment

Finally, there is *seasonal unemployment* that is related to jobs that depend on seasonal activities. This includes the extra workers hired for the holidays, for vacation season, and for crop harvesting. Seasonal jobs end when the short-term demand for workers ceases.

Enrich

Research the highest rate of unemployment in the last five years. What economic factors contributed to a high unemployment rate?

Activity

The unemployment rate in September of 2009 was 9.8%. Plot annual rates from 2009 to the present.

Vocabulary

Explain the difference between *frictional unemployment* and *structural unemployment*.

Discuss

List jobs affected by seasonal unemployment. Rank the jobs in the order of predominance in your community.

Note

The underemployment rate is also referred to as *U6* and is considered the broadest measure of unemployment.

Reflect

Do you know anyone who is unemployed? What are the challenges of unemployment?

Discuss

How does unemployment affect the economy?

Discuss

How do teens contribute to GDP?

Underemployment

In addition to the unemployed, a percentage of the labor force will be *underemployed*. **Underemployment** refers to workers who are employed only part time or who are "over qualified" for their jobs. They are the skilled workers who hold jobs requiring few skills. Some of these workers are underemployed by choice, but most cannot find work at their skill or educational level.

Continuing prosperity and stability require the workforce and other productive resources to be employed at full capacity. This is one of the goals government seeks to achieve through its economic policies.

Factors Affecting Economic Policies

The economy is incredibly complex and difficult to understand and predict. The primary and difficult challenge for government is to soften the ups and downs of the economy. Government policies are intended to increase growth and employment and to keep inflation low. Another goal of government, covered in Chapter 4, is to ensure the proper balance of trade in world markets.

Fiscal Policy

Fiscal policy refers to the federal government's taxing and spending decisions. Government often uses fiscal policy to stimulate the economy in periods of recession and high unemployment. Fiscal policy can also slow economic activity in periods of inflation or rising prices. The government's taxing and spending decisions are made in Congress. They are driven by economic indicators and analysis of the economy.

Gross Domestic Product

The economy is described in terms of many indicators. The best measure of economic growth is the gross domestic product (GDP). The **gross domestic product** measures the value of all goods and services produced by a nation during a specified period. The real GDP is the GDP adjusted for inflation.

The GDP includes the following:

- *personal consumption expenditures*—consumer spending
- *gross private domestic investment*—money businesses invest in buildings, equipment, technology, innovation, and inventory
- *net exports of goods and services*—the value of the goods and services exported minus the value of goods and services imported from other countries
- *government consumption expenditures and gross investment*—government spending

The U.S. Department of Commerce's Bureau of Economic Analysis (BEA) calculates the GDP each quarter. The growth or decline in production is measured by the change in the real GDP from one quarter to the next. Although the GDP is calculated quarterly, it is expressed as an annual rate.

For example, the chart in 2-3 shows the GDP figures from the first quarter of 2007 until the second quarter of 2009. The drop in GDP at the end of 2008 reflects the severe economic problems the U.S. was experiencing. At the end of 2008, GDP decreased at an annual rate of 6.3 percent. This was the largest drop in GDP in a quarter century.

A falling GDP indicates a weakening economy. When the GDP declines for two or more consecutive quarters, the economy is said to be in recession. A rising GDP indicates economic growth, or the beginning of a recovery from recession. An unexpected spurt in GDP may indicate that the economy is overheating and inflation could result.

Gross Domestic Product		
(billions of dollars)		
Seasonally adjusted at annual rates		
Year	Quarter	GDP
2007	1	13,795.60
	2	13,997.20
	3	14,179.90
	4	14,337.90
2008	1	14,373.90
	2	14,497.80
	3	14,546.70
	4	14,347.30
2009	1	14,178.00
	2	14,143.30

U.S. Bureau of Economic Analysis—Rev. 8/27/09

2-3

The GDP is shown in billions of dollars. Note the drop in GDP starting in the fourth quarter of 2008.

Consumer Price Index

The **consumer price index (CPI)** measures the movement of prices. It is a measure of the average change in prices over time for selected goods and services. It sometimes is called the "cost of living index." The CPI measures price changes for a bundle of goods and services purchased by average consumers against the prices for the same goods and services in a base period.

Here is how it works. The base period, which is 1982 through 1984, has an index number of 100. Price movements are stated as a percentage change from that index number. For example, the August 2008 CPI for all items was 214.46. This means $2.14 was needed in 2008 to buy what would have cost $1.00 in 1983.

The CPI measures price changes by collecting data from over 57,000 households and 19,000 establishments in 85 areas across the country. A weakness in the CPI is that it does not include real estate prices, income tax and other taxes, or social security paid by individuals and businesses. These expenses represent some of the greatest price increases for consumers.

The CPI is used to measure cost of living changes and to adjust wages for workers who are covered by *collective bargaining* agreements. These are contracts between employers and labor unions. A **labor union** is a group of workers who unite to negotiate with employers over issues such as pay, health care, and working conditions. CPI is also used to determine increases in social security and pension benefits to reflect cost of living increases.

Activity

List goods commonly purchased by teens. Research the average price of each item today. Then research the average price of each item 15 years ago. How have prices changed?

Linking to... History

Adam Smith and John Maynard Keynes

Two economists instrumental in shaping modern economics were Adam Smith (1723-1790) and John Maynard Keynes (1883-1946). The ideas of Smith and Keynes continue to foster debate about the role of government in the economy today.

Adam Smith lived at the dawn of the industrial revolution. Previously, most people lived in rural areas and produced most of what they needed themselves. The industrial revolution brought people to cities to work in factories. Factory workers became part of an assembly line, each specializing in a small task that contributed to a finished product.

In his book, *The Wealth of Nations*, Smith hailed specialization, or *division of labor,* that created greater economic efficiency, mass production, and markets for goods. He argued that a free market economic system was superior to other systems because it harnessed a powerful force that motivated people: self-interest. In a free market economy, people have the freedom to do what is best for themselves and wind up doing what is best for the economy.

For example, in order to maximize profits, producers avoid wasting resources. To increase earnings, workers learn new skills. This give and take between people acting in their own self-interest is the "invisible hand" that runs the economy. Smith opposed government interference in the economy.

John Maynard Keynes witnessed WWI and the Great Depression. He and others saw the depression as a failure of Smith's "invisible hand" theory. The economy was damaged and only government intervention saved it. New government programs created jobs and stimulated the economy. Spending on WWII created new demand that finally lifted the U.S. out of the depression.

In his book, *The General Theory of Employment, Interest, and Money,* Keynes argued that economic stability and prosperity depends on government playing a role in the economy.

Enrich

Research the government response to the recession in 2008 and 2009. What actions did the government take to stimulate the economy?

Fiscal Policy During Periods of Recession and Inflation

As mentioned earlier, a recession is a period of slowing economic activity. Overall economic activity declines. To stimulate demand for goods and services during a recession, government takes actions to increase the amount of money in circulation. With more money available, economic activity tends to expand. Government may increase spending to stimulate the economy. It may also lower taxes to leave more money for consumers and businesses to spend, which also increases demand. Businesses expand to meet the increased demand. Economic growth and expansion results.

Inflation occurs when demand is greater than supply. Increased demand drives up the prices of limited supplies. To combat inflation, government may increase taxes and reduce its own spending. This takes money out of circulation, reduces demand, and slows economic activity. Such action should help control inflation and bring prices down.

Monetary Policy

Monetary policy refers to actions the *Federal Reserve Board* takes to change the supply of money and credit. The *Federal Reserve Board* is part of the **Federal Reserve System**, also called the *Fed*. Created by Congress in 1913, this system is comprised of the Board, 12 Federal Reserve Banks, and the Federal Open Market Committee. The Fed regulates the nation's money supply and banking system. It uses the following three tools to manage the supply of money and credit.

Reserve Requirements

The level of reserves mandated by the Fed is the cash that banks and other financial institutions must set aside rather than lend to customers. It is expressed as a percent of their deposits. For example, suppose the reserve requirement is 10 percent. A bank that has $10 million in deposits from its customers can only lend $9 million. The other million must stay on deposit. High reserve requirements reduce the amount of money available for lending. As a result, the supply of money and credit falls. Low reserve requirements have the opposite results.

Discount Rate

The *discount rate* is the interest rate Federal Reserve Banks charge commercial banks for credit when they borrow. This affects the rates that banks charge consumers and businesses. A high discount rate discourages bank borrowing and reduces lending activities. This lowers the amount of money in circulation. Low discount rates have the opposite effect. One of the first steps the Fed takes to address an economic slowdown is to lower the discount rate. This makes credit available at a lower cost and permits businesses to expand and consumers to buy more goods and services. In periods of inflation the Fed is likely to increase the discount rate.

Open Market Operations

Open market operations refer to the Fed's buying or selling of Treasury securities in the marketplace. Treasury securities are debt obligations of the U.S. Treasury that include treasury bonds, notes, and bills. When the Fed buys these securities it increases the money supply. When the Fed sells government securities, the money supply shrinks because the dollars paid for these securities are no longer in circulation.

Easy Versus Tight Money

When the Fed follows an "easy" monetary policy, money and credit are readily available. Interest rates are relatively low. Under these conditions, consumers and businesses tend to spend. They buy or build more homes when interest rates for home mortgages are lower. Companies borrow more money for expanding their businesses. Entrepreneurs borrow

Vocabulary

Differentiate between *fiscal policy* and *monetary policy.*

Enrich

Research the names and locations of the 12 Federal Reserve Banks.

Enrich

Interview a representative of a local financial institution to learn how reserve requirements govern operations of the institution.

Enrich

Find recent examples of government's fiscal and monetary decisions. Discuss the impact of government actions.

money to start new businesses. Farmers borrow to buy machinery and land to produce more crops. All of these activities stimulate the economy and create jobs. However, if too much money is pumped into the economy through Federal Reserve policies, inflation may result.

In times of inflation, the Fed turns to "tight" monetary policy. It increases reserve requirements, raises the discount rate, and sells government securities. These actions reduce the money supply and discourage the use of credit. As economic activity slows, price increases tend to level off or fall.

It may sound simple for the Fed to speed up or slow down the economy, but maintaining a balance between supply and demand is no easy task. All the parts in the puzzle are constantly changing. When facing stagflation, the Fed's job becomes even more challenging. If it tightens the money supply, which is the sure cure for inflation, it risks further slowing the already depressed economy. In addition, it can take months for monetary policies to bring about the desired changes. Finding the right balance and the right timing is critical and complicated. Government policymakers must be extremely careful in wielding their power.

Sometimes the government enacts policies that make a bad situation worse. For example, during part of the 1930s, the government followed a tight monetary policy. Some economists say this policy may have led to a deepening of economic troubles that became the Great Depression. The Depression did not end until the government pumped millions of dollars into the economy through a vast jobs program. The entry of the U.S. into World War II boosted demand for military weapons, uniforms, machinery, and many other goods and services that created jobs and economic growth.

Overall, government fiscal and monetary policies moderate the ups and downs in the business cycle. The government's goal is to create longer periods of prosperity with less severe downturns and upswings in the economy. The government's attempts to control recession and inflation are outlined in 2-4.

Taxing and Spending

Government taxing and spending decisions make a significant impact on the overall economy. These decisions determine the amount of taxes individuals and businesses will pay. The decisions also determine the services that government will provide in return.

The circular flow diagram of the economy in 2-5 is similar to one presented in the previous chapter. However, this diagram incorporates the government's role. The inner circles, in black, show how government participates in the flow of goods and services as well as money. Producers/sellers provide goods and services to government and receive payment in return. Consumers/workers provide labor and capital for government and receive payment in return. Producers/sellers and consumers/workers receive programs, goods, and services from government for which they pay taxes. A **tax** is a fee imposed by government on income, products, or activities, and paid by citizens and businesses.

Fiscal and Monetary Policies			
Economic Conditions	**Likely Fiscal Policy**	**Likely Monetary Policy**	**Expected Results**
Inflation– A period of rising prices.	• Increase tax rates leaving consumers and business less to spend. • Reduce government spending to cut the amount of cash flowing into the system.	• Raise reserve requirements, so less money and less credit are available. • Increase the discount rate, making credit more expensive. • Sell government securities, drawing money out of circulation.	• Lower credit availability. • Less money in circulation. • Reduced spending. • Lower demand. • Falling production. • Slowing economy.
Recession– A period of economic slowdown and unemployment.	• Lower taxes, giving consumers and businesses more money to spend. • Increase government spending to pump more money into the economy.	• Lower reserve requirements, permitting banks to lend more money. • Lower the discount rate, making credit more affordable. • Buy government securities, pumping money into the economy.	• Increase availability of money and credit, which increases spending, which increases demand, which increases production, which leads to business expansion and jobs.

2-4

The government uses fiscal and monetary policies to alter economic conditions.

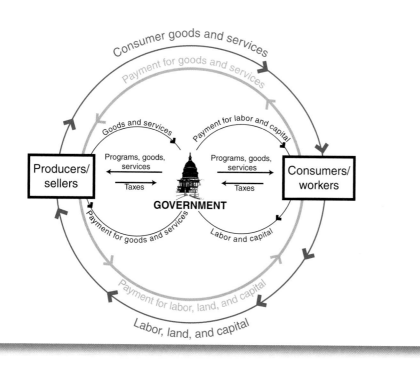

2-5

A circular flow of goods, services, and money takes place within the economy. This chart shows how government participates.

Enrich

Find out what tax laws were passed by the legislature and presented for the president's signature in recent years. Discuss their impact on taxpayers, business, and the economy.

Resource

It's the Law, Activity A, WB

Discuss

How do you feel about government redistribution of income? What needs do you think we should pay for in this manner?

Tax revenues pay for government operations. These include expenses connected with Congress, the court system, presidential offices, law enforcement, and a host of federal agencies and commissions. Taxes also pay for public goods and services that private citizens and businesses cannot or do not produce. At the federal level, these include national defense, social welfare programs, education, highways, transit systems, environmental protection, and certain areas of research and development.

At the local and state levels, tax revenues pay for government operations and for public goods and services closer to home. These include schools, libraries, hospitals, roads, airports, parks, and fire and police protection. Citizens and businesses "buy" these goods and services from government with tax dollars.

Government spending of tax revenues creates demand for goods and services. For example, government pays for public schools with tax dollars. Private contractors build the schools with materials produced by private industries. This spending feeds money into the system, creates demand for goods and services, sparks business activity, and creates jobs.

During periods of inflation, government spending has a negative impact on the economy. It increases demand in the marketplace. When the combined demands of government and consumers are greater than the economy's capacity to produce, prices go up. This is why reductions in government spending help fight inflation by reducing demand.

Redistribution of Income

When government chooses to tax those who have more money to provide for those who have less, it redistributes income. One way to achieve this goal is through a *progressive tax*. This means those with higher incomes pay a higher rate of tax than those with lower incomes. The federal income tax system is progressive.

The government redistributes income through *transfer payments*. Transfer payments include income and benefits that the government provides for individuals and households in the form of social programs. The three most prominent programs are Social Security, unemployment compensation, and Temporary Assistance to Needy Families (TANF). These benefits are paid largely by taxing those who do not receive them.

A *subsidy* is a form of transfer payment that gives financial assistance to a business or entity, such as the arts, education, or health care. It may come in the form of a direct payment, a tax benefit, or some other advantage. The government pays billions of dollars in subsidies each year. The principal goal of subsidies is to benefit the public in some way.

For example, government may subsidize small farmers so they can compete with corporate-owned farms. A subsidy paid to milk producers guarantees them a reasonable profit and ensures a supply of milk for consumers. Many farmers who grow subsidized crops—including corn, wheat, cotton, soybeans, and rice—also get checks from the government. The flow of money in these cases is from taxpayers to those receiving the payments.

Deficit Spending and the National Debt

Often the cost of government programs and services is greater than the tax revenues it collects. Just as consumers borrow or use credit to pay their bills, the government borrows money to cover its expenses. The money is raised by the sale of Treasury and savings bonds to individuals, companies, and foreign countries.

Deficit spending is the amount the federal government spends each year beyond the amount it receives in revenues. When the government receives more than it spends, it is called a *surplus*.

Over the years, deficit spending and government borrowing have created a huge debt. Each year's deficit increases this debt. The **national debt** is the total amount of money the government owes at a given time. Like consumers, the government must pay interest, or fees, to borrow money.

The money paid in debt interest leaves less to pay for health care, education, environmental protection, defense, or other needs. When government borrows excessively, there is less credit available for business expansion, home mortgages, and other business and consumer needs. Dollars spent by government are dollars that are not available to the private sector where growth generally is created.

You and other taxpayers end up paying for the debt. As government spending and debt increase, revenues and taxes must also increase. High levels of government spending and national debt threaten future economic growth and represent a huge burden on future generations.

It is critical to keep a healthy balance between government participation and private enterprise if the U.S. economy is to stay a free market economy.

Vocabulary

Define deficit spending and describe its economic consequences.

Note

Investigate how federal government revenues, expenditures, and debt have changed over the past 10 years. Was it more or less than you expected?

Discuss

Can you give examples of government involvement in the areas of regulation, taxation and spending, and economic policy?

ECONOMICS in ACTION

The National Debt

In 2008, total federal, state, and local government spending came to more than 36 percent of GDP. The interest on this debt was one of the largest expense items in the federal budget. It came to approximately $261 billion or 9 percent of the federal budget. This amount was three times more than the amount spent on education, training, and employment.

After 2008, the deficit soared much higher. In 2009, the Congressional Budget Office predicted the deficit would be more than $1.8 trillion. The office predicted annual deficits of more than $1 trillion for years to come.

A growing national debt burdens both government and citizens. Eventually, taxpayers must pay for the debt.

Discuss

What is the appropriate level of government regulation? Discuss the cost/benefit relationship of regulations.

Enrich

Find out current corporate compliance rates in various areas. Compare them to rates in other years. How do such costs affect business operations?

Reflect

How have these laws directly affected you?

Vocabulary

Define the terms *perfect competition, monopoly,* and *oligopoly*. Discuss their meanings under the antitrust laws.

Enrich

Find examples of local monopolies and discuss how they differ from businesses that must compete.

Government Regulations

Almost every phase of business and economic activity falls under some form of government regulation. For instance, the simple hamburger sold across the nation is subject to thousands of local, state, and federal regulations. Rules cover everything—fat content of the meat, ingredients in the ketchup, advertising slogans, hiring practices, wages, restaurant inspections, disposal of trash, etc.

The earliest regulations were drafted mainly to promote fair competition and to ensure public well-being and safety. The regulations focused on preventing practices that interfered with fair competition. They were also aimed at protecting consumers from unfair and possibly harmful practices in the marketplace.

Fair Competition

Free competition is one of the hallmarks of a market economy. It works best when there are many sellers offering similar products. Competition between producers results in greater innovation, better service, and lower prices for consumers. It also results in the most efficient allocation of resources for the economy. This type of market structure is called **perfect competition**. It exists as a goal but is never fully achieved.

The opposite of perfect competition is monopoly. **Monopoly** refers to a single seller or producer of a given product or service. Since it has no competition, a monopoly business can charge high prices. There is little incentive to improve production efficiency or the products and services themselves.

Another threat to perfect competition is oligopoly. **Oligopoly** occurs when a few large companies dominate an industry. Oligopolies today include the music, communications, and automobile industries, among others.

The *antitrust laws* were passed to promote competition and fair trade and to prevent trade restraints in the marketplace. The best-known antitrust laws are

- The *Sherman Antitrust Act of 1890* prohibiting monopolies.

- The *Clayton Antitrust Act of 1914* prohibiting price fixing and other unfair trade practices.

- The *Federal Trade Commission Act of 1914* creating the Federal Trade Commission. This commission was given the power to investigate unfair or deceptive trade practices and to enforce compliance with lawful practices.

Although monopoly is illegal, exceptions have been made for some industries. For example, cable television companies were allowed to monopolize cable service in particular areas. It was impractical to have two or more companies rigging wires and cables throughout a community. Also when a drug company develops a new product, it becomes the sole provider of the drug for a period of time. During this period of no competition, the company earns high profits. In this way, it is reimbursed for the costly process of bringing a new drug to market.

Oligopoly is legal, but the companies in an oligopoly are not allowed to make secret agreements among themselves. This is called **collusion**. Companies often collude to shut out smaller competitors and to engage in *price fixing*. Price fixing occurs when two or more businesses in an industry agree to sell at a set price and eliminate competition.

The Public's Well-being and Safety

In 1906 the Congress passed laws regulating the labeling of food and drugs and to ensure that meat was inspected before it could be sold. In 1913 the Federal Reserve System was established to oversee banking activities.

The Great Depression of the 1930s brought widespread unemployment and business failures. In response Congress passed new laws that increased government's power to intervene in the economy. New legislation provided for unemployment benefits, retirement income, and insured bank deposits. It also regulated the sale of securities and gave workers the right to form unions, 2-6.

Government involvement in the economy continues to grow. Today we have more than 100 regulatory agencies. Regulations that ensure public well-being and safety include laws in the areas of:

- equal opportunity
- fair labor practices
- workplace safety
- environmental protection

Activity

Complete the sentence "There ought to be a law..." with a description of specific protection consumers need today. Discuss answers in class.

Activity

Contact your representative's office for information on the progression of a bill from proposal to enactment.

Note

Investigate how the administrative costs of federal government regulation have increased in the last 30 years. Why is this?

Enrich

Trace the history of government regulation in one of the areas listed on pages 53 and 54 over the past 25 years.

Enrich

Investigate and discuss consumer protection legislation at the state and local levels.

2-6

The National Labor Relations Act of 1935 gave workers the right to form unions. Unions help workers, such as assembly line employees, achieve fair wages and good working conditions.

Government & Public Administration

Elected Representatives— State or Federal

Representatives are elected officials who serve as legislators at the state or federal level. They serve a leadership role in government by making decisions, analyzing government regulations and policies, and enacting new laws and regulations.

- pure foods, drugs, and cosmetics
- product safety
- truth in advertising and labeling
- truth in lending and saving

The Food and Drug Administration, the Environmental Protection Agency, the Consumer Product Safety Commission, and many other government agencies administer these regulations.

Costs of Regulation

Government regulations have a major impact on the economy. For example, every phase of the auto industry is regulated by government, from the manufacturer to your local service garage. Regulations cover working conditions, employee benefits, car warranties, auto servicing, registration and licensing, insurance, and advertising. Important and necessary as they are, federally mandated safety features, pollution controls, and fuel economy requirements add hundreds of dollars to the price of a new car.

Federal laws are passed by Congress in the U.S. Capitol, and signed into law by the President, 2-7. Regulations may be necessary to protect consumers and to ensure fair business practices. However, as the number of regulations and regulatory agencies increases, so does the cost to government, business, and ultimately consumers.

The scope of regulations and the paperwork required also add to the cost of regulating. Historically, government regulations were directed at a specific product or industry. Today, laws, such as the Occupational Safety and Health Act (OSHA) and the Consumer Product Safety Act (CPSA), apply to almost every existing business and product. Overall regulations also require more record keeping and paperwork than in the past.

Complying with government regulations is costly for businesses. Some question the wisdom of regulations that severely restrict industries from remaining competitive. In 2005 small firms with 20 or fewer employees paid an average annual cost of $7,647 per employee to comply with federal regulations. For larger businesses with 500 or more employees, compliance costs were $5,282 per employee. This does not include government expenses for enforcement and for the agencies created to enforce laws.

The impact of both inflation and recession is greater when excessive regulations cut into productivity and dramatically add to the cost of doing business.

2-7

Legislators present bills to be enacted in the Capitol where they are voted upon by Congress and then presented to the President to be signed into law.

Case Study: Government Regulation

Jake's Bread Factory

Jake worked for many years in a bakery. Eventually, he opened his own business. He baked high-quality breads and rolls. The business was successful and demand soared.

Jake wants to enlarge his plant, buy improved equipment, and hire more help to increase production. However, the expansion will make his business subject to more government regulations:

- Mandatory safety equipment and materials.
- Employee health and retirement benefits.
- New content and nutritional labeling.
- Packaging specifications.
- More inspections by the city health department.
- Additional and more detailed record keeping connected with these regulations.

Jake will have to raise prices to cover the costs associated with the additional regulations. If the demand for bread falls, the cost of meeting the regulations may become too high. He might be forced to close his business. If Jake decides not to expand, the jobs he would have created and the increased productivity will not benefit the economy.

Case Review

1. Regulations ensure Jake uses wholesome ingredients and is fair and honest with employees and customers. How much and what type of regulation do you feel is necessary to achieve these goals?
2. Some people argue for more regulations, stronger consumer protection, and broader government powers. How do you feel? What evidence can you find to support or oppose this position?
3. Critics of government regulations claim the cost is too high. They argue money spent to comply with regulations reduces the amount available for capital improvements. The cost is ultimately passed on to consumers in the form of higher prices. How do you feel? What evidence can you find to support or oppose your view?

Health Science

Occupational Health and Safety Specialists

Occupational health and safety specialists inspect workplaces and recommend ways to reduce and eliminate disease or injury. They look for biological, chemical, physical, and radiological hazards and identify ways to increase workers' safety. Specialists are employed by federal, state, and local government agencies.

Government Agencies Serving Consumers

Government agencies assist consumers by establishing and enforcing laws and regulations at the local, state, and federal levels. They protect consumers from unsafe products and unethical business practices. They represent consumer interests in many areas.

At the local and state levels, government agencies provide information, protection, and many other services. The agencies regulate food standards and sanitation practices, credit and insurance transactions, and business and trade practices. They also govern the licensing and certification of such groups as medical professionals, hospitals, nursing homes, funeral homes, lawyers, and others who serve the public.

Following is a list of several key federal government agencies with a brief description of their primary functions. All of these agencies have Web sites that fully describe their functions and services.

The *Department of Agriculture (USDA)* is one of the largest federal agencies. Its various departments and services relate to food production, economics, and international trade. In the interests of consumers, the USDA researches the nutrient content of food and ways to improve the quality and food safety of crops and livestock. It also provides food assistance to needy consumers and nutrition education to the public.

The *Department of Energy (DOE)* works toward a reliable, affordable, and clean energy supply for the nation. To achieve that goal, current programs focus on: biomass research and development, alternative energy sources such as wind and solar, and the potential of clean coal power. Other DOE priorities include the development of non-petroleum fuel sources for vehicles and better fuel economy, and more energy-efficient homes, appliances, and electronics.

The *Department of Labor (DOL)* promotes the welfare of wage earners, improves working conditions, and advances employment opportunities. This department enforces labor laws that include minimum wage, child labor, anti-discrimination, maximum working hours, and safety and health regulations. It also administers the Bureau of Labor Statistics and the Occupational Safety and Health Administration (OSHA).

The *Department of Health and Human Services (HHS)* serves the needs of citizens from birth to old age through a variety of programs and assistance. It administers financial aid programs, promotes public health, and works to control drug and alcohol abuse. HHS supervises and coordinates the work of many offices including the Centers for Medicare & Medicaid, the Office of Public Health and Science, the National Institutes of Health, the Centers for Disease Control and Prevention, and the Food and Drug Administration.

The *Food and Drug Administration (FDA)* protects the public against impure and unsafe foods, drugs, cosmetics, and other hazards. It operates national centers for drug evaluation and research, food safety and applied nutrition, and veterinary medicine.

The *Social Security Administration (SSA)* manages the federal government's retirement, survivors and disability insurance, and the supplemental security income programs.

The *Department of Housing and Urban Development (HUD)* supervises programs related to housing needs, fair housing opportunities, and community development. It administers mortgage insurance to promote home ownership, rental assistance for low- and moderate-income families, housing safety standards, urban renewal programs, and federal real estate laws.

The *Consumer Product Safety Commission (CPSC)* protects the public against risk of injury from consumer and children's products, 2-8. It sets safety standards for products and researches the causes and prevention of product-related injuries and deaths.

The *Federal Trade Commission (FTC)* promotes free and fair competition by preventing deceptive practices, false advertising, and unfair trade practices in the marketplace. It enforces consumer protection legislation in a variety of areas including consumer credit transactions, packaging and labeling, product warranties, and truth in advertising.

The *Securities and Exchange Commission (SEC)* enforces fair and full disclosure of financial data about securities being offered for sale. The SEC also protects investors against fraud when buying or selling securities. It regulates security exchanges and associations, investment companies, brokers, dealers, and investment counselors.

The *U.S. Department of the Treasury* manages the finances of the federal government. It collects taxes and other payments that are owed to the government. It pays the nation's bills, borrows money if necessary, prints and distributes currency, regulates national banks, guards the country's gold and silver, and investigates financial crimes and crimes involving the use and distribution of alcohol and tobacco.

The *Federal Communications Commission (FCC)* regulates communications by telephone, television, radio, cable, wire, and satellite.

Specific Laws Protecting Consumers

In addition to the many agencies that serve and protect consumers, a host of federal, state, and local laws addresses consumer protection. A few of the many federal laws that protect you and all consumers in the marketplace include:

- Product Packaging Protection Act of 2002
- Fair and Accurate Credit Transactions Act of 2003
- Food Allergen Labeling and Consumer Protection Act of 2004
- Bankruptcy Abuse Prevention and Consumer Protection Act of 2005
- Dietary Supplement and Nonprescription Drug Consumer Protection Act of 2006

With all this government protection and regulation, abuses and unfair play still exist in the marketplace, though they are not the rule. Most businesses, like most people, want to do the right thing. Still, new ways to work the system with advantages to the seller at the expense of the consumer will continue to surface. When you enter the marketplace, be prepared to use your best judgment.

Reflect

What government regulations have affected you as an employee?

Resource

Government Agencies and *Their Functions*, Activity C, WB

Reflect

When have your consumer interests been served and protected by a federal government agency?

Resource

Chapter 2: Government and the Economy, Teacher's PowerPoint Presentations CD

2-8

The Consumer Product Safety Commission provides recall information and safety alerts for children's products, such as infant car seats.

Chapter Summary

In our economic system, the most fundamental role of government is to provide the legal and institutional environment and the economic policies that permit and encourage productive economic activity. The system is based on the rule of law and leads to political and economic stability. This is what gives businesses and individual citizens the confidence to enter the marketplace as producers, workers, and consumers.

Government also plays other important roles in the economy. It controls the money supply and levies taxes to pay for government operations and public services. These fiscal and monetary policies keep our economy stable and prosperous. Government enacts legislation to promote open and fair competition and to protect consumer interests in the marketplace.

Government protects your consumer interests and rights in countless ways. Specific laws cover almost every possible type of consumer product and transaction. Government agencies and departments serve and protect consumers at federal, state, and local levels. Laws and regulations cover everything from the purity of your food and water, to the air you breathe, and the money you borrow. As a consumer, you will want to be aware of the laws that protect your interests and the government agencies serving you.

Review

1. What is government's fundamental role in a free market economy?

2. Name three other functions of government in our economy.

3. Name and describe the four parts of the business cycle.

4. Name three signals of a recession.

5. How does inflation hurt consumers and businesses?

6. What is stagflation?

7. Name and describe three types of unemployment.

8. List three consequences of rising unemployment and underemployment rates to families.

9. What is fiscal policy and how can it be used to stimulate or slow down the economy?

10. What is monetary policy and how can it be used to stimulate or slow down the economy?

11. Name three ways national debt hurts the economy.

12. What is the purpose of antitrust laws?

13. Name six government departments or agencies that serve and protect consumers.

Critical Thinking

14. How can too much government interference in the economy have a negative impact? What is too much? What is necessary?

Answers to *Review*

1. to provide the legal and institutional environment and the economic policies that permit and encourage economic activity

2. (Name three:) Set economic policies; make tax and spending decisions; control the money supply; regulate business and economic activity.

3. contraction—a period of slow or no growth; trough—when a contraction stops; recovery—when business activity grows again; peak—height of recovery

4. (See page 39.)

5. It decreases the value of a dollar.

6. a period of slow growth and high inflation

7. (See pages 41–42.)

15. In your state, how much sales tax do you pay for every dollar you spend? How does the government use this money?

16. What choices has your community made in recent years in the use of public funds or tax revenues to meet public needs and wants for such services as education, police protection, street repairs, parks, and recreation?

17. What public goods do you and your family routinely use and enjoy?

18. How do laws that prohibit monopolies protect the consumer's right to choose?

19. What are the costs of regulation for government and for business and in what way do consumers pay these costs?

20. What has been your experience with consumer protection agencies and laws?

Academic Connections

21. **Reading.** Read the business section of *The Wall Street Journal* or another major newspaper for one week and summarize the financial and economic state of the economy.

22. **Social studies.** Make an appointment to visit a local government official of your village, city, or county. Find out how local taxes are assessed in your community and what services they provide. Summarize your findings for the class.

23. **History.** Some Americans are strongly opposed to almost any government intervention in the economy. How did they view the enlarged role of the government during the economic crisis that began in the fall of 2008? Research the press coverage at that time and share your findings with your class.

24. **Social studies, writing.** Many people believe that media oligopolies threaten American democracy. Do a few large companies control the newspapers, radio and television stations, and publishing houses in your community? Do some research to either confirm or deny this and write an article for the school or local newspaper.

MATH CHALLENGE

25. This chapter uses graphs to present statistical information. A graph is used to depict the unemployment rate over time. A line graph shows fluctuations in the business cycle over time. For each of the following, state what type of chart would best express the information.
   A. Show fluctuations in the rate of inflation over the past 25 years.
   B. Show the proportion of new U.S. citizens who came from each of the world's continents.
   C. Show total taxes collected by the federal government during the past 10 years.

Tech Smart

26. Use the Internet to find the current U.S. unemployment rate, GDP, CPI, and Federal Reserve discount rates. Cite your sources.

10. (See pages 45–46.)

11. (Name three:) less money to pay for programs and services; less credit; less money available to the private sector; increased taxes, negative impact on future growth and stability

12. to promote competition and fair trade and to prevent trade restraints in the marketplace

13. (Name six: Refer to "Government Agencies Serving Consumers" section in text.)

Answer to *Math Challenge*

25. A—line graph; B—pie chart; C—bar graph

8. (List three:) losing homes; going into debt; losing employer-provided health benefits; developing health problems such as stress-related illnesses, depression, and substance abuse

9. It is the government's taxing and spending decisions. To stimulate the economy, government spends more and lowers taxes. To combat inflation, government increases taxes and reduces spending.

CHAPTER 3

Consumers in the Economy: An Overview

Reading for Meaning

Skim the review questions at the end of the chapter first. Use them to help you focus on the most important concepts as you read the chapter.

standard of living

GDP per capita

labor productivity

prosperity

durable goods

investment

asset

income tax

sales tax

property tax

CHAPTER OBJECTIVES

After studying this chapter, you will be able to

- **relate** your consumer economic activities to your financial well-being and to the state of the overall economy.

- **explain** how economic conditions affect job opportunities and standard of living.

- **summarize** how consumer spending influences overall economic conditions in a market economy.

- **describe** the impact of consumer and government borrowing on the economy.

- **give examples** of ways consumer economic problems arise from market characteristics.

- **outline** consumer economic problems that result from consumer mistakes.

Central Ideas

- The economic decisions of consumers impact the overall economy.
- Smart consumers avoid the pitfalls that a market economy can create.

Y ou live in a market economy. Your economic activities, such as spending and voting, all make a difference. You are fortunate to live in a market economy with its freedom and many advantages. However, living in a market economy can present problems and challenges. Making wise choices and managing money carefully are important skills for consumers in the marketplace.

This chapter provides a brief overview of consumer activities as they relate to the U.S. economic system. In Unit 2 of this text, individual topics and their connection to your personal finances will be covered in greater detail.

Economic Activities of Consumers

The economic activities of consumers play a vital role in a market economy. Consumers earn, spend, borrow, and save. They invest their dollars. They share financial risks through insurance. They pay taxes and vote for the candidates who support policies and programs that will affect the economy. The way consumers perform these activities determines how well they live and how well the economic system works.

3-1

Certain career choices require many years of education and training. Advanced education often leads to greater earning potential.

Earning Your Way

A market economy permits you to choose the fields in which you work. You can also choose the level of education and training you want to attain, 3-1. Those choices largely determine your job opportunities and earning power.

The ability to find work depends on job skills, experience, and education. It also depends on your career choice and the demand for workers in your chosen field. Qualified people who want to work in high-demand fields are likely to find employment and earn a comfortable income.

Once hired, job performance helps determine how far and how fast a worker will advance. Hard work and the ability to work well with others are important qualities in almost every field. In today's fast-changing world, it also is important to continually update job-related skills.

As you advance on the job, your income and your personal *standard of living* should increase. **Standard of living** is the overall level of comfort of a person, household, or population as measured by the amount of goods and services consumed. If your income rises faster than prices, more goods and services will be available to you and your standard of living will rise. For most people, that translates into a higher quality of life. Your earning power and job performance are directly related to your standard of living.

Earnings and the Economy

Besides determining your personal wealth, your earning activities contribute to the nation's wealth. The *national standard of living* is the level of prosperity in the country. It is measured by income levels and the ability of citizens to acquire necessary goods and services. These include housing, food, health care, education, transportation, and communications. As a nation, the United States has one of the highest standards of living in the world.

GDP Per Capita. There are different ways to measure a nation's standard of living. Many economists use *GDP per capita*. As you will recall, GDP, or *gross domestic product*, is a measure of the market value of all final goods and services created in an economy during a given time period. *Per capita* simply means *per person*. **GDP per capita** is the market value of final goods and services produced per person. It is the national GDP divided by the number of people in the country. GDP is usually adjusted for inflation and stated in dollars.

When GDP per capita is high or rising, incomes are rising and more goods and services are available to each citizen. This indicates that people are consuming more and their standard of living is rising. On the other hand, when GDP per capita is falling, it indicates falling incomes. Fewer goods and services are available and being consumed. A lower GDP signals a lower standard of living for a nation's people.

There are some problems with using GDP per capita to measure standard of living. It assumes that everyone gets an equal share, although that is false in reality. Also, GDP as a measure of output does not account for unpaid work, such as housework, child care, and volunteer work. However, despite these problems and others, GDP per capita is the most common way to measure living standard.

Labor Productivity. Economists also use *labor productivity* as an indicator of a nation's economic health or *prosperity*. **Labor productivity** is the value of the goods and services a worker creates in a given time. High labor productivity indicates a healthy economy. To raise labor productivity, businesses and governments must invest in productive resources, such as technology, factories, and the education and training of workers. Top-performing workers using efficient tools and technology increase their own earnings. Their high productivity also boosts the nation's wealth by raising GDP.

It is clear that your earning activities plus those of all others in the job market make a huge impact on the economy. At the same time, the state of the economy affects your earning potential. Economic conditions influence the number of jobs that are available, the type of work in demand, and salary levels. Demand in job markets is ever changing.

Discuss

How do you think the standard of living varies from person to person?

Resource

Understanding a Market Economy, Activity B, WB

Discuss

How does productivity increase wealth of the individual and the nation?

Activity

Research the median income of families in the U.S. Is it higher or lower than you expected? Next, research the average income. How do these numbers compare?

Market Researchers

Market researchers help companies understand what types of products people want and at what price. They gather data on competing products, successful methods of marketing and distribution, and future sales potential. Their evaluations help companies decide whether to expand product lines or develop new ones.

Spending and the Economy

A market economy permits you to make your own spending choices. The way you make those choices determines what your money will buy. Getting the most satisfaction for the dollars you spend requires careful choices in the marketplace.

Your spending decisions help create a demand for the goods and services you buy. You contribute to the profit and success of the business from which you buy. Your individual spending may not be major in creating a demand for specific products or in supporting one business over another. However, as a group, you and other consumers determine the success or failure of specific goods, services, and businesses.

Consumer confidence is a key factor in determining the state of the economy. When consumers believe the economy is strong or improving, they tend to spend more. This creates a greater demand for goods and services. Businesses expand to meet the increased demand. As they expand, they create more jobs. This creates a sense of **prosperity**. Times of economic prosperity can be defined as periods of growth and financial well-being. They are marked by high employment, job security, and overall stability.

When consumers are doubtful about the economic future, they spend and borrow less. This lowers the demand for goods and services. Businesses slow down because sales decline. Jobs are harder to find. Workers are laid off. These conditions can lead to a recession, or a period of economic slowdown. As discussed in Chapter 2, a recession is marked by rising unemployment, falling demand, slowed production, and declining economic activity.

Saving Your Money

People think of savings as money that is put aside for the future. However, anything that improves a person's financial position is considered savings. This includes the cash value of a life insurance policy, home

ECONOMICS in ACTION

Consumer Confidence

Consumer confidence is a key indicator of the state of the economy. It is based on a survey that asks people in 5,000 U. S. households how they view their financial well-being, spending power, job opportunities, and confidence in the future. Researchers at the nonprofit Conference Board process their answers and reduce them to a number.

The Consumer Confidence Index is a value between 0 and 100. By following the index from month to month, researchers gauge whether consumers are more or less optimistic. A high number indicates optimistic public opinion. To see current Consumer Confidence Index values, check the Conference Board Web site at www.conference-board.org.

improvements, and the purchase of durable goods. Furniture, appliances, and cars are called **durable goods** because they have lasting value. Savings such as these increase your financial well-being as long as you do not spend beyond your ability to pay.

Saving and the Economy

In a market economy, the money you and other consumers transfer to financial institutions is pumped back into the economic system, 3-2. It is loaned to businesses and other consumers to pay for business growth, building construction, and the purchases of homes. Savings used this way help generate more jobs, greater productivity, and a growing economy. Therefore, the health of the economy is closely related to the *savings rate*, or the amount of money people save.

Borrowing to Spend

Each time you use a credit card or charge account or take out a cash loan, you are borrowing. These are forms of *consumer credit*. This is a tool that lets you buy now and pay later. There are good reasons to borrow. Borrowing is sometimes the only way consumers can pay for major purchases, such as a house, car, or college education. Saving enough money to pay for these large expenditures all at once is difficult. Credit can also help you pay for unexpected expenses, such as a large medical bill.

In most cases, you pay a fee for using credit. Credit is costly in another way, too. When you use credit, you spend future income. This means part of your future earnings must be used to pay what you owe. The use of credit reduces future income. People who do not monitor and control their borrowing can get into serious financial trouble. Chapter 9 discusses both the sound and risky uses of credit.

Activity

List durable goods that are considered savings because they contribute to financial welfare and security.

Discuss

Why are the savings of consumers necessary to the health of the economy and prosperity for all?

Discuss

What impact does consumer installment credit have on the economy?

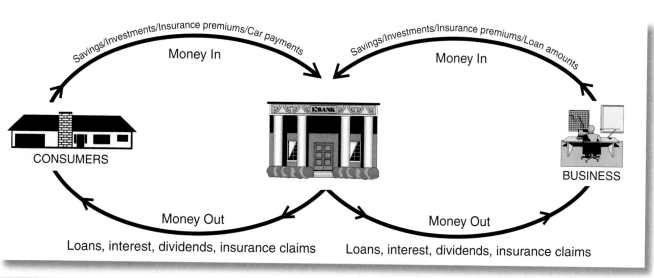

3-2
This diagram shows the flow of money in and out of financial institutions—banks, credit unions, and insurance companies.

Discuss

How does the overall use of consumer credit affect the forces of supply and demand?

Discuss

How does the present use of credit carry the seeds of an eventual economic downturn?

Discuss

What does it mean to "share risks" through insurance?

Borrowing and the Economy

Consumer borrowing has two important effects on the economy. It increases the amount of money in circulation, and it increases the demand for consumer goods and services. For example, when you borrow, you have more money to spend. As you and other consumers use borrowed money, you increase consumer demand in the marketplace.

When the economy is in a recession, the use of credit can help increase consumer demand. Consumer spending, whether with cash or with credit, stimulates the production of goods and services. This is why the Federal Reserve System may lower interest rates and encourage the use of credit during a recession. It helps stimulate growth.

Consumer borrowing can have a negative impact on the economy when the supply of money increases faster than the supply of goods and services. This causes prices to rise, and inflation is the result.

Another reason for the cautious use of credit is its long-term effect. Unfortunately, the overuse of credit carries the seeds of an eventual economic downturn because the credit used today must be repaid with tomorrow's dollars. That means tomorrow's dollars will be paying today's debts rather than supporting future demand. Using credit increases immediate demand, but it decreases future demand. Economic prosperity is threatened if many people are deeply in debt.

Insuring Against Financial Risks

Insurance is a risk-management tool or a way to protect yourself against certain financial losses. When you buy insurance, you and other buyers pay a fee to own an insurance policy. A policy is a document that

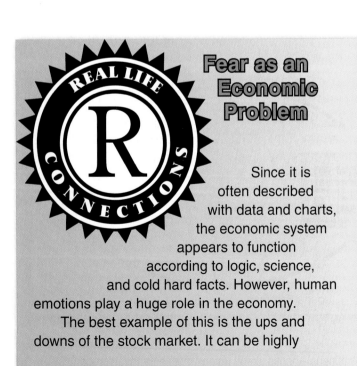

Fear as an Economic Problem

Since it is often described with data and charts, the economic system appears to function according to logic, science, and cold hard facts. However, human emotions play a huge role in the economy.

The best example of this is the ups and downs of the stock market. It can be highly volatile, fluctuating with consumer confidence and anxiety. The feelings and behavior of consumers can cause economic upturns and downturns. When consumers are optimistic about the economy, they spend more money, which boosts the economy. When they are feeling anxious or pessimistic, they curtail their spending, which depresses the economy.

The U.S. economic system is built on faith and trust. For example, millions of people put their money into banks because they trust that it will be safe there. The banks make money by taking in deposits and lending to businesses and other consumers. If anything should happen to frighten large numbers of depositors, they can demand their money and a bank failure can result.

outlines the specific terms, the risks covered, and the payments that must be made.

You share financial risks related to life, health, and property. For example, suppose you and 5,000 others buy health insurance. If you must go to the hospital for an illness, the insurance premiums of those who do not need to be hospitalized will help pay your expenses, 3-3. Insurance companies invest the insurance payments of all policyholders. These payments and their earnings are used to pay the bills of policyholders who suffer financial losses. The number of people who suffer losses at any given time is much smaller than the number of policyholders in the insurance pool. Many types of insurance are available. They will be covered in detail in Chapter 10.

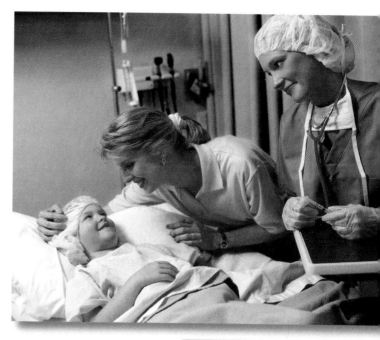

Insurance and the Economy

Insurance strengthens the overall economic stability of the nation. It spreads financial risks and stabilizes income in the face of serious financial losses. Social insurance programs contribute to social stability. These government programs include Social Security, Medicare, Medicaid, unemployment insurance, and workers' compensation. They provide income, medical care, and other services to citizens who are retired, ill, disabled, or unemployed.

In addition, insurance companies invest billions of dollars of insurance payments in business enterprises each year. This investment contributes significantly to the strength of the economy. Personal insurance needs are covered in detail in Chapter 10.

Investing for the Future

When you have saved enough money to provide for emergencies and some goals, you will want to think about investing your money. An **investment** is an asset you buy that increases your wealth over time, but carries the risk of loss. An **asset** is an item of value you own, such as cash, stocks, bonds, real estate, and personal possessions. Consumers invest money to improve their financial position and increase their future economic security. The purpose of investing is to make more money than you invest. Investments include financial instruments such as stocks, business ownership, valuable items, and real estate.

Investments usually give consumers a greater return on their money than savings. However, the risk of loss is greater for investments than for savings accounts. The desire for profit motivates people to invest. Investors hope to eventually sell their investments at a higher price than they paid for them. However, there is the chance that they will lose part or all of their investment. That is why it is important to do careful research before you invest. Greater detail on investing your money will be covered in Chapter 12.

3-3

Health insurance will help pay this patient's medical bills.

Discuss

How does insurance contribute to a person's overall economic stability? How does it protect individuals?

Vocabulary

Differentiate between *saving* and *investing*.

Enrich

Interview a local business owner to learn how he or she obtained financing to start, operate, and expand the business. Relate this to consumer saving and investing.

Investment and the Economy

Consumer investments pay for a large share of business growth and activity. Businesses use the money to help purchase new plants and equipment. Investments also help pay for the research and development of new technology and the marketing of new products and services. Economic development and growth are directly related to the investments and savings of individuals as described in the following example.

If an airline company wants to expand its service, it can issue new stock for sale to the public. When investors buy the stock, the company gets the money it needs to buy new planes. Companies building the planes create jobs. Operating the planes creates more jobs, better service for consumers, and a profit for the airline.

If the company continues to make a good profit, the price of its stock may rise. This encourages more investors to buy stock in the company with the hope of making a profit. Investors make money on the investment and workers receive more job opportunities. The company makes money on the new planes and consumers benefit from more flights and better service. Investment dollars start this type of chain reaction in businesses of all types, 3-4. The benefits of investment ripple through the economy.

Paying Taxes for Government Services

In the previous chapter, you learned that the government provides many of the goods and services that citizens want and need. These include the military, highways, the judicial system, schools, and parks. Tax revenues pay for the many government departments, agencies, and programs and the services they provide.

Local, state, and federal governments levy different types of taxes. They include

- **income tax**—a tax on the earnings of individuals and corporations. It is levied by the federal government and most state governments.

- **sales tax**—tax added to the price of goods and services you buy.

- **property tax**—a tax that is paid on real estate owned by individuals and corporations.

In the U.S., voters indirectly decide what they want to "buy" from government. They decide the level of taxes they will pay for their purchases. For example, citizens vote for more taxes every time they vote for a new school, more police protection, or a new highway. They vote for higher taxes every time they vote for a

3-4

This diagram shows how consumers and business work together through consumer investments to keep the economy going.

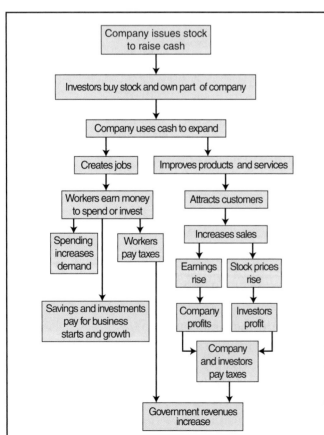

candidate who advocates new government programs without reductions in government spending.

Taxes, Government Spending, and the Economy

As you learned in the last chapter, government economic policies play an important role in the overall economy. The government's spending of tax dollars stimulates the economy. It creates demands for goods and services that are usually met by private businesses.

Government spending can also harm the economy. It can drive prices up and cause inflation. When the government spends more than it receives in tax revenues, it must borrow money. Year after year of deficit spending increases the national debt. U.S. citizens ultimately pay for government spending and the national debt through taxes.

When government increases taxes, it tends to depress the economy because it reduces the amount of money available for business activity. Taxes and government spending are discussed in more detail in Chapter 7.

Economic Problems of Consumers in a Market Economy

A market economy offers you, the consumer, both the privilege and the challenge of making free economic choices. You are free to choose how to earn a living and what to do with your money. You can choose to pay cash or use credit. You can decide to spend or save. Free choice offers you the opportunity to decide for yourself how to get the most satisfaction from your money.

Free choice does not guarantee satisfaction. Certain characteristics of a market economy can complicate choices. Following are some of these characteristics.

Confusing Variety of Products

Businesses compete with one another in a market economy. As a result, the same or similar goods and services are sold by a wide variety of outlets. Choosing a reliable seller and finding the best product for the best price is a challenge. It is necessary to learn something about the sellers as well as the products and services you buy.

A market system also supports the development of countless new products and ideas. The system rewards producers who give consumers what they want. As a result, the variety of goods and services found in the marketplace is extensive. Consider all the fabrics, styles, and colors of clothing you can buy. Ponder the many sizes, models, and features of cars. Count the specialties in medical care and the number of choices in home furnishings. Think of the many forms of consumer credit, types of insurance, and ways to save and invest money. Even the many flavors, types, and brands of ice cream can make choosing difficult.

Customer Support Specialist
Customer support specialists are employed by companies to serve as a direct point of contact for customers. They interact with customers and are responsible for ensuring that customers receive appropriate, courteous service and help with questions and concerns.

The choices open to consumers make it possible to meet almost every need. However, these many options also make it a challenge to choose intelligently. Careful comparison shopping, particularly for costly purchases, is one way to reduce the confusion and make satisfying choices.

Questionable Selling Methods

In a system where the survival of a business depends largely on attracting consumer dollars, selling plays an important role. Businesses want to sell as much as possible at the highest price they can get. With this goal in mind, most businesses advertise and market their goods and services aggressively.

While most businesses are honest and fair, some may use questionable selling methods to increase their sales and profits. Techniques such as high-pressure selling, less-than-truthful advertising, contests, and "free" offers can encourage you to buy for the wrong reasons. Too often, factual information is not part of a sales pitch. You need to focus on what is important to you before making purchases.

Keep in mind that deliberately deceptive advertising and other dishonest business practices are illegal. If you question the ethics of a store or selling method, contact the local Better Business Bureau, the chamber of commerce, or the nearest office of the Federal Trade Commission. You have the power through these agencies to fight back.

Conflict of Interest

To a certain extent, buyers and sellers want different things. Suppose you are in the business of selling cell phones. You want to sell as many phones at the highest price you can get. You want to be able to pay your business expenses and make a good profit.

When you are buying a cell phone, you want the phone that best fits your needs at the lowest possible price. You want to have money left over to spend for other items. In other words, sellers want the highest price they can get, while consumers want the best quality at the lowest price.

The free-market system helps resolve the conflict of interest between sellers and buyers. Both wages earned by the seller and prices paid by the buyer are tied to the forces of supply and demand. Everyone depends on these forces to achieve the proper balance between wages and prices. The system strives to create a supply of goods and services to meet demand at prices that will keep the producer in business and the buyer able to buy.

Consumer Mistakes Leading to Problems

For a variety of reasons, consumers sometimes make poor choices when presented with the many options offered by a market economy. These choices can lead to economic problems. Following are some common consumer mistakes.

Public Information Coordinators

Public information coordinators serve as advocates for businesses, associations, and other organizations. They build and maintain positive relationships with the public by working closely with print or broadcast media. They also handle tasks such as organizing special events and mediating conflicts.

Lack of Planning

Some of the worst consumer economic problems are caused by lack of planning. When consumers fail to plan ahead, they lack direction for their spending. They do not set goals for the use of income or build savings for future needs. Lack of planning also makes it difficult to control the use of credit.

Consumers who do not plan ahead often have trouble paying routine monthly bills. They can even have difficulty buying groceries to make nutritious meals at reasonable prices. Clothing buys that can be incorporated into a person's wardrobe require planning. Buying a car to meet needs for transportation and fit the budget requires planning. Planning is also necessary to have money available for occasional expenses, such as birthday gifts, insurance payments, vacations, and taxes, 3-5.

Poor planners often find it difficult to save enough for big expenses, such as a car, a home, education, or retirement. They often end up making purchases that do not meet needs and wants. Careful planning is the only way you can take charge of your own financial well-being. It allows you to match the highs and lows of expenses with the highs and lows of income over a lifetime.

Enrich

Role-play a situation depicting a conflict of interest between a seller and buyer.

Discuss

Give examples of how the market economy resolves the conflict of interest between seller and buyer.

Discuss

What can happen when consumers fail to plan ahead?

Reflect

What consumer mistakes have you made as a result of failing to plan?

Case Study: Consumer Mistakes

Poor Planning

Lamont has a pay-as-you-go cell phone. He figures the 1,000 minutes he purchased would last a month. However, he burns through the minutes in three weeks and does not have the money to buy more.

Sarah's friends are taking a trip together during spring break. She intends to go too, but blows her savings on a new jacket.

Ken gets a job and opens a savings account at a bank. He plans to deposit his paycheck and eventually buy a car with his savings. However, a few days after payday, he has nothing left to deposit.

Case Review

1. How does poor planning affect each person?
2. What would you have done differently in each case?
3. What did Ken do right? How did his good intentions go wrong?

3-5

With proper financial planning, you will be not only able to afford a vacation, but also to relax and enjoy the time away.

Activity

Select five consumer products or services and list the information you would need before deciding to purchase them.

Activity

Select one major consumer product and collect a variety of readily available information on it.

Discuss

Do you find it difficult to ask salespeople questions? Why or why not? When is talking to salespeople helpful? When is it *not* helpful?

Reflect

Can you think of impulse purchases you made that turned out to be mistakes? Were there consequences?

Failure to Use Information

The failure to thoroughly investigate and to ask questions concerning a future purchase can lead to disappointment and even big mistakes. For instance, Mariko signs up for an $800 online course in communications. She does not finish the course because the assignments take more time and hard work than she expected. It also is difficult to get help from the school because she gets a different instructor every time she has a question. She drops the course and loses her $800.

These types of situations are avoidable when consumers seek and use available information. Reliable facts can be found for almost every product and service you want to buy. When reliable information is not available for a given product or service, you will be wise to make another choice. Sources of information abound, and the Internet can retrieve consumer information in seconds. Salespeople and other consumers who have used specific products and services can be helpful, too.

The fastest and easiest way to get information is to ask questions. Make it your rule to ask first and buy later. Getting the facts first is especially important where health, safety, or large amounts of money are involved. Making uninformed choices can be costly, disappointing, and even dangerous.

Impulse Buying and Overspending

Even informed consumers sometimes indulge in impulse or thoughtless spending. Others habitually overspend, which can lead to debts that are difficult to repay.

If you are like most consumers, you sometimes buy things without thinking about your needs and goals or the consequences of spending.

Case Study: Consumer Mistakes

Buying on the Spur of the Moment

Ginny buys a pair of shoes because they are on sale. They are the right size, the right price, comfortable, and attractive—but they are red. She has nothing to wear with red shoes.

Rafael goes to the grocery store for a loaf of bread. He ends up spending $18 for groceries he did not plan to buy.

Althea sees a TV commercial for an exercise machine and dials the toll-free number. When the machine is delivered, she has lost interest and sticks it in the closet.

Case Review

1. Have you ever made similar mistakes? How might you have avoided them?
2. What could each person have done to spend more wisely?
3. Who do you think made the most foolish purchase? Why?

When done regularly, this type of spending can consume a sizable amount of money. Thoughtful spending will leave more dollars for the needs and wants that are truly important to you.

Overspending happens most frequently with credit cards. When spending cash, you cannot spend more than you have. You think more carefully before making a purchase. A budget or spending plan can help you control spending and stay within your means. Details on planned spending and the use of credit will be covered in later chapters.

Poor Communication

Most businesses want to know the likes, dislikes, wants, needs, and problems of their customers. Failure to speak up, ask questions, and complain when necessary can be costly. An open line of communication can lead to greater satisfaction with products, services, and sellers.

Consider this example. Charlene calls to request servicing for her furnace. She is told that a repairperson could come on Monday afternoon. Since Charlene works during the week, she takes Monday afternoon off to let the repairperson into her house. She is docked $80 from her paycheck. Later she learns that the repair could have been done on Saturday or in the evening. Better communication would have saved money. If Charlene had requested a different day or time, she would not have lost pay.

Activity

Draft letters to business or government expressing approval or disapproval or asking for information.

Resource

Identify the Consumer's Mistake, reproducible master 3-2, TR

Resource

Chapter 3—Consumers in the Economy: An Overview, Teacher's PowerPoint Presentations CD

Chapter Summary

Consumers play an important role in the functioning of a market economy. In a free market economy, consumers influence outcomes directly. Consumer behavior also affects overall economic conditions and prosperity, or the lack of it.

While a market economy offers freedom and many advantages to consumers, it also presents problems and challenges. For example, the vast selection of goods and services available in the marketplace can make choosing difficult. Selling methods of merchants often pressure consumers to buy what they do not need. There is a natural tension between the seller who wants to make money and the buyer who wants to get the most for money spent.

In some cases, consumers create their own problems in the marketplace. Lack of planning, failure to seek needed information, impulse spending, and poor communication can result in faulty buying decisions and poor money management. You need to be aware and alert to avoid such common mistakes.

Review

1. How can a person's income affect his or her personal standard of living?

2. How does consumer spending affect the state of the economy?

3. How does the use of credit affect immediate consumer demand?

4. Why does the overuse of credit eventually lead to an economic downturn?

5. What role do consumer savings and investments play in the overall economy?

6. What type of tax is paid on real estate owned by individuals and corporations?

7. What questionable selling methods do some businesses use to increase their sales and profits?

8. Explain the conflict of interest between consumers and sellers in a market economy.

9. Name four common ways consumers create problems for themselves in a market economy.

10. Describe how poor communication can result in problems for consumers.

Critical Thinking

11. How do consumer savings and investments support business growth and expansion?

12. Explain how savings, investments, and insurance premiums serve as the source of credit for consumers and businesses. Illustrate your explanation with a chart or drawing showing the flow of money.

Answers to Review

1. As a person's income increases, his or her personal standard of living will probably rise.

2. Increased consumer spending creates demand and helps promote a healthy economy. Decreased consumer spending lowers demand and contributes to the slowing of business and economic activity.

3. It increases the amount of money in circulation and the current demand for consumer goods and services.

4. The credit used today must be repaid with tomorrow's dollars, so tomorrow's dollars will be paying debts rather than supporting future demand.

5. The money consumers save and invest finances business growth, government programs, and other economic activity. It contributes to economic prosperity.

6. property tax

7. high-pressure selling, deceptive claims, contests, and free prizes

13. What industries suffer most when consumer spending is down? For example, what happens to the housing and construction industry? What related industries are likely to suffer? What industries seem to suffer the least during a recession?

14. What consumer problems do you consider most serious? What do you think can be done about them? What consumer problems have you experienced? How might you have avoided them?

15. Describe the consequences of impulse buying and habitual overspending.

Academic Connections

16. **Social studies.** Using travel guides, almanacs, and the Internet, make a chart comparing the standard of living in the U.S. with that of another country. Include information on price comparisons for similar goods and services.

17. **Speech.** Create a short video of consumers in the marketplace, such as shopping at a sale or buying groceries. Focus on the economic problems they may encounter in a market economy.

18. **Research, writing.** Research and report on the economic impact of the attack on the World Trade Center in 2001. Discuss which industries were most affected. Describe the effects on jobs, consumer spending, government spending, and taxes.

19. **Social studies, research.** Research a period of economic prosperity in the United States. What events led to this period? What events caused an eventual downturn?

MATH CHALLENGE

20. A country's standard of living, or level of prosperity, is measured by GDP per capita. Using the figures for GDP and population, calculate the GDP per capita for each of the following countries.
    A. India: GDP = $1.209 trillion; population = 1.17 billion
    B. Guatemala: GDP = $67 billion; population = 14 million
    C. France: GDP = $2.499 trillion; population = 64.3 million

Tech Smart

21. Use the Internet to find the most current GDP and total population for each of the following countries:
    - Ethiopia
    - China
    - United States

8. Sellers try to sell at the highest possible price, while consumers try to buy the best quality at the lowest price.

9. lack of planning, failure to use reliable information, impulse buying and overspending, poor communication

10. (Student response should include an example of how a consumer lost money due to poor communication.)

Answer to *Math Challenge*

20. A. $1,033
    B. $4,785
    C. $38,864

CHAPTER 4

The Global Economy

Reading for Meaning

Read the chapter title and write a paragraph describing what you know about the topic. After reading the chapter, summarize what you have learned.

economic globalization

international trade

imports

exports

specialization

comparative advantage

economies of scale

migrants

multinational corporation

outsourcing

offshore outsourcing

capital

cartel

exchange rate

balance of payments

trade deficit

trade surplus

free trade

trade barrier

European Union (EU)

North American Free Trade Agreement (NAFTA)

World Trade Organization (WTO)

CHAPTER OBJECTIVES

After studying this chapter, you will be able to

- **outline** advantages and disadvantages related to globalization.
- **explain** why countries specialize and how this leads to international trade.
- **analyze** the effect of multinational companies on the global economy.
- **describe** the relationship between currency strength and the balance of trade.
- **cite** examples to show how international trade affects the overall economy, businesses, workers, and consumers.
- **describe** what you can do to develop the skills needed to succeed in a global economy.

Central Ideas

- Globalization is the growing economic interconnectedness of people around the world.

- Globalization presents new opportunities and dilemmas.

After silencing a Chinese-made alarm clock, an American consumer gets dressed in jeans made in Thailand and a T-shirt manufactured in Israel. Breakfast is cereal sprinkled with California raisins made from grapes picked by Mexican migrant farmworkers. Before leaving, the consumer brushes his teeth with toothpaste made in a Nigerian factory by employees of an American corporation. Once outside, he gets into a vehicle made in the U.S. by a Japanese automaker. He drives to work at a multinational corporation with offices in 30 countries.

Like this fictitious consumer, you live in a world that is becoming increasingly globalized. *Globalization* refers to the process of becoming worldwide in scope. **Economic globalization** is the flow of goods, services, labor, money, innovative ideas, and technology across borders. It is changing the way people communicate, shop, and conduct business.

In recent decades, globalization has intensified. You will need to keep up with this new global environment. Understanding it will help you to hold your own in the job market and in the marketplace.

Flow of Goods and Services

One of the major forces behind globalization is international trade, 4-1. **International trade** is the buying and selling of goods and services across national borders and among the people of different nations. It has been going on for thousands of years. Many of the earliest travelers were traders looking for natural resources, new products, and new markets for their goods. They created trade routes that crisscrossed continents and oceans.

Most trade today occurs between businesses in different nations. Government and individuals are not directly involved. However, governments do regulate and set the parameters for international trade. You will read more about government's role in trade later in the chapter.

4-1

Container and cargo ships carry traded goods between the U.S. and its trading partners.

Linking to... History

The Silk Road

One of the most famous trade routes was called the Silk Road, created around 100 BC. It was a network of roads that connected Europe, North Africa, and Asia. Caravans of traders exchanged gold, glass, perfumes, and other Western goods for the East's silk, ceramics, spices, and iron. People, plants, animals, ideas, knowledge, and culture also flowed back and forth.

International trade is discussed in terms of *imports* and *exports*. **Imports** refer to the goods and services that come into a country from other countries. The *importer* purchases these goods and services. **Exports** are the goods and services grown or made in a particular country and then sold in world markets. The *exporter* is the party who sells these goods or services.

Discuss

What is the difference between merchandise imports and exports and service imports and exports?

What Is Traded

For many people, the subject of trade conjures images of giant containers being loaded and unloaded from ships at American ports. This is the trade in products or goods. As you will recall from Chapter 1, goods are physical items—foodstuffs, furniture, toys, computers, car parts, and all other items on store shelves. More than half of the world's imports are intermediate goods that are used to produce other goods.

Trade in services, or work performed, makes up about 20 percent of world exports. These services are provided by businesses in industries including banking, transportation, insurance, law, telecommunications, and entertainment. This sector is rapidly increasing as more professional services in research, consulting, and information processing are needed.

Money also flows between nations. This includes investments. Foreign investors buy U.S. treasury bonds. U.S. companies pay their workers living in foreign countries. You will read more about this later in the chapter.

Law, Public Safety, Corrections & Security

Customs Inspectors

Customs inspectors enforce laws governing imports and exports. They inspect cargo, baggage, and articles worn or carried by people, vessels, vehicles, trains, and aircraft entering or leaving the United States.

Why Trades Occur

Two parties trade with each other because each expects to benefit from the transaction. One party receives a product or service and the other receives payment. You probably make dozens of trades a day. For example, if you go to a bakery and give the clerk some money, you receive a blueberry muffin in return.

Buying what you need is easier and more efficient than trying to make all the items yourself. The same is true for countries. No country can produce all the goods and services that its people and businesses want. However, it can provide a range of products and services. Then it can trade these for whatever it cannot produce. This is called **specialization**. The types of goods and services that countries specialize in depend on the following factors.

Natural Resources, Climate, and Geography

Climate, geography, and access to natural resources vary from one country to another. These factors determine in part what a particular country can and cannot produce.

For example, the tropical climate of Costa Rica makes it an ideal place to grow bananas. Thailand and Indonesia produce most of the world's rubber. Bolivia has the largest stores of the lithium used in batteries. The vast natural gas fields of Russia supply that country with more natural gas than it needs. Likewise, Saudi Arabia has vast reserves of oil. The climate and geography in parts of the U.S. make it well suited to grow much of the world's corn, wheat, and soybean crops, 4-2. Each country's excess can be exported.

On the other hand, climate, geography, and natural resources can limit what a country can produce. A tropical climate or a desert cannot produce the variety of foods that its people want. Even the U.S., a country with varied climate and geography, cannot grow enough coffee and cocoa to meet consumer demand. Whatever cannot be produced in sufficient quantities to meet demand must be imported.

4-2

The United States exports grain to countries with less plentiful corn, wheat, and soybean crops.

Available Human Resources

The quality of the labor force in a particular country determines what it can and cannot produce. For example, what is the literacy rate? Does a large share of the population have computer skills? How many colleges, universities, and specialized training programs are available?

Industries that require a highly skilled workforce would not take root in a country where most workers are uneducated and unskilled. In these countries, most jobs would be low paying, such as those in the garment-making industry and low-skilled factory work.

Other labor force factors include pay scales and cost of living. Shoes and clothing are examples of labor-intensive products that are made by workers in other countries. These workers generally earn less than U.S. workers who do the same jobs. For example, a worker in an Asian factory may make only $5 a day for a 14-hour workday.

To take advantage of lower labor costs, some companies move their manufacturing operations overseas. The products are then imported into the U.S. for sale.

Consumer Preferences

Some products are imported because they are specialties of particular countries or regions. These products can be made just as efficiently in the importing country. However, the foreign-made products offer style and performance qualities that consumers prefer. This has been the case in high-fashion clothing from European designers, high-performance automobiles from Japan and Germany, and a variety of electronic products primarily from Asia.

Comparative Advantage

If a nation could produce all the goods and services its citizens and businesses need, there are still advantages to trade with other nations. An economic concept called *comparative advantage* explains why. **Comparative advantage** is the benefit to the party that has the lower opportunity cost in pursuing a given course of action. The opportunity cost of a choice is the value of the best option or alternative given up.

The following example explains how this works. Suppose a doctor and a nurse staff a small medical office. The doctor sees 20 patients a day. Each appointment is billed at $100. The nurse is paid $250 per day to run the office.

The doctor is more efficient than the nurse at both treating patients and running the office. Can the doctor save money by firing the nurse and doing both jobs? Looking at opportunity costs provides an answer. Without a nurse, the doctor has less time to see patients. There would be five fewer patients seen. The doctor's fees, which total $2,000 at 20 patients, would be reduced by $500.

For the doctor, the opportunity cost of managing the office is $500. However, the nurse is paid half that amount. It makes financial sense for the doctor to treat more patients and hire a nurse to manage the office.

When individuals, businesses, or nations specialize in the activities for which their opportunity costs are lowest, everyone benefits. Countries tend to export what they produce most efficiently. They import the goods and services produced more efficiently in other countries. When nations trade with each other, consumers gain more choices and lower prices.

One of the reasons for comparative advantage is an economic concept called **economies of scale**. The cost of producing one unit of something declines as the number of units produced rises. The costs of production are spread over more units. If a business can sell more of a product by expanding into overseas markets, it can take advantage of economies of scale.

U.S. Trade

The U.S. is a dominant power in global economic markets. According to the U.S. Bureau of Economic Analysis and the U.S. Census Bureau, the U.S. exported an estimated $1.83 trillion worth of goods and services in 2008. During that same year, the U.S. imported $2.52 trillion worth of goods and services.

Discuss

Give examples of specific products that are imported because of consumer preference.

Vocabulary

Ask a student volunteer to summarize the concept of comparative advantage.

Resource

Comparative Advantage, Activity A, WB

Resource

How Comparative Advantage Works, reproducible master 4-1, TR

Discuss

How do you think U.S. exports affect other countries?

Enrich

Research and write a report about a controversial U.S. export, such as violent movies or fast foods. Why did a foreign government or its citizens protest or ban the product? Do you agree or disagree?

Note

Categories of U.S. import goods, from largest to smallest, are: industrial supplies, consumer goods, capital goods, agricultural products. Categories of U.S. export goods, from largest to smallest, are: capital goods, industrial supplies, consumer goods, agricultural products.

Resource

Understanding Migration: An Interview, Activity B, WB

With less than 5 percent of the world's population, the U.S. produces over 20 percent of the world's total output. In recent years, the people and businesses of the U.S. have sold between 10 and 12 percent of their total output in world markets.

The U.S. is the world's largest importer and a major market for more than 60 countries. Millions of people across the globe depend on the U.S. for their livelihoods. When the U.S. economy falters and consumers close their wallets, factories on the other side of the world shut down and workers lose their jobs.

The U.S. was once the world's largest exporter of manufactured goods. However, this is no longer true. According to the U.S. Census Bureau's Foreign Trade Division, the U.S. imported about $338 billion worth of goods from China in 2008. This is almost five times the worth of U.S. goods exported to China. This has created a trade imbalance that you will read more about in the following pages.

The U.S. imports more manufactured goods than it exports, 4-3. However, it exports more services than it imports, 4-4. The U.S. has a trade surplus in services and a trade deficit in goods. Top U.S. trading partners for both imports and exports are listed in 4-5.

U.S. Commerce		
Category	**Imports**	**Exports**
Industrial Supplies	Crude oil	Organic chemicals
Consumer Goods	Automobiles, clothing, medicines, furniture, toys	Automobiles, medicines
Capital Goods	Computers, telecommunications equipment, motor vehicle parts, office machines, electric power machinery	Transistors, aircraft, motor vehicle parts, computers, telecommunications equipment
Agricultural Products	Cocoa, coffee, rubber	Soybeans, fruit, corn

4-3

The U.S. has a trade deficit for goods, meaning it imports more than it exports.

U.S. Service Exports
Financial services—investing and insurance services
Information services—computer consulting, data processing
Other services—architectural design, construction, engineering, legal, advertising, marketing, accounting, management, technical training, travel, tourism, entertainment, and transportation services

4-4

These are just a few examples of U.S. service exports.

A high percentage of what is consumed in the U.S. is produced in the U.S. However, products and services that cannot be provided in sufficient quantity or quality at the desired price are imported. Imports represent dollars flowing out of the country.

Flow of Labor

In addition to increasing the movement of goods and services between countries, globalization increases the flow of labor. People who move from one place or country to another are **migrants.** Today almost 1 in 40 people in the world are migrants. Some are refugees or asylum-seekers who flee their birth country because of persecution. They may be members of a minority ethnic or religious group who are denied basic rights by their government. Millions of people cross borders to escape war, economic crisis, and natural disasters. Some leave to escape rampant crime and corruption.

However, many are economic migrants seeking better opportunities to work and earn a living wage. The gap between wealth and poverty in countries is a major cause of migration, both legal and illegal. For example, a Mexican can earn on average nine times more working in the United States than working in Mexico.

The developed countries, such as the United States, are beacons for people seeking economic opportunities. More than 30 million people, or 11 percent of the U.S. population, were born in another country. Most recent migrants came from Latin America, Asia, and the Caribbean.

As American businesses open offices and factories in foreign countries, a growing number of Americans are becoming economic migrants. However, their numbers are much smaller than the number of migrants coming into the U.S.

Impact of Multinationals

Much of globalization is driven by the growth of multinational corporations. A **multinational corporation** is a business that operates in more than one country. Some multinationals are so large that their assets are greater than the GDPs of entire countries. These large companies have greatly increased the amount of global trade.

Multinationals are created when several companies in different countries are combined. An example of a multinational corporation is Johnson & Johnson. With corporate headquarters in New Jersey, it is comprised of 250 subsidiary companies in 57 countries. A *subsidiary* is a business that is controlled by another business.

Top U.S. Trade Partners	
Exports	**Imports**
Canada	Canada
Mexico	China
China	Mexico
Japan	Japan
Germany	Germany
United Kingdom	United Kingdom
Netherlands	Saudi Arabia
Korea	Venezuela
Brazil	Korea
Belgium	France

Source: Foreign Trade Division, U.S. Census Bureau

4-5
These are the top nations the United States trades with in the world market, ranked by 2008 U.S. total value of goods.

overnment & Public Administration

Consular Officers
Consular officers receive and review applications for nonimmigrant visas. They also provide a range of services to American citizens overseas.

Resource
Multinational Corporations,
reproducible master 4-2, TR

American multinationals employ millions of people in their subsidiaries across the globe. Also, millions of Americans work for U.S.-based subsidiaries of multinational corporations headquartered elsewhere. For example, Japanese auto maker Toyota had 38,340 employees in North America in 2005. Before the economic downturn in 2008, Toyota had plans to build a $1.3 billion plant in Mississippi. Multinationals have altered world trade in important ways that are discussed in the following sections.

One Product, Many Origins

A product label that reads *Made in the U.S.A.* or *Made in China* only tells part of the story. Many of the world's largest companies operate across the borders of several countries. The parts and labor that go into the production of almost anything today come from many different countries.

Take a popular brand of a smart phone, for example. Researchers at the University of California in Irvine found 451 parts in a 2005 model. Each part was traced back to the supplier who made it and to the country where it was made. The hard drive was traced to an electronics manufacturer in Japan. This manufacturer used factory workers in China and the Philippines. Other parts were traced back to companies located in the U.S., Korea, and Taiwan.

Researchers found that the manufacture of smart phones created 41,000 jobs around the world. About 14,000 of these were in the U.S., consisting of marketing, design, engineering, and retail sales jobs. The 27,000 overseas jobs were mostly low-paid manufacturing jobs.

Outsourcing occurs when companies move sections of their business to other companies or to their own subsidiaries. **Offshore outsourcing** refers to moving sections of a business to another country. It usually occurs because a business wants to take advantage of lower labor costs, productive resources, and other benefits in other locations, 4-6. When an American company moves a piece of its operations to another country, it creates jobs in that country. Often those jobs offer better opportunities than the workers previously had.

While outsourcing can offer companies substantial cost savings and greater productivity, it can result in job losses for workers at home. These newly unemployed workers may be forced to take lower-level jobs with less pay and fewer benefits or to relocate themselves. Retraining and upgrading skills often are necessary to find new jobs. This is one painful reality of globalization.

4-6

Labor-intensive industries, such as the textile industry, have moved to Africa and Asia where the cost of labor is cheaper.

Case Study: The World Economy

Profit Squeeze

Walter owns a small business in Illinois. In recent years the cost of running his business has increased across the board. The cost of doing business threatens to reduce profits to the point that it is not worth Walter's time, effort, and investment to keep his business going.

Walter has two options. He can either increase his prices or he can decrease his production costs. Nothing about Walter's business requires him to be located in Illinois. Cost savings is the chief advantage of moving all or part of a business to a country with low-cost labor and a favorable tax structure. In addition, there would be far less government interference and oversight.

Unfortunately, if Walter decides to do this, his 70 employees will be left jobless. Relocating them would be impossible.

Case Review

1. Do you think Walter is justified in moving his business to another country? What other alternatives might he have?
2. If Walter decides to move the business, what do you think he should do about the employees he must let go? Has he a responsibility to them?
3. What do you think could be done in the United States to encourage businesses to stay in the country? How does the economy suffer when businesses leave?

Flows of Capital Investment

The growth in multinational corporations has increased the flows of capital, money, and investments around the world. **Capital** is money used to generate income or to invest in a business or asset. Many economists believe that this flow, rather than the flow of goods and services, is the most powerful force driving globalization today.

Money flows from one country to another when a parent company builds a factory overseas or lends money to a foreign subsidiary for expansion. One-third of global trade today is the movement of raw materials, goods, services, and product parts from one subsidiary of a multinational to another.

Another type of international investment occurs when investors buy or sell the stocks and bonds of foreign companies. Investors include individuals, businesses, and groups of people who pool their money in pension and

Note

In the past, most international investment was: A) aid given by developed countries and international aid organizations to developing nations, or B) commercial loans made by banks to foreign governments and businesses.

Discuss

How are you affected by the exchange rate?

Reflect

Have you had any experience with foreign currency?

Activity

Ask students to find the current exchange rate of the U.S. dollar and the currencies of five nations of their choice.

Enrich

Invite a speaker from a local bank to discuss the foreign exchange market and factors that impact the supply and demand for U.S. dollars and its exchange rate.

mutual funds. These funds are then used for international investments. You will read about stocks, bonds, and mutual funds in Chapter 12.

Collusion and Cartels

Many multinational corporations have achieved worldwide dominance in their industries. For example, some large agribusiness companies control the world market for seeds and other agricultural products. The enormous wealth and power of some corporations gives them significant influence over governments and global trade policies.

Chapter 2 covered several forms of market control. Monopoly occurs when one firm controls the entire market for a particular good or service. An oligopoly exists when a few large companies control an industry and set prices.

A **cartel** is a group of countries or firms that control the production and pricing of a product or service. It has the same economic effect as a monopoly. An example of a cartel is the Organization of Petroleum Exporting Countries, or OPEC. OPEC nations collude to set prices for oil by controlling the supply. Their decisions determine market prices and, ultimately, the amount you pay for fuel to run your car and heat your home.

International Monetary System

When people in the same country buy and sell goods to one another, they use the same currency. In the U.S., that is the dollar. However, when buyers and sellers are in countries that use different currencies, they must first figure the value of one currency in relation to the other. This involves the *foreign exchange market,* or *foreign currency market.*

The Foreign Exchange Market

Different types of currency are bought and sold on the foreign exchange market. A currency, like a product, has a price. The **exchange rate** is the value of one currency compared to another. The exchange rate tells you how much you must pay in dollars to buy a unit of foreign currency.

Exchange rates are constantly changing. Buyers and sellers in the foreign exchange market generally set currency values. The currencies of countries that are politically and economically stable are more desirable to investors. The more desirable a currency is, the greater the demand for it.

Also, the value of a nation's currency can be affected by changes in interest rates. The higher an interest rate, the greater is the return on an investment. Higher interest rates draw foreign investors and this increases the demand for a currency.

Buying and Selling U.S. Dollars

The foreign exchange market affects your life every day. It determines how much you pay for the goods and services you rely on. However, most

Chapter 4   The Global Economy   **85**

people only learn of the foreign exchange market when they travel to another country, 4-7. The foreign exchange rates are available on the pages or Web sites of business publications.

For example, someone who is going to Canada may need to exchange American dollars for Canadian money. If the exchange rate is $1.10 Canadian for each U.S. dollar, a traveler should get $110 Canadian for each $100 U.S., minus fees. You can exchange money at banks, airports, and currency exchanges. Airports usually charge the highest fees. A number of online currency conversion calculators are available, including the Universal Currency Converter at www.xe.com.

Businesses must also use the foreign exchange market when conducting business in other countries. For example, suppose a business located in China wants to buy road-building equipment from a U.S. company in Peoria, Illinois. The equipment costs $500,000. To make the purchase, the Chinese need to convert their currency, the Yuan Renminbi (RMB), into USD, or U.S. dollars. How much Chinese currency do they need to convert?

Suppose that the foreign exchange rate on the day of purchase is:

1 USD (U.S. dollar) = 6.835 RMB (Chinese currency).
500,000 USD = 3,417,500 RMB. They may need a little extra to cover fees.

However, when U.S. businesses buy Chinese products, they do not have to convert dollars into Chinese currency. This is because many countries, including China, accept the USD because of its stability relative to other currencies. The USD is the *international reserve currency*.

4-7

American tourists and business travelers get more for their money when the U.S. dollar is strong.

Trade and Exchange Rates

The value of a nation's currency, including the USD, goes up and down with the demand for it in other countries or in world markets. At times, the value of U.S. dollars is high, or strong.

When the dollar is strong,

- goods and services imported into the U.S. cost less. This raises demand for imports. When the value of the dollar is high compared with the currency you are buying, you get more for your money. Your dollars go further when you travel in that country.

- foreign buyers must pay more for exports from the U.S., so they buy less. When the dollar is strong, foreign investors must pay more for U.S. companies, real estate, and stock, so they tend to invest less.

> **Note**
>
> The mortgage/banking crisis and global recession shook the world's confidence in the U.S. economy. Some world leaders suggested changing the international reserve currency to something other than the U.S. dollar.

Case Study: The World Economy

Talia Makes a Switch

Talia is a freshman in college. She wants to work on immigration issues after graduation. The ability to speak Spanish would be an advantage in her chosen field. She wants to apply for a study abroad program in Spain so she can become fluent in the language.

Unfortunately, the cost of the program increased and the value of the U.S. dollar dropped. The airfare also increased more than 30 percent because fuel prices have risen. It looks like a semester in Spain is no longer an option.

Though she is disappointed, Talia is still determined. She is considering several options including a summer program rather than a full semester. She could also choose a semester in a South American country where the dollar goes further and the airfare would be lower.

Case Review

1. Which alternative would you choose if you were Talia? What are the pros and cons of study abroad programs? Would one of these opportunities interest you?
2. Why does the falling value of the dollar increase the cost of going to other countries?
3. How does the value of the dollar affect prices at home such as gasoline, imported products, travel, and food?
4. Why does a devalued dollar attract foreign visitors to America? How does it affect students from abroad studying in the U.S.?

Discuss

What is the impact on trade when the dollar is strong? when it is weak?

When the dollar is weak,

- goods and services imported into the U.S. cost more. This reduces demand for imports. Traveling in other countries costs more because dollars buy less.

- foreign buyers pay less for exports from the U.S., so they buy more. Foreign citizens, businesses, and governments get more for their money when they invest in the U.S. They tend to invest more.

Exchange rates change daily. They are published regularly and can be found in travel sections as well as the financial pages of most major newspapers.

The U.S. Trade Deficit

To understand international trade, you need to know the meaning of *balance of trade*. This is the difference between total imports and total exports of goods and services. These numbers are recorded in the **balance of payments**. This is an account of the total flow of goods, services, and money coming into and going out of the country. When a country buys, or imports, more products than it sells, a **trade deficit** develops. The country has an *unfavorable balance of trade*. If it sells, or exports, more than it buys, the country has a **trade surplus**. The country then has a *favorable balance of trade*.

The United States has run a substantial trade deficit since 1976. It imports more goods and services than it exports, 4-8. Currently the U.S. runs the largest deficit and China runs the largest surplus among worldwide trading nations.

The deficit makes it possible for China and other nations to accumulate more U.S. dollars. With accumulated dollars, these nations can buy more U.S. goods, services, and assets such as real estate, securities, and businesses.

The U.S. actually needs more foreign investors to buy treasury bills, corporate securities, and real estate to help pay off the growing national debt. However, many economists feel that, in the long run, this is not a healthy situation. They feel that trade deficits and budget deficits coupled with the growing national debt weaken the U.S. economy and its leadership position in the world.

Vocabulary

Contrast the terms *trade deficit* and *trade surplus*.

Enrich

Ask students to research the amount of the current U.S. trade deficit.

Activity

The U.S. trade deficit decreased during the severe recession of 2008. Ask students to explain why.

Note

The balance of payments includes two accounts. The current account is a record of all transactions related to the import or export of goods and services. The capital account is a record of transactions related to the purchase or sale of assets such as stocks, bonds, companies, and real estate.

Government's Role in Global Trade

Governments regulate trade. Government trade policies are often described as *free trade* or *protectionism*. **Free trade** is a policy of limited government trade restrictions. Individuals and businesses are generally

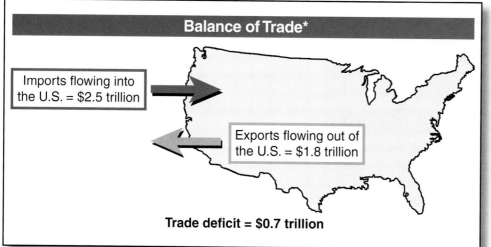

Balance of Trade*

Imports flowing into the U.S. = $2.5 trillion

Exports flowing out of the U.S. = $1.8 trillion

Trade deficit = $0.7 trillion

4-8

The flow of money out of the U.S. to pay for imports exceeds the flow of money into the country to pay for exports. This is the trade deficit.

* 2008 figures from the U.S. Dept. of Commerce, Census Bureau, Foreign Trade Division

free to buy and sell goods and services from people and businesses in other countries. Governments generally favor free trade that opens markets for the goods and services they export. Imports may be restricted. Trade restrictions are often called *protectionism*. It is designed to protect businesses at home from foreign competition.

Why Nations Favor Free Trade

Theoretically, trade among nations benefits all the trading nations. Therefore, everyone benefits when tariffs and other impediments to trade are kept to a minimum. Some of the arguments for free trade have been discussed earlier in this chapter. In summary, free trade is beneficial because it

- stimulates growth and raises productivity and living standards in the countries that open their economies to world markets.

- allows countries to specialize in those goods and services they produce most efficiently and trade for those that they produce less efficiently, 4-9. This is the comparative advantage argument.

- produces a greater variety of goods and services at lower prices as a result of worldwide competition and innovation. Consumers enjoy a greater selection of goods and services at lower prices.

- generates more innovation and product improvements as a result of competition and the international exchange of ideas and technologies.

- creates new investment opportunities stemming from capital flows across international borders.

- promotes cooperation and peaceful relations among nations who become trading partners. When a country needs and wants goods and services produced in other nations, there is a strong incentive to maintain relations.

Why Nations Favor Restricted Trade

Nations, including the U.S., restrict trade for various reasons.

- ***To protect domestic industries.*** Governments often seek to protect home-based industries from foreign competition.

4-9
Some countries produce and export automobiles, which increases competition.

- *To protect the jobs of workers.* Labor, capital, and materials often cost less in other countries compared with the U.S. Foreign companies can offer their goods at lower prices. If these goods are allowed into the U.S. marketplace, U.S. companies making similar goods could not compete. This could drive them out of business and lead to job losses.

- *To reduce dependence on single sources of necessary items.* For example, the U.S. depends on OPEC sources of oil. These oil-producing countries can cut the supply of oil or raise prices, causing serious problems in the U.S.

- *To control the distribution of products or technology that can threaten national security.* For example, the export of technological know-how and materials that could be used to build weapons to attack the U.S. are restricted.

- *To address unfair trade practices.* For example, importers may engage in *dumping*. This refers to the sale of imported products at lower prices than those charged in the domestic market for similar products. Once the imported products dominate the market and drive the domestic producers out of business, the importer raises the price. The government of the importing country may tax these imports to raise their prices so domestic companies can better compete.

Critics of free trade have other arguments. In the U.S., they claim that free trade increases the U.S. trade deficit in world markets as the U.S. continues to import more than it exports. Others say it benefits larger companies and developed nations at the expense of smaller businesses and emerging nations. They claim it also threatens cultural identity and individuality as large international corporations replace smaller, less competitive local businesses.

How Governments Restrict Trade

The government can limit opportunities for foreign companies to sell their products or services on an equal footing with domestic companies. *Protectionism* refers to government policies that restrict trade. Protectionist policies can backfire as other countries retaliate by imposing their own trade barriers.

Trade Barriers

Government policies can discourage imports through *trade barriers*. A **trade barrier** is any action taken to control or limit imports. There are several types of trade barriers.

- A *tariff* is a tax on imports that makes them more expensive to consumers. It is intended to make U.S. products more cost competitive with imports.

- An *import quota* is a limitation on the number or quantity of imports allowed into the country.

Discuss

How do government subsidies affect trade? Why are they sometimes controversial?

Activity

Using government sources, identify products that are subsidized by the U.S. government and the dollar amounts of the subsidies.

Vocabulary

Define *European Union* and explain why this group is important.

Enrich

Using at least four sources, investigate ways NAFTA has affected consumers, workers, businesses, and the economies of the three nations for better or worse.

- A *non-tariff barrier* is a type of regulation, such as environmental quality regulations or a U.S. safety requirement.

- An *embargo* is a law used by a government to prohibit trade with a particular country for political reasons.

Subsidies

Subsidies, which were discussed in Chapter 2, are another form of protectionism. A *subsidy* is a payment, tax break, or other incentive paid by government to a local business or industry. Subsidies allow businesses to offer their goods for sale at lower prices. This enables the goods to compete successfully with foreign products. Subsidies are often attacked for creating an unfair advantage for the business receiving the incentive.

For example, suppose an electronic company in another country receives subsidies from its government. The company ships its products to the U.S. Since the company receives subsidies, it can charge less for its products than a U.S. company making similar products. The U.S. company cannot afford to meet the low selling price. Eventually, the majority of customers buy the cheaper import and the U.S. company goes out of business.

Currency Manipulation

Currency manipulation refers to action taken, usually by a government or central bank, to increase or decrease the value of a specific currency. The value of the U.S. dollar is determined by the forces of supply and demand in the foreign currency exchange markets. This is true of most other currencies as well. When a nation sets the value of its currency without regard for the market, it is said to be "manipulating its currency."

If a nation artificially lowers the value of its currency, it can gain competitive trade advantages. The International Monetary Fund prohibits currency manipulation for the purpose of gaining unfair trade advantages. When a nation's currency is weak, its exports become cheaper in world markets. Its imports, however, become more expensive. As a result, the country tends to increase its exports and decrease its imports. This creates a trade surplus. A weak currency also invites more foreign investment into the country. This often translates into new factories, new jobs, and more products for export.

For trading partners, the consequences include trade deficits and unfair competition in domestic markets. For example, in recent years China has kept its currency artificially low, 4-10. This allows China to sell its products in the U.S. at lower prices than similar products manufactured in this country. In some industries, this unfair advantage can drive firms out of business. American workers lose their jobs. In addition, the U.S. trade deficit with China continues to grow and China's trade surplus with the U.S. increases. These low-priced imports are a short-term advantage for U.S. consumers, but it is not a healthy situation for the U.S. economy long-term.

Trade Organizations and Agreements

The United States has existing trade agreements and partnerships with a number of other individual nations and regions of the world. The goal of these agreements is to create economic benefits and opportunities for all participating nations as a result of free trade and investment across their borders. Figure 4-11 lists some of the many trade organizations in the world today.

The **European Union (EU)** is the largest trade sector in the world, surpassing any individual country. As of 2008, the EU had the largest GDP. According to the World Trade Organization, it was the largest importer and exporter of goods and services. Also as of 2008, 27 nations belonged to the EU. Fifteen of these countries share a common currency called the *euro*.

North American Free Trade Agreement (NAFTA) between the U.S., Canada, and Mexico lowered trade barriers and opened markets among the three countries. Canada and Mexico are top trading partners of the U.S. and trade has increased dramatically among the three nations.

4-10

The currency of the People's Republic of China is the Yuan RMB.

Trade Organizations		
Abbreviation	**Organization**	**Country Members**
ASEAN	Association of South East Asian Nations	Brunei Darussalam, Burma (Myanmar), Cambodia, Indonesia, Laos, Malaysia, Philippines, Singapore, Thailand, Vietnam
CAFTA-DR	Central America-Dominican Republic Free Trade Agreement	Costa Rica, Dominican Republic, El Salvador, Guatemala, Honduras, and Nicaragua
EU-27	European Union-27	Austria, Belgium, Bulgaria, Cyprus, Czech Republic, Denmark, Estonia, Finland, France, Germany, Greece, Hungary, Ireland, Italy, Latvia, Lithuania, Luxembourg, Malta, Netherlands, Poland, Portugal, Romania, Slovakia, Slovenia, Spain, Sweden, United Kingdom
NAFTA	North American Free Trade Agreement	U.S., Canada, Mexico
OPEC	Organization of the Petroleum Exporting Countries	Algeria, Angola, Ecuador, Indonesia, Iran, Iraq, Kuwait, Libya, Nigeria, Qatar, Saudi Arabia, United Arab Emirates, Venezuela
SADC	South African Development Community	Angola, Botswana, Democratic Republic of Congo, Lesotho, Malawi, Mauritius, Mozambique, Namibia, Seychelles, South Africa, Swaziland, Tanzania, Zambia, Zimbabwe

Source: International Trade Administration, U.S. Dept. of Commerce.

4-11

These are some of the many trade organizations around the world.

The "Anti-Globalization" Movement

Some people and groups do not view international trade agreements and groups positively. The label *anti-globalization* describes individuals and groups who oppose globalization. These include labor, environmental, and human rights groups all over the world.

Many of these groups say that they are not against globalization. They object to a type of globalization driven by the needs of wealthy countries and multinational corporations. They charge that trade agreements and global economic institutions put profits above the well-being and livelihood of people. For example, critics of NAFTA say it hurts small farmers, especially in Mexico. Lowered trade barriers opened the Mexican market to U.S. agribusiness. Unable to compete with cheap imports, many Mexican farmers lost their livelihoods and became migrants.

The basic goal of many groups in the anti-globalization movement is to promote social justice and human rights. They especially work for the elimination of inequities between the poor and the rich around the world.

World Trade Organization

Most governments believe that fair and open trade among nations benefits all. Governments, even friendly allies, constantly negotiate trade terms with one another. Disputes often involve access to markets. Trade disputes arise over certain policies and practices that create unfair competition, in the view of at least one country.

Issues of protectionism and unfair trade are controversial and complicated. They often involve more than economic considerations. Trade restrictions, or trade sanctions, are political weapons that can be used against the economies and governments of other countries.

The General Agreement on Tariffs and Trade (GATT) was formed after World War II by the Allied nations to aid post-war recovery. This is a set of international agreements that promote free and fair trade among nations. GATT agreements attempted to reduce the use of tariffs, quotas, and other trade restrictions.

In 1995, the **World Trade Organization (WTO)** was created to expand the work of the GATT. The WTO is an international organization that mediates trade disputes among 151 member nations and establishes trade practices that are acceptable and fair to all nations. WTO agreements are signed by practically every trading nation in the world. Besides trade in goods, the WTO is also involved in the regulation of trade in services, inventions, and intellectual property.

Other Important Global Organizations

Besides the WTO, many of the world's nations have come together in other organizations and forums to achieve mutual goals. These goals include the establishment of world peace, elimination of hunger, poverty, and disease, and sustainable growth and development. Many of the groups, which often work together, directly or indirectly influence trade and global economics.

World Bank

The World Bank has a membership of 186 countries. Its primary mission is to fund specific projects that promote economic development, reduce poverty, and raise living standards. To this end, the Bank provides financial and technical assistance to developing countries. Financial assistance consists of grants and low- or no-interest loans. For more information, check out its Web site at www.wto.org.

International Monetary Fund (IMF)

The primary mission of the International Monetary Fund is to oversee the international monetary system. It works to stabilize exchange rates and eliminate trade barriers. Its 184 member countries are advised on how to better manage their economies. The IMF also helps member nations head off and resolve economic crises.

Like the World Bank it provides loans and technical assistance to countries. However, unlike the World Bank, these monies are not intended to fund specific projects, but to stabilize the overall economy of the country and promote growth. The IMF Center is located in Washington D.C. Its Web site is www.imf.org.

G20

The Group of Twenty Finance Ministers and Central Bank Govenors (G20) is a forum for 19 countries plus the European Union. Besides the United States, the G20 countries are Great Britain, Japan, Italy, France, Russia, Canada, Germany, Australia, Argentina, Brazil, China, India, Indonesia, Mexico, Saudi Arabia, South Africa, South Korea, and Turkey. The heads of state of G20 countries meet annually to discuss issues ranging from health and the environment to trade and terrorism. The leadership role rotates among the member countries.

United Nations (UN)

The United Nations, headquartered in New York City, is an international organization of 192 member countries, 4-12. When it was created after WWII, its primary purpose was to maintain peace and security in the world. The UN is known as the entity that provides humanitarian assistance in areas ravaged by war and natural disasters. It is a forum where member countries can condemn political aggression and human rights violations. Its programs promote better living standards for people around the world. For more information about the UN, go to www.un.org.

4-12

The United Nations headquarters is located in New York City.

Discuss

Compare and contrast the main goals of the WTO, World Bank, IMF, and the UN.

Activity

Choose one of the organizations listed on this page and research its origins. When was it founded and why? How has the organization's mission changed over time?

Note

In 2009, the G8, which consisted of wealthier, mostly Western nations, stopped regular meetings. Its policy making functions were taken over by the G20. This reflects the growing importance of emerging-market and developing countries in the global economy.

Globalization and You, the Student

Globalization presents advantages and disadvantages, hopes and fears, pros and cons. It dramatically affects economic conditions and trade in every nation. Both consumers and producers operate in world markets. This is why it is important to understand the role of globalization in your economic life.

For example you are already buying goods and services from other countries. As a worker, the goods or service your company produces will likely be sold in other countries. You may work for a multinational corporation at some point in your life. Your managers and coworkers may be foreign-born. You will be competing for jobs with workers around the world.

As a Worker

Globalization affects you as a worker because it influences demand for both goods and services. This, in turn, influences job creation and opportunities. Increased exports mean growth, and growth means jobs.

For example, when an American company gains access to foreign markets and competes successfully in the sale of its products and services, the company will grow and expand. It will need more workers. There will be more jobs. This also is true when foreign companies open plants or offices in the United States. This creates new jobs in the U.S.

As a worker, you may be unfavorably affected if you work in areas that are subject to foreign competition. Foreign competition may also lead to a loss of jobs for U.S. workers in certain sectors. When U.S. companies must compete with popular imports, as happened with the auto market in recent years, U.S. workers may lose their jobs. In some industries there also may be layoffs and shifts in employment as a result of offshore outsourcing.

Jobs commonly outsourced are those in the manufacturing industries. However, service and professional jobs, especially those in information technology, are also being outsourced. For example, when you call a computer company's service department, the person who answers is often a half a world away. Accountants living in another country can prepare taxes. X-rays and other test results can be read and interpreted by non-American medical professionals.

What You Can Do

You need to be prepared for employment in a global market and for the changing cultural and political landscape that lies ahead of you. Here are a few ideas.

- **Continue your education.** Completing high school and getting postsecondary education and training are more important than ever. With offshore outsourcing and the Internet, competition for jobs is global. Jobs for the uneducated and unskilled are moving to places where workers are paid a small percentage of a U.S. worker's salary.

Discuss

How can foreign competition affect the U.S. job market? Is this a reason for buying domestic products?

Reflect

What have you done to prepare yourself for the global job market? What can you do?

Resource

Imports Scavenger Hunt, Activity C, WB

Hospitality & Tourism

Interpreters

Interpreters translate or interpret written or oral communication into another language. They need to be sensitive to the cultures associated with the languages they translate.

The more education and professional and technical skills you develop, the more opportunities and security you will gain.

- **Consider science- and math-related occupations.** The U.S. currently imports workers to fill many jobs that require science and math backgrounds. There is a great need for workers who have solid foundations in these subject areas, 4-13.

- **Keep your skills sharp.** After you enter the work world, keep the door to education open. Stay informed about trends in your field. Take advantage of retraining and educational opportunities on and off the job. Go back to school to learn new skills.

- **Learn a foreign language.** Fluency in almost any foreign language will become a key asset in the work world. Those who become proficient in Chinese (Mandarin) and other Asian languages, Russian, or Arabic will open doors to job opportunities around the world.

- **Learn about world affairs.** Regularly read newspapers, magazines, and Web sites that report extensively on international affairs and foreign policy issues. Seek out books about areas of the world that interest you. Tune in to radio and television programs broadcast from other countries.

- **Travel or live abroad.** Enroll in a student exchange program. Spend a summer working, studying, or doing volunteer work abroad. Visit relatives and friends who live in other countries. Learn about other cultures while having the adventure of your life. As the world grows more interconnected, global issues will become more important to everyone.

4-13
Workers who have education and training in science and technology fields will have better job opportunities in the future.

Resource

Chapter 4—The Global Economy, Teacher's PowerPoint Presentations CD

The citizens of every nation will become in a sense citizens of the world. Common interests will include policies governing the use and sharing of resources, environmental concerns, and controlling terrorism. Other issues include broad access to necessary medicines and health care services, alleviating poverty, and educating citizens for life in a global society.

As the globe grows smaller, the United States will have to decide whether it will become more involved with other nations in a variety of areas. Nations will need to cooperate with one another in addressing issues such as the environment, poverty, terrorism, AIDS, and disaster recovery. Peace keeping in areas of conflict will continue to call for international cooperation.

The future is likely to hold both more cooperation and more competition in global markets. There will need to be international agreements on the use of world resources. You will also likely see a continued increase in the exchange of ideas and developments in the fields of science and technology.

Chapter Summary

Economic globalization is the increasing economic interconnectedness among governments, businesses, and citizens of the world. Goods and services, money, labor, technology, and ideas all move rapidly across national borders. International trade plays an essential role in economic systems. It influences supply and demand, prices, competition, consumer choice, and government policies. It affects job opportunities and living standards.

As nations trade with each other, they export those goods and services they can produce efficiently and in abundance. They import goods and services they cannot produce efficiently or in adequate quantities to meet the nation's needs.

The exchange rate refers to the value of one nation's currency compared to another. The value of a currency goes up and down with the demand for it in world markets. The strength of a nation's currency affects its trading position in the world.

The balance of payments refers to the difference between a country's total imports and exports. When a nation imports more than it exports, it develops a trade deficit. If exports are greater than imports, a surplus develops. When a domestic industry cannot compete successfully with imports, there is a tendency to protect the domestic industry with some form of trade restraint. The goal of world trade organizations and agreements is to promote fair trade among nations for the benefit of all.

Review

1. What is economic globalization?

2. What is the role of specialization in trade between nations?

3. How does comparative advantage affect trade with other nations?

4. What are migrants and what role do they play in globalization?

5. What is the role of multinational corporations in globalization?

6. What is the difference between outsourcing and offshore outsourcing?

7. Why does the value of the dollar go up and down in relation to other currencies?

8. Explain the difference between a trade deficit and a trade surplus.

9. List two advantages and two disadvantages of free trade.

10. What is protectionism? What forms can it take?

11. List three ways international trade affects you.

Critical Thinking

12. How does the current value of the dollar affect U.S. trade with other nations?

13. Discuss the current U.S. account deficit and its consequences. What steps can the country take to reduce this deficit?

Answers to *Review*

1. the flow of goods, services, labor, money, innovative ideas, and technology across borders

2. No country can produce all the goods and services that its people and businesses want. However, it can provide a range of products and services and trade these for whatever it cannot produce.

3. Comparative advantage is the benefit to the party that has the lower opportunity cost in pursuing a given course of action. When individuals, businesses, or nations specialize in the activities for which their opportunity costs are lowest, everyone benefits. Countries tend to export what they produce most efficiently. They import the goods and

14. What are some of the immediate advantages and disadvantages of free trade?

15. If you were to lose your job to offshore outsourcing, what steps would you take to find a new job and recover financially? What do you think your employer and the government could and should do to assist you?

16. Outline what young people can do today to prepare for working in a global economy and to protect themselves against future job dislocations. What can you do personally?

Academic Connections

17. **Social studies, speech.** Trace the history of trade agreements over the past 50 years and present an oral report on your findings.

18. **Research, writing.** Write a paper on the European Union's origin and goals. Also discuss the EU's position in world trade. Include problems the EU nations experienced in converting to a single currency, and the advantages it has created in trade with other nations and in tourism.

19. **Social studies, research, writing.** List at least three trade agreements of the U.S. with other nations. Research and discuss the pros and cons of these agreements.

services produced more efficiently in other countries. When nations trade with each other, consumers gain more choices and lower prices.

4. Migrants are people who move from one place or country to another. They cause a flow of labor to countries with job opportunities.

5. Large multinational companies have greatly increased the amount of global trade.

6. Outsourcing occurs when companies move sections of their business to other companies or to their own subsidiaries. Offshore outsourcing refers to moving sections of a business to another country with lower labor costs and productive resources and advantages.

7. The value of a nation's currency goes up and down with the demand for it in other countries and in world markets. The value of the U.S. dollar moves up and down depending on economic conditions in the U.S. and around the world.

8. When a country imports more products than it exports, the country has a trade deficit and an unfavorable balance of

20. **Speech.** Debate international trade, with teams taking sides for and against open markets. Discuss some of the problems and disputes that have arisen among nations over trade policies.

MATH CHALLENGE

21. You want to buy two books published only in the U.K. The cost of the books is £17.98. The current exchange rate is $1 = £0.60797.
    A. What is the cost of the books in U.S. dollars? (Round up to the nearest cent.)
    B. Shipping from the U.K. is £9.97. What is the total cost of your purchase including shipping in U.S. dollars?

Tech Smart

22. Research current exchange rates for various currencies against the U.S. dollar. Include the British pound, Japanese yen, Indian rupee, Canadian dollar, Mexican peso, Chinese yuan, and the euro.

23. Using the Internet, look up and compare the U.S. economy with that of three other nations. Compare the following factors: type of government, gross domestic product (GDP), income per capita, literacy rate, significant natural resources, growth and inflation rates, annual exports and imports, and cost of living.

trade. If it exports more than it imports, the country has a trade surplus and a favorable balance of trade.

9. (List two of each. Student response. See pages 88–89)

10. Government policies that restrict trade include trade barriers, subsidies, and currency manipulation.

11. (List three. See page 94.)

Answers to Math Challenge

21. A. $29.57
    B. $45.97

Unit 2
Managing Your Finances

In This Unit

Achieving financial security requires lifetime planning. You can start by identifying the values and goals that are most important to you. By planning, acting, and evaluating, you can manage your income and assets to create an effective money management plan. This, along with other financial tools discussed in this unit, can help you acquire and manage your financial resources throughout your lifetime.

CHAPTER 5

Making Smart Decisions

Reading for Meaning

Examine the photograph shown here and the list of key terms. What clues do they convey about the chapter topics you will study?

management

values

value system

ethic

goal

priority

standard

cost-benefit
   principle

marginal benefit

marginal cost

decision-making
   process

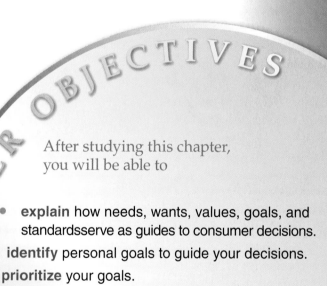

CHAPTER OBJECTIVES

After studying this chapter,
you will be able to

- **explain** how needs, wants, values, goals, and standardsserve as guides to consumer decisions.
- **identify** personal goals to guide your decisions.
- **prioritize** your goals.
- **identify** the resources available to you.
- **plan** the use of resources available to you.
- **use** the decision-making process.
- **apply** management principles to help you achieve important goals.

Central Ideas

- Careful decisions and wise use of resources can help you achieve your financial goals.

- Reviewing the success or failure of past decisions helps you make better decisions.

Managers

Managers perform a broad range of duties. They coordinate and direct the many support services that allow organizations to operate efficiently. Specific duties vary in degree of responsibility and authority.

Resource

Values: What Is Important to You? color lesson slide, TR

Y ou are the manager of your life. Many factors depend on how well you do your job. For example, by managing your time, you accomplish more of what you want to do, 5-1. By managing your financial resources, you control the dollars that pass through your hands.

Management is the process of organizing and using resources to achieve predetermined objectives. It involves identifying resources, setting goals, making decisions, solving problems, and evaluating results. Developing good management skills can help you achieve all the goals you set for yourself.

The Personal Side of Consumer Choices

Some people always seem to know what they want and where they are going. They seem to know what is important and what is not worth serious attention. This sense of direction and purpose is often a key factor separating the people who achieve what they want from those who do not. Developing this sense of direction and purpose requires a clear understanding of personal needs, wants, values, goals, and standards.

Importance of Needs and Wants

As discussed in chapter 1, *needs* are those items you must have to survive. Examples include your basic physical needs for food, clothing, and shelter. Psychological needs include feelings of safety, security, love, acceptance, approval, and success.

Wants, on the other hand, are items you would like to have. They are not essential for life. For instance, you may want to buy a new cell phone or a completely new wardrobe. However, you can survive without achieving these wants.

Importance of Values

Values are a person's beliefs about what is important and desirable. They influence the way you live and think as well as your decisions, actions, and behavior. Values differ among people. Some of the important values for many people are a loving family, loyal friends, good health, a meaningful career, financial security, and inner peace. Do you support these values? Which other values are important to you?

Values govern and direct your life even if you are unaware of them. Identifying and choosing your values will give you a sense of control.

5-1

When you determine how to spend your time, you are managing your life.

Case Study: Making Decisions

What Do You Value?

As long as Reyna can remember, her family has been short of money. Her only spending money is what she earns from babysitting. Most of her clothes come from her older sister. She believes that having money is just about the most important thing in life. She intends to have plenty of it when she grows older and tries to be part of the "rich crowd" at school. Reyna thinks people who have money are really better than others.

Terrence has little respect for money because his family has always had plenty. He expects to attend one of the better universities in the country after high school graduation. His grades are good, and his family can afford any college he chooses. He doesn't really want to go, but he knows it will be easier than fighting his family about it. He believes there are more important things in life than money, but doesn't know where to search for them.

Carlos is 25 and works in a service station. He wants to marry Angelique, but Angelique's father says she is accustomed to having what she wants. He wonders if Carlos is ready for the financial responsibilities of marriage and supporting a family. Carlos wonders if he should find a better-paying job, or if he would be happier with someone who has values more similar to his own.

Case Review

1. What is most important to Reyna? to Terrence? to Carlos?
2. In what ways do you think Reyna, Terrence, and Carlos might change their views about money in the future?
3. How do their views differ from your own? To what extent do you agree with each of them?

Some people need to make a list of everything important to them before they know what their values are. When you give the list some thought, you will probably find that your family, friends, education, and life experiences all influence your list of values. As you meet new people and have new experiences, what is important to you may change. As life unfolds, your values may change, too. Some become more important and others less so.

As you continually make different decisions, you eventually create a *value system*. A **value system** guides your behavior and provides a sense of direction in your life. For example, good school performance may score

Reflect

What does management mean to you, and how do you manage your life and money?

Discuss

How can management skills put you in control?

Resource

Money Worry Meter, reproducible master 5-1, TR

Discuss

How do you distinguish between needs and wants? Cite some examples.

Resource

BeLEAVE in Your Values, transparency master 5-2, TR

Activity

Trace your recent choices and typical behavior back to a value system and discuss how value systems develop.

high in your value system. If so, you will try to participate in class, complete your homework, and prepare for exams. If loyalty to friends is high in your system, you will help your friends when they need you. If popularity ranks higher than loyalty, you may find it difficult to stand by an unpopular person or cause.

Importance of Ethics

A closely related concept is ethical behavior. An **ethic** is a moral principle or belief that directs a person's actions. Ethics often conform to accepted standards of right and wrong. Ethical behavior involves honesty, fairness, reliability, respect, courage, tolerance, civility, and compassion. These and other qualities make people's lives with each other peaceful and safe.

Ethical behavior is expected from businesses and government, as well as from individuals. The opposite of ethical behavior is *unethical behavior.* Unethical behavior is usually considered wrong and may even be illegal. Unethical behavior includes stealing office supplies from an employer, surfing the Internet on company time, and returning used merchandise to a store. Other examples include a business that releases toxic waste into the environment and government officials who use their office for financial gain.

Importance of Goals

A **goal** is an objective you want to attain. Usually goals are closely related to values. For example, if health and fitness rank high on your list of values, you may set goals to establish a personal fitness program, avoid drugs, and eat nutritious foods. If you rank education high, some type of career preparation program would become an important goal. This goal might motivate you to begin a savings program to pay for advancing your education. You might also commit extra hours to homework in preparation for further schooling.

Linking to... History

Crisis of Ethics

Unethical behavior played a large role in the financial crisis of 2008/09. Some consumers lied about their income so they could qualify for large mortgage loans. Eager to make money from loans, some financial institutions encouraged consumers to take on too much debt. Other business people sold investments that were riskier and worth less than investors were led to believe. Many corporate leaders collected large salaries while their companies went bankrupt or received taxpayer money to stay in business.

Much of this behavior could be described as unethical. It was driven by the desire for financial gain at the expense of others.

You can set goals for almost anything in life, and there are different types of goals. You may set "to be" goals, "to do" goals, and "to have" goals.

"To Be" Goals

These goals are related to personality and character. You might want to be smart, popular, entertaining, reliable, laid-back, or competitive. This group of goals also includes career choices. You may want to be a teacher, an airline pilot, a scientist, or an artist, 5-2.

"To Do" Goals

These goals cover the endless list of things you might want to accomplish. You may want to learn to play the piano or speak a foreign language. You may decide to go to college, travel, or get a job as soon as possible. You may want to see a particular movie or make the basketball team. Perhaps your goal is to clean out your closet and organize your life. These are all "to do" goals.

"To Have" Goals

These goals are easy to identify and continually change. You may want a new watch, a car, your own phone, a personal media player, or concert tickets. These goals include the endless list of routine purchases such as socks and toothpaste. These goals also include higher-priced items for which you need to plan and save.

Timing of Goals

Financial goals can also be classified by their time schedules. *Short-term goals* are those that you want to reach within the next weeks or months, but within a year. For instance, saving enough money to buy a new coat may take several months. *Medium-term goals* are those that may take one to three years to achieve. These may include buying a new bike or musical instrument. *Long-term goals*, such as completing school, starting a career, getting married, or buying a house, may take several years to achieve.

Evaluating Goals

No one has enough resources to reach all of his or her goals at one time. You can get the most from your resources by planning how and when to use them. You will gain more control over your life and achieve the goals most important to you.

5-2
Career choices, such as becoming a health care professional, are "to be" goals.

Vocabulary

Define and discuss *greed, wealth, poverty, affluence,* and *materialism* as they relate to the meaning of money in life.

Vocabulary

Distinguish between *values* and *goals* and discuss the relationship of one to the other.

Activity

Divide a page into three columns and list your "to be," "to do," and "to have" goals.

It is helpful to not only identify your goals, but to also rank them in order of importance. This helps you direct your time, energy, and money to the goals that are most important to you. As you set and rank your goals, ask yourself the following key questions:

Is the goal realistic and possible? Getting all As is a realistic goal for some, not for others. Buying a car in two years is possible for some, but not everyone. The important thing is not to let the impossible stand in the way of the possible. Make an effort to set realistic goals for yourself. What are some possible goals? Which are most important to you?

Can you break the goal into smaller goals? Many goals, especially medium- and long-term goals, can be challenging. You can tackle them by breaking them down into smaller, more-achievable goals. For example, saving $500 for summer camp may sound impossible. There are only five months until the money is due. However, you can focus on the smaller goal of saving $100 each month or even $25 each week. You will be even more motivated if you reward yourself for each milestone achieved.

Can progress toward the goal be measured? Progress toward a goal should be measurable in dollars, grades, hours, points, or something else. Otherwise, you cannot judge your progress. For example, if your goal is to get an A or B in a class this semester, you can measure your progress weekly by tracking your grades for homework, quizzes, and exams. If your goal is to buy something, such as a laptop computer, you measure progress by the number of dollars you save. Seeing progress motivates you to continue working hard.

What will the goal cost in time, money, and effort? After thinking it through, you may decide that some objectives are not worth what it takes to achieve them. For example, if you want to start a new business, a careful look at the time and the risks involved might change your mind.

Will you still want the goal by the time you are able to reach it? For instance, a high school senior may want a scooter for getting to and from school. If it requires a year or more of savings, the need may vanish by the time the money is available. The need for a car may become more important.

It pays to set worthwhile, realistic goals. Attaining them can give you a sense of satisfaction and accomplishment. On the other hand, working toward unrealistic goals can cause frustration. Aiming at the impossible can prevent you from reaching what is possible.

Interdependent and Conflicting Goals

People generally have several goals at one time. Goals may be *interdependent*. This means you have to achieve one goal in order to reach another. For instance, you need to finish high school before going to college. You need to complete training before starting a career. You need to complete driver education before getting a driver's license.

Goals sometimes conflict with one another. For example, Alfonso has $800. He wants to buy a used car and take a one-week trip with his friends. He does not have enough money for both. Alfonso must decide which of these *conflicting* goals he values more.

Judy also has conflicting goals. She wants to be on the girl's basketball team, which practices each day after school. At the same time, she wants to keep her part-time job after school. Judy cannot reach both her goals. She must decide which is more important to her.

Life is full of conflicting goals and difficult choices. When your goals conflict, your priorities and values will help you choose wisely.

Establishing Priorities

A **priority** is a goal or value that is given more importance than other goals and values. To *prioritize* is the process of ranking several items in their order of importance. It is helpful to identify what is important to you and rank each item from most to least important. This helps you direct your time, energy, and money to whatever you most want to achieve—your priorities.

Whenever you decide one thing is more important than another, you are making a priority judgment. If you think it is important to enjoy your work, you may choose a job you like over a higher-paying job that does not appeal to you. When you think about your own priorities, what would you put at the top of your list?

Reflect

When have you been in a situation similar to Maurice? How do you determine your priorities when you have too many things on your plate?

Resource

Psychological Aspects of Money, Activity C, WB

Resource

Your Financial Tendencies, Activity D, WB

Case Study: Making Decisions

A Matter of Priorities

Maurice wants the male lead in the school play. The problem is that rehearsal is held for two hours every weekday afternoon for the next three months. If he gets the lead, he must quit his after-school job at a service station. If he quits now, the station manager probably wouldn't hire him for full-time summer work. Maurice desperately needs the income to help his family pay medical bills.

Since he is a senior, this is Maurice's last chance to be in a high school production. The best actors in the spring play are sometimes chosen for Summer Theater. This often leads to a career in drama, which Maurice has always wanted.

Case Review

1. What is the trade-off if Maurice decides to keep his job?
2. What is the opportunity cost if he decides in favor of the play?
3. What other alternatives might Maurice have?
4. How would you resolve Maurice's goal conflict if this were your decision?

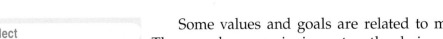

Reflect

What standards govern your choices and behavior? How would you describe your personal and family standard of living?

nufacturing

Quality Control Technicians

Quality control technicians ensure that manufactured products or services adhere to a defined set of standards. They follow plans or procedures to improve production or service.

Some values and goals are related to money and financial matters. These can have a major impact on the choices you make in the marketplace and in your personal life. The case studies about Reyna, Terrence, and Carlos present three different viewpoints about the importance of money. Reading them may help you understand how values, goals, and priorities affect behavior and financial choices.

Standards of Quality and Excellence

A **standard** is an established measure of quantity, value, or quality. The word *standard* is used in many different ways. Electrical products must meet certain safety standards before they receive a seal of approval. People who want to work in professions such as law and medicine must meet certain skills and knowledge standards before they can enter those professions.

Individuals develop their own personal standard of living. This living standard is expressed by the "to be," "to do," and "to have" goals that each achieves.

You set standards for the way you want to live, what you want to do, and the goods and services you want to buy. These standards depend on your values and goals. They often vary from situation to situation. For instance, if a big, perfect picture is a top priority when you buy a television, you may only settle for the best. Your standards for a TV would be high. However, suppose you just want a small TV that fits the corner of a work space. Your standards would call for something smaller and less pricey.

What degree of quality do you seek as you work toward your goals? Do you strive for As and Bs in school, or are you satisfied with Cs? See 5-3.

Do you practice a piece of music until you can play it without any mistakes, or are you satisfied playing it reasonably well? The answers to these questions can reveal some of your standards. Having a clear understanding of your standards, priorities, and goals will help you make wise financial decisions.

Identifying Resources

Resources are tools you can use to reach goals. As discussed in chapter 1, there are two types of resources—human and nonhuman. *Human resources* are those resources you have within yourself. They include energy, knowledge, experience, skills, talents, motivation, imagination, and determination. Other people and their skills are also human resources.

Nonhuman resources are external, such as money, time, and equipment. It is easy to overlook some of these. People often do not see their possessions as resources or as a means to achieving goals. Consider the resource value of a computer, camera, car, time, and other things available for your use.

5-3

If your goal is to graduate from college, then you may set high standards for the grades you achieve now.

Do not overlook public resources such as libraries, parks, recreational facilities, schools, and public transportation. Very often you can use public services to bring you closer to the goals you wish to achieve. For instance, can you think of ways to reach a specific goal by using a local library? the park district? public transportation?

Everyone has different amounts and types of resources. To be a good manager, you need to identify all the resources available to you. As you consider how to use your resources, keep the following tips in mind:

Resources are scarce. The amount of available time, energy, money, land, and other resources is limited. By planning, you can make the most of them.

Resources are manageable. You can manage resources to meet specific goals. For example, saving money or using credit lets you buy costly items you cannot purchase with a single paycheck. Planning your errands to follow direct routes and avoid backtracking saves time and fuel. Reading a book when you are on a bus or in a waiting room makes idle time productive.

Resources are related to one another. You can often combine several resources to reach a specific goal. For example, you might use both savings and credit to buy a big-ticket item, such as a car. In addition, one resource may be needed to produce or make use of another. You could use your talent and skills to get a job and earn money. Finally, you can use one resource to make up for the lack of another. For example, if you have plenty of time and little money, you can check several stores for the best values before buying.

Practicing good resource management will help you reach your goals. The following are some questions to consider:

- Which of your resources are plentiful and which are scarce?

- Can you combine several resources for more effective use of each?

- How can you use your human resources to make up for what you are missing?

Making Financial Decisions

Every day you make countless decisions—big, small, important, and unimportant. Some are so routine that you hardly use any thought at all. Think about today. Before you left home, you decided when to get up, what to wear, what to eat, when to leave home, and how to get to school.

Every day people face big and little problems. They make promises and cannot keep them. They are supposed to be in two places at the same time. They run out of money before payday. Instead of thinking and planning, they relied on one of the following:

- *Acting out of habit.* Do you automatically get your favorite foods for lunch every day? Do you sit with the same group for lunch? Do you shop in a few favorite stores?

- *Acting on impulse.* Have you bought a pair of shoes on sale, even if they did not really fit? Did you ever go to a movie you did not care to see just because your friends were going?

Resource

Your Resources, Activity B, WB

Discuss

What are some examples of managing resources to meet specific goals?

Reflect

When have you used one resource to make up for the lack of another?

Discuss

How would you answer the questions on this page to help you plan the use of resources?

Reflect

How would you answer these questions about the circumstances in which you have made decisions?

Discuss

What types of decisions do you think require a more thoughtful approach?

Resource

Rational Decision Making, Activity E, WB

Discuss

In what ways do you manage your life? Cite examples.

- *Failing to act.* Have you settled for unemployment by not applying for summer jobs until they were all taken? Have you earned a poor grade by not studying for an exam? Have you been broke when you needed money because you failed to save?

You have probably used all these ways at one time or another. For some choices, these methods work just fine. However, the financial decisions in your life carry lasting consequences. Given their importance, these decisions call for systematic choices.

Cost-Benefit Principle

Economics gives you tools to make wise choices. One of the most basic of these tools is the **cost-benefit principle**, or *cost-benefit analysis*. Cost-benefit analysis is a method of weighing the costs against the benefits of an action. It shows that you should take an action or make a purchase only if the benefits are at least as great as the costs.

For example, if you want to take a vacation in another state, you may need to decide whether to drive or fly to your destination. Suppose you determine that flying costs $350 more than driving. However, it also saves you eight hours of driving time. You would ask yourself: Is the benefit of saving eight hours worth the cost of $350? The choice depends on the value you place on time saved and on how much money you can comfortably spend. The choice will be different for different people.

This principle applies to economic decisions of individual consumers, businesses, and governments. Is the benefit worth the cost?

Marginal Analysis

Marginal analysis is a powerful decision-making tool. It takes into account the added benefit, versus the added cost, of one more unit of a product. The change in total benefit of using one additional unit is the **marginal benefit**. The change in total cost of using one more unit is the **marginal cost**.

For example, suppose you are hungry and buy a slice of pizza. It tastes so good, you buy another and another. Will the second piece bring as much satisfaction as the first piece? Probably not, because you are less hungry. The third piece will be even less satisfying. Eventually you stop eating. You would probably be willing to pay more for that first piece than for the second, more for the second than for the third.

Eventually you stop eating because you get little or no benefit since your stomach is full. The marginal benefit of using each additional unit of something tends to decrease as the quantity used increases. This is called the *law of diminishing marginal utility*. The law applies to thrill rides, ice cream, movie tickets, and many other experiences and purchases.

A Commonsense Rule

Even before applying laws of economics to help make financial decisions, one rule is obvious. People should not spend more than they can

ECONOMICS in ACTION

Marginal Analysis

Marginal analysis can help business owners use their resources in the best way possible. For example, suppose five workers in a toy factory produce 100 large, stuffed teddy bears per day. Each worker makes 20 teddy bears apiece. They sew the toy's arms, legs, torso, and head separately. Then they stuff the parts and sew them together. The sewing room has five heavy-duty machines.

The plant manager hires two more workers, but does not buy new machinery. She reasons that time used to stuff the pieces can be done away with the sewing machines. This should leave some machines free for the new workers to sew more teddy bears. The seven workers handle the new work arrangement well and produce 20 teddy bears apiece or 140 daily.

This success inspires the manager to add one more worker, but she doesn't get the results she expects. The number of teddy bears produced daily is only 152, not the 160 she expected. Workers average only 19 teddy bears apiece. They must stand in line to use equipment, which slows them down. The manager realizes that increasing total production by only 12 teddy bears daily does not cover the cost of the eighth worker.

By using marginal analysis, businesses can determine the right number of workers needed to maximize their profits.

---

afford. In other words, the key to financial well-being is spending less than you earn. An expression for this behavior is *living within your means.* It is the only way to have financial peace of mind.

Financially mature individuals realize they cannot afford everything they want. Consequently, they establish priorities and plan carefully. They make sure their needs are covered before wants are satisfied. If there are family responsibilities, the needs of the family generally come before the wants of individual family members.

Financially responsible people know they are accountable for their financial future. They develop a clear understanding of their financial situation before making decisions that involve current or future money matters.

Systematic Decision Making

When deciding important matters, a systematic or rational *decision-making process* can help you arrive at the best course of action. This **decision-making process** is a method of choosing a course of action after evaluating information and weighing the costs and benefits of alternative actions and their consequences. It involves five steps, 5-4.

Steps in the Decision-Making Process		
Step	**Keyword**	**Approach**
1	Problem	Define the problem or challenge.
2	Alternative	Explore alternatives.
3	Choose	Choose the best alternatives.
4	Act	Act on the decision.
5	Evaluate	Evaluate the decision.

5-4
The five steps of the decision-making process can help you solve problems effectively.

Resource

Planning, Activity F, WB

Reflect

What obstacles come between you and your goals?

Activity

Select a goal you want to achieve and identify the obstacles and resources related to it.

1. *Define the problem to be solved or the issue to be decided.* You need a clear idea of the challenge before you can find the best solution. What is the problem? Perhaps you never have time to exercise. Identifying this problem can lead you to set an achievable goal, such as finding an hour each day for exercise.

2. *Explore all alternatives.* Analyze possible solutions to your problem. If you need to find an hour to exercise, identify and cut back on time killers. Can you free up an hour by limiting your Internet surfing and TV watching? Can you rearrange your schedule to gain time? Is there an after-school activity you can drop, or can you combine some of your activities?

3. *Choose the best alternative.* After considering all alternatives, decide on which best fits your situation. It may be one alternative or some combination.

4. *Act on your decision.* You must carry out your plans. For example, if you decide to rearrange your schedule, write a plan for the new routine. Make every effort to follow it for a few days to see how it works. You may need to make some adjustments. If you decide to limit phone time, it may help to tell friends when you are taking calls and when you are not available. Find reminders and aids to help you stick to your new schedule.

5. *Evaluate your solution or decision.* Evaluation is an ongoing process. As you carry out your plan, evaluate your progress toward your intended goal. Is the plan of action working? How can you improve it? The evaluation process can help you stay on track and make future decisions.

Managing Resources to Reach Goals

Whether you run a big corporation, an average household, or your own personal affairs, you need management skills to get things done. Management skills put you in control. You make the decisions. You carry them out. You benefit from the right choices and occasionally suffer from the mistakes.

You have seen that decision making is an important part of management. However, management involves more than making decisions and solving problems. Management is a three-part process: planning, acting, and evaluating.

The Planning Phase

A job well planned is a job half done. This familiar saying points out the importance of the planning phase of management. Whether you want to reach a career goal or decide what clothes to wear, some forethought or planning helps. Deciding what to wear to school may involve very little conscious planning. Choosing what to wear to a wedding or a job interview takes more thought. Building an appropriate wardrobe for your lifestyle can be a major planning challenge.

The planning phase of management involves identifying goals, obstacles, and resources.

- Start with your goals. What do you want to get or achieve?
- Next, consider the obstacles. What stands between you and your goals? What must you overcome?
- Then list your resources. What can you use to overcome the obstacles and reach your goals? Include personal resources, such as energy, creativity, determination, special skills, and talents.

Two management plans are shown in 5-5. Listed under each goal are the obstacles and resources related to it. Try putting together a similar plan for achieving something you want such as a summer job, a racing bike, or a part in a school play.

The Action Phase

Planning is of little value without action. The action phase of management involves putting your resources to work to overcome the obstacles that stand between you and your goals. Success in this phase depends on two key characteristics—determination and flexibility.

Human Services

Customer Service Representatives
Customer service representatives interact with customers to provide information. They respond to inquiries about products and service, and handle and resolve complaints.

Reflect

Can you think of situations in your life when determination or lack of it has made a difference?

Achieving Goals by Overcoming Obstacles		
Goal	**Obstacles**	**Available Resources**
To complete an English assignment on time	time limitations lack of interest in the topic difficulty getting started tough grading by the English teacher	two free hours after school each day the public library reference room knowledge of the topic and where to go for information detailed instructions from the English teacher writing and computer skills a computer determination to finish on time and get a good grade
To become president of the student body	the popularity of the other candidates difficulty in contacting all the voters limited time before the election lack of organization among the supporters	knowledge of the job and its demands experience in student government organizational skills public speaking skills reputation for leadership energy and enthusiasm for planning and running the campaign knowledge of what the voters want broad support from both student body and faculty friends who are willing to help run the campaign use of school computers and graphics programs the desire to win

5-5

Listing your goals, obstacles, and resources give you perspective on what you can accomplish.

Discuss

How can the ability to be flexible contribute to reaching important goals? Give examples.

Reflect

Can you think of things you would do differently if you had a second chance? How can careful evaluation of past events help you improve in the future?

Reflect

Consider plans or actions you have taken to reach an important goal. Evaluate your plans or actions using the questions listed in Chart 5-6.

Resource

Chapter 5—Making Smart Decisions, Teacher's PowerPoint Presentations CD

Determination helps you stay focused on the final goal and stick with the project to the end. Determination is especially necessary when something happens to change your plans. For instance, when working on a tough math assignment, you may feel like giving up. With determination, you keep working until the problem is solved.

Flexibility helps you adjust to new and unexpected situations. It helps you find ways to revise and improve your plans.

Imagine that you have two goals for the weekend: earn money for a camping trip and write a book report. You have a babysitting job on Saturday and plan to spend Sunday afternoon on the book report. When you are called to babysit for much longer than expected, you revise your plans. You write the report while babysitting when the children are asleep. This frees up time for something else on Sunday. Flexibility can work to your advantage in all kinds of situations.

The Evaluation Phase

Evaluation is a continuous function. Through evaluation, you assess your progress as you go through all stages of the management process. Evaluation also improves your management skills for future projects. Ongoing evaluation can help you develop better ways of using resources to reach goals. Consider what worked and what did not in your planning. How can you do better next time? See 5-6 on the process of evaluation.

The Process of Evaluation		
Evaluating Plans	**Evaluating Actions**	**Evaluating Results**
What are the goals?	Is the plan working?	Were the goals achieved?
What obstacles stand in the way?	Is there steady progress toward the goals?	Was achieving the goals worth the effort and resources used?
What resources are needed?	Are resources being used to their best advantage?	Are results satisfactory?
Are the needed resources available?	Are top priority goals getting top priority attention?	What key factors contributed to reaching or failing to reach the goals?
Are the goals realistic, given the obstacles and resources?	Is there room for improvement in the original plans? What adjustments can be made?	What were the weaknesses in the plans and actions? What were the strengths?
Are the goals worth the effort and resources required to attain them?	Have new or unexpected developments created the need to change the original plans? What changes are needed?	How can future plans be improved?

5-6

Evaluation is an important part of effective management.

Making smart decisions will help you sucessfully manage your finances.

Chapter Summary

Knowing yourself may be the most important requirement when it comes to making intelligent choices. Competent consumers base decisions on personal needs and wants—on the values, ethics, and goals that are most important to them. Goals for spending and well-established priorities can guide you to choices that give lasting satisfaction.

Management involves using resources (what you have) to reach goals (what you want). It starts with identifying available resources. There are two types of resources—human and nonhuman. Resources are limited, manageable, and related to each other. The process of management also requires making decisions and solving problems.

Economic decision-making tools include cost-benefit analysis and marginal analysis. Perhaps a more important tool is commonsense. It reminds you to live within your means so you can enjoy financial well-being now and in the future.

When aiming at specific goals, a systematic decision-making process helps consumers make intelligent choices. It is a five-step process. Making the best use of resources in management is a three-step process. It calls for planning, acting, and evaluating.

Review

1. Name and describe the three types of goals that differ by the amount of time it takes to reach them. Give an example of each.

2. How are standards related to values and goals?

3. How does the cost-benefit principle apply to decision making?

4. Give an example of why marginal benefit and marginal cost should be considered in decision making by consumers. Do the same for producers.

5. List the five steps of the decision-making process.

6. What three factors should be identified in the planning phase of management?

7. What two key characteristics determine success in the action phase of management?

8. What are the two purposes of evaluation in management?

Critical Thinking

9. Why are values and goals different for different people? Why and how are values and goals likely to change throughout your life?

10. Why is it important to establish priorities to guide your consumer and life choices?

Answers to *Review*

1. long-term goals, medium-term goals, short-term goals (Examples are student response.)

2. Standards are based on goals and values.

3. Cost-benefit analysis states that you should take an action or make a purchase only if the benefits are at least as great as the costs.

4. When the marginal cost is greater than the consumer's marginal benefit, they should stop purchasing the product. Producers can determine how many workers they need for maximum production, and at what point more workers fail to increase production.

11. Why do a person's standards vary from one situation to another?

12. What are your most important and valuable human and nonhuman resources?

13. Apply the decision-making process to an important decision or short-term goal you are facing. Describe the decision, list the alternatives, choose the best alternative, act on the choice, and evaluate the results. Discuss how this process could help you with key decisions and problems in your future.

Academic Connections

14. **Social studies.** Discuss how the decision-making process might help in establishing local, state, and federal government policies.

15. **Writing.** Write a paper in which you list several of your goals. Then identify each as a "to be," "to do," or "to have" goal and explain your reasoning.

16. **Speech.** Role-play examples of decisions people make
    A. just to please someone else
    B. on the spur of the moment
    C. by failing to act

Math Challenge

17. College can be a huge expense. Many college students receive grants, scholarships, and loans that help reduce costs. However, for this exercise, assume that you and your parents will be paying the entire cost.

    A number of Web sites offer online calculators that provide estimates of college costs. Use one of these sites to figure out how much you will need for college. (One example is the College Board's site at www.collegeboard.com/student/pay/index.html. Click on the financial calculator for college costs.) Determine how much you will need to save per month.

Tech $mart

18. When you picture yourself as an adult, what standard of living would you like? How much money will you have to earn to achieve this lifestyle? The Jump$tart Coalition for Personal Financial Literacy developed an online questionnaire to help you answer this question. Go to www.jumpstart.org/realitycheck. Answer a series of questions about your future lifestyle choices. Then let the online calculator tell you how much income you would need to achieve this standard of living.

    The site also gives examples of occupations that earn the required amount of income. How much income would your standard of living require? What are a few of the occupations you might choose to earn this income?

5. (1) Define the problem to be solved or the issue to be decided. (2) Explore all the alternatives. (3) Choose the best alternatives. (4) Act on your decision. (5) Evaluate your solution or decision.

6. goals, obstacles, and resources

7. determination and flexibility

8. to assess your progress and to improve your management skills for future projects

Personal Finance: An Overview

Reading for Meaning

Skim the chapter by reading the first sentence of each paragraph. Use this information to create an outline of the chapter before you read it.

financial literacy

budget

income

expense

fixed expense

variable expense

philanthropy

cash flow statement

net worth statement

net worth

liability

wealth

family life cycle

demographics

family crisis

recordkeeping

CHAPTER OBJECTIVES

After studying this chapter, you will be able to

- **prepare** a budget tailored to income and needs.
- **prepare** cash flow and net worth statements.
- **plan** family finances for different stages in the life cycle.
- **give examples** of economic, demographic, cultural, and technological factors that can impact financial planning.
- **explain** ways to deal with a financial crisis.
- **identify** important financial and legal documents to keep on hand.

Central Ideas

- Enjoying financial security throughout life is an achievable goal.
- Budgets and other financial planning tools can help people achieve financial security.

The average high school graduate can expect to earn just over one million dollars in a lifetime, according to statistics. College graduates will earn more than two million. However, no matter how much you earn, your needs may not be met if resources are not used wisely.

Financial planning is an ongoing process designed to take you from where you are to where you wish to be financially. It is a way to take control of your financial resources and future. The ultimate purpose of financial planning is to reach important goals and achieve a sense of financial security for life. *Financial security* is the ability to meet essential needs without taking on more debt than you can repay.

Preparing Financial Statements

Reaching financial security is the result of planning. Before you learn to plan, though, you must achieve financial literacy. **Financial literacy** is the understanding of the basic knowledge and skills needed to manage financial resources. Having financial literacy means you are aware of different financial management options and the way each functions. With this knowledge, you can be confident as you manage your money, credit, accounts, and investments. You feel secure in your ability to make these resources work for you.

Tailoring a Budget to Income and Needs

Planning allows you to meet changing needs and goals over your lifetime. It begins with managing day-to-day expenses. A *budget* can help you make the most of your money and avoid financial problems. A **budget** is a spending plan for the use of money over time based on goals and expected income. The purpose of a budget is to take control of your money and spending. Creating a simple, workable budget involves these basic steps.

Financial Goals		
	When Wanted	**Estimated Cost**
Short-Term		
Boots	In 2 months	$ 65
Christmas gifts	In 3 months	$ 100
Summer trip	In 9 months	$ 350
Medium-Term		
Laptop computer	In 1 year	$ 500
Used car	In 2 years	$ 6,000
Long-Term		
College expenses	In 5 years	$32,000

6-1

Organizing your goals on a chart similar to this can help direct your spending and saving to whatever is most important to you at a given time.

1. Establish Financial Goals.

Well-thought-out goals can help you direct your dollars to those things you consider most important. Make a list of your financial goals. (Chapter 5 covered goal setting in detail.) Include short-, medium-, and long-term goals, 6-1. For example, the goal of getting money for a movie this weekend is fairly immediate. Saving enough money for a week-long camping trip next year with friends is a medium-term goal. A new car or future education are long-term goals. They require saving over a period of time.

Keep in mind that financial goals change over the years. At this moment, your goals may include saving money for a personal media player, a car, travel, or college. However, as you experience college, work, and perhaps marriage and parenthood, your financial goals will evolve.

2. Estimate and Total Your Income.

Determine your budget period. The period—weekly, biweekly, or monthly—depends on when you receive most of your income. **Income** is any form of money you receive, such as an allowance, a paycheck, and gains from an investment. If you receive a weekly allowance, for example, it makes sense to budget on a weekly basis. If you receive a regular paycheck and pay monthly bills, it may be easier to work with monthly figures.

Estimate your income during a typical budget period. Using a worksheet such as the one in 6-2, write your best estimate of how much money you normally receive from each income source. Total the estimates and write it at the bottom of the sheet. This is your estimated total income for a budgeting period.

3. Estimate and Total Your Expenses.

After figuring your income, the next step is figuring your expenses. An **expense** is the cost of goods and services you buy. It helps to classify your expenses as *fixed or variable* expenses.

Fixed Expenses. A **fixed expense** is a set cost that must be paid each budget period. Fixed expenses may include

- rent or mortgage payments
- tuition
- insurance premiums
- loan payments (auto, educational)

Discuss

How are financial goals likely to change over the years? How do you think your goals will be different five or ten years from now?

Activity

Using a chart similar to 6-2, estimate income you expect to receive next month.

Discuss

How can an up-to-date estimate of income help you reach goals?

Estimating Income

Week or Month of _____

Income Sources	Estimated	Actual
Jobs		
Babysitting	$ 25	$
Yard work	$ 40	$
Part-time at Pizza Parlor	$ 200	$
Allowance	$ 40	$
Gifts	$ 10	$
Total Income	**$ 315**	**$**

6-2

Use a form similar to this one to estimate expected income. Review your estimates and fill in with actual figures to stay up-to-date on the amount you have to spend and save.

These expenses tend to increase in number and amount as you move into adult years. As a rule, fixed expenses must be paid when due. Therefore, it is important to list them first.

Variable Expenses. A **variable expense** is a cost that changes both in the amount and time it must be paid. These expenses can often be pared down or cut. When people are short of cash, variable expenses are the first expenses they will scrutinize. Variable expenses include

- food
- clothing
- medical expenses
- entertainment

Most teenagers receive the basic necessities from their families and spend their money on *discretionary expenses.* These expenses do not involve basic needs. They include music, snacks, computer games, and movies. For adults, discretionary expenses often include vacations, gifts, expensive clothing, and other unnecessary goods and services.

Clothing can be both a necessary and a discretionary expense. For example, buying a basic coat to keep you warm during cold weather is a necessary expense. However, a pricey designer coat is a discretionary expense because a less expensive coat would do.

Using the worksheet in 6-3 as a guide, list the general categories for your fixed and variable expenses in the far left column. For example, write *Snacks, Clothes,* and so forth. Then write down how much you spend on each.

Estimating Expenses			
Week or Month of _____			
Expense Items	**Due Dates**	**Estimates**	**Actual**
Fixed Expenses			
Bus pass	_____	$ 15	$_____
Lunches	_____	$ 90	$_____
Savings	_____	$ 15	$_____
Variable Expenses			
Snacks	_____	$ 20	$_____
Movies/concerts/events	_____	$ 40	$_____
Clothes	_____	$ 50	$_____
CDs/music files	_____	$ 25	$_____
Gifts	_____	$ 20	$_____
Magazines	_____	$ 15	$_____
Grooming aids	_____	$ 25	$_____
Total Expenses	_____	$ 315	$_____

6-3

Make adjustments to your variable expenses when you are short of cash.

Building Savings into Your Budget

It is wise to include savings in your budget. Save a small amount regularly in a special fund. This way, you will have cash available if an unexpected expense arises. Everyone needs an *emergency fund* when unexpected expenses occur. These can include a hefty car repair bill, unexpected medical expenses, or a home repair cost. An emergency fund is also an important financial cushion to have in case of job loss or some other disruption to income.

With savings, you can plan ahead for major expenses and medium- and long-term goals. For example, to prepare for a camping trip, estimate how much money you will need and the time you have to get it. Suppose the trip will cost $360 and it is five months away.

- How much do you need to save per month? Divide $360 by 5, the number of months. If you save $72 each month, you will have enough.

- How much do you need to save per week? Divide $360 by 20, the number of weeks in five months. If you save $18 each week, you will have enough.

You can use this method to plan for any expense if you know the amount you need and when you need it.

In the future, when you have money left over after expenses, saving that money can increase your resources. Later chapters cover many more ways to preserve and increase your financial resources. Chapter 9, for example, discusses the use of credit to meet goals and manage the peaks and valleys of income and expenses. Chapters 11 and 12 discuss savings in more detail, as well as investments that can improve your financial circumstances.

Charitable Giving as an Expense

Many people voluntarily contribute money or items of value to charities. A charity usually refers to an organization that aids the poor, the homeless, the sick, and others in need. **Philanthropy** is the act of giving

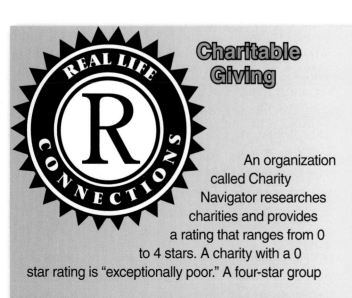

Charitable Giving

REAL LIFE CONNECTIONS

An organization called Charity Navigator researches charities and provides a rating that ranges from 0 to 4 stars. A charity with a 0 star rating is "exceptionally poor." A four-star group is "exceptional." You want to choose highly rated charities because they make the best use of your contributions. You also want to choose charities with programs that are growing.

By typing the name of a charity into www.charitynavigator.org, you can get a detailed report that tells you how much money it collects and spends. The group's "efficiency rating" is based on how much it spends on programs versus administrative costs and fund-raising. Charity Navigator gives the salaries of heads of charities. A "capacity rating" is based on the growth of revenue and programs.

money, goods, or services for the good of others. You may want to make charitable giving a regular expense in your budget. In addition to helping others, you often get a tax deduction.

Be watchful when giving to charities. Some groups pose as charities but use the funds they collect to enrich themselves. Other groups are genuine but use too much money for nonprogram costs. It pays to do some research before you give.

To determine how much you can give, consider your income, expenses, and outstanding debts. Until you have an income high enough to support charitable giving, you can always volunteer your time and energy.

4. Analyze Current Income and Spending.

Taking a close look at your record of income and spending is an important step in money management. It is easy to overestimate income and underestimate expenses. A detailed record of spending almost always turns up some surprises and some unnecessary spending. Inspect your record of income and expenses. Are your income figures accurate? Subtract your expenses from your income for each budget period. Do you come out even? Do you have money left over for goals?

If you have nothing left or if you are "in the hole," you will need to find ways to increase income or cut expenses. To increase income, explore these possibilities.

- Can you earn extra money by handling more responsibilities at home or for your neighbors? Can you go grocery shopping, wash windows, or reorganize closets and cabinets?

- Can you get a part-time job if you do not have one? Look for help wanted ads. Can you get ideas from family, friends, coaches, and counselors? Have you overlooked any job opportunities?

- If you have a job, can you negotiate an increase in wages? Can you work more hours without sacrificing the time you need for school-work and other important activities?

To reduce spending, study your record of expenses.

- Start with your discretionary expenses. Can you eliminate something? reduce the cost of an item? get something for free? For example, perhaps you can make a gift instead of buying one. You can cut back on music downloads and text messaging. You can read your favorite magazines at the library instead of buying them.

- Look at expenses you list under the fixed and variable categories. These expenses may be necessary, but can you reduce their cost by making substitutions? For example, maybe you can bring your lunch from home instead of buying it. Try a generic shampoo instead of an expensive brand.

- Can you cut any expenses unrelated to your priorities and goals? For example, if good health is a priority, you can stop buying soda and potato chips.

After you figure out how to stretch your income to cover your needs, you can move to step 5.

5. Prepare a Trial Budget.

At this point, it is time to bring together your goals, income, and expenses into some form of a plan. A plan reduces the temptation to spend carelessly. The form in 6-4 illustrates one way to organize a budget. You may wish to draft a similar form for your own financial planning.

Keep these records over a period of time so you can review your financial situation now and then. The important thing is to put your budget in writing and keep it up-to-date as you go along. The tips in 6-5 can make a budget work better.

Fill in the "Planned" column of the worksheet using the estimated calculations you made in 6-3. This is your trial budget.

6. Put Your Budget Into Action.

Once your budget is set up, you need to spend and save according to plans. Keep your budget handy and refer to it often. When the budget period ends, fill in the amounts for actual income and expenses. When an actual expense is greater than the amount you budgeted, identify the

Budget		
Week or Month of _____ **October** _____		
Income	**Planned** $___315___	**Actual** $_____
Expenses		
Fixed Expenses	$___120___	$___120___
Bus pass	$___15___	$___15___
Lunches	$___90___	$___90___
Savings	$___15___	$___15___
Variable Expenses	$___195___	$___195___
Snacks	$___20___	$___17___
Movies/concerts/events	$___40___	$___39___
Clothes	$___50___	$___55___
CDs/music files	$___25___	$___23___
Gifts	$___20___	$___20___
Magazines	$___15___	$___13___
Grooming Aids	$___25___	$___28___
Total Expenses	$___315___	$___315___

6-4

You could use a form similar to this for your trial budget. Use your estimates of income and expenses, financial goals, and record of spending in making up your trial budget.

Quick Tips to Better Budgeting

- Keep it simple.
- Write it down.
- Be specific.
- Be flexible.
- Be disciplined.
- Keep it all together.
- Be prepared for the unexpected.

6-5

When planning a budget, keep these tips in mind.

Cash Flow Statement	
Week or Month of October	
	Actual
Income (Cash Inflows)	
Part-time jobs	$265
(Babysitting, yard work, pizza parlor)	
Allowance	$ 40
Gifts	$ 10
Total Income	**$315**
Expenses (Cash Outflows)	
Fixed expenses	$120
(Bus pass, lunches, savings)	
Total Fixed Expenses	**$120**
Variable expenses	$145
(Snacks, clothes, cell phone, grooming aids/makeup, movies/concerts/events	
Total Variable Expenses	**$145**
Total Expenses	**$265**
Net Cash Income	**$ 50**

6-6

A cash flow statement shows your actual income and expenses.

cause. Did you ignore the plan? Was there an unexpected expense? Was your estimate too low? If your estimate was too low, adjust your budget to better reflect actual costs.

7. Evaluate Your Budget Periodically.

From time to time, it is wise to review your money management plan to make sure it is working for you. You can expect your financial plans to change with significant events in your life. These include going to college, starting a new job, leaving home, getting married, having children, or changing jobs.

Consider these questions as you evaluate your budget.

- Is your financial plan working? Is your money doing what you want it to do?
- Are you reaching important goals?
- As you achieve goals, do you set new ones?
- Are you controlling your spending?
- Has your income or pattern of spending changed significantly?
- Are there changes in your life that call for adjustments in your financial planning?

When revisions are needed, make the necessary changes and update your budget. Recheck in a week or two to see if the new entries are an improvement. If you monitor your finances carefully, your income will work well for you over the years.

Preparing a Cash Flow Statement

A **cash flow statement** is a summary of the amount of money received as well as the amount paid out for goods and services during a specific period. A cash flow statement is also called an *income and expense statement*.

The cash flow statement shown in 6-6 appears very similar to the budget statement shown earlier. However, there are important differences. In the cash flow statement,

- income is called *Cash Inflow*
- expenses are called *Cash Outflow*

- the term *Actual* heads the column of figures instead of *Planned*

The cash flow statement goes beyond the budget to reflect actual money inflow and outflow for the month. Prepared at the end of the budget period, it shows real income and spending, not what was planned for the month.

To get accurate figures for the statement, record cash inflows and outflows in an Income and Expense Log, 6-7. The log is also called a *personal spending diary*. Record any money you receive plus any you spend. For example, write "Snacks," "Clothes," and so forth to record expenses. Then write down how much you spend on each. Also report exactly how much money came in. Do this until you reach the end of your budget period.

With a cash flow statement in hand, you can prepare a budget for the next month more quickly. You will find that careful recording of cash inflows and outflows leads to more accurate budgeting.

Preparing a Net Worth Statement

It is wise to evaluate your total financial situation at least annually. A *financial* or *net worth statement* can help you do this accurately. A **net worth statement** is a written record of your current financial situation. Your **net worth** is the difference between what you own and what you owe. It measures your financial standing at a particular point in time.

This may not seem important now, but as you move into the adult world, your circumstances can change rapidly and tracking your finances can become complicated.

As you revise this statement, you see the progress you are making toward your goals. The net worth statement helps you chart your financial future. On it, you list *assets* and *liabilities* and subtract what you owe from what you own to determine net worth, 6-8.

Business, Management & Administration

Bookkeepers

Bookkeepers update and maintain accounting records. They calculate expenditures, receipts, accounts payable and receivable, and profit and loss. They may also handle payroll, make purchases, prepare invoices, and keep track of overdue accounts.

Discuss

How do you think each of the pointers in 6-5 could improve your money management skills and budgeting success?

Reflect

Can you think of situations in your life or in your family that called for changes in the use of money and in financial plans for the future?

Reflect

How would you answer the questions on page 126 to help you evaluate your success and progress in using a budget?

Income and Expense Log			
Date	**Item**	**Income**	**Expense**
9/10 Fri.	Bus fare—round-trip		$4
	Lunch		$5
	Snack		$2
9/11 Sat.	Babysitting	$20	
	Snack		$3.50
	School supplies		$17
	Movie ticket		$7
9/12 Sun.	Gift from uncle	$10	
	New sneakers		$34

6-7

Keeping a detailed log of your income and spending will help you develop a more accurate and realistic budget.

Discuss

What is the value of an up-to-date net worth statement? When might you use it?

Resource

Your Net Worth, Activity D, WB

Activity

Using a form similar to 6-8, determine where you stand financially. Suggest to your family you should complete the form for personal and confidential use.

Net Worth Statement

Assets

Liquid Assets:

Cash on hand	$_____
Cash in savings, checking, and money market accounts	_____
Cash value of insurance	_____
Other	_____
Total Liquid Assets	$_____

Investment Assets:

Stocks and bonds	$_____
Mutual funds	_____
Individual Retirement Accounts	_____
Other	_____
Total Investment Assets	$_____

Use Assets: (market values)

Auto	$_____
Home	_____
Furniture and equipment	_____
Other	_____
Total Use Assets	$_____

Total Assets	$_____

Liabilities

Current Liabilities:

Credit cards and charge account balances due	$_____
Taxes due	_____
Other	_____
Total Current Liabilities	$_____

Long-term Liabilities:

Auto loan	$_____
Home mortgage	_____
Other	_____
Total Long-term Liabilities	$_____

Total Liabilities	$_____
Net Worth (total assets less total liabilities)	$_____

6-8

A net worth statement helps you determine your net worth at a given point in time.

Assets

An *asset* is an item of value you own, such as cash, stocks, bonds, real estate, and personal possessions. Assets are divided into three categories.

- *Liquid assets* include cash and savings that quickly and easily convert to cash.

- *Investment assets* include stocks, bonds, and invested funds that are set aside for long-term goals, such as the education of children or retirement needs.

- *Use assets* include a home, auto, personal possessions, and other durable goods that enrich your life through use.

Assets tend to change in value from year to year so you will want to list them at their *current* or *market value*. This is their estimated worth at the time you make your net worth statement.

Vocabulary

Explain the meaning of the italicized words and give examples of each.

Reflect

What are some liabilities you expect to have in the future? What are some liabilities you hope to avoid having?

Discuss

What images come to mind when you hear the word *wealth*?

Liabilities

A **liability** is a financial obligation that you currently owe or will owe in the future. Liabilities include unpaid bills, credit card charges, mortgages, personal loans, and taxes. These are divided into two categories:

- *Current liabilities* are items due soon, usually within the year. They include medical bills, taxes, and unpaid bills from credit cards and charge accounts.

- *Long-term liabilities* include obligations to be paid over a long period of time, such as a home mortgage or auto loan.

Your Net Worth

Subtract liabilities from assets to arrive at your net worth. If you own more than you owe, you have positive net worth. This means that you can meet your financial obligations. You may also have assets you can use to meet financial goals that go beyond your obligations.

Wealthy individuals will have assets far in excess of their liabilities. The term **wealth** refers to an abundance of assets that are accumulated over time. It includes investments, property, a business, and other items of value that contribute significantly to financial security and a high standard of living and giving.

If your net worth is a negative figure, your debts exceed your assets. You need to find ways to reduce expenses or increase income. Start with a careful look at expenses. Try to reduce or eliminate all the items that are not essential. Pay off credit debts and do not take on more credit obligations. Consider ways to increase income by working more hours or assuming more responsibilities on the job. A job change or additional training may also lead to higher income in some situations. In some families unemployed family members may be able to find work that pays. Take every possible measure to create a positive net worth.

Discuss

What does the term *life cycle* mean to you? How does it relate to financial planning and security?

Activity

Study 6-9 and relate it to your family's situation and stage in the life cycle.

Reflect

How does your family's financial life compare to that outlined in this chart?

Planning Family Finances

As you enter the adult world, your money management activities will expand. Teens eagerly await the day when they can afford to live on their own. Once independent, their eyes are opened to the many expenses they must handle that were previously paid by their parents. Managing finances well to remain independent becomes their number one challenge.

Often young adults who are newly independent try to hold down costs by sharing living expenses with one or more friends. After a period of living with others or on their own, many adults eventually form families. Their financial responsibilities increase dramatically. There are family as well as personal expenses to cover. Perhaps the most important factors affecting your adult budgeting decisions will be your age and the stage you occupy in the family life cycle.

Family life cycle refers to the stages a family passes through from formation to aging. Your goals and needs, as well as earning and spending patterns, will change with each stage. Becoming familiar with these patterns can provide you with a framework for your own financial planning. See 6-9.

Financial Aspects of the Family Life Cycle		
Stages in the Family Life Cycle	**Career and Income Characteristics**	**Typical Expenses and Obligations**
Beginning Stage		
Marriage Getting started as a couple Establishing a home	Finishing education Making career decisions Entering the workforce Low or no income, with gradual increases	Living expenses Tuition and/or repayment of education loans Auto loan payments and insurance Life, health, and other insurance Home furnishings Savings and retirement contributions Income tax
Expanding Stage		
Birth/adoption of first child The infant years	Increasing income and job responsibilities One or two full-time incomes Decreased income if wife leaves work for childbearing	Child care and baby equipment Education fund Increased insurance coverage Prenatal, birth, and postnatal health care Income taxes Retirement contributions

6-9   (Continued.)

Career and income characteristics along with typical expenses and obligations tend to follow a general pattern at different stages of the life cycle.

Developing Stage		
Toddler, preschool, and elementary school years: Children become primary focus	Job advancement likely Increasing income Increasing job responsibilities	Move to larger living space Additional home furnishings Property and income tax increases Increased living expenses Retirement contributions
Adolescent years: Involvement in school activities Preparation for launching stage	Continuing job advancement or possible career change Possible return of mother to the workforce Income still increasing	School expenses for extracurricular activities Savings and investments Savings for education Charitable contributions Travel Adolescents' spending Income and property taxes

Launching Stage		
Children leave home Parents adjust to "empty nest"	Heavier job responsibilities Peak performance years Income may peak as well Benefits may increase Retirement planning becomes a priority	Home improvements or new, smaller home Replacement furnishings Education and tuition costs Travel Retirement savings Income and property taxes Weddings of children

Aging Stage		
Parents focus on each other Children marry Grandchildren arrive Elderly parents may require care	Job responsibilities and earnings begin to level off Retirement and estate planning take form	Travel, recreation, and adult education Care for aging parents Increased savings and investments Gifts to help children get established Income and property taxes Long-term care insurance
Retirement years: Establishing new routines, interests, and hobbies Grandparenting	Part-time or volunteer work Social Security income Income from retirement savings Wills and estate plans are revised as needed	Health insurance Possible relocation to a retirement area Travel Health care and medications Taxes Long-term care

6-9

(Continued.)

Discuss

How is planting a tree similar to financial planning?

Discuss

How do you think values, goals, and priorities are likely to change as people move through the various stages of the life cycle? To what extent do they stay the same?

Beginning Stage

From age 18 to the late 20s, young people are getting established on the job and in life. Those who marry begin the first stage of the family life cycle, called the *beginning stage.* Income for most young adults starts low and gradually increases with time on the job. Two-income couples enjoy the benefits of combined incomes. People who marry later may have established careers and higher incomes.

Expenses at this time are likely to include education, college loans, home furnishings, and insurance. The down payment on a home is often the largest single expense of young couples. Other major expenses include an auto, savings, or contributions to a retirement fund. Couples need to revise their savings and investment programs to meet their changing needs as they move to later stages in the life cycle.

Case Study: Making Plans

Looking Ahead

Maria and Tony plan to be married in six months. Maria is a nursery school teacher, and Tony is a welder. Their combined annual income is almost $60,000.

During their first few years of marriage, Maria and Tony plan to buy a house and some furniture. Tony owns a car. They both use credit cards, but have little debt.

After four to five years, they hope to start a family. Maria wants to work as a substitute teacher until their children reach school age. By then, Tony's income may be higher. His work benefits include health care coverage, and life and disability insurance.

Case Review

1. What expenses will this couple likely have in the first year or two of marriage?
2. What steps do Maria and Tony need to take now in order to drop to one steady income when children come?
3. What big expenses are likely to come with the purchase of a home? with their first child? with later children?
4. What contributions should Maria and Tony make for unexpected emergencies and expenses?

Expanding Stage

For adults under age 40, life is often characterized by job advancement, rising income, and increasing responsibilities. With the birth or adoption of the first child, couples enter the *expanding stage* with all its joys and responsibilities.

If one spouse leaves the workforce to raise children, income declines. At the same time, expenses increase. Child-related expenses include child care, children's clothing, baby equipment, toys, and medical expenses. With children may come the decision to move to a larger home, 6-10. This is a good time to review and expand insurance protection. An educational fund for children may be started. It is important to draw up a will, too.

Developing Stage

School-age children and adolescents bring a new set of circumstances for families. Family life tends to revolve around the children and their school life. Expenses include a larger clothing budget, sports and hobby equipment, lessons and tutoring, allowances, and savings for future education. Another expenditure for some is a second car.

During this stage, a spouse who left the workforce may return either to satisfy career goals or to supplement income. This may require at least a brief return to school to update education and skills. While income may still climb during parenting years, expenses grow as well. They include housing, insurance, taxes, education, savings, and retirement planning.

6-10
The arrival of children will call for major adjustments in financial planning.

Launching Stage

Parents in their 40s and 50s share another set of common experiences. Families enter this stage as the children leave home for college, jobs, or homes of their own. During these years, job advancements often bring higher incomes. Earnings may peak. It is also a time when some may seek a job or career change.

Many families at this stage need extra income to cover college expenses and retirement savings. Retirement planning is critical.

In some families, this is a time when aging parents become a concern. Those in this situation are often called the "sandwich generation." Parents find themselves "sandwiched" between college-bound teens and their own aging parents. Both financial and emotional demands are great when this happens.

Discuss

What child-related expenses can you name?

Reflect

What traits do you think will characterize your finances in the next 10 to 12 years?

Discuss

What financial and other difficulties can you identify for the "sandwich generation"?

Reflect

What do you expect your life to be like financially as you move from the young adult stage to age 40?

Discuss

How do values, goals, and standards tend to affect family economics and consumer decisions?

Discuss

How do you think life and financial circumstances for older adults who are still working differ from those who are retired? Cite examples.

Aging Stage

From the late 50s to retirement, people often need to adjust to new events. Earnings level off. Aging parents may require attention and assistance. Children have left home, creating the "empty nest." Many parents become grandparents. Married couples often renew their focus on each other. They may choose to travel or become more active in the community.

Individuals and couples often focus on retirement planning during these years. Empty-nest families may choose to move to a smaller home and simplify their lives for retirement. Those caring for elderly parents may face heavy health and nursing-care costs. Couples need to have reliable health insurance and consider buying long-term care insurance for themselves. At this stage, estate planning is important. It is also the time to review and revise wills.

For most people, this stage marks formal retirement. Some retirees seek part-time work or volunteer opportunities. For many, free time is a welcome luxury. It is a good time to downsize, live more simply, and conserve energy and income. Those in good health may travel more. Grandchildren are frequently important at this time of life.

Income and most living expenses usually decline during retirement years. Security and comfort depend on the financial planning that occurred in earlier stages. For those who have not planned, the retirement years can bring financial hardship as income drops. Serious spending cutbacks may be required, especially as medical costs rise. Retired adults need to review wills and estate plans. They should go over the provisions in each with their adult children.

Variations in the Cycle

Not every family follows the stages of the family life cycle in order, 6-11. The number of children and spacing between them can cause the cycle to vary from family to family. Some families skip, overlap, or repeat stages of the family life cycle. For example, couples that do not have children skip the expanding, developing, and launching stages. Parents with children in school could have more children. This would cause an overlap of the developing and expanding stages. Single parents who remarry may repeat stages with their new spouses.

As family conditions change, financial planning concerns change, too. For example, single individuals, childless couples, single-parent families, and divorced or separated people have these added considerations.

Singles and Childless Couples

Singles and couples with no dependents do not have the expenses related to childrearing, such as school and medical expenses. Both groups may spend more throughout the life cycle on travel, leisure, and other extras. Some may choose to give more to charitable causes. Both groups often feel a greater responsibility to help their aging parents.

Stages of the Family Life Cycle

Beginning Stage	Expanding Stage	Developing Stage

Couple marries.	The first child is born.	Children start school.

Launching Stage	Aging Stage

Children begin moving away from home.	Parents retire.

Variations in the Cycle

A childless couple goes through the beginning and aging stages only.	A single parent in the expanding stage could repeat the beginning stage with a new spouse.	A couple with children in school could have another child, causing an overlap of the expanding and developing stages.

A couple in the launching stage could adopt a child after an older child has left home, returning to the expanding stage.	In an extended family, a couple in the aging stage might not be alone after they retire.

6-11

Not all families proceed through all stages of the family life cycle in the same way.

Single-Parent Families

Females lead most single-parent families. Their income is typically less than that of two-parent families and single-parent families led by males. Saving and planning for future security is sometimes difficult as these families struggle to meet current expenses. Government and community services and assistance can be very helpful for single-parent families.

Case Study: Making Plans

The Single Life

At 28, Myra has no plans to marry and no children. She is a top-notch photographer and earns $50,000 annually. She also receives outstanding benefits through her job, including health, disability, and life insurance. Myra's parents are in good health and they both work. Her two brothers have jobs and families of their own. Myra lives in a rented apartment and is thinking about buying a home, something she has always dreamed.

Case Review

1. What changes in Myra's situation could alter her financial needs and plans?
2. Suppose one of Myra's parents becomes ill, resulting in financial problems. How could this affect Myra's financial plans?
3. Suppose Myra's brother and his wife die in an accident and Myra is named guardian of their children. How might this change her financial plans?
4. What are some financial steps Myra should take before purchasing a home? What steps should she take after becoming a homeowner? What additional expenses will home ownership bring?
5. What are some key differences in financial planning for those with and without dependents?
6. How does an individual's age relate to financial planning and decisions?

Discuss

What do you see as the primary financial concerns of divorced couples?

Separated and Divorced People

Separated and divorced people face a unique set of financial concerns. They may have the following expenses: legal fees, alimony, child support, and property settlement costs. The costs of establishing and maintaining two homes rather than one is another expense, especially if there are children. A divorce or separation may require additional furnishings and moving costs.

No matter what your situation will be, it is wise to begin a savings and investment program and to insure against financial risks early in your adult life. These two steps are the foundation of financial security in later life. Savings can cover unexpected expenses and emergencies and help to reach goals. Insurance protects against major disasters. With both, you can feel reasonably comfortable with your financial situation. Start with a personal savings plan. The longer you save, the more you will accumulate.

Financial Decisions in a Changing World

Besides the family life cycle, other important factors and forces will impact your life. These include economic, social, cultural, and technological forces. Individually and together, these factors will cause you to redefine your financial needs, priorities, and goals.

The Economy and Your Finances

When the economy is on the upswing, people are generally optimistic. Businesses make money, grow, and hire more workers. People who want work can find good jobs. Most consumers who want to can find a job. Their future income is fairly secure and they can pay their bills. If they plan carefully, they can even save and invest for the future. However, when the economy is plagued by problems, such as recession, inflation, or unemployment, managing your finances becomes even more important and challenging.

Recession, a period of slow or no economic growth, can have a major impact on personal money management. This is especially true for those who are out of work or whose incomes are stagnant. Recessions spread uncertainty and pessimism over the entire economy. Consumers spend less and save more if possible. Businesses cut back and unemployment rises.

Discuss

What are some ways inflation and recession might affect you and your family in the use and management of money?

Activity

Research and report on periods of recession in the United States.

ECONOMICS in ACTION

Severe Recessions Hit Home

When recessions hit the U.S. economy, the impact is felt in millions of homes across the country. Young adults struggle with finding work as businesses shed jobs and curtail growth. Financial institutions make fewer loans. Long-term goals, such as increasing one's education and buying a home, must be put on hold.

When people lose their jobs or have their hours reduced, entire families feel the pain. Many lose the health insurance that was provided through their jobs. Unemployment often pushes many families out of their homes.

Loss of income means lifestyle changes for almost everyone. There is less money and much more anxiety. Retirement savings drop with the stock market. People who were retired or nearing retirement are forced to work beyond their planned retirement age, if they can find work.

Inflation, or a period of rising prices, also relates to personal money management. As prices go up, the value of a dollar goes down. If income does not rise at the same rate that prices rise, buying power is reduced. Consumers cannot buy as much or save as much. Financial planning and saving can help consumers cope with challenging economic conditions.

Demographics and Your Finances

To some extent, the way you manage your money and your life in the years ahead will depend on *demographics*. **Demographics** refer to the statistical characteristics of the population. *Vital statistics* include records of births, deaths, and marriages. *Social statistics* include population breakdowns by age, sex, and race with geographic distributions and growth rates.

Other social-economic statistics concern education levels, income levels, employment, religion, crime, immigration, and ethnic representation. A current almanac is a good place to look for the latest demographic statistics. Recent demographic trends have an impact on the overall economy, and in turn, on the financial life of consumers. Consider some of the following trends and their economic implications:

- Couples are marrying and having children later in life.

- The percentage of single-parent families is growing, 6-12.

- The average age of the overall population is increasing.

- Educational requirements for jobs are rising and job markets are changing.

- Skilled workers are in greater demand.

- More young adults are living at home with their parents.

- The number of unmarried adults is increasing.

- More mothers are working away from home.

- The number of births to single mothers is increasing.

All these and other factors will affect your financial future.

6-12

The growing number of single-parent families is one demographic factor that has affected the economy.

Culture and Your Finances

Most urban areas include a variety of racial and ethnic groups. Each group makes an impact on consumer attitudes and buying habits, community services, schools, and many other consumer and family issues.

Relationships and marriages between people of different races, cultures, and religions are on the increase. This creates a blending of ethnic traditions, religious beliefs, languages, and concepts of "family." Cultural and ethnic traditions affect many everyday choices and routines. They may dictate the role each partner plays in the family, who makes financial and spending decisions, whether both partners work, how the family uses credit, and how the family manages its money.

Technology and Your Finances

New developments and discoveries in communications, medicine, science, and other areas change the way we live in the world. For example, medical advances may result in a longer, healthier life for you and others. New findings on healthful lifestyles include fitness routines, nutritious diets, and stress reduction. You now know how to improve your own health and quality of life. However, living longer makes financial planning even more critical. Your savings must sustain you over a longer life span.

Technology brings other changes in the way you live and deal with financial matters. For example, the Internet has altered the way people buy goods and services. You can buy everything from groceries to autos to movie tickets online. Information technology can bring you the latest information from around the world about consumer products, services, and issues. Money management software brings you up-to-the-minute tools for managing money and performing many financial tasks online. You can do your banking, bill paying, investing, and fund transfers online in your own home, 6-13. The Internet brings an international marketplace to your fingertips.

Activity

Write a research report on how handling financial transactions was different 100 years ago.

Discuss

Debate the positive and negative effects of technology on family income.

Discuss

How often do you buy items using the Internet? How often do you bank online? Do you think this will change over time?

6-13
With a computer and an Internet connection, you can manage your finances almost anywhere.

Reflect

How would you describe a financial crisis?

Activity

Search current newspapers and magazines for stories of family crisis. Discuss possible ways of dealing with the different situations. How might the individual crisis differ for families at different stages in the life cycle and how might the coping mechanisms differ?

Advanced technology creates new markets and brings more and cheaper goods and services to consumers. It also creates new jobs in many fields. Unfortunately it also has fueled *offshore outsourcing* in some fields. This is the business practice of moving factories and jobs overseas and across borders to take advantage of cheap labor and business-friendly government regulations. As a result, many American workers must compete for jobs with lower-paid workers in other countries. This has caused layoffs and unemployment, especially among those who work in manufacturing and information technology industries. Today and in the future, the higher-paying jobs will require higher levels of education and training. Education has never been more important than in today's economy.

Working Through Financial Problems

You can often avoid financial trouble by living within your means and keeping debt under control. This involves taking responsibility for your life, including your financial choices and decisions.

Preparation will help you weather a crisis situation if it arises. Getting the best education and job training possible are ways to be prepared. With a good education and job skills, you are better able to find work and advance on the job. Staying current in your field through continuing education and training programs also helps. Usually higher earnings and greater job security result.

An emergency fund equal to several months' pay is another way to prepare for the unexpected. The amount of money needed in the fund differs from one person to another. However, it should equal your monthly income multiplied by the number of months you are likely to be out of work. In some cases, such as during a recession or if you work in a competitive field, the emergency fund should equal as much as eight to ten months of pay.

Preventive measures also help. Those discussed here and in other chapters include

- sound money management
- practical credit controls
- regular savings
- insurance protection
- reasonable caution in financial matters
- regular discussions of financial matters with household members old enough to understand the fundamentals of money management

Prevention, when possible, is the most painless way to deal with potential disasters.

Unexpected Crisis

There may be times when financial disaster strikes because of circumstances beyond your control. A **family crisis** is a major problem that impacts the future of the family and its lifestyle. Examples include job loss, divorce, death, disability, serious illness, and natural disaster. When such events occur, you may need to make some serious changes in your financial planning and behavior. If debt problems reach the crisis stage, you must take drastic steps to correct the situation.

In many cases, you should start by discussing the problem with adult members of the household, including older children. Make sure that everyone understands the potential impact on their standard of living and what they can do to help. For example, college-bound teens may need to consider work/study programs or a community college near enough to live at home while going to school. Knowing they have a stake in resolving the crisis will encourage cooperation of all family members and reduce conflict.

Make a list of financial and non-financial resources available to you. In analyzing your situation, consider the following steps you can take to minimize negative financial or other consequences.

- Accept and acknowledge the crisis.
- If debt is a part of the crisis, contact creditors promptly.
- Avoid making any new credit purchases.
- Look for affordable credit and financial counseling.
- Adjust spending habits and cut expenses.
- Look for every possible source of income.
- Ask unemployed family members to seek work.
- Check the availability of assistance from your extended family, employers, insurance, government programs, and community or charitable organizations.
- Sell some assets, such as real estate, investments, autos, and valuable possessions.
- As a last resort, consider bankruptcy.

Some situations may call for the help of professionals such as health care providers, family counselors, financial advisors, and lawyers to determine the full scope of the crisis.

Keeping Important Documents

As you enter the world of work and adult responsibilities, certain documents and papers will become important in managing your affairs. It is important to find a safe place for these documents and to set up a system so you can find them, 6-14. The process of setting up and maintaining an organized system for your financial affairs is called **recordkeeping**.

You will need these documents for a variety of financial and legal transactions and purposes. You may need to refer to your records when you do the following:

- apply for jobs
- make budget and financial planning decisions

Discuss

When and how might you use each of the listed documents?

- prepare and file income tax returns
- make loss estimates and insurance claims
- verify bill payments, tax deductions, insurance claims, and property ownership

Documents and Records You May Need

Personal

- Birth/marriage/death certificates
- Passports
- Adoption and custody papers
- Military papers
- Separation agreements
- Divorce degree
- Social Security card
- Citizenship papers

Employment

- Résumés
- Copies of completed job applications
- Employment contracts
- Letters of recommendation
- Employment benefit information and documents
- College transcripts and training certificates

Finances

- Budget
- Financial statements
- Bank statements
- Canceled checks
- Credit card and charge account statements and records of payment
- Loan papers and receipts of payments

Insurance

- Original policies
- List of premium amounts and due date
- Claims information
- List of policies, numbers, company names, and types of coverage
- List of beneficiaries and amounts of expected benefits
- Medical history with names of physicians and record of current prescriptions

Taxes

- Copies of past tax returns
- Record and receipts of deductible expenses
- Record of taxable income
- Paycheck stubs
- W-2 Forms

Property

- Lease/mortgage papers
- Property tax statements and receipts of payments
- Deeds and title papers to property
- Inventory of personal possessions with purchase prices, estimated value, and photos of valuables
- Warranties and instruction manuals
- Service and repair records
- Bills of sale and receipts of payments for valuable purchases
- Receipts for improvements of real estate property
- Appraisals of real estate and valuables

Savings and Investments

- Purchase and sale records for stocks, bonds, and mutual funds
- Investment certificates
- Savings and account records

Estate Planning

- Will (original and copies)
- Individual Retirement Account (IRA) statements
- Pension information
- Social Security records
- Retirement plan documents

Keeping these documents organized and handy will help you be a better manager.

- file for employee or Social Security benefits
- make savings and investment decisions
- work on retirement and estate planning
- draw up a will
- settle an estate

Key Lists to Keep Current and Available

Along with important documents and records, you should keep several lists handy to help manage your financial affairs. Important information should be readily available to the person who would handle your financial and legal affairs if you were unable to do so. Make a list of the following items and keep it in a secure place:

- *savings and checking accounts* with account numbers, names on each account, name of financial institution where each account is located

- *credit card and charge accounts* with account numbers, name of issuer, expiration dates, and names of persons authorized to use each account

- *PINs (personal identification numbers)* for cash or debit cards and passwords for online accounts

- *securities and investment records* including stocks, bonds, mutual funds with identifying numbers, names of issuers, estimated values, purchase prices and dates, names of brokers, and location of certificates and accounts

- *other records* including wills and trusts, insurance policies with claims information, mortgage papers, other loan contracts, tax records, property deeds and titles, pension plans and employee benefit documents, Social Security and Medicare records

- *names, addresses, and phone numbers* for lawyers, investment brokers, physicians, insurance agents, financial advisers and consultants, executors, guardians, business partners or co-owners, real estate brokers, and others who should be consulted in the management of your legal and financial affairs; names and contact information for people named in your will

- *property, possessions, and valuables* with their location, estimated market value, appraisals, details of their purchase, and intentions for their disposition

- *household product information and warranties* to explain product features, use and care, and servicing options

- *instructions for the management of your affairs*, including provisions for your dependents, disposal of your property and possessions, and other wishes you want carried out

A good record-keeping system will be simple and convenient. You will need to keep many of these records and lists readily available in a secure home file. Use a desk drawer, file cabinet, or box to keep important papers together in one place.

Reflect

What type of record-keeping procedure do you use? How do you think accurate and complete records could help you manage your money better?

Discuss

What type of filing system can you develop for keeping documents in order and available as needed?

Enrich

Locate samples of documents and records listed and create a display file.

Reflect

Which of the items on the key lists apply to you? How would you use this information?

Activity

Share this list of lists with your parents. Discuss what information they keep on file and how you could tap into it, if necessary, in their absence.

Activity

Determine which types of information to keep in a safe-deposit box and which you need readily available in a home file.

Discuss

What are some uses of financial records and receipts that are not necessarily related to budgeting?

Activity

Review and briefly outline the steps to rational decision making and the steps to making the best use of resources.

You may want to safely keep important documents, such as insurance policies, in a safedeposit box at a financial institution with copies in your files. All this will be more important as you find yourself dealing with the details of adult life.

Information that is stored on your computer should also be organized and saved. This may include contracts; past tax forms; and e-mail correspondence with employers, insurance companies, product manufacturers, and others. Set up an online filing system. For example, create a file to hold all your correspondence with a health insurer.

To prevent losing important documents if your computer fails, create backup copies. You also need to install security software to protect yourself from thieves who target financial information on unprotected computers.

Scheduling Bills

If you lose track of your bills, you run the risk of paying them late or not at all. Set aside a basket, box, or drawer where you immediately put every bill that comes in. If you do not receive a bill that you expected, contact the source right away. Thieves sometimes take mail and use the financial information it contains to steal from unsuspecting people.

Keep track of due dates. Many people pay bills on a regular schedule, such as every Sunday night or at the end of the month, 6-15. The due dates and your paydays will dictate your bill scheduling. You can pay bills online or by mailed check. You may not have enough in your checking account to pay all of your bills in one sitting. Pay the bills that are due first. Bill paying is easier if you keep stamps, address labels, and envelopes on hand.

Keeping Budgeting Records

Keeping organized records can help you stay within your budget and make adjustments as needed. It is helpful to keep these records over a period of time so you can review your financial situation now and earlier.

Keep your budget with other money management material. Then you will have all the information when you want to evaluate and make necessary revisions in your financial planning. Your files should contain financial records related to your income, spending, and savings. Income records to keep include

- paycheck stubs
- statements of interest earned on savings accounts
- records of dividends
- amounts of cash gifts, tips, and bonuses

If you receive cash for a job, such as lawn work or babysitting, keep a written account of what you are paid. Spending records include

- canceled checks
- receipts from bills paid
- statements from credit accounts
- cash register receipts

Receipts are especially important for fixed expenses, such as loan payments, and for major purchases, such as a road bike. Receipts for these items serve as proof of payment. They may be needed for warranty services or settling disputes.

You need not save receipts for minor purchases, such as cosmetics or movie tickets. However, if you have trouble staying within your budget, you may want to record all purchases for a while. Then you will have a clear idea of where your money goes. Also, keep receipts for any purchases you may need to return, exchange, or have serviced. Proof of purchase is often required for these transactions.

Financial records are an important part of your money management. In later years, you will need detailed records for savings, credit transactions, investments, real estate, taxes, and insurance.

Discuss

How can you expect money management procedures to become more complicated as you enter adult life?

Resource

Chapter 6—Personal Finance: An Overview, Teacher's PowerPoint Presentations CD

6-15
Keeping track of your bills and their due dates will help you pay them on time and avoid late fees.

Chapter Summary

Achieving financial security requires financial literacy and lifetime planning. A budget can guide you through financial decisions.

As you enter the adult world, your money management activities will expand. A periodic net worth statement charts progress and is an important tool. Financial goals and priorities change as people move through the stages of the family life cycle.

You will not only find personal finances more involved, but you will discover that the world around you will affect your economic life as well. Demographic and cultural factors will affect your financial decisions. Technology will change the way you live and earn and spend. The changing economic climate will affect your earning power, job choices, and financial life.

Attention to warning signals can help you avoid serious financial problems. Another component of achieving financial security is learning to deal with crises. Coping methods are vital tools to use when faced with unexpected financial setbacks.

It also becomes increasingly important to develop a system for keeping necessary financial and legal documents. Knowing what to keep and where to file different papers can be a significant help in managing your financial and legal affairs over your lifetime.

Review

1. Give three examples of each kind of expense: fixed and variable.

2. What financial facts are included in a net worth statement?

3. What are three types of assets?

4. Name two types of liabilities.

5. Identify the five stages of the family life cycle and a typical feature of each.

6. Name three events in life that call for a change in financial plans.

7. Name four ways to prevent financial crises.

8. What are the steps families can take to cope with financial disaster?

Critical Thinking

9. Why do you think people often delay serious financial planning?

10. What are the advantages of beginning savings and investment programs at an early age? What are the consequences of putting off saving until age 30? age 40? age 50?

Answers to Review

1. (List three of each. Student response.)

2. assets, liabilities, and net worth

3. liquid, investment, and use assets

4. current and long-term liabilities

5. beginning stage, expanding stage, developing stage, launching stage, aging stage (Features are student response.)

6. (Name three:) going to college, starting a new job, leaving home, getting married, having children, changing jobs

7. (Name four:) sound money management practices, practical credit controls, regular savings, insurance protection, reasonable caution with financial matters, regular discussions of financial matters with adult household members

8. accept and acknowledge, contact creditors, avoid new credit purchases, seek counseling, adjust spending habits and cut expenses, look for new sources of income, check availability of assistance, sell some assets, consider bankruptcy

11. How do you think financial security, financial insecurity, and financial crises affect each of the following groups?
    A. Single individuals with no dependents and no sources of income other than their own earnings.
    B. Married couples with no children.
    C. Married couples with dependent children.
    D. Retired couples.

12. How would a financial crisis in your family affect you personally?

13. Cite an example of ways each of the following can influence personal and family money management and lifestyles.
    A. The economy.
    B. Demographics.
    C. Cultural and ethnic traditions.
    D. Technology.

Academic Connections

14. **Social studies.** Research local government agencies and community organizations that offer assistance to individuals and families who are facing financial hardships. Develop a brief directory of available services.

15. **Research, writing.** Choose one of the following topics. Write a three-page report using at least five reliable sources of information.
    - The role of savings in achieving financial security.
    - Dealing with financial crises.

16. **Research, speech.** Interview two couples: one that has been married less than 5 years and one that has been married more than 15 years. Ask the couples to list some of the adjustments people need to make in financial planning and decisions when they marry.

Math Challenge

17. Lena Chang, 23, lives alone in a rented apartment. She earns $2,300 a month after taxes and payroll deductions. She has a savings account containing $1,500. She also owns $2,000 in stocks and some jewelry worth about $1,000. Her largest asset is a car that could sell today for $10,000. She still owes $15,000 on a student loan.

    Her monthly expenses include
    - $250 savings
    - $750 rent
    - $250 student loan payment
    - $250 utilities
    - $200 gas, car insurance, and registration
    - $230 groceries
    - $50 donations to a charity
    - $350 extras such as entertainment, eating out, and clothing

    Create a net worth statement for Lena. Is her net worth statement positive or negative?

Tech $mart

18. Find the Web sites of three private charitable organizations that you may want to support someday. Check out each organization on www.charitynavigator.org for an evaluation of its effectiveness. What group does each organization serve? What types of contributions, besides money, might be needed?

19. Investigate online several available money management software programs and outline the key features of one of them. Discuss ways money management software could help you with financial planning and management over your lifetime.

Answer to *Math Challenge*

17. negative

CHAPTER 7

Reading for Meaning

Before reading a new section, study any charts and tables. This will increase your understanding of the material.

Income and Taxes

earned income

wage

minimum wage

piecework income

salary

commission

tip

bonus

compensation

employee benefit

gross income

payroll deduction

FICA (Federal Insurance Contributions Act)

net income

unearned income

interest

entitlement

Social Security

Medicare

disability

Medicaid

Form W-4

Form W-2

tax deduction

exemption

tax credit

CHAPTER OBJECTIVES

After studying this chapter, you will be able to

- **identify** different types of income and employee benefits.
- **relate** taxation to government spending.
- **list** goods and services government provides.
- **identify** different types of taxes.
- **identify** common tax forms.
- **describe** basic procedures for filing a tax return.
- **explain** the purposes and function of the Social Security system.

Central Ideas

- The taxes of many make it possible for government to provide public goods and services that benefit all.

- Taxes reduce each individual's income and wealth.

Vocabulary

List, define, and differentiate among different forms of income.

Reflect

What are your current sources of earned income?

Activity

Research the current rate for minimum wage.

Discuss

What are the advantages and disadvantages of being paid piecework income or a salary?

Vocabulary

Differentiate between *commission* and *tips*.

Income gives individuals spending money. Taxes give the various levels of government their spending money, which is called *revenue*. A major way for government to raise revenue is by taxing each person's income as well as items they buy or own. The government then uses that revenue to provide public goods and services that benefit all. As a teen, you use some of those goods and services now, such as schools, libraries, parks, highways, and police protection. As an older adult, you will use other types of public goods and services, such as Social Security benefits.

In this chapter, you will examine different types of income and taxes and the ways different levels of government use your taxes. The chapter also discusses procedures for paying income and Social Security taxes. Important issues related to tax legislation are outlined. Finally, you will learn about Social Security benefits and some of the concerns that may prompt changes both in Social Security benefits and the way we pay for them.

The Many Forms of Income

There are many ways to acquire income, but for most, employment is the primary way. A person can also receive income from sources other than work, and that income may likewise be subject to taxation.

Money Earned from Work

Earned income is the income you receive from employment. As you enter the workplace, you will learn that income from work can have the following forms.

Wages

A **wage** is payment for work and is usually computed on an hourly, daily, or piecework basis. A wage is paid on a schedule—often every week, every two weeks, or every month. For example, an hourly wage is a set amount paid for each hour worked. Eligible workers who put in more than 40 hours per week must recieve overtime pay at least 1½ times their hourly rate.

Many unskilled and beginning workers are paid the *minimum wage*. The **minimum wage** is the lowest hourly wage employers can pay most workers by law. Workers who frequently receive minimum wage include food preparers in fast-food restaurants, store salespeople, and workers at a car wash. Contrary to popular belief, most minimum wage workers are adults, not teens.

Piecework income is a wage based on a rate per unit of work completed. For example, garment workers may be paid by the number of garments completed. They must, however, receive at least the minimum wage.

Government sets and enforces the minimum wage through the Fair Labor Standards Act of 1938 (FLSA). Periodically, lawmakers pass legislation raising the minimum wage so it keeps pace with cost-of-living increases. See www.dol.gov to check the current minimum wage. Some states require a higher minimum wage than the federal wage. If there is both a state and a federal minimum wage, workers get whichever is higher.

Some employees are exempt from receiving the full minimum wage. For example, workers under the age of 20 who are receiving job training can be paid less. However, this is only during their first 90 consecutive days on the job. High school students enrolled in career education classes can sometimes be paid less than full minimum wage. Your state's department of labor can answer questions about wage requirements.

Salary

Salary is payment for work that is expressed as an annual figure. It is paid in periodic equal payments. The payment period is usually weekly, biweekly, or monthly. For example, the salary for a job may be listed as $50,000 a year. A worker does not receive a lump sum payment of $50,000. Instead, the salary is divided into equal payments at regular intervals during the year.

Salaried workers are expected to put in as much time as it takes to do the job. Therefore, teachers, managers, supervisors, and professionals are not paid overtime.

Commission

A **commission** is income paid as a percentage of sales made by a salesperson. Some people may work on a commission-only basis. Others may receive a combination of base salary plus commission. Salespeople who usually work on commission sell cars, real estate, insurance, and other goods and services.

For a salesperson on commission, making many sales means income goes up. If customers do not buy, income shrinks. For many salespeople, income varies from month to month and year to year. A good salesperson generally earns more in commissions than in salary.

Tips

A **tip**, or gratuity, is money paid for service beyond what is required. A customer leaves a tip as a reward for good service. Tips are also given as incentives for workers to provide good service. This money belongs to workers, not their employers. This form of income is common for waiters, taxi drivers, hairdressers, and other service-industry workers, 7-1.

Payroll Accounting Clerks

Payroll accounting clerks collect, calculate, and enter data that determines employee paychecks. They update payroll records when base salary, tax exemptions, and benefit deductions change. They also compile summaries of earnings, taxes, deductions, leave, disability, and nontaxable wages for each employee.

7-1
Tips are a form of income and are subject to taxation.

Employee Benefits Specialists

Employee benefits specialists oversee programs available to employees. Such benefits include health insurance, parental leave, wellness, and retirement programs, among others. These specialists help employees take full advantage of the benefits paid completely or partly by their employer.

In some cases, tip-earning employees are also entitled to a minimum wage. It is less than the standard minimum wage. However, if a worker's total earnings are below the standard minimum wage, the employer is required to pay the difference.

Bonus

A **bonus** is money added to an employee's base pay. It is usually a reward for performance or a share of business profits. Bonuses are incentives to encourage workers to perform better. Bonus income is usually based on worker performance, length of time with the company, or company performance.

Employee Benefits

So far, this chapter has discussed forms of monetary compensation. **Compensation** is the payment and benefits received for work performed. Some of the most valuable forms of payment to workers are not monetary. An **employee benefit**, or *fringe benefit*, is a form of nonmonetary compensation received in addition to a wage or salary. Employee benefits offer important financial advantages.

The availability of employee benefits and other extras depends on the company and type of work. While these are not dollar-income items, they contribute significantly to the financial well-being of workers and their families. Common types of employee benefits include the following:

- paid vacation and holiday time from work
- paid sick leave
- life and health insurance
- retirement savings plan

Your employer can help you save money for the future. An employer-sponsored retirement savings plan is an investment program. One example is a 401(k) plan for corporate employees. Money is deducted from employee paychecks and placed into a savings fund before pay is taxed. Employers sometimes match employee contributions. However, with a few exceptions, money must stay in the account until retirement to avoid taxes and penalties. (Chapter 12 will present more information about these and other valuable financial resources.)

Business Profit Income

A growing proportion of the U.S. workforce is self-employed. Unlike employees, who perform services for their employer, the self-employed work for themselves.

This category of workers includes many entrepreneurs in the trades, such as plumbers, carpenters, and painters. Artists and consultants are often self-employed. A teenager who has a part-time job mowing lawns is self-employed.

The form of income they earn is called *profit* or *self-employment income.* One of the drawbacks of being self-employed is that you must arrange and pay for your own employee benefits. Some of these benefits, especially health care, are costly when purchased by individuals. Another disadvantage is that you must pay the entire cost of your Social Security and Medicare taxes instead of half the cost.

Payroll Deductions

The dollar figure on your paycheck is not the same as the dollar figure you are told when hired for a job. **Gross income** is wages or salary before payroll deductions. A **payroll deduction** is a subtraction from your gross income. Common payroll deductions are

Discuss

Discuss the advantages and disadvantages of being self-employed.

Activity

Interview a self-employed worker. What do they like and dislike about being self-employed?

Vocabulary

Differentiate between *gross income* and *net income.*

Case Study: A Taxing Situation

Unmet Expectations

Alvira is a high school junior looking for a summer job. She loves animals. This led her to a local veterinarian. Luckily, the vet was looking for an office assistant. She needed someone to assist in handling the animals that came in for treatment, grooming, and boarding. Alvira would work 30 hours and earn $240 per week. She would get paid every two weeks.

Alvira's first paycheck was much lower than the $480 she expected. Her paycheck stub showed the following payroll deductions: $29.76 for FICA, $6.96 for Medicare tax, $62.10 for federal withholding tax, and $28.80 for state income tax. Alvira was shocked and disappointed to receive only $352.38. Still, she had the job she wanted and felt it was pretty good money anyway.

Case Review

1. Do these figures surprise you? What has been your experience with jobs and payroll deductions?
2. Do you think it is fair for Alvira to pay $127.62 in taxes every two weeks? Why or why not?
3. What benefits does Alvira receive from the money she pays in taxes? Does she receive any direct benefits? What services that she enjoys are paid by tax dollars?
4. What information from her paycheck stub will be important when Alvira files her income tax return?

Activity

Find out if your city charges income tax. What is the rate?

Reflect

Have you received a paycheck for work with similar deductions? How do you feel about the amount that comes out of your pay? Discuss.

- *Social Security tax, or* **FICA (Federal Insurance Contributions Act),** *and Medicare.* It is 7.65 percent of earnings. Employers pay half of the FICA taxes for each employee.

- *federal withholding tax.* It varies with employee earnings and eligibility for tax benefits.

- *state withholding tax.* It varies with employee earnings and from state to state.

- *city withholding tax.* Some cities charge income tax.

- *other benefits.* These may include health care, dental, vision care, and other insurance that employees purchase through their employers.

Net income, or *take-home pay*, is your gross income (plus bonuses, if you get them), minus payroll deductions. See the paycheck stub in 7-2. In a pay period, the worker earned a total of $1,113.73 in wages and overtime pay. This is gross income, but the worker's net pay is only $827.70. Net income is reduced by payroll deductions collected by the employer and sent to government authorities and insurance companies. Deductions can lower a paycheck by 20 percent or more.

By law, workers are required to pay Social Security and withholding taxes. These topics are discussed in greater detail later in this chapter.

Money Earned Outside Work

Earned income is earnings from employment. **Unearned income** is earnings from sources other than work. It includes

Town Department Store	**Employee** Kristy A. James	**SSN** 987-65-4321
	Pay Period 3/8/XX to 3/21/XX	
	Pay Date 3/27/XX	**Net Pay** $827.70
	Check No. 12341234	

Earnings	Hrs.	Current	YTD	Deductions	Current	YTD
REGULAR	80.00	1113.73	5923.12	FICA	69.06	494.17
OVERTIME			1872.99	MEDICARE	16.15	115.58
				FED. TAX	116.17	880.89
				STATE TAX	52.40	347.68
				HEALTH	32.25	225.75
TOTALS	80.00	1113.73	7796.11		286.03	2064.07

7-2

This paycheck stub shows some of the common payroll deductions from income.

- interest paid on savings and bonds. **Interest** is paid by financial institutions, businesses, and government in exchange for the use of customers' money.

- earnings from investments or selling assets

- rent, or regular fees paid for the use of property

- Social Security and retirement account payments

- inheritance, awards, and gifts

- alimony

- unemployment compensation

Taxes on unearned income vary. Most sources are taxed. Some are taxed at higher rates than others.

The Importance of Taxes

The government generates revenue by taxing its citizens and businesses. Tax revenue is used to run the government. However, since its resources are limited, government must make choices. So, like individuals and families, government creates a budget for spending. The budget reflects the priorities and goals of the government and its people.

At present, most taxpayers spend a sizable share of their dollars to pay their income, Social Security, and other taxes. It is to your advantage to know what your tax dollars buy and how the tax system works.

Paying for government operations, facilities, and services is the primary purpose of taxes. The government provides goods and services that benefit the public. Examples include fire and police protection, schools, highways, airports, parks, and water and sewage treatment.

Besides providing goods and services necessary for society, legislators may raise or lower taxes to achieve one of the following goals.

Stabilizing the economy. The government may use taxes to promote economic stability, fight inflation, or slow a recession. (Chapter 2 discusses this in more detail.)

Addressing social challenges. Some tax dollars are used to provide services and opportunities for the aging and other populations in need. Food stamps, housing subsidies, and veterans' educational benefits are examples of such programs. A less obvious but very important way that government addresses social needs is by supporting an economy that raises the country's standard of living. Less government assistance is needed when people have the ability to improve their financial situation.

Influencing behavior. By removing taxes from some items and taxing others, government tries to change peoples' behavior. For example, the government allows taxpayers to deduct certain charitable donations. This lowers the donor's taxes and encourages giving. The government adds tax on alcohol and tobacco products, which increases their cost and discourages their use.

Discuss

How many services and facilities can you name that are financed by taxes?

Reflect

In what ways do you think taxes have influenced behavior and spending for your family?

Example

Bring a newspaper or magazine article on government spending, taxation, or borrowing to class.

Resource

Spending Tax Dollars, Activity A, WB

Federal Government Spending

Taxation is the primary source of revenue for both federal and state governments. Approximately 57 percent of all tax dollars goes to the federal government. In those years when the government spends more than it collects, it must borrow money. This is called *deficit spending*, and it increases the national debt. Sources of the federal government's revenue and expenditures are shown in 7-3.

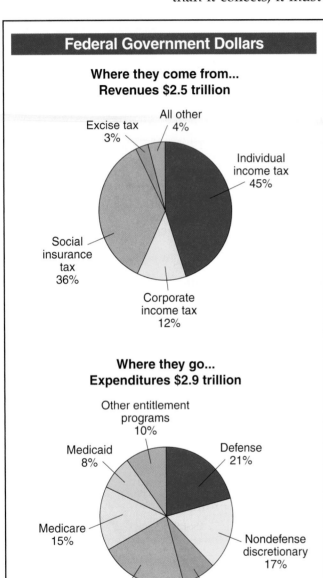

Federal Government Dollars

Where they come from...
Revenues $2.5 trillion

All other 4%
Excise tax 3%
Individual income tax 45%
Social insurance tax 36%
Corporate income tax 12%

Where they go...
Expenditures $2.9 trillion

Other entitlement programs 10%
Medicaid 8%
Defense 21%
Medicare 15%
Nondefense discretionary 17%
Social Security 21%
Interest on national debt 8%

Congressional Budget Office, 2008 Budget

7-3

This chart shows where federal government revenues come from and where they go. When expenditures exceed revenues, the government must borrow money, creating an increase in national debt.

Mandatory Expenses

Each year the federal government spends over 60 percent of its total budget on *mandatory expense* items. A mandatory expenditure is a commitment the federal government has made. It must pay these expenses. If there are not enough tax dollars to support it, the government must borrow the money to meet these commitments.

About 60 percent of mandatory expenditures are entitlements. An **entitlement** is a government payment or benefit promised by law to eligible citizens. The largest entitlement program is Social Security, followed by Medicare.

Social Security is a federal program that provides income when earnings are reduced or stopped because of retirement, serious illness or injury, or death. In the case of death, benefits are provided to survivors of the deceased. Benefits are funded by a payroll tax on workers' income and matching contributions from employers.

Medicare is a federal program that pays for certain health care expenses for older citizens and others with disabilities. A **disability** is a limitation that affects a person's ability to function in major life activities. Medicare is funded by payroll taxes and administered by the U.S. Department of Health & Human Services.

Medicaid is a government program that pays certain health care costs for eligible low-income individuals and families. It is administered by state governments. Funding comes from state and federal tax revenues.

Other entitlement programs include federal employee retirement benefits, veterans' pensions and medical care, nutrition assistance, unemployment compensation, and housing assistance. Any reductions or changes in these programs require new legislation.

Interest on the national debt is also a mandatory expense item. This interest must be paid, even if the government must borrow money to pay it.

Linking to... History

The Growing National Debt

When the financial system was near collapse in 2008, the government pumped billions of dollars into ailing financial institutions. When the economy failed to turn around, the government spent billions more the following year. Although many agreed that spending was necessary, it created an even larger national debt.

A *national debt* results from continued deficit government spending over time. In January 2009, the national debt was over $10.6 trillion, or almost $35,000 per citizen.

In recent years, the growing national debt has alarmed both legislators and taxpayers. The national debt includes money owed by the government to Social Security, Civil Service Retirement, Military Retirement, Medicare, and other trust funds. It also includes debt held by the public in the form of government securities. In addition, the country owes billions of dollars to foreign investors and nations holding U.S. treasury securities or dollars. Taxpayers must pay interest on the debt.

Across the country, citizens are calling for controls on government taxing and spending. However, at the same time, they want more Social Security benefits, broader health care coverage, better schools, safer streets, and increased national security.

Debt reduction is particularly important to you, the young citizens of the nation. You will inherit today's debt, so it is in your best interest to

- decide what services you want from the government and how much you are willing to pay for them
- vote intelligently for candidates and policies that promote sound taxing and spending

The interest is paid to financial institutions, foreign investors and governments, and individuals who buy government securities. In essence, these institutions and individuals lend money to the federal government and taxpayers pay the interest.

Discretionary Expenses

A discretionary expenditure is an expense item that can be adjusted according to needs and revenues. National defense and nondefense discretionary spending are the two main categories. Money for national defense is used to equip the armed forces and pay for military personnel, research, and technology. When the nation goes to war or enters a military conflict, defense spending is increased.

Nondefense discretionary spending includes the cost of government operations and a wide array of programs. The federal government also provides funds to state and local governments for certain programs.

State and Local Government Spending

Both taxation and government spending vary widely from state to state and city to city. However, the sources of revenues and categories of expenditures are similar.

Activity

Study and discuss Figure 7-3 to learn more about where federal government revenues come from and where they go.

Resource

Reflections on Government Spending, reproducible master 7-1, TR

Resource

Federal Government Dollars: Where They Come from... and *Federal Government Dollars: Where They Go...*, color lesson slides, TR

Activity

Develop a list of at least ten ways to reduce government spending. Discuss pros and cons of each suggestion.

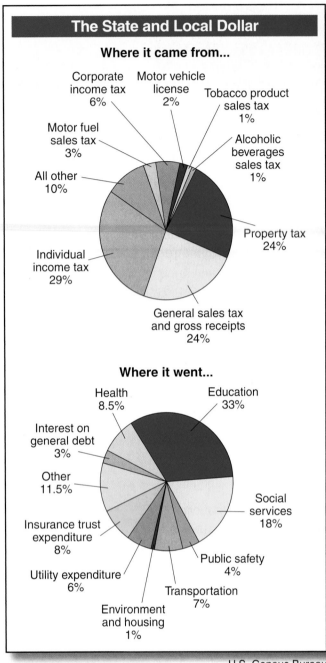

The State and Local Dollar

Where it came from...

- Corporate income tax 6%
- Motor vehicle license 2%
- Tobacco product sales tax 1%
- Motor fuel sales tax 3%
- Alcoholic beverages sales tax 1%
- All other 10%
- Property tax 24%
- Individual income tax 29%
- General sales tax and gross receipts 24%

Where it went...

- Health 8.5%
- Education 33%
- Interest on general debt 3%
- Other 11.5%
- Social services 18%
- Insurance trust expenditure 8%
- Utility expenditure 6%
- Public safety 4%
- Environment and housing 1%
- Transportation 7%

U.S. Census Bureau

7-4

This chart gives you some idea of revenues and spending at the state and local levels.

Reflect

When and how have you benefited from the services shown in Figure 7-4?

Sales, real estate, and personal property taxes make up a large part of state and local revenues. Most states and localities also rely on personal and corporate income tax for a large share of their revenues. These taxes are used mainly to pay for public education, highways, and public assistance programs run by the state. Figure 7-4 shows government taxing and spending at the state and local levels.

Types of Taxes

Different types of taxes apply to different taxable items including income, purchases, property, and wealth. More than one government body can tax the same item. For example, all levels of government have the power to tax personal income.

Direct and Indirect Taxes

One tax classification has to do with how taxes are paid. *Direct taxes* are those paid directly to the government by the taxpayer. Personal income tax is a direct tax. *Indirect taxes* are taxes *levied*, or imposed, on one person or entity, but shifted to or paid by another. Sales tax is one example. It is imposed on the seller of goods and services, but paid by the consumer.

Progressive, Regressive, and Proportional Taxes

Another classification of taxes has to do with how the tax rate is applied. A *progressive tax* imposes a higher tax rate on those with higher incomes. Income tax is one type of progressive taxation. As earners' incomes increase, their tax rates increase. In recent years, tax rates ranged from 10 to 35 percent. Progressive tax rates change with new tax laws. However, lower rates always apply to lower incomes, and rates increase as income increases.

A *regressive tax* has the effect of imposing a higher tax rate on those with lower incomes. A *proportional tax* imposes the same tax rate on all individuals or entities regardless of differences in income or ability to pay. Sales tax is one example of proportional tax in that the same rate is applied to purchases of all consumers. However, it also is considered a regressive tax in that it takes a higher percentage of income from consumers with lower incomes.

For example, two consumers buy a computer for $1,000. Both pay a 7 percent sales tax that comes to $70. The tax is proportional since both pay the same rate. However, if one buyer has an annual income of $30,000 and the other has an annual income of $60,000, the sales tax could be considered regressive because the $70 sales tax represents a higher percentage of the lower income.

What Is Taxed?

The major categories of taxable items are income, purchases, property, and wealth. You pay two types of taxes on money you earn—Social Security and income taxes. You have already learned about Social Security and Medicare taxes. You also will pay a variety of other taxes as you earn, spend, save, invest, buy a home, start a business, and finally when you die. This section describes some of these taxes.

Personal income tax—levied on money you receive from income. When people compute their taxes in April, they may find they owe more or less than was deducted from their pay. This results in additional payments or a refund. Income tax may be levied by state and local governments as well as the federal government.

Purchase tax—levied by state and local governments on purchases of goods and services. All but five states have a general *sales tax* on the goods

Activity

Make a list of buildings and facilities in your community paid for with tax dollars.

Resource

Town Revenues and Spending, reproducible master 7-2, TR

Resource

The State and Local Dollar: Where It Came from... and *The State and Local Dollar: Where It Went...,* color lesson slides, TR

Discuss

How do state and federal government taxation and expenditures differ?

ECONOMICS in ACTION

Lost Government Revenue

During an economic recession the revenues that federal, state, and local governments receive from various forms of taxes are affected. For example, many businesses close or lay off workers. Some workers are forced to take job furloughs, or unpaid leave. As the incomes of individuals and businesses fall, so does government's share of that income in the form of income taxes.

Sales tax revenues also drop. Unemployment or worry about job loss causes consumers to scale back spending. State and local governments that rely heavily on revenue from sales taxes must make do with much less.

Most state and local governments also depend on property tax revenues to fund education, social programs, law enforcement, and much more. During the latest recession, millions of homeowners fell behind in mortgage payments. The banks that provided the mortgage loans took over these homes and sold many at less than previous market values.

The market value of a home is, in part, dependent on the sale prices of nearby homes. When a home is sold at a low price, the market value of nearby homes often decreases. When home values drop, so does property tax revenue. With less money coming in, many local governments were forced to cut spending.

At the same time that tax revenues fall during a recession, the need for government services increases. For example, unemployment creates increased demand for social services. In some areas, cities must spend more on law enforcement to enforce evictions caused by foreclosures.

and services people buy. In many states, food and drugs are exempt from this tax. This eases the burden of sales tax on the poor.

Excise tax—levied by federal and state governments on the sale and transfer of certain items. Examples include cigarettes, alcoholic beverages, air travel, telephone services, gasoline, firearms, and certain luxury items.

Property Tax—levied on property you own. It includes *real estate property tax* and *personal property tax*. Real estate tax is based on the value of land and buildings owned. This is an important source of revenue for local and state governments. Rates vary greatly from area to area and state to state. *Personal property taxes* are assessed in some states on such items as cars, boats, furniture, and other assets.

Wealth tax—levied on assets. There are two main types of wealth taxes.

- Estates worth over a certain amount are subject to *estate tax*. This is a tax imposed by the federal government on assets left by an individual at the time of his or her death. It must be paid out of the estate before assets are distributed.

- *Gift tax* is levied by the federal government on donors or givers who transfer assets over a given amount to others. The regulations regarding gift tax change from time to time when new tax laws are passed.

Paying Income Taxes

The Internal Revenue Service, or IRS, is the government agency responsible for collecting federal income taxes. Each year, taxpayers must file a tax return with the federal government. A tax return is a report containing information used to calculate taxes owed by the taxpayer. Tax returns must also be filed with state and city governments in many areas. Not filing a tax return is a crime, as is providing false information on a tax form.

Your Employer's Role

The federal income tax system is built on a pay-as-you-earn concept. This means a working person pays taxes paycheck-by-paycheck instead of in one lump sum each year. State and local income taxes usually work this way, too.

When you begin a job, your employer will ask you to fill out a **Form W-4**. This form is called the Employee's Withholding Allowance Certificate, 7-5. It tells your employer how much to withhold from your paychecks as payroll deductions. Employers send this money to the IRS. Social Security and Medicare taxes are also withheld from your pay.

The amount of income tax withheld from your paycheck depends on how much you earn and the number of allowances you claim. A worksheet comes with the Form W-4 to help you figure out your personal withholding allowances. Taxpayers may take an allowance for themselves and for each of their dependents. The more allowances you claim, the less tax will be withheld from your paycheck by your employer.

-------- Cut here and give Form W-4 to your employer. Keep the top part for your records. --------

Form **W-4**	**Employee's Withholding Allowance Certificate**	OMB No. 1545-0010
Department of the Treasury Internal Revenue Service	▶ **For Privacy Act and Paperwork Reduction Act Notice, see page 2.**	20**XX**

1 Type or print your first name and middle initial	Last name	2 Your social security number
Kristy A.	James	987 65 4321

Home address (number and street or rural route)	3 ☒ Single ☐ Married ☐ Married, but withhold at higher Single rate.
1027 Cedar Street	Note: *If married, but legally separated, or spouse is a nonresident alien, check the "Single" box.*
City or town, state, and ZIP code	4 If your last name differs from that on your social security card,
Franklin, IL 65432	check here. You must call 1-800-772-1213 for a new card. ▶ ☐

5	Total number of allowances you are claiming (from line **H** above **or** from the applicable worksheet on page 2)	5	2
6	Additional amount, if any, you want withheld from each paycheck	6	$
7	I claim exemption from withholding for 20XX, and I certify that I meet **both** of the following conditions for exemption:		
	• Last year I had a right to a refund of **all** Federal income tax withheld because I had **no** tax liability **and**		
	• This year I expect a refund of **all** Federal income tax withheld because I expect to have **no** tax liability.		
	If you meet both conditions, write "Exempt" here . . . . ▶	7	

Under penalties of perjury, I certify that I am entitled to the number of withholding allowances claimed on this certificate, or I am entitled to claim exempt status.

Employee's signature
(Form is not valid
unless you sign it.) ▶ *Kristy A. James*   Date ▶ *January 2 20XX*

8 Employer's name and address (Employer: Complete lines 8 and 10 only if sending to the IRS.)	9 Office code (optional)	10 Employer identification number

Cat. No. 10220Q

7-5

Employees complete the Form W-4. It provides information employers use to determine how much federal tax to withhold from paychecks.

Each year, by the end of January, you will receive a **Form W-2** from each employer, 7-6. This is called a Wage and Tax Statement and is usually mailed to your home. It states the amount you were paid during the previous year. It also gives the amounts of income, Social Security, and Medicare taxes withheld from your income during the year.

You will receive a *Form 1099-MISC* if you received income from self-employment, royalties, rent payments, unemployment compensation, and other sources.

Preparing Your Return

You will need the following records and forms to prepare your return correctly:

- Form W-2 from each of your employers
- all 1099 forms
- other records of income, such as from tips
- Social Security number for yourself and household members
- copies of your tax returns from the previous year you filed
- forms and instructions from the IRS
  See 7-7 for other records you may need.

Reflect

What experiences have you had completing tax forms?

Discuss

What is the point of keeping accurate records?

Resource

Income Tax Return, Activity B, WB

a Employee's social security number 987-65-4321		Safe, accurate, FAST! Use IRS e-file		Visit the IRS website at www.irs.gov/efile.

b Employer identification number (EIN) XX-XXXXXXX	1 Wages, tips, other compensation 28956.98	2 Federal income tax withheld 3020.42

OMB No. 1545-0008

c Employer's name, address, and ZIP code Town Department Store 111 Broadway Avenue Franklin, IL 65432	3 Social security wages 28956.98	4 Social security tax withheld 1795.56
	5 Medicare wages and tips	6 Medicare tax withheld 419.90
	7 Social security tips	8 Allocated tips

d Control number	9 Advance EIC payment	10 Dependent care benefits

e Employee's first name and initial Last name Suff. Kristy A. James	11 Nonqualified plans	12a See instructions for box 12
	13 Statutory employee ☐ Retirement plan ☐ Third-party sick pay ☐	12b
1027 Cedar Street Franklin, IL 65432	14 Other	12c
		12d
f Employee's address and ZIP code		

15 State Employer's state ID number IL XX-XXXXXXX	16 State wages, tips, etc. 28956.98	17 State income tax 1362.40	18 Local wages, tips, etc.	19 Local income tax	20 Locality name

Form **W-2** Wage and Tax Statement   **20XX**   Department of the Treasury—Internal Revenue Service

Copy B—To Be Filed With Employee's **FEDERAL** Tax Return.
This information is being furnished to the Internal Revenue Service.

7-6

A Form W-2 shows how much an employee was paid during a year and what payroll deductions were taken.

Other Helpful Records for Filing Taxes

- Canceled checks and receipts for deductions or credits entered on your tax return
- Itemized bills and receipts for deductible expenses
- Bills and receipts for permanent home improvements
- Records of interest paid on home mortgages
- Real estate closing statements
- Investment records including purchase and sale dates, prices, gains, losses, and commissions

7-7

You need certain records, receipts, and documents to help you fill out tax return forms.

Choosing a Tax Form

When filing a tax return you will use one of three common forms: *1040EZ, 1040A,* or *1040.* These forms and many others are updated each year. They are available on the IRS Web site, or at public places such as libraries and post offices. The tax instruction booklet tells you which form to use.

Long form. Form 1040 must be used by taxpayers with an income over a certain amount or with itemized tax deductions. A **tax deduction** is an expense that can be subtracted from taxable income. *Itemize* means to list your tax deductions. You should use the long form when adjustments to income, itemized tax deductions, and tax credits can reduce your taxes.

You may want to consult a tax specialist to help you complete the forms and determine what expenses you can deduct.

Short form. Young workers usually use less complicated forms. Form 1040EZ and Form 1040A are relatively easy to complete and file, 7-8. These two forms may only be used by taxpayers whose income falls within certain limits and who choose not to itemize tax deductions.

Department of the Treasury—Internal Revenue Service

Form 1040EZ

Income Tax Return for Single and Joint Filers With No Dependents (99) **20XX**

OMB No. 1545-0074

Label
(See page 9.)

Use the IRS label.

Otherwise, please print or type.

Presidential Election Campaign (page 9)

Your first name and initial	Last name
Kristy A.	James
If a joint return, spouse's first name and initial	Last name
Home address (number and street). If you have a P.O. box, see page 9.	Apt. no.
1027 Cedar Street	
City, town or post office, state, and ZIP code. If you have a foreign address, see page 9.	
Franklin, IL 65432	

Your social security number
987 : 65 : 4321

Spouse's social security number

▲ You **must** enter your SSN(s) above. ▲

Checking a box below will not change your tax or refund.

Check here if you, or your spouse if a joint return, want $3 to go to this fund . . . ▶ ☐ **You**   ☐ **Spouse**

Income

Attach Form(s) W-2 here.

Enclose, but do not attach, any payment.

1	Wages, salaries, and tips. This should be shown in box 1 of your Form(s) W-2. Attach your Form(s) W-2.	1	28,956	98
2	Taxable interest. If the total is over $1,500, you cannot use Form 1040EZ.	2		
3	Unemployment compensation and Alaska Permanent Fund dividends (see page 11).	3		
4	Add lines 1, 2, and 3. This is your **adjusted gross income.**	4	28,956	98
5	If someone can claim you (or your spouse if a joint return) as a dependent, check the applicable box(es) below and enter the amount from the worksheet on back.			

☐ **You**   ☐ **Spouse**

If no one can claim you (or your spouse if a joint return), enter $8,950 if **single;** $17,900 if **married filing jointly.** See back for explanation. 5 | 8,950 | 00

6	Subtract line 5 from line 4. If line 5 is larger than line 4, enter -0-. This is your **taxable income.** ▶	6	20,006	98

Payments and tax

7	Federal income tax withheld from box 2 of your Form(s) W-2.	7	3,020	42
8a	**Earned income credit (EIC)** (see page 12).	8a		
b	Nontaxable combat pay election. 8b			
9	Recovery rebate credit (see worksheet on pages 17 and 18).	9		
10	Add lines 7, 8a, and 9. These are your **total payments.** ▶	10	3,020	42
11	**Tax.** Use the amount on **line 6 above** to find your tax in the tax table on pages 28–36 of the booklet. Then, enter the tax from the table on this line.	11	2,603	00

Refund

Have it directly deposited! See page 18 and fill in 12b, 12c, and 12d or Form 8888.

12a	If line 10 is larger than line 11, subtract line 11 from line 10. This is your **refund.** If Form 8888 is attached, check here ▶ ☐	12a	417	42
▶ b	Routing number		
▶ c	Type: ☐ Checking ☐ Savings		
▶ d	Account number		

Amount you owe

13	If line 11 is larger than line 10, subtract line 10 from line 11. This is the **amount you owe.** For details on how to pay, see page 19. ▶	13		

Third party designee

Do you want to allow another person to discuss this return with the IRS (see page 20)? ☐ **Yes.** Complete the following. ☑ **No**

Designee's name ▶	Phone no. ▶ ( )	Personal identification number (PIN) ▶

Sign here

Joint return? See page 6.

Keep a copy for your records.

Under penalties of perjury, I declare that I have examined this return, and to the best of my knowledge and belief, it is true, correct, and accurately lists all amounts and sources of income I received during the tax year. Declaration of preparer (other than the taxpayer) is based on all information of which the preparer has any knowledge.

Your signature	Date	Your occupation	Daytime phone number
Kristy A. James	3/10/XX	Sales Clerk	(123) 123-4567
Spouse's signature. If a joint return, **both** must sign.	Date	Spouse's occupation	

Paid preparer's use only

Preparer's signature ▶	Date	Check if self-employed ☐	Preparer's SSN or PTIN
Firm's name (or yours if self-employed), address, and ZIP code ▶		EIN	
		Phone no. ( )	

For Disclosure, Privacy Act, and Paperwork Reduction Act Notice, see page 37.   Cat. No. 11329W   Form **1040EZ**

7-8

The 1040EZ is the simplest income tax return form.

Example

Obtain copies of Forms 1040EZ, 1040A, and 1040 for review and discussion.

Discuss

Which taxpayers are most likely to use each tax form?

Vocabulary

Define key tax terms and use each in a sentence.

Other restrictions are outlined in the instructions that come with each IRS form.

Figuring Taxable Income

No matter which form you choose, the goal is to figure how much taxes you owe. First, calculate your income for the past year. This includes wages, salaries, tips, interest payments, unemployment compensation, and investment income. The numbers come from Forms W-2 and 1099. The less income you earned, the lower your taxes should be.

Adjustments and adjusted gross income. Fortunately, your taxes are not calculated based on gross income. The good news is your income can be reduced by adjustments. *Adjustments* are other expenses that reduce taxable income. This helps to reduce the amount of tax that must be paid. The IRS instruction forms indicate who is entitled to which adjustments. For example, students or their parents can deduct the interest paid on student loans. You arrive at adjusted gross income by subtracting your adjustments from your total income.

Exemptions. You can further reduce your taxable income by subtracting allowable exemptions from your gross income. An **exemption** is a tax benefit that reduces the amount of income that is taxed. The amount of money allowed for each exemption follows the rate of inflation. The exemption is phased out when income exceeds a certain amount.

Tax deductions. A *standard deduction* is the set amount you may deduct from gross income before determining tax. The deduction amount is set by law and varies according to the taxpayer's filing status (single, married, head of household). Like the personal exemption, the amount allowed for the standard deduction is adjusted each year. According to the IRS, two of three taxpayers take the standard deduction. After subtracting the amount of either your itemized tax deduction or standard deduction, you arrive at taxable income.

Tax rates and allowable tax deductions and exemptions tend to change with each new tax law. In recent years, taxable income in the lowest income bracket was taxed 10 percent, while that in the highest income bracket was taxed 35 percent.

Figuring Taxes Owed

Once you calculate your taxable income, you can figure if the tax withheld from your paychecks by your employer was enough to cover what you owed. Check the IRS tables to determine how much someone with your taxable income is required to pay, 7-9.

Tax credits. You can reduce the amount of taxes you owe with tax credits. A **tax credit** is an amount you can subtract from the taxes you owe, if you are eligible. It is a greater advantage than an exemption or tax deduction subtracted from taxable income. For example, the government might offer a tax credit to consumers who purchased a plug-in or electric motor vehicle. Tax advisors or the IRS can tell taxpayers which tax credits might be available to them.

11,000

If Form 1040EZ, line 6, is—		And you are—	
At least	But less than	Single	Married filing jointly
		Your tax is—	
11,000	11,050	1,253	1,103
11,050	11,100	1,260	1,108
11,100	11,150	1,268	1,113
11,150	11,200	1,275	1,118
11,200	11,250	1,283	1,123
11,250	11,300	1,290	1,128
11,300	11,350	1,298	1,133
11,350	11,400	1,305	1,138
11,400	11,450	1,313	1,143
11,450	11,500	1,320	1,148
11,500	11,550	1,328	1,153
11,550	11,600	1,335	1,158
11,600	11,650	1,343	1,163
11,650	11,700	1,350	1,168
11,700	11,750	1,358	1,173
11,750	11,800	1,365	1,178
11,800	11,850	1,373	1,183
11,850	11,900	1,380	1,188
11,900	11,950	1,388	1,193
11,950	12,000	1,395	1,198

14,000

If Form 1040EZ, line 6, is—		And you are—	
At least	But less than	Single	Married filing jointly
		Your tax is—	
14,000	14,050	1,703	1,403
14,050	14,100	1,710	1,408
14,100	14,150	1,718	1,413
14,150	14,200	1,725	1,418
14,200	14,250	1,733	1,423
14,250	14,300	1,740	1,428
14,300	14,350	1,748	1,433
14,350	14,400	1,755	1,438
14,400	14,450	1,763	1,443
14,450	14,500	1,770	1,448
14,500	14,550	1,778	1,453
14,550	14,600	1,785	1,458
14,600	14,650	1,793	1,463
14,650	14,700	1,800	1,468
14,700	14,750	1,808	1,473
14,750	14,800	1,815	1,478
14,800	14,850	1,823	1,483
14,850	14,900	1,830	1,488
14,900	14,950	1,838	1,493
14,950	15,000	1,845	1,498

17,000

If Form 1040EZ, line 6, is—		And you are—	
At least	But less than	Single	Married filing jointly
		Your tax is—	
17,000	17,050	2,153	1,751
17,050	17,100	2,160	1,759
17,100	17,150	2,168	1,766
17,150	17,200	2,175	1,774
17,200	17,250	2,183	1,781
17,250	17,300	2,190	1,789
17,300	17,350	2,198	1,796
17,350	17,400	2,205	1,804
17,400	17,450	2,213	1,811
17,450	17,500	2,220	1,819
17,500	17,550	2,228	1,826
17,550	17,600	2,235	1,834
17,600	17,650	2,243	1,841
17,650	17,700	2,250	1,849
17,700	17,750	2,258	1,856
17,750	17,800	2,265	1,864
17,800	17,850	2,273	1,871
17,850	17,900	2,280	1,879
17,900	17,950	2,288	1,886
17,950	18,000	2,295	1,894

20,000

If Form 1040EZ, line 6, is—		And you are—	
At least	But less than	Single	Married filing jointly
		Your tax is—	
20,000	20,050	2,603	2,201
20,050	20,100	2,610	2,209
20,100	20,150	2,618	2,216
20,150	20,200	2,625	2,224
20,200	20,250	2,633	2,231
20,250	20,300	2,640	2,239
20,300	20,350	2,648	2,246
20,350	20,400	2,655	2,254
20,400	20,450	2,663	2,261
20,450	20,500	2,670	2,269
20,500	20,550	2,678	2,276
20,550	20,600	2,685	2,284
20,600	20,650	2,693	2,291
20,650	20,700	2,700	2,299
20,700	20,750	2,708	2,306
20,750	20,800	2,715	2,314
20,800	20,850	2,723	2,321
20,850	20,900	2,730	2,329
20,900	20,950	2,738	2,336
20,950	21,000	2,745	2,344

7-9
Federal tax tables show how much is owed based on taxable income.

Filing on Time

Your Form W-2 tells you how much tax was withheld from your paychecks last year. If you paid more taxes than you owed, you get a refund. If you paid less tax than you owed, you must make up the difference with a payment to the IRS.

Follow the steps outlined on the tax form you are using. If you owe taxes, write your check or money order for the amount, payable to the Internal Revenue Service. Be sure the check includes your name, address, Social Security number, and daytime phone number. Sign your return and mail it to the IRS office indicated in the form.

The final date for filing federal taxes for the previous year is April 15. If that date falls on a Saturday, Sunday, or legal holiday, taxes are due on the next business day. Returns must be postmarked no later than the due date. Filing and paying late may result in penalties.

Reducing your taxes by claiming legitimate adjustments, tax deductions, and credits is called *tax avoidance*. It is a legal way to avoid paying unnecessary taxes. Failing to declare all income or falsifying deductions, adjustments, or credits are forms of *tax evasion*. This criminal offense can carry heavy penalties.

State and Local Tax Forms

Forty-three states collect personal income tax. Rates vary from state to state and are usually based on adjusted gross income, taxable income, or some other figure taken from your federal return. Filing deadlines usually

Vocabulary

Distinguish between *tax avoidance* and *tax evasion*.

Enrich

Contact your state's office of revenues for information on state taxation. Discuss.

correspond with filing of federal tax forms. The departments of revenue for your state and municipality can provide the information you need on state and local income, property, and other taxes.

Electronic Filing

Electronic filing (e-filing) allows you to file your income tax returns online. E-filing can be simple and quick. For those who expect a tax refund, online filing usually provides a faster refund than filing a paper return. You can use the IRS e-file program on your computer or with the help of a tax professional.

If your return is relatively complicated, you may want help. You can use an Authorized IRS e-file Provider. This person will help you prepare and e-file your return. You sign your return with a self-selected personal identification number (PIN) and pay any taxes you owe, either with a credit card or a direct debit from your bank.

To access details and filing instructions for e-filing, go to www.irs.gov/efile. This site provides all the information you need to file your return online quickly and conveniently.

Sources of Tax Information and Assistance

Many places offer help in tax planning and filing your return. As income increases, finances become more complicated. You may want to find professionals to advise you on tax matters. Several sources of assistance are listed below.

Internal Revenue Service (IRS)

Tax rates and laws change from year to year. The IRS publishes free instruction booklets annually, available online or at your nearest IRS office. These materials may also be available at your local library and post office. Once you have filed a return, you will receive a tax package at the beginning of each year from the IRS. It will provide instructions for filing.

Check your local phone directory for the IRS number to call for publications and advice on specific tax questions. The IRS operates a system of recorded phone messages with tax information on a variety of questions. The agency also offers a Web site at www.irs.gov and a toll-free hotline for specific questions. Walk-in service is available at some IRS offices across the country.

Tax Preparation Services

If your taxes become complicated by investments, deductions, or other financial circumstances, you may want to call a professional to help prepare your tax return. Services of this type range from one-person offices to nationwide firms specializing in tax preparation.

Many tax attorneys and certified public accountants specialize in tax matters. They may prepare your tax return for your signature, based on records and receipts you provide. Some tax preparers guarantee to pay penalties resulting from errors they make. However, the taxpayer has the ultimate legal responsibility for any errors and any penalties for late payment.

Tax Preparation Guides and Software

Each year, several excellent tax guides are available for purchase. They are also available at many public libraries. Most news and financial periodicals run articles on tax filing, too. These appear in the weeks and months before April 15 each year.

A variety of computer software programs provide tax information and advice, 7-10. They can reduce the time required to complete your return. After the first year, you simply update the figures and details on your return. This simplifies recordkeeping. Reliable computer tax programs provide annual updates covering changes in the tax laws.

Tax Preparation Professionals

Professional tax preparers complete tax forms for individuals and businesses. Usually they have an accounting or finance background. These professionals continually stay abreast of the latest changes in state and federal tax guidelines.

IRS Audits

A *tax audit* is a detailed examination of your tax returns by the IRS. In 2007, the IRS audited approximately one percent of the more than 139 million returns filed. If the IRS audits your return, you have to prove the accuracy of your reported income, tax deductions, adjustments, credits, and other details on your tax return. This is when good recordkeeping comes in handy.

It pays to know your rights as a taxpayer if your return is audited. The Internal Revenue Service Reform Act of 1998 guarantees taxpayers due process in their dealings with the IRS. You are expected to answer the IRS agent's questions honestly and completely, providing documentation when necessary. You may take an accountant, attorney, or tax preparer with you to the audit session.

7-10

Using a reliable tax software program can simplify the process of completing a return.

The IRS must provide a detailed statement of your rights and the IRS's obligations during the audit, appeals, refund, and collection process. You have the right to make an audio recording of any audit interview conducted by the IRS. If you disagree with the outcome of a tax audit, you have the right to a conference at the Regional Appeals Office. From there, you can take your case to the U.S. Tax Court, the U.S. Court of Federal Claims, or even the U.S. Supreme court. In the end, you have to pay any additional taxes, interest, and penalties that are assigned.

Tax System Reform

When the federal income tax system was created in 1914, the tax code was 14 pages long. Today the U.S. tax code contains thousands of pages of complex rules and provisions. The IRS publishes over 450 tax forms and almost 300 forms to explain them. There are also 50 state tax systems and over 80,000 local taxing agencies. Each has its own set of laws and regulations.

As the cost of providing government services increases, taxes increase. As legislators periodically revise and review the tax code, the tax system becomes more and more complex. In recent years, tax reform legislation has occupied both state and federal lawmakers. Citizens concerned about rising taxes have pushed for measures that limit new taxes.

The federal tax code changes periodically. Congress struggles to meet the need for revenues with a level of taxation voters will accept. Legislators propose new tax laws to increase revenues, to make the tax burden fairer, and to achieve desired economic outcomes.

Tax Legislation

Since major changes in tax policies can cause major changes in the economy, any new tax legislation needs to be thought out carefully. Here are some issues that are considered when new tax proposals and policies are evaluated.

Effectiveness. Will a new or changed tax law produce adequate revenues? Tax revenues should be great enough to achieve the goals of the tax proposal. Ideally, revenues should be considerably higher than the cost of administering, enforcing, and collecting the taxes. The federal income tax system spends approximately 50 cents for every $100 it collects, which is very cost efficient.

Fairness. Is the tax fair? To be fair, a tax must fit the taxpayer's ability to pay. Tax rates should be no greater than required for essential government services and operations. In addition, the burden should be distributed fairly among taxpayers. Generally, those with similar incomes and resources should be taxed at the same rate. Fairness in taxation is not a new issue. It has been a concern throughout history.

Impact. Is the economic impact of tax legislation minimal or beneficial? Almost all tax legislation shapes the economy to some degree. Tax laws should achieve positive economic goals or at least keep negative results to a minimum. For example, a tax on gasoline can lower demand and slow the depletion of oil reserves. This may discourage unnecessary driving and reduce auto pollution. Since it is spread among many taxpayers, a gasoline tax achieves a reasonable degree of fairness, though it is harder on lower income taxpayers, particularly if they commute to work.

Tax laws should not cause major economic problems or seriously interfere with the forces of supply and demand. For example, an increase in federal income tax during a recession would lower consumer demand at a time when the economy needs the stimulus of greater demand. Eliminating the tax advantages of retirement accounts could reduce savings rates at a time when savings are needed for business growth and expansion.

Paying Social Security Taxes

Franklin Roosevelt signed the Social Security Act into law in 1935. Medicare became part of the law in 1965. The Social Security Administration

Case Study: A Taxing Situation

Ending Deficit Spending

Leslie is a new congresswoman. She ran on a campaign promise to put an end to deficit spending. She knows ending deficit spending requires both higher taxes and less spending. Here are some of her ideas and the opposition she faced.

Increase gasoline taxes by 25 cents per gallon. This, too, is seen as unfair to low-income taxpayers. Transportation industries also opposed it because of increased operating costs.

Cut spending for all government agencies by five percent. Almost every agency objects, claiming they need more money, not less.

Reduce spending for national defense by five percent. The Defense Department and advocates of a strong military object to weakening American defenses. Others say it will lead to unemployment of defense industry workers.

Case Review

1. What does Leslie's experience tell you about the problems involved in trying to control government spending?
2. What ideas can you propose for increasing government revenues? What opposition would your ideas meet?
3. What government services would you give up to help reduce deficit spending?

manages the Social Security program. Today, the program covers almost everyone who works. The tax is figured as a percentage of an employee's income and deducted from gross income. FICA, or Federal Insurance Contributions Act, is the law that requires the collection of Social Security payroll taxes.

Workers and their employers split FICA taxes. Each pays 7.65 percent—6.2 percent for Social Security and 1.45 percent for Medicare. The self-employed pay the entire tax. All income is taxed for Medicare. However, there is a cap on the amount of income that is subject to Social Security taxes. The IRS publishes this figure each tax year.

Employers deduct FICA taxes from each employee's paycheck. They add their share of FICA tax and pay the total to the government under the employee's name and Social Security number. The amount of Social Security tax deducted appears on an employee's paycheck.

Activity

If you receive a paycheck for part-time work, find the FICA amounts withheld.

Reflect

Do you know your Social
Security number? When have
you used it for identification?

Example

Contact your local Social
Security office for a copy of an
application form for a Social
Security card.

Enrich

Find out the current
requirements for receiving
different levels of Social Security
benefits.

Discuss

Who would be eligible for
different types of Social Security
benefits?

Your Social Security Number

A Social Security number serves two major purposes. The Social Security Administration uses this number to keep a record of your covered earnings. These earnings determine the amount you will eventually receive in retirement, disability benefits, or benefits to your survivors if you die. The Internal Revenue Service also uses your Social Security number as a taxpayer identification number on all tax returns and IRS forms.

Today most parents apply for a Social Security number for their children. It is needed to claim a child as a dependent on income tax returns, to open a bank account, to buy savings bonds, and to obtain health insurance coverage. When giving the information required for a birth certificate, parents are asked whether they wish to apply for a Social Security number. Normally the hospital will provide all the information needed to do this. Applications also are available online at www.socialsecurity.gov.

No two Social Security numbers are the same. Your number is yours alone. It prevents your records from getting mixed up with the records of someone else who may have the same name. If you lose your card or change your name, contact the nearest Social Security office for a new card. Safeguard your Social Security number. Do not carry it with you or give it out unnecessarily. Criminals can use this number to steal your identity and damage your finances.

Social Security Benefits

When you begin working, your Social Security taxes pay for the benefits others receive. When you retire, or if you become disabled or die, other workers pay Social Security taxes to cover benefits to you and your family. Before a worker or a worker's family can receive benefits, the worker must have paid Social Security taxes for a certain length of time.

As you work, you earn Social Security credits—usually four per year. The amount you must earn to receive a credit has been increased several times. The number of credits required to receive Social Security benefits varies. Most workers need 40 credits or ten years of work to qualify for benefits. Younger workers who become disabled may require fewer credits to qualify.

The benefit amount depends on the worker's age and average earnings over a period of years. Here are the types of benefits the Social Security program provides.

Retirement Benefits

Workers become eligible for full retirement benefits at age 67. Early retirement can begin as early as age 62, but you only receive about 70 percent of retirement benefit payments. Benefits may also be made to these members of a retired worker's family:

- unmarried children under 18 (under 19 if full-time high school students) or over 18 with a serious disability beginning before age 22

- spouse who is age 62 or older

Case Study: A Taxing Situation

A Time to Collect

Horace and Mandy Khan raised two children. Their youngest child left home last year. Horace is just turning 65 and Mandy is 62. Horace worked 42 years for the same company and can now retire with full pension. Mandy worked part time when the kids were young and full time for the last 10 years. They always paid Social Security taxes when they were working. With retirement near, they look to their Social Security benefits for part of their retirement income.

Horace's earnings over the past five years have been between $40,000 and $50,000 annually. Mandy earns between $25,000 and $30,000 each year. Horace's pension will pay him $2,000 each month. Mandy has no retirement plan through her employer.

Case Review

Contact your local Social Security office or go online to answer the questions.

1. Approximately how much can Horace and Mandy expect in Social Security retirement benefits each month?
2. Can Mandy collect anything for the Social Security tax she paid during her working years?
3. Will the Khans be required to pay income tax on their Social Security benefits?
4. How will monthly payments change if Horace dies? if Mandy dies?

- spouse of any age if caring for a retired worker's child under age 16 or disabled

Disability Benefits

A worker who becomes disabled before retirement age may receive disability benefits. Getting these benefits often involves an extensive application process. A worker must present concrete evidence that disability prevents him or her from earning a living. The Social Security Administration will review a worker's medical records and other information to determine eligibility. Monthly disability benefits may also be paid to a worker's family members.

Discuss

What is involved in applying for Social Security benefits?

Resource

Social Security, Activity D, WB

Discuss

If more money is going out of the Social Security system than is coming in, what problems can you see ahead?

Survivors' Benefits

If a worker dies, benefits may be paid to certain members of the worker's family. A single, lump-sum payment may also be made when a worker dies. This payment usually goes to the surviving spouse. Monthly benefits may be paid to these members of a deceased worker:

- unmarried children under age 18 (19 if full-time high school students) or over 18 if severely disabled, with the disability occurring before age 22

- spouse 60 or older (50 if disabled)

- spouse at any age who is caring for a worker's child under age 16 or disabled

- spouse 50 or older who becomes disabled

- parents who depend on the worker for half or more of their support

Benefits for Divorced People

An ex-spouse can be eligible for benefits on a worker's record under certain circumstances. This eligibility does not affect the amount of benefits the worker and the worker's family are entitled to receive. To qualify for benefits, an ex-spouse must satisfy these requirements:

- married to the worker at least 10 years

- at least 62 years old

- not eligible on his or her own or on someone else's Social Security record

Social Security benefits do not start automatically. When a person becomes eligible, he or she must apply for them at the nearest Social Security office. The Social Security administration calculates benefits and issues monthly payments. The administration also calculates possible future benefits based on current earnings. However, calculations cannot be exact for young workers far from retirement age.

It is a good idea to check your Social Security record every few years to make sure your earnings are being credited to your record. You can get a free postcard form at any Social Security office for this purpose.

Retirees need to contact the Social Security office in their area several months before retirement. This will give the office plenty of time to calculate benefits and begin payments as soon as retiring workers are eligible.

Social Security System Reform

The sound future of Social Security depends on responsible fiscal action today. People are living longer lives. By 2030, there will be almost twice as many Americans of retirement age as there were in 1999. Presently, about three workers pay Social Security taxes for every beneficiary. By 2030, there will be only two workers to every beneficiary. While the system has some reserves, benefit payments will exceed tax collection around 2013 unless Social Security reforms are enacted soon.

If benefit payments exceed tax collection, the Social Security trust fund will be depleted. There will be no money in the fund to support all the persons who have paid into it. Dealing with this problem will require increasing taxes, decreasing benefits, or both. In the 1980s, Congress called for taxing some retirees' benefits and raising the retirement age. This was done, but it was not enough. Among the other solutions proposed are plans to

- reduce the automatic cost-of-living allowance (COLAs) increases in benefits

- raise taxes on benefits to higher-income recipients

- cut benefits for higher-income recipients

- raise the retirement age again

- increase Social Security tax contributions

- invest Social Security trust fund surpluses in the stock market

- permit individuals to invest a portion of their Social Security taxes in personal retirement accounts

As policy makers work toward reform, it will be important to provide dependable benefits regardless of changes in the economy and financial markets. Benefits must continue for the retirees, people with disabilities, and low-income individuals who currently receive payments. One of every three people getting benefits in the current system is *not* a retiree.

Continued funding of the system will likely require increasing revenues and reducing benefits. It also will require fiscal responsibility, a curb on deficit spending, and a reduction of the national debt. It will be in your best interest to keep up with new developments in Social Security reform as it relates to both taxes and benefits. It is your money at both ends—paying and receiving.

Discuss

How do you think new legislation pertaining to Social Security will work? What would you recommend if more needs to be done?

Resource

Chapter 7—Income and Taxes, Teacher's PowerPoint Presentations CD

Chapter Summary

People earn income from work or other sources, such as interest on savings. Government taxes both individual and corporate income. Taxes pay for government operations, services, and programs, including Social Security, Medicare, and Medicaid. The government must borrow money when spending exceeds tax revenues.

Taxpayers are required to file an annual income tax return. This involves keeping necessary records and receipts and preparing income tax forms. The federal tax code changes frequently as Congress struggles to meet the need for revenues with a level of taxation voters will accept.

Social Security provides income when earnings stop for certain reasons. Generally, employers and employees each pay half of the Social Security tax on total income. As the number of people collecting Social Security increases and the number of workers paying into the system decreases, reforms must be made to keep the program funded.

Review

1. What is an employee benefit?

2. What is the difference between gross income and net income?

3. How does government spending relate to taxation?

4. Give three examples of public goods and services that your taxes buy.

5. What is the greatest mandatory federal government expenditure?

6. Name the four major types of taxes that provide most state and local government revenues.

7. Explain the difference between a progressive tax and a regressive tax.

8. When you become employed, your employer will ask you to fill out a _____ for tax withholding purposes.

9. What effect does raising the number of allowances on a Form W-4 have on net income?

10. What are the three common forms for filing taxes?

11. Explain how to figure taxes owed.

12. True or false. The IRS typically audits about 25 percent of all personal income tax returns.

13. What are the two major purposes of Social Security numbers?

Critical Thinking

14. Compare and contrast progressive and regressive taxes.

15. What government services would you be willing to pay higher taxes to support? Why?

Answers to *Review*

1. a form of nonmonetary compensation received in addition to a wage or salary

2. Gross income is the total amount you earn before any deductions for taxes, Social Security, company benefits, etc. Net income is gross income minus payroll deductions.

3. Tax revenue is used to pay for government operations, facilities, and services. When the government spends more than it collects, it must borrow money or raise taxes.

4. (Give three:) fire and police protection, schools, highways, airports, parks, water and sewage treatment, libraries, national defense, Social Security, Medicare

5. the Social Security program

6. sales tax, personal and corporate income tax, property tax

7. A progressive tax imposes a higher tax rate on those with higher incomes. A regressive tax imposes a higher tax rate on those with lower incomes.

16. If you had the task of reducing federal government spending, what programs or services would you cut or eliminate and why?

17. What do you see as the consequences of continued deficit spending
    - for yourself and your family?
    - for continuing government services and programs?
    - for business and industry?
    - for the United States and its position in the world politically and economically?

18. Why is Social Security reform necessary?

19. What actions would you recommend for strengthening the Social Security program? Why?

Academic Connections

20. **Research.** Find out the current amount of the national debt. Prepare a brief report discussing how the national debt affects the economy and you as a citizen.

21. **Research, writing.** Visit the IRS Web site and research the following items. Write a two-page summary of your findings.
    - Services the IRS provides for taxpayers.
    - Questions and problems taxpayers most frequently bring to the IRS.
    - Available advice and publications on filing federal tax returns.
    - Recent and pending legislation that affects individual and corporate income taxes.
    - Tax audits—reasons returns are audited and the procedure.

22. **Financial literacy, reading.** Obtain copies of tax Forms 1040EZ, 1040A, and 1040. Compare the three forms. Learn the meaning of any terms appearing on the forms you do not understand.

23. **Research, speech.** Visit Web sites of the IRS and the SSA. Report to the class on the information and publications available from each agency.

MATH CHALLENGE

24. You live in an area that has a general sales tax rate of 8.5 percent on most purchases. How much sales tax would you pay for the following goods and services from area stores?
    A. $150 jacket
    B. $30 hair cut
    C. $2 magazine

    The tax rate in a neighboring county is 7 percent. How much can you save on each item by crossing the county line to do your shopping?

Tech Smart

25. Using the latest federal income tax tables on the IRS Web site, look up the income tax figure for each of the following:
    - a single person whose taxable income is $38,000
    - a married couple filing a joint return with a taxable income of $100,000

26. Compare IRS Free File with an authorized e-file software program. Use a spreadsheet to record each program's income restrictions, fees, and customer support.

8. Form W-4

9. Claiming more allowances will increase net income.

10. Form 1040EZ, Form 1040A, Form 1040

11. First, calculate taxable income. Next, use tax tables to determine how much tax you are required to pay at your income level. Finally, subtract any tax credits from the amount of taxes you are required to pay.

12. false

13. The Social Security Administration uses Social Security numbers to keep a record of people's covered earnings.

The Internal Revenue Service uses Social Security numbers for taxpayer identification.

Answer to _Math Challenge_

24. A. $12.75; savings of $2.25
    B. $2.55; savings of $0.45
    C. $0.17; savings of $0.03

CHAPTER

8

Financial Institutions and Services

Reading for Meaning

After reading the chapter, outline the key points and compare your outline to the text. This will help you retain what you have read and identify what needs to be read again.

commercial bank

Federal Deposit
  Insurance
  Corporation
  (FDIC)

savings and loan
  association

credit union

National Credit Union
  Administration
  (NCUA)

mutual savings bank

electronic funds
  transfer (EFT)

automated teller
  machine (ATM)

ATM card

endorse

bank statement

cashier's check

certified check

money order

traveler's checks

CHAPTER OBJECTIVES

After studying this chapter, you will be able to

- **identify** different types of financial institutions.
- **select** the financial services that will best meet your needs.
- **use** ATM and debit cards responsibly.
- **manage** a personal checking account.
- **write** and endorse checks correctly.
- **calculate** a checkbook balance.

Central Ideas

- Financial institutions are vital to the economy because they make financial transactions possible.

- A checking account is a basic tool to help you manage your financial resources.

Resource

Key Financial Services, color lesson slide, TR

Resource

Financial Talk, reproducible master 8-1, TR

Resource

Your Financial Opinion, reproducible master 8-2, TR

Reflect

What experiences have you had with financial institutions?

Resource

Where Do Deposits Go? transparency master 8-3, TR

The economic system could not function without financial institutions. These institutions—including commercial banks, savings and loan associations, and credit unions—are financial go-betweens. They keep money flowing throughout the economy among consumers, businesses, and government.

When people deposit money in a bank, that money does not sit in a vault. The bank lends the money to other consumers and businesses. The dollars may be loaned to consumers to help finance new cars, homes, college tuition, and other needs. Businesses may borrow the money for new equipment and expansion. State and local governments may borrow to build new highways, schools, and hospitals. The interaction that financial institutions create between consumers, businesses, and governments keeps the economy alive, 8-1.

Without financial institutions, consumers would probably keep their cash under a mattress or locked in a safe. Money could not circulate easily. The nation's money supply would shrink. Funds would not be available for consumer spending. Demand for goods and services would fall. Businesses could not get the money to modernize plants and develop new products. The economy would slow down. Jobs would become scarce. As you can see, the economy depends on the flow of money and the services financial institutions provide.

This chapter looks at the many types of financial institutions and services and describes different types of checking accounts and special checks. Later chapters cover other services of financial institutions. Credit

8-1

Financial institutions keep money flowing through the economy among consumers, businesses, and government.

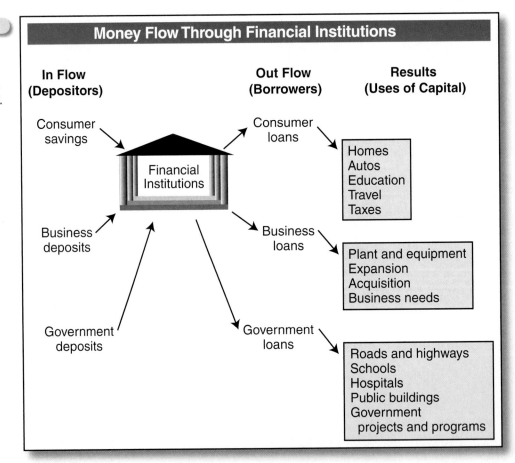

is discussed in Chapter 9, savings accounts in Chapter 11, and investment services in Chapter 12.

Types of Financial Institutions

In the past, financial institutions were more specialized. Each type of institution offered a distinct set of services to a specific set of customers. Deregulation, computer technology, and recent economic conditions have made these institutions more alike. Following are brief descriptions of financial institutions and their services.

Commercial Banks

A **commercial bank** is owned by stockholders and operated for profit. Its primary functions are to receive, transfer, and lend money to individuals, businesses, and governments. Commercial banks are often called full-service banks. They offer a wide variety of services.

These banks may be chartered by the federal government or by a state government. Federally chartered banks are called national banks and may use the word *national* in their names. These banks must comply with federal banking regulations. State chartered banks are regulated by state banking commissions.

The **Federal Deposit Insurance Corporation (FDIC)** is a U.S. government agency that protects bank customers by insuring their deposits. It also examines and supervises financial institution policies and operations. Its goal is to help maintain consumer and business confidence in the banking system. To do this, the FDIC insures bank deposits. This guarantees that depositors are protected if their bank fails or cannot repay deposits on demand. See 8-2.

In the past, the FDIC insured $100,000 of a customer's total deposits in a given bank. This amount has been temporarily increased to $250,000 until the end of 2013. Then, in 2014, it will revert to $100,000.

Suppose a depositor has $240,000 in savings and $10,000 in a checking account at the bank. All $250,000 would be returned by the FDIC to its owner if the bank were unable to pay. On the other hand, if the person has $256,000 in checking and savings deposits, FDIC insurance covers all but $6,000.

It is possible for that customer to have a separate type of account at the bank (such as a business account). In this case, the total of the customer's accounts is insured up to $250,000. If the person opens an account at another bank, the FDIC also insures this account for $250,000.

8-2

Accounts in commercial banks are insured by the FDIC.

ECONOMICS in ACTION

A Banking System Breakdown

The U.S. economy depends on the flow of money and the services financial institutions provide. When that flow stops, all parts of the economy are negatively affected. Such an event began in the fall of 2008.

Many financial institutions in the United States and around the world lost billions of dollars on risky real estate loans and other investments. Some of them, including banks and big Wall Street financial firms, failed. Other firms were weakened and taken over by stronger companies. Still others received funds from the federal government to help them stay in business.

Even with billions of dollars pumped into the banking system by the federal government, money did not circulate freely. Banks drastically reduced lending, triggering a downward spiral in the economy. Many consumers could not get loans for cars, homes, or other needs. Businesses could not borrow to expand, meet payrolls, or pay for inventories. They grew cautious and cut spending. Firms focused on survival by cutting spending as well as their workforce.

Unemployment grew to new highs. Even consumers who had jobs lost confidence and cut their spending. Demand for goods and services fell. Many businesses posted losses, and eventually some failed. The economy went into a serious recession.

Savings and Loan Associations

Savings and loan associations (S&L) are financial institutions that previously only made mortgage loans and paid dividends on depositors' savings. Today savings and loan associations offer most of the services commercial banks do. They may be state or federally chartered. There are two types of savings and loans.

- Mutual savings and loan associations are owned by and operated for the benefit of their depositors. These depositors receive dividends on their savings.

- Stock savings and loan associations are owned by stockholders. Like commercial banks, these companies operate for profit.

Credit Unions

A **credit union** is a nonprofit financial cooperative owned by and operated for the benefit of its members. Its services are offered only to members. Membership is available through affiliation with an employer, a union, religious organization, community organization, or some other group.

Since credit unions are not-for-profit organizations, they pay no federal income taxes. Members often run them, and operating costs may be relatively low. For these reasons, successful credit unions can lend funds to members at slightly lower rates than other financial institutions. They may also pay slightly higher interest rates on savings. Today, larger credit unions are run by professional management. They offer most of the services banks and other financial institutions provide.

Credit unions may be either federally or state chartered. The **National Credit Union Administration (NCUA)** grants federal charters and supervises credit unions across the country. NCUA also insures deposits in all federally chartered and many state chartered credit unions.

Mutual Savings Banks

A **mutual savings bank** is owned by its depositors. After deducting operating costs and cash for reserves, earnings are divided among depositors. These earnings are dispersed in the form of dividends. Traditionally, mutual savings banks received and paid dividends on deposits and made home mortgage and improvement loans. Now, they, too, offer a wider variety of financial services.

Only state governments charter mutual savings banks. They exist in only 17 states, mostly in the northeast.

Choosing a Financial Institution

When choosing a financial institution, consumers generally look for checking, savings, investment, and credit services. Before opening an account, it is wise to do some research. Web sites of banks and other institutions have information about their services and fees. To assess whether an institution has a helpful staff, you may want to visit it in person.

Compare local banks, credit unions, savings and loan associations, and other providers of financial services. Find the place that best serves your current and ongoing financial needs. Once you choose a financial institution, it pays to establish a good working relationship. Make your financial needs known and learn how the institution can help you manage your money.

Check-Cashing Services

Check-cashing services are not financial institutions, but businesses that provide certain financial services for a fee. People who turn to check-cashing services generally have no bank account and need cash immediately. Financial experts advise consumers to avoid check-cashing services for two reasons. They are not federally insured and they charge high fees, which quickly surpass bank fees. By contrast, many banks offer free checking and low-cost services if the account balance stays above a certain level. Many check-cashing services also make payday loans, which are even more costly. For most consumer needs, bank accounts are less costly and more reliable than check-cashing services.

Bank Examiners

Bank examiners ensure or enforce compliance with laws and regulations governing banking transactions. They examine and verify the accuracy of financial institutions' records.

Safety

Before you open an account, find out if the banking institution is insured by the federal government. A sign stating "Insured by FDIC" or "Insured by NCUA" should appear by the front window or near each teller station.

You can learn if an institution is FDIC-insured by checking the Federal Deposit Insurance Corporation's Web site at www.fdic.gov. Access its *Bank Find* feature and provide the name and address of the banking institution you want to check. When customer deposits are federally insured, it means the bank, savings and loan, or credit union is regularly checked. The institution must pass ongoing examinations into its financial holdings, operations, and management.

Services of Financial Institutions

Today many of the services offered by financial institutions are provided through *electronic funds transfers.* An **electronic funds transfer (EFT)** refers to the movement of money electronically from one financial institution to another. These electronic transactions occur much faster than check and cash transactions. You may find some of the following electronic services helpful in managing your money.

Automated Teller Machines

An **automated teller machine (ATM)**, also called *cash machine*, is a computer terminal used to transact business with a financial institution. See 8-3. An **ATM card** allows customers to withdraw cash from and make deposits to their accounts using an ATM. The card is coded with account

Linking to... History

U.S. Department of the Treasury

In 1789, Congress created the Department of the Treasury to manage government finances and to promote the growth and stability of the economy.

Alexander Hamilton, a Founding Father and economist, was the first Secretary of the Treasury. He is credited with helping to create a strong federal government and central banking system.

Some specific functions of the Treasury Department are

- produce U.S. bills and coins
- collect taxes, duties, and other payments to the government
- pay the government's bills, borrowing money when necessary
- advise the President on economic matters
- supervise financial institutions
- guard against threats to the U.S. economic system
- enforce finance and tax laws
  For more information, visit www.treasury.gov.

information and protected by a *personal identification number* or *PIN*. Terminals are located at financial institutions and other convenient locations. They are usually available 24 hours a day. ATM cards are discussed in more detail later in the chapter.

Direct Deposits or Withdrawals

Customers using this service can arrange to have paychecks, social security checks, and other payments deposited directly into their accounts. They can also pay bills without writing and mailing checks. Recurring bills—car payments, insurance premiums, utility bills, and others—can be automatically paid. Money can be transferred from a checking to a saving account each month, creating an automatic savings program. All these transactions are recorded and included in monthly bank statements. Using EFT in these ways can make managing money more convenient.

Point-of-Sale Transfers

POS, or point of sale, is the place a transaction was made. A *point-of-sale transfer* occurs when you move money from your account to pay for a purchase. This requires the use of a debit card. First, the merchant scans your card. Then the amount of the purchase immediately transfers from your bank account to the merchant's account. This allows you to purchase merchandise without checks, cash, or credit.

Online Banking Services

Many consumers find online banking more convenient than traditional banking. They can conduct banking business from home 24 hours a day. The bank assigns user identification numbers and security codes that allow customers to gain access to their accounts online. These codes must be kept confidential so no one else can use the accounts. Online banking allows customers to do the following:

• check their account balance

• review their account history

• arrange and schedule electronic bill payment

• confirm any direct deposits, withdrawals, and transfers

If you are interested in online banking, ask your financial institution whether it is available. This electronic service requires online access and a checking account.

A number of personal financial software programs take advantage of online banking. Three highly rated programs are *Quicken*, *Microsoft Money*,

8-3
ATMs are a convenient way to access funds in bank accounts.

Discuss

What do you see as the advantages of ATMs?

Enrich

Evaluate each of the listed services at a local financial institution.

Discuss

What are the advantages of using online banking? Are there any disadvantages?

Webmasters

Webmasters develop
Web sites for financial
institutions that deliver
services of the institution,
such as online bill
payment and 24-hour
banking services. They
also make financial sites
secure for online banking.

and *Moneydance*. Also, many banks and brokerage firms offer their own personal finance programs for customers to download free of charge.

These programs can make managing your finances and keeping important records much easier. While each program has unique features, most of them allow you to do the following:

- access bank and brokerage accounts
- pay bills online
- balance your bank statements
- set up a personal budget based on your income, goals, and expenses
- keep a detailed record of spending
- keep detailed tax records
- plan ahead for major expenditures
- access money management and investment information from reliable sources
- transfer funds from one account to another

Case Study: Using Dollars and Sense

What About Online Banking?

For her birthday, Alyssa received a new computer that was faster and performed more functions than her old one. She was eager to experiment with all the new things she could do. Alyssa had a checking account at a local bank. She wanted to pay her bills and track her account from home.

Alyssa visited her bank's Web site to research its online services. Then she signed up for the service. After selecting her user ID and security code, she accessed her account online.

Alyssa directed her rent and insurance premiums to be paid online. She would pay her other bills as she received them. Alyssa also decided to have her paycheck deposited directly to her account. All in all, Alyssa felt she had gained new control over her financial affairs.

Case Review

1. Would you conduct your financial business online?
2. What questions would you ask before signing up for online banking services?
3. What are some of the advantages of online banking? Can you identify any disadvantages?

Overdraft Protection

An *overdraft* is the act of writing a check for an amount greater than the balance of the account. With overdraft protection service, a financial institution will honor a check written by you even if it exceeds your account balance. Banks normally charge a $25 or higher fee for each overdraft. Customers can avoid overdrafts by managing their accounts well.

Although overdrafts are not encouraged, some banks offer overdraft protection. This involves automatically moving money from the customer's savings account to the checking account to cover the amount of the check. You can ask the bank about its policies as well as its fees or charges for this service.

Stop Payment

Upon your request, a financial institution will refuse to honor a check you wrote. This service is useful if a check is lost or stolen and you want to prevent others from cashing it. Stop payment is also useful when you have a grievance concerning goods or services paid for by check. A charge generally applies for this service, but it may be well worth the cost.

Drive-Up and Mail-In Services

Many financial institutions offer customers the convenience of making deposits and withdrawals by mail or at drive-up windows. Drive-up banking may even be available at times when the lobby is closed.

Safe-Deposit Boxes

Some financial institutions rent boxes in their vaults for the storage of valuables. Jewelry, birth records, insurance policies, and other important items are often kept in safe-deposit boxes. This is an important feature if you need a safe location for valuable or irreplaceable items. Rental charges for these boxes vary.

Financial Counseling and Special Programs

Specialized services may include a trust department, tax reporting assistance, and financial planning. Additional offerings may include money market funds, and mortgage loans. There may be associated fees.

Personal Checking Accounts

When earning a regular income, the first financial service many people need is a checking account. It offers a safe place to keep your money. It provides a convenient way to buy goods and services and pay bills, 8-4. It provides a record of deposits and receipts of payments. Responsible use of checking accounts aids in money management. It also helps you build a sound credit rating.

Enrich

Outline your needs for financial services.

Activity

Contact a local bank and interview a representative about these topics. Would you choose this bank?

Discuss

What are some of the ways people use personal checking accounts?

8-4

A checking account is the most common way of paying bills.

Bank Tellers

Bank tellers help customers use their checking, credit card, escrow, investment, loan, and savings accounts. They also sell savings bonds, accept payment for customers' utility bills and charge cards, process certificates of deposit, and sell traveler's checks.

Accounts and Services

Look for financial institutions that offer the accounts and services you want in a checking account. Consider the following features.

Restrictions and Penalties

Ask about minimum balance requirements, withdrawal limitations, and penalties for overdrafts or late payments on credit accounts. These items can increase the cost of services and make managing your money more complicated.

Fees and Charges

Ask about all fees and charges associated with the type of account you want. These may include a maintenance fee, charges for ATM use, low-balance penalties, check-writing fees, and check-printing costs. These charges can vary among institutions and different types of accounts. Higher minimum balance accounts usually reduce or eliminate these fees.

Interest Rates

Compare the interest rates on interest-bearing checking accounts. In addition, examine the rates charged to borrow money or use a bank credit card. Look for high yields on savings and low rates for using credit.

Convenience Services

Look for financial institutions that make banking and other financial transactions easy for you. Services that save you time and effort include convenient hours, ATMs in various locations, online banking, and credit cards.

Checking Account Types

Financial institutions use different names to describe checking account services they offer. The best account type for you depends largely on the amount you can deposit, the number of checks you expect to write each month, the account features you want, and the fees associated with the account. For interest-bearing accounts, your choice also depends on the interest rate that deposits earn.

When you shop for a checking account, the following questions can help you make the best choice:

- Is there a minimum deposit requirement? If so, what is it?
- What are the charges if the balance drops below the minimum?

- What are the fees per month and per check?

- Does the institution offer an interest-bearing checking account? If so, what is the interest rate and the minimum balance required?

- What other services are offered in connection with different types of accounts?

- What fees are charged for different services and accounts?

Three common types of checking accounts—basic, interest-bearing, and lifeline—are described here.

Basic Checking Account

This type of account permits you to deposit and withdraw your money and write checks. It usually requires a minimum balance to avoid service charges. If you fall below this minimum, you are charged a fee. There also may be a monthly service charge and a fee per check. Fees vary from one financial institution to another. A basic account may be a good choice if you write many checks and can keep the minimum balance.

Interest-Bearing Checking Account

This is a combination savings and checking account. Your money earns interest, and you can write checks on the account. In credit unions, these accounts are called *share drafts*. In banks and savings and loan associations, they are called *negotiable orders of withdrawal* or *NOW accounts*. Financial institutions offer this account with varying interest rates, minimum-balance requirements, and service charges.

Lifeline Checking Accounts

These relatively new accounts are intended for low-income customers. In some states, banks are required by law to make these accounts available. They feature low minimum-deposit and minimum balance requirements, low monthly fees, and limits on the number of checks that may be written per month.

Opening a Checking Account

Opening a checking account requires only a few simple steps. Certain restrictions may apply if you are under 18 years of age. Some banks require a parent or guardian to be on the account with you.

When you open an account, you are asked to sign a signature card. This is the only signature the financial institution will honor on checks and withdrawal slips. Over the years, you will sign contracts, Social Security forms, tax forms, and other documents. Sign your name the same way on all these documents to avoid confusion, 8-5.

Activity

Apply these questions to different checking accounts offered by local financial institutions to determine which account would best meet your needs.

Enrich

Define and describe the pros and cons of each type of checking account listed.

Enrich

Determine what specific needs each type of checking account is designed to meet.

Bank Checking Draft Signature Card

Submit one card to establish an optional check redemption privilege which allows you to write checks against your account.

Name of Account _____

Account Number _____ Date _____

The registered owner(s) of this account must sign below. By signing this card, the signatory(ies) agree(s) to all the terms and conditions set forth on the reverse side of this card.

_____   _____
Signature   Signature

_____   _____
Signature   Signature

Institutional Accounts: Joint Tenancy Accounts:

❏ Check here if any two signatures are required on checks   ❏ Check here if both signatures are required on checks

❏ Check here if only one signature is required on checks   ❏ Check here if only one signature is required on checks

---

8-5

When you open a checking account, you will be asked to sign a card with the signature you intend to use for all your financial and legal transactions.

Enrich

Role-play a consumer opening a checking account in a financial institution.

Discuss

What are the benefits of having a joint account? What are the dangers?

If you want someone else to have check-cashing privileges on your account, he or she also needs to sign a signature card. This may be helpful if you want someone else to be able to access your account in the event that you are unable to do so. If you share an account with a parent or a spouse, it becomes a *joint account*. This requires a clear understanding of who will write checks and how records of transactions will be kept.

When you open a checking account, you receive a small book of starter checks. These starter checks are blank but show your account number. You use them until your personalized checks arrive. They will be printed with your name, address, and account number, 8-6. The checkbook includes a *register* for keeping track of your transactions, 8-7.

Managing the Cards Linked to Your Account

You may be offered credit, debit, and ATM cards when you open a checking account. (Credit and credit cards are described in more detail in the next chapter.)

Inquire about the service fees associated with using your ATM and debit cards and any limits applying to their use. To avoid errors in your account balance, record all transactions and fees in your checkbook register. Keeping your receipts will also help. If used wisely and responsibly, these cards can provide you with greater financial flexibility.

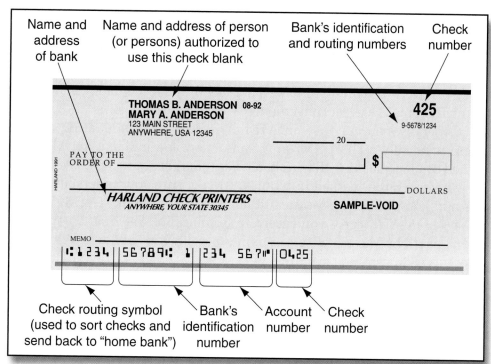

Name and address of bank

Name and address of person (or persons) authorized to use this check blank

Bank's identification and routing numbers

Check number

THOMAS B. ANDERSON 08-92
MARY A. ANDERSON
123 MAIN STREET
ANYWHERE, USA 12345

425
9-5678/1234

20

PAY TO THE ORDER OF

$

HARLAND CHECK PRINTERS
ANYWHERE, YOUR STATE 30345

SAMPLE-VOID

DOLLARS

MEMO

⑈1234⑈ 56789⑈ 1 234 567⑈ 0425

Check routing symbol (used to sort checks and send back to "home bank")

Bank's identification number

Account number

Check number

8-6

Your personalized checks include information financial institutions need to process checks correctly.

RECORD ALL CHARGES OR CREDITS THAT AFFECT YOUR ACCOUNT

NUMBER	DATE	CODE	DESCRIPTION OF TRANSACTION	PAYMENT/DEBIT (−)	✔ T	FEE (IF ANY) (−)	PAYMENT/ CREDIT (+)	BALANCE $
	3/1		Opening balance		00		100 00	100 00
								100 00
101	3/2		Lee's Grocery	15 32				15 32
			Groceries					84 68
	3/3		Cash withdrawal	20 00				20 00
								64 68
102	3/4		The Book Shelf	11 75				11 75
			Calendar					52 93
	3/6	DC	No Limits	35 13				35 13
			Jeans					17 80
	3/8	D	Deposit				130 00	130 00
								147 80
103	3/9		Lee's Grocery	18 35				18 35
			Groceries					129 45
	3/11	AP	Unified Utilities	23 07				23 07
			Electric bill					106 38
	3/14	DC	Mary's Dept. Store	34 60				34 60
			Navy shirt					71 78
104	3/16		Richard's Records	21 20				21 20
			CD					50 58
	3/22	D	Deposit				130 00	130 00
								180 58
105	3/26		Lee's Grocery	47 58				47 58
			Groceries					133 00
	3/29		Cash withdrawal	30 00				30 00
								103 00
106	3/30		Dr. Harvey	65 00				65 00
			Dental checkup					38 00
	4/1	D	Deposit				130 00	130 00
								168 00
			Service charge	5 00				5 00
								163 00

8-7

Make a point of recording all your checks, debits, ATM transactions, and deposits in your checkbook register.

Activity

Find the illustrated information on a personalized check. Discuss uses of this information.

Discuss

Why is it important to keep track of the checks you write in the checkbook register?

Discuss

Why is it important to keep your PINs private? What can happen if you don't?

Discuss

What is the difference between an ATM card and a debit card? How is each used?

Discuss

What safety guidelines apply to ATM use?

ATM Cards

An ATM card allows you to get cash from your account at any time. ATMs are located at banks, malls, airports, grocery stores, and other places. ATM cards can also be used at machines in other cities, states, and countries. This is a great convenience when you are traveling.

Generally, you may use an ATM owned by your bank at no charge. There is usually a charge for any transaction you make at an ATM not owned by or affiliated with your bank. Fees charged for using an ATM card vary; however, they can add up quickly. Make sure you understand these fees and know which ATMs are affiliated with your bank's network.

With an ATM card, you receive a unique PIN. Safeguard your card and your PIN so no one else can gain access to your account. When you insert an ATM card, the machine will ask you to enter your PIN. Then you will enter information about the transaction you want to make. With the push of a few buttons, the ATM processes your request and delivers cash and accepts your deposits. For your own protection when using the ATM, follow the safety tips listed in 8-8.

Debit Cards

Banks usually offer a combined debit and ATM card. You can use the debit card at ATMs and any business that accepts credit cards. When you make a purchase, you present the card or swipe it through an electronic scanner. Then you enter your PIN to authorize the payment. The purchase amount is subtracted immediately from your checking account.

Using a debit card is similar to writing a check because the purchase amount comes directly from your checking account. Be sure you have an adequate balance in your account to cover your debits. If your account is overdrawn, you will be charged a fee.

8-8

Since money is withdrawn at ATMs, this makes them a target for crime. Follow these tips to use ATMs safely.

Safety Tips for Using an ATM

- **Memorize your personal identification number (PIN).** Do not tell anyone your PIN or carry it with you. If someone stole both your card and PIN, they would have complete access to your account.

- **Protect your privacy.** Do not let anyone see you enter your PIN. If a friend is standing too close, politely ask the person to step back. If a stranger is too close, cancel your transaction and use the ATM at another time.

- **Watch for suspicious people.** Criminals may target ATMs as easy places to steal money. Before approaching, see if anyone is standing around. If so, use another machine or return later.

- **Use an ATM in a well-lighted area.** Generally avoid nighttime use, but if necessary, choose a machine in a grocery store or other high-traffic area. If at the bank at night, choose a drive-up ATM rather than a walk-up machine.

- **Make transactions at walk-up ATMs quickly.** Approach the ATM with your card out and ready. Then, leave the area immediately and count your money later.

Credit cards, debit cards, and ATM cards offer several advantages. They eliminate the need to carry large amounts of cash. They allow you to access your money any time of day or night. They let you purchase goods and services in places where checks are not accepted.

Making Deposits

To deposit money in your account, fill out a *deposit slip* as a record of the transaction. A deposit slip states what is being deposited—currency, coins, or checks—and the amount of each item, 8-9. Follow these steps when filling out a deposit slip:

1. Write the date.

2. Enter the amount of money being deposited in checks, currency, and coins. If you need more room, you may continue listing checks on the back of the deposit slip.

3. Total the amount of currency, coins, and checks to be deposited. Write this number after the word *Subtotal*.

4. If you want to withdraw cash at the same time you make a deposit, enter the amount after the words *Less cash received*. You must sign the slip if you want cash back from your deposit.

5. Subtract the amount in *Less cash received* from the *Subtotal*.

6. Enter the actual amount deposited after *Total deposit*.

7. Record the deposited amount in your checkbook register.

When you make a deposit in person, you receive a receipt. If you deposit by mail, the bank sends you a receipt. When you make deposits at an ATM, you receive a receipt detailing the transaction and showing the current balance in your account. Save your receipts to help balance your checkbook.

Activity

Obtain a deposit slip from a financial institution and fill it out following the steps given.

Enrich

Interview an adult who gets paychecks direct deposited. Does the adult prefer this method? Why or why not?

Note

Many banks require photo identification if you are receiving cash back from a deposit.

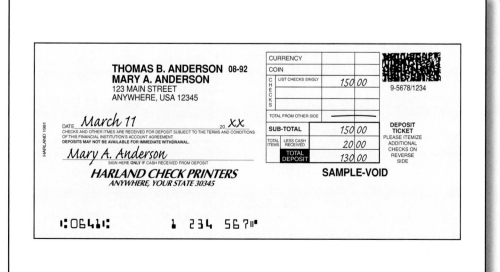

8-9
A deposit slip is a record of money you put into your account.

Endorsing Checks

Vocabulary

Differentiate between the three types of endorsement.

Discuss

When would you use each type of endorsement?

Example

Obtain blank checks from a financial institution for demonstration and practice in writing a check.

Before you can cash or deposit a check made out in your name, you must *endorse* it. To **endorse** a check, sign your name on the back of the check in the space indicated for a signature. There are three ways to endorse a check:

- *Blank endorsement.* This requires only the signature of the payee. The *payee* is the person to whom the check is written. A check endorsed this way may be cashed by anyone. For your protection, use this type of endorsement only at the time and place you cash or deposit a check.

- *Restrictive endorsement.* A check with this type of endorsement may be used only for the specific purpose stated in the endorsement. *For deposit only* is a common restrictive endorsement. It is often used when banking by mail or depositing at an ATM.

- *Special endorsement.* This is used to transfer a check to another party. Only the person named in the endorsement can cash the check. To use a special endorsement, write *Pay to the order of _____* (the name of the party to receive the check). Sign your name as it appears on the check.

Writing Checks

A blank check has important information on it. This information helps financial institutions process checks correctly. For checks to be processed, they must also be written correctly. When writing a check, enter the following items in the correct spaces. See 8-10.

1. date

2. name of the payee—the person, business, or organization receiving the check

8-10

Write checks neatly and carefully to avoid mistakes.

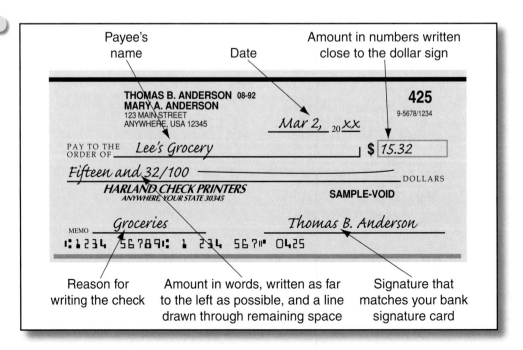

3. amount of the check in numbers

4. amount of the check in words

5. reason for writing the check, after the word *Memo*, if you want a record

6. your signature, which should look like that on your bank signature card

For your own protection, write checks in dark ink. If you make a mistake, destroy the check and write a new check. Do not make corrections on the check.

When you write a check, record the check number, date, payee, and amount in your checkbook register. Subtract the check amount from your balance. Record a destroyed check by writing its number and the term *void*. When you make a deposit, also record the date and amount of the deposit and add it to your balance. If you follow these guidelines, you will always know how much money is in your account.

Balancing Your Checkbook

Once you open a checking account, you will generally receive a bank statement each month online or in the mail. A **bank statement** is a record of checks, ATM transactions, deposits, and charges on your account, 8-11.

Resource

Banking Basics, Activity B, WB

Activity

Give a line-by-line explanation of the items listed on this statement.

Resource

Checking Accounts, Activity C, WB

8-11

A bank statement is a record of all deposits, checks, charges, and other transactions involving your account during the statement period.

National Bank
Anytown, U.S.A.

ACCOUNT NUMBER
123-45-67-8
PAGE 1
NO. OF CHECKS 10

THIS STATEMENT DATE AND BALANCE		DEBITS AMOUNT	NUMBER	SERVICE CHARGE
3/31/XX	$48.73	$246.29	10	5.00

LAST STATEMENT DATE AND BALANCE		CREDITS AMOUNT	NUMBER	
2/28/XX	$50.02	$250.00	2	

STATEMENT OF ACCOUNT

Sarah Student
2647 Evergreen Drive
Anytown, U.S.A.

DAY	REF	CHECKS AND OTHER DEBITS AMT	REF	CHECKS AND OTHER DEBITS AMT	DEPOSITS AND OTHER CREDITS	DAILY BALANCE
3/2	488	15.32				34.70
3/4	489	25.00				9.70
3/9	490	5.25				4.45
3/11					130.00	134.45
3/15	ATM, National Bank	80.00				54.45
3/16	492	23.07				31.38
3/21	493	18.35				13.03
3/23					120.00	133.03
3/25	494	34.60				98.43
3/26	495	12.20				86.23
3/28	496	7.50				78.73
3/30	497	25.00				53.73
3/30		5.00		SERVICE CHARGE		48.73

Reflect

What can happen if you do not balance your checkbook often? How would you feel if a check you wrote bounced?

Activity

Ask a parent how often he or she balances the checkbook register. Is this often enough to catch a mistake that could lead to an overdraft?

Activity

If you have a checking account, go through these steps to balance your account when you receive your next statement.

This statement usually begins with a summary of your account. It will tell you the beginning balance, the total amount of checks and other payments, the total of deposits and credits, and the ending balance. The summary will be followed by a detailed listing of

- checks paid, with the date, number, and amount of each

- other items paid, such as withdrawals, fees, and bills you authorized the bank to pay for you

- deposits and credits, with the dates, descriptions, and amounts

Canceled checks or photocopies of checks paid from your account may be enclosed with the statement. The first step in balancing your checkbook is to compare the canceled checks with those recorded in your checkbook register. Compare the deposits in your register with those on the statement and any receipts you may have. Check ATM transactions and fees recorded in your register against those on the statement. If the statement shows any service charges, subtract these from the balance shown in your register. Contact your bank if the statement lists questionable fees or items of which you have no record.

Next, account for the checks, ATM transactions, and deposits you made that have not yet appeared on your statement. There is a worksheet on the back of most bank statements for this, 8-12. On the worksheet, follow these steps:

1. On the first line, write the closing balance as shown on the bank statement.

8-12

This type of worksheet and directions for balancing an account will appear on the back of most bank statements.

BALANCING WORKSHEET

MONTH _March --_ , 20 _XX_

BANK BALANCE shown on this statement $ __48.73__

ADD+ $ __125.00__

DEPOSITS made but not shown on statement because made or received after date of this statement.

TOTAL $ __173.73__

SUBTRACT–

CHECKS OUTSTANDING .... $ __68.40__

BALANCE...............$ __105.33__

The above balance should be same as the up-to-date balance in your checkbook.

CHECKS AND DEBITS OUTSTANDING
(Written but not shown on statement because not yet received by Bank.)

NO.		
498	28	40
499	15	00
ATM	25	00
TOTAL	68	40

2. List all deposits you made that are not on the statement.

3. Add the amounts from steps 1 and 2. Write the total.

4. List by number and amount any checks and ATM withdrawals not included on the statement. Add these amounts together and enter the total at *Checks outstanding*.

5. Subtract the amount in step 4 from the amount in step 3 and enter the *Balance*.

The balance on your worksheet should match the current balance in your checkbook register. If they do not agree, go through the above steps very carefully to check your math. If the figures still do not agree or come close, you may want to contact your bank for help.

Special-Use Checks

In addition to personal checks, other types of checks can be used to transfer funds from payer to payee. Each serves a special purpose. They are available from most financial institutions, usually for a fee.

Cashier's Check

You buy a *cashier's check* from the bank and use it to make a payment to another person. A **cashier's check** is drawn by a bank on its own funds and signed by an authorized officer of the bank. The bank guarantees payment.

Certified Check

A **certified check** is a personal check with a bank's guarantee the check will be paid. When a bank certifies a check, the amount of the check is immediately subtracted from your account. A certified check is used to make a payment to a payee who does not accept personal checks.

Money Order

A **money order** is an order for a specific amount of money payable to a specific payee. People who do not have checking accounts may use money orders to send payments safely by mail. Money orders are sold in financial institutions, U.S. post offices, and other convenient locations.

Traveler's Checks

People who travel and do not want to carry large amounts of cash often use **traveler's checks**. They can be cashed at many places around the world. If the checks are lost or stolen, they can be replaced at the nearest bank or by the agency selling them. Keep a record of check numbers separate from the checks. You need identifying numbers to replace lost or stolen checks. Sign the checks only at the time you cash them.

Chapter Summary

Financial institutions aid the flow of money in the economy. For consumers they provide key money management services. These include checking, savings, and credit accounts. Most institutions also provide online banking, 24-hour ATMs, and other services to make banking more convenient.

A checking account is the first financial service needed by most consumers. Types of checking accounts include basic, lifeline, and interest-bearing checking accounts. Each meets different consumer needs. Shop around and ask questions before choosing a specific account and financial institution.

Managing a checking account involves certain basic skills—making deposits, writing and endorsing checks, and balancing your account each month.

You may also want to look into the variety of other financial services designed to help consumers manage their money. It pays to shop around for a financial institution offering the services and personal attention you need.

Review

1. What is the primary function of financial institutions in the economy?

2. Name and briefly describe three common financial institutions serving consumers.

3. Describe an electronic funds transfer (EFT) and how it relates to your financial transactions.

4. What are the conveniences of automatic teller machines (ATMs)?

5. What financial transactions can be handled with an online account?

6. When might you need overdraft protection or a stop payment order?

7. List four fees frequently connected with a checking account.

8. Name and describe the three types of checking accounts.

9. What is the purpose of endorsing a check?

10. Name and describe four special-use checks.

Critical Thinking

11. If a person prefers to pay for everything with cash, is a checking account needed?

12. If you had the choice of opening a checking account in a bank or a credit union, which would you choose? Explain your reasoning.

13. Describe three smart ways to use and manage an ATM machine and card.

14. When would a person probably use a cashier's check? a certified check? traveler's checks?

Answers to *Review*

1. to aid the flow of money throughout the economy

2. (List three:) commercial banks, savings and loan associations, credit unions, mutual savings banks (Descriptions are student response.)

3. An electronic funds transfer (EFT) refers to the movement of money electronically from one financial institution to another. These electronic transactions occur much faster than check and cash transactions.

4. Terminals are located in convenient places and are sources of cash 24 hours a day.

5. checking an account balance; reviewing account history; arranging and scheduling electronic bill payment; confirming any direct deposits, withdrawals, and transfers

6. overdraft protection— when a check written by you exceeds your account balance; stop payment order—when a check is lost or stolen, or when you have a grievance concerning goods or services paid by check

Academic Connections

15. **Research.** Examine three financial institutions in your area and develop a checklist for comparing their services.

16. **History, writing.** Investigate the beginning and the development of one of the following: ATM machines; online banking; or traveler's checks. In a written report, trace your topic from its beginning to the present day usage.

17. **Research, speech.** Research EFT systems, how they originated, and how they benefit consumers. Present your findings to the class.

18. **Social studies, writing.** Examine consumer banking and banking services in an industrialized country of your choice. Write a report on your findings.

MATH CHALLENGE

19. Balance a checking account that recorded the following activity since the last statement.

    Deposits: $25.00 and $120.00

    Checks: $25.00, $8.50, and $98.00

    ATM withdrawals: $20.00

    There was a $3.00 bank fee for using an ATM outside the bank's network, and the last statement's balance was $250.00. How much is in the account?

Tech Smart

20. Using presentation software, make an electronic presentation that shows how to write and endorse a check. Be sure to cover the three types of endorsement.

21. Search the Internet to find three local banks. Access each bank's Web site and examine the requirements for opening a basic checking account with no limit on the number of checks written. Using a computer program, graphically compare each bank's requirements. (Some banks may offer more than one type of account.) Explain which bank and account you prefer and why.

22. Imagine that you manage a local bank with six outlets and ATMs at each. Your bank also has ATMs at city hall and the local shopping mall. Working as a Web designer, create a home page that welcomes new customers and announces the bank's locations and basic services. (Assume the bank offers all the services discussed in the chapter.) What words and images would you use? Share your creation with the class.

7. maintenance fee, charges for ATM use, low-balance penalties, check-writing fees, and check-printing costs

8. basic checking accounts, interest-bearing checking accounts, lifeline checking accounts (Descriptions are student response.)

9. Endorsement gives a person title to the check and the right to cash or transfer it.

10. cashier's checks, certified checks, money orders, traveler's checks (Descriptions are student response.)

Answer to *Math Challenge*

19. $240.50

CHAPTER

9

Credit

Reading for Meaning

Read the chapter two times. During the first reading, jot down sentences you do not understand. During the second reading, use your notes to focus on areas you need to review more carefully.

credit

creditor

contract

default

principal

annual percentage rate (APR)

closed-end credit

secured loan

collateral

cosigner

open-end credit

creditworthy

credit report

credit card

grace period

repossession

foreclosure

lien

garnishment

bankruptcy

loan shark

easy-access credit

payday loans

pawnshop

rent-to-own

title loan

CHAPTER OBJECTIVES

After studying this chapter, you will be able to

- **explain** the advantages and disadvantages of using credit.
- **identify** the different types of consumer credit.
- **describe** how to establish a sound credit rating.
- **define** the key terms in credit contracts and agreements.
- **compare** credit terms and charges.
- **outline** the steps involved in managing credit.
- **identify** steps to take in resolving credit problems.
- **summarize** the laws that govern the use of credit.

Central Ideas

- Credit is a powerful financial management tool.
- Serious financial problems result from the misuse of credit.

In a cash transaction, you hand over money in exchange for goods or services. Like cash, credit is a medium of exchange. **Credit** allows you to buy goods or services now and pay for them later. More specifically, it is an agreement between two parties in which one party, the **creditor**, supplies money, goods, or services to the other. In return, the receiving party, or the borrower or debtor, agrees to make future payment by a particular date or according to an agreed-upon schedule.

Credit is more costly than cash because fees are usually added to the amount owed. It is costly in another way, too. When you use credit, you spend future income. This means part of your future earnings must be used to pay what you owe. The use of credit reduces future income.

Governments, businesses, and consumers use credit. Credit plays an important role in personal economics. Used carefully and wisely, it can help people get more of the things they need when they need them. Misused credit can lead to financial disaster. It is important for your own financial well being to learn how to manage your credit dollars.

Consumer credit also plays an important role in the economy. It provides the extra buying power needed to support mass production and distribution of goods and services. Therefore, credit helps make more goods and services available to consumers at lower prices.

Understanding Consumer Credit

All credit is based on trust. The creditor believes there is a high likelihood the borrower can and will pay what is owed. For example, suppose you go out to eat with friends. One friend does not have enough money and asks to borrow some of yours. If you trust that friend and can spare the money, you will probably lend it, 9-1.

Credit also has an element of risk. When you lend a friend money, a DVD, or a shirt, you risk that he or she will not return it. An unpaid debt between friends can harm a friendship. If a friend does not pay you back, you will probably not lend to him or her again.

Although a car loan is more complicated, it also depends on the creditor trusting that the borrower will repay the debt. The creditor takes a risk, but that risk is minimized in several ways. Before the loan is made, the borrower must sign a **contract**, a legally binding agreement between the borrower and the creditor. The contract states the terms of the car loan. If the borrower **defaults**, or fails to pay the debt, the creditor can take the borrower to court and even take back the car.

9-1

People usually feel comfortable lending to friends they trust because they believe the debt will be repaid.

Borrowers must pay creditors for the cost of making credit available and for the risk involved in possible defaults. Payment takes the form of interest and other finance charges. This means that a borrower repays not only the **principal**, or amount borrowed, but also the finance charges stated in the contract. That makes buying with credit more costly than paying cash.

Before making credit available, a creditor reviews the borrower's financial history. Just as you may not lend money to someone who does not repay debts, creditors will not lend to a person with a poor credit reputation. Before making a loan offer, creditors already know the likelihood of the borrower defaulting on the loan. If risk of default is high, most reliable creditors will not lend. Less reputable creditors may lend, but with a much higher finance charge and unfavorable terms.

Reasons to Use Credit

You will find it smart to use credit in some situations, but not in others. Several advantages of using credit are listed here.

- *Use of goods and services as you pay for them.* Being able to wear a coat or drive a car as you pay for it can be a big plus. This is a common reason for using credit.

- *Opportunity to buy costly items that you may not be able to buy with cash.* Many people find it difficult or impossible to save enough to pay for a car or hospital bill in one payment. With credit, you can buy goods and services as you need them and pay for them over a

Reflect

What has been your family's experience with consumer credit?

Discuss

How does the availability of consumer credit help to launch new products?

Discuss

What products, other than computers, can you name that were supported by the use of consumer credit?

Linking to... History

Role of Credit in the Computer Industry

Consumer credit can help launch a new product. For example, when personal computers first hit the market, prices were high and sales were low. In 1981, around 750 thousand personal computers were being used in homes across the country. By 1991, the number had increased to almost 28 million.

Today, approximately 75 percent of U.S. households have personal computers and Internet access. Since 1980, personal computers improved dramatically. They are more powerful, efficient, and user-friendly. They are also smaller and less expensive. The vast array of software available continues to grow.

Most buyers used some form of consumer credit to pay for their personal computers in the early 80s. The use of credit made it possible for

more people to buy. Increased consumer demand supported mass production and distribution while lowering unit production costs. Manufacturers passed on these savings to consumers in the form of lower prices. Growth in the computer industry also financed research and development.

Lower prices sparked even more sales. The industry grew rapidly, bringing exciting job opportunities. More people were hired to sell and service personal computers. New businesses emerged to produce, sell, and rent software and accessories for these computers.

In the case of personal computers, credit stimulated consumer demand and business growth. It helped maintain a healthy balance between supply and demand. Without consumer credit, the industry would have grown less rapidly. Prices would have stayed higher and sales lower. Fewer jobs would have been created and fewer people employed.

Reflect

What uses of credit do you think justify the cost of using it?

Discuss

What advantages does the use of credit offer consumers?

Discuss

Why do you think these reasons for using credit can make good financial sense?

Discuss

What problems can you see in using credit for these reasons?

Enrich

Cite examples of each of the disadvantages of using credit.

Enrich

Interview a creditor to find out what it costs to make credit available to consumers.

period of time. Borrowing is sometimes the only way consumers can pay for major purchases, such as a car.

- *Source of cash for emergency or unexpected expenses.* Even the best money managers face the unexpected. Credit can offer temporary help.

- *Convenience.* Credit eliminates the need to carry large amounts of cash. It provides a record of purchases. It usually simplifies telephone, mail, and Internet shopping as well as necessary returns and exchanges.

- *Sales.* Credit allows you to take advantage of sale prices on goods or services you need when you do not have enough cash at sale time.

- *Long-range goals.* Credit can help consumers make purchases that are part of a long-range financial plan, such as paying for education, furniture, or a vacation.

Drawbacks of Credit Use

To use credit wisely, you need to be aware of its drawbacks as well as its benefits. Consider the negatives when you are deciding how and when to use credit. Here are some disadvantages of using credit:

- *Reduction of future income.* By using credit, you spend future income. You thereby reduce the amount of money you can spend later.

- *Expense.* Using credit usually costs money. The more credit you use and the more time you take to repay, the more you will pay in finance charges. This reduces the amount you will have to spend for other goods and services.

- *Temptation.* Credit makes it easy to spend money you do not have. It can be difficult to resist buying what you cannot afford or can do without when you have ready credit.

- *Risk of serious consequences.* Failure to pay debts on time and in full can cause serious financial problems. You will read about these later in this chapter.

Cost of Credit

When you borrow $10 from a friend, you probably repay the friend an even $10. If you charge purchases or borrow cash in the marketplace, you usually pay finance charges. You pay these charges because it costs businesses money to grant you credit.

The creditors who do not have cash on hand borrow the money to make credit available. When they borrow, they must pay interest. Creditors with cash on hand lose the chance to invest it when they use their money to give you credit. In a sense, they are investing in you, and the interest you pay is their return on investment.

Creditors must also pay the costs of opening and servicing credit accounts. These costs include employees, facilities, and the materials needed to lend money, send out bills, and record payments.

When consumers fail to pay on time or in full, the creditors' costs go up. The expenses of collecting overdue debts and absorbing the losses of unpaid accounts add up quickly. As a result, the price of credit goes up for all consumers, even those who pay on time.

Case Study: Using Credit

The Credit Game

Chiyo graduated from college recently and has a steady job. She wants the convenience of charging purchases, so she opens a credit card.

Chiyo's first credit card bill is almost $600. Since she did not keep track of her charges, the bill is a surprise. Her paycheck is only $1,035 a month after deductions. After paying rent and other expenses, she has only $30 left to pay on her credit account each month.

Chiyo didn't need most of the credit card purchases. It takes her 24 months to pay off the debt. She pays over $118 in finance charges.

Damian looks at credit as a useful tool. He realizes the importance of establishing credit so he can get loans in the future. Besides, he doesn't think it is realistic to buy everything with cash.

Although Damian is happy to have his credit card, he is a little afraid of it. His family had some debt problems when he was younger.

Damian uses his credit card sparingly and keeps track of his charges. He limits his overall debt to an amount he can repay. He uses credit only for things he really needs. His first purchase is a pair of waterproof boots he buys on sale. Damian uses his credit card because he doesn't have enough cash. If he waited until payday, the boots would no longer be on sale. By using credit wisely, Damian saves $20.

Case Review

1. How does offering credit work in the interest of sellers?
2. How can the use of credit work for consumers? How can it create problems?
3. What advice would you give Chiyo for the future use of credit?
4. What did you learn from Damian's example?
5. How can consumers enjoy the benefits and avoid the problems of using credit?

Finance Charges

The finance charge is the total dollar cost of credit. It is the dollar amount paid for credit. A finance charge has two parts: interest and fees.

For example, a $1,000 loan may have a finance charge of $50, which is $10 in fees and $40 in interest. When you apply for credit, the interest you pay depends on the *annual percentage rate (APR)*, the amount of credit used, and the length of the repayment period. Here is how these factors work to determine the cost of credit.

Annual Percentage Rate

The finance charge you pay for the use of credit is expressed as a percentage. An **annual percentage rate (APR)** is the annual cost of credit a lender charges. The higher the APR, the more you pay. For example, the interest for a $500 loan repaid in 12 monthly payments would cost

- $50.08 at 18 percent
- $58.72 at 21 percent
- $67.36 at 24 percent

Amount of Credit Used

The more you charge or borrow, the more interest you pay. For example, the interest on a loan repaid in 12 monthly payments at an annual percentage rate of 18 percent would cost

- $50.08 for a $500 loan
- $110.01 for a $1,000 loan
- $220.02 for a $2,000 loan

Length of the Repayment Period

The more time you take to repay the money you borrow, the more interest you will pay. For example, the interest on a $500 loan at 1.5 percent per month (18 percent per year) would cost

- $50.08 if repaid in 12 monthly payments
- $99.44 if repaid in 24 monthly payments
- $150.88 if repaid in 36 monthly payments

Types of Credit

There are many types of consumer credit and ways to categorize them. The following are widely used terms you should know.

Closed-End Credit

Closed-end credit refers to a loan that must be repaid with finance charges by a certain date. These loans are given for a specific purpose, and

include car loans, student loans, and most home loans, 9-2.

Loans are granted by commercial banks, credit unions, finance companies, insurance companies, and credit card agencies. When you take out a loan, you sign a contract stating the amount of the loan, the interest rate, length of the loan, and other provisions of the agreement.

A **secured loan** requires collateral. **Collateral** is property that a borrower promises to give up in case of default. If you fail to pay as agreed, the creditor may take the property to settle the claim against you. You may pay lower finance charges on a secured loan because the creditor takes less risk when collateral is pledged. The car is collateral in an auto loan.

An *unsecured loan* is made on the strength of your signature alone. You sign a contract and promise to repay according to terms of the agreement. It is difficult to obtain a loan of this type unless you have a strong credit rating. If you have nothing to pledge as collateral, you still may be able to get a loan if you have a cosigner. A **cosigner** is a responsible person who signs the loan with you. By signing the loan, the cosigner promises to repay the loan if you fail to pay. Unsecured loans usually have higher interest rates than secured loans.

Most closed-end credit is offered in the form of installment loans. An *installment loan* lets you borrow a given amount of money and repay it with interest in regular installments. Finance charges vary with the size of the loan, the interest rate, and the repayment period. Interest rates vary with different lenders and with the collateral pledged.

9-2

Home loans are a type of closed-end credit that homeowners repay by a certain date.

Open-End Credit

Open-end credit allows the borrower to use a certain amount of money for an indefinite period of time. As long as the borrower makes payments on a schedule, pays any finance charges, and stays within the borrowing limit, he or she can continue to use the credit.

One example of open-end credit is a credit card. Retailers, merchants, banks, credit agencies, and other businesses that issue credit cards to consumers offer open-end credit. Terms may differ slightly with different creditors and in different states.

Two common types of open-end credit are regular charge accounts and revolving credit accounts. A *regular charge account* lets you charge goods and services in exchange for your promise to pay in full within 25 days of the billing date. You receive a bill or statement each month. If you pay on time, there is no finance charge.

Vocabulary

Distinguish between a *secured loan* and an *unsecured loan*.

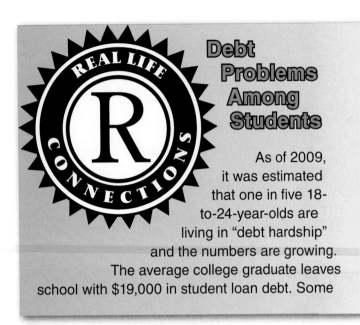

Debt Problems Among Students

As of 2009, it was estimated that one in five 18- to-24-year-olds are living in "debt hardship" and the numbers are growing. The average college graduate leaves school with $19,000 in student loan debt. Some students have as much as $40,000. Those in professional schools such as law, medicine, and dentistry may incur debts as high as $100,000 by graduation. Credit card debt may add another $3,000 to $7,000 to these obligations. The fact is more students drop out of college today for financial concerns than for academic failure. Students should try to explore every possible way to pay for their education without incurring excessive debt. They should consider savings, scholarships, low-tuition schools, work/study programs, part-time jobs, government aid programs, and other means of paying for education and training.

Activity

Explain the difference between a regular charge account and a revolving account.

Note

Outstanding consumer credit for credit cards and other revolving credit has increased dramatically over the past 20 years. How do you account for this increase?

Reflect

Which of the steps for establishing a credit rating have you already taken?

A *revolving credit account* offers you a choice of paying in full each month or spreading payments over a period of time. If you choose not to pay in full, there is a finance charge.

You must make at least the minimum payment each month. For small balances, the minimum payment is usually a set amount, such as $10. For larger amounts of credit, the minimum payment is usually a percentage of the unpaid balance.

A typical revolving credit account places a limit on the total amount you may owe at any one time. You may make any number of purchases at any time as long as you do not exceed your credit limit. This type of credit is available through many retailers and through issuers of credit cards, such as Visa, MasterCard, and Discover. They can be used to buy goods and services from any seller who honors the card you carry.

Establishing Credit

You may find it difficult to get credit at first. This is because creditors want evidence that you can and will pay your debts. Here are some steps you can take to build a sound financial reputation.

1. *Start with a job.* Prove that you can earn money.

2. *Open a savings account.* Saving regularly shows a responsible attitude toward financial matters. Your savings also may serve as collateral for a loan.

3. *Open a checking account.* A well-managed checking account shows you have experience in handling money.

4. *Apply to a local department store or a gasoline company for a credit card.* If you are granted credit, make small purchases and pay promptly. This will give you a record of steady payments.

If you have never used credit, you will need to establish a credit rating from scratch.

Your Credit Rating

Creditors decide whether or not to grant people credit based on their credit ratings. A *credit rating* is the creditor's evaluation of your willingness and ability to pay debts. It is measured by the three Cs:

- *Character*—based on your reputation for honesty and your financial history. The person who has a record of paying bills on time and of assuming financial responsibility will rate high on character.

- *Capacity*—your ability to earn money and pay debts. It is measured by your earning power and employment history.

- *Capital*—your financial worth. People with land, a home, cars, savings, or anything of value have capital. Capital gives a person a more favorable credit rating.

A **creditworthy** applicant is judged to have the assets, income, and tendency to repay debt.

The Credit Report

How do lenders get the information to evaluate a consumer's creditworthiness? They look at the application and whether the prospective borrower has a job. They may contact references listed on the application. An important factor is the length of the credit history. If you are unemployed or never have used credit, it may be difficult to get a loan or credit card.

Most lenders also turn to *credit reporting agencies*. A *credit reporting agency*, or credit bureau, is an organization that collects information about the financial and credit transactions of consumers. Businesses notify the credit reporting agencies when a consumer opens a new account, closes an account, or skips or makes late payments.

There are three major national credit reporting agencies: Equifax, Experian, and TransUnion LLC. Once you begin to use credit, you will automatically establish a record at a credit-reporting agency. These agencies sell credit reports to creditors.

A **credit report** is a record of a person's credit history and financial behavior. It includes every credit account ever opened and outstanding balances on current credit accounts. It also lists negative information such as *delinquent* or late payments and overdue taxes. The information on credit reports from the different agencies does not always match up. Carefully review your credit report and check key information in each section, 9-3. If you find errors, contact the credit reporting agency for instructions on filing a dispute.

Your credit report largely determines whether you can get credit when you need it. With a poor report, you will have trouble getting credit and may have to pay higher finance charges.

Resource

Credit Worthiness Survey,
Activity B, WB

Vocabulary

Define and explain the *three Cs*
of a credit rating.

Reflect

Would you be considered
creditworthy?

Resource

Credit Report Sample,
reproducible master 9-1, TR

9-3
A credit report shows if a person has used credit wisely.

How to Read a Credit Report	
Section	**What to Check**
Personal Information	Verify your personal information, such as your name, address, phone number, date of birth, and Social Security number.
Credit Summary	This section summarizes your revolving and installment accounts and any home loans. Check the balances and your total amount of outstanding debt.
Account Information (also called *Credit Items*)	Make sure all accounts listed belong to you. This section may be lengthy, but it is important to check all details for accuracy, including payment history, balance, and account status. Late payments and accounts taken over by collection agencies appear in this section.
Public Records (also called *Negative Information or Items*)	Any bankruptcies, garnishments, or liens are shown here. Ideally, this section should be blank.
Inquiries (also called *Credit History Requests*)	Look over the list of creditors that recently viewed your credit report. Applying for a credit card, taking out a loan, submitting an apartment application, or applying for insurance can trigger inquiries.

Note

Credit reporting agencies use different names for the sections of credit reports. Figure 9-3 shows commonly used section names.

Enrich

Access the Web sites of each of the three credit reporting agencies to learn how they operate, what services they provide, and how to access your credit record. Discuss findings in class.

Resource

Credit Account Application, transparency master 9-2, TR

Reflect

What has been your family's experience with credit cards? Do you see them as an asset or a liability?

Credit Scores

Creditors also evaluate creditworthiness by looking at *credit scores*. A credit score is a numerical measure of a loan applicant's creditworthiness at a particular point in time. It is generated primarily by credit reporting agencies.

Your credit score may differ from one credit reporting agency to another. Each agency has access to different information and uses different mathematical formulas to calculate scores. However, the scores for the same person are usually similar. A credit score is based on the following:

- *Bill paying.* You score high here if you have a record of paying your bills on time.

- *Debt-to-credit-limit ratio.* Your debt is the total of all you owe on credit cards, car loans, home loans, and so forth. Your credit limit is the total amount you are allowed under credit card maximums and your original loan amounts. A lower ratio is best.

- *Credit history length.* The longer you have used well-managed credit card accounts, the better.

- *Recent credit application.* Several applications for new credit accounts can have a negative effect on your credit score.

- *Different types of credit.* Having a mix of loans and credit cards is slightly favored over using only one type of credit.

The higher a credit score, the greater a person's creditworthiness. However, what is considered a good credit score varies. For example, the credit-reporting agency Experian uses a scoring system based on letters, such as the grades you receive in class, 9-4.

What one creditor considers a good score may not be good enough for another. What a creditor considers a good score today may be too low for that same creditor tomorrow. When credit is tight, creditors look for higher credit scores before granting a credit request. A person's credit score changes as his or her financial history and obligations change.

> ### Credit Score Ratings
>
> This is how Experian rated credit scores in early 2009.
>
> - **A: 901 to 990.** Consumers in this group have a low risk of defaulting on loans and lenders offer them the best rates and terms.
> - **B: 801 to 900.** Consumers in this group have managed their credit well and are offered good rates and terms by lenders.
> - **C: 701 to 800.** Lenders may consider consumers in this group for loans, but often require more information.
> - **D: 601 to 700.** Consumers in this group have a higher default rate. Lenders may give them credit, but only at a higher interest rate.
> - **F: 501 to 600.** Consumers in this group have a high risk of defaulting on loans. Lenders will often deny them credit. If they get credit, they pay higher interest rates.

Getting a Credit Card

Credit cards are most often used to buy goods and services on a time-payment plan. You pay for the purchase later, plus interest. Some credit cards may also be used to obtain cash. There are three common types of credit cards:

- *General-purpose cards*, such as Visa or MasterCard, are issued by banks, credit unions, and other financial institutions. You can use these cards around the world at the many places where they are accepted. Very often, you can also obtain cash at automated teller machines using these cards. They carry a credit limit and require minimum monthly payments. Finance charges and other fees vary.

- *Company or retail store cards*, issued by service stations, local merchants, or chain stores, permit you to charge purchases only with the merchant issuing the card. Normally, you have a credit limit and are required to repay a minimum amount each month. Finance charges vary.

- *Travel and entertainment cards* usually require you to pay the entire balance each month. Some cards allow you to pay over a longer period for travel- and vacation-related expenses such as airfare, tours, cruises, and hotel bills. On these balances, you usually pay a high interest rate and must make minimum monthly payments.

9-4

In early 2009, the U.S. average credit score, according to Experian, was 692.

Activity

Obtain application forms for Visa, MasterCard, and Discover cards to study and compare.

Resource

Credit Application, Activity C, WB

Reflect

Does your family use travel and entertainment credit cards?

How Credit Cards Work

This example illustrates how a typical credit card is used. Valerie opens a revolving charge account at a local department store. She is issued a credit card. In May, she charges $85 on her credit card. This amount is more than she wants to pay in June when the bill comes. She decides to pay the minimum payment of $10. During June, she charges another $15 worth of merchandise.

In July, the bill totals $91.13. This includes the $75 unpaid balance from June, a 1.5 percent finance charge of $1.13, and $15 for new purchases.

Case Study: Using Credit

Ty's "Deal"

Ty is buying a motorcycle. He's so excited about his new bike that he closes the deal right away and finances with the seller.

He rides away on his new bike feeling great until he runs into his friend Sara. She explains how credit charges differ from lender to lender. The chart below compares Ty's deal with two other sources for a $2,000 loan financed over a 24-month period. Failing to shop for credit was an expensive mistake.

Comparing Credit Sources			
	Ty's Deal	Source 1	Source 2
Annual Rate	15%	10%	12%
Monthly Payment	$96.35	$92.01	$93.75
Total Payments (monthly × 24)	$2,312.40	$2,208.24	$2,250.00
Down Payment	$250.00	$250.00	$250.00
Total Paid	$2,562.40	$2,458.24	$2,500.00
Finance Charges (total payments less $2,000)	$312.40	$208.24	$250.00

Case Review

1. What should Ty have done before financing through the seller of the motorcycle?
2. How much money could Ty have saved by financing at a 10 percent annual rate?
3. How many months would you take to pay off a loan of this type? How would this affect your finance charges?
4. How much time would you be willing to spend looking for the best loan terms?
5. How would you have handled Ty's situation differently?

Now Valerie can continue to make minimum payments or pay her account in full.

Since Valerie's credit limit is $1,000, she can continue to charge merchandise until her unpaid balance reaches that limit. As her unpaid balance goes up, so will the minimum monthly payment and the finance charge.

Making minimum payments increases the cost of credit and the amount of time it will take to pay it off. Pay off the balance in full each month to avoid finance charges.

Shopping for a Credit Card

Shopping for credit is as important as shopping for the goods and services you buy with it. When you want to borrow cash or use credit to finance a purchase, shop around for the best credit terms. The more you borrow, the more you pay. The higher the annual percentage rate, the more you pay. The longer you take to repay, the more you pay in credit charges.

The Contract

When you apply for credit, you will be asked to fill out a credit application form like the one in 9-5. This form helps creditors evaluate your financial standing and credit rating.

Using credit involves certain responsibilities for you and the creditor. These are spelled out in credit contracts and agreements. The terms outlined in a written agreement are legally binding. They can be enforced in courts of law if you or the creditor fails to carry out the terms of the contract. It is very important to understand exactly what you are agreeing to do before you sign any contract.

Read the contract thoroughly. Be sure all blank spaces have been filled. None should be left open for someone to fill later. Make sure the annual percentage rate and the dollar cost are stated clearly and accurately. Ask questions if there are any terms you do not fully understand.

Study the contract to find out what action the creditor can take if you pay late or fail to make a payment. Also find out if you can pay in advance. If so, check to see if part of the finance charges will be refunded.

Contract Clauses to Avoid

Watch for an *acceleration clause* that allows the creditor to require full and immediate payment of the entire balance if you miss a payment or fail to abide by the terms of the contract.

For a home loan or an installment loan, find out whether the contract calls for a *balloon payment*. This is a final payment considerably larger than the regular monthly or periodic payments and it is required to retire the loan. If a balloon payment is required, find out the amount and your options if you are unable to make this final payment. Can you refinance? If so, under what terms?

Be wary of *add-on clauses* that allow you to buy additional items before paying in full for goods you have already purchased. The clause may allow

9-5

This application form helps creditors evaluate your credit worthiness. Note the questions on the form.

Discuss

What should you do if you do not understand the terms in a credit contract?

Activity

List the information needed to complete a credit application form.

Resource

Understanding Credit Disclosures, reproducible master 9-3, TR

Activity

Search the Internet for information on credit card offers from financial institutions. Find disclosures available on the financial institution Web sites. Compare the disclosures from two sources.

BELK CREDIT APPLICATION

EMPLOYEE NO.   DATE

Type of Account Requested:
☐ INDIVIDUAL   ☐ JOINT

PLEASE TELL US ABOUT YOURSELF

FIRST NAME (TITLES OPTIONAL)   MIDDLE INITIAL   LAST NAME   AGE

STREET ADDRESS (IF P.O. BOX — PLEASE GIVE STREET ADDRESS)   CITY   STATE   ZIP

☐ OWN   ☐ LIVE WITH RELATIVE   MONTHLY PAYMENT   YEARS AT PRESENT ADDRESS   HOME PHONE NO.   NO. OF DEPENDENTS
☐ RENT ☐ OTHER $ (   )

PREVIOUS ADDRESS   CITY   STATE   ZIP   HOW LONG

NAME OF NEAREST RELATIVE NOT LIVING WITH YOU   RELATIONSHIP   PHONE NO. (   )

ADDRESS   CITY   STATE

NOW TELL US ABOUT YOUR JOB

EMPLOYER OR INCOME SOURCE   POSITION/TITLE   HOW LONG EMPLOYED YRS.   MOS.   MONTHLY INCOME $

EMPLOYER'S ADDRESS   CITY   STATE   TYPE OF BUSINESS   BUSINESS PHONE (   )

MILITARY RANK (IF NOW IN SERVICE)   SEPARATION DATE   UNIT AND DUTY STATION   SOCIAL SECURITY NO.

SOURCE OF OTHER INCOME (Alimony, child support, or separate maintenance need not be revealed if you do not wish to have it considered as a basis for repaying this obligation)   SOURCE   INCOME $ ☐ MONTHLY ☐ ANNUALLY

AND YOUR CREDIT REFERENCES ARE

NAME AND ADDRESS OF BANK/SAVINGS AND LOAN   ☐ CHECKING ☐ SAVINGS ☐ LOAN   PREVIOUS BELK OR LEGGETT ACCOUNT? ACCOUNT NO. HOW IS ACCOUNT LISTED?   ☐ YES ☐ NO

List Bank cards, Dept. Stores, Finance Co.'s, and other accounts:

NAME	ACCOUNT NO.	BALANCE	PAYMENT
		$	$
		$	$
		$	$
		$	$

INFORMATION REGARDING JOINT APPLICANT

COMPLETE THIS AREA IF   ☐ JOINT ACCOUNT IS REQUESTED   ☐ YOU ARE RELYING ON SPOUSE'S INCOME OR CREDIT HISTORY TO OBTAIN CREDIT

FIRST NAME   MIDDLE INITIAL   LAST NAME   AGE   RELATIONSHIP   SOCIAL SECURITY NO.

JOINT APPLICANT'S ADDRESS IF DIFFERENT FROM APPLICANT
ADDRESS   CITY   STATE   ZIP

JOINT APPLICANT'S PRESENT EMPLOYER   ADDRESS   HOW LONG EMPLOYED YRS.   MOS.

BUSINESS PHONE (   )   POSITION/TITLE   MONTHLY INCOME $

YOUR SIGNATURE PLEASE   Store Stamp Below

I have read and agree to the Terms and Conditions of the Belk Retail Charge Agreement as set forth on attached. Belk is authorized to investigate my credit record and exchange credit experience with other creditors and Credit Reporting Agencies. This information is given to obtain credit, and is true and complete.

FOR OFFICE USE ONLY

Letter _____
CB. RPT. _____
EMP. VER _____

Applicant's Signature   Date

Joint Applicant's signature
(required if joint applicant section completed)   Date

DATE	EMP.	#CARDS	T/C	CR/LN.	APPROVED

the seller to hold a security interest in the items purchased first until you pay for later purchases in full. For example, you buy a washer and dryer, but before paying for them you add a refrigerator. The seller can hold title to the washer and dryer until you also pay for the refrigerator.

Read credit contracts thoroughly with particular attention to possible fees, penalties, and consequences of failing to carry out all the terms of the agreement. Do not sign until you fully understand all the terms and the obligations you are assuming.

Disclosures

By law, credit card offers must include certain disclosures or credit terms, 9-6. Before accepting and using any of these cards, you need to read the fine print on any contract you sign and ask questions. Knowing the exact cost of credit can help you compare finance charges and find the best

Annual percentage rate (APR) for purchases	2.9% until 11/1/XX after that, 14.9%
Other APRs	Cash-advance APR: 15.9% Balance-Transfer APR: 15.9% Penalty rate: 23.9% See explanation below.*
Variable-rate information	Your APR for purchase transactions may vary. The rate is determined monthly by adding 5.9% to the Prime Rate.**
Grace period for repayment of balances for purchases	25 days on average
Method of computing the balance for purchases	Average daily balance (excluding new purchases)
Annual fees	None
Minimum finance charge	$0.50

Transaction fee for cash advances: 3% of the amount advanced

Balance-transfer fee: 3% of the amount transferred

Late-payment fee: $25

Over-the-credit-limit fee: $25

* Explanation of penalty. If your payment arrives more than ten days late two times within a six month period, the penalty rate will apply.

** The Prime Rate used to determine your APR is the rate published in the Wall Street Journal on the 10th day of the prior month.

Adapted from the brochure *Choosing a Credit Card*,
Board of Governors of the Federal Reserve System

9-6
On credit card application forms, disclosures are usually shown in a box similar to this one.

deal. It also helps you decide how much credit you can afford to use. The application should include the following information.

Annual Percentage Rates

The APR must be disclosed. This is the finance charge on unpaid balances. There is usually one rate for purchases and a higher rate for cash advances.

The issuing companies often offer an attractive "introductory rate" that lasts only three to six months, after which you pay the considerably higher regular rate. In this case, it is important to check how long the introductory rate lasts and what the regular rate is.

In addition, know the terms of the rate. Can the credit card company raise the rate for any reason, such as missing a payment on this card?

Variable-Rate Information

Interest rates can be fixed or variable. A *variable interest rate* fluctuates with the ups and downs of the economy. It can start out low and reset to a higher rate. A *fixed interest rate* stays the same, although under certain conditions such as a late payment, it can change.

Resource
Calculating Finance Charges, transparency master 9-4, TR

Vocabulary
What is *APR*?

Activity
Use the Internet to research current APRs on credit cards.

Discuss
What is an *introductory rate*?

Vocabulary
Differentiate between a variable interest rate and a fixed interest rate.

Grace Period

A **grace period** is the time between the billing date and the start of interest charges. You have that time to pay the full balance without interest.

In a few states, a grace period is mandatory on any new charges made each month. Interest may only be figured on outstanding balances from the prior month. There are no interest charges on credit card balances that are paid in full by the due date each month.

Method of Computing the Balance

It is important to understand how interest is calculated. If you pay less than the full amount owed each month, you will pay interest on the unpaid balance. Creditors compute interest charges in different ways. Their methods can result in very different actual finance charges, 9-7. You need to read the fine print on credit agreements and monthly statements to learn what methods are used to calculate interest. Creditors are required by law to provide an explanation.

Annual Fee

Find out whether you must pay an annual fee for the privilege of using the card. These fees can be as much as $50 or more. It pays to look for cards with low or no annual fees.

Other Fees

It pays to know what extras can be charged to your account and how you can avoid these charges. These may include fees for

- late payments

- exceeding your credit limit

- cash advances

- balance transfers

Shop around for the best credit card deal. You can compare cards, interest rates, fees, and features online as well as by contacting individual credit card issuers.

Rewards

You may want to find out whether there are any perks or rewards associated with using a certain credit card. These may include cash-back offers, no-interest introductory offers, credits for purchases of certain goods and services, and other incentives. You want to weigh the value of any rewards against the costs and fees associated with each card.

Subprime Credit Cards

Subprime credit cards are cards offered to people who have a poor credit history. Often they carry very high interest rates, large annual fees, sign-up fees, participation fees, late payment penalties, and other charges.

Calculating Interest on Revolving Credit Accounts

- *Average Daily Balance*. The creditor starts with the beginning balance for each day in the billing period and subtracts any payments or credits to your account on that day. Then the balances for each day in the billing cycle are totaled. The total is divided by the number of days in the cycle to arrive at the average daily balance. Interest charges are figured on that amount. New purchases may or may not be added to the daily totals. This is the most common method of computing charges.

- *Adjusted Balance*. The creditor determines the balance by subtracting payments or credits received during the billing period from the outstanding balance at the end of the previous billing period. Purchases you make during the current billing period are not included. This is the most favorable method for consumers but rarely used by creditors.

- *Previous Balance*. The creditor computes interest charges on the amount you owed at the end of the previous billing period. Payments, credits, and new purchases during the current billing period are not included.

- *Two-Cycle Balances*. The creditor calculates interest charges on average daily balances and account activity over the last two billing cycles. This is the most costly method for the consumer. There is pending legislation that would prohibit two-cycle balances.

9-7

Actual finance charges can vary depending on the method used to calculate interest.

The credit limits are generally low—$250 to $300. Some card issuers limit the credit to an amount equaling the deposit made in a collateral savings account. In other words, if you deposit $300, that is your credit limit; deposit $5,000 and that is your limit.

Subprime cards generally are easy to get, but very costly. For example, you are issued a card with a $300 limit. It comes with a sign-up fee of $85, a monthly participation fee of $8, and an annual fee of $50. This leaves $157 of credit. Terms vary with different credit card issuers. Be wary because you almost always lose more than you gain with a subprime credit card. It is better to deal only with reputable creditors.

Discuss

Which method of calculating interest is most beneficial for the consumer? for the creditor?

Discuss

What are the consequences of using credit without planning?

Reflect

How would you describe your financial personality?

Managing Your Credit

Credit can make it possible for you to spend more than you earn—temporarily. With careful planning, credit can help you get more of the things you want when you want them. Without planning, credit can create serious, long-lasting financial and legal problems. The following tips will help you handle credit responsibly.

Know Your Financial Personality

A close look at your financial personality can help you decide when and if you can use credit safely. Your financial personality is a combination of your attitudes about money and your spending patterns. You express your financial personality by the way you handle cash and credit.

Reflect

Do you know someone who is an impulse shopper?

Discuss

What are some of the financial personalities displayed in recent movies?

Reflect

Based on these questions, is credit a safe tool for you to use?

Discuss

Name ways consumers can keep track of spending.

Financial personalities vary greatly. Some people spend money freely. Others find it hard to part with a dollar. Some think through each purchase, while others buy on impulse. What are your money attitudes and habits?

- Do you find it easy to control spending?
- Do you save regularly?
- Do you follow a spending plan?
- Do you consider purchases carefully, particularly major purchases?
- Do you pay bills promptly?
- Do you buy only what you can afford?
- Do you make long-range financial plans?
- Do you handle financial matters with confidence?
- Do you see credit as a tool to use with care and caution?

If you answered "yes" to most of these questions, credit is probably a safe tool for you to use.

Keep Track of Spending

Since many credit problems result from poor money management, the development of good management skills outlined in Chapter 6 can help you avoid serious credit problems. This includes creating a budget or spending plan. Try not to use more credit than you can pay off each month. You only pay interest charges if you roll over a balance to the next month.

Since overspending is easy with a credit card, it is important to keep track of your charges and account balance. Save your receipts. You may want to keep a paper or an electronic log of credit charges so you always know how much you have spent. If you have more than one card, keep track of the total credit spent on all cards.

ECONOMICS in ACTION

Excessive Credit and the Economy

Excessive use of credit can throw the economy off balance and foster inflation. When consumers use credit to buy goods and services, it increases the demand for whatever they are buying. If the demand increases faster than the supply, prices will increase. When government and business join consumers in the excessive use of credit, demand surpasses supply and inflation results. The economy is weakened and fewer job opportunities exist.

Remember Alternatives to Using Credit

Usually you have three alternatives to using credit. You may choose

- not to buy

- to pay with savings

- to postpone buying now, and buy later with cash

The choice you make will depend on what you want to buy and what you want to achieve with your cash and your credit. Here are some questions to help you evaluate your choices.

How important is making the purchase? If you can do without something, you might be wise to not buy it. Is having the purchase now instead of later worth the extra price you pay for credit?

Are you willing to use all or some of your savings to buy now? Unless you have planned to use money you have saved to make the purchase, reducing or eliminating your savings could be risky. Often it is difficult to replace the savings used for unplanned purchases. You may be left unprepared for unexpected emergencies or financial difficulties.

Can you save your money and buy later? This will depend on how long you can wait to make the purchase. It will also depend on your ability to save money. Many people find it easier to make monthly credit payments than to put money in savings.

By waiting and saving, you may miss the satisfaction or pleasure of having what you want now. For example, suppose you want to take a vacation with friends. They are leaving next month for a week at the beach. According to your savings plan, you need three more months to save enough money for the trip. If you wait three months, you will not be able to share the vacation with your friends. In this case, you may decide to use credit to help you finance the vacation.

On the other hand, waiting may help you get more satisfaction from a purchase. Suppose you want to buy a pool table. You want it now, but you do not have enough money. Also, you are not sure what type of pool table you want. You decide to wait and save. As you are saving, you do some comparison shopping. You decide what features you want and where to get the best deal. When you finally buy the pool table, your satisfaction is greater than if you had rushed into a credit purchase. A waiting period can make the purchase more valuable to you.

Check Monthly Statements

You get a *monthly statement* for each credit card account. These statements are another form you need to study and understand, 9-8. In addition to the date, amount, and business related to each purchase, the statement should tell you the following:

- date that payments are due

- minimum payment due

- new balance and previous balance

- total amount of new purchases, fees, and advances

Resource

Alternatives to Credit, color lesson slide, TR

Reflect

What alternatives can you name to using credit?

Activity

Compare the statement in 9-8 with statements your parents receive. Do you find the same information?

Activity

Review the credit card statement in Figure 9-8 and find the information listed.

The total amount you can charge to your account.

The amount of credit available in your account.

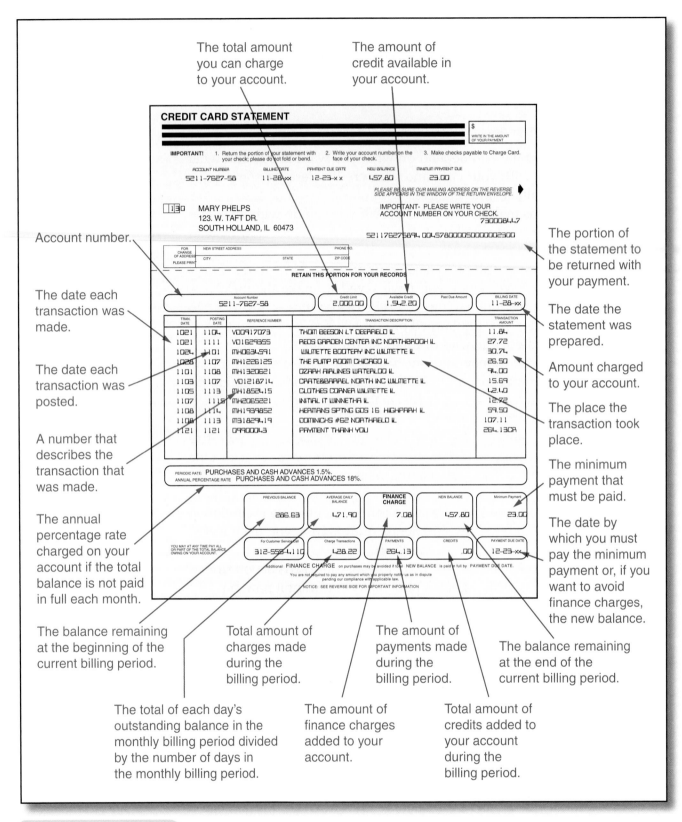

Account number.

The date each transaction was made.

The date each transaction was posted.

A number that describes the transaction that was made.

The annual percentage rate charged on your account if the total balance is not paid in full each month.

The balance remaining at the beginning of the current billing period.

The total of each day's outstanding balance in the monthly billing period divided by the number of days in the monthly billing period.

Total amount of charges made during the billing period.

The amount of finance charges added to your account.

The amount of payments made during the billing period.

Total amount of credits added to your account during the billing period.

The portion of the statement to be returned with your payment.

The date the statement was prepared.

Amount charged to your account.

The place the transaction took place.

The minimum payment that must be paid.

The date by which you must pay the minimum payment or, if you want to avoid finance charges, the new balance.

The balance remaining at the end of the current billing period.

9-8

This statement explains the information you will find on monthly credit card bills.

- finance charges as a dollar amount, as well as the periodic and corresponding annual percentage rate

- total amount of payments and credits

- total amount of credit available on the account

Check the statement each month against your own record of charges, payments, and credits.

Check Your Credit Report Regularly

If you make a habit of checking credit reports regularly, you can correct any errors before they cost you a loan, an apartment, or even a job. Checking these reports is the best way to make sure no one has applied for a loan or credit card in your name.

By law, you are entitled to receive one free copy of your credit report from each of the major credit reporting agencies every 12 months. You may receive the report in paper or electronic form. To order your reports, go to www.annualcreditreport.com.

If you find an error or an incomplete entry in a credit report, make sure you correct it right away. Go to the agency Web site for instructions on how to challenge negative information. You will need to contact the agency and provide copies of any documents that back up your claim.

Report Lost or Stolen Cards

If a person's credit cards are lost or stolen, the law offers some protection. The cardholder is responsible for only $50 in charges per card if someone else uses the cards. However, if a cardholder notifies the companies that issued the cards before someone else uses them, the cardholder cannot be held responsible for any charges.

Be sure to report credit card thefts or losses as soon as possible by phone. Follow up with a letter or an e-mail. It is a good idea to keep a list of your credit cards on hand. Include the name of the issuer, account numbers, and telephone number for each card.

Handling Credit Problems

Used unwisely, credit can lead to serious financial difficulties. Chart 9-9 lists some of the danger signals that warn credit users of trouble ahead.

The consequences of having a poor credit report are severe and impact more than the ability to get credit. A person with a low credit score may

- be unable to get loans and credit cards

- pay higher interest rates for credit

- have fewer housing choices because landlords check credit reports and reject people with low scores

Credit Warning Signals

- Stalling one creditor to pay another.
- Receiving past due notices with billing statements.
- Paying only the minimum required each month.
- Charging more each month than the amount you can pay.
- Not paying off credit account balances.
- Routinely running out of money before payday.
- Using credit cards or cash advances for everyday living expenses.

9-9
Beware of these warning signals when using credit.

- have fewer job prospects because employers avoid job candidates with financial problems

- pay higher insurance premiums

Accurate negative information, such as missed or late payments, may remain on your report for seven years. Bankruptcies may remain for 10 years.

When debtors fail to pay, lenders and businesses will try to recover what they are owed. Following are some of the actions they may take.

Collection Agencies

When debts go unpaid, businesses and creditors often hire collection agencies. A *collection agency* is a business that specializes in debt collection. Often it is paid with a portion of the money collected. In order to get full payments from you, collection agencies use every lawful means possible. The nonstop pressure they apply causes many debtors to pay in full.

Repossession of Property

Repossession is the taking back of collateral when a borrower fails to repay a loan. For example, companies that repossess autos may tow the cars away without notice. The cars are auctioned and the money goes toward paying the debt.

Perhaps the most serious type of repossession is *foreclosure*. **Foreclosure** is the forced sale of a property. The property, usually a home, is taken back by the lender because the debtor failed to make loan payments. The residents receive a court order to remove their possessions and leave by a specific date.

Liens Against Property

A **lien** is a legal claim on a borrower's property by a creditor who is owed money. For example, if a person fails to pay state taxes, the state can put a lien on his or her home. To sell or take out a loan on the home, the debtor must pay off the lien first.

Garnishment of Wages

The court may order *garnishment* of a debtor's earnings. **Garnishment** is a legal procedure requiring a portion of the debtor's pay to be set aside by the person's employer to pay creditors. This reduces the amount of the debtor's paychecks. Some employers fire employees who have repeated garnishments.

Repossession Agents

Repossession agents are often contracted by creditors who cannot recover money owed to them. They locate or recover personal property, such as cars, boats, and appliances, sold under a security agreement.

Bankruptcy

When financial circumstances are desperate, some debtors have little choice but to file for personal *bankruptcy*. **Bankruptcy** is a legal state in which the courts excuse a debtor from repaying some or all debt. In return, the debtor must give up certain assets and possessions. The *Bankruptcy Act* allows debtors to file "Chapter 7" or "Chapter 13" bankruptcy.

- *Chapter 7 Bankruptcy.* The court declares the person unable to meet financial obligations. Most debts are discharged or forgiven. This is also referred to as *straight bankruptcy*. The court then takes and sells the debtor's property and possessions. Proceeds from the sale are divided among the creditors. The law exempts certain assets and possessions: a small equity in a home, an inexpensive car, and limited personal property.

- *Chapter 13 Bankruptcy.* This plan permits debtors with regular incomes to pay all or a portion of their debts under the protection and supervision of the court. The court sets up a three- to five-year repayment schedule. It also establishes the monthly amount to be paid toward debts. Once the court accepts the debtor's petition, creditors may not take action against the debtor. This plan has three advantages over straight bankruptcy. The debtor fulfills credit obligations, keeps most of his or her own property and possessions, and maintains a reasonably sound credit rating.

Some types of debt cannot be wiped out by declaring bankruptcy. These include most student loans, alimony, child support, and many types of taxes.

The consequences of filing bankruptcy can haunt a debtor for many years. Once a court declares that people are bankrupt, a report stays in the credit records for 10 years. They may be denied loans or credit cards, or only be granted credit at inflated interest rates. They may be denied a job, a business loan, insurance, or housing by anyone who sees their credit report.

Bankruptcy, even for unavoidable reasons, often carries a stigma. People who file bankruptcy may be viewed as dishonest or untrustworthy. They may be considered irresponsible for not paying their debts. For these reasons, bankruptcy is a last resort.

The Easy-Access Credit Trap

You have probably heard the term **loan shark.** It refers to someone who loans money at excessive rates of interest. They usually use predatory lending tactics and offer easy-access credit. **Easy-access credit** refers to short-term loans granted regardless of credit history at high interest rates. Even people who are poor credit risks can get these loans if the practice is considered legal in their state. Easy-access credit includes the following:

- **Payday loan.** These are short-term, high interest loans that must usually be repaid on the borrower's next payday. Repayment is guaranteed by the borrower's personal check at the time of the loan or by

Vocabulary

What is a *debt collection agency*?

Discuss

What is the most serious type of repossession?

Discuss

What mishaps or bad habits can lead to credit problems?

Vocabulary

Distinguish between *Chapter 7* and *Chapter 13* bankruptcy filings.

Enrich

Research the history of the U.S. court system and bankruptcy. Summarize your research in a slide show presentation.

Reflect

Have you or someone you know been a victim of predatory lending?

Enrich

Research state laws limiting payday loans.

Discuss

What are the advantages and disadvantages of rent-to-own?

Reflect

Have you ever had trouble paying a debt you owe?

access to the borrower's bank account. Payday loans carry extremely high finance charges, but some states have laws that limit them.

- **Pawnshops.** A pawnshop is a business that gives customers high-interest loans with personal property, such as jewelry, held as collateral. Some pawnshops offer payday loans, too.

- **Rent-to-own.** This is an arrangement in which a consumer pays rent for the use of a product and eventually owns it. The advantage is little or no initial payment. The disadvantage to the consumer is paying much more than the product's purchase price by the time the final payment is made.

- **Title loan.** A short-term loan is made using a borrower's car as collateral. The cost of these loans is high and the borrower risks losing his or her car.

Here is an example of how easy-access credit differs from legitimate sources of credit. Suppose you borrow $1,000 by using a credit card cash advance. The APR is 21.99 percent. That is equivalent to a monthly interest rate of 1.833 percent (APR divided by 12). If you repaid the money in a month, you would pay an $18.33 finance charge.

Contrast that to what you would pay if you borrowed from a payday loan company. Finance charges are often $15 or more for every $100 borrowed. At $15, you would pay $150 to borrow $1,000. To get the loan, you write a check for $1,150. You get $1,000 and must pay this back in two weeks.

If you do not have the money, like many borrowers, you can roll the loan over for another two weeks for an additional finance charge. You owe the lender another $150. After one month, you have paid $300 in fees. What is the annual equivalent of this interest rate? If you continued to roll over the loan for a year, the APR would be 350 percent, or $3,600!

Inform Creditors

If you have trouble paying your bills, notify creditors promptly. Many reputable creditors will work with you. They may help you by renegotiating repayment schedules, or setting up a repayment program you can handle. They may be willing to extend your repayment schedules to lower the size of your monthly payments. Of course this will cost you more in credit charges in the long run, but it may help you get through a difficult period.

The quicker you realize you are having financial problems, the quicker and easier it will be to correct them. It pays to tackle these problems before they get beyond your control.

Get Credit Counseling

With a sound financial spending and savings plan, some people can correct their own financial problems. However, when financial problems get out of control, it is time to look for outside help. Following are some possible options. Be cautious of "credit doctors" and for-profit credit repair clinics that promise to fix your credit rating for a fee. These companies promise what no one can deliver. Read on for more reliable options.

Debt Counselors

Debt counselors help clients resolve financial difficulties. They provide financial counseling about debt, credit, money management, budgeting, and housing issues.

One reliable source of help for people with credit problems is a *credit counseling service*. A credit counseling service is an organization that provides debt and financial management advice and services to people with debt problems at little or no cost. The National Foundation for Consumer Credit sponsors several hundred credit counseling services throughout the United States and Canada. The credit counseling services, with the support of local merchants and financial institutions, offer aid in two forms.

The service helps a debtor with a stable income work out a practical financial program for repaying debts, 9-10. The service also helps the debtor plan and control current expenses to avoid further debts.

When debtors are very deep in debt, the counseling service offers another alternative. It tries to arrange new repayment plans with creditors. If creditors agree, the debtor gives the counseling service a set amount from each paycheck, and the service pays the creditors. Credit counseling services of this type help about five of every six applicants.

9-10
Credit counselors help clients develop a plan to get out of debt.

Finding a Reputable Company

Unfortunately, some of the businesses that claim to be nonprofit credit counseling services are not. These include debt negotiation or debt adjusting businesses that charge high fees. The fees cause their clients to fall deeper into debt.

A company that charges high fees or demands that the debtor pay them rather than their creditors should be avoided. Debtors should pay little or nothing for the help they receive. Claims that are too good to be true indicate a problem. This might be a guarantee that they can make debt disappear or dramatically reduce total debt. Also be suspicious of those who claim an ability to remove accurate negative information from credit reports.

Consumers can contact their local consumer protection agency to get a referral to a reputable consumer credit counseling service. The U.S. Trustee Program of the Department of Justice maintains a list of credit counseling agencies approved for prebankruptcy counseling. The list is found on their Web site. It also is a good idea to check with the local Better Business Bureau or the state attorney general's office for reports of consumer complaints against specific companies.

Activity

Contact the National Foundation for Consumer Credit for information on counseling services.

Activity

Search the Internet for the location of the nearest Consumer Credit Counseling Service.

Consumer Credit Legislation

Over the years a number of federal laws have been passed to protect consumers when they use credit. The key points of the most important credit legislation are outlined in the following sections.

Truth in Lending Law

The *Truth in Lending Law,* passed in 1969, requires creditors to tell consumers what credit will cost them before they use it. Under this law, credit contracts and agreements must include

- the amount financed or borrowed
- the total number, amount, and due dates of payments
- the finance charge in dollar amount and annual percentage rate
- all charges not included in the finance charge
- penalties or charges for late payment, default, or prepayment
- a description of any security held by the creditor

For merchandise purchased on time, creditors must provide additional information. This includes a description of the merchandise, the cash price and the deferred payment price, and the down payment or trade-in. The Truth in Lending Law also prohibits creditors from issuing credit cards you have not requested.

Equal Credit Opportunity Act

The *Equal Credit Opportunity Act,* passed in 1975, prohibits credit grantors from discriminating against consumers on the basis of sex, marital status, race, national origin, religion, age, or the receipt of public assistance. This means credit can be denied only for financial reasons and not for any of the factors listed above. When applicants are turned down, creditors must provide a written explanation of why credit was denied.

Fair Credit Reporting Act

Passed in 1971 and revised in 1977, the *Fair Credit Reporting Act* requires accuracy and privacy of information contained in credit reports. If you are refused credit because of information supplied by a credit reporting agency, this law gives you the right to

- receive the name and address of the reporting agency that sent the report
- find out from the reporting agency what facts are on file, the source of the information, and who has received the information
- require a recheck of any information you find to be false
- receive a corrected report if errors are found
- require the agency to send the corrected report to all creditors who received false information

Fair Credit Billing Act

The *Fair Credit Billing Act,* passed in 1975, protects consumers against unfair billing practices. It outlines the procedures to follow in resolving billing errors or disputes. The law requires creditors to send customers a written explanation of steps to take when questions arise concerning bills. The customer has 60 days after receiving a bill to notify the creditor of an error, 9-11. The creditor must answer within 30 days. Within 90 days, the creditor must either correct the bill or explain if it is accurate. Creditors may take no collection action on amounts in question until billing disputes are resolved. However, the customer must pay any amount not in question.

Electronic Funds Transfer Act

Electronic Funds Transfer (EFT) systems use electronic impulses to activate financial transactions instead of cash, checks, or paper records. The *Electronic Funds Transfer Act* protects consumers in these transactions by

- prohibiting the distribution of unrequested EFT cards. You receive a card only if you ask for it.

- requiring issuers of EFT cards to provide cardholders with written information outlining their rights and responsibilities for the card and its use.

- limiting to $50 the liability for unauthorized transfer. The cardholder must notify the issuer of card loss or misuse within two business days.

- requiring issuers to provide cardholders with printed receipts of EFT transactions.

- requiring issuers to promptly investigate and correct EFT errors.

9-11

Under the Fair Credit Billing Act, customers have a certain amount of time to resolve billing disputes.

Fair Debt Collection Practices Act

Passed in 1978, the *Fair Debt Collection Practices Act* protects consumers against unfair methods of collecting debts. According to this law, debt collectors may not

- reveal or publicize a debtor's debt to other people

- contact debtors at inconvenient times (before 8 a.m. or after 9 p.m.) or places (such as work)

- use threats or abusive language

- make annoying, repeated, or anonymous phone calls

Discuss

What are the most important rights of credit card holders?

Discuss

What is the main goal of the Bankruptcy Abuse Prevention and Consumer Protection Act?

Activity

Research a famous person who has filed for bankruptcy. How did bankruptcy affect his or her life?

Resource

Chapter 9—Credit, Teacher's PowerPoint Presentations CD

- make false or misleading statements about the collector's identity or the consequences of nonpayment
- collect unauthorized fees or charge debtors for calls and telegrams

Preservation of Consumers' Claims and Defenses Ruling

The *Preservation of Consumers' Claims and Defenses Ruling* was issued by the Federal Trade Commission. It protects debtors from being forced to pay for goods and services when they have a legitimate dispute with the seller of those goods or services.

This applies when a retailer sells consumer credit obligations or contracts to a third party creditor. The consumer then owes the third party. If the goods or services purchased with credit are unsatisfactory, the debtor still owes the third party rather than the seller. For this reason, the seller does not feel obligated to correct any problems with the goods or services.

This ruling greatly limits the "holder-in-due-course doctrine." That doctrine says the holder of a consumer contract has a right to collect a debt regardless of any unfair practices on the part of the seller.

Here is an example to show how the rule protects you. Suppose you buy a $500 TV from the Viewing Center. You sign an installment contract calling for 18 monthly payments. The Viewing Center offers credit through a sales finance company. Therefore, you owe the finance company rather than the seller.

After the television is delivered, you find that it does not work. You can get sound but no picture. When you complain, the seller refuses to correct the problem. You threaten nonpayment. The seller says that is not the Viewing Center's problem because you owe the finance company.

You complain to the finance company, but they tell you the television is the seller's responsibility. Legally, you owe the finance company regardless of the seller's performance.

The Preservation of Consumers' Claims and Defenses Ruling protects you in this type of situation. Under the ruling, you have a right to a legal defense in court if you refuse to pay a creditor because you have a dispute with a seller.

Bankruptcy Abuse Prevention and Consumer Protection Act

The main goal of federal law, passed in 2005, was to make the bankruptcy system fairer to both debtors and creditors. However, it has been criticized for disproportionately benefiting the credit card industry.

It made filing for Chapter 7 bankruptcy more difficult. Those who are allowed to file must pass a "means test" that takes into account factors such as income and assets. Those who do not pass the means test must file for Chapter 13 bankruptcy that requires some repayment of debt. Another provision of the law requires debtors to get credit and financial counseling before filing for bankruptcy.

Chapter Summary

Using credit has both advantages and disadvantages. Knowing when to use it and understanding the different types of credit can help consumers enjoy the benefits of using credit and avoid credit problems. Credit use impacts a person's credit rating. Credit reporting agencies use credit scores to summarize a person's payment history, debt owed, and credit account use.

Opening a credit card and using it responsibly is one way to build a good credit rating. When shopping for a credit card, read each contract carefully, know the clauses to avoid, and compare disclosures. Before using credit, consider other alternatives. Some ways to avoid credit problems include tracking spending, checking monthly statements, reviewing credit reports annually, and reporting lost or stolen cards.

Consumers can resolve credit problems by informing creditors when serious financial problems arise and seeking credit counseling. Federal laws protect consumers in many ways, including requiring creditors to disclose the cost of credit, preventing unfair billing practices, and regulating debt collection methods.

Review

1. How does a credit transaction differ from a cash transaction?

2. List three advantages and three disadvantages of using credit.

3. What three factors determine the amount you pay in finance charges?

4. Explain the difference between closed-end and open-end credit. Give an example of each.

5. What steps can you take to build a sound credit rating?

6. What is the function of a credit reporting agency?

7. What factors influence a person's credit score?

8. What contract clauses should be avoided when applying for a credit card? Explain each clause.

9. Explain the difference between variable interest rates and fixed interest rates.

10. What are subprime credit cards?

11. What are some alternatives to using credit?

12. How can consumers obtain free copies of credit reports? How often are free copies available?

13. What are the advantages of filing bankruptcy under Chapter 13 instead of Chapter 7?

14. How can credit-counseling services help debt-troubled individuals and families?

15. What is the purpose of the Equal Credit Opportunity Act?

Critical Thinking

16. How can the use of credit have a positive influence on the economy?

17. How can the use of too much credit contribute to inflation?

18. Suppose you buy a 10-speed bike using credit. After two weeks, the bike only runs on five speeds. Although the bike has a two-year warranty, the seller refuses to do anything about the problem. Your credit contract has been sold to a finance company and the seller has been paid. Describe your rights if you refuse to pay the creditor.

19. How can your financial personality help you decide when and if you can use credit safely? How would you describe your financial personality?

20. Why do you think so many students and young people today are incurring so much

---

Answers to *Review*

1. cash—you hand over money in exchange for goods and services; credit—you receive goods and services and pay later

2. (List three of each:) advantages—use goods and services as you pay for them; buy costly items you cannot pay for with cash; access to cash for unexpected expenses; convenient; take advantage of sales; make purchases for a long-range plan; disadvantages—reduces future income; finance charges; temptation to overspend; risk of serious financial problems

3. the amount of credit used, the annual percentage rate, and the length of the repayment period

4. closed-end—the borrower must repay the borrowed amount by a certain date; open-end—the borrower can use a certain amount of money for an indefinite period of time. (Examples are student response.)

5. Get a job, open a savings and checking account, get a credit card, make small purchases, and pay promptly.

6. Collect information about consumer financial transactions; compile credit reports; sell reports to lenders.

7. bill paying, debt-to-credit-limit ratio, credit history length, recent credit application, different types of credit

8. acceleration clause—allows creditor to require full and immediate repayment of the balance if a payment is missed; balloon payment—requires a large final payment to retire the loan; add-on clause—permits seller to hold security interest in items purchased until all charges are paid in full

9. Variable rates fluctuate; fixed rates stay the same.

10. They are offered to those with a poor credit history and have high interest rates, many fees, and low credit limits.

11. Do not buy; pay with savings; buy later with cash.

12. At www.annualcreditreport.com. Consumers can get one free copy from each major credit agency every 12 months.

13. The debtor fulfills credit obligations, keeps most property and possessions, and maintains a reasonably sound credit rating.

14. They help debtors develop repayment plans.

15. to prohibit credit grantors from discriminating on the basis of sex, marital status, race, national origin, religion, age, or the receipt of public assistance

debt? What are some steps that could be taken to deal with this problem?

Academic Connections

21. **Financial literacy, math.** Suppose you want to buy a $600 television on credit. Find out what the credit terms would be if you obtained the credit from the seller, a cash loan, or a credit card. Find out about finance charges, annual percentage rate, monthly payments, length of the repayment period, and late payment charges. Where would you get the best deal?

22. **Financial literacy.** Ask a representative from a credit-counseling agency to speak to your class about how to use credit wisely. Prepare a list of questions to ask the speaker. You may want to include some of the following:
    A. What are the most common problems connected with the use of consumer credit?
    B. What are the most common causes of credit problems?
    C. How can consumers avoid credit problems?
    D. How can credit counseling help consumers with financial problems?

23. **Financial literacy, writing.** Pick up an application for a credit card or charge account from a local bank or store. Fill it out and explain why creditors require the information requested on the application.

24. **Writing.** Write a definition of the following and explain how each could affect your use of credit.
    - acceleration clause
    - balloon payment
    - add-on clause
    - repossession
    - garnishment

25. **Research, social studies.** Research the current status of debt among college students and young adults. Report your findings to the class and discuss possible remedies.

Math Challenge

26. Fiona's credit card balance is $5,000. The APR is 18 percent and the minimum payment is 5 percent of the balance. What is the minimum payment due? How much of the minimum payment goes to interest? to the principal? If Fiona makes the minimum payment this month and does not use her card to make any more purchases, what will her balance be next month? What is next month's minimum payment due?

Tech $mart

27. Find out how consumer financial behavior affects credit scores. Go to www. vantagescore.experian.com and find the Credit Score Illustrator tool. Explore the different consumer scenarios.

28. Go to www.consumercredit.com and find the Credit Card Interest Calculator. Use the calculator to illustrate the benefits of paying more than the minimum due on a credit card. Enter the following numbers into the calculator:
    Dollar amount charged: 1,000
    Annual interest rate: 18
    Minimum payment percent: 4
    Leave *minimum payment* blank and compute the results.
    Reset the calculator and enter the following numbers:
    Dollar amount charged: 1,000
    Annual interest rate: 18
    Minimum payment: 50
    Leave *minimum payment percent* blank and compute the results.
    How much time and money can you save by paying more than the required 4% each month?

Answer to *Math Challenge*

24. monthly interest rate = 1.5% (18% ÷ 12); minimum payment due = $250 (5,000 × 5%); interest paid = $75 (5,000 × 1.5%); principal paid = $175 (250 − 75); next month's balance = $4,825 (5,000 − 175); next month's minimum payment due = $241.25 (4,825 × 5%)

CHAPTER 10
Insurance

Reading for Meaning

After you read the chapter, test your comprehension of new vocabulary. Write a sentence using each vocabulary word.

risk
risk management
dependent
policyholder
premium
deductible
fee-for-service plan
coinsurance
inpatient
managed care plan
co-payment
health savings account (HSA)
exclusion

preexisting condition
beneficiary
term life insurance
whole life insurance
endowment insurance
appraisal
depreciation
bodily injury liability
property damage liability
no-fault auto insurance

CHAPTER OBJECTIVES

After studying this chapter, you will be able to

- **explain** how insurance protects individuals from financial risk.
- **outline** the different types of private health insurance coverage.
- **describe** types of government-sponsored health insurance programs.
- **explain** the purpose of disability insurance.
- **distinguish** among the various types of life insurance.
- **outline** the key factors to consider when buying home insurance.
- **select** auto insurance coverage to meet individual needs.

Central Ideas

- Risk management is an important component in financial planning.
- Insurance is a tool that protects against certain financial losses.

Life involves risk. **Risk** is a measure of the likelihood that something will be lost. Some risks are predictable—you will sometimes get sick and you will grow old. Other risks are unpredictable. These include serious illnesses or injuries, car accidents, house fires, and theft. Some events can limit your ability to earn a living or wipe out your assets. When you earn income, own property, and accumulate savings, these are too important to lose.

Financial security depends in part on risk management. **Risk management** is the process of measuring risk and finding ways to minimize or manage loss.

Managing Risk

There are four strategies for dealing with risk. You have probably used several of them.

- *Avoidance* is avoiding risk. For example, if a trail marker warns "Do not go beyond this point!" hikers avoid injury by obeying the warning. There may be hazards beyond the sign.

- *Reduction* is a strategy of minimizing risk because you cannot always avoid it. For example, a reduction strategy for staying healthy is washing your hands often to eliminate disease-causing germs. Wearing a seat belt while driving is a reduction strategy that lowers the chance of injury or death in the event of an accident.

- *Retention* refers to assessing risk and making financial preparations for possible future loss. It is also called *self-insurance.* For example, a person may set aside money in a savings account in case he or she loses a job. Retention strategies do not work as well when potential losses are very high.

- *Transfer* is the shifting of risk. You do this by joining a big pool of people and transferring your risk to an insurance company. The company invests the fees you pay and uses earnings to pay claims of insured persons. If you have an accident or another setback, the insurance company pays for your losses. There is little probability that large numbers of people will need payouts at the same time.

Risk Managers

Risk managers identify potential problems and predict their probability of occurring. They suggest ways of appraising and controlling risk and minimizing its effects. Their input helps to determine the amount people pay for insurance.

Insurance Protection

The main purpose of insurance is to provide protection against specific types of financial losses. A sound insurance program begins by assessing the risks you face. Consider the losses that could damage or destroy your financial security, then take steps to protect yourself with appropriate insurance.

Events that could put your finances at risk include illness or injury, accidents, death, and property losses, 10-1. The purpose of insurance is to pay for losses that would be difficult or impossible for you to cover. A careful look at the risks you face and a plan for managing them with insurance and other resources are basic steps in any financial plan.

The type and amount of insurance needed varies from person to person. It depends on the risks being covered, the amount available to pay for losses, and the financial obligations of the insured persons. For example, a childless unmarried person generally needs less coverage than a head of a family with several children. Protection needs increase with each new dependent and with increased assets. A **dependent** is an individual who relies on someone else for financial support, such as a child, a spouse, or an elderly parent.

When you buy an insurance policy, you become a **policyholder**. You pay a set amount of money, called a **premium**, to the insurance company on a regular basis. The premiums you and other policyholders pay are invested by the company to earn money. Both premiums and earnings are used to pay insurance claims. A *claim* is a bill submitted to the insurance company for payment.

Types of insurance that protect against financial risks include health, disability, life, home, and auto. These are discussed in different sections of this chapter.

10-1

Insurance can help you cover unexpected expenses, such as rebuilding a home after a flood.

Private Health Insurance

Health insurance offers protection by covering specific medical expenses created by illness, injury, and disability. Today, approximately 35 percent of health care costs are paid by private plans offered by insurance companies. Many of these plans are available through employers.

Participants in private insurance plans usually pay a monthly premium plus a deductible. A **deductible** is the amount you must pay before insurance begins to pay. For example, if your deductible is $500 annually, you must pay for health care services until you reach a total of $500, at which time the insurance company begins paying.

Most private insurance programs are group plans sponsored by employers, unions, and other organizations. Individuals may also purchase private health insurance, but it usually costs more and provides less coverage than group plans.

Resource

Health Insurance Terms, reproducible master 10-2, TR

Activity

Research fee-for-service insurance. What are its advantages and disadvantages?

Fee-for-Service Plans

Fee-for-service plans pay for covered medical services after treatment is provided. You can usually go to any licensed health care provider or accredited hospital of your choice, 10-2.

You are responsible for a deductible and coinsurance. **Coinsurance** is a percentage of the service cost that patients pay. For example, if a medical service costs $100 and the coinsurance is 20 percent, your cost would be

$20. In a fee-for-service plan, you pay the $100 at the time of the medical service. Either you or the doctor's office submits a claim to the insurance company. You then receive a reimbursement, or repayment, of $80.

If you have fee-for-service coverage, learn how to file claims and file them promptly. Keep the name and phone number of your plan handy, with membership numbers and other information you may need to receive services and file claims.

Fee-for-service plans generally offer basic and major medical coverage. Basic coverage includes prescriptions, hospital stays, and inpatient tests. An **inpatient** is a person whose care requires a stay in a hospital. Basic coverage also pays for some doctor's visits, outpatient procedures and certain other medical services.

Major medical coverage typically covers the costs of serious illnesses and high-cost procedures and injuries. Often fee-for-service plans combine basic and major medical protection in one policy called a *comprehensive plan*.

10-2

In a fee-for-service health insurance plan, you have the freedom to go to any licensed health care provider you like.

Discuss

List the advantages and disadvantages of managed care.

Activity

Interview someone who is enrolled in an HMO. Does this person like his or her health care system?

Managed Care Plans

Managed care plans contract with specific doctors, hospitals, and other health care providers to deliver medical services and preventive care to members at reduced cost. Your choice of service providers is limited to those who participate in the plan, except for necessary referrals to specialists outside the plan.

You and/or your employer pay a set amount in monthly premiums. You also pay any required deductibles, coinsurance, or co-payments. A **co-payment** is a flat fee the patient must pay for medical services. Co-payments are due at the time of service. For example, when you have a doctor's appointment or a prescription filled, you pay the co-payment at that time. Co-payment amounts are determined by your health care plan.

Three forms of managed care are health maintenance organizations (HMOs), preferred provider organizations (PPOs), and point-of-service (POS) plans.

Health Maintenance Organizations (HMOs)

These organizations provide a list of participating physicians from which you choose a primary care doctor. This doctor coordinates your health care and carries out routine exams and treatments. The plan normally covers only treatment provided by doctors who participate in the plan. If you go outside the plan for care, you pay part or the entire bill.

Normally, you must go through your primary care doctor for a referral to a specialist if you require specialized treatments, consultations, or procedures. Your primary care doctor and a referral specialist from the HMO will determine which treatments and procedures are covered.

Reflect

Would you choose a PPO plan? Why or why not?

Preferred Provider Organizations (PPOs)

These organizations arrange with specific doctors, hospitals, and other caregivers to provide services at reduced cost to plan members. You receive services at lower cost by going to participating caregivers, but you may go outside the plan if you are willing to pay the extra cost. For example, the plan may pay 80 percent of the cost of care within the plan and only 60 percent outside the plan. This offers you more choice than an HMO.

Case Study: Life Plans

It's Negotiable

Maurice was elected to represent his union. In three months, he will take part in negotiating a new contract with company management. One of the union demands is maintaining the cost of health care insurance for union members and their families. Currently, union members pay 15 percent of premiums while the company pays 85 percent.

The company wants to increase the cost union members pay to 20 percent. Carmela, a company spokesperson, argues that health care costs are rising dramatically and the company can no longer afford the current coverage. She also argues that health care costs are passed on to customers, making the company less competitive and possibly risking its future. She also points out other companies within the industry have a 20–80 split.

Case Review

1. Should companies be financially responsible for the health care of employees and their families?
2. Should employees be responsible for paying a portion of their own health care costs?
3. What types of problems might occur in an employer-sponsored health program?
4. How might health care programs differ for large and small companies?
5. What health care provisions should employees be aware of in case they lose or change their jobs?

Point-of-Service (POS)

These plans connect you with a primary care doctor who participates in the plan and who is your "point of service." That doctor supervises your care and makes referrals as necessary to participating or nonparticipating specialists.

POS plans combine features of both HMOs and PPOs. There usually is no deductible and co-payments are limited if you see doctors within the plan. You may also choose health care providers outside the plan, but a deductible may apply and co-payments are higher.

Health Savings Accounts

A **health savings account (HSA)** is a tax-advantaged savings account available to people enrolled in qualified *High Deductible Health Plans (HDHPs).* In an HDHP, the patient pays a high deductible before the insurance begins to pay. However, the monthly premiums are usually lower than other types of plans.

If you have an HSA, you may contribute pre-tax dollars into the account. The maximum annual amount you can contribute is adjusted each year. Current HDHP deductible amounts and HSA contribution levels are available on the U.S. Treasury Department Web site.

You may use savings in the account to pay for health care costs. Unused funds in the account may accumulate tax-free. However, if you use funds for purposes other than health care costs, you will incur tax penalties.

An HSA can save you money three ways. The high deductible feature in your health care coverage makes premiums less expensive. You can deduct the amount you contribute to your HSA, thus reducing your taxes. The unspent savings in your account are allowed to accumulate tax-free until you need them to pay health care expenses.

You may be able to set up an HSA through your employer. If your employer does not offer these accounts, you may be able to establish one on your own. For a list of companies that offer HSA-eligible plans in your state, go to www.HSAInsider.com.

COBRA

If you are covered by an employer-sponsored group plan and leave your job, you are likely to lose your health care coverage. In this case, you may be entitled to continue your health benefits under the *Consolidated Omnibus Budget Reconciliation Act (COBRA).*

This law gives qualified workers the right to continue their group coverage for a limited period of time. However, you must pay the premiums for continuing coverage. For information on COBRA and its possible benefits, contact the nearest U.S. Department of Labor office.

Individual Plans

People who are not eligible for COBRA, those who are between jobs, and the self-employed may purchase health insurance on their own.

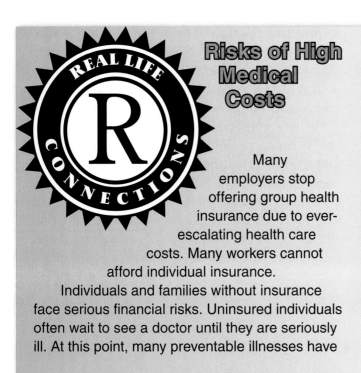

Risks of High Medical Costs

Many employers stop offering group health insurance due to ever-escalating health care costs. Many workers cannot afford individual insurance.

Individuals and families without insurance face serious financial risks. Uninsured individuals often wait to see a doctor until they are seriously ill. At this point, many preventable illnesses have escalated and treatment options are less effective and more costly. High medical bills are one of the top reasons people file for bankruptcy.

Uninsured mothers often do not get adequate prenatal care. Uninsured children may fall behind in school because of frequent, untreated illnesses. Even with government-sponsored health insurance, many older adults cannot afford prescription drugs. They may skip doses or cut back on other necessities, such as food, to pay for prescriptions.

In recent years, politicians, medical associations, insurance companies, and employers have worked on overhauling the country's health care policies. The goal is to reduce costs, yet make health care available and affordable to all U.S. citizens.

These individual policies are more expensive and more exclusive than group plans. Premiums for an individual can be as much as $800 a month. Families often pay more than $1,000 a month.

Many families and individuals cannot afford these premiums, so they go without health insurance. However, it is risky to go uninsured. A serious illness or injury can easily wipe out a person's life savings, assets, or business.

Many health insurance companies sell individual plans. An application process includes filling out a medical history questionnaire and sometimes submitting to medical tests or a complete physical exam. Healthy young applicants are usually accepted. However, people suffering from serious injuries, illnesses, or chronic physical or mental health problems may be denied coverage. If they are accepted, they pay high premiums.

These plans may contain many exclusions. **Exclusions** refer to medical services that are not covered. Examples include dental care or treatment of preexisting conditions.

A **preexisting condition** is an illness or an injury you had before signing up for health care insurance. Generally, these conditions are not covered by a new plan for a stated period of time, if at all.

Coverage for Young Adults

Many health insurance plans cover the policyholder's children until they reach a certain age. Full-time college students can usually remain on their parents' plan. However, once they leave college, change their student status to part-time, or get married, they may no longer be eligible, 10-3. Eligibility requirements vary from state to state.

Many colleges offer student medical insurance for major medical expenses. For routine health problems, students can visit free and low-cost campus

Reflect

Which of these factors do you think will be most and least important to you when you are selecting health care coverage in the future?

Activity

Research typical examples of preexisting conditions. As a class, create a list.

Reflect

Do you have health insurance? Do you have your own policy or are you covered under your family's plan?

health and mental health clinics. People who do not go to college often get health coverage through an employer. However, health coverage is usually not available to part-time, temporary, and contract employees.

Many young people pass up health coverage because of high monthly premiums and deductibles. Healthy young people may not want to pay for health insurance, but serious illness is always a possibility. Also, accidents are a leading cause of injury and death among young adults. Experts recommend carrying major medical insurance to at least pay for hospitalization, tests, and surgery in case of serious illness and injury.

10-3

Many young adults may remain on their parents' health insurance plans until they graduate college or reach a certain age.

Discuss

Why is it important for young people to have health insurance?

Activity

Visit your state insurance department Web site. What information is available to consumers?

Discuss

What are the factors to consider when evaluating health insurance plans?

Long-Term Care

Long-term care insurance covers certain costs of care in a nursing home, an assisted living facility, or at home. The plan pays for the assistance needed by a person with a chronic illness or disability who cannot safely live alone.

Older consumers are the primary purchasers of long-term care insurance. Plans vary in cost and the services provided.

Choosing a Plan

Many different types of private insurance programs are available. If you are looking for an individual plan, it pays to shop around. Your state insurance department Web site may offer consumer information and assistance.

If you have access to a group plan through your employer or some other affiliation, you can usually sign up during an *enrollment period*. At this time, policyholders can also change plans or renew coverage. Carefully review the insurance materials provided and choose the plan that meets your needs.

In evaluating health insurance plans, consider the services covered, the choice of health care providers, and the costs.

Services

No plan will pay for all your medical expenses or cover all the services you may need. *Maximum benefits* refer to the maximum paid for specific types of treatment or the maximum number of days care is covered. For example, payment for mental health care may be limited to $1,000 annually; the number of days in a hospital may be limited as well.

Plans also may require preauthorization and utilization reviews for certain services. A *preauthorization* is a requirement to obtain approval from the plan before receiving certain procedures and treatments. A *utilization review* is an insurance company's examination of requests for medical treatments and procedures to make sure they are covered and the patient truly needs them.

Be sure to find out if preauthorizations and utilization reviews are required. Look for coverage of the services that are most important to you. These may include the following:

- inpatient hospital services

- outpatient surgery

- office visits

- preventive care and screenings

- maternity care and well-baby care

- medical tests

- emergency room care

- physical therapy

- x-rays

- mental health services

- drug and alcohol abuse treatment

- prescription drugs

- home health care

Choice

Some plans allow you to choose your doctors, regardless of where they practice or their hospital affiliation. Other plans limit you to participating health care providers. Consider the following questions:

- How important is it to choose your own doctor and hospital or continue with the providers you already use?

- What health care providers, including doctors, hospitals, and labs, participate in the plan? Where are they located?

- What are the provisions for seeing a specialist if you believe you need one?

- Can you change doctors without prior approval if you are dissatisfied with your primary care physician?

Cost

Make sure you know the answers to the following questions before choosing a plan:

- What premiums must you pay?

- Is there a deductible? If so, how much is it? Which services are subject to the deductible?

Claims Investigators
Claims investigators handle insurance claims when a company suspects fraudulent or criminal activity, such as arson, falsified claims, staged accidents, or unnecessary medical treatments. They often perform surveillance work.

Activity

Obtain several copies of health insurance policies. What services are covered under each?

Reflect

What health insurance services are most important to you?

Activity

Answer each of the questions under the heading "Choice." Based on your answers, what type of health insurance plan is best for you?

Enrich

Invite a human resources manager to speak to your class. Discuss the cost of health insurance for employers and employees.

Activity

Research the average cost of health care for consumers in the United States and in other countries. How do the costs compare?

Discuss

Name five ways to lower health care costs.

Reflect

Which of these practices does your family follow in the attempt to minimize spending on personal health care?

- What are the costs of using non-participating providers and facilities?

- What health costs should you be prepared to pay? Check any exclusions, service limitations, or restrictions on preexisting conditions that may apply to you.

- What portion of charges must you co-pay? Do co-payments apply to every medical service you receive or only to specific items such as office visits and prescription drugs?

- In a managed care program, find out whether co-payments are higher if you go outside your health care plan for treatment.

Figure the total cost of the premiums you would pay together with the deductible. Certain plans have lower premiums, but higher co-payments or deductibles. Others may have the reverse. Very often you can reduce monthly premiums by choosing a plan with a higher deductible. This can save you money if you typically require only routine health care services.

You can control your health care costs by developing habits that make the most of your health care dollars. See 10-4.

Government-Sponsored Health Insurance

The government offers health insurance to certain eligible people, including older adults, people with disabilities, low-income families, and children. What each person pays, if anything, depends on various factors.

Ways to Lower Health Care Costs

- Make good health a priority. Follow a balanced approach to diet, exercise, sleep, stress control, and accident prevention.
- Find out what free or low-cost health services and programs are available through your school, employer, community, and government.
- Know exactly what expenses your health insurance covers, keep accurate records, and file claims promptly for covered expenses.
- Discuss fees and prices with health care providers. Cost-conscious patients can often avoid unnecessary expenses.
- Lower hospital costs by asking for outpatient care, if possible, and minimum hospital stays.
- Get a second opinion before agreeing to non-emergency surgery or costly procedures.
- Obtain necessary authorizations before receiving treatments to be sure they are covered by your insurance.
- Keep track of out-of-pocket spending on health care expenses. If these are more than a certain percentage of your income, they may be tax deductible.

10-4

Individuals can lower the cost of health care by following these recommendations.

Medicare

Medicare covers specific health care expenses for eligible citizens age 65 and older. It also covers those under age 65 with certain diseases or disabilities. The government funding for Medicare comes from payroll taxes. Four different parts of Medicare provide coverage for specific services.

Part A—Hospital Insurance

Part A helps pay for inpatient care in hospitals and skilled nursing facilities up to a specified number of days. It does not cover long-term care, but it covers some home health care and hospice care. *Hospice care* is for people with a terminal illness.

Most people do not pay a monthly premium for Part A coverage if they paid Medicare taxes while working. Employers and employees each paid half the premiums, while self-employed people paid the full amount.

A deductible must be met before Medicare will pay for hospital stays. If a patient needs care beyond the specified number of days allowed for home health, hospice, and skilled nursing care, the patient is responsible for paying certain costs. Current deductible rates and patient costs are available online at www.medicare.gov.

Part B—Medical Insurance

Part B is a voluntary program that helps pay for a variety of health care costs. These include doctors' fees, outpatient hospital services, home health services, certain tests, and other health care costs. To obtain Part B coverage, enrollees must pay a monthly premium.

Patients also pay an annual deductible each year before Part B will pay for services. In addition, patients pay coinsurance for certain services. For example, patients pay 20 percent of the cost for a physical therapy session. Premiums, deductibles, and coinsurance rates change periodically.

Part C—Medicare Advantage Plan

Private health insurance companies contract with Medicare to provide this type of plan. Medicare Advantage Plans combine Part A and Part B benefits under one plan. Some people prefer this type of plan because it simplifies enrollment and payment procedures. In most cases, prescription drug coverage is also included. Plans vary in coverage and costs.

Part D—Prescription Drug Coverage

Part D helps to lower prescription drug prices and protect against higher future drug prices, 10-5. Those who enroll in this program pay a monthly premium. Private insurance companies provide the coverage. There are a variety of plans offered and subscribers choose the one that best suits their medical needs.

Discuss

Who is eligible for Medicare?

Enrich

Investigate the monthly premium and deductible for people in Medicare's medical insurance program.

Vocabulary

Describe the services covered under Medicare Parts A, B, C, and D.

Enrich

Bring to class several recent articles on health care reform. Discuss pros and cons of proposals outlined.

Medigap Insurance

This helps pay for health care costs not covered by Medicare, such as co-payments and deductibles. Private insurance companies sell this type of protection—not the government. Usually, this insurance is only available for patients who have both Medicare Parts A and B.

It is available in up to 12 standard benefit packages that provide varying degrees of coverage. The broader the coverage is, the higher the premium. It pays to shop carefully for a reputable, reliable insurance company with a good record of customer service.

Medicaid

Medicaid is a health insurance program for eligible low-income persons and those with certain disabilities. It is a state-administered program financed by federal and state tax revenues.

Patients apply for Medicaid at public aid offices within their state. The services provided vary from state to state. Most Medicaid programs pay for inpatient and outpatient hospital services, clinic care, X-rays, and laboratory services. Some states also pay for family planning, home health care services, dental and eye care, and other medical needs.

10-5

Medicare Part D helps patients pay for prescription drugs.

Children's Health Insurance Program (CHIP)

Many American families earn too much to qualify for Medicaid, but not enough to afford private health insurance premiums. The *Children's Health Insurance Program (CHIP)* gives federal funds to states to provide health insurance coverage for children ages 18 and younger. The program rules vary slightly among states. Taxes on cigarettes and other tobacco products fund the program.

Disability Insurance

Disability insurance pays a portion of income lost to a worker who is unable to work for a prolonged period because of illness or injury. Many people do not think they need disability insurance. However, the loss of income because an inability to work can be financially devastating.

Disability insurance may replace as much as 60 to 70 percent of the income normally earned. The two types of disability insurance are short term and long term. Short-term coverage normally requires a waiting period of up to 14 days and provides coverage for up to two years. Long-term coverage may have a waiting period of several weeks or months and it pays for a number of years or for life.

Many employers provide limited disability insurance to their workers as a benefit. The employer pays the premium for these group plans. If an employee wants a higher level of insurance through the group plan, he or she may be able to pay for it. Consumers may buy this type of coverage independently if they are not part of employer health care plans or other insurance programs.

Shop carefully if you are buying disability insurance because plans vary greatly from company to company. Important questions to ask when buying disability insurance include

- *What benefits are promised?* How much money will you receive?

- *What is the waiting period?* Benefits do not start immediately. There is a waiting period of weeks or months. If you opt for a longer waiting period, your insurance premium will often be lower.

- *How long are benefits available?* The length of time a person can receive benefits varies. This can be a few years, until retirement, or for a lifetime.

- *Can the policy be canceled by the insurer?* A *non-cancelable clause* means that the insurance company cannot cancel your coverage so long as you pay the premiums. A *guaranteed renewable clause* means that you can renew the coverage with the same benefits but usually at a higher cost.

You may have to give up some of the features you want to get an affordable premium. For example, lowering the amount of the benefit or lengthening the waiting period will reduce the premium you must pay.

Vocabulary

Differentiate between short-term and long-term disability coverage.

Discuss

Do you think employers should be required to provide disability insurance to their workers?

Discuss

Name four questions to ask when buying disability insurance.

Vocabulary

Define a *non-cancelable clause* and a *guaranteed renewable clause*.

Linking to... History

Occupational Safety and Health Administration

The *Occupational Safety and Health Act of 1970* requires employers to provide a safe working environment and safety training for their employees. The Occupational Safety and Health Administration (OSHA) is the government department that sets and enforces safety regulations and health standards for workers. Since the agency was created in 1971, injuries have declined by 42 percent and occupational deaths have dropped 62 percent. Still, over 5,000 employees lose their lives on the job each year.

OSHA provides workplace inspection, training, and education programs. It also enforces the law. The penalty for violating an OSHA standard can range as high as $70,000, depending on the seriousness of the violation. Workers are also required to adhere to OSHA health and safety standards. Not doing so can result in injured coworkers and job termination.

Discuss

What is the role of life insurance in financial planning?

Enrich

Interview or invite to class an insurance agent to learn more about the different types of life insurance.

Discuss

When does a person need to obtain life insurance?

Discuss

When is term insurance the best choice?

Workers' Compensation

Workers' compensation insurance is another type of disability insurance. It provides a safety net for workers with work-related illnesses or injuries. It covers medical care and pays for a portion of lost wages. It also pays for medical treatment and rehabilitation that injured workers may require.

When workers are permanently disabled, they may receive benefits for life. If injuries and illnesses are fatal, workers' compensation provides death benefits to survivors.

Employers in every state are required to provide some form of workers' compensation insurance. Employees must file claims through their employers to apply for workers' compensation. Each state has its own laws and time limits for filing claims. Applicants must prove they are disabled and usually must submit to examinations by insurance company doctors. To find out more about your state's workers' compensation laws, check with the state workers' compensation board.

Life Insurance

The right life insurance choices can help provide financial security for you and your family. Life insurance protects dependents from loss of income and other expenses after the death of the insured person. The larger your financial responsibilities, the more important it is to have adequate coverage. Life insurance is especially important if you have a spouse, children, or elderly parents who depend on your income.

When an insured person dies, the face value of his or her policy is paid to the beneficiary. The *face value* is the amount for which the policy is written. A **beneficiary** is a person or organization named by the policyholder to receive assets after the policyholder's death.

The three traditional types of life insurance are term, whole life, and endowment. Each is available in slightly different forms and with different features.

Term Life

Term life insurance provides protection only for a specific period of time. This may be one, five, ten, or twenty years or until a specified age. When the term ends, so does the protection. Term policies often include a renewable option that allows you to renew the coverage at the end of the term, but at higher rates.

The advantage of term insurance is that it offers the most protection for your insurance dollar. Policies offering only protection cost less than policies with savings features. For those who really need insurance and cannot afford high premiums, term coverage may be the best choice.

Whole Life

Whole life insurance provides basic lifetime protection so long as premiums are paid. Whole life insurance is also called *straight life insurance*.

The face amount is paid to the beneficiaries upon death of the insured. The coverage builds cash value over the years. *Cash value* is the amount of money a policyholder would receive if the policy were surrendered before death or maturity.

You may be able to borrow against the cash value of whole life insurance at a relatively low interest rate. However, until repaid, benefits are reduced by the amount of the loan. You also can surrender the policy for its cash value if you want to change or eliminate coverage. New types of whole life insurance were developed in recent years to meet today's needs and demands. The new types include variable life, adjustable life, and universal life.

Discuss

Why do you think there are several types of life insurance on the market?

Case Study: Life Plans

A Death in the Family

Robb's father died suddenly during Robb's senior year in high school. The death left his family in a state of emotional and financial shock.

Robb's father was only 42 years old and in fine health. His income was good, but benefits were limited. The family received $30,000 from a pension plan and $25,000 from a life insurance policy. The benefits plus $7,500 in savings wasn't enough for their family of four with no income and three teenagers to educate.

Now the family must sell their home and look for cheaper housing. Robb was accepted by a college and planned to go in the fall, but will have to delay college plans or go part-time for now.

Robb figures he must work full-time after graduation to help support his family. His mother, once a teacher, plans to teach full-time after taking some required courses. His younger sisters will have to babysit and find other jobs to earn spending money for clothes and extracurricular activities.

Case Review

1. Could Robb's family have planned better to minimize or eliminate some of these financial problems? Name at least five steps they could have taken.
2. What else can the family do at this point to meet and overcome the financial hardships they face?
3. What government and community agencies and programs could be helpful to a family in their situation?

Limited Payment Policies

Limited payment policies offer lifetime protection. They call for premium payments over a stated period of time, such as 20 years, or until you reach a certain age. During the payment period, premiums are higher and cash value builds faster than for standard whole life coverage.

Variable Life

Variable life insurance premiums are fixed. Your insurance protection is combined with an investment feature. The face value varies with the performance of the fund in which the premiums are invested. However, the face amount may not fall below the original amount of the insurance. These policies guarantee a minimum death benefit. The benefit may be higher than the guarantee, depending on the earnings of the premium dollars invested.

The advantage of this type of life insurance is the possibility of gaining earnings when the value of the fund rises. The main disadvantage is it may not offer the best of either insurance or investment opportunities.

Adjustable Life

You can revise an adjustable life insurance policy as your needs change, 10-6. Within limits, you may raise or lower the premiums, face value, and

10-6

Parents may wish to increase their life insurance coverage when they have a child. Adjustable whole life insurance allows policyholders to change coverage when needed.

premium payment period. Coverage may start with term insurance for a given amount, premium, and term. All these may change as needed. Flexibility is the key advantage of adjustable life coverage. The need to constantly monitor coverage may be a disadvantage.

Universal Life

Universal life insurance permits the adjustment of premiums, face value, and level of protection. In addition, it offers an investment feature. The cash value is invested to earn interest at current market rates. An annual statement shows the current level of protection, cash value, and interest earned. The statement also includes a breakdown of how premiums are allocated to protection, investment, and expenses.

An advantage of universal life is flexibility, both in the amount of the premiums and in the level of protection. Earnings also keep pace with current market rates. If interest rates go down, however, your earnings decrease. You pay no taxes on the accumulated interest until you cash in your policy. This can be an advantage for persons in high income tax brackets.

Endowment Insurance

Endowment insurance pays the face value of the policy to beneficiaries if the insured dies before the endowment period ends. It pays the face amount to the insured if he or she lives beyond the endowment period.

The advantage of endowment insurance is the combination of protection and savings. It is a type of investment. Disadvantages are the high premiums and possible tax consequences.

Selecting the Protection You Need

Each person's needs are unique. The life insurance coverage that is right for one person or family may be wrong for another. Finding the type and amount of protection that works best for you requires careful planning.

The amount and type of life insurance protection you need depends on two key factors: your present and future earning power and your financial responsibilities and obligations.

Amount of Protection

Protection is often based on the amount of earnings that would be lost if the insured died prematurely. It is also matched to the needs of survivors for whom the insured is financially responsible. These needs depend on the number of survivors, their marital status, their earning power, and their lifestyles.

Other factors to consider include the share of family income provided by the insured and income available from other sources. Careful analysis

Discuss

Why do insurance needs vary from family to family?

Discuss

How are insurance needs related to the number of children or other dependents in a family?

Enrich

Apply the factors discussed to your family situation to determine what insurance protection would be appropriate for you.

Reflect

What, if any, type of insurance protection does your family receive through an employer?

Discuss

How might insurance needs change at different stages in the life cycle?

Discuss

What are the advantages of each of these life insurance features?

Resource

Life Insurance: How Much Is Enough? color lesson slide, TR

is needed to determine the amount of protection to buy. Consider the following factors to decide how much coverage you need.

- *Ages and financial needs of those depending on your income.* Dependents may include aging parents or relatives as well as a spouse and young children.

- *Amount of money your dependents would need to maintain their standard of living without your income.* Ideally, money would be left to cover a home mortgage and everyday living expenses. It might also cover major future expenses such as college education for children.

- *Other sources of income that would be available for dependents.* Would dependents be able to draw on Social Security benefits, savings, employee benefits, or their own earnings? You want enough coverage to fill the gap between what is available from other sources and what your dependents would need.

- *Amount of cash needed to pay burial costs and unpaid debts.* Even if you are single with no dependents, you need enough life insurance to take care of these costs. Then your financial obligations will not burden your parents or other relatives.

Types of Protection

You can buy life insurance in a variety of forms and with many special benefits. The decision depends on how much coverage you need, what you can afford to spend, and the special features you want.

Group insurance may be available through your employer, union, or another group to which you belong. As a rule, group coverage costs less than an individual policy for the same amount of coverage. Very often, group coverage is provided as a fringe benefit where you work. The employer may pay all or part of the premium. If you rely on group protection, look for a conversion clause. This permits you to convert to an individual policy without proof of insurability if you should leave the group.

Individual policies, though more expensive, generally can be tailored to the policyholder's needs. Features to consider when choosing life insurance protection include the following:

- *Guaranteed renewability* allows you to keep coverage in force at the end of a term without new evidence of insurability. Premium rates increase with each new term.

- *Double indemnity* provides for double benefits if death is the result of an accident. This may also be called an *accidental death benefit.*

- *Disability benefit* provides for a waiver of premiums if the insured becomes permanently and totally disabled. While this provision often is available as a feature on a life insurance policy, more comprehensive separate disability coverage is usually desirable.

- *Convertible provision* permits you to convert or exchange a term policy for another form of protection without new evidence of insurability.

Case Study: Life Plans

Life Insurance for Coni

Coni is 23 and just started her first job after college. She is single with no dependents. Both Coni's parents are living. A $150 credit card balance and a $1,500 car loan are her only major financial obligations other than her apartment lease.

When Coni is 25, her father dies. His retirement funds leave just enough money for her mother to make ends meet. Coni's mother could become financially dependent on her if she outlives her source of income.

At 28, Coni marries Arend. Arend has no dependents. That year, Coni is promoted at work. At 30, Coni has their first child. Two years later, she has a second child. She works part-time until the children reach school age. This reduces her income temporarily. Coni and Arend start setting aside money for the children's college costs.

When Coni and Arend reach their mid-forties, the children are in high school. They will start college in three and five years. Coni's mother is in a nursing home, and Coni is paying most of the bills. Both Coni and Arend are working and are at the peak of their careers. They expect their salaries to remain fairly stable during the remaining 20 years of work.

Now Coni and Arend are in their mid-fifties. Both children graduated from college. Coni's mother passed away. Coni and Arend begin to consider travel and retirement.

Case Review

1. When Coni was single and both her parents were alive, do you think she needed life insurance? Explain.
2. When Coni's father died, what changes should she have made in her insurance program? Why?
3. What type of insurance program would you recommend for Coni and Arend when they married? Why?
4. What insurance and other financial planning would be suitable for a couple with young children?
5. How would Coni and Arend's financial planning change when they reached their forties?
6. What changes do you think they should make in their insurance program now? Why?

Insurance Representatives

Insurance representatives interact with agents, insurance companies, and policyholders. They handle much of the paperwork related to insurance policies, such as sales, policy applications, and changes and renewals to existing policies.

Finally, consider how life insurance fits into your overall plan for future security and eventual retirement. Future financial security depends on the right mix of savings, insurance, and investments. Some people plan to use insurance as a form of savings. In this case, be sure the earnings on your insurance match or exceed those on other forms of savings and investments.

Choosing a Company, Agent, and Policy

Select a company that is respected within the insurance industry, by its policyholders, and by people in the financial field. Check whether the company has a reputation for settling claims fairly and promptly. Also be sure the company is licensed to operate in your state.

You can research and compare life insurance companies by reviewing *Best's Insurance Reports*. This can be found in most public libraries or online at www.ambest.com. You also can check out an insurance company through your state insurance department.

Look closely at policies that offer the benefits and options important to you. Be sure to compare the premiums charged by different companies for the same types and amounts of coverage. If you are considering whole life insurance, compare the cash value accumulation rates. Additional information on buying life insurance is available from a number of financial publications and online.

The life insurance agent you choose is also important. Very often, the agent is the key to the quality of service you receive. All states require a special license to sell life insurance. Initials following an agent's name indicate completion of specific studies in the insurance field. *CLU* indicates a Chartered Life Underwriter. *ChFC* indicates a Chartered Financial Consultant. *LUTCF* indicates a Life Underwriters' Training Council Fellow. Members of the National Association of Life Underwriters subscribe to the ethical standards of that group.

Choose an agent who can clearly explain the different types of coverage and benefits available. A good agent advises you honestly about the type and amount of coverage you need. He or she also helps you evaluate your coverage as your needs and finances change. Finally, a responsible agent handles policy revisions and claims promptly.

Once you choose a company and an agent, select a policy. Talk honestly with your agent as you discuss your needs.

After you buy a policy and it is delivered to you, review it carefully. Be sure the policy you are given is the one you chose. If the policy does not meet your expectations, most companies allow you to return it within ten days without obligation. As you review the policy, check to see that it states the following:

- Name of the company.
- Name of the insured and the beneficiaries.
- Type of coverage.
- Amount of coverage and benefits.
- Amount and due dates of premiums.

- Terms for borrowing money against accumulated cash value, if applicable.

- Schedule of cash value accumulation, if applicable.

- Benefits and options of the policy.

Be sure to ask questions about any terms, provisions, or sections you do not understand. Once you are insured, inform your family and beneficiaries of the coverage and the location of the policy.

Discuss

What type of protection does homeowner's liability coverage provide? Give examples of what is and isn't covered.

Enrich

Obtain a copy of a homeowner's insurance policy and study both coverage and exclusions.

Home Insurance

Once you invest in a home of your own, you want to protect it with insurance. Homeowner's insurance provides coverage for liability and property damage under certain conditions. It provides two basic types of coverage: property protection and liability protection.

Property coverage insures you against damage to or loss of dwelling and personal property and possessions, such as clothes and furnishings. It may also pay for additional living expenses if you should need to move out of your home because of damage to the property. The specific losses covered depend on the type of policy you buy.

Liability coverage protects you if others are injured on your property. For example, if someone falls and is hurt in your home, liability coverage pays for any loss incurred.

This coverage also protects you if you, your family, your pets, or your property accidentally damages the property of others. It pays for the legal costs of defending yourself if you are sued because of injuries or damages. Limits on this coverage generally run around $100,000. You can buy additional coverage either in an umbrella policy or extended liability policy. An *umbrella policy* is an insurance policy that covers loss amounts that are higher than those covered by primary policies.

Amount of Coverage

The first step in buying the right homeowner coverage is to find out how much it would cost to rebuild your home. This may be more or less than the price you paid for the home or the amount it would bring if you sold it today. The cost of rebuilding your home depends on local building costs and the type of home you own.

Your insurance agent may be able to help you calculate building costs, or you may need an appraisal. An **appraisal** is an estimate of the current value of property. A qualified appraiser should make an appraisal. Once you arrive at an appraised value, buy enough insurance protection to cover the cost of replacing your home. Today most insurance companies recommend enough insurance coverage to rebuild your home if it should be completely destroyed.

To keep insurance coverage up-to-date, inform your insurance agent of any major home improvements you make. You also may want to add an inflation-guard clause to your policy. This automatically adjusts policy renewal coverage to reflect current rebuilding costs.

Read the policy to learn what coverage is provided for personal possessions. It generally is limited to 50 percent of the amount of coverage on the home, but may be higher. Compare the contents limit with the total value of your possessions. If coverage is not adequate, you should talk to your insurance agent about increasing protection.

Knowing whether your personal property is insured for replacement cost or actual cash value is also important.

- *Actual cash value* is the replacement cost minus depreciation. **Depreciation** is a decrease in the value of property as a result of age or wear and tear.

- *Replacement value* covers the cost of replacing what you lose without deducting depreciation.

For example, a five-year-old TV set, even in good condition, is no longer worth what you paid for it, or what a new similar set would cost. If the set were stolen, actual cash value recovery would not pay for a new one. If it were insured for replacement value, you could recover the full cost of a new TV set of comparable quality. Obviously, it pays to insure possessions for replacement rather than actual cash value, though it costs from 10 to 15 percent more.

When insuring home and possessions, make a complete inventory of your belongings. Include the purchase date and price for costly items. It is a good idea to take photos or videos of each room. This helps you remember the contents and establish your claims in case of major losses, 10-7.

Cost of Home Insurance

Be sure to call or visit with representatives from several companies to comparison shop before you buy insurance. Compare company reputations for honoring and prompt processing of claims. The cost of protecting your home and personal possessions depends primarily on four factors:

- *Type and amount of coverage.* The higher the amount of protection purchased and the more perils covered, the higher the premium will be. A policy with replacement value coverage is more expensive than one with cash or market value protection.

- *Size of the deductible.* The higher the deductible is, the lower the insurance premium will be.

- *Risk factor where you live.* The type of home you own and its location influence premium rates. For example, you pay more for fire protection on a frame house than on a brick house. You pay more for protection against theft and vandalism in high-crime areas than in low-crime areas.

- *The insurance company.* The cost of insurance premiums varies from company to company.

- *Opportunity for discounts.* Check with your insurance agent to see if you qualify for premium reductions for more than one policy with the

Filing a Home Insurance Claim

Follow these steps to file a claim on your home insurance.

1. Report any burglary or theft to the police immediately.

2. Notify your insurance agent or company promptly by phone with a written follow-up report. Determine exact coverage your policy provides and find out whether the loss exceeds the deductible. Ask about details of filing a claim and about records and estimates you may need to file a claim for repairs or replacements.

3. Make temporary repairs and take necessary steps to prevent further damage. Keep receipts and records of expenses involved for reimbursement.

4. Make a list of lost or damaged articles with estimated replacement costs and confirming records of purchase and replacement prices.

5. Keep records and receipts for living expenses if damage to your property requires you to find a place to live while repairs are being made.

6. Provide your insurance agent or company with the necessary receipts, records, and information required to handle and settle your claim.

7. Check your policy to find out what steps are involved in settling a claim. If you are dissatisfied or have questions concerning the final settlement, discuss matters with your agent or the claims adjuster.

8. If you find a settlement unsatisfactory or are not satisfied with your insurance company's handling of your complaint, you can contact your state insurance department or call the National Insurance Consumer Helpline for assistance.

Insurance Information Institute

10-7

These guidelines can help you file a home insurance claim.

company such as home and auto coverage. Also, check if discounts are available for devices such as a smoke detector or burglar alarm, for nonsmoker policyholders, or for long-term policyholders. These discounts can reduce your homeowner premiums considerably.

When you are ready to buy home insurance, take time to study the types and amounts of coverage available. Then find an informed, reputable insurance agent or broker who can advise you on the type and amount of coverage you need. Ask friends and business associates about their experience with insurance agents and companies.

A.M. Best & Company rates insurers for financial stability. The ratings are published in *Best's Insurance Reports: Property-Casualty*. This publication is available in the reference section of most public libraries and online at www.ambest.com. Your state insurance department may also help you evaluate a company's service and complaint record. In addition, you can find information online about home insurance coverage, companies, and rates.

Enrich

Study and discuss the information in 10-7. Identify the information and documentation you would need to file a claim.

Enrich

Investigate the types of information that are found in *Best's Insurance Reports Property–Casualty*. Report your findings in class.

Renter's Insurance

Renter's insurance covers losses due to damage or loss of personal property and possessions. These include jewelry, electronics, furniture, bedding, and so forth. The landlord carries coverage on the dwelling itself.

Discuss

How does renter's insurance differ from homeowner's insurance?

Discuss

What situations call for special floaters or endorsements to provide insurance protection?

Resource

Shopping for Auto Insurance, Activity D, WB

Renters should look for a policy with liability insurance. If guests were harmed in a rental home, liability insurance would cover any expenses incurred by the resident.

College students living in a dorm or renting an apartment may need renter's insurance, a floater, or an endorsement to protect their possessions. A *floater* is a form of insurance that covers specific items wherever you take them. It "floats" with possessions such as a musical instrument or a laptop computer.

An *endorsement* is an attachment to existing insurance coverage, such as a family policy to protect a computer, a television, and other expensive items taken to college.

Auto Insurance

Auto insurance gives policyholders coverage for liability and property damage under specified conditions. When you own or lease a car, you take certain personal and financial risks. If you are involved in a car accident, you may be required to pay thousands of dollars for injuries and property damage, 10-8. If you are in an accident where you are at fault or claims are filed against you, it can cost thousands of dollars in legal fees as well as damages. Practically no one can afford the financial risks of extensive property damage, serious injury, or death without insurance coverage.

All 50 states have *financial responsibility laws* that require drivers to show proof of their ability to pay stated minimum amounts in damages

10-8

Having adequate auto insurance is important. Car accidents can cost thousands of dollars for repairs, medical expenses, and legal fees.

after an accident. Most states also have *compulsory auto insurance laws* that require car owners to buy a minimum amount of bodily injury and property damage liability insurance in order to legally drive their cars.

When you are ready to buy auto insurance, shop carefully to get the coverage you need at the best price. An auto insurance policy may include several types of coverage for the insured individual or family.

Types of Auto Insurance

Of the six basic types of auto insurance coverage, two are liability coverage. They pay other parties for losses you cause. The other auto policies pay you, the insured, for losses outlined in the policy.

Bodily injury liability is coverage that protects you when you are responsible for an auto accident that results in the injury or death of other parties. **Property damage liability** protects you when you are responsible for an auto accident in which the property of others is damaged.

These policies cover the policyholder, family members, and any person driving the car with the owner's permission. They pay damages to the other parties involved in an accident you cause. Both types of liability coverage pay the legal fees for settling claims. They also pay for damages assessed against you, up to limits stated in the policy. These damages include injuries to other parties or damage to the property of others.

Medical payments or *personal injury protection (PIP)* pays you, the insured, for medical expenses resulting from an accident in your car, regardless of who is at fault. It covers you and any person injured in or by your car.

Collision insurance pays you for damage to your car due to an auto accident or collision with another car or object.

Comprehensive physical damage insurance pays you for loss or damage to your car resulting from fire, theft, falling objects, explosion, earthquake, flood, riot, civil commotion, and collision with a bird or animal.

Uninsured and underinsured motorist insurance pays you for injuries caused by an uninsured or hit-and-run driver. It covers insured persons driving, riding, or walking. It covers you if injured as a pedestrian. It also covers passengers in the insured person's car.

Auto Insurance Costs

Auto insurance is a costly service. Coverage for young drivers is particularly high because statistically they have more accidents. Adding a teenage driver to a family policy may increase the insurance premium by as much as 75 percent.

The guidelines in 10-9 can help you select the automobile insurance you need. The cost of auto insurance depends on the following factors.

Driver Classification

Driver classification is determined by the age, sex, and marital status of the driver. Driving record and habits are also considered.

Suggestions for Buying Automobile Insurance

1. Decide on the types and amounts of coverage you need. If you now have a policy, review your coverage and its cost before renewal time.
2. Check with several reputable insurers. Keep in mind the least expensive coverage is not necessarily the best for you. Consider such things as the company's reliability and its reputation for service, including claims handling. If you're in doubt about a company, check with your state insurance department.
3. Consider the amount you would save by paying a higher deductible. You may find it pays in the long run to take care of small losses yourself.
4. Check with your agent regarding your eligibility for premium discounts.
5. Consider special coverages or higher policy limits if you frequently drive other commuters to work or groups of children to school or special events.
6. Consider reducing or dropping collision coverage as cars get older.

10-9

These guidelines can help you select auto insurance.

Statistically, young, single males are involved in more serious accidents than other classes of drivers. Therefore, they tend to pay the highest insurance premiums. If a young man marries, his insurance costs may decrease because, statistically, married men have fewer serious accidents than single men. Rates for women, single and married, are lower than for males.

A poor driving record tends to increase premiums as does a record of previous claims and costly settlements. When your driver classification changes, so might your insurance rates.

Rating Territory

The number and amount of claims an insurance company processes in your area determines rates for auto insurance. Premiums are higher in frequent claim areas such as big cities and high traffic districts.

Premium Discount Eligibility

Some companies offer discounts to drivers who

- have a safe driving record
- get good grades (if still in school)
- are nonsmokers
- install antitheft devices and air bags
- are over a certain age
- have two or more cars on a policy
- have a positive credit report

Check with your insurance company about possible discounts.

Insured Car's Year, Make, and Model

Cars that are costly to repair or that are favorite targets of thieves cost more to insure. Premiums are higher for luxury, sports, and new cars than for standard models and older cars. For older cars, collision insurance may not be cost effective.

Cars that require expensive repairs and parts generally cost more to insure. Very popular models cost more to insure than more ordinary cars. Check the insurance costs for different models before buying a car.

Deductible Amount

Increasing the deductible amount can reduce premiums for collision and comprehensive damage coverage. Increasing your deductible from $250 to $500 could save you 15 to 30 percent on your premium. The higher the deductible is, the lower the premium will be.

Coverage Amount

The more protection you buy, the higher the premium will be. However, the cost per dollar of coverage is usually less for more coverage. For example, a $100,000 policy costs less per dollar of coverage than a $50,000 policy. Just remember to buy the amount of coverage you need. A reliable agent can help you decide.

Insurance Company

Premium rates and service for the same coverage may vary greatly from company to company. It pays to shop carefully. You may be able to save by combining different coverages into one policy rather than buying each separately.

To compare insurance costs, check the cost of coverage you need with several reliable insurance companies. Once you buy auto insurance, read your policy carefully and know what coverage you carry.

It also is a good idea to keep the policy and records of premium payments and claims together in one place so you can find them as needed. You also must carry proof of your insurance coverage in your vehicle in most states. See 10-10 for procedures to follow at the scene of an accident and in filing an insurance claim.

No-Fault Auto Insurance

No-fault auto insurance eliminates the faultfinding process in settling claims. When an accident occurs, each policyholder makes a claim to his or her own insurance company. Each company pays its own policyholder regardless of who is at fault. No-fault insurance is designed to simplify and speed up payments to accident victims. It also acts to lower insurance rates by reducing costly court trials to determine fault.

Activity

Visit www.iihs.org for information on injury, collision, and theft loss experience by car make and model.

Enrich

Explain how deductibles work and investigate how much premiums decrease as deductibles increase.

Enrich

Interview an insurance agent for advice on deciding what amount of auto insurance coverage to buy.

Enrich

Research the no-fault laws in your state.

Resource

Life Plans, reproducible master 10-3, TR

Auto Accidents and Insurance Claims

At the Scene of an Accident

- Stop your car safely beyond the accident and out of traffic. Turn on flasher or warning light.
- Assist the injured, but do not move anyone unless absolutely necessary.
- Administer any first aid you are qualified and trained to provide.
- Stay calm and help others to do the same.
- Get help as fast as possible. Call or have someone call the police and an ambulance if needed.
- Provide police with information they request.
- Ask for a copy of the police report.
- Write down 1) names, addresses, and phone numbers of those involved in the accident and of any witnesses, 2) license number, make, and model of cars involved, 3) driver's license number of drivers involved, 4) insurance company and identification number of each driver involved, and 5) names and badge numbers of police officers and other emergency assistants.
- For a collision with an unattended or parked auto, try to find the owner. If unsuccessful, leave a note with your name, number, and address. Damages over a certain amount must be reported to the police in most states.

Filing an Insurance Claim

If your car is involved in an auto accident; if it is damaged by fire, flood, or vandalism; or if it is stolen, follow these steps in filing a claim for your losses.

- Phone your insurance agent or a local company representative as soon as possible to report the incident.
- Ask the agent how to proceed and what forms or documents are needed to support your claim. These may include medical and auto repair bills and a copy of the police report.
- Obtain and provide the information the insurer requires. Cooperate fully with your insurance company in the investigation and settlement of claims.
- Turn over copies of any legal papers you receive in connection with the accident and losses you are claiming. If you are sued or claims are brought against you, the insurance company will provide legal representation for you.
- Keep copies of any paperwork and documents you submit with your insurance claim.
- Keep records of any expenses you incur as a result of an automobile accident. They may be reimbursed under the terms of your policy.

Note: If involved in an accident, it is unlawful to leave the scene without proper notification if there is injury, death, or property damage over a certain amount. Check the laws on reporting accidents in your state.

10-10

Follow these steps if you are involved in an auto accident and must file an insurance claim.

Enrich

Review listed procedures to follow at the scene of an accident. Role-play accident situations, carrying out these procedures.

State legislators decide whether their state adopts a no-fault insurance plan and what form it takes. Most states with a no-fault plan have a combination no-fault and liability insurance. The no-fault pays for claims up to a set amount called a *threshold*. However, in most states individuals can sue for additional damages when an accident involves severe injuries, death, or major medical bills. Liability insurance pays for damages over and above the threshold amount.

High-Risk Drivers

It can be difficult for individuals with poor driving records to buy insurance. Insurers consider these drivers too great a risk. In such cases, it may be possible to obtain coverage through an assigned risk plan. This is a state-supervised program in which high-risk drivers are assigned to insurance companies. The companies are required to provide coverage, but premiums are considerably higher than for those with better driving records.

Enrich

Investigate your state's assigned risk plan to learn what coverage is available and what it costs.

Resource

Chapter 10—Insurance, Teacher's PowerPoint Presentations CD

Chapter Summary

The types of insurance protection consumers typically buy cover health, disability, life, home, and auto. Protection needs in these areas vary with every individual and family. It pays to shop carefully for the best coverage at the best price.

The high cost of medical care makes it important to investigate all options for obtaining health insurance. Older citizens and certain groups may be eligible for government insurance programs such as Medicare and Medicaid. Disability insurance protects against financial loss if the policyholder becomes disabled and can no longer work.

Adequate life insurance coverage guarantees income for the policyholder's survivors. It is particularly important for those who are financially responsible for a spouse, children, or others. Term life, whole life, and endowment insurance are three main types of protection against the loss of income as a result of the death of a wage earner. Life insurance may also offer investment features.

Once you own a home, you need insurance to protect it. A reliable insurance agent can help you select the type and amount of coverage you need. Costs depend on the type and amount of coverage you buy, the deductible amount, the risk factors where you live, and the opportunity for discounts.

Carrying adequate auto insurance is a major responsibility of car owners. Different types of coverage protect against the different risks individuals assume as a car owner. The cost of insurance depends on many factors, including your driving record, where you live, and the type of car you drive.

Review

1. Give two examples of financial risks that insurance can protect against.

2. Explain how HMO, PPO, and POS health insurance plans differ.

3. How can a health savings account (HSA) save you money?

4. List three disadvantages of individual private health insurance plans.

5. What factors should be considered before enrolling in a health insurance plan?

6. What are the differences between Medicare and Medicaid?

7. What is disability insurance and how does it work?

8. What are the differences between term life, whole life, and endowment insurance?

9. What are two key factors that determine the amount of life insurance to buy?

10. What four major factors determine the cost of home insurance?

11. Which type of insurance coverage pays for damage your car causes someone else's property if you are responsible for the accident?

12. List five factors that determine auto insurance costs.

Critical Thinking

13. Outline the health care costs typically covered by health insurance.

14. Explain and give examples of the following terms as they apply to health insurance.
    A. preexisting
    B. exclusions
    C. co-payments
    D. deductibles

15. What are the advantages of long-term care insurance and who needs it?

16. Name and describe the different types of whole life insurance.

17. List four factors you should consider when selecting a life insurance company and agent.

18. Explain the types of coverage home insurance policies provide.

Answers to *Review*

1. (Give two:) health care costs due to illness or injury; loss of income due to disability or death; loss of property due to natural disaster, accidents, or theft

2. HMO—only covers services by providers in the plan, must have a primary care doctor; PPO—costs are lower for providers in the plan, costs are higher for providers outside the plan; POS—primary care doctor acts as "point of service" and makes referrals, costs are lower for providers in the plan, costs are higher for providers outside the plan

3. High deductible makes premiums less expensive; contributions qualify for tax deductions; unspent savings accumulate tax-free.

4. (List three:) high premiums; extensive application process; many people are denied coverage; many exclusions

5. services, choice, and cost

6. Medicare is for people over age 65 and people with certain diseases or disabilities. It is a federal program funded by payroll deductions. Medicaid is for people with low incomes or disabilities. It is a joint federal and state program funded by tax revenues.

7. Disability insurance pays a portion of income lost if a person is unable to work because of an injury or illness.

Short-term and long-term insurance offer benefits for different periods of time. Usually, there is a waiting period before benefits begin.

8. Term life provides protection only for a specific period of time, with no savings features. Whole life provides basic lifetime protection and builds cash value over the years. Endowment pays the face amount of the policy to beneficiaries if the insured dies before the endowment period ends. It pays the face amount to the insured if he or she lives beyond the endowment period.

9. (Give two:) age and financial needs of dependents; amount of money needed for dependents to maintain their living standard; other sources of income for dependents; cash needed to pay burial costs and unpaid debts

10. the type and amount of coverage, the size of the deductible, the risk factor where you live, the insurance company

11. property damage liability

12. (List five:) driver classification; where you live; eligibility for premium discounts; the year, make, and model of the car; the amount of the deductible; the amount of coverage; opportunity for discounts

19. What kinds of auto insurance coverage do you or your family carry? How might the family coverage and costs change if you are added to the policy as a new driver? How might the cost change for one vehicle if you raise the deductible and lower liability coverage limits?

20. How does no-fault auto insurance work?

Academic Connections

21. **Financial literacy, research.** Use the Internet to research disability and long-term care insurance offered by three major insurance companies. Find out about coverage, costs, and factors to consider in deciding whether and how much of this type of coverage someone might wish to consider at different stages of life.

22. **Research, speech.** Describe the life insurance needs of the following family. The husband is 30 years old and earns $55,000 a year. The wife is 29 years old and earns $40,000 a year. Both have secure jobs, excellent health, and health insurance through their employers. The couple has two children, ages four and two, and no other dependents. Their financial goals include a larger home, an education for their children, and a comfortable retirement income. Talk to a life insurance agent in your community. Ask what type of life insurance is recommended for this family and why. Describe how life insurance decisions relate to investment and other financial decisions. Report your findings to the class.

23. **Math.** Make a list of personal possessions you would take if you went away to college. Estimate the value of each item and calculate the total value. Contact your family's insurance agent. Based on the value of your possessions, how much would it cost to insure them?

24. **Financial literacy, math.** Use the Internet to obtain no obligation rate quotes for renter's insurance at two different companies. Find out how much you would pay a year for a renter's policy in an area where you would like to live. Choose the same coverage options for both quotes. Investigate the claims record and reputation of each company. Compare the policies or coverage. Which company appears to offer the best coverage and service for the least amount of money?

25. **Reading.** Obtain an auto insurance policy to study and analyze. Underline the most important phrases and circle any terms you do not understand. Discuss the policy in class, explain the coverage it provides, and define the circled terms.

Math Challenge

26. Tyrone visits his doctor because he has abdominal pain. The doctor examines Tyrone and sends him to the outpatient testing center at a local hospital for an abdominal scan. Given the following information, how much will Tyrone pay out of his own pocket for the doctor's visit and test? How much would it cost Tyrone if he didn't have insurance?

Doctor's visit: $125

Abdominal scan: $1,600

Tyrone's Insurance Coverage

Deductible: $250 per year (Tyrone has paid $75 toward his deductible.)

Co-payments: $30 per doctor visit; $10 for generic drugs; $30 for brand-name drugs (Co-payments do not count toward the deductible.)

Tech Smart

27. The law requires that drivers carry certain types and amounts of auto insurance. These requirements vary among states. Using the Internet, find the legal requirements in your state. Do you believe they are sufficient? What changes would you make? Why?

Answer to *Math Challenge*

26. Tyrone owes $30 for the office visit. Since he has not paid his deductible, Tyrone must pay $175 ($250 – $75) of the cost of the abdominal scan. The total cost for Tyrone is $205 ($30 + $175). If Tyrone did not have insurance, the doctor's visit and test would cost him $1,725.

CHAPTER 11

Savings

Reading for Meaning

Examine the charts before you read this chapter. Write down questions you have about them. Try to answer the questions as you read.

simple interest

compound interest

Rule of 72

tax exempt

tax deferred

annual percentage
   yield (APY)

certificate of deposit
   (CD)

U.S. savings bond

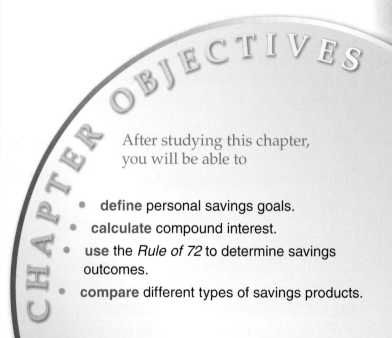

CHAPTER OBJECTIVES

After studying this chapter,
you will be able to

- **define** personal savings goals.
- **calculate** compound interest.
- **use** the *Rule of 72* to determine savings outcomes.
- **compare** different types of savings products.

Central Ideas

- A savings plan is an essential piece of an overall financial program.
- Compound interest helps your savings grow over time.

Vocabulary

Define *savings* and *savings plan*.

Resource

Your Saver Profile, Activity A, WB

Discuss

What are some consequences of *not* having a savings plan?

*S*aving is setting money aside for future use. A *savings plan* is a strategy for using money to reach important goals and to advance your financial security. Creating a savings plan involves a careful look at your current finances and your important objectives.

Money is a limited resource. Every decision to spend or save has an opportunity cost. The money you spend today cannot meet tomorrow's needs and wants. The opportunity cost of current spending is reduced future spending power. Current spending also costs you the opportunity to earn interest on savings.

Using interest-earning opportunities can help your savings grow. To make the most of your savings dollars, learn how interest is calculated. Compare savings products and services at different financial institutions and choose the type that best meets your needs.

Creating a Savings Plan

A personal savings plan is a vital part of an overall financial plan. A savings plan consists of creating an emergency fund, setting goals for savings, and choosing a combination of savings instruments to meet your needs. First, you need to have money that can be set aside for savings.

Budget for Saving

Review the money management section in Chapter 6. Follow the steps outlined to create a simple, workable money management plan. This will give you an in-depth look at your current finances. It will also tell you how much money you can use to start a savings program. Once you budget for savings, the following strategies can help you make your savings grow:

- *Pay yourself first.* Rather than waiting until all bills are paid before the leftovers go into savings, feed your savings first. Budget for savings. Put it into your spending plan. Make this a regular part of your bill-paying routine. When you receive extra money—a gift, a bonus, a tax refund—add it to your savings.

- *Use direct deposit.* Many employers can deposit employees' paychecks directly into their bank accounts. A portion can go into a savings account. This strategy is another way to pay yourself first.

- *Let your savings grow.* Your savings will not build up if you are constantly dipping into it. Except for withdrawing money to pay for the savings goals you set, stay out of your savings. If the temptation is too great, perhaps you can choose a savings plan that makes withdrawal difficult.

- *Reduce spending, increase saving.* Keep a spending log as described in Chapter 6. This will show you where your money goes. Look for places where you can cut spending and add to your savings. The chapters in Unit 3 give tips for saving money on your purchases.

Create an Emergency Fund

The first savings goal is to build an emergency fund. An emergency fund is savings you can easily access in case of a job layoff, illness, or unexpected expense. Since most emergencies are unplanned, the money should be available to use right away.

The amount of money in this fund varies depending on your needs. However, a common guideline is that you keep enough money in the emergency fund to cover living expenses for six to eight months. This would include rent or mortgage payments, car and other loan payments, taxes, utilities, food, and all other expenses.

Discuss

List events that might cause a person or family to use emergency fund money.

Enrich

Outline your savings goals and objectives by answering these questions.

Set Goals for Saving

Once you have an emergency fund, you can save for other things. It is easier to save if you have clearly defined goals, 11-1. Begin with a list of what you want to achieve with your money. What would persuade you to give up spending now so you can save enough for the future? Your savings goals need to be

- *realistic.* Consider your income and expenses, your life situation, and any likely changes. Set up financial goals that you can achieve based on these realities. For example, suppose you can save $300 monthly and you want to buy a car within two years without getting a loan. A used car is realistic while a new luxury car is not. What are your goals? Are they objectives you can achieve?

11-1

Planning ahead can help you achieve long-term goals, such as paying for a college education.

- *specific and measurable.* Outline your goals in exact terms. "Putting together $1,200 for a ski trip next winter" is more specific than "saving money to travel sometime in the future." Likewise, "saving $50 per month to buy a computer next summer" is more specific than "putting money aside in case you need it next year." What specific goals do you and your family want to reach in the near or distant future?

- *time related.* Put your goals and objectives into a time frame. When will you need your savings? This will vary for different goals.

It is never too soon to start saving for the goods and services you want for your future. Once you know what you want your money to do for you, you can take realistic steps to reach your financial goals.

Maximizing Savings

There are many different places to save your money. Saving money in a financial institution, such as a bank or credit union, provides a safe place

Financial Managers

Financial managers at financial institutions are responsible for directing bank operations and overseeing the management of the products and services offered to customers. They may also resolve customer problems, oversee investments, and manage employees and departments.

to keep money and a way to earn interest. You can maximize your savings by considering the following:

- *Total amount deposited.* Obviously, the more you deposit, the more interest you earn.

- *Interest rate.* The higher the interest rate, the more you stand to gain.

- *Time span of deposit.* The longer money remains in savings without withdrawals, the more you accumulate.

- *Interest type.* There are two types of interest. **Simple interest** is computed only on the *principal* or the amount of money originally deposited. The principal does not include interest earned. **Compound interest** is figured on the money deposited plus the interest it earns. The interest previously earned is included in the total before new interest earnings are computed. Earning interest on the interest makes money grow faster.

- *Frequency of compounding.* The more often interest is compounded, the faster savings grows. Compounding may be done on a daily, quarterly, monthly, or semi-annual basis. Over time, compound interest increases the value of your savings. This concept is known as the *time value of money.* See 11-2.

11-2

The dual effects of time and compound interest add value to savings.

Watch Your Savings Grow			
Weekly Savings at Different Interest Rates, Compounded Monthly			
Weekly Amount:	**Number of Years**		
	10	**20**	**30**
$10 4.5%	$ 6,550	$ 16,814	$ 32,897
25	16,375	42,035	82,243
50	32,750	84,069	164,486
$10 5.5%	$ 6,910	$ 18,871	$ 39,576
25	17,274	47,176	98,940
50	34,548	94,353	197,880
$10 6.6%	$ 7,294	$ 21,243	$ 47,914
25	18,236	53,107	119,786
50	36,472	106,214	239,572
$10 7.7%	$ 7,707	$ 23,984	$ 58,361
25	19,267	59,959	145,903
50	38,533	119,918	291,807
$10 8.8%	$ 8,148	$ 27,155	$ 71,491
25	20,371	67,888	178,729
50	40,741	135,776	357,459
Original Amounts Saved:			
$10	$ 5,200	$ 10,400	$ 15,600
25	13,000	26,000	39,000
50	26,000	52,000	78,000

Calculating Compound Interest

Calculating compound interest involves several steps.

1. Multiply the deposit by the annual interest rate.

2. Divide the answer from Step 1 by the rate of compounding. For monthly compounding, divide by 12; for quarterly, divide by 4; for semi-annual, divide by 2; for daily, divide by 365.

3. Add the answer from Step 2 to the deposit amount. The result is the new balance with interest.

These steps are shown in Chart 11-3, which calculates monthly compounding. For example, the savings plan shows a single deposit of $100 and an annual interest rate of 5 percent. Therefore, the deposit amount at the end of Month 2 is $100.84.

Future Value Tables

A future value table provides an easy way to calculate compound interest earnings at different interest rates and times. Future value tables usually show compound interest earnings for either a series of equal annual deposits or a single deposit, 11-4.

Calculating Compound Interest			
Month	**Step 1** Deposit × Annual Interest Rate	**Step 2** Step 1 Answer ÷ Rate of Compounding	**Step 3** Deposit + Step 2 Answer = New Balance with Interest
1	$100 × 5% = $5	$5 ÷ 12 = $0.42	$100 + $0.42 = $100.42
2	$100.42 × 5% = $5.02	$5.02 ÷ 12 = $0.42	$100.42 + $0.42 = $100.84
3	$100.84 × 5% = $5.04	$5.04 ÷ 12 = $0.42	$100.84 + $0.42 = $101.26
4	$101.26 × 5% = $5.06	$5.06 ÷ 12 = $0.42	$101.26 + $0.42 = $101.68
5	$101.68 × 5% = $5.08	$5.08 ÷ 12 = $0.42	$101.68 + $0.42 = $102.10
6	$102.10 × 5% = $5.11	$5.11 ÷ 12 = $0.43	$102.10 + $0.43 = $102.53
7	$102.53 × 5% = $5.13	$5.13 ÷ 12 = $0.43	$102.53 + $0.43 = $102.96
8	$102.96 × 5% = $5.15	$5.15 ÷ 12 = $0.43	$102.96 + $0.43 = $103.39
9	$103.39 × 5% = $5.17	$5.17 ÷ 12 = $0.43	$103.39 + $0.43 = $103.82
10	$103.82 × 5% = $5.19	$5.19 ÷ 12 = $0.43	$103.82 + $0.43 = $104.25
11	$104.25 × 5% = $5.21	$5.21 ÷ 12 = $0.43	$104.25 + $0.43 = $104.68
12	$104.68 × 5% = $5.23	$5.23 ÷ 12 = $0.44	$104.68 + $0.44 = $105.12

11-3

After one year, a single deposit of $100, earning an annual interest rate of 5 percent compounded monthly, will increase to $105.12.

Resource

Calculating Compound Interest, Activity B, WB

Discuss

What difference does the frequency of compounding make on savings?

Activity

Visit a financial institution Web site. How often is interest compounded on money market deposit accounts?

Future Value of $1 (Single Deposit)

Years	Annual Interest Rate							
	1%	2%	3%	4%	5%	6%	7%	8%
1	1.0100	1.0200	1.0300	1.0400	1.0500	1.0600	1.0700	1.0800
2	1.0201	1.0404	1.0609	1.0816	1.1025	1.1236	1.1449	1.1664
3	1.0303	1.0612	1.0927	1.1249	1.1576	1.1910	1.2250	1.2597
4	1.0406	1.0824	1.1255	1.1699	1.2155	1.2625	1.3108	1.3605
5	1.0510	1.1041	1.1593	1.2167	1.2763	1.3382	1.4026	1.4693
6	1.0615	1.1262	1.1941	1.2653	1.3401	1.4185	1.5007	1.5869
7	1.0721	1.1487	1.2299	1.3159	1.4071	1.5036	1.6058	1.7138
8	1.0829	1.1717	1.2668	1.3686	1.4775	1.5938	1.7182	1.8509
9	1.0937	1.1951	1.3048	1.4233	1.5513	1.6895	1.8385	1.9990
10	1.1046	1.2190	1.3439	1.4802	1.6289	1.7908	1.9672	2.1589
11	1.1157	1.2434	1.3842	1.5395	1.7103	1.8983	2.1049	2.3316
12	1.1268	1.2682	1.4258	1.6010	1.7959	2.0122	2.2522	2.5182
13	1.1381	1.2936	1.4685	1.6651	1.8856	2.1329	2.4098	2.7196
14	1.1495	1.3195	1.5126	1.7317	1.9799	2.2609	2.5785	2.9372
15	1.1610	1.3459	1.5580	1.8009	2.0789	2.3966	2.7590	3.1722
16	1.1726	1.3728	1.6047	1.8730	2.1829	2.5404	2.9522	3.4259
17	1.1843	1.4002	1.6528	1.9479	2.2920	2.6928	3.1588	3.7000
18	1.1961	1.4282	1.7024	2.0258	2.4066	2.8543	3.3799	3.9960
19	1.2081	1.4568	1.7535	2.1068	2.5270	3.0256	3.6165	4.3157
20	1.2202	1.4859	1.8061	2.1911	2.6533	3.2071	3.8697	4.6610
25	1.2824	1.6406	2.0938	2.6658	3.3864	4.2919	5.4274	6.8485
30	1.3478	1.8114	2.4273	3.2434	4.3219	5.7435	7.6123	10.0627
35	1.4166	1.9999	2.8139	3.9461	5.5160	7.6861	10.6766	14.7853
40	1.4889	2.2080	3.2620	4.8010	7.0400	10.2857	14.9745	21.7245
50	1.6446	2.6916	4.3839	7.1067	11.4674	18.4202	29.4570	46.9016

11-4

This table shows the future value (with compounding) of a single deposit of $1.

For example, find the future value of a single $100 deposit after 5 years at a 6 percent interest rate. Look along the "5 years" row to the number in the "6%" column. Multiply 1.3382 by $100. The $100 deposit would be worth $133.82.

Suppose you made a single deposit of $1,000 instead of $100. To find the future value after 5 years at 6 percent interest, multiply by $1,000. The $1,000 would grow by $338.20.

Rule of 72

If you do not have a future value table, you can use the **Rule of 72** to estimate the amount of time or interest it will take for your savings to double in value.

To calculate the number of years in which your savings will double, divide 72 by the rate of interest. For example, if you deposit $1,000 at a rate of 4 percent, divide 72 by 4. The result is 18. In 18 years your $1,000 will be worth approximately $2,000.

To find the annual interest rate needed to double your savings, divide 72 by the number of years. For example, if your savings was in an account for 20 years, divide 72 by 20. The result is 3.6. Your savings must be in an account paying 3.6 percent for it to double in 20 years.

Consider Inflation and Taxes

Due to inflation, a dollar buys less this year than it did last year. The inflation rate varies from quarter to quarter and year to year. An inflation calculator tells you how much buying power a sum of money will lose between two points in time. One such calculator is available on the Bureau of Labor Statistics Web site.

When planning for the future, keep in mind that inflation reduces the value of your savings. The goods and services you wish to buy with your savings next year will cost more money than they cost today. Try to find a savings plan that pays higher interest than the rate of inflation.

Taxes also erode savings. Taxes on the money you earn can take 25 percent or more of your income. You minimize taxes by putting money into tax-exempt or tax-deferred savings.

- **Tax exempt** refers to earnings that are free of certain taxes. Certain savings accounts for education expenses are tax exempt.

- **Tax deferred** refers to a type of savings in which taxes on principal and/or earnings are not due until the funds are withdrawn. Retirement savings accounts are a common example—taxes are deferred until withdrawals begin at retirement.

When you can reduce or defer taxes on the money you save, you accumulate more money over time. Many employers offer tax-exempt or tax-deferred savings plans. Retirement plans help employees by allowing them to shift some of their current income to the future.

You must pay taxes on the interest earned by your savings. After the end of the year, you should receive a 1099-INT form from each financial

Resource

Truth in Savings Act,
transparency master 11-2, TR

Discuss

How does the Truth in Savings
Act protect consumers?

Vocabulary

What is the *APY*? What is its
use?

Discuss

Which of these factors would
you consider most and least
important when shopping for a
savings account?

institution that holds your savings. It will state the total interest you earned that year. You need to report this amount when filing your taxes.

Savings Choices

You can choose from a variety of savings products and plans. Compare the options and decide which will bring you the highest earnings and most advantageous opportunities for your savings, 11-5. You may want to start your search online. Many financial institution Web sites outline the rates, terms, fees, and services available with different savings products.

The *Truth in Savings Act* requires financial institutions to provide clear information about the costs and terms of interest-earning accounts in uniform terms. The purpose of the Truth in Savings Act is to help you compare savings products and make informed decisions. The Act requires advertising and any materials describing savings products to include the

- minimum amount required to open the account

- interest rate

- annual percentage yield (APY) and the period during which that APY is in effect. The **annual percentage yield (APY)** is the rate of yearly earnings from an account, including compound interest.

- minimum deposit, time requirements, and other terms the saver must meet to earn the stated APY

- description of any fees, conditions, and penalties that could lower the yield

As you compare savings products and plans, it is important to make sure your money is safe. As explained in Chapter 8, the Federal Deposit Insurance Corporation (FDIC) insures deposits in many financial institutions up to a certain amount. The National Credit Union Administration (NCUA) insures deposits in most credit unions.

Choosing a Savings Product

To decide which form of saving is best for you, consider the following questions:
- How much can you save regularly each week or month?
- When and how often do you expect to deposit money?
- When and how often do you expect to withdraw savings?
- Are you willing and able to deposit $1,000 or more for 90 days or longer?
- Do you have a specific goal, such as an amount you want to save within a given time?
- Are you saving for a specific purpose or purchase?
- Is it important to be able to convert savings to cash quickly and conveniently?

11-5

You must look carefully to find the savings account that will make the most money for you.

Linking to... History

Federal Insurance on Deposits

In 1929, the U.S. stock market crashed, sending the country into what is known as the Great Depression. During the depression, many customers lost their savings and investments in failed financial institutions. Others went to their banks and withdrew all of their money in what is described as a "run on the bank." This caused more financial institutions to fail.

The Federal Deposit Insurance Corporation (FDIC) was created to prevent similar events from happening again. This agency is responsible for protecting consumer deposits and promoting confidence in the banking system. Banks contribute to an insurance fund administered by the FDIC. If a bank fails, the FDIC draws money from this fund to pay back all insured deposits. For more information about the history of the FDIC, visit www.fdic.gov.

Another important consideration is liquidity. *Liquidity* refers to the ease with which an asset can be converted into cash without losing value. You may want part of your savings to be "ready money" for emergencies or other needs. However, you often earn more interest on money you agree to leave on deposit for longer periods of time.

For top earnings on your savings, look for the

- *highest annual interest rate.* The higher the rate, the more interest your money will earn.

- *highest APY.* The higher the rate, the more your money will earn.

- *most frequent compounding of interest.* The more frequently interest is compounded, the more interest your savings will earn.

- *shortest interest periods.* Interest periods may be monthly, quarterly, semiannually, or annually. Generally, shorter interest periods offer more flexibility for depositing and withdrawing money without loss of interest.

- *fewest restrictions and penalties on the account.* These can affect both your earnings and your use of the account. For example, savings accounts may involve a minimum deposit or balance requirements.

- *lowest fees.* Even small fees can add up over time. A financial institution may charge a fee every time you write a check on an account, for example.

Make sure you find out when interest is credited to your account. If you withdraw savings just before interest is credited, you may not receive the full interest on your savings. To address this problem, some financial institutions offer a *grace period*. During this time, you can receive full earnings on deposits or withdrawals. The grace period often extends from five days before to five days after the crediting date. You may withdraw or deposit money during the grace period and still receive interest for the entire period.

Resource

Your Savings Program,
Activity C, WB

Enrich

Invite a representative from a financial institution to discuss and explain different types of savings accounts and methods of calculating interest.

Discuss

What are the advantages of opening a savings account?

Discuss

How does a money market account work?

Reflect

What experience have you or your family had with online-only savings accounts?

Savings Accounts

Regular savings accounts pay interest and allow you to make deposits and withdrawals. At credit unions, savings accounts are called share accounts. Savings accounts generally offer the lowest interest earnings of all savings options. They also have the most liquidity of savings options.

Two common types of savings accounts are passbook savings and statement savings. With passbook savings, you receive a book to record deposits and withdrawals. With the more popular statement savings, you receive regular statements of deposits, withdrawals, and balances. Savings accounts may include a debit card, an ATM card, or online banking.

Many financial institutions offer special purpose savings accounts. These accounts encourage consumers to set aside money in a separate account for specific purposes. In some cases interest on these accounts is tax free or tax-deferred, allowing savings to accumulate at a faster pace. Special savings accounts may be used to save for college tuition, vacations, or other goals.

Money Market Deposit Accounts

Money market deposit accounts pay higher interest rates than savings accounts. These accounts are liquid. However, money market accounts require higher minimum balances than savings accounts, usually from $100 to $2,500. They also offer limited check writing and money transfer privileges.

Online-Only Savings Accounts

Internet banks provide banking services online. Customers access the bank's Web site to make electronic deposits and withdrawals, transfer funds, or check account balances. Internet banks have minimal operating expenses because they do not maintain or staff physical banks or branch offices. Their lower overhead costs allow them to pay higher interest rates on savings accounts.

The higher yield is the primary advantage of online-only savings accounts. It is easy to compare Internet banks and the yields they offer online. Questions to consider when shopping for online banking include:

- How do rates and yields compare from bank to bank?

- How easily and quickly can you withdraw your money if you need it?

- How do you make deposits?

- Are accounts covered by the FDIC?

- Does the bank have reliable online security for your personal information?

- How prompt and thorough is the bank in answering your questions and concerns?

- Can you easily link your online account with your local bank to make transfers?

Case Study: Using Dollars and Sense

A New Way to Save

After he gets a summer job, Morton's mom convinces him to open a savings account at the bank she uses. The earnings are unimpressive. While surfing the Internet, Morton comes across ads for online high-yield savings accounts.

Morton learns these accounts pay higher interest than his savings are earning. Some also offer auto loans and home mortgages at relatively low rates.

Morton is a little nervous about committing his savings online. However, the Internet banks he investigates are covered by FDIC insurance. After some more checking, he opens an online-only savings account. The procedure is simple because he can transfer funds electronically from one bank to the other.

Case Review

1. What do you think of Morton's decision to move his savings into an online-only account?
2. Go online to investigate online-only savings accounts. Compare two or three accounts at different Internet banks and answer the following questions:
- What are some of the features of these accounts?
- How do online-only savings accounts differ from the accounts the local bank offers?
- What are some of the advantages and disadvantages of online-only savings accounts?
- How can you open an online-only savings account?

- What other banking services are available in addition to savings accounts?
- Do you feel comfortable and confident dealing with the banking institution?

There can also be some disadvantages to consider if you are interested in online-only savings accounts. For example, you cannot establish a personal banking relationship as with your local bank or credit union. Every

time you call with a question or problem you are likely to talk to a different person.

There also may be a lag time both for deposits and withdrawals to clear. This can be a problem in an emergency when you need cash immediately. Finally, you may run into technical difficulties with the bank's computer system or your own. In this case your account information and funds may be inaccessible until the problem is solved.

Certificates of Deposit

A **certificate of deposit (CD)** requires you to deposit a given amount of money for a set period of time or term. When the term is up, you can keep your money in the CD, deposit it in another CD, or take it out. A CD is sometimes called a *time deposit* or *time account*.

Certificates of deposit may offer a fixed annual rate of interest or a variable or floating interest rate. A variable rate moves up and down with market rates. Usually it is tied to a specific market rate, such as the rate on U.S. Treasury Bills.

Since CDs require you to commit your money for a period of time, they pay a higher rate of interest than money market and savings accounts. The longer you agree to hold a CD, the higher the rate of interest you can earn. For example, a six-year CD will yield a higher annual rate of interest than a two-year CD.

CDs are not liquid. In order to get the highest interest earnings, you must leave your money in the CD until the term is up. This term may be as little as one month or as much as seven years. If CDs are cashed before the time period is over, a significant amount of interest is lost. Also, there is a penalty for early withdrawal.

When shopping for a CD, make sure you ask these questions:

- What is the current APY?

- What is the maturity date?

- What is the dollar amount of earnings if you hold the certificate to maturity?

- What happens to the CD at maturity? Will your money earn interest at the regular savings account rate? Will it be automatically reinvested in another CD? Will the financial institution hold it with no interest until hearing from you? Will you receive notice of the maturity in advance? This gives you time to decide how to put the money to work again.

U.S. Savings Bonds

U.S. savings bonds offer another secure way to save your money. When you buy a **U.S. savings bond**, you are loaning the government money for a minimum of one year. On the specified date, the government repays the loan with interest. You are limited to a maximum purchase of $5,000 per year for each type of bond. The two types of U.S. savings bonds are the

I Savings Bond and the *EE Savings Bond*. They are issued in both paper and electronic form. U.S. savings bonds can be purchased at most financial institutions, online, and through employers' payroll deduction plans.

I Bonds are sold at face value in denominations ranging from $25 to $5,000. In other words, a $50 I Bond sells for $50. I Bonds pay a fixed interest rate plus a semiannual inflation add-on rate. The Secretary of Treasury determines the fixed interest rate. The interest rate in effect at the time of purchase applies for the life of an I Bond.

The inflation rate is based on the *Consumer Price Index*, a figure that represents prices consumers pay for goods and services. Every six months, the inflation rate on I Bonds changes. When interest rates are low and inflation is not a threat, the return on I Bonds is relatively low. However, they are good insurance against inflation.

EE Bonds are sold in denominations ranging from $25 to $5,000. Paper EE Bonds are also available in a $10,000 denomination. Electronic EE Bonds are sold for face value. Paper EE Bonds are sold for half of their face value. For example, a $50 bond is sold for $25.

EE Bonds earn a fixed interest rate. The rate is based on market yields of *Treasury Notes*, a type of government-backed investment, and other considerations related to savings bonds. New rates are announced every six months. When you buy an EE Bond, the current interest rate will apply for the life of the bond. Interest is compounded semi-annually.

You can redeem I and EE Bonds within 12 months, but you will lose three months interest if you do. There is no penalty for redemption after five years. You can defer federal income tax on interest earnings until you cash the bonds. Other tax benefits may apply if the bonds are used to finance education. To learn more about U.S. savings bonds, go to www.treasurydirect.gov.

Activity

Pick up information on series EE bonds at a local financial institution. Read and discuss what you learn.

Resource

Chapter 11—Savings, Teacher's PowerPoint Presentations CD

Chapter Summary

Steps to financial security begin with a savings plan. Saving provides money for emergencies and for purchases you may need to make in the relatively near future. Setting personal savings goals will help you decide where and how to save your money.

It is a great advantage to begin your savings program when you are young. The longer your savings accumulate the more they earn. Compound interest helps your savings grow more quickly.

Several types of savings products are available to get you started. Key features to look for when deciding when and where to save include the annual interest rate, the annual percentage yield (APY), the lowest fees, and the fewest restrictions on savings accounts.

In addition to savings accounts you may choose to save through special purpose accounts, money market accounts, CDs, or U.S. savings bonds. These types of savings are usually a part of an overall financial plan.

Review

1. What are three points to consider when setting goals for savings?

2. What does it mean to "pay yourself first?"

3. What determines the amount of interest you earn on your savings?

4. How do simple and compound interest differ?

5. An account earning 5.50 percent annual interest will earn the most if it is compounded a) quarterly, b) monthly, c) daily.

6. Explain the Rule of 72.

7. What are four factors to look for when comparing potential earnings on savings options?

8. Explain what the APY is and how it is used in reference to savings accounts.

9. What is an online-only savings account and why does it usually pay higher interest than regular accounts?

10. Name and describe the two types of U.S. savings bonds.

Critical Thinking

11. Outline your own short-, medium-, and long-term savings goals. Discuss how they are likely to change as you pass through the life cycle stages discussed in Chapter 6.

12. Study the following savings options and list the advantages and disadvantages of each:
    *   Regular savings accounts
    *   Money market deposit accounts
    *   Online-only savings accounts
    *   Certificates of deposit
    *   U.S. savings bonds

Answers to *Review*

1. Set goals that are realistic, specific and measurable, and time related.

2. You budget some money for savings before spending any.

3. the amount deposited; the interest rate; the length of time the money is in savings; the interest type; the frequency of compounding

4. Simple interest is computed only on the principal; compound interest is figured on the money deposited plus the interest.

5. C

13. Assume you have $1,000 you can save for one to three years. Compare savings options at three or more financial institutions. Determine which institution will pay the highest rate of interest for your money. Also find out how much you could expect to earn in one, two, and three years. In a short report, explain which savings option you would choose and why.

14. Research and compare different college savings plans. Develop a guide to use for establishing your own savings for college with your family.

Academic Connections

15. **Speech, writing.** Interview a representative at a financial institution near you to learn what types of savings accounts and services are offered. Pick up literature on different savings programs and determine which you would find most attractive if you had $200 to $500 to put in savings. Prepare a brief report for the class on your experience.

16. **Research.** Conduct an online survey of money market deposit accounts. Choose three or four of these accounts to discuss in class. Include the overall advantages and disadvantages of money market deposit accounts, the range of interest rates paid, and account services.

17. **Financial literacy, writing.** Develop a "saver's guide" covering places to save, types of savings accounts, safety and liquidity of saved funds, and questions to ask before committing your money to an account.

18. **History, math.** Interview your parents, an aunt or uncle, your grandparents, or other older adults to learn what they paid for common items when they were your age. Check out earlier prices for an ice cream cone, a movie, shoes, cars, TV sets, haircuts, etc. Calculate the percentage difference between earlier prices and today's costs. Discuss findings with the class.

MATH CHALLENGE

19. Use the Future Value Table, Figure 11-4, to find the amount of interest you would earn if you put $4,500 in a savings account for 35 years at an annual interest rate of 3 percent.

20. Calculate the number of years it would take to double a $10,000 deposit in a savings account earning 3 percent interest.

Tech $mart

21. Suppose you have three accounts with the details below at a bank in your community. Use the EDIE calculator at www.fdic.gov/edie/index.html to determine how much of the savings is insured by the FDIC.

    Checking Account: $5,000, Single—No beneficiaries, Non-interest bearing checking account

    Money Market Deposit Account: $45,000, Single—No beneficiaries, Interest-bearing account

    Certificate of Deposit: $150,000, Single—No beneficiaries, Interest-bearing account

6. To estimate the number of years it will take for savings to double in value, divide 72 by the interest rate. To estimate the annual interest rate needed to double savings, divide 72 by the number of years the money is saved.

7. (List four:) annual interest rate, APY, frequency of compounding, length of interest periods, restrictions and penalties, fees

8. The APY is the rate of yearly earnings from an account, including compound interest. Financial institutions must state the APY when describing earnings on savings. This allows consumers to compare accounts at various institutions.

9. It is an Internet account that allows electronic deposits and withdrawals and transfer of funds. Internet banks pay higher interest because they have low overhead and do not maintain and staff banks or branches.

10. (See "U.S. Savings Bonds" on pages 274–275.)

Answers to *Math Challenge*

19. $8,162.55 ($12,662.55 – $4,500)

20. Use the Rule of 72. 72 ÷ 3 percent = approx. 24 years

CHAPTER 12

Investing and Estate Planning

Reading for Meaning

Read the review questions at the end of the chapter before you read the chapter. Keep the questions in mind as you read to help identify key information.

appreciation

capital gain

stock

dividend

common stock

preferred stock

securities exchange

stockbroker

bond

mutual fund

net asset value (NAV)

money market fund

bull market

bear market

investment portfolio

diversification

prospectus

dollar-cost averaging

annuity

estate

executor

will

trustee

living will

trust

probate court

CHAPTER OBJECTIVES

After studying this chapter, you will be able to

- **explain** the role of investments in overall financial planning.
- **identify** the various types of investment choices.
- **read** and understand market quotations.
- **explain** the role of real estate in an investment plan.
- **describe** factors to consider when choosing investments.
- **identify** retirement investment options.
- **explore** the basics of estate planning including wills and trusts.

Central Ideas

- Investments create wealth that meets long-term financial goals.
- Investing offers the opportunity to earn relatively high returns but it is not without risk.

Resource

The House that Financial Planning Built, color lesson slide, TR

Reflect

What has been your family's experience with making investments?

Reflect

How would you describe your future investment goals?

Discuss

How might a person's place in the life cycle influence investment decisions?

*I*nvesting is purchasing a financial product or valuable item with the goal of increasing wealth over time, in spite of possible loss. Investments generally offer greater returns or profit on your money than savings. However, they also present an element of risk.

As you read in Chapter 11, savings deposited at insured financial institutions are guaranteed against loss. Investments are not insured. When you invest, you risk losing some or all of your money. Careful investing for long-term financial goals reduces risk. Gains usually exceed losses over time.

Deciding to Invest

Understanding when to put money into savings and when to invest will help you make sound financial decisions. You are ready to invest when you meet all the following conditions:

- You pay your essential living expenses and have money left over.

- You do not have excessive debt.

- You are not paying finance charges, which may be higher than any earnings on an investment.

- You have adequate insurance protection.

- You have emergency savings of six to eight months of living expenses.

It is a good idea to set aside a given amount to invest every week or every month.

An investment plan is an important step to meeting long-term goals and achieving financial security. People invest for many reasons:

- *To increase wealth.* Many people invest with the intention of holding onto the investment and allowing its value to grow over time. Growth, or **appreciation**, refers to an increase in the value of an investment. Various types of investments grow at different rates.

- *To earn a steady income.* Some types of investments disperse earnings on a regular basis through checks sent to investors. Other types of investments offer continuous interest payments to investors. Owners of rental property, for example, can earn income from rents collected from tenants.

- *To beat inflation.* Inflation reduces the value of money and the return on investments. Due to inflation, a dollar will buy less next year than it did this year. To beat inflation, the rate of return needs to be higher than the rate of inflation.

- *To take advantage of tax benefits.* Some investments are tax exempt or tax deferred, such as certain retirement accounts. Also, capital losses can be deducted when calculating taxes. A *capital loss* occurs when an investor loses money because the selling price of an investment is less than the purchase price. **Capital gain** is income earned

Case Study: Making Plans

Money from the Keyboard

Cotelia is an outstanding pianist. She studies on scholarship at a local music center and attends a music camp in the summers. She wants to take lessons with the best music teachers to reach her potential as a serious pianist. She hopes to play with symphony orchestras around the world some day.

To fulfill her dreams, she will need a lot of money. However, her family is not wealthy. Cotelia plans to earn and save as much as possible. In her free time, she earns money by performing at parties and other events. In the past year, she earned about $1,800.

Cotelia thinks she can earn even more money by performing with several musician friends. They want to form a musical group and perform at concerts, dances, and parties. They believe they can earn a lot over the next few years.

Case Review

1. How would you advise Cotelia to save and invest her earnings over the next five years?
2. What might she be inclined to do with her money if she did not have these objectives—or if her family could afford to pay for her future study?
3. How do objectives like Cotelia's influence earning efforts, and savings and investment decisions?
4. What are some ways young people with other interests and talents can earn and invest for future goals?

when the selling price is greater than the purchase price. The government taxes capital gains.

Tax reduction strategies vary greatly from investor to investor and from year to year as tax laws change. Certain investments are especially important for those in high tax brackets. It pays to look for a competent tax accountant, lawyer, or financial planner for advice in this area.

- *To preserve wealth in unstable economic times.* Both investments and cash can lose value quickly during times of inflation or political and economic instability. Choosing a variety of investments helps protect your investments during periods of economic uncertainty.

Consider your reasons for investing when developing an investment plan. For example, if earning income is important to you, look for investments that pay steady earnings and show high yields. If growth is more important, invest in companies that put earnings back into research, development, and expansion.

Selecting investments to meet your goals and objectives requires careful study. Investments are characterized by these four factors:

- *Degree of volatility* refers to quick and unexpected changes in value or price. The change can be either positive or negative. Volatile investments can present greater uncertainty as to risk and to return.

- *Potential rate of return* is the expected earnings on an investment for a given period of time. It is often expressed as a percentage. Look for investments that show a history of growth.

- *Level of risk* is the degree to which an investment may deviate from its expected return. Low-risk investments generally offer lower profits but more security. High-risk investments offer the possibility of big gains, but also big losses. Most investments fall somewhere between these extremes.

- *Liquidity* is the ease with which you can convert an investment to cash without serious loss. High-liquidity investments are actively traded on the stock market. Less liquid investments, such as antiques, coins, gold, and real estate, are more difficult to sell.

Your investment goals and objectives will change over time depending on your earning power and your stage in the life cycle. *Risk tolerance* is the amount of uncertainty you can handle. It is connected to your level of comfort with the possibility of loss. Each person needs to determine his or her own emotional and financial risk tolerance and choose investments accordingly.

For short-term goals, use the savings instruments discussed in Chapter 11. The advantage of investing for a long-term goal is having many years before you will need your money. This allows you to keep money invested during the ups and downs of the economy and to achieve gains over time.

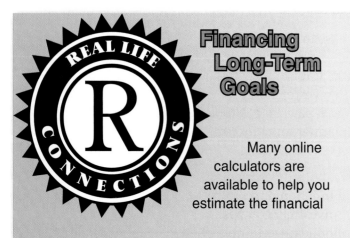

Financing Long-Term Goals

Many online calculators are available to help you estimate the financial investment needed to reach long-term goals. Here are some examples:

- College education:
  http://apps.collegeboard.com/fincalc/college_cost.jsp
- Retirement: www.calcxml.com/do/ret02
- New business start-up:
  www.homebiztools.com/startup.htm

Check out these sites and try the calculations.

Types of Investments

A *security* is a type of investment issued by a corporation, government, or other organization. The most popular investments—stocks, bonds, and mutual funds—are securities. Real estate and valuable goods can also be investments. Valuable goods include rare, pricey items, such as gold, gems, and antiques.

Stocks

A **stock** is a share in the ownership of a corporation. Stockholders have *equity* in the company and share in the profits after debts, taxes, and operating expenses are paid. Corporations sell stock to pay the costs of business start-ups, continuing operations, and expansion.

Stockholders make money in several ways:

- *Dividend income.* A **dividend** is a portion of a company's earnings paid to stockholders. Dividends are distributed when declared by the company's board of directors. Instead of paying dividends to investors, some companies put profits back into the company in the hope of increasing its growth and stock value.

- *Increased stock value.* Investors purchase stock when they believe it will appreciate or rise in value. Then they can either sell it at a profit now or hold onto it for further gains. Investors make money when they buy low and sell high.

- *Stock splits.* A corporation may decide to split its stock to create more shares. When this happens the price per share goes down initially, but shareholders receive more shares. This generally increases the demand for and the price of the stock. Investors who owned stock before the split profit because they own more shares, which are likely to increase in value.

Stock Classifications

The two basic types of stock are *common* and *preferred*. Companies may issue other classes of stock, each with its own contractual rights.

Owners of **common stock** earn dividends declared by the company. They can also vote in the election of company directors and on other matters presented at shareholder meetings.

Owners of **preferred stock** receive regular dividends at a set rate. In addition, they have first claim on assets in the event of a company failure. However, preferred stock owners do not have voting privileges.

Being a stockholder does not make you responsible for any of the company's debt if it goes out of business. The company's creditors cannot come after stockholders for payment.

However, if a company closes its doors, stockholders may lose their investment in the company, along with any profits. The first in line for payment from the company's assets are creditors. Next, preferred stockholders' claims are met. Only then are the claims of common stockholders met.

Example

Bring *The Wall Street Journal* to class to read and discuss the financial news.

Vocabulary

Distinguish between *common stock* and *preferred stock*.

Resource

Evaluating Stocks, Activity A, WB

Resource

Stock Activity, reproducible
master 12-1, TR

Vocabulary

Distinguish between *income
stock* and *growth stock*.

Discuss

Rate the types of stocks listed
from most to least risky.

Since it is paid first, preferred stock is a more conservative, safer invest-ment with less risk than common stock.

The price of common stock usually moves up and down more than preferred stock. However, preferred stock typically does not increase in value as much as common stock.

Besides the common or preferred labels, you may see stock described in one or more of the following ways:

- *Blue-chip stocks* are from large and historically successful compa-nies. They are more expensive, but considered safe investments with moderate returns.

- *Income stocks* are issued by companies that pay above-average divi-dends to investors. These stocks are for investors, such as retirees, who want a regular source of income.

- *Growth stocks* are from companies that put a premium on long-term growth. Most or all profits are put back into the company and often there are no dividends. Growth stocks are for investors who plan to buy and hold their stocks for long term gains.

- *Defensive stocks* are issued by companies whose sales are relatively stable across the ups and downs of the economy. These companies often sell necessities—food, health care, and utilities.

- *Cyclical stocks* are from companies whose sales are sensitive to eco-nomic ups and downs. The companies provide goods and services that consumers buy when economic conditions are good. Consumers spend less in these areas during economic downturns, 12-1.

12-1

Auto manufacturing companies have cyclical stock. In economic downturns, consumers buy less cars, manufacturing slows, and stock value declines. In prosperous times, car sales often increase, manufacturing picks up, and stock value rises.

- *Penny stocks* are issued by companies with questionable sales forecasts. They are inexpensive, but risky. However, if the company becomes successful, investors can get above-average returns. Penny stocks can cost as little as a few cents or as much as $10 per share.

Additional stock categories exist, each presenting different levels of risk and volatility. Choosing a combination of stocks with varying degrees of risk can reduce overall risk.

Stock Trading

Stocks are bought and sold in several ways. Most securities are bought and sold on securities exchanges or over-the-counter markets. It also is possible to buy through an initial public offering. Some companies also sell their stock directly to the public.

Securities Exchanges

A **securities exchange** is a formal market where securities are bought and sold by stockbrokers. A **stockbroker** is an agent who buys and sells securities for clients. Brokers are licensed by the National Association of Securities Dealers to trade securities. Usually stockbrokers charge a commission on both "buy" and "sell" transactions.

In a securities exchange, the buyers and sellers themselves do not meet. The issuers of the securities are not involved in these transactions and receive no money from them. A securities exchange is sometimes called a *stock market*. One of the major international exchanges is the New York Stock Exchange (NYSE) Euronext.

The *National Association of Securities Dealers Automated Quotations (NASDAQ)* is an American-based electronic network for trading securities. NASDAQ lists the securities of more than 3,000 companies worldwide. International securities exchanges make it easier and less expensive to invest in foreign companies.

Over-the-Counter (OTC) Markets

Stocks that are not listed on securities exchanges can be bought and sold at over-the-counter (OTC) markets. OTC markets are virtual markets where dealers and brokers conduct business through an electronic network of computers and telephones. Other types of securities are also traded on OTC markets. OTC markets lack many of the rules and regulations imposed on brokers in securities exchanges. Investors need to be especially alert when trading OTC stock because there can be a high level of risk involved. The largest OTC markets in the U.S. are NASDAQ's Over the Counter Bulletin Board (OTCBB) and PinkSheets.

Initial Public Offering (IPO)

An initial public offering is a company's first sale of stock to the public. Companies usually make an initial public offering to raise capital for expansion or to become publicly traded. The company works with one or more investment banks that help determine the type of stock to issue, the price, and the best time to make the offering. The banks charge a commission to sell the securities to investors. The money raised from the sale of IPO stock, minus the bankers' commission, goes to the company. IPO stocks can be risky investments because the company is often a young business without a long track record of success.

If investors want to resell their IPO stocks, they do it on a secondary market. A securities exchange is a secondary market.

Stock Quotations

You can follow the ups and downs of stocks by checking daily stock quotations. Stock quotations, or listings, appear in the financial section of *The Wall Street Journal* and other major newspapers, 12-2. Listings are also available on the Internet. To find a particular stock, you need to know the ticker symbol, or the abbreviation used for the company.

Stock quotes contain valuable financial information. The current yield (Yld%) and the price/earnings ratio (PE) help investors determine the health or weakness of a company and the value of its investments.

Stock Quote										
52 Weeks		Stock	Div	Yld%	PE	Vol 100s	Hi	Lo	Last	Chg
Hi	Lo									
19	13	Corp.X	0.50	3.00	28	19409	17.13	16.00	16.50	−0.25

52-Week Hi/Lo: Highest and lowest prices paid per share over the past year.

Stock: Company name or the stock's ticker symbol.

Div: Dividend paid per share of stock over past year. There will be no number if the stock does not pay dividends.

Yld%: Yield percentage or rate of return on one share of stock; calculated by dividing the annual dividend (Div) by the current price of the stock.

PE: Price/earnings ratio is the price of a share of stock divided by earnings per share for the last 12 months. Low-risk stocks usually have low PE ratios. Speculative and high-growth stock ratios are often much higher.

Vol 100s or **Sales 100s:** Previous day's volume, or total number of shares traded, quoted in hundreds. (For the above listing, sales totaled 1,940,900 shares.)

Hi: Highest price paid per share on previous day.

Lo: Lowest price paid per share on previous day.

Last or **Close:** Final price paid per share on previous day.

Chg: Compares the final price paid per share today with that paid the previous day. A positive number indicates a price increase; a negative number indicates a price decrease.

12-2

Stock quotations provide essential information for investing in securities and following those you own.

Bonds

A **bond** is a certificate of debt issued by a corporation or government. When you buy a bond, you are lending money to the issuer of the bond. Until the bond matures, you, the bondholder, are a creditor. The issuer owes you the amount of the loan plus interest on the bond's face value.

Information stated on a bond includes the following:

- *Maturity date* is the date a bond or other obligation is due to be paid.

- *Face value* is the amount for which a bond is issued and on which interest payments are figured. At maturity, the bondholder receives the face value.

- *Yield* is the percentage of a return on an investment.
  Other important terms relating to bonds include the following:

- *Coupon rate* is the annual interest the issuer promises to pay on the face value.

- *Market value* is the amount for which a bond sells. It may be more, less, or the same as the face value.

- *Current yield* is the annual interest or coupon rate divided by the market price of a bond.

Types of Bonds

The three major issuers of bonds are corporations, municipalities, and the federal government.

Corporate bonds are issued by businesses that need money to operate and expand. The quality, coupon rates, and yields of these bonds vary with the financial soundness of the issuing corporation. Yields and market prices move up and down as market interest rates change.

Most corporate bonds are bought and sold by brokers. Some bonds are bought and sold on securities exchanges and are listed in newspapers and online. High-grade corporate bonds are considered safer investments than stocks because they are debt instruments. If a company goes bankrupt, it must pay its debts first.

Municipal bonds are issued by state, county, and city governments. Coupon rates and yields depend on market rates and the financial soundness of the issuing municipality. Interest on these bonds is exempt from federal income tax and in some cases state and local taxes as well. This makes municipal bonds attractive to upper income investors in high tax brackets.

Most municipal bonds are bought and sold by brokers. Some municipalities may allow investors to purchase bonds directly from the local government. Corporate and municipal bond listings are in the financial section of major newspapers and online. Look for certain key information when reviewing bond quotations, 12-3.

Discuss

How do you explain the fall in bond prices when interest rates rise and the rise in bond prices when interest rates fall?

Discuss

What is one of the key advantages of buying municipals?

Vocabulary

Differentiate among *corporate*, *municipal*, and *federal government bonds*.

Reflect

What buildings and facilities in your area were financed by municipal bonds?

Enrich

Use the financial pages of a current newspaper to find the yield, coupon rate, market value, and current yield for a given bond.

Bond Quote

Issuer Name	Symbol	Coupon	Maturity	Rating	Close	Change	Yield %
Bank ABC	B. ABC	2.250%	Mar 20XX	Aaa	100.985	−0.073	1.861
Corp. Y	COR.Y	8.500%	May 20XX	A	106.695	2.375	7.520
Z Corp.	Z.CO	2.250%	Mar 20XX	Aaa	101.042	−0.041	1.839

Symbol: Abbreviated name of the issuing corporation.

Coupon: The annual interest paid on the bond. Coupon rates generally are higher on lower quality bonds to reward buyers for taking greater risks.

Maturity: The date the bond is due.

Rating: The quality/risk rating of the bond. As the risk increases, the ratings decline from the highest quality or safest rated, Aaa or AAA, to the lowest quality rated, C or D.

Close: The closing price of the bond at the end of the day. Prices are usually shown as a percentage of the face value.

Change: Compares the closing price with the price paid the previous day. Some quotes show the change in increments of 1⁄32.

Yield: The actual return on investment. Calculations are based on the coupon rate and the current market value of the bond.

12-3

Corporate bond quotations provide the information you need to track bond yields and prices in the marketplace.

Activity

Find Moody's and Standard and Poor's bond ratings in the library. What do you think accounts for different ratings?

Enrich

Find the bond quotations in the newspaper and explain the information provided.

Corporate and municipal bonds are rated for quality and risk. The first four rating categories—AAA, AA, A, and BBB—are recommended for conservative investors. The other four categories—BB, B, C, and D—are considered too risky for average investors.

U.S. government bonds are issued by the U.S. Treasury and are the safest bonds you can buy. When you buy one, you lend money to the federal government. Treasury bills, notes, and bonds sell in increments of $100.

- *Treasury bills (T-bills)* are short-term debts with maturities ranging from a few days to 52 weeks. They are the most actively traded government debt. Treasury bills sell for less than the face value. They do not pay interest before maturity. You pay less than $100 for a T-bill and receive the full $100 at maturity. The difference between the price you pay and the amount you receive at maturity is the interest.

- *Treasury notes and Treasury bonds* are sold at auction and carry a stated interest rate. Buyers receive semiannual interest payments. Treasury notes are short-term securities with maturities of two, three, five, seven, or 10 years. Bonds are long-term investments with maturities of 30 years. Both notes and bonds are sold in increments of $100. The actual price you will pay for these securities depends on the interest coupon and the yield at auction. These may be paper

ECONOMICS in ACTION

Credit Ratings Agencies

Credit ratings organizations evaluate debt securities, such as bonds, and rate them according to risk. Investors use the ratings to help guide investment choices.

The U.S. Securities and Exchange Commission designates certain agencies as Nationally Recognized Statistical Ratings Organizations (NRSOs). To be considered an NRSO, the agency must reveal its method used to determine ratings. Some of the most well-known NRSOs are Standard and Poor's Ratings Services, Moody's Investor Services, and Fitch, Inc.

Critics question the objectiveness of ratings organizations. NRSOs have been accused of giving high ratings to risky securities to please issuers who pay for the rating services. When agencies receive payment from the corporations whose securities they are rating, critics cite a conflict of interest.

In the future, the SEC may establish stricter rules and regulations for NRSOs to prevent conflicts of interest.

certificates or entered into an electronic account. Today most are sold electronically.

- *U.S. savings bonds* were discussed in Chapter 11.

Mutual Funds

A **mutual fund** is created by pooling the money of many people and investing it in a collection of securities. Professional managers at investment firms select the securities that make up a mutual fund.

Inexperienced investors often start with mutual funds because of three key advantages:

- *Professional management.* Mutual funds are managed by professional investors who follow the markets carefully and are assisted by a team of researchers.

- *Diversification.* Mutual funds offer diversification in a single investment. As mentioned earlier, when you invest in several securities, you spread your risks.

- *Liquidity.* Mutual fund shares are easy to buy and sell.
  Mutual funds also have some drawbacks:

- *Management fees.* Mutual fund managers charge fees to pay for research, administration, sales, and other expenses. Usually the fees are near industry averages. However, some management fees are extremely high and cut into your earnings significantly. These costs must be paid even if the fund performs poorly.

Vocabulary

Explain the differences among *treasury bills*, *notes*, and *bonds*.

Reflect

What do you see as the advantages of investing through a mutual fund?

Vocabulary

Distinguish between an *open-end mutual fund* and a *closed-end fund*.

Discuss

What types of investment goals are different types of funds designed to meet?

Enrich

Investigate and report on buying and selling mutual funds.

- *Lack of control.* You give up control over the selection and timing of your investments. The fund managers make these decisions.

- *Minimum investment.* Many mutual funds require a minimum investment of $1,000 or more.

Types of Mutual Funds

The two basic types of mutual funds are closed-end or open-end. A *closed-end fund* offers a fixed number of shares. These shares are traded like stocks on securities exchanges and secondary markets. You buy and sell shares in these funds through investment brokers, not through an investment company.

The *open-end fund* has an unlimited number of shares. It sells and redeems shares at their net asset value. Current market value or **net asset value (NAV)** is the fund's assets minus its liabilities. The *value per share* is the NAV of the fund divided by the number of shares outstanding.

Most mutual funds are open-end funds. Open-end mutual funds may be load or no-load funds. *Load funds* charge a commission or "load" of up to eight percent of the amount you invest when you buy shares. The average commission is three to five percent. *No-load funds* do not charge fees when you buy shares. However, you may be charged fees when you sell or redeem your shares.

Several different types of mutual funds are available.

- *Income funds* buy conservative bonds and stocks that pay regular dividends. Their primary goal is to provide current income.

- *Balanced funds* invest in common stock, preferred stock, and bonds. Their goal is to provide a low-risk investment opportunity with moderate growth and dividend income.

- *Growth funds* invest in securities that are expected to increase in value. They emphasize growth over income, but involve more risk.

- *Specialized funds* invest in securities of certain industries or sectors, such as all technology or all health care companies. They may also invest in certain types of securities, such as all municipal bonds or common stock. Some concentrate on foreign securities.

Mutual funds are often divided into families. Each fund has its own name and investment objectives. Mutual fund quotations display the names of individual funds listed within each family group, 12-4.

A **money market fund** is a type of mutual fund that deals only in high interest, short-term investments, such as U. S. Treasury securities, certificates of deposit, and commercial paper. *Commercial paper* is a short-term note issued by a major corporation. The funds are managed and sold by investment companies, brokerage firms, and other financial institutions.

The interest earned, minus management fees for operating the fund, is passed along to the depositors. Interest rates on money market funds go up and down with money market rates.

Investing in money market funds has many advantages. These funds provide small savers with high yields when interest rates are high. They

Mutual Fund Quote				
Fund	**NAV**	**Chg**	**YTD %** **return**	**3-yr %** **chg**
Fund Company 123				
BalFundA	9.89	0.01	28.1	−4.7
SpecFundB	31.72	0.02	28.6	1.2

Fund: Name of the fund company that sells the funds, followed by the names of individual funds offered.

NAV: The dollar value of one share of the mutual fund.

Chg: Difference between the day's NAV and the previous day's NAV.

YTD (Year to Date) %: The percentage gain or loss since the first trading day of the year.

3-yr % chg: The fund's total gain or loss over the past three years, indicated as a percentage.

12-4

Mutual funds quotes appear in the financial pages of major newspapers and online.

can be liquidated at any time since they have no term or maturity date. No interest penalties apply for early withdrawals. They can be used as collateral for loans.

Money market funds have some disadvantages, too. The rate paid on money market funds changes daily. If money market rates drop, so does the rate of return. A minimum investment of $1,000 or more may be required. Unlike money market deposit accounts, the savings instrument discussed in Chapter 11, money market funds are not FDIC-insured.

Factors Affecting Returns

In a market economy, the laws of supply and demand determine the price of stocks and many other investments. *Supply* is the amount of a product or service producers are willing to provide. *Demand* is the quantity of a product or service consumers are willing to buy. Both supply and demand are closely connected to price.

Certain information can help predict investment returns, including economic indicators, current events and trends, and data about particular economic sectors, industries, and companies.

Business Cycle Fluctuations

When the economy is growing, most businesses and investors do well. However, when economic growth slows, many businesses and investors lose money as sales decline. Cyclical industries are more sensitive to the ups and downs of the business cycle. The performance of these companies is often tied to interest rates, fuel costs, and products that are not immediately essential to the consumer. The stock issued by companies within these industries is categorized as cyclical.

Activity

Outline the advantages and disadvantages of depositing money in money market funds.

Resource

Mutual Funds and Money Market Funds, Activity B, WB

Discuss

How do stocks, bonds, and mutual funds differ?

Being aware of the ups and downs of the economy can help investors make wise choices. The Chapters in Unit 1 discussed some economic indicators that help economists assess the health of the economy. These include the unemployment rate, GDP, consumer price index, and consumer confidence. These statistics are released by government economists and other groups on a regular basis.

Interest Rate Fluctuations

Fluctuations in interest rates affect the value of securities and other investments. Bonds and real estate are directly affected by interest rate ups and downs. For example, as interest rates rise, bond prices fall. This is because investors can receive higher returns by investing in bonds with the new higher rates. Conversely, as interest rates fall, bond prices rise. Real estate sales increase as interest rates fall and suffer when they rise. Business growth generally is more robust when interests rates are low and suffers when rates increase.

Stock Market Fluctuations

Bull and *bear* are terms used to describe the strength or weakness of the stock market. **Bull market** is an extended period of consumer confidence and optimism when stock prices rise. The sense of optimism often encourages the exploration of other investment opportunities, including real estate and valuable goods.

Bear market is an extended period of uncertainty and pessimism when stock prices fall. It occurs when investors feel insecure and uncertain about the economy. Fearing further drops in the value of their investments, they often sell them. However, this is often a buying opportunity because prices are low.

Product Innovation

Historically, investors who financed winning products in their infancy, such as the automobile, microwave oven, and cell phone, made handsome profits. Those who invested in products that did not succeed lost their money. Most investors fall somewhere between high profits and big losses.

Business failure is caused by many factors ranging from poor management to new competition and government regulations. Technological advancement can cause new companies and industries to spring up, while making outdated companies obsolete.

Government Actions

Actions by government can impact the value of an investment positively or negatively. Product recalls, new regulations, and increased taxes often have a negative impact on company stock. Trade barriers protecting companies from foreign competition often improve the outlook of stock in protected industries.

Exchange-Rate Risk

For investors who trade securities of companies in other countries, the currency exchange rate needs to be considered. It may be necessary to exchange dollars for another currency. Dividends and gains or losses may be presented in foreign currency. The ups and downs of the exchange rate, whether buying or selling, become a potential risk for the investor.

Real Estate

Buying *real estate* (land or buildings) is another way to invest for future profit. This type of investment usually requires enough money for a down payment plus a long-term loan.

For most people, buying a home is their first experience in real estate. When the real estate market is strong, owning your home can increase your net worth and protect against inflation. Property usually increases in value over time. Still, most financial experts advise thinking of a home first in terms of a place to live and second as an investment.

Buying land or buildings for investment purposes is not for amateurs. Before investing in real estate for profit, buyers need to know about property values and property management. They also need to learn about mortgages, down payments, taxes, titles, insurance, and the legal aspects of leases and property ownership. These considerations are described in Chapter 18.

REITs and Real Estate Mutual Funds

Purchasing stock in a *Real Estate Investment Trust (REIT)* is a way to invest in real estate without the complications and financial commitment of owning property. A REIT is a company that owns profit-earning real estate, such as apartments, shopping malls, office buildings, or hotels. Mortgage REITs specialize in buying and selling mortgage-backed securities.

The government requires that REITs distribute most of their profits to shareholders through dividends. Shares of many REITs are traded on securities exchanges.

Real estate mutual funds are another way to indirectly invest in real estate. Funds may include a mixture of securities from REITs, commercial developers, and other types of real estate companies.

Investing in REITs and real estate mutual funds requires less capital and offers more liquidity than purchasing property. Changes in interest rates, housing prices, and demand for housing can affect the rate of return. As with other securities, investors should research before investing and carefully review prospectuses and annual reports.

Valuable Goods

People have collected precious goods and objects for thousands of years and continue to do so today. These items can be attractive investments because their value is not eroded by inflation as paper money can be. Valuable goods include the following:

Real Estate Appraisers
Real estate appraisers estimate the value of land and buildings, ranging from residential homes to major shopping centers. They write detailed reports on their research observations and explain reasons for arriving at their estimates.

Discuss

What are some of the risks and benefits of investing in real estate?

Enrich

Interview a real estate broker in your area about property values and the prospects for real estate investments.

Activity

Make a list of professionals you may need help from when buying real estate. Outline the services each offers.

- *Collectibles* are objects purchased for the pleasure of ownership and because they are expected to increase in value. Common collectibles include rare coins, books, stamps, art, antiques, sports memorabilia, and vintage automobiles.

- *Precious metals* include gold, silver, platinum, and other metals. People buy them in the form of pieces of jewelry, coins, bars, or ingots from banks and dealers. An *ingot* is a bar of metal that is sized and shaped for easy transportation and storage.

- *Precious gemstones* include diamonds, emeralds, sapphires, and others. They are collected as stones or as pieces of jewelry.

Consider the risks before you choose these investments. They are less liquid than stocks, bonds, and mutual funds. Like real estate, valuable goods can be difficult to sell quickly. When collectors are ready or forced to sell these assets, they sometimes must accept less than what they originally paid. These valuable goods can also be hard to store and protect from damage and theft.

Judging the worth of valuable items is often difficult unless you have expert knowledge and considerable experience. Only then are you safe in purchasing these items from dealers and online auction sites. Before buying valuable goods for investments, consult a reputable professional with experience in estimating value. Ask for a formal appraisal before making a significant investment in collectibles.

Prices for precious metals, particularly gold, silver, platinum, and copper, are posted on business Web sites. Prices for these goods are often volatile.

Keep in mind there is no guaranteed return on investment in valuable goods. Putting money into a savings account generates interest. Over time, investing in securities usually pays off. Historically, real estate goes up in value. The rate of return on collectibles and precious metals and gems is less predictable.

Choosing Investments

An **investment portfolio** is a collection of securities and other assets a person owns. Successful investors diversify their portfolios. **Diversification** refers to spreading risk by putting money in a variety of investments. Building a diversified portfolio involves gathering information, considering strategies, and selecting investment methods.

Sources of Information

Check the following sources before choosing an investment. Consult a professional for advice on complex investments. Financial experts can help in areas where you do not feel confident and competent on your own, 12-5.

Financial Experts		
Job Title	**Description**	**Credentials**
Accountant	• Keep, audit, and inspect financial records of individuals and businesses • Prepare financial reports and tax returns	**CPA (Certified Public Accountant)** indicates an accountant is certified by the American Institute of Certified Public Accountants.
Financial Planner	• Assist consumers in forming a financial program • Give advice on insurance, savings, investments, taxes, retirement, and estate planning	**CFP (Certified Financial Planner)** indicates completion of training and certification administered by The Certified Financial Planner Board of Standards, Inc. **ChFC (Chartered Financial Consultant)** may be used by those who have completed additional education and training with the CFP Board. Financial planners are not required by law to be certified or licensed.
Investment Broker-Buyer	• Buy and sell securities and other investment products	Must be registered with the Securities and Exchange Commission (SEC) and the Financial Industry Regulatory Authority (FINRA).
Registered Representative	• Salespeople who work for broker-buyers, commonly known as brokers	Must be registered with FINRA and licensed by the appropriate state securities regulator.
Investment Adviser	• Provide information and advice on different types of securities	Advisors managing over $25 million in client accounts must be registered with the SEC. Advisors managing less must be registered with the state securities regulator.

For more information, visit www.finra.org/investors.

12-5

Consulting an experienced professional can help in managing financial and legal matters.

Online Resources

Today's technology allows you to use the Internet to view important investment information. In the recent past, this type of information was only available to brokerage firms and investment analysts. Investment-related Web sites provide useful information about individual securities and market movements. On company Web sites, look at investor information or press releases to evaluate the company's investment potential.

The U.S. Securities and Exchange Commission (SEC) is the government agency that regulates the securities industry. Its mission is to combat fraud as well as ensure the securities markets operate efficiently and fairly. All publicly traded companies are required to file financial statements and documents with the SEC. The SEC manages the EDGAR database and keeps it up-to-date as a guide for investors. Visit www.sec.gov to explore this database.

Enrich

Discuss when to engage the services of each expert listed in Figure 12-5.

Enrich

Research the Financial Industry Regulatory Authority (FINRA). Discuss the goals and objectives of the organization.

Activity

Visit the Web site of a company that issues stock. What information is available for investors?

Annual Reports

Most corporate Web sites offer access to annual and quarterly reports. These sources give a good picture of current and predicted market performance.

One piece of information in annual reports—earnings per share (EPS)—is especially important. When earnings per share increase from year to year it is an indication the company is doing well. *Earnings per share* is the total corporate earnings, after taxes, divided by the total number of shares.

Prospectuses

A **prospectus** is a legal document that gives a detailed description of a security. When an investor buys a security, the issuer must provide a prospectus. You may also get a copy mailed to you if you are considering buying a security. A prospectus can usually be found on a company's Web site or the SEC's EDGAR database.

A prospectus lists company officers, describes business history and operations, and outlines plans for the future. It also includes the following financial information:

- *Risks.* This section spells out the ways an investor can lose money by investing in the security.

- *Performance summary.* This indicates how the investment has performed and how its performance compares with that of similar investments. Past performance does not necessarily indicate future results.

- *Fees and expenses.* This section outlines any fees or commissions you must pay when buying, selling, or redeeming shares.

- *Management.* This section identifies the qualifications and experience of the directors and officers of the company or fund.

Market Quotations

Stock, bond, and mutual fund quotations, or listings, contain important financial information, including records of past and current performance. Market information on securities appears in the financial section of *The Wall Street Journal* and other major newspapers. For up-to-the-minute information, review listings on the Internet.

Investment Strategies

Smart investing is a balancing act. It requires balancing risks against returns, 12-6. Younger investors can usually take more risks than older investors. A young investor has many wage-earning years ahead. However, as people get closer to retirement, they need to choose more conservative investments to preserve principal and provide income.

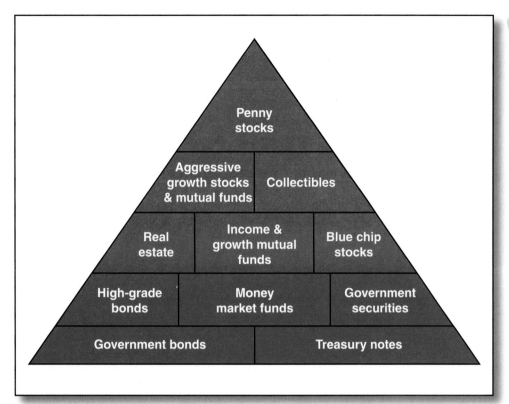

12-6
High-risk investments, at the top of the pyramid, have a greater chance of earning high returns. Low-risk investments, at the base of the pyramid, usually have low returns.

Investing at an early age allows you to benefit from two common investment strategies: *buy and hold* and *dollar-cost averaging*.

Buy and Hold

Buy and hold is the strategy of buying securities and holding them for long term gains as opposed to frequent trading. An investor using this strategy stays invested during market fluctuations. Investors who sell stocks when they drop in value lose money. Investors who hold onto stocks usually gain in the long run.

If your stock earns dividends, you will earn money over the years you own the stock. Also, if you hold a stock for a period of time, the company may split its stock, thus increasing your holdings.

Buy and hold does not mean buy and forget. You need to check your investments periodically to know how well they are performing. When an investment is not performing well it may be time to sell and reinvest in a more promising company. Consult an accountant or tax professional to evaluate the tax implications of selling.

Dollar-Cost Averaging

Dollar-cost averaging is a strategy of investing a fixed dollar amount at regular intervals, such as monthly, without regard to the price of the investment at the time you buy it. You end up buying more shares when the price is low and fewer when it is high. This buying strategy eliminates the risk of investing a lump sum when it may not be the best time to buy.

Discuss

What investment in Figure 12-6 is considered the highest risk? the lowest risk?

Vocabulary

Describe the buy and hold and dollar-cost averaging investment strategies.

Discuss

Discuss the importance of monitoring an investment's performance.

Linking to... Math

How Dollar-Cost Averaging Works

The following example illustrates dollar cost averaging. Investor A buys $1,000 worth of Stock X. At $25 a share, the chart shows that Investor A bought 40 shares. Using dollar-cost averaging, Investor B buys $250 worth of Stock X every month.

The stock's price drops over the next three months. By the fourth month, the 40 shares of Stock X purchased by Investor A would sell for $800—a loss of $200. However, after four months, Investor B owns 51.7 shares of stock. Investor B's shares would sell for $1,034—a gain of $34.

Month	Price/Share	Investor A		Investor B	
		Investment	# Shares	Investment	# Shares
1	$25	$1,000	40	$250	10
2	$20			$250	12.5
3	$15			$250	16.7
4	$20			$250	12.5
Total		$1,000	40	$1,000	51.7

Finance

Brokerage Clerks
Brokerage clerks compute and record data pertaining to securities transactions. They may also take customer calls, create order tickets, record a client's purchases and sales, and inform clients of changes to their accounts.

Dollar-cost averaging offers the added advantage of convenience. You can set up an automatic payment and make it a part of your overall budget. It helps you make a habit of investing amounts of money you can afford. You can invest as little as $25 monthly. Brokerage firms, mutual funds, and retirement accounts all offer opportunities for dollar-cost averaging.

Buying Securities

Once you have decided on a few specific securities you wish to buy, there are several ways to acquire them.

Brokerage Firms

To buy stocks, bonds, and other securities, you may open an account with a brokerage or securities firm. The main mission of a brokerage firm is to buy and sell for its customers. The fee you pay for these services is called a commission.

You make an application to open an account with a firm. Once your application is accepted, you call your broker with your orders to buy and sell. Most firms also offer online services.

Full-service brokerage firms maintain research departments to follow market trends and individual securities. In addition, they provide investment advice, portfolio management, and other services. The commission you pay covers the cost of trading and support services provided by the firm. Both experienced and beginning investors can benefit from the expertise of full-service brokerage firms.

Discount brokerage firms execute orders to buy and sell securities, but offer few other services. For instance, a discount brokerage does not offer investment advice. The commission is considerably lower than that of a full-service broker. However, you will need to do your own research and investment planning when you buy from a discount broker. Some experienced investors may prefer to use discount brokers to save money on commissions.

Online brokerage firms have hundreds of online brokers available to help consumers buy and sell securities. Use the following guidelines when investing through an online brokerage firm:

- *Check online brokers carefully before becoming involved.* Make sure the people you deal with are reputable and legitimate. You can check out brokers and securities firms with your state securities regulator or the nearest SEC office.

- *Print information on any investment you are considering.* You also may want to obtain other written material, such as a prospectus, an annual report, and recent company news. Study this information carefully. Before placing an order, know exactly what you are buying and what risks are involved.

- *Obtain and keep written confirmations of your buy-and-sell orders and their completion.* File all your investment records and information in a safe place where you can locate them easily. You will need these records to file your tax returns.

- *Follow your investments' performance.* Prices can rise and fall swiftly in active markets. When you invest directly online, no one will be supervising your account. This makes it essential to follow market trends and prices of securities you own. You want to buy and sell at the most advantageous times.

When you buy and sell securities online or by phone, you will need to use certain types of orders to conduct your trades.

- A *market order* instructs your broker to buy or sell a stock at the best price available. The price may be higher or lower than when you placed the order. Stock prices can change between the time you place an order and the time it is executed.

- A *limit order* instructs your broker to buy or sell a certain stock at a set price or better. If the broker cannot buy or sell at the price you request, the order will not be executed.

- A *stop order* instructs your broker to buy or sell a stock when and if it reaches a specific price. It will be carried out only when stock reaches the target price. This type of order helps you protect your gains and limit losses.

The brokerage firm keeps a record of your transactions. You should receive a statement outlining your account activity periodically, usually every month. You will also receive year-end statements and forms for filing income tax returns.

Activity

Research brokerage firms in your area. Are there any reputable firms potential investors could contact?

Activity

Search the Internet for discount brokerage firms. What services are offered?

Reflect

If you wanted to invest, would you consider online trading? Why or why not?

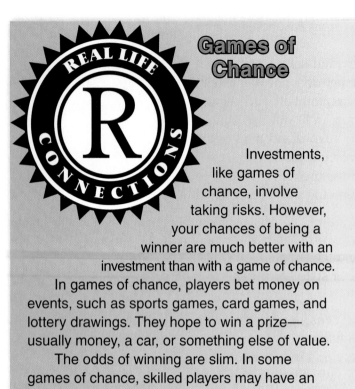

Games of Chance

Investments, like games of chance, involve taking risks. However, your chances of being a winner are much better with an investment than with a game of chance.

In games of chance, players bet money on events, such as sports games, card games, and lottery drawings. They hope to win a prize—usually money, a car, or something else of value.

The odds of winning are slim. In some games of chance, skilled players may have an edge. However, chance or luck is the only usual determinant of who wins and who loses. Of the many thousands of people who buy tickets for a state lottery, for example, sometimes there are no winners. Losers, however, always lose money.

Games of chance, especially gambling, are restricted by law. Those who invest in extremely risky investments are called speculators. Speculation refers to taking high risks in the hope of making big profits.

However, choosing to invest carefully is a wise financial decision. When you buy an investment, you get something in return—a home, a stock certificate, or a treasury bill. Sound investments held over time tend to increase in value. Profiting from an investment depends on the investor's financial knowledge and discipline, not merely on chance.

Enrich

Contact the National Association of Investors Corporation. Inquire about investment clubs in your area.

Discuss

Name the advantages and disadvantages of investing in DRIPs.

Investment Clubs

An *investment club* is a group of people who work together to learn about securities and to invest their pooled funds. Most investment clubs become legal partnerships for the purpose of filing income tax and meeting Internal Revenue Service requirements.

Members attend regular meetings (usually monthly), pay dues, and elect officers. The members decide by vote the amount of the dues each person will pay per month. Members research and follow stocks under consideration or in the club's portfolio. They also buy and sell securities by vote of the majority.

An investment club can be a good way to start investing. It offers the opportunity to invest on a small scale while learning. If you can find a few friends who are interested in learning to invest, you may want to consider forming an investment club.

The National Association of Investors Corporation provides information on starting and running a successful club. You also will find similar information from the Securities and Exchange Commission and Investment Club Central.

DRIPs

A Dividend Reinvestment Plan (DRIP) offers a way to bypass brokers and commissions and invest directly in a company. Dividends are automatically reinvested. Many companies offer DRIPs to the public.

To enroll in one of these plans, you need to become a stockholder by purchasing at least one share of stock in your own name. Once enrolled, most companies allow you to invest small amounts routinely. Some even offer a 3 to 5 percent discount from the current market price of the security. Automatic weekly or monthly stock purchases can often be made in amounts as little as $25.

When you wish to sell shares it may take a few days to complete the transaction. There may also be a fee for selling. You need to keep careful records of dividends, gains, and losses for income tax purposes.

Investing for Retirement

Retirement planning is a key element of financial security. Recent trends indicate more people are retiring earlier and living longer. Early retirees could need income for as long as 20 to 30 years. Providing income for this many years requires early planning, careful investment, periodic review, and proper adjustments to meet changing needs. Starting a retirement investment plan early is the most effective way to provide enough money on which to live after retiring.

You may be able to draw on a variety of income sources for later years. Social Security is a government program financed by joint contributions from workers and employers. While Social Security is not intended to be your sole source of income, it will be an important piece of your retirement picture. For more detailed information on what you can expect from Social Security, see Chapter 7.

The other income sources you may rely on include retirement programs offered by employers, personal retirement plans, and annuities.

Employer-Sponsored Retirement Plans

Some employers sponsor retirement programs for their employees. These programs vary greatly, but all must meet the standards set forth in the Employee Retirement Income Security Act (ERISA). This 1974 law sets standards for pension and retirement plans to guarantee that workers receive entitled benefits.

Vesting requirements are an important part of this act. *Vesting* gives you a legal right to an increasing portion of the money your employer reserves in your name. Vesting schedules are usually gradual. Typically, after seven to ten years, you will be fully vested. It is particularly important if you leave the company for another job or if you are laid off.

401k

A *401k* is a well-known employer sponsored retirement plan. The plan is funded with your own before-tax salary contributions and often with matched contributions from your employer. Employer contributions can take different forms, such as employee stock ownership, profit sharing, deferred-compensation plans, or cash.

Reflect

In what types of retirement accounts or programs does your family participate?

Resource

The Rewards of Saving Early, transparency master 12-2, TR

Vocabulary

Describe the importance of vesting in employer-sponsored retirement plans.

Vocabulary

Distinguish between *IRAs* and *SEPs*.

Discuss

Who is eligible for an IRA or a SEP?

Discuss

How does an annuity work and when is it a good choice?

Typical 401k plans offer several different investment options, including stocks, bonds, or money market funds. Diversifying investments will minimize risk. Financial experts usually recommend choosing more aggressive investments if you have many years before retirement. In later years, conservative investments should predominate.

Investing in 401k plans is one of the better ways to save for retirement, especially when employers match contributions. The great advantage of a 401k is the tax-deferred growth of your savings. Plans can vary greatly from employer to employer. They can also be affected by changing tax laws.

When job hunting, one important area to explore is the type of retirement plan(s) offered to employees. Having a job you love plus a reliable retirement plan is the ideal combination.

Personal Retirement Plans

You may also place part of your earnings in a personal retirement fund. You can start a personal retirement plan at most financial institutions.

When opening a personal retirement account, it is important to choose a sound, reputable financial institution. This institution should provide personal counselors and easy-to-understand guides that inform you of the many issues to consider. Money deposited in a personal retirement plan is usually invested in stocks, bonds, and mutual funds.

IRAs

An *Individual Retirement Account (IRA)* is a personal retirement investment account with tax benefits. There are many types of IRAs. Traditional and Roth are two common types. By contributing money to a traditional IRA, taxpayers avoid paying taxes on contributions and earnings until they withdraw the funds at retirement. Some IRA contributions can be deducted from current taxable income. Contributions to a Roth IRA are taxed, but withdrawals are usually tax free.

Self-Employed Plans

Self-employed individuals can open a Simplified Employee Pension (SEP) plan. Tax-deductible contributions are limited to a percentage of earned income. Earnings grow tax deferred until money is withdrawn at retirement.

A *Keogh plan*, also called an *H.R. 10*, is another type of personal retirement plan for the self-employed. Tax-deductible contributions are limited to a set percentage of earned income. The allowable percentage changes periodically. The interest earned on Keogh accounts is not taxed until retirement. Retirement may begin as early as 59½.

For the latest information and regulations on these personal retirement plans, visit the Internal Revenue Service Web site at www.irs.gov.

Annuities

An annuity is another form of personal retirement planning. An **annuity** is a contract with an insurance company that provides regular income for a set period of time, usually for life. Some annuities also provide death benefits. Investors make payments into an annuity over many years or in one large payment. Both the money invested and the interest it earns accumulates in the annuity.

The principal and earnings on an annuity are not taxed until money is either withdrawn or paid out at a future time. Annuities with reputable insurance companies are considered safe, reliable investments. However, investors should shop around and compare costs, fees, and interest rates.

Resource

Last Will and Testament,
Activity C, WB

Vocabulary

Describe what is meant by an
estate and *estate planning.*

Estate Planning

Estate planning is part of an overall financial plan. An **estate** refers to the assets and liabilities a person leaves when he or she dies. It includes property, savings, investments, and insurance benefits. *Estate planning* is the active management of these assets with directives for managing and distributing them when the owner dies.

Goals of an Estate Plan

An estate plan allows people to

- decide long before their death how they want their assets managed afterward.

- provide for their dependents.

- minimize tax liabilities.

- name an executor to oversee the management of their affairs upon their death. An **executor** is a person appointed to carry out the terms outlined in their will. If a person dies without naming an executor, the court will appoint one.

- assign a *power of attorney*, which is a legal document giving the person they choose the power to act for them regarding their financial and legal matters.

- prepare a will.

Wills

A **will** is a legal document stating a person's wishes for his or her estate after death. In most states, people must be at least 18 to make a will and must be "of sound mind." This means they must know what they are doing and be mentally competent.

A will guarantees disposal of an estate according to the wishes of the deceased person, 12-7. This makes settling an estate simpler for beneficiaries, usually family members. Friends may be listed as beneficiaries, as well as a favorite charity, a college, or some other organization.

What Wills Should Include

Generally, it is wise to ask a lawyer for advice on what to include in a will and to draw up the document. A will should do the following:

- *Name beneficiaries,* the people or groups who will receive assets. Assets include personal property and real estate, money, securities, jewelry, and family heirlooms. It should clearly outline a person's wishes for the transfer of his or her property.

- *Name an executor,* the person who will manage the affairs of the estate. He or she pays off funeral expenses, medical bills, taxes, and other liabilities. The executor also performs other duties outlined in the will.

- *Name a guardian,* the person responsible for the care of any beneficiaries who are young children. A guardian may also manage an estate on behalf of the dependents, or a trustee may be named to do this. A **trustee** is a person or institution named to manage assets on behalf of the beneficiaries.

A will must be signed in the presence of witnesses. If you change your will after it has been signed, an amendment called a *codicil* is added. The codicil must also be signed in the presence of witnesses. If you need to make major changes in an existing will, you may wish to write a new will. In this case it is important to add a clause that cancels all previous wills and codicils.

The cost of a will varies. The more complex the estate, the more expensive the will may be. You can write your own will. A do-it-yourself kit that contains basic information and sample formats may cost less than $20. However, this is unwise for large estates, situations with many tax issues, or when there are complicated instructions for distributing assets.

Since legal requirements for wills vary from state to state and may change with new laws, consulting an attorney is a wise choice. This is especially true for people who own their own businesses or have estates that total more than $1 million. Attorney fees vary and consumers can usually arrange a free consultation with a lawyer. Your local American Bar Association can refer you to an attorney who can help.

When people die without a will, it is called dying *intestate.* When there is no will, property is divided according to state laws. This is not ideal because it can take a lot of time and the government decides how to distribute assets.

The Living Will or Healthcare Proxy

The **living will,** or *healthcare directive,* is a statement of instructions for specific medical treatment if a person becomes unable to make medical decisions. The primary purpose is to make known what medical treatments you do or do not wish to receive in the face of terminal injury or illness. It outlines your desires about medically prolonging your life. This is a serious and very personal step to take. It needs to be discussed with family members, loved ones, and your physician.

Trusts

In addition to a will, you may need one or more trust agreements, particularly if your estate is complicated or if you wish to make special arrangements for its settlement. A **trust** is a legal document that gives a named trustee the authority to manage the assets in an estate on behalf of the beneficiaries.

When you create a trust, you become the *grantor*. As grantor, you transfer assets to the trust. You name a trustee to manage the assets according to terms outlined in the trust. You also name the beneficiaries who are to receive the assets.

You can establish either a living trust or a testamentary trust. A *living trust*, set up during your lifetime, can provide for the management of your assets before your death and for the distribution of assets as directed after your death. Prior to death you may serve as grantor, trustee, and beneficiary of the trust.

A *testamentary trust* is set up under the terms of your will and becomes effective when you die. Normally, drawing up a trust agreement calls for the services of a competent lawyer who is familiar with estate planning.

Purposes of Trusts

Trusts are used to achieve different goals. People can use a trust to

- provide income and asset management for beneficiaries
- set forth specific provisions for the support and education of minor children or dependents with disabilities
- have a plan in place for managing financial affairs if they should become incapacitated or unable to manage for themselves
- minimize estate and gift taxes
- protect their privacy and avoid probate court

Probate court is the government institution that processes a deceased individual's will and estate. The probate procedure requires

- proof the will is valid
- an inventory and identification of the deceased person's assets and property
- property appraisals
- settlement of debts and taxes
- distribution of property according to terms of the will

Probate can be a costly and time-consuming process that involves paperwork, court appearances, and lawyers. Probate fees are paid out of the estate before assets are distributed. The process can take several months, a year, or longer. The executor of the estate must manage the assets during this period. These proceedings are a matter of public record. You can establish a trust to avoid this lengthy and costly process.

Discuss

What financial circumstances call for a trust in addition to a will?

Vocabulary

Describe the *probate procedure*.

Resource

Chapter 12—Investing and Estate Planning, Teacher's PowerPoint Presentations CD

Case Study: Making Plans

Final Decisions

Kelly and Jerome owned a very successful office supply business. Over the years, they made enough money to buy a house, raise two children, travel, and retire in comfort.

Sadly, Jerome died just a few years after they retired. Not only had Kelly lost her husband, she also faced a sea of financial confusion. Neither Kelly nor Jerome could face the thought that one of them would die, so they had not planned accordingly.

Since there was no will, Jerome's estate was divided according to state law. Half of his property went to their children. The amount Kelly received did not allow her to live comfortably for long. She had no legal right to the money the children inherited. Since Kelly and Jerome also did no tax planning, Kelly had to pay taxes that could have been avoided.

Case Review

1. When does it become important to draw a will and look to estate planning?
2. Why is a will important even to those who do not have large amounts of money or property?
3. What are some estate planning steps that can ease financial burdens following the death of a loved one?
4. What are some consequences of dying without a will when one leaves young children behind?
5. What advice would you have given to Jerome and Kelly before they reached retirement age?

Chapter Summary

Investing money offers the opportunity to accumulate more money to meet future needs and goals. Investment choices include stocks, bonds, and mutual funds. Higher risk investments frequently offer the possibility of greater gains—and greater losses than less risky choices. No matter where you put your money, it is smart to investigate before you invest.

Real estate is another way to invest. It can bring handsome profits but also involves considerable risks. Investing in real estate is not for amateurs. You need to do your homework and seek the advice of reliable professionals.

Building an investment portfolio begins with defining objectives and gathering information. Choosing where to invest is an important step. Finally, consulting a reputable financial advisor can help you make sound decisions.

Early planning for retirement is the key to living comfortably in the later years. Today, people are living longer and retiring sooner, which makes early retirement planning even more important.

Estate planning is a part of financial planning that requires careful consideration. This includes drawing up a will and possibly a trust to direct the distribution of assets upon one's death.

Review

1. Define *investing*.

2. List three reasons people choose to invest.

3. What are the key characteristics to consider when choosing an investment?

4. Where are stocks bought and sold?

5. What information on a stock quotation helps investors determine the value of the investment?

6. What is the main difference between a bond and a stock?

7. What are the three main types of bonds?

8. Why do mutual funds offer more diversity than buying individual stocks and bonds?

9. Name and describe one factor affecting investment returns.

10. Name and describe two ways to indirectly invest in real estate.

11. What is a prospectus and what should it tell you?

12. Explain the purpose of brokerage firms and describe three types.

13. Name two sources of retirement income.

14. What retirement plans are designed for self-employed persons?

15. Name the primary objectives of estate planning.

Critical Thinking

16. If you were going to invest in stocks, would you buy common or preferred stock? Which is more likely to increase in value? Which do you think is the better investment? What are the advantages and disadvantages of each?

17. Research and discuss the pros and cons of international securities exchanges.

18. Compare the three types of bonds. Which type of bond would you prefer to buy? Why?

19. What are the advantages and disadvantages of investing in a mutual fund?

20. What should you consider before buying shares in a mutual fund?

21. Name five reliable sources of information on stocks, bonds, and mutual funds.

22. Compare the advantages and disadvantages of buying and selling investments through brokerage firms, investment clubs, and DRIPs.

23. Describe employer sponsored and personal retirement plans, their characteristics, and their tax advantages.

24. Describe the possible consequences of dying without a valid will.

25. If you were to write a will today, what would it contain? How might it change if you were 30 years old, single, and earning $60,000 annually? if you were 30, earning the same amount, and married? with children?

Answers to *Review*

1. Purchasing a financial product or valuable item with the goal of increasing wealth over time, in spite of possible loss.

2. (See page 282.)

3. volatility, rate of return, level of risk, liquidity

4. at securities exchanges; at over-the-counter markets; through an initial public offering

5. The current yield and price/earnings ratio.

6. A bond is a certificate of debt issued by a corporation or government. A stock is a share in ownership of a corporation.

7. corporate, municipal, U.S. government

8. A mutual fund is a collection of several securities bundled into a single investment.

9. (See "Factors Affecting Returns" on pages 291–293.)

10. (See page 293.)

11. (See page 296.)

12. (See pages 298–299.)

13. (Name two:) Social Security, employer-sponsored retirement plans, personal retirement plans

14. Simplified Employee Pension (SEP) plan, Keogh plan

Academic Connections

26. **Financial literacy, writing.** Choose two mutual funds. Review their prospectuses. Write a paper comparing their objectives and historical rates of return.

27. **Financial literacy, math.** Assume you have $2,500 to invest in any way you choose. Establish goals and objectives for your investments. Interview a stockbroker or an investment adviser for information on the types of securities and investment strategies available. Choose the securities you would buy and locate the quotes in a financial newspaper or online. Develop a system for charting their ups and downs in the market. Explain your choices in terms of your objectives and follow your "investments" for at least two months. At the end of that period, evaluate your choices in terms of performance and meeting your investment goals.

28. **Financial literacy.** Form a team of classmates and develop a plan for investing $5,000 over the length of this course. Use the Internet, current financial publications, and books on financial planning for information on developing your plan. Factors to identify and consider include your objectives, types of investments, expected returns, risk tolerance, liquidity, and diversification. Describe your plan in terms of these factors. In the final week of class, compare your team's plans with those of other teams in the class.

29. **Research, speech/writing.** Go online to investigate one of the following topics. Give an oral or written report on what you learn.
    - Stocks
    - Mutual funds
    - Government bonds
    - Security exchanges—NYSE Euronext and NASDAQ
    - Investment clubs

30. **Research, speech.** Interview an officer in a financial institution about retirement accounts. Find out what types of accounts are available. Discuss the advantages of opening a retirement account when you are in your early twenties. Report your findings to the class.

31. **Social studies.** Investigate the laws in your state regarding persons dying without a will. Report on the laws related to distribution of assets, naming of an executor, naming of a guardian, taxation of assets, and other specifics stated in the law.

32. **Research, writing.** Write a three-page report on retirement planning, the living will, or wills and trusts in estate planning. Use at least five reliable sources of information.

MATH CHALLENGE

33. How many shares of stock would you own at the end of one year if you invested $1,000 each quarter at the following stock prices? Use dollar-cost averaging and round your answer.

First quarter	$20/share
Second quarter	$25/share
Third quarter	$30/share
Fourth quarter	$35/share

Tech $mart

34. Look up a publicly traded stock on www.nasdaq.com or www.nyse.com. Record the daily closing value for two weeks. Compare the value on day one with the value on day 14. How did the stock perform?

Answer to *Math Challenge*

33. In the first quarter, 50 shares are purchased; in the second, 40; in the third, 33 (rounded); in the fourth, 29 (rounded). The total number of shares purchased is 152.

15. Decide how to divide assets; provide for dependents; minimize tax liabilities; name an executor; assign a power of attorney; draw a will.

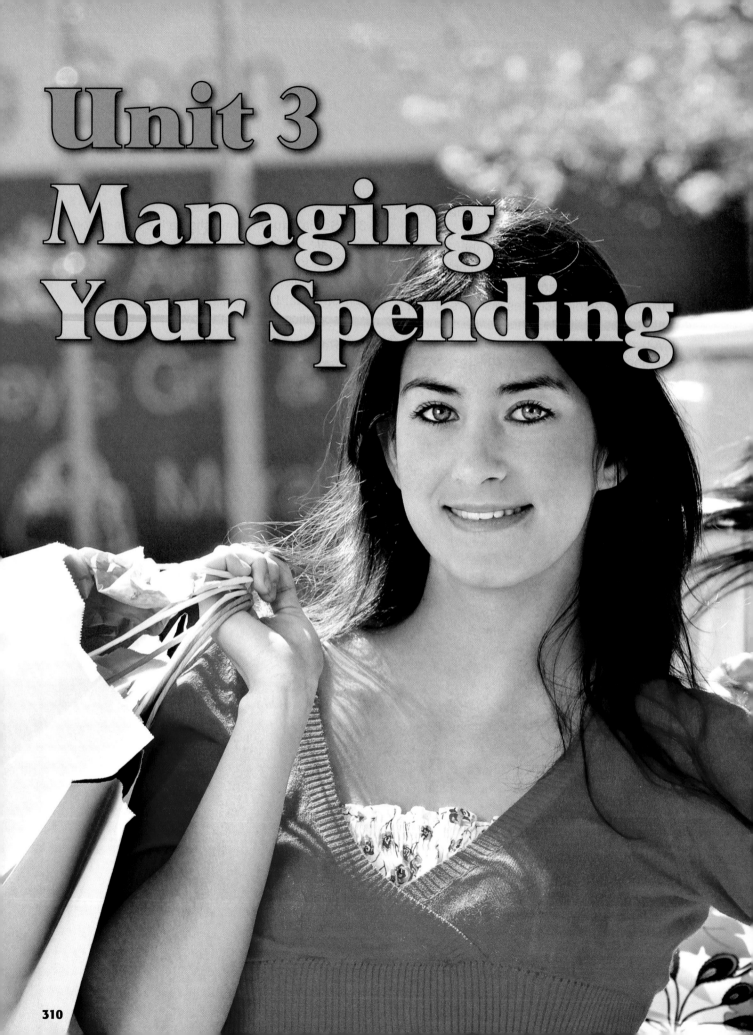

Unit 3
Managing Your Spending

In This Unit

As a consumer, you make decisions every day related to routine spending for food, clothing, health, and personal needs. Most consumers also face some big spending decisions involving the choices of transportation, housing, and products and services for their homes. You want your money to go far in the marketplace. This involves knowing your rights and fulfilling your responsibilities as a consumer. Acquiring smart shopping skills—knowing where to shop and how to find information about products and services, for example—will help you make wise decisions.

CHAPTER

13

Smart Shopping Basics

Reading for Meaning

What are some of your most and least successful shopping experiences? What did you learn from these experiences? Keep this in mind as you read this chapter.

retail store

nonstore seller

telemarketing

t-commerce

e-commerce

consumer
  cooperative

advertising

comparison
  shopping

warranty

full warranty

limited warranty

implied
  merchantability

implied fitness

extended warranty

work order

CHAPTER OBJECTIVES

After studying this chapter, you will be able to

- **evaluate** various types of sellers in the marketplace.
- **identify** reliable sources of consumer information.
- **describe** shopping tools for consumers.
- **list** guidelines for making rational shopping decisions.

Central Ideas

- To save money and build wealth, you must spend less than you earn. Being a smart shopper helps you accomplish that.

- Shopping choices are almost endless. Weighing the choices carefully involves rational decision making.

Smart shopping can make $50 seem like $100. If you develop shopping skills, you can buy far more than an unskilled buyer who spends the same amount of money. As a smart shopper, you will get greater satisfaction for your dollars. Your shopping experiences will be rewarding rather than frustrating.

Shopping smart is largely a matter of understanding the marketplace, knowing what you want, using reliable information, and making sound decisions. There are countless places to shop and items to buy. Choosing from so many alternatives can be a challenge. Knowing what you want and seeking out reliable consumer information can help you make the right buying decisions.

Places to Shop

The marketplace is where buyers and sellers meet to exchange goods, services, and money. In a free enterprise economy, the marketplace has certain characteristics that set it apart from markets in other economies. It is characterized by free economic choice, the profit motive, and competition. Within the framework of these three characteristics, the forces of supply and demand create a vast arena of sellers and buyers.

The marketplace is made up of many sellers and places to shop. You can shop at neighborhood stores, shopping centers, downtown shopping areas, and even in your own living room. Each place you shop has different characteristics and offers different advantages and disadvantages.

Linking to... History

Shopping and the Economy

Except for a few brief periods, the late twentieth and early twenty-first centuries were prosperous times for most Americans. Unemployment and inflation were low. Climbing stock market levels created wealth for most investors. Homeowners benefited from rising property values. Taxes were low.

During the prosperous times, Americans spent more than they saved. Consumer spending was high and people used credit to buy more goods and services. In 2008, the U.S. economy went into recession. Businesses suffered and laid off workers. Unemployment climbed.

Consumers stopped spending and focused on paying off debt and saving money. People delayed major purchases with hopes of better times ahead. Although saving is a good financial strategy for individuals, strong consumer spending is crucial to the health of the U.S. economy in a recession. It makes up about 70 percent of the gross national product.

American consumers contributed to a global economic boom. During the recession, imports slowed. Other countries cut production and their workforces. Hotels and restaurants around the world struggled without American tourists. When Americans stopped shopping, the impact was felt thousands of miles away.

Neighborhood Stores

Neighborhood stores may offer convenience and personal service, but selection often is limited by a store's size and space. Prices may be higher because of the small sales volume and the high cost of operating a small business.

The small stores in your immediate area are a good choice when you are in a hurry or you want personal service. You may also feel some sense of loyalty to these stores because you know the owners and sales staff. In addition, they depend heavily on your business. Often they will go out of their way to take care of your needs.

Shopping Centers

Shopping centers range from small strip malls with eight or ten stores to huge malls with several major department stores and a variety of specialty shops. Advantages of these centers include a broad selection of goods and services selling at competitive prices.

In the larger malls, it is possible to shop for a wide variety of goods and services at one time and often under one roof. Many malls offer special attractions and promotions to bring in more customers. Easy parking is a plus at most shopping centers.

Downtown Shopping Areas

Downtown shopping areas in bigger cities offer some of the same advantages of shopping centers. However, stores are usually more spread out and it is not as easy to go from one to another. In most major cities, parking is a challenge and an expense, but public transportation is usually readily available.

Leading department stores are a big draw for city shoppers. Cultural and sporting events, hospitals, clinics, and professional offices and services are often located in the area. This makes it possible to combine shopping with other activities. For those who work in the city, it may be one of the more convenient places to shop.

At-Home Shopping

At-home shopping can be done through door-to-door sellers, catalogs, telephone, television, and the Internet. In many ways, shopping at home is the most convenient way to buy what you need if you make careful choices and avoid returns and exchanges.

The technology of the Internet and television brings worldwide markets into your living room. These technologies let you shop and compare products 24 hours a day, seven days a week—whenever it is convenient for you. You can buy through online auctions and catalogs from both local companies and from sellers in distant places. This type of shopping saves the time, energy, and fuel required to go to stores and malls.

Reflect

Are there neighborhood stores where you frequently shop? What do you like about these stores?

Reflect

Do you live near a downtown shopping area? What draws you to a downtown area to shop?

Discuss

What are the advantages and disadvantages of at-home shopping?

However, you do not "see" the seller and you cannot physically inspect the merchandise prior to purchase. When you buy from a distance, it is important to be familiar with the seller and the products sold. Remember to add shipping and handling costs to the price of your purchases. Returns and exchanges usually are at the buyer's expense. You will learn more tips for shopping from a distance in the next chapter.

Types of Sellers

The marketplace is made up of sellers who do business in different ways. It includes different types of retail stores and a variety of nonstore sellers such as door-to-door sales, catalogs, telemarketers, electronic sales via television and the Internet, and consumer cooperatives.

Retail Stores

Retail stores sell goods and services directly at their place of business. Retailers include department stores, specialty shops, superstores, warehouse clubs, discount stores, factory outlets, and resale shops. Stores may be independently owned and centered in one region, or they may be chain stores located across the country. Many of these retailers also operate active catalog and Internet businesses.

Department Stores

Department stores sell a wide variety of goods and services in a single store. Merchandise is divided into departments that seem like small shops within the larger store. Sections include clothing for men, women, and children. Cosmetics, linens, home decor, shoes, jewelry, and housewares are some of the other departments. These stores offer the convenience of one-stop shopping plus a variety of customer services.

Specialty Stores

Specialty stores sell a specific type of merchandise or services such as shoes, toys, health foods, books, or gifts. Barbershops and beauty salons also are examples. Generally, the salespersons in these stores are well informed about products and services, 13-1.

13-1
A specialty shop selling bicycles may offer services such as custom bike fittings and free tune-ups.

Superstores and Warehouse Clubs

Superstores and *warehouse clubs* offer advantages to consumers, but they threaten local neighborhood stores that cannot compete with their pricing or large volume of merchandise. These stores are often in shopping

Case Study: Shopping Solutions

The Purpose Guides the Choice

Tony is captain of his high school tennis team. He hopes to go to college on a tennis scholarship. Tony's tennis racket cracked so he needs to replace it. Selecting a new racket is an important purchase for him.

Tony knows exactly what features he wants. He needs a racket with the right grip, weight, balance, flexibility, and durability. He shops carefully.

After looking in several stores, Tony buys a top-of-the-line racket from a specialty store. The tennis pro at the store checks the grip for Tony and strings the racket with just the right tension. The racket is expensive, but Tony pays for the best because he needs it for his level of the game.

Catina wants to play tennis because some of her friends play. She doesn't know if she will like the game or how much she will play. She doesn't want to spend a lot of money.

Catina goes to a sporting goods superstore. She asks to see an inexpensive racket that will be good enough for learning the game. She buys a medium-quality racket for a reasonable price. The racket works very well for her.

Case Review

1. How do you think price is related to quality and features in a product?
2. What quality and price factors might influence your choice of
   - a winter coat?
   - a computer?
   - a game system?
   - suntan lotion?
   - a musical instrument?
   - a car?
3. What types of sellers would you go to for each of the items listed above?
4. What are some consequences of failing to consider how you will use a product when you make a buying choice?

malls or on the outskirts of town. Some superstores specialize in specific products such as electronics, sporting goods, foods, or building and office products. Others sell a wide variety of merchandise similar to the department stores.

Discuss

What types of products do you shop for in discount stores?

Reflect

Do you shop at factory outlets? What do you like about this type of store?

Resource

Rating the Sellers, Activity A, WB

The warehouse clubs sell memberships to customers who want buying privileges. They usually offer a wide variety of merchandise at relatively low prices. Their offerings may include prescription drugs, auto services, travel packages, and more.

Discount Stores

Discount stores sell certain lines of merchandise at lower prices than other stores. They can afford to do this because they buy in large quantities and often limit customer services such as deliveries, credit, and returns. Most discount stores are self-serve operations with few salespeople. They may offer real bargains on some items, but it pays to compare prices because they do not always offer the best buys.

Factory Outlets

Factory outlets are owned by merchandise manufacturers or distributors. They sell directly to consumers rather than through wholesalers or other retailers. Very often, a variety of factory outlets will be located in an outlet mall, usually in an outlying area. Merchandise featured at outlets may include overstocks and items that did not sell in other stores. Factory outlet prices are usually lower than prices for the same merchandise in other retail stores.

Resale Shops

Resale shops sell used merchandise at greatly reduced prices. Extras such as warranties, guarantees, exchanges, and credit privileges are rare, but prices are likely to be exceptionally low. It is important to inspect used merchandise carefully to be sure items are in good condition. Clothing, household items, and furniture are among the items typically sold in resale shops. There are several types:

- *Resale shops* buy merchandise from individuals, sell it to customers, and keep the profit.

- *Thrift shops* usually sell donated merchandise. They are operated by churches, hospitals, or charitable organizations for the benefit of those they serve.

- *Consignment shops* accept merchandise to sell and pay the owners a percentage when the items are sold.

Nonstore Sellers

Direct marketers, also called **nonstore sellers**, sell goods and services in different ways and from different locations. They include door-to-door salespersons, catalogs, telemarketers, electronic sales via television or Internet, consumer cooperatives, and vending machines.

These methods of selling goods and services offer advantages, but it is important to check the reliability and legitimacy of the seller before buying. It can be difficult to locate a distant seller if there are problems after the sale.

Door-to-door Salespersons

Door-to-door salespersons are sellers who come to your door and offer the convenience of buying at home. It can be a plus to see certain products such as home furnishings or decorating items in the home before buying. It also can be an advantage when you are considering goods or services that need to be demonstrated or discussed before you decide to buy them.

Before opening your door to a seller, ask to see identification, a selling permit or license, and a company connection. If you buy, obtain a written copy of all details of the sale such as delivery dates, model numbers, price, warranties, and credit terms. Also obtain a contact name and number for after sale follow-up if there are any problems with the purchase.

Catalogs

Catalogs allow you to order goods and services featured on their pages. It is important to check the reliability of the seller before buying and to understand the policies on returns or exchanges. Also consider shipping costs, both for orders and possible returns. Add any costs involved to the purchase price to figure the final cost to you.

Telemarketing

Telemarketing is a form of selling that involves the seller phoning you to promote the purchase of goods or services. You can buy everything from toys to insurance to burial plots by telephone. Telemarketers may call you at inconvenient times with offers that do not interest you. Consumer protection laws require telemarketers to clearly state the company and caller name, the purpose of the call, and the type of goods or services being offered.

If you do not wish to receive calls from telemarketers you can place your phone number on the National Do Not Call Registry by calling 888-382-1222 or by going online at www.donotcall.gov. Telemarketers are not allowed to call registered numbers. In addition, they may not call before 8:00 a.m. or after 9:00 p.m. or misrepresent the goods and services they are selling.

T-Commerce

T-commerce refers to shopping on television. *Television shopping networks* are TV marketplaces. Sellers display and sell their goods and services on TV broadcasts around the clock. Most networks also offer featured items online along with a full Internet catalog of other items for sale.

Sellers market their merchandise on TV using commercials that include a number to call for more information or to purchase. Whether by network or commercial, you can see the product, order by phone, pay by credit card, and have the item delivered to your home.

Discuss

What types of goods and services are you likely to buy from a door-to-door salesperson?

Discuss

What are the pros and cons of buying products from a mail order catalog? What types of goods might you buy this way?

Examples

Have students offer examples of polite ways to handle unwanted telemarketing calls.

Interactive television or ITV lets you use your remote control to make purchases. If you see a TV commercial for a pizza or a piece of fitness equipment, you can buy it instantly by using your remote control to place your order.

E-Commerce

E-commerce refers to buying and selling goods and services online. You can access thousands of retail sites online to buy almost everything you can buy offline.

Offerings include books, clothing, food, furniture, vacation and business travel, automobiles, investments, cosmetics, and prescription drugs, 13-2.

Internet Auctions

Internet auctions are markets where sellers offer items for sale to the highest bidder. In some cases, the seller will set a "reserve price" that is the lowest acceptable price for the item. Each auction is announced and bidding closes at a preset time. The highest bidder for each item in the auction "wins." Items with reserve prices are sold if the highest bid exceeds that price.

In person-to-person Internet auctions, buyers and seller connect at the close by e-mail or telephone to arrange payment and delivery. In business-to-person auctions, the auction site controls payment and delivery arrangements. Before you buy or sell at an Internet auction site, order or download a copy of the Federal Trade Commission publication *Internet Auctions, A Guide for Buyers and Sellers.*

13-2

Busy consumers can use e-commerce to save time. Online grocery stores offer a wide selection and convenient home delivery.

Consumer Cooperatives

Consumer cooperatives are nonretail associations owned and operated by a group of members for their own benefit rather than for profit. Members contribute services and dues to participate in the association. Goods and services usually sell at lower prices than in retail stores. However, the selection of merchandise and customer services are limited to what the membership can provide.

Vending Machines

Vending machines started primarily as places to buy snacks and soft drinks. Today, a large variety of merchandise is available through vending machines, including food, cosmetics, clothing items, grooming supplies, and jewelry.

Vending machines offer the advantages of easy, fast purchases and often are available 24 hours, seven days a week. However, since the actual vendor or seller is not present, dissatisfaction with items purchased from a vending machine can be difficult to resolve.

Consumer Information Sources

There is no substitute for reliable information when you go shopping. As goods, services, and markets become more varied and complex, knowledge is ever more important. Common sources of consumer information on specific goods and services include other consumers, advertisements, labels and hangtags, product rating and testing organizations, salespeople, and the Internet. Knowing how to find, evaluate, and use available information can help you become a smarter shopper.

Other Consumers

Most people get information about products and services from friends, relatives, neighbors, and other people they know. When was the last time you bought something because a friend had it? Friends often provide information about everything from new trendy fashions and exciting movies to computer games and electronic products. Friends can provide valuable information about their experiences with a product, a service, or a seller.

Consumer reviews of products and services have become a prominent feature on the Internet. Many consumers rely on reviews to guide their buying decisions. Products and services frequently reviewed include hotels, restaurants, and autos. Bookseller sites often allow readers to post book reviews. Consumer reviews have expanded to include all types of services, including those of doctors and other professionals.

Reviews are available on company Web sites, independent rating service Web sites, and government or consumer advocacy Web sites. Many of these sites are free. Others charge a fee or require membership to access evaluations.

Enrich

Research the availability of consumer cooperatives in your area. What are the advantages and disadvantages of participating in a consumer cooperative?

Discuss

How would you relate the phrase "Knowledge is power" to shopping skills?

Activity

Select a product or service you want to buy and collect reliable information about it.

Emotional Triggers for Spending

For many people, shopping is a fun social pastime. For some it is an unwelcome necessity. For others, shopping is a way to cope with stress, sadness, or low self-esteem. Sometimes, shopping to meet emotional needs causes people to spend more than they can afford. Routine overspending leads to financial problems.

Sometimes people overspend because they seek approval from others. For example, you probably know someone who bought an overpriced pair of sneakers or jeans because everyone else was wearing them. *Peer pressure* is the power a social group has over someone who seeks the group's approval and acceptance.

Another type of pressure to buy is exerted by *role models*, or the people you admire and strive to imitate. A role model can be a parent or other relative, a teacher, a coach, or even a politician. It can be a celebrity, such as a famous athlete or model. Many fads start when famous people adopt them.

When people follow the spending decisions of others, they often make spending mistakes, especially the mistake of overspending. They also buy things they do not need.

Advertising messages often suggest that acquiring possessions brings success, happiness, and satisfaction. However, for most people, being involved and participating in meaningful activities offers a more reliable path to happiness and fulfillment. Hobbies, volunteer work, and sports can relieve stress, build self-esteem, and provide joy and contentment.

Copywriters

Copywriters work with artists to conceive, develop, and produce effective advertisements. They create the written message in print ads, posters, brochures, and Web pages as well as the scripts of radio and television spots.

Advertisements

Advertising is probably the most readily available source of information about goods, services, and sellers. **Advertising** is a paid message touting the attributes of something in order to convince consumers to buy it. Advertising comes in many formats including ads in magazines, commercials on television, pop-ups on the Internet, and billboard images. Most ads contain some useful information. You can usually count on advertising to

- introduce new products and services
- keep you up-to-date on existing products
- give changing price information
- tell where to find advertised items

To make the best use of ads and commercials, concentrate on the facts. Look and listen for specifics on brands, features, and prices. Keep in mind when looking for the "facts" that advertising is intended to promote and sell goods and services.

Labels and Hangtags

Information on labels and hangtags tells you about the content, quality, performance, care, and maintenance of various products. This information helps you select, use, and care for products. The law requires specific facts to appear on the labels of certain products.

The Federal Trade Commission requires that all clothing labels give clear and complete care instructions. Clothing and textile products must be labeled with fiber content, identification of the company name or manufacturer, and country of origin. When reading clothing labels and hangtags, you will find the brand name of the product. Also look for information about materials and quality work used in the product.

Food packages must carry a list of ingredients, the name and address of the manufacturer, quantity by weight, number of servings, and specific nutritional information. For food products, note the nutritive values, grade and quality levels, expiration dates, and storage instructions.

Drugs and cosmetics are labeled with ingredients, directions for use, and cautions against misuse. Laundry supplies, household cleaning agents, pesticides, and herbicides must be labeled with directions for safe use and disposal. They should contain cautions or warnings against hazards of misuse.

Look for age-of-user advice on toy labels, such as "suitable for ages 4 to 6" or "not recommended for children under three." New cars must be labeled with certain price and fuel economy information.

In addition, many manufacturers voluntarily provide useful information on labels, such as recipes and serving suggestions on food packages. Regardless of the product you are buying, its label can be an important source of practical, reliable information.

Activity

Bring to class five print advertisements and underline the facts in each.

Enrich

Write a page summarizing the value of advertising as a source of consumer information.

Reflect

What has been your experience with using labels for product information?

Enrich

Research legislation related to the labeling of different products. Find examples of labeling required by law.

Enrich

Collect and display labels from different types of products for study and discussion.

Testing and Rating Services

The testing and rating of consumer goods and services provides valuable guides for shopping. You can use testing and rating information to evaluate features and compare different models and brands of products and services. This helps you make purchase decisions that will best meet your needs. Two common forms of testing and rating results are seals of approval or certification and ratings in consumer publications.

Seals usually rate products as "certified," "approved," "tested," or "commended." The same organizations that test products issue seals for the products that meet their standards. A common seal is shown and explained in 13-3.

The Consumers Union publishes *Consumer Reports* magazine, which carries ratings of tested products and services. The magazine provides comparative buying information to help consumers shop wisely.

Before using testing and rating information, you need answers to the following questions:

- *Who sponsored or conducted the testing?* Consider the qualifications, interests, and intentions of the testing organization. For example, *Consumer Reports* does not get revenue from advertising sales. This allows it to be more unbiased in its reporting compared with groups that rely on advertisers. Can you expect the ratings to be honest and objective, or are they designed to help promote the product?

- *What features and performance standards were tested?* Be sure features and performance standards that are most important to you are included in the testing and rating.

13-3

This seal indicates that an appliance meets specific performance and safety standards.

The Seal	Where It Is Found	What It Means
(UL) Underwriters Laboratories, Inc.	On appliances, computer equipment, furnaces, heaters, fuses, smoke detectors, fire extinguishers, and thousands of other products.	Products passed initial tests and periodic factory evaluations, indicating they continue to meet UL standards for safety.

Resource

Rating Product Tests, Activity B, WB

Activity

Look for the UL seal on products your family owns.

Enrich

At the library, compare the types of information provided in *Consumer Reports* and *Consumers Research Magazine*.

Activity

Look up ratings on a product you want to buy. How helpful do you find the ratings and information provided?

Reflect

What seals of approval or product ratings have you relied on when shopping for consumer products?

- *Under what conditions were tests run, and what test methods were used?* Check to see if products were tested for the type of use you will give them. For example, suppose TV reception was tested under ideal laboratory conditions and you live where there is a lot of interference. The test results may not be your best guide.

- *What do the test results mean?* Read explanations of seals and ratings carefully to find out exactly what they mean.

- *When were products tested, and which models were included?* Products tested one year could improve or become less desirable the next year, particularly in product lines where research brings about frequent changes. If you use test results and ratings as a guide, be sure they include the actual models you are considering.

- *What factors are important to you that are not included in testing?* Consider price, availability, credit terms, delivery, installation, and reputation of the seller. None of these will be covered by product testing and rating services.

Salespersons

Knowledgeable salespeople can be one of your best sources of information on the products and services they sell. They should know how different brands and models compare and what features are most important. They should also know when new merchandise is expected, when sales are scheduled, and a host of other facts that can help you make sound buying decisions.

Of course, not all salespeople are well informed and helpful. Their job is to sell the merchandise as well as to please the customer. Some do a better job than others.

Be fair and considerate with salespeople, especially in stores where you shop regularly. You are likely to get better service and more reliable information. For example, a salesperson who likes you may tell you of an upcoming sale, call you when new merchandise arrives, or give you a straight answer when you need an opinion about a product.

The Internet

The Internet is one of the most complete, up-to-date sources of consumer information available. You can

- compare product prices, features, and availability
- check the reliability of sellers, order merchandise, and file complaints
- access both private and government agencies that protect your interests

Online brokers offer shopping search engines called "bots" that search the Web for the best values for different products. You select a category and then type in the name of the product to find comparative prices and features. The Internet mall offers a great many features and advantages to time-pressed shoppers.

Making Shopping Decisions

Every shopping decision has an opportunity cost. Since money is a limited resource, spending it now means giving up the opportunity to spend it later. Consumers who realize this and look at the costs and benefits of different spending alternatives come out ahead.

Smart shopping depends on rational decision making. To be a smart shopper, you need well-defined goals and a clear view of your resources. Review the section on rational decision making in Chapter 5. Apply this process to shopping for goods and services.

A spending plan based on sound decisions works to your advantage both for routine shopping and big purchases. Spending plans need to fit into an overall budget tailored to your specific income and needs. This type of planning gives you a framework for making decisions and can help you avoid impulse buying. A clear picture of your needs can also help you choose the best quality level for different purchases, 13-4. Finally, planning can help you stay within price ranges you can afford.

Best quality	Medium quality	Lower quality
Top of the line. Upper price range. The most and best features.	Medium price range. Standard features. Customary materials, design, and performance.	Lowest price range. Very few features. Adequate materials, design, and performance.
Buy when:	**Buy when:**	**Buy when:**
Top quality and performance are needed for frequent or extended use. You can afford the best and owning it is worth the cost.	Medium quality suits your purpose and is affordable. The best is not necessary for the amount of use it will get. Durability, practicality, and reasonable price are important. Extra features are not required.	Lower quality suits your purpose. The item will be used only occasionally or temporarily. The item will be outdated or outgrown soon. The item is necessary and it is all you can afford.

13-4
The way you will use a product and your budget will determine what quality level to buy for different products.

Case Study: Shopping Solutions

Planning Is the Key

Sheri and John want a long list of things for their new apartment. Each time they walk through a store, they see something to buy.

As a result, Sheri and John make foolish purchases and buy items they could postpone. Now they must do without some things they really need. For example, they have an electric knife but no toaster. They have many sofa pillows but a cheap lumpy mattress. They have mismatched furniture—Sheri bought a green flowered chair the same day John bought a blue plaid sofa.

Sheri and John see their mistakes when they evaluate their finances and their apartment. They decide to review their needs and set goals. They plan key purchases by deciding which items are most important. They also estimate the cost of each purchase. This plan is an overall guide to shopping and spending. Financial planning helps Sheri and John make sound shopping decisions.

Case Review

1. How can random spending create money problems?
2. How can well-established goals help people make better shopping decisions?
3. How might your goals for the next three to five years influence your shopping decisions?
4. It is easy to see the value of a spending plan for major purchases. How can an overall plan improve shopping skills for small purchases and routine spending?

Enrich

Develop a buyer's guide for consumers to follow when shopping for products.

You need a variety of shopping skills to carry you through the marketplace with confidence. Certain guides apply to shopping in general, while others apply specifically to buying products, buying services, or shopping at sales.

General Shopping Tips

Here are some general shopping guides to help you get value for your dollars.

- *Deal only with reliable businesses and business people.* Countless consumer problems arise each year as a result of trading with dishonest sellers and being "taken in" by shady selling schemes.

- *Compare products, services, and places to shop.* Check prices, quality, performance, and anything else that is important to you for a specific purchase. Find out about the sellers' operating policies concerning returns, exchanges, credit, and customer satisfaction. Check repair policies, especially for products that are very expensive to replace.

- *Consider the value of time and energy as well as money.* For example, suppose the price of a product is lower in a shopping center than in a neighborhood store. Getting to the shopping center would take more time, energy, and gasoline. When you weigh these disadvantages against the potential savings, is it worth it?

- *Do your homework before buying expensive goods and services.* If you are unfamiliar with a product or service, take time to learn more about it before you shop. Basic knowledge of prices, ratings, and recommended features can help you make informed decisions.

- *Report unfair or dishonest business practices to appropriate organizations and authorities.* Places to look for action or assistance are listed in 13-5. Consumer protection offices of local and state governments and the state attorney general's office can also help resolve customer-seller conflicts. In some cases, law enforcement agencies depend on the help of citizens to track down wrongdoers in the marketplace. By contacting the proper authorities, you can help put dishonest sellers out of business.

- *Handle money with care whether you shop with cash or credit.* Keep receipts and sales slips for possible returns or exchanges. When using credit, be sure to keep track of purchases and limit total charges to an amount you can pay on time with ease. When paying by mail, send a check or money order, never cash. This is safer and it gives you a record of the payment. Take care to keep track of both cash and credit cards as you shop.

- *Deal fairly and honestly with others in the marketplace.* Look to the guidelines in 13-6 as you come in contact with various businesses, salespeople, professionals, and other shoppers. You will get more respect and better service by being honest, courteous, and fair.

Reflect

When have you used any of these shopping tips? Did they work well for you?

Activity

Access at least three of the sources listed in 13-5 and describe the types of information and assistance each provides.

Enrich

Draft a letter to one of the organizations listed in Figure 13-5 to report an unfair or dishonest business practice. Discuss when such a letter might be needed and the types of information it should include.

Resource

What Goes into a Smart Purchase? color lesson slide, TR

Online Sources of Consumer Information and Assistance	
Center for Democracy and Technology	www.cdt.org
U.S. National Better Business Bureau	www.us.bbb.org
Federal Citizen Information Center	www.info.gov
Federal Trade Commission	www.ftc.gov
Food and Drug Administration	www.fda.gov
Internet Scam Busters	www.scambusters.org
National Do Not Call Registry	www.donotcall.gov
National Fraud Information Center	www.fraud.org
U.S. Postal Inspection Service	www.uspis.com

13-5

These agencies and organizations offer information and assistance with consumer problems and complaints.

Fairness Guide

With Salespeople	With Professionals
Show courtesy to salespeople and others who serve you in the marketplace.	Respect the expertise, training, and education a professional person offers. Understand that professionals are selling their time; do not waste it.
Wait your turn when stores are crowded and salespeople are busy.	Be on time for appointments or give plenty of notice if you must be late or cancel.
Avoid shopping just before closing time.	Pay promptly unless you have made credit arrangements.
Ask for salespeople who have been helpful in the past, and thank them for their help.	Call during office hours except when emergencies require off-hour calling.
Handle merchandise with care to avoid soiling or damaging it.	Remember, in most cases, you are in partnership with the professionals who serve you. Working together is the best way to achieve mutual goals.
Return merchandise to its proper place after you handle it.	
Inform salespeople if you come across damaged or broken products.	
Be as free with compliments for good service as you are with complaints for poor service.	
With Other Shoppers	**With Businesses**
Wait your turn when several shoppers want help at the same time.	Let merchants and manufacturers know what you like or dislike about their products, services, and policies.
Avoid pushing, shoving, raising your voice, and blocking aisles or doorways.	Make necessary returns and exchanges promptly, particularly when merchandise is seasonal.
Control children, pets, and shopping carts.	Be businesslike about handling problems and registering complaints.
Respect the needs and belongings of other shoppers.	Avoid damaging merchandise or making unfair returns, exchanges, or demands.

13-6

Fairness in the marketplace is a two-way street that both businesses and consumers travel.

Discuss

What steps do you take to be fair in the marketplace? Can you think of fairness pointers that are not in Figure 13-6?

Resource

Shopping Courtesy, Activity C, WB

Shopping for Goods

When you buy merchandise, inspect it first. Look products over carefully. Read labels, hangtags, seals, and manuals. Look for information about the price, quality, and performance features. Also consider any extra costs for delivery, installation, upkeep, and servicing of goods. Be sure to know exactly what you are buying and the quality you are getting.

For certain goods, it may pay to buy in quantity. For example, soap at three bars for $2.75 is a better buy than a dollar each. When buying in large quantities, make sure the merchandise will keep. Only buy what you can conveniently use and store.

As you shop for goods, remember the options available to you. Compare different stores as well as products to find the best values. You may be able to save a lot of money by *comparison shopping*. **Comparison shopping** is the process of gathering information about products and services to find the best quality or usefulness at the best price.

Knowing what features, performance requirements, quality, and price range you want gives direction to your shopping. It will also help you evaluate quality and performance.

Warranties

A written **warranty** guarantees that a product will meet certain performance and quality standards. The warranty provides for specific remedies if the product does not live up to stated promises. Warranties are included in the purchase price.

Warranties can guide consumers both in the purchase of products and in later needs for service and satisfaction. By law, consumers have the right to read product warranty promises before they buy.

The basic types of written warranties are *full* and *limited*. A **full warranty** must provide the following:

- free repair or replacement of defective products or parts

- repair or replacement within a reasonable time

- no unreasonable demands on the customer as a condition of receiving repairs or replacement

- replacement if a number of attempts at repair fails

- transfer of coverage to a new owner if the product changes hands during the warranty period

A **limited warranty** provides service, repairs, and replacements only under certain conditions. The customer may need to pay labor costs or handling charges. It may cover repairs only and not replacement. It may also require return of the product to the seller or authorized service center for warranty servicing.

Most warranties cover products for a stated period of time, such as 90 days or one year. Warranties do not protect against failure caused by customer misuse of a product.

In addition to the written warranty, most products carry unwritten implied warranties of merchantability and fitness. **Implied merchantability** means that a product is what it is called and does what its name implies. A computer printer must print documents; a heater must produce heat. The product must be in working order.

Implied fitness means that a product must be fit for any performance or purpose promised by the seller. If a salesperson or hangtag suggests roller skates for outdoor use, they must be fit for outdoor skating. Implied warranties apply to the condition of a product at the point of sale. They cover defects that are present but may not be obvious at the time of purchase.

You may need a proof of purchase to receive warranty service, so be sure to keep the sales receipt, warranty, and model number of the products you buy. To make the best use of a product warranty, read it carefully.

- How long does coverage last?

- Does it cover the entire product or only parts of the product?

- What performance and characteristics are guaranteed?

Vocabulary

Differentiate between *full warranty* and *limited warranty*.

Example

Bring product warranties to class to read and discuss.

Reflect

What has been your experience with product warranties?

Vocabulary

Explain *implied merchantability* and *fitness* and find examples of each.

Discuss

What are some steps warranties might require of consumers to obtain warranty coverage?

Enrich

Develop a guideline for consumers on evaluating and using warranties.

Discuss

What is an extended warranty and how does it differ from a regular warranty?

Reflect

When would you consider buying an extended warranty?

Discuss

How can you evaluate extended warranties and decide whether or not to pay for this extra protection?

- Is the labor to repair the product included?
- Who is responsible for carrying out warranty promises?
- What must the consumer do to receive warranty benefits?

Extended Warranties

When you buy major appliances, autos, or electronic products, you often are offered a *service contract* or **extended warranty** for an additional cost. The contract covers servicing for a product, if needed, during the term of the contract.

An extended warranty may offer more protection than you need and it can be expensive. It covers servicing and repairs that may be required after the warranty expires. In some cases the extended warranty duplicates protection that comes with the product. Before you buy this type of protection consider the following questions:

- What is the cost of an extended warranty or service contract? Must you pay a deductible?
- What is covered by the agreement and what must you do to obtain the services promised? Must you provide proof of periodic maintenance in order for the warranty to be honored?
- Does the extended warranty cover services already guaranteed in the original warranty?
- What would repair services cost without an extended warranty? What would it cost to simply replace the product if it fails? It may be cheaper to replace the product than to buy the extended warranty.
- Who and where do you call for service? If you have time, check them out with a consumer protection group, such as the Better Business Bureau.
- Can you buy the service contract at a later date or after the warranty expires?

If you want to buy this type of protection you may want to buy it directly from the manufacturer rather than the retailer or other third party. Compare the available sources of protection.

Used Merchandise

In some cases, you can meet your needs with used instead of new products. For example, an apartment can be furnished with used furniture for a small fraction of the price you would pay for new. Items people often buy secondhand include sports equipment, baby clothing, musical instruments, furniture, and autos.

Secondhand stores, auctions, army surplus stores, garage sales, and online and printed classified ads all offer opportunities for buying used items in good condition. Usually there are no guarantees on used products so it pays to examine goods with great care before buying. Be especially careful when buying items for infants and children. Make sure the item was not recalled by the manufacturer because of a safety hazard. Some items such as infant and child car seats should not be purchased used because they may have hidden damage from car accidents.

You can also look for giveaways, especially free furniture and other hard-to-move items. People who must move may be forced to give away possessions that could not be sold quickly. Others like the idea of recycling their belongings and keeping them out of landfills.

Shopping for Services

Buying services is different from buying goods. When you buy a product, you can see it, inspect it, try it on, or handle it. After using a product once, you can usually expect it to be the same each time you buy it.

When buying a service, you do not really know what you are getting until after you receive it. For the most part, you buy on faith. Therefore, it is important to check the reputation of any business or person who offers a service. Try to talk with former customers. Find out if they are satisfied with their service.

Most services require special knowledge or skills. Examples are dental and medical care, auto and household repairs, and legal and financial advice. When buying such services, carefully investigate the person's qualifications and the reputation of the business. Check out the person's education and training, experience, and membership in professional organizations. Choose only qualified professionals whom you can trust to do a good job, 13-7.

Know or find out who performs the service. Ask how long the service takes, how much it costs, and what the price includes. For expensive services, such as auto repairs and home improvements, get several written estimates from different sources. Compare estimates carefully, reading all the details. Look for reasonable price estimates along with assurance the job will be done right, on time, and with appropriate guarantees.

Also give a clear and complete description of the service you want. For example, when you get a haircut, describe the type of cut you want or bring a picture of the style. If you do not know what you want, ask for advice. Professionals who know their fields can give you valuable information.

Work Orders and Contracts

Work orders and contracts are common when buying services on your car or home or other work that is performed over a period of time. A **work order** requests service and describes the work that will be performed. For expensive or lengthy service jobs, a contract may be signed. A contract for services should include

- the name, address, phone number, and license number of the service provider

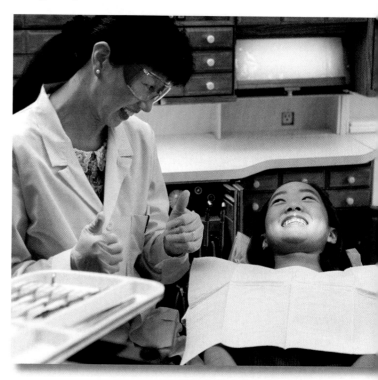

13-7

Search for a licensed and experienced provider with whom you feel comfortable for services such as medical and dental care.

- a description of the work to be done and materials to be used

- the starting and estimated completion dates

- the total cost and a schedule of payments

- a description of the grounds for terminating the contract by either party along with the consequences of termination

Ask to see a copy of the service provider's liability insurance certificate if it is applicable. If a building permit is required, ask the service provider to apply for it in his or her name. Be sure to thoroughly inspect the work before paying in full or signing a completion certificate.

Shopping at Sales

There are several guidelines to follow when shopping at sales events.

- ***Do not let price reductions tempt you to buy what you do not want or will not use.*** For example, a $90 jacket on sale for $35 is no bargain if it does not fit. A half-price banana split is no bargain if you are trying to lose weight.

- ***Look for possible flaws and see if they will affect your use of the product.*** Very often you cannot return or exchange sale items. If a product is marked "second," "irregular," or "as is," it may be flawed in some way.

- ***Figure the cleaning or repair costs if items are soiled or damaged.*** For example, suppose a $150 white coat is marked down to $110 but is soiled and needs dry cleaning. Add the cost of dry cleaning to the sale price before figuring your bargain.

- ***Find out store policies on sale items before you buy.*** Does the store allow returns or exchanges on sale items?

- ***Try to plan your purchases to match the timing of sales.*** Seasonal sales usually offer the best buys. Knowing when to expect price cuts on certain products and services can help you plan your purchases to get the best values for your dollars, 13-8. Check ads and store mailings to know what is on sale in your area.

The Right of Refusal

It pays to exercise the "right of refusal" when sellers offer items you do not need, do not want, or cannot afford. As long as the economic system guarantees free economic choice, no one can make you buy what you do not need or want. You always have the ultimate right of refusal. Use this right to protect your financial interests.

On a larger scale, consumers need the right of refusal to maintain control of demand in the marketplace. Consumers have the power to strengthen the demand for what they buy and to weaken the demand for what they refuse. Thus, the economic system, as well as your own financial welfare, depends on the intelligent use of the power of refusal.

Shopping Guide for Seasonal Sales

January	February	March
Watch for: Postholiday sales Preinventory sales January "white" sales *Best buys:* Winter clothing, coats, bedding, linens, furniture, floor coverings, toys, sports equipment, home appliances	*Watch for:* Lincoln's, Washington's and Presidents' Day sales Valentine's Day specials *Best buys:* China, silverware, glassware, rugs and floor coverings, TVs and sound equipment, sportswear and sports equipment, furniture and home furnishings, housewares, used cars, mattresses	*Watch for:* Spring promotionals *Best buys:* China, glassware, garden supplies, housewares, laundry appliances, spring clothing, infants' wear, shoes, skates, ski equipment, luggage

April	May	June
Watch for: Warm weather sales *Best buys:* Clothing, fabrics, lingerie, hosiery, ladies' shoes, home clean-up/fix-up supplies	*Watch for:* Mother's Day sales Memorial Day specials *Best buys:* Outdoor furniture, luggage, jewelry, auto tires and accessories, bedding, lingerie, clean-up/fix-up supplies, TVs	*Watch for:* Father's Day sales Bridal and graduation gift specials *Best buys:* Floor coverings, bedding, lingerie, hosiery, sleepwear, clothing, women's shoes

July	August	September
Watch for: 4th of July sales *Best buys:* Fabric, furniture, summer clothes, sportswear and equipment, computers, indoor and outdoor furniture, swim wear	*Watch for:* Summer clearances Back-to-school sales *Best buys:* Luggage, sports equipment, bedding, furniture, outdoor furniture and garden supplies, school supplies, air conditioners and humidifiers, lawn equipment	*Watch for:* Back-to-school specials *Best buys:* Outgoing year's car models, auto accessories, china, glassware, fall fashions, housewares, bikes, grills, consumer electronics, paint, shrubs and trees

October	November	December
Watch for: Columbus Day specials *Best buys:* Major appliances, furniture, women's coats, fall/winter sportswear, last of outgoing year's car models, bikes, school clothes, silverware	*Watch for:* Election, Veterans, and Thanksgiving Day specials *Best buys:* Shoes and boots, blankets, bedding, kitchen appliances, china, glasswear, holiday gifts, toys, new cars, computers	*Watch for:* Holiday gift and toy promotions Postholiday sales Storewide clearances *Best buys:* Cars, resort and cruise wear, men's and children's wear, coats, TVs

13-8

This shopping calendar can help you time purchases to get the best sale prices. Shopping skills are the keys to shopping smart.

Chapter Summary

Smart shopping is a skill almost anyone can develop. It involves knowing about different places to shop and different types of sellers. The marketplace offers consumers many opportunities to comparison shop and find the goods and services they want at the best prices.

Collecting, evaluating, and using information as it applies to different purchases is part of smart shopping. Smart shopping also calls for rational decision making and a personal spending plan. Specific suggestions apply to buying products and others apply to buying services. Shopping at sales calls for another set of techniques to get the best bargains.

Review

1. Name three common locations where you can buy goods and services.

2. Name five types of sellers.

3. What are some advantages and disadvantages of buying from a door-to-door salesperson?

4. Distinguish between t-commerce and e-commerce. What are some advantages and disadvantages of this type of shopping?

5. How do consumer cooperatives differ from retail stores and other nonstore sellers? What are the advantages and disadvantages of joining a consumer cooperative?

6. What can shoppers learn from the information on labels and hangtags?

7. Name three questions you should answer before using testing and rating information.

8. How can a spending plan help you make smart shopping decisions?

9. Name five tips for making rational shopping decisions.

10. Describe the major difference between buying products and buying services.

11. When you buy a product with a warranty, what information do you need to keep with the warranty?

12. List five questions consumers should ask before purchasing an extended warranty.

Critical Thinking

13. In what ways have technological developments changed the marketplace in the past 20 years?

14. What sources of information have you found most helpful when buying goods and services? Why were they helpful?

Answers to *Review*

1. (Name three:) neighborhood stores, shopping centers, downtown shopping areas, at home

2. (See pages 316–321.)

3. advantages—convenience, opportunity to see merchandise in the home where it will be used; disadvantages—you must be careful to check the credentials of these sellers; it may be hard to locate a disreputable salesperson if the merchandise is not delivered or if it is unsatisfactory

4. (See pages 319–320.)

5. Consumer cooperatives are formed, owned, and operated by a group of members for their mutual benefit. Advantage—generally lower prices than retail stores; disadvantage—limited selection of goods and services

6. the content, quality, performance, care, and maintenance features of the product

7. (See pages 323–324.)

8. It can help you avoid impulse buying, choose the best quality level for different purchases, and stay within your price range.

15. How do you decide what to buy? How do needs, prices, and quality affect your shopping decisions?

16. How can well-established needs and goals help you make sound decisions as you shop?

17. Describe your most successful shopping experience. Describe your most disappointing shopping experience. Why was one successful and the other disappointing?

Academic Connections

18. **Financial literacy.** List at least five products that you expect to buy in the near future. According to the shopping guide for seasonal sales, what month of the year would you most likely find the best price for each item?

19. **Financial literacy, research.** From your product list above, choose one that costs $200 or more. Make a list of the characteristics and features you want this product to have. Then check brand names and prices for this product at three or more stores and online. What differences do you find in quality and price from one brand to another and from one seller to the other?

20. **Writing.** Develop a list of guidelines to follow when shopping for products or services online and on television.

21. **Social studies.** Make a directory of government and private agencies that provide consumer protection and assistance with problems in the marketplace.

22. **Research.** Investigate service contracts and extended warranties on the Internet to answer the following questions.
    - When, if ever, does buying a service contract make sense?
    - What are the advantages and disadvantages of an extended warranty?
    - What do sellers and manufacturers have to gain from selling service contracts?
    - What should consumers know before buying a service contract or extended warranty?

MATH CHALLENGE

23. Store A has flip-flops on sale at two pairs for $5.50. Store B has them on sale for 25% off their normal price of $3.50 a pair. Store C gives you one free pair of flip-flops if you buy a pair at the regular price of $5.
    A. How much do the flip-flops cost per pair at each store?
    B. What store has flip-flops at the lowest price per pair?
    C. What is the worst deal?

Tech Smart

24. Use comparison shopping to find the best deal. Search the Internet for several sellers of three products or services you want to buy. Write down the name of each seller, the price charged, and any additional charges such as shipping and taxes. Identify the best deal.

9. (See pages 326–327.)

10. When buying a product, you can see what you are getting. When buying a service, you do not know exactly what you are getting until after you receive it.

11. proof of purchase, sales receipt, warranty, and model number

12. (See pages 329–330.)

Answer to *Math Challenge*

23. A. Store A—$2.75 each; Store B—$2.63 each; Store C—$2.50 each
    B. Store C
    C. Store A

Consumers in the Marketplace

Reading for Meaning

Has a salesperson ever tried to sell you something you didn't really want to buy? How did you manage the situation? What do you wish you had known at the time?

product placement

infomercial

direct mail advertising

buying incentive

loss leader

rebate

bait and switch

pyramid scheme

chain letter

sweepstakes

lottery

skill contest

identity theft

spam e-mails

phishing

caveat emptor

consumer advocate

binding arbitration

small claims court

class action lawsuit

lawsuits

CHAPTER OBJECTIVES

After studying this chapter, you will be able to

- **explain** how consumers can take advantage of various selling methods.
- **identify** different types of advertising and marketing techniques.
- **identify** reliable sources of consumer information and protection.
- **recognize** and guard against various forms of financial fraud.
- **write** an effective letter to resolve a consumer problem.
- **outline** steps to take in resolving consumer disputes.
- **describe** the rights and responsibilities of consumers.

Central Ideas

- Consumers need a set of basic skills to navigate the marketplace.

- Businesses use a variety of methods to sell products to consumers.

- Consumers need to know what options they have for protecting themselves against fraudulent practices.

- Consumers are guaranteed certain rights in the marketplace, but they also have responsibilities to know and exercise these rights.

Some consumers seem to know what they want. They find goods and services they need at prices they can afford. They manage their resources well and avoid costly mistakes. Others tend to make the wrong choices. They are often "taken in" by dishonest merchants. They sometimes take on too much debt. They never seem to be in control of their finances.

Most people probably fall somewhere in between the confident, competent consumer and the uncertain, inexperienced "victim." You can be either type. However, confidence and competence pay big dividends in the marketplace.

There is a basic set of skills you need to make the most of your consumer dollars. It starts with a clear understanding of the methods sellers rely on to make you want their goods and services. It also will be important to recognize and protect yourself against fraudulent practices in the marketplace. Now is the time to start mastering the art of consumer self-defense.

In addition, you need to learn where to find reliable information about products and services, consumer legislation, and economic conditions. Finally, it is important to know your consumer rights and responsibilities. The laws and government agencies that protect your rights were discussed in Chapter 2. Your specific rights along with the corresponding responsibilities are outlined later in this chapter.

Selling Methods

When you enter the marketplace to buy goods and services, remember that businesses are there to sell and make a profit. You enter to buy at the best price. The purpose of the market is to arrive at a transaction and price that is acceptable to both seller and buyer.

To increase sales and profits, businesses use a number of selling methods. Advertising, a trained sales staff, buying incentives, special sales, and available credit are all designed to encourage customers to buy. As a consumer, you can make these selling methods work for you as long as you know their main purpose is to sell goods and services, 14-1.

Advertising: Getting the Message to You

Advertising is any public announcement promoting a product or service for sale. Businesses advertise to sell goods, services, ideas, and images.

14-1

Smart consumers use selling methods such as advertising and sales to help them purchase items they need for lower costs.

They spend billions of dollars annually to put their messages before you. Every day you are exposed over and over again to advertising in its many forms. Advertisements appear in newspapers and magazines, on television and the radio, in Web sites and blogs, in direct mail, on clothing, and on billboards.

The goal of the advertiser is to send the message and increase sales. As sales of a product increase, the production costs per unit go down. In general, this is good for consumers because the product can be sold for a lower price. Advertising can also create the desire for unnecessary products and services.

Through advertising, sellers tell you about their products and services. Keep in mind that only positive information about a product or service is likely to appear in an ad. Although law prohibits false and misleading advertising, you still should expect some exaggerated claims. It pays to develop a healthy skepticism when it comes to analyzing advertisements.

Common Advertising Appeals

Sellers use many advertising techniques to convince you to buy their products. Many of them can be put into one or more of the following categories.

- *Insecurity appeal* taps into consumers' fears of being excluded, unpopular, or unappealing to the opposite sex. Examples include commercials for mouthwashes, teeth whiteners, deodorants, and diet aids. Ads for cosmetics and women's clothing may succeed by making girls and women wish to imitate models and appear more attractive.

- *Testimonials* show "real people" recommending a product or service. For instance, a woman may talk about the time she saves by using a particular cleaning product. The "real people" are usually actors and actresses.

- *Celebrity endorsements* use famous personalities to promote products. Examples include a golf pro endorsing a credit card company and a famous actress selling her own perfume.

- *Sex appeal* uses attractive models to grab consumers' attention. An example might be a beautiful woman draped over a car.

- *Bandwagon* techniques try to convince the public that a product is fashionable or trendy—everyone is buying it. An example might be an ad that shows groups of kids playing with a toy. Kids feel that everyone else has this toy and they should have it too.

- *Puffery* uses exaggerated claims about a product or service. These include ads that make statements such as "best in the U.S.," "life changing," and "even surpasses designer brands."

- *Nostalgia* is associating a product or service with the "good old days," childhood memories, or a time when life was simpler and more satisfying. For example, a commercial showing a family eating soup on a cold day hopes to link the soup to family love and togetherness.

- *Humor* involves using a funny character, picture, or situation to get your attention. These include a talking duck and a juggling banker.

- *Statistics* that are shocking or provocative also may be used in advertisements. For instance, "200,000 germs lurk in your toilet" may be part of a pitch for a toilet cleaner.

Product Planners
Product planners are responsible for the entire life cycle of a product. They are involved in the acquisition, distribution, internal allocation, delivery, and final disposal of a product.

Example
Find and display advertisements using each of the techniques described. Discuss the appeals in class.

Resource
Advertising Techniques, Activity A, WB

Resource
Selling Methods, Activity B, WB

Case Study: Winners and Losers

Advertised Specials

Coletta and Tyrell have been married for three months. Coletta does most of the food shopping. Before shopping, she flips through the newspaper. The food section tells her what foods are plentiful and gives her ideas for meals. The supermarket advertisements allow her to compare food prices. She saves money by buying advertised specials and by clipping coupons for items she plans to buy. Coletta is a winner.

Tyrell has a weight problem. One day Tyrell sees an ad titled "Eat your way slim and trim." The product is Weight Losers Chocolate. The ad says eating a chocolate bar before meals and in place of snacks will curb the appetite. Tyrell buys a large supply of the miracle candy.

However, the candy doesn't taste like candy, hot fudge sundaes, or anything else Tyrell likes. He eats the diet snack for a few days, but it doesn't satisfy his cravings. Soon the candy winds up in the trash can. Tyrell loses money, not pounds.

Case Review

1. How did advertising influence consumer demand for goods and services in Coletta's case? in Tyrell's case?
2. How did Coletta use advertising to her own advantage? How was Tyrell's approach different?
3. What makes an ad misleading, false, deceptive, or unfair? How can consumers protect themselves from this type of advertising? What does the government do? What can reputable businesses do?
4. What advertisements have you seen that would help you make a rational buying decision? What ads can you name that make false or misleading promises? What are some ways to tell the difference between the two?

Reflect

When have you been a victim in the marketplace?

- ***Green ads*** associate the use of a product or service with saving the planet, conserving resources, or some other environmental benefit. Key words may include *natural, organic, pure,* and *healthful.* This type of ad might include shampoo called *pure* and *natural* with the bottle pictured in front of a spectacular waterfall.

Advertising images often have little or nothing to do with the product being sold. For example, a beautiful woman has little to do with a soft drink. A scenic countryside has little to do with the automobile industry that produces cars. An athlete has little to do with a brand of clothing. These are illustrations of the *association principle* at work. By using an image that has positive associations—attractiveness, popularity, power, natural beauty—advertisers hope to link desirable traits to their products, 14-2.

Finding new ways to reach potential customers has presented challenges to advertisers. Bombarded by so many commercial messages, consumers have become cynical about advertising. It is harder for advertisers to get consumers' attention. **Product placement** is a means of showing a brand name product or its trademark in movies and television programs. This happens when you see an actor or actress driving a particular car or drinking a specific soft drink on-screen. Very often advertisers pay movie studios to put products in a scene.

Many of these techniques are not really harmful, but it pays to look more closely at the product, not the advertising appeals. For example, what does it mean when an advertiser says a product is *new and improved, better*

14-2
You may be tempted to buy athletic shoes endorsed by your favorite athlete, even if he or she does not use them professionally.

Advertising and Children

Children in the U.S. are bombarded by thousands of ads every day. These include ads on television, the Internet, magazines, and billboards. They appear as logos on cars, in sports venues, and on the T-shirts of their favorite celebrities.

Younger children are especially vulnerable to advertising messages. They have not developed the ability to distinguish between the truth and a sales pitch.

The advertising of certain products and services is blamed for many problems of children and adolescents. Ads for fast-food restaurants, sugar-filled sodas, and fatty foods are blamed for childhood obesity. Ads that use sex appeal are said to contribute to teen pregnancy and low self-esteem among girls. Concerns that tobacco advertising encouraged teen smoking led to laws that limited these ads.

Parents, consumer advocates, pediatricians, and other groups have severely criticized much of the advertising directed at minors. These groups call for laws to regulate both the content and volume of this advertising.

Many advertisers say their messages are not as powerful as critics suggest. They resist regulation, claiming they are self-regulated and they follow an industry code of ethics with regard to advertising to minors. They also point out that advertising is a form of free speech and guaranteed by the First Amendment.

What do you think of this controversy? Do you think advertising has that much influence on children and teens? Have advertisers ever gone too far? What role should parents take in guiding their children's response to advertising?

Activity

Find the words *free, one time offer,* and *valued at* in print advertisements. Bring the advertisements to class for discussion.

Enrich

Contact the nearest Better Business Bureau for a copy of the "Code of Advertising" booklet.

Reflect

When have you been influenced by advertising to buy something you did not want or need or could not afford?

than ever, a free trial, or *economy size*? Look beyond these vague descriptions when you make buying decisions.

Helpful Information

There is an art to reading an ad or hearing a commercial. Look for the following information:

- factual descriptions of the products or services offered for sale
- listing and demonstration of special product features and qualities
- statement of differences between advertised items and similar goods and services on the market
- details on prices, availability, places to buy, special offers, and terms of sale

Words that should alert you to possible deception are *free, one-time offer,* and *valued at*. When an offer sounds too good to be true, you can be almost sure that it is.

The Better Business Bureau publishes a "Code of Advertising." This booklet sets standards for advertising. Businesses that belong to the Better Business Bureau should follow this code. A copy of the booklet is available from your local bureau or online at www.us.bbb.org.

Infomercial

The **infomercial** is a form of paid television programming designed to sell a service, product, or idea. It is sometimes called a *direct response television advertisement (DRTV)* because the aim is to sell directly to the viewer via interactive television or by telephone.

Infomercials are usually program-length advertisements. The format often resembles actual television programming, and the products or services being promoted are demonstrated. Some common products you may see in an infomercial include cosmetics, exercise equipment, kitchenware, electronics, health care devices, and weight loss programs.

Frequently the advertisements will offer easy payments and risk-free trials. They also claim that availability is limited to encourage viewers to "buy now." Infomercials can offer valuable product information and demonstrations. However, consumer advocates recommend a thorough investigation of the infomercial sponsor, product or service, and advertising claims.

Sellers try to show their products and services in the best light possible. If you remember this, advertising can help you as well as the seller. You win when you look for useful information in ads. You lose when you let ads persuade you to buy what you do not want, do not need, or cannot afford.

Direct Mail Advertising

Direct mail advertising is another method sellers use to promote products and services. This is often called *junk mail*. It includes advertising circulars, catalogs, coupons, and other unsolicited offers that arrive

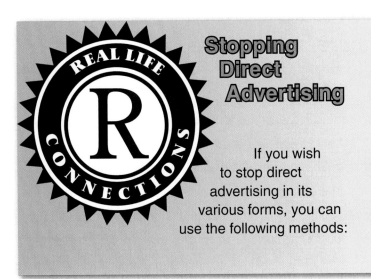

Stopping Direct Advertising

If you wish to stop direct advertising in its various forms, you can use the following methods:

- For telemarketing, register your phone number online at www.donotcall.gov or call 1-888-382-1222 and ask to have your number removed from call lists.

- For direct mail, register your name and address online at www.dmachoice.org and ask to have your name deleted from direct mail marketers lists.

- For e-mail, register online with www.dmachoice.org/enos to opt out of receiving unsolicited advertising e-mails.

through mail or another delivery service. Fund-raising is also carried out through direct mail.

Direct business-to-consumer advertising comes via telephone and e-mail as well. Some consumers find this direct approach helpful, while many consider it a nuisance.

Special Sales and Promotions

Businesses hold special sales and promotions to attract customers and increase sales. When price reductions and promotions increase sales and profits, they benefit the seller. When you buy goods and services you need on sale, you benefit as well. However, if you let reduced prices persuade you to buy what you do not need, you lose. To take advantage of sales and promotions, shoppers need to

- know what they need and want with or without sales

- stay within preset price limits for given items, buying only what they can afford

- stick to an overall spending plan and not be sidetracked by price reductions, especially for major purchases

- anticipate reduced prices on products and services they intend to buy, such as preseason specials and end-of-season sales, 14-3

- control the urge to buy what they do not need or want just because it is on sale.

It is in your best interest to know the meaning of the following terms frequently used to attract customers and sell merchandise.

> **Reflect**
>
> When have you purchased a sale item because of a reduced price and found it to be a false savings?
>
> **Activity**
>
> Name two or three items you intend to buy and describe how you might manage to buy them on sale using each of these pointers.

14-3

It's always a plus if you can buy what you want on sale.

Case Study: Winners and Losers

It's in the Bag

Morris is a high school senior. He and a friend are planning a cross-country camping trip right after graduation and Morris needs a sleeping bag. While searching for a bargain online, he finds a Web site advertising a good selection of sleeping bags at reduced prices. The Web site belongs to a store that has a location in town that carries the same merchandise. At the store, Morris buys a $150 down sleeping bag that is marked down to $100. Morris saves $50.

Susan sees the same Web site with marked down sleeping bags. She has never been camping, but figures she will go someday and will need a sleeping bag. She heard that down sleeping bags are the best. Susan picks up her paycheck and heads for the sports shop. She buys a $120 bag reduced to $80. Susan doesn't see how she can go wrong with a bargain like this, although it eats up most of her paycheck. Susan never does go camping. The sleeping bag sits in her closet in its original wrapping. She loses her $80.

Case Review

1. What advantages do sales and promotions offer shoppers?
2. What experiences have you had buying goods and services during special promotions and sales?
3. Why was the purchase of a sleeping bag on sale a bargain for Morris and a costly mistake for Susan?
4. Why are people so often tempted to buy at a sale even if the goods and services do not meet real needs?

Vocabulary

Explain the meaning of the different types of sales and discuss the potential savings each offers. What are some tips for shopping at different types of sales?

- *Clearance sale*—indicates a reduction from previous prices on merchandise the seller wants to "clear" or sell, usually to make room for new merchandise.

- *Closeout sale*—refers to products that are no longer being produced and have been discontinued by the supplier or manufacturer.

- *Going-out-of-business sale*—refers to sellers who are actually closing their business and are selling goods at reduced prices to hasten the closing. Keep in mind that sellers who are not closing may use the phrase "going-out-of-business" just to get customers into the store.

- *Introductory offer*—indicates new merchandise selling at a price that will increase after the initial offer.

- *Liquidation*—refers to the sale of merchandise at reduced prices in order to aid in converting inventory to cash. This is another term that is often misused.

Buying Incentives

Buying incentives are offered by sellers to help sell goods and services. Trading stamps, coupons, contests and games, rebates, premiums, and prizes are all forms of buying incentives. They are often found in magazines or newspapers. Sometimes these incentives come with the purchase of goods and services. You benefit from this form of selling as long as you limit purchases to the goods and services you would ordinarily buy or try. You lose if you buy something you do not really want just to get stamps, use a coupon, or win a "free" prize.

Cents-off and two-for-one offers, bargain buys, and other forms of special pricing are also buying incentives. Some sellers offer loss leaders to bring customers into the store. A **loss leader** is an item priced at or below cost to attract buyers who will then purchase other merchandise.

Another type of buying incentive, usually used for expensive items, is the rebate. A **rebate** is a cash back offer to buyers. For example, a seller may advertise a $75 rebate on the purchase of a $600 television set. Ideally, the buyer sends the proof-of-purchase to the manufacturer and receives the $75 rebate. However, rebate offers usually come with rules, regulations, deadlines, and sometimes complicated instructions the buyer must follow. Before you buy on the strength of a rebate, study the offer carefully.

Various buying incentives can offer real savings to alert shoppers. These shoppers know which price reductions are real and which purchases truly meet their needs.

Packaging and Display Tools

Experts have carefully planned every aspect of a product's presentation, from its color and size to its name and labels. Before a product or service goes on the market, these aspects have been studied and tested. Often groups of consumers are used to evaluate products before they go on the market. They are called *focus groups.*

Once a product is ready for sale, sellers make even more calculations about which locations in which stores will bring the most sales. Take a walk through a large supermarket or drug store. Study the packages and product displays. Note how many items seem intentionally placed to attract your attention. Can you identify some of the eye-catching techniques used?

Studies indicate that items placed at floor level attract the least notice. When the same products are raised to waist level, sales increase by almost 60 percent. At eye level, they jump almost 80 percent.

Products you are likely to buy on impulse will usually be placed in spots near the checkout counter. These may also be in display racks in the aisles where you can pick them up with ease. Staples in the supermarket, such as dairy products, breads, meat, poultry, and produce, will be located well into the store. Nonessentials will be near the front. This way, you are

Visual Merchandise Managers

Visual merchandisers are responsible for designing and implementing window and in-store displays for both online and brick and mortar retail stores. Visual merchandisers create displays that maximize the space of the store while appealing to the senses of their target customers.

Resource

Bait and Switch, color lesson slide, TR

Reflect

When have you been drawn to a product because of a display or package?

drawn into and through the store. Then you are apt to see and buy more products than you intended.

Packaging can be a powerful selling tool. Notice the color, shape, size, and labels on the packages that attract you most in your walk through the store. You will feel the urge to reach for some products more than others. See if you can figure out what draws you to different packages.

In addition to appearance, packages may sell for their convenience features or their ecological claims. Ecological selling terms include *recyclable* and *earth friendly*. Convenience innovations include "boil-in-the-bag" foods, juice boxes, squeezable bottles and tubes, pull-tab cans, and spray containers.

Consumer Credit

Businesses may offer credit to make it easier for customers to buy more and higher-priced goods and services. Credit is good for sellers because it increases sales, 14-4. It can be good for consumers, too, when they use it with forethought and planning. More on the pros, cons, and intelligent use of credit appears in Chapter 9.

Deceptive Selling Techniques

Certain deceptive selling methods, though illegal, still exist in the marketplace. These include

- false or misleading statements about products, services, prices, or guarantees

- advertising sale items that are not actually available for sale

- falsely using statements such as *special price* or *clearance price* when items are not actually selling at reduced prices

- making false or misleading statements regarding guarantees

Bait and Switch

Bait and switch selling is a common deceptive practice. This technique involves advertising an item at a very attractive price to attract customers. When the customer comes to buy, the seller claims to be out of that item. Instead, the seller presents a more expensive substitute.

Bait and switch is against the law. If you find a business using this technique, you should report it to the Federal Trade Commission or your state consumer fraud agency.

14-4

Shoppers often favor stores where they have charge accounts. Credit privileges can increase sales.

Pyramid Schemes

Another common deceptive practice is the use of **pyramid schemes**. These scams call for each participant to buy into the plan for a given amount of money. Then each participant must sign up a certain number of additional participants to do the same. The promoters of these schemes promise huge profits in a short time for simply handing over your money and getting others to join you. The only way you can move up and collect the promised profits is to recruit new participants who will recruit others. The many at the bottom of the pyramid end up paying money to the few at the top. The promises almost always are exaggerated and false.

Eventually the pyramid collapses because there can never be enough new investors to pay off all the earlier investors. Many of these schemes are promoted online. Pyramid schemes are illegal and should be reported to the Federal Trade Commission. Warning signs of pyramid schemes include

- the promise of quick easy money and high returns on your investment
- the requirement of a large initial investment to participate
- no available money-back or exit plan
- unknown promoter or company making the offer and no detailed information available
- profit dependent on recruiting new members into the plan
- a sense that the program is not legitimate

When you enter the marketplace, it pays to be alert and to look to your own best interests. The best way to avoid unfair selling methods is to trade only with reputable businesses and sellers. They will be concerned about their reputation, repeat sales, and keeping you as a happy returning customer.

Chain Letters

Chain letters are letters or e-mails that generally promise big returns for little effort. A simple chain letter or e-mail includes a list of names and addresses. You are asked to send something, such as a postcard or a dollar, to the first person on the list. Then you remove the first name on the list and add your own name to the bottom.

You make a specified number of copies of the letter with the names and instructions and send them to your friends. The letter promises that you will receive a specified number of whatever you send in return. Very often these letters involve a get-rich-quick scheme, an emotional plea, or some incredible return for your efforts. There may also be a threat of consequences for breaking the chain.

These letters can be a nuisance and a waste of time. When they involve money or valuable items and promise big returns, they are considered a form of gambling and are illegal. They will certainly never make you rich, lucky, healthy, or whatever else they may promise.

Discuss

List some current sweepstakes you know of. What are the prizes in each case? What is advertised by the sweepstakes? What do you have to buy to take part?

Reflect

Have you ever known anyone who won a lottery? What are your chances of winning a lottery in your state?

Discuss

Do you know of anyone who has had his or her identity stolen? What steps did the victim have to take to undo the damage?

Sweepstakes, Lotteries, and Games of Skill

Sweepstakes are a form of advertising in which the chance to win items of value or prizes is offered to consumers with no purchase or entry fee required to participate. These offers usually come via direct mail, the Internet, or television. Prizes range from relatively small items such as personal media players, digital cameras, and smart phones to vacations, cars, cash, and dream homes.

Lotteries are similar to sweepstakes, except prizes are awarded to participants by chance in exchange for some form of payment. Most states run lotteries to help fund government operations.

Skill contests also offer the opportunity to win prizes, but the winners are determined by skill instead of chance. There may be an entry fee or purchase required to enter the contest. Law regulates these types of promotions, but you also need to be alert on your own behalf. Find out the sponsor, prizes, odds, and what you must do to participate. Before you enter a sweepstake, lottery, or game of skill for a chance to win prizes,

- look for a full description and an estimate of the value of any prize or winning

- read and be sure you understand all the rules, including small print

- know exactly what is required to participate

- know all the fees, charges, or expenses involved in participating

Protection Against Financial Fraud

Financial fraud consists of crimes related to credit card accounts, electronic fund transfers, identity theft. Financial fraud also includes other unauthorized uses of bank, credit, Social Security, or investment accounts. These types of crime are on the rise, and they can be devastating. You can protect yourself both through prevention and by quick action if you become a victim.

Identity theft is the crime of stealing someone's personal information and using the information to commit theft or fraud. This can happen when someone steals a person's credit cards, bank and investment account numbers, or Social Security number. If someone steals your information, he or she can use it, and your name, to access funds in your bank or investment accounts. The thief could also write checks on your bank account, make charges on your credit cards, and sign up for cellular phone service.

Identity theft is increasing rapidly. Victims can incur serious financial losses. They also have the inconvenient and time-consuming task of stopping the theft and reestablishing their credit, 14-5. The costs of just undoing the damage can be substantial.

Identity theft is often committed online using pop-up messages or spam e-mails. **Spam e-mails** are usually sent by a company to a variety of e-mail addresses as a form of advertising. These e-mails are not requested by the recipient and are often unwanted. However, spam e-mails can also be sent by criminals as phishing schemes.

Phishing is a crime committed online with messages that seek personal information. The phisher claims to be a business where the consumer has an account, such as a bank or credit card company. The message will ask the receiver to confirm, update, or verify the account by giving sensitive personal information. This usually includes Social Security numbers, credit card numbers, passwords, bank account information, or other financial data. The phishing e-mails usually look official. If you provide the information, the phisher will use it to sell your identity or to run up bills and commit other crimes in your name. It is important not to reply to the e-mail or click on any link provided.

The loss or theft of a wallet can present similar problems if credit cards and identifying information end up in the wrong hands. Following are a few steps you can take to protect yourself against this type of crime before you become a victim:

14-5
Discovering that your identity has been stolen means spending a lot of effort to reverse the damage to your credit.

- Do not carry your Social Security card or give it out if other ID will be enough. You may have to disclose your Social Security number when you get a new job, file tax returns, open a credit account, and apply for insurance or financial aid. If your school uses Social Security numbers on student identification cards, ask if something else can be used.

- Do not throw away credit card receipts or monthly statements without first shredding them. Shred anything with your name and account number on it.

- Do not give your Social Security, bank account, or credit card numbers to anyone without knowing that the information will be secure. Also make sure the request for the information is necessary and authentic.

- Periodically order a copy of your credit report from a credit-reporting agency. Promptly resolve any errors or negative results in the report.

- Carry only the credit cards you really need and use.

- Make photocopies of all the items in your wallet—front and back of cards. This will be very helpful if your wallet is lost or stolen and you need to notify creditors.

- Keep a list of all your credit cards with account numbers, expiration dates, and toll-free customer service phone numbers. You will need this information in case of loss or theft.

Discuss

How often do you receive spam or phishing e-mails? How do you handle these cases?

Discuss

Do you know of anyone who ever responded to a phishing e-mail? What were the consequences?

Reflect

When was the last time you wanted to complain about a consumer product or service? What did you do about it?

Resource

Consumer Complaints, Activity C, WB

Activity

Select three companies and find out to whom different types of complaints and correspondence should be addressed.

If you become a victim of identity theft or lose a wallet, move quickly to minimize the damage. Call credit card companies and accounts promptly to report missing cards and follow the call with written confirmation. Contact your bank as well if you are missing checks or ATM cards. File a police report if you are a victim of theft. It also is a good idea to report your missing credit cards and identifying information to the three national credit-reporting agencies. (Their contact information is given in Chapter 9.)

If your Social Security card or number has been stolen, contact the Social Security Administration's fraud line at (800) 269-0271 or www.ssa.gov. Two other places to turn for help are

- the Federal Trade Commission's Identity Theft Clearinghouse at (877) 438-4338 or www.consumer.gov/idtheft
- the Identity Theft Resource Center at www.idtheftcenter.org

Consumer Self-Defense

Looking after your own interests is an essential consumer skill. Most sellers are honest and reputable, and most products are what they claim to be. However, there are times when consumers need to apply the principle of **caveat emptor**. This means *let the buyer beware*—the risk in the transaction is on the buyer's side. If you have any question about a seller's reliability or the quality of a product, proceed with caution. This is particularly true when a sizable amount of money is involved or when you are signing a contract.

Self-defense also involves following up when products and services do not meet your expectations or the sellers' claims. It calls for settling differences with sellers and seeking the help of third-party consumer advocates when necessary. **Consumer advocates** are individuals or groups who promote consumer interests in areas such as health and safety, education, redress, truthful advertising, fairness in the marketplace, and environmental protection. Finally, consumer self-defense may require legal action when all else fails.

Successful Complaining

What do you do when a product fails or you are overcharged because of a billing error? What if repairs do not actually fix your car or a salesperson is rude? To address any of these problems, you need to complain to the right person in the right way. The art of complaining is an essential self-defense tool.

Simple exchanges and returns of unsatisfactory merchandise can often be handled by taking purchases back to the seller and explaining your dissatisfaction. Most reliable merchants take care of simple matters on the spot. Here are a few suggestions when problems are more involved or complicated:

- *Put it in writing.* When your complaint is serious, put it in writing. Explain the problem clearly, rationally, and briefly. Include important facts, figures, and dates along with copies of receipts, 14-6.

(Your Address)
(Your City, State, Zip Code)
(Date)

(Name of Contact Person)
(Title)
(Company Name)
(Street Address)
(City, State, Zip Code)

Dear (Contact Person):

On (date), I purchased (or had repaired) a (name of product with serial or model number or service performed). I made this purchase at (location and other important details of the transaction.)

Unfortunately, your product (or service) has not performed well (or the service was inadequate) because (state the problem).

Therefore, to resolve the problem I would appreciate your (state what you want—repair, replacement, refund, apology, etc.). Enclosed are copies (copies, NOT originals) of my records (receipts, guarantees, warranties, canceled checks, contracts, model and serial numbers, and any other documents).

I look forward to your reply and a resolution to my problem, and will wait (set a time limit) before seeking third-party assistance. Please contact me at the above address or by phone at (home or office numbers with area codes).

Sincerely,

(Your Name)
(Your Account Number)

14-6

This sample complaint letter shows what information to include when writing about a consumer problem with a product or service.

- *Be prompt.* Do not wait weeks or months to act. Put your case in writing right away and send the letter using registered mail. The receiver must sign for a registered letter, and the sender receives a record of its delivery.

- *Address the right source.* Direct your complaint to the right person and place. If an adjustment requires approval from higher up, the department or store manager is the person to see. Contact the credit department for billing errors and other credit problems. Complain to the top management of a company if a problem is serious or is not solved at lower levels. For names and addresses of local businesses and organizations, check the business's Web site or your local phone book. To find the

Activity

Using this format, complete a letter about a specific product or service you have found unsatisfactory.

Discuss

What are some reasons for putting a complaint in writing?

Discuss

What are some guidelines to follow if you complain via e-mail?

names of officers of large business firms, use *Standard and Poor's Register of Corporations* available online or in most public libraries.

- *Be specific and factual.* Clearly identify the product or service in question and describe the problem. Include the date and place of purchase, the product name and model number, and the purchase price. Include your account number or the last four digits of your credit card number if the purchase was charged.

- *Be reasonable.* You are more likely to get a satisfactory response if you state your problem reasonably and sympathize with the reader. For example, you might write, "I realize it takes time to correct a computer error, but…" or, "I know it must be difficult to give one-day service on appliances, but…" Threatening or sarcastic letters rarely lead to satisfactory solutions.

- *Suggest a solution.* You may not always get your way, but it helps to outline the solution you are seeking. Do you expect a repair, a replacement, a refund, or an apology?

- *Be businesslike.* Put your grievances and transactions with business firms in writing. Keep a written record of phone conversations with the date, the name of the other party, and promises made or action to be taken. Keep important receipts and records together. You may need to furnish papers or documents such as sales slips, bills, receipts, warranties, and previous correspondence. Send copies of these papers and keep the originals.

- *Be persistent.* Most problems can be solved with one letter directed to the right person. However, if you do not get the desired results, write a follow-up letter. Enclose a copy of earlier correspondence and indicate a date by which you expect some action. If a third letter is necessary, include copies of the previous letters and outline the action you will take if the matter is not settled by a certain date.

Consumer Advocates

If you cannot settle differences directly with sellers, it is often helpful to contact an outside party or organization, such as a consumer advocate. Government agencies that offer consumer assistance and services were listed and described in Chapter 2. Figure 14-7 is a listing of Web sites for key government agencies that assist consumers in different areas.

When dealing with dishonest and fraudulent business practices, contact the appropriate government regulatory agency. Most federal agencies will have local or regional offices. In addition, local and state governments provide regulatory and law enforcement functions to deal with fraud in the marketplace. Check your telephone book for names and numbers of consumer advocacy agencies that assist consumers in your area. Most major city phone books provide a separate listing of government services.

Nongovernment consumer advocacy comes from a variety of sources and offers a range of services to consumers. The advocacy groups fall primarily into the following categories:

- United States Department of Agriculture: www.usda.gov
- Consumer Product Safety Commission: www.cpsc.gov
- Environmental Protection Agency: www.epa.gov
- Federal Trade Commission: www.ftc.gov
- Food and Drug Administration: www.fda.gov
- Health and Human Services: www.hhs.gov
- Housing and Urban Development: www.hud.gov
- National Institutes of Health: www.nih.gov
- United States Postal Service: www.usps.gov
- United States Department of Transportation: www.dot.gov
- United States Department of Justice: www.usdoj.gov
- Securities and Exchange Commission: www.sec.gov
- Social Security Administration: www.ssa.gov

14-7

These Web sites will connect you to key government agencies that serve and protect consumers.

Enrich

Develop a consumer directory of local organizations and government agencies to which consumers can turn with problems and complaints.

Enrich

Interview someone at your local Better Business Bureau. Ask how many and what kinds of complaints the BBB receives. How do they handle these complaints?

Activity

Contact the nearest office of the CPSC for information on the agency's function and recent actions.

Enrich

Contact the nearest Better Business Bureau for a copy of the "Code of Advertising" booklet.

Activity

Visit each of these Web sites to learn what information they provide.

- *Better Business Bureaus (BBBs).* These are nonprofit organizations supported largely by local businesses. They promote ethical business practices, and in some cases, offer dispute resolution programs. Call a local BBB to learn what assistance and services it offers consumers.

- *National Consumer Organizations.* Consumer interest groups offer a variety of services. They advocate for consumer causes, and provide educational materials and information on products and services. Many of these groups work actively for better consumer protection and services, 14-8.

- *Trade Associations and Dispute Resolution Programs.* Companies that produce or sell the same types of goods and services may belong to an industry association. These associations often act as go-betweens for the companies they represent and consumers. They provide consumer

- American Association of Retired Persons (AARP): www.aarp.org
- Consumer Federation of America (CFA): www.consumerfed.org
- Consumers Union: www.consumersunion.org
- Consumer World: www.consumerworld.org
- Federal Reserve Education: www.federalreserveeducation.org
- Identity Theft Resource Center: www.idtheftcenter.org
- Internet Scam Busters: www.scambusters.org
- National Consumers League: www.nclnet.org
- National Foundation for Credit Counseling: www.nfcc.org
- National Consumer League's Fraud Center: www.fraud.org

14-8

This chart lists some of the better known nongovernment organizations that serve and protect consumers.

information on products and services and may offer dispute settlement programs. Most of these associations have Web sites.

- *Corporate Consumer Departments.* Many companies operate consumer affairs departments that deal with consumer concerns and resolve disputes. When you cannot get satisfaction with a seller, you can contact the consumer affairs department at the company headquarters. Very often these departments have toll-free numbers and Web sites.

Difficult Cases

Some problems require some form of legal action. However, legal action is costly and time consuming, and a favorable outcome is not guaranteed. For these reasons, most consumers consider it only as a last resort. Options depend on the nature of the problem and the amount of money involved. These options include binding arbitration, small claims court, a class action lawsuit, or an individual lawsuit.

Binding arbitration is a method of settling disagreements through an objective third party. Once both parties agree to arbitrate, each presents his or her case to the arbitrator to resolve. The arbitrator's decision is final and legally binding. Arbitrators are chosen from a pool of volunteers or professionals depending on the program. Binding arbitration is quick, low cost, and relatively simple and informal.

Small claims court offers a simple, prompt, and inexpensive way to settle minor differences involving small amounts of money. Procedures are relaxed with consumers normally representing themselves without a lawyer. They collect and bring documentation and evidence to support their cases. Claim amounts are limited to a maximum of $1,200 in some states and up to $5,000 in others. Since procedures vary from state to state, contact your local courthouse for more information.

Class action lawsuits are legal actions in courts of law brought by a group of individuals who have been similarly wronged. In these cases, the courts permit members of a common class to pool their grievances. They can then sue for damages on behalf of the entire class or group. One example is a group of consumers who have been similarly harmed or defrauded. Laws governing this type of lawsuit vary from state to state.

Individual **lawsuits** are civil actions brought by a person (a plaintiff) against another party (the defendant). The plaintiff claims to be damaged, or negatively impacted, from actions by the defendant. He or she seeks a legal remedy to be determined by the court. If the plaintiff is successful, a judgment will be entered in his or her favor. The judgment may involve court orders to enforce the plaintiff's rights or award damages to the plaintiff. The court may also issue an order to prevent or compel specific action by the defendant.

The Informed Consumer

Unfortunately, the information you need to be an informed consumer includes constantly changing facts and figures. Products, services, laws, and economic conditions can change a great deal from year to year. It is to your advantage to stay up-to-date. Following are some pointers on where to look for consumer information and how to evaluate and use it.

Community Resources

To be an informed consumer, you need to know what data sources are available to you. Figure 14-9 lists some of the resources available in most communities. The people, places, and organizations listed can provide valuable information to help you make wise economic decisions in the marketplace.

A valuable resource that is sometimes overlooked is the newspaper. Almost every daily and weekly newspaper offers articles and advertisements related to consumer issues. Most newspapers are also available online.

The Internet

The Internet opens a whole world of consumer information and resources. You can find product information, the latest on consumer laws and protection, and comparison shopping data. Credit and financial information, health and medical news, and other helpful data are also available. You can research and buy almost anything online.

When using the Internet for information, shopping, or personal business, take care to check the reliability of sources and sites. It is important to follow a few basic guidelines for dealing with distant merchants whether they are selling online or by telephone, mail order catalogs, or television.

Reflect

What information or services have you used from any of the sources listed in Figure 14-9?

Activity

Ask each student to contact a different source from Figure 14-9 to learn what information and services are offered.

Discuss

How can the Internet help you be a more informed consumer?

Community Resources*	
People	**Organizations**
Bankers	Bankers associations
Business people	Better Business Bureau
Credit managers	Chambers of commerce
Customer service managers	Consumer organizations
Financial advisers and planners	Trade associations
Insurance agents	**Government Agencies**
Stockbrokers	Consumer Information Center
Places	Consumer protection agencies
Brokerage houses	Extension Service
Courthouses	Federal Communications Commission
Financial institutions	Federal Trade Commission
Insurance companies	Food and Drug Administration
Libraries	Internal Revenue Service
Real estate firms	Social Security Administration
Small claims court	
*Most of these resources can be accessed online.	

14-9
Knowing and using the resources available in your community will help you make intelligent consumer decisions.

Dealing with Distance Sellers

Discuss

How often do you deal with distance sellers? Do you like or dislike making purchases from distance sellers? Why?

Reflect

If you make purchases online, do you always check to make sure the site is secure before entering personal payment information?

Activity

Print out and bring in privacy policies from Web sites of three different online sellers. Discuss their similarities and differences in class.

To make the most of shopping with a seller who does not have a local store, follow these guidelines:

- *Understand what you are buying, from whom you are buying, and all the details of the sale.* Find out the name and physical location of the company. Before you buy, ask questions about the company and its products and services. If you have doubts about the quality of the company or its products, check with the organizations listed in 14-7 and 14-8. Use the checklist in 14-10 to mark off what you need to know before completing a telephone, Internet, television, or catalog purchase.

- *Maintain your security when shopping online.* Buy only from secure sites. Secure site addresses show an icon such as a lock at the bottom right corner of the browser window. If you pay by credit card, you may want to have one card with a low credit limit that you use only for online and other distance purchases.

- *Check the seller's privacy policy before giving your credit card number or other information.* Find out what information about you the site collects, how it is used, and how it is protected. Most reliable sites have an easily accessible "privacy statement" explaining their policies. *Caution: When buying online, provide only the information required to complete transactions. This should not include passwords, Social*

14-10

Use a checklist/form similar to this one before you make a major purchase.

Consumer Checklist

___ Date _____

___ Name of the salesperson _____

___ Name, address, and phone number of the company _____
_____

___ Description of the product or service _____
_____

___ Identifying model and order numbers _____

___ Purchase price _____ Sales tax _____

___ Cost of handling and shipping _____

___ Total cost _____

___ Delivery date _____ Delivery method _____

___ Seller's policies regarding returns, exchanges, refunds _____
_____

___ Terms of any warranties _____
_____

___ Terms of any credit agreement _____
_____

___ Customer service contract _____ Phone number _____

Security numbers, birth dates, bank account numbers, or other personal and financial information.

- **Keep a complete record of each transaction.** Get any information in writing so you have a record of the transaction if you need it. Ask to have a copy of your orders e-mailed to you with confirmation numbers and details of the order. Save and print information on your order—date, delivery promises, merchandise descriptions, prices, guarantees, model numbers, and shipping charges.

- **Pay by credit card.** Credit cards offer the advantages of easier returns and exchanges, convenience in resolving problems, and the protection of consumer credit laws.

- **Know your rights.** Consumer protection laws apply to online transactions. Contact the appropriate law enforcement agency if you have problems. See 14-7 and 14-8 for a listing of agencies and organizations that offer consumer protection and assistance.

- **Take your time.** Do not let sellers rush you into a buying decision, particularly for costly items. Study the offer. Discuss it with a person you trust if you have any doubts or questions. Compare similar offers from other sellers.

- **Do not fall for the unbelievable.** If an offer sounds too good to be true, it probably is not true. Check out "good deals" before you buy.

Regardless of what you are buying, deal only with reputable sellers who are fair and honest with customers. This is the best way for you to protect your interests. The checklist in 14-11 can help you evaluate the many sellers in the marketplace.

Evaluating Consumer Information

After identifying reliable sources of information, you may want to begin a consumer information file. This will put the latest facts and figures at your fingertips when you need them. You can then use material in your file to make intelligent consumer decisions. You will need to evaluate articles and booklets to see what is worth keeping. The following guidelines will help you evaluate materials.

Use Reliable and Informed Sources

A reliable source on one subject may not be the best place for facts on other topics. For example, a banker may give sound financial advice,

Evaluating Sellers

1. Are policies concerning returns, exchanges, and refunds reasonable?
2. Is advertising believable? Are goods and services available at advertised prices?
3. Are salespeople helpful without being pushy?
4. Can you get straight answers to questions about products, services, and store policies?
5. Does the seller belong to the local chamber of commerce, Better Business Bureau, or other associations that set standards for fair business practices?
6. Do prices and services compare favorably with those of other sellers?
7. Have people you know had favorable experiences dealing with the seller?
8. Do you get prompt, courteous attention when you have questions, problems, or complaints?
9. Does management accept responsibility for the actions of salespeople and other employees?
10. Does the seller have a good reputation in the community?

14-11

These questions can help you evaluate the reliability and fairness of sellers. Several *no* answers should warn you away from a seller.

but know nothing about buying furniture. A medical association can tell you how to find a doctor, but not how to buy a car. The Food and Drug Administration can tell you how to read a nutrition label, but not how to judge auto repair services.

Determine the Primary Purpose of the Information

Is it intended to inform the buyer or to sell a product, service, or idea? Both news articles and advertisements can offer helpful information, but advertisements generally present only positive facts.

Evaluate the Usefulness of the Information

Look for material that is up-to-date and easy to understand. Read to see if recent developments on the product or subject are discussed. Consider whether the data is complete. Does it tell what you need to know about products, services, features, quality, performance, warranties, and prices?

Once you begin collecting consumer materials, you will need to organize the information for easy use. Find a drawer or box large enough to hold all the materials you collect. Then sort according to subject matter. As you gather new materials, add them to your file. Periodically review what you have filed and discard information that is no longer current or useful. If you keep information electronically, organize it by folders.

Consumer Rights and Responsibilities

In a message to Congress in 1962, President John F. Kennedy outlined four basic consumer rights. Since 1962, four more rights have been added. The eight rights are

- the right to safety
- the right to be informed
- the right to choose
- the right to be heard
- the right to satisfaction of basic needs
- the right to redress
- the right to education
- the right to a healthful environment

Today, these eight consumer rights have been endorsed by the United Nations and affirmed by Consumers International, a worldwide consumer organization. (See www.consumersinternational.org.) Each of these rights carries responsibilities. Together they form the basis for fairness in meeting consumer needs.

Safety: Rights and Responsibilities

The right to safety means protection against the sale and distribution of dangerous goods and services. The government plays an important role in protecting consumers.

However, responsibilities for safety also rest with consumers. For example, it is up to the consumer to read and follow directions that come with a product, especially those that can present hazards with misuse. These include electric and gas appliances, household chemicals, and yard equipment. Care in the safe use, storage, and disposal of potentially dangerous products is also a key consumer responsibility, 14-12. Consumers have a responsibility to report product-related health and safety problems promptly to the seller and the manufacturer. If the problem is serious, such as a shock from an electric product, consumers should also inform the proper government agency. The agency can take prompt action to prevent an injury or accident for other consumers. The Consumer Products Safety Commission handles problems involving hazardous products. The Food and Drug Administration deals with issues related to food, drug, and cosmetic products.

14-12

These labels are required on products containing hazardous substances.

Truthful Information: Rights and Responsibilities

Consumers are entitled to accurate information on which to base their choices and buying decisions. The most common sources of consumer information include advertising, product labels, warranties, articles in newspapers and magazines, salespeople, and other consumers. Government protects the consumer's right to information through various agencies and laws. For example, it requires labels with specific information on certain products. Contracts and agreements are also required to provide specific information for the consumer. In addition, government prohibits false and misleading advertising.

With this right comes the consumer responsibility to seek, evaluate, and use available information on products, services, and sellers. Before you buy, investigate a seller's policies on sales, returns, and exchanges. It also pays to check a store's reputation for honesty and fair play, to evaluate advertising claims and product performance, and to compare quality and prices.

Choice: Rights and Responsibilities

Consumers have the right to choose the goods and services they buy and the places they shop. To have free choices, the market must provide a number

of sellers offering a variety of goods and services at competitive prices. Laws protect consumers' free choice in the marketplace by prohibiting practices such as monopoly and price fixing.

Consumers are responsible for carefully choosing those products and services that will best meet their needs at prices they can pay. Choosing is not always an easy matter. The average supermarket alone carries over 15,000 items with a wide variety in almost every product category. This calls for informed and careful decisions, 14-13.

The responsibilities of choice go beyond the goods and services you buy. Consumers also have an obligation to deal only with reliable, reputable businesses. This is for their own protection and for the overall good of the marketplace. Every buying choice expresses approval of the purchase and the seller. Consumers need to be aware of the message they send with their choices and their money.

14-13

Consumer choice in a market economy is well illustrated in the modern supermarket. Each department offers an abundance of choices.

Reflect

What do you really know about the stores where you shop?

Discuss

How can consumers avoid being overwhelmed by the available choices in the marketplace?

Discuss

What examples can you give of messages consumers send when they spend?

Reflect

When and how have you made your voice heard by a business or government agency?

A Voice: Rights and Responsibilities

When consumers have legitimate problems or concerns, they have the right to speak up, be heard, and expect results. This requires that both business and government respond.

Consumers are responsible for speaking out and expressing their concerns to appropriate business and government representatives. This means learning and using appropriate and effective means of communication. Consumers need to develop the ability to compliment and complain. Let businesses know what you like and want, as well as what you dislike.

Satisfaction of Basic Needs: Rights and Responsibilities

Consumers have the right to access goods and services that satisfy their basic needs. These include adequate food, shelter, clothing, health care, education, and sanitation. The basics should be available to all consumers. To satisfy basic needs, you need both enough income to purchase essentials and a marketplace that provides them.

Governments play a major role both in defining basic needs and ensuring that all citizens are able to satisfy them. The U.S. government provides public housing and social programs, Medicare and Medicaid, Social Security, tax-supported schools and hospitals, and sewer and sanitation systems. However, providing these for everyone is an ongoing challenge.

Responsibility for satisfying basic needs rests also with consumers themselves. For example, it is up to the consumer to put essential needs ahead of other items when spending. It is the consumer's responsibility to learn about and take advantage of basic services provided by government and the marketplace. It is up to consumers to get the training and education that will enable them to earn a living wage.

Redress: Rights and Responsibilities

The consumer has a right to receive a fair settlement of disputes. This includes some form of compensation for misrepresentation, shoddy goods, or unsatisfactory services.

Here again, consumers share some of the responsibilities. They need to present their disputes clearly to the appropriate authorities and make their demands reasonable. The section on consumer self-defense outlines ways to take responsibility for settling disputes.

Consumer Education: Rights and Responsibilities

A consumer has a right to consumer education. This refers to some training and mastery of the knowledge and skills needed to make informed, confident choices in the marketplace. It also includes achieving an awareness of basic consumer rights and responsibilities.

You are fulfilling a part of the responsibility by taking a consumer education or personal finance course and reading this book. There are many other opportunities for consumers to learn the skills they need to function to their own advantage in the marketplace.

Healthful Environment: Rights and Responsibilities

A consumer has a right to live and work in an environment that is nonthreatening to the well-being of present and future generations. This right calls for pure water and air, safe and responsible waste disposal, preservation of natural resources, and respect for the earth and overall environment.

Chapter 23 outlines environmental concerns along with consumer rights and responsibilities connected to environmental issues.

Activity

Draft a letter to an appropriate government agency commenting on a consumer issue.

Discuss

When might a consumer need to exercise the right of redress? What does this mean?

Activity

Find articles in news magazines on recent consumer-related legislation proposed and passed.

Activity

Outline this chapter and review the most important points.

Resource

Chapter 14—Consumers in the Marketplace, Teacher's PowerPoint Presentations CD

Chapter Summary

Sellers use a variety of methods to encourage consumers to buy. Customers who understand selling methods can use them to their advantage. For example, advertising provides information of use to consumers. Buying incentives may offer unique opportunities to try new products at special prices. Sales and promotions offer price reductions. Credit offers a way to buy now and pay later.

Knowing how to complain effectively is an essential consumer skill. Getting results involves stating your case and presenting important details to the appropriate person in a businesslike manner. Learning the key sources of reliable product information is also part of being a competent consumer. It pays to keep a well-organized file of useful data to use when making choices in the marketplace.

As a consumer, you enjoy certain rights and carry certain responsibilities. For example, you are entitled to safety in the marketplace—safe products and services. However, you are responsible for using products as directed and for heeding safety precautions and warnings. You have the right to be heard and the responsibility to speak out when you have a problem with products or services or sellers.

Review

1. What is the primary purpose of advertising?

2. List and describe four advertising techniques.

3. List four types of information to look for in advertisements.

4. What is a loss leader?

5. Why are supermarket staples, such as dairy products, breads, meat, poultry, and produce, usually located well into the store?

6. List and describe three deceptive selling techniques.

7. Explain how identity theft occurs.

8. List five guidelines to follow when making a complaint.

9. List three guidelines to follow when evaluating consumer information.

10. List and describe four of the consumer rights.

Critical Thinking

11. How might you use the selling methods of businesses to your own advantage? Give examples.

12. What points should you consider when evaluating consumer information?

Answers to Review

1. to sell goods, services, ideas, and images

2. (Describe four:) Insecurity appeal taps into consumers' fears about being excluded, unpopular, or unappealing to the opposite sex. Testimonials are "real people" recommending a product or service. Endorsements are paid promotions by famous personalities. Sex appeal uses attractive models to sell. Bandwagon techniques try to convince the public a product is fashionable or trendy. Puffery describes exaggerated claims advertisers sometimes make about a product or service. Nostalgia is associating a product or service with childhood memories

or a time when life was simpler and more satisfying. Humor involves using a funny character, picture, or situation to get your attention. Statistics are often shocking or provocative. Green ads associate the use of a product or service with an environmental benefit.

3. descriptions of the products or services offered for sale; listing and demonstration of special product features and qualities; statement of differences between advertised items and similar goods and services on the market; details on prices, availability, places to buy, special offers, and terms of sale

13. When have you or your family complained about a product or service? What was the problem? How did you resolve it?

14. What course of action would you take if you could not get a serious consumer problem solved by the seller or manufacturer?

15. Start collecting material for a personal consumer information file. Concentrate on collecting information that applies directly to you as a consumer and to products and services you buy.

Academic Connections

16. **Social studies.** How many of the consumer resources listed in 14-9 are available in your community? Contact several of them to learn what services they offer consumers. Discuss findings in class.

17. **Research, speech.** Research a consumer issue of your choice on the Internet, or shop for a specific product online. Report findings to the class.

18. **Reading.** Read through magazines and newspapers, studying the advertisements. How much useful information can you find among the ads? Which ads give little or no information but appeal to your emotions?

19. **Writing.** Imagine your latest bill for your cell phone service contains charges you know you did not incur. Write a billing dispute letter using the following information: Mr. Sinclair Low, Customer Service Manager, Great Phones Company, 111 Hollywood Dr., Louisville, Illinois 60477.

MATH CHALLENGE

20. A bike shop has a bicycle on clearance sale for $265. That same bike is available from a Web-based business for $220. The sales tax rate for both is 6%. The Internet business charges $30 for shipping and handling. The bike shop bicycles are assembled free of charge. The bike available online is shipped unassembled. It costs $35 to have someone put it together. Which is actually a better deal?

Tech $mart

21. Review the types of advertising claims described in this chapter. Find examples of four of them on the Internet. One source might be Web sites of organizations that award accomplishments in advertising, such as the Clio Awards (www.clioawards.com).

4. an item priced at or below cost to attract buyers who will then purchase other merchandise

5. You are drawn into and through the store, where you will see and buy more products than you intended.

6. (Describe three:) false or misleading statements; advertising sale items that are not actually available; falsely claiming that an item is selling at a reduced price; making false or misleading statements regarding guarantees; bait and switch (advertising an item for sale, then claiming to be out of the item and substituting a more expensive item); pyramid schemes (buying into a plan for a given amount of money and signing up a certain number of additional participants to do the same); chain letters, which promise big returns for forwarding the letter to other people; sweepstakes

7. The thief steals a person's credit cards, bank and investment account numbers, or Social Security number and uses it to access the person's bank accounts, open a bank account, write checks, make charges on credit cards, and sign up for cellular phone service.

8. (List five:) Put it in writing. Be prompt. Address the right source. Be specific and factual. Be reasonable. Suggest a solution. Be businesslike. Be persistent.

9. Use a reliable and informed source for the type of information you need; determine the primary purpose of the information; evaluate the usefulness of the information.

10. the right to safety, the right to be informed, the right to choose, the right to be heard, the right to satisfaction of basic needs, the right to redress, the right to education, the right to a healthful environment (Descriptions are student response.)

Answer to *Math Challenge*

20. Bike Shop: $265 + $15.90 tax = $280.90

Internet: $220 + $13.20 tax + $25 shipping and handling + $35 assembly charge = $293.20

CHAPTER

15

Spending for Food

Reading for Meaning

Create a graphic organizer to illustrate factors you should consider when shopping for food. Add to the graphic organizer as you read the chapter.

nutrients

fiber

Dietary Guidelines for Americans

MyPyramid

impulse buying

convenience foods

brand name products

generic products

point-of-sale

standard of identity

nutrition facts panel

universal product code (UPC)

unit price

open dates

pull date

freshness date

expiration date

pack date

inspection stamps

food grades

organic food

produce

CHAPTER OBJECTIVES

After studying this chapter, you will be able to

- **identify** nutritional needs and the best food sources of essential nutrients.
- **plan** nutritious, appetizing meals and snacks.
- **demonstrate** how to read and use nutrition facts labels in planning meals and evaluating nutritional value of different foods.
- **establish** a food budget based on individual needs and resources.
- **evaluate** food stores to determine where to shop for the best prices, selection, and quality.
- **list** the basics of safe food handling and storage.
- **explain** the use of food labels, unit pricing, open dating, and government grading.
- **identify** healthful choices to select when eating out.

Central Ideas

- Government-issued guides such as MyPyramid can help you choose nutritious foods.

- Meal management can help you get the most from your food dollars.

Over your lifetime, you will spend thousands of dollars each year feeding yourself and your family. It pays to learn the basics of smart food shopping early in life. This requires knowing nutritional needs, making wise food choices, and following a well-planned budget. Handling food safely and selecting nutritious meals in restaurants also contribute to good health.

Planning Nutritious Meals and Snacks

Before you can plan healthful meals and snacks, you need to know the foods and nutrients your body requires. Then you can select nutritious foods with confidence. The food you eat affects the way you look, feel, and function. Eating the right foods can help you stay healthier and live longer. Learning to plan nutritious meals has a positive effect on your health. Learning to shop for the best food values can have a positive effect on your budget.

Nutrients You Need

Nutrients are chemical substances found in foods. They furnish energy, build and maintain body tissues, and regulate body processes. You need six types of nutrients: proteins, fats, carbohydrates, vitamins, minerals, and water. Chart 15-1 lists the functions and sources of these key nutrients.

Fiber is also essential for good health. It is the indigestible or partially digestible part of plants. It helps move food and digestive by-products through the large intestine and promotes good digestion. Whole grains, fruits, and vegetables are good sources of fiber.

Linking to... Science

Sugar and Your Teeth

You probably know that eating sugary foods can result in cavities, but do you know why? Bacteria that live in your mouth feed off sugar. The bacteria then produce acid that eats away at the enamel on your teeth, causing cavities. The more often you eat foods high in sugar, the more the bacteria will feed. This is why it is important to limit your intake of sugary foods, brush your teeth often, and especially brush after eating or drinking sugary substances. The less time the sugar stays in your mouth, the less acid is produced. Avoiding sugary foods that stick to your teeth, such as caramel, is especially important.

Key Nutrients		
Nutrient	**Functions**	**Sources**
Vitamins **Vitamin A**	Helps keep skin clear and smooth Helps keep mucous membranes healthy Helps prevent night blindness Helps promote growth	Liver, egg yolk, dark green and yellow fruits and vegetables, butter, whole milk, cream, fortified margarine, ice cream, cheddar-type cheese
Thiamin **(Vitamin B-1)**	Helps promote normal appetite and digestion Helps keep nervous system healthy Helps body release energy from food	Pork, other meats, poultry, fish, eggs, enriched or whole-grain breads and cereals, dried beans, brewer's yeast
Riboflavin **(Vitamin B-2)**	Helps cells use oxygen Helps keep skin, tongue, and lips normal Helps prevent scaly, greasy areas around mouth and nose Aids digestion	Milk, all kinds of cheese, ice cream, liver, other meats, fish, poultry, eggs, dark leafy green vegetables
Niacin **(a B vitamin)**	Helps keep nervous system healthy Helps keep skin, mouth, tongue, and digestive tract healthy Helps cells use other nutrients	Meat, fish, poultry, milk, enriched or whole-grain breads and cereals, peanuts, peanut butter, dried beans and peas
Vitamin C	Helps wounds heal and broken bones mend Helps body fight infection Helps make cementing materials that hold body cells together Promotes healthy gums and tissues	Citrus fruits, strawberries, cantaloupe, broccoli, green peppers, raw cabbage, tomatoes, green leafy vegetables, potatoes and sweet potatoes cooked in the skin
Vitamin D	Helps build strong bones and teeth Helps maintain bone density	Fortified milk, butter and margarine, fish liver oils, liver, sardines, tuna, egg yolk, sunshine
Vitamin E	Acts as an antioxidant although exact functions are not known	Liver and other variety meats, eggs, leafy green vegetables, whole-grain cereals, salad oils, shortenings, and other fats and oils
Vitamin K	Helps blood clot	Organ meats, leafy green vegetables, cauliflower, other vegetables, egg yolk
Protein	Builds and repairs tissues Helps make antibodies, enzymes, hormones, and some vitamins Regulates fluid balance in the cells Regulates many body processes Supplies energy when needed	Complete proteins: Meat, poultry, fish, eggs, milk and other dairy products, peanuts, peanut butter, lentils Incomplete proteins: Cereals, grains, vegetables

(Continued.)

15-1

A well-balanced diet provides the body with the six types of nutrients: vitamins, proteins, fats, carbohydrates, minerals, and water.

Key Nutrients *(continued)*		
Nutrient	**Functions**	**Sources**
Fat	Supplies energy Carries fat-soluble vitamins Protects vital organs Insulates the body from shock and temperature changes Adds flavor to foods Provides essential fatty acids	Butter, margarine, cream, cheese, marbling in meats, nuts, whole milk, olives, chocolate, egg yolks, bacon, salad oils, dressings
Carbohydrates	Supplies energy Provides bulk and fiber in the form of cellulose (needed for good digestion) Helps the body digest fats efficiently	Sugar: Honey, jam, jelly, sugar, molasses Fiber: Fresh fruits and vegetables, whole-grain cereals, and breads Starch: breads, cereals, corn, peas, beans, potatoes, pasta
Minerals **Calcium**	Helps build bones and teeth Helps blood clot Helps muscles and nerves function properly Helps regulate the use of other minerals in the body	Milk, cheese, other dairy products, leafy green vegetables, and fish eaten with the bones
Phosphorous	Helps build strong bones and teeth Helps regulate many body processes Aids metabolism	Protein and calcium food sources
Iron	Combines with protein to make hemoglobin Helps cells use oxygen Aids metabolism	Liver, lean meats, egg yolk, dried beans and peas, leafy green vegetables, dried fruits, enriched and whole-grain breads and cereals
Water	Is a basic part of blood and tissue fluid Helps carry nutrients to cells Helps carry waste products from cells Helps control body temperature	Water, beverages, soups, and most foods

15-1

(Continued.)

Dietary Guidelines for Americans

The **Dietary Guidelines for Americans** were developed by the U.S. Departments of Agriculture and Health and Human Services. They provide advice for choosing nutritious foods and maintaining a healthful lifestyle. Recommendations cover the following eight areas.

- *Adequate nutrients within calorie needs.* No one food contains all the nutrients your body needs. Therefore, it is important to eat a variety of nutrient-dense foods every day staying within recommended calorie limits. Try to choose foods that are *nutrient-dense*. These foods are high in nutrients compared to the amount of calories they contain.

- *Food groups to encourage.* Include fruits, vegetables, whole grains, and fat-free or low-fat milk products in your daily diet.

- *Weight management.* Maintain a healthy weight by balancing calorie intake with calories expended. Weight extremes can cause serious health problems, including anorexia and obesity. Both of these conditions contribute to other health problems.

- *Physical activity.* Participate in a total of at least 30–60 minutes of physical activity every day. This can include routine physical activities such as doing chores and taking stairs as well as planned exercise. This activity can be done in increments and accumulated throughout the day. Increments should be at least 10 minutes in duration.

- *Fats.* Limit high-fat foods and avoid saturated and trans fatty acids. Choose foods containing unsaturated and monounsaturated fatty acids such as fish, nuts, and vegetable oils. See 15-2.

- *Carbohydrates.* Choose fiber-rich fruits, vegetables, and whole grains to keep the digestive system healthy. Limit intakes of sugar and sweeteners, which can cause weight gain. Restrict foods and beverages that contain sugar and starch.

Discuss

What role does nutrition play in overall well-being and good health?

Reflect

How many of these recommendations do you follow? Where do you need to improve your eating habits?

Enrich

Find information on recommended weight for your height, body type, sex, and activity level.

Activity

Identify sugar- and sodium-containing ingredients on product labels. Then check nutrition labels to find the specific sugar and sodium content in several foods.

Enrich

Investigate and report the reasons for cautions against saturated fats and cholesterol, sugars, and salt and sodium.

Fat Facts on Food Labels

Definition (per serving)

fat free—less than 0.5 gram of fat

light or lite—one-third fewer calories or half the fat

low calorie—40 calories or fewer

low fat—3 grams or fewer of total fat

low saturated fat—1 gram or less of saturated fat

low cholesterol—20 milligrams or fewer of fat and 2 grams or fewer of saturated fat

reduced fat—at least 25 percent less fat

15-2

This chart defines the terms used in fat labeling.

Resource

MyPyramid, transparency
master 15-2, TR

Resource

Planning with MyPyramid,
Activity B, WB

- *Sodium and potassium.* Avoid sodium, but get plenty of potassium. Too much sodium, or salt, in the diet can lead to heart disease. A potassium-rich diet can help prevent high blood pressure.

- *Food safety.* Prevent foodborne illnesses by careful handling, preparation, and storage of foods. Food safety guidelines are discussed later in this chapter.

MyPyramid

MyPyramid is a tool developed by the U.S. Department of Agriculture for developing your own personal eating plan. It encourages people to both eat nutritious foods and get plenty of physical activity to maintain a healthful weight.

MyPyramid is made up of six colored triangles, 15-3. Five of them represent the major food groups: grains, vegetables, fruits, milk, and meat and beans. The narrowest triangle represents oils. All foods are

15-3

MyPyramid helps you understand how to personalize eating plans for good health.

represented because people must eat a variety of foods to obtain all the needed nutrients.

- *Grains.* At least half the grains you eat should be whole grains, which have the most fiber and nutrients.

- *Vegetables.* Vegetables can be divided into subgroups, including dark green, orange, dry beans and peas, and starchy. It is important to eat a variety of vegetables because each subgroup contains different nutrients.

- *Fruits.* Choose a wide variety of nutrient-rich fruits and juices. The best forms to eat are fresh, dried, and canned in water or juice. Avoid fruits with added sugars, including those canned or frozen in syrup.

- *Milk.* As often as possible, choose low-fat or fat-free milk products. These include fat-free milk, part skim cheese, and low-fat or fat-free yogurts. Limit high-fat choices such as pudding and ice cream.

- *Meat and beans.* This group includes meat, poultry, fish, eggs, dry beans, nuts, and seeds. Try to select items from this group that are lower in fat. These include fish, lean meat, skinless poultry, and dry beans.

- *Oils.* Because oils are high in calories, try to eat them sparingly. Avoid trans fats and limit saturated fats. More healthful oils include those from olives, nuts, avocados, and some fish. Oils contain fatty acids, some of which are necessary for health.

Recommended Amounts

How much of each food group should you eat? The answer varies from person to person and is based on your age, gender, and activity level. These factors determine your calorie needs. To find out the ranges that are best for you, check the MyPyramid Web site, www.mypyramid.gov. You will need to answer a few easy questions to get meal-planning advice tailored to your needs.

Before You Shop for Food

Some knowledge of the factors that affect food prices can help you stretch food dollars. It can help you anticipate price trends and plan ahead to take full advantage of good buys.

A food budget can also be an important shopping guide. It focuses attention on what you need to buy and prevents impulse buying and overspending. **Impulse buying** refers to unplanned or "spur of the moment" purchases.

Finally, a plan for meals and snacks with some ideas for leftovers can make you a better shopper. It gives direction to your choices and reduces waste and costly mistakes.

Activity

Divide a sheet of paper into five columns, one for each food group, and list your favorite foods under each heading. Plan several menus using your favorites.

Discuss

Suggest ways to limit your intake of oils.

Activity

Keep track of foods you eat for one week and compare your diet with the recommendations.

Enrich

Contact a nutritionist or the American Dietetic Association to learn how vegetarians can get adequate protein, B-vitamins, and iron in diets without meat, poultry, or fish.

Food Spending in Hard Times

Food shoppers address financial hardships in a variety of money-saving ways. They go to less-expensive eateries or choose cheaper menu items, if they go out at all. The restaurant industry suffers when consumers stay away.

Grocery shoppers use more coupons, watch for specials and sales on weekends, and follow their shopping lists closely. They buy less-expensive forms of foods, such as frozen rather than fresh and canned rather than frozen. Many shop for generic products rather than brand names and buy fewer deli items.

Growing vegetable gardens become popular, as well as canning and freezing food. A financial downturn also causes greater reliance on food stamps, soup kitchens, and food banks.

Resource

Food Prices, Activity C, WB

Enrich

Search for current articles and events that influence the price of different foods today. Discuss.

Enrich

Investigate recent nutritional discoveries and announcements that tend to change eating habits and, as a result, food prices.

Activity

Brainstorm a list of ways consumers can affect the price and supply of different foods.

Activity

See if you can predict price trends that are likely to follow certain current events.

Factors Affecting Food Prices

When the supply of food is greater than demand, prices fall. When demand is greater than supply, prices rise. Rising prices tend to encourage production and increase supply, thus lowering demand. Falling prices tend to discourage production and decrease supply, thus increasing demand. Prices tend to go up and down until price equilibrium is reached. That occurs when supply and demand for a given product at a given price are in balance.

A look at the supply and demand for beef illustrates their relationship to beef prices. Suppose a supplier pays $3.00 per pound for rump roast, and tries to sell it for a profit at $5.00. Perhaps consumers feel that $5.00 per pound is too expensive and do not buy it. If the supply at that price becomes greater than the demand, prices will fall. They will continue to fall until the low prices encourage more consumers to buy more roast. Eventually this increasing demand will meet the supply.

If the demand increases so much that it becomes larger than the supply, roast beef prices will rise. They will continue to rise until the high prices encourage producers to increase the supply. Eventually the increasing supply will meet the demand. Many factors besides price can affect the supply and demand of food.

- *Increased grain exports reduce the U.S. supply of grain.* This increases the price of grain for cattle producers and the cost of raising cattle. To cover increased costs, cattle producers hold out for higher prices when selling their cattle, thus raising the price to consumers, 15-4.

- *Flooding reduces crop production and increases feed prices for livestock.* This raises the cattle producers' costs and may reduce the supply of cattle, thus raising consumer prices.

- *Cattle producers refuse to bring beef to market because of low prices.* This boycott lowers the supply of beef and increases the price of existing supplies.

- *A meat packers' strike also reduces the supply of beef and increases price.* If the strike is settled by higher wages, another hike in the price of beef would occur to cover increased labor costs.

- *Food experts praise the nutritional value of poultry and fish over red meat.* This lowers the demand for beef and its price will fall. At the same time, demand for poultry and fish will rise along with their prices.

- *Consumers boycott beef.* This decreases demand so price will eventually fall. If demand continues to drop so producers cannot make a profit, supply will decrease, too. Then, when the boycott ends, both demand and beef prices will be high until the supply catches up with the demand.

- *The price of poultry decreases.* A reduction in the price of poultry would also affect the price of beef. With lower poultry prices, some consumer demand for beef would shift to poultry. Lower demand for beef would cause its price to fall.

- *The minimum wage is increased.* An increased minimum wage would increase the cost of raising, butchering, and delivering beef to consumers. The price of many food products would go up to cover increased labor costs.

- *Higher taxes reduce the amount of money consumers have to spend.* The demand for beef would drop and its price would fall as well. Lower beef prices would bring demand and supply into balance.

- *Lower taxes increase the amount of money consumers have to spend.* This could increase the demand for beef and its price would rise. Prices would remain higher until the supply increased to meet demand.

15-4
Heavy exports of wheat tend to reduce supplies for domestic use. This in turn increases the cost of grain and products made with grain.

Establishing a Food Budget

Individuals and families spend different amounts for food. How much you spend depends on your income, living expenses, food needs, and personal preferences. Generally, higher-income families spend a relatively small portion of total income for food—around 10 to 15 percent. Low-income families sometimes spend as much as 40 percent of income or more for food.

When planning a food budget, consider nutritional needs, resources, and preferences. To determine a reasonable amount of money to allow for food, answer the questions below.

- *What are the ages and activity levels of household members?* The amount of food you need depends on the makeup of your family. A family of four with two athletic teenage boys may eat twice as much as a young couple with two toddlers.

Hospitality & Tourism

Food and Beverage Managers
Food and beverage managers oversee food and beverage inventory and budget control. They assist with menu planning and make sure prepared dishes meet quality and safety standards.

Reflect

Does your family follow any type of food budget? How do you think a food budget could help control food costs?

Reflect

How do the answers to the questions on this page relate to the amount your family spends for food?

Discuss

How do age and activity level influence the amount and type of foods a person needs?

Enrich

Compare the prices of ten food products at different types of stores. Discuss price variations from store to store.

- *What special dietary needs must be met?* Weight control, infant feeding, illness, pregnancy, and special diets for medical reasons influence food choices and costs. Consider special needs in your family when making a food budget.

- *What personal and family preferences will affect food choices?* Eating habits, cultural or ethnic traditions, and food likes and dislikes all need to be considered when planning menus and shopping for food. Depending on your needs and where you live, favorite foods may be hard to find and expensive.

- *How much do you entertain and eat away from home?* The type and amount of entertaining you do will affect the amount you spend for food. Eating away from home may cut grocery store bills, but it will probably increase overall food spending. Meals away from home almost always cost more than similar meals prepared at home.

- *Where do you normally shop?* Small neighborhood stores and convenience marts have a low sales volume and must pay relatively high prices for the foods they sell. Therefore, they charge higher prices than large supermarkets. Large markets and chain stores buy in large volume because they have high-volume sales. They can charge lower prices and still make a reasonable profit.

- *How skilled are you at food shopping and preparation?* Experienced shoppers usually get far more from food dollars than new shoppers. Consumers who prepare most foods at home can save money. Those who eat out frequently or buy prepared and convenience foods will spend more money feeding their families.

Since food is a flexible expense, you can often adjust your food budget to the amount of money available. You can eat steak, go to your favorite restaurant, or throw a party when your pockets are full. You can stay home and eat canned tuna when you need money for car repairs, medical bills, or other pressing expenses.

Before you go to the store, plan your food purchases. Shop with a grocery list and a spending limit in mind. Record what you actually spend each week. If your spending exceeds the amount you planned without a good reason, you will need to adjust your food choices and control impulse buys.

Planning Food Purchases

Planning what to buy before shopping helps you get what you want and avoid costly impulse spending. Experienced shoppers may plan meals mentally. Beginners usually need to sketch weekly menus and snack plans on paper. All shoppers will do better with a written shopping list. The following are some tips for effective planning:

- Check food pages and ads in local papers and store Web sites for prices, specials, and menu ideas. Try to plan around foods that are in season or on sale.

- Outline meal, snack, and leftover plans for the week.

- Refer to recipes for ideas and ingredients you will need, 15-5.

- Keep a running shopping list. Add items as you run short. Include foods you need for planned meals and specials you want to buy.

- Use coupons from newspapers, magazines, and Web sites for products you intend to buy.

- Make wise use of **convenience foods**, which are partially prepared or ready-to-eat foods. They are great time-savers on busy days and less costly than eating out.

Advance planning is designed to guide you purposefully through the store. It is not meant to prevent you from getting good buys that are not on your list. If you see sale items you know you will use, revise your plans on the spot and make substitutions. Buy a new product you want to try if the price is right.

Brand Name Versus Generic Products

Brand name products have distinctive packaging and are identified with one manufacturer. **Generic products** are plain-labeled, no-brand grocery products. They may have irregular shapes and sizes, less flavor, or varied color or texture. However, they are just as wholesome and nutritious as brand name foods. Generic products cost less than other brands because less money is spent on packaging and advertising.

In planning whether to buy generic products, think about how you are going to use them. If you dislike the appearance of generic green beans, you may want to add them to a casserole where appearance is less important. When serving green beans as a side dish, you may decide to use a higher-quality brand.

When You Shop

There are many sources of information that lead to food values. Knowing how to use this information can help you make wise choices and control spending. Point-of-sale information is available in stores. Newspaper pages and ads, nutrition labels, cookbooks, and food magazines all provide information you can use when planning meals for your family. You also can access volumes of information online.

15-5
When planning a trip to the grocery store, check recipes ahead of time to see what you need.

Activity

Collect food product coupons. Discuss the savings the coupons represent and which ones you would actually use.

Activity

List five favorite high-priced foods and five low-cost substitutes.

Activity

Compare three generic products with brand name equivalents. What differences do you find?

Government & Public Administration

Health and Sanitary Inspectors

Health and sanitary inspectors examine establishments where foods are manufactured, handled, stored, or sold. They enforce legal standards of sanitation, purity, and grading.

The Food Store

Prices, selection, and quality of foods, as well as customer services, vary from store to store. Finding grocery stores with good buys may take a little comparison shopping. After trying a number of food stores, differences in quality and selection may become obvious to you. You may realize that one store carries better quality meats than another. Still another store may have a better selection of fresh fruits and vegetables. Therefore, you may decide to shop at certain stores for certain items. If your time is limited, you may choose to do most of your shopping in a supermarket that features many departments in one store. In some regions, farmers' markets and seasonal roadside stands are popular choices, 15-6.

To save both time and money, try to make one major food shopping trip a week. It is best to do your weekly shopping at a time when you can go alone and when you are not hungry. For the bulk of your food buying, it is a good idea to shop in the same one or two stores most of the time. You will get to know the store well enough to find what you want quickly.

Do not be afraid to ask for what you want and to return what is not satisfactory. If the cut of meat you want is not available on the shelf, ring for help and request it. If you arrive home with a food showing signs of spoilage, take it back immediately for credit or exchange. Since food stores want your business, they will usually try to keep you satisfied. You'll be a welcomed customer wherever you shop by following the guidelines outlined in 15-7.

Point-of-Sale Shopping Aids

As you shop, look for aids that can save you time and money and help you make appropriate selections. These are called **point-of-sale** or in-store shopping aids. Information and tools to assist consumers include food labels, the universal product code, unit pricing, open dating, and government inspection and grading information. Each of these offers advantages to the consumers who understand how to use them.

Food Labels

Food labels tell you exactly what you are buying. Some information on food labels is required by law. Other information, such as cooking directions and recipe ideas, is given voluntarily by food manufacturers to help consumers use and enjoy their products. Following is the information required by law on every food label:

15-6

Farmers' markets generally offer a selection of fresh seasonal fruits and vegetables.

- common name of the food and its form (whole, chopped, diced, etc.)

- net contents or net weight

Supermarket Shopping Code

1. Return empty bottles and plastics for recycling to designated areas.
2. Do not block aisles.
3. Avoid unnecessary handling of fresh fruits and vegetables.
4. Notify management of accidental spills and breakage so they may be promptly cleaned up.
5. Complete shopping before entering a checkout line.
6. Follow posted directions for express lines.
7. Present cents off coupons for credit only for the items actually purchased.
8. Have payment and coupons ready when entering the checkout line to avoid delays and inconvenience to other customers.
9. After transferring purchases to the car, return grocery carts to the designated area.

15-7

Simple courtesy helps take the hassle out of grocery shopping.

- name and address of the manufacturer, packer, or distributor
- list of ingredients in descending order of amounts present

A listing for canned tomato sauce may read, "Ingredients: tomatoes, salt, dextrose, spices, onion powder, and garlic powder." The tomatoes are present in the largest amount by weight and garlic powder in the least amount by weight. Any additives used in the food must be listed and the word *artificial* must be stated if flavors are artificial.

A number of common food products are made according to a **standard of identity** set by the FDA. These foods contain ingredients in preset amounts. They have standard names, such as ice cream, ketchup, and mayonnaise. All ingredients in these foods must be listed on the label.

Most food products are required to carry a **nutrition facts panel**. This label must include certain information listed in a certain order. The label, 15-8, must list

- serving size in both household and metric measures
- servings per container
- calories per serving and calories from fat
- Percent Daily Values in grams or milligrams for
    - total fat, saturated fat, and trans fat
    - cholesterol
    - sodium
    - total carbohydrate including dietary fiber and sugars
    - protein
    - percentages of Daily Values for vitamin A, vitamin C, calcium, and iron per serving; amounts of other vitamins and minerals may also be listed

Resource

Choosing Where to Buy Food, Activity D, WB

Activity

In a five-minute brainstorming session, list nonfood items that are commonly sold in supermarkets.

Discuss

When you go to a food store, how many items do you typically buy you did not intend to buy? How might this affect a food budget?

Reflect

Does your family do most of its shopping in the same two or three stores? What advantages does this offer?

Enrich

Role-play situations between a customer and a store employee involving the return of unsatisfactory food items.

Discuss

How might failing to follow the supermarket shopping code aggravate other customers and store employees?

Activity

List all the point-of-sale shopping aids you can find in a local supermarket. Discuss.

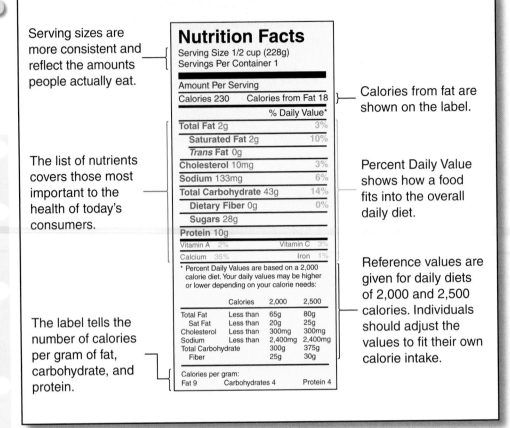

Serving sizes are more consistent and reflect the amounts people actually eat.

The list of nutrients covers those most important to the health of today's consumers.

The label tells the number of calories per gram of fat, carbohydrate, and protein.

Calories from fat are shown on the label.

Percent Daily Value shows how a food fits into the overall daily diet.

Reference values are given for daily diets of 2,000 and 2,500 calories. Individuals should adjust the values to fit their own calorie intake.

Universal Product Code

The **universal product code**, or *UPC*, is the series of black and white lines, bars, and numbers that appears on products for sale. See 15-9. The symbol is part of a computer checkout system. The UPC is designed to save time and labor costs. It shortens checkout time and allows customers to use self-checkout.

15-9

Most supermarkets scan UPC symbols to check out grocery items by computer.

Some stores provide scanning stations so customers can check prices as they shop. During checkout, a clerk passes each item over a computer scanner. From the UPC symbol, the computer identifies the name and size of the item and records the information. Then the computer transmits the price to the cash register. The price and description of the item are printed on the customer's receipt. This code also helps retailers adjust inventories and reorder items as needed.

The UPC speeds up the checkout process and reduces the chance of human errors. It also helps store managers know which products sell best.

This computer checkout system eliminates the need to mark the price on every item. Instead, prices appear on the shelves where items are displayed. A change in the price of a product can simply be entered into the computer. This reduces labor costs and makes food stores more efficient, thus holding down food prices.

Unit Pricing

Consumers can use unit pricing in comparing similar items to find the best buy. The **unit price** of a product is based on the cost per unit, weight, or measure. A product's unit price is usually listed on the shelf label where the product is displayed, 15-10.

This type of pricing lets you compare food prices at a glance. To make use of unit pricing when shopping, remember to compare

- the price per unit of a product, such as early June peas, to different brands and sizes of the same product

- the price per unit of different forms of a product, such as canned versus frozen peas

- the price per unit of a product to a similar product, such as canned peas versus green beans

Figure 15-10 shows a comparison of different sizes of grape juice. The unit prices tell you the cost per ounce of grape juice in a small jar is 4.63 cents. The cost per ounce of juice in a larger jar is 4.05 cents. The larger size jar is the better buy if you will use all of it.

Discuss

What do you see as the pros and cons of using the UPC?

Note

Use unit pricing activities to reinforce students' math skills.

Activity

Use unit pricing in a local food store to make the comparisons described.

15-10

Unit pricing helps shoppers compare costs of different quantities and brands of food.

Vocabulary

Distinguish among the various types of dating used on food product labels.

Reflect

When have you used the date on a product as a guide to buying or using the product?

Vocabulary

Distinguish between inspection stamps and food grades. Discuss the use and value of each.

Open Dating

Open dating helps you select fresh and wholesome foods. **Open dates** indicate when the foods should be used for best quality, flavor, and nutritive value. Many food manufacturers date perishable and semi-perishable foods. Except for baby formula, there is no federal law requiring open dating. However, over 20 states require open dating for some foods.

The dates on food items most often refer to the pull or sell date. The **pull date,** or *sell by date*, is the last day a product should be sold. This date allows some time for safe home use and storage. For example, if a milk carton is dated Jan. 15, you should be able to keep it refrigerated at home a few days beyond January 15. Dairy products, meats, and poultry are often stamped with pull dates.

Products may carry other dates. A *best if used by date*, or **freshness date**, is the last day you can expect a product to have peak quality. This date often appears on bakery products, such as breads, rolls, doughnuts, and cakes. It also appears on prepackaged fresh vegetables. Sometimes these foods are sold at reduced prices after they pass the freshness date. Foods are safe to eat for a few days beyond their freshness date, but they will not be at peak quality.

Other food items may be stamped with an expiration date or a pack date. An **expiration date** refers to the last day a product should be used. Baby formula and yeast often carry expiration dates. The **pack date** is the day the product was processed or packaged. Canned foods are often marked with a pack date.

When you are not sure what the date on a food package means, ask a few questions. Food store employees should be able to explain dating codes. To benefit from open dating,

- determine whether the date on food products is the pull, freshness, expiration, or pack date

- buy only the products you can use before the expiration date or within a few days of the pull or freshness date

- notify store management when you find items on the shelves after their pull date

- store foods properly at home and use them within a reasonable period of time

Government Inspection and Grading Programs

The United States Department of Agriculture (USDA) regulates the inspection and grading of foods you buy. **Inspection stamps** tell you the foods are wholesome and safe to eat. This means they have been processed and packaged under sanitary conditions. **Food grades** indicate the quality of foods.

Although most government inspection programs and all grading programs are voluntary, many food manufacturers and packers have their foods inspected and graded. Certain foods, such as meat and poultry, must be federally inspected before they can be sold and shipped across state lines. Products that carry government inspection and grade markings include raw meat, raw poultry, processed meat and poultry products, eggs, and dairy products.

Organic Foods

Most food stores today feature organic foods, particularly in the produce, meat, and dairy sections. **Organic foods** are produced without manufactured fertilizers, pesticides, growth stimulants, genetic engineering, and other banned processes. Organic meats and poultry must come from animals raised without the use of growth hormones, antibiotics, or feed made from animal parts. The only drugs that may be used are those that treat sick animals.

Organic foods are always more expensive than non-organic counterparts. They are more costly to produce and bring to the market. The USDA Organic stamp may be used only on foods that are certified at least 95% organic, 15-11. Organic foods are generally no more nutritious than other foods. However, they are often purchased by consumers who are concerned about the effects of pesticides, growth stimulants, and genetic engineering.

Buying Food Online

In some areas, you can do your food marketing on the Internet. Buying food online offers the advantages of shopping at any time of day or night and having groceries delivered to your door. Some large supermarkets

USDA

15-11

Foods that are certified as organic by the USDA may carry this stamp.

Commercial Food Photographers

Commercial food photographers take photos that show food looking its best. They spend hours planning each photo's lighting, props, and setting. When the food is in place, photographers shoot quickly to avoid melting, drying, shriveling, and other reactions to hot lights.

Activity

Visit a food store and list the many foods featured in the dairy section. Review the labels and nutritive values of these products.

Vocabulary

Find the terms *pasteurized*, *homogenized*, and *fortified* on dairy products you buy.

Activity

Visit a food store and find at least five different forms of milk and milk products. Discuss the uses of each.

Activity

Compare the prices of different forms of milk sold in a local store.

Activity

Read the labels of several dairy dessert products for information on fat content and nutrition.

offer online and telephone shopping. In some urban and suburban areas, independent non-store marketers sell food and groceries only online.

Though online services vary, the basic operation is similar for all. The seller maintains a warehouse of food and grocery products. The customer selects staples and products listed in the online menu, which usually has categories similar to those in the supermarket. These will include dairy products, produce, meats and poultry, canned goods, frozen foods, and general grocery supplies. Most sites also offer weekly specials.

Customers click items they want, filling their online shopping carts, and pay with a credit card. The seller delivers the order within a specified time period. While delivery and other fees may be involved, many consumers claim they save money because they do less impulse buying and more planning. People with disabilities, parents with infants, and those who dislike grocery shopping appreciate this convenience.

Buying Specific Foods

Knowing how to judge the quality and nutritional value of specific foods is essential to getting your money's worth in the supermarket. Following are some general guides to follow when shopping in different departments within the food store.

Dairy Products

Dairy products are one of the best sources of calcium and are excellent sources of other essential nutrients including protein, phosphorus, and vitamins A, B-2, and D. You can choose from a wide variety of dairy foods, such as milk, cheese, ice cream, and yogurt.

Milk and Milk Products

Fresh milk is popular for drinking and many other uses. You can buy it fat-free or with three different levels of fat content: low-fat 1%, low-fat 2%, or whole, which is over 3% fat. All forms of milk contribute the same nutrients except for fat. Flavored milk drinks are also available. Cultured buttermilk and yogurt are other milk products found in the dairy section of food stores.

Concentrated milk products include canned evaporated milk and sweetened condensed milk plus nonfat dry milk. These are usually used in recipes and are not interchangeable.

Cream is available with fat content ranging from a small amount to 40%. Cream products include half-and-half, light cream or coffee cream, light whipping cream, and heavy whipping cream. Also available are sour half-and-half and sour cream.

Ice cream is a frozen dessert with high fat and sugar content. Lower-fat varieties are also available.

Cheese

Cheese is a dairy food that is made from a concentrated form of milk or cream. Nutrients, color, texture, aroma, flavor, and cost vary with each of the many varieties of cheese. When buying cheese, compare the prices of various forms of the same type of cheese. Sliced, cubed, shredded, or grated cheese usually costs more than the same quantity of cheese sold in a solid piece.

Butter

Butter is a dairy product made from the fat or cream of milk. Commonly sold in sticks, butter is available salted or unsalted. Whipped butter costs more than regular butter. National brands and higher grades cost more than house brands and lower grades. Butter is usually more expensive than margarine, which is a widely used butter substitute. Margarine is made from vegetable oils and is not a dairy product.

Eggs

Eggs are high in protein and can be served as a less-expensive substitute for meat. They also provide B vitamins, iron, phosphorus, and vitamins A and D. Since egg yolks are high in cholesterol, many health experts recommend using whole eggs or yolks in moderation.

A variety of egg products are available at most food stores. They are similar to whole eggs in the nutrients they provide. These can be found in the dairy section near whole eggs.

The price of eggs depends on their grade and size. Higher grades and larger sizes are more expensive. Government grades are based on the appearance of the egg yolk, white, and shell. The three grades are U.S. Grade AA, U.S. Grade A, and U.S. Grade B. Most stores sell only Grade AA or A eggs.

When shopping, select eggs with clean, uncracked shells, 15-12. Shell color has nothing to do with quality, nutritive value, or flavor.

Meats

Beef, veal, pork, and lamb are the most commonly chosen meats. All are high in protein as well as phosphorus, iron, copper, and B vitamins. Different cuts vary in tenderness, size, and amount of fat and bone. The

Enrich

Write a report on how butter differs from margarine in terms of nutrition, price, forms, and uses.

Enrich

Research and report on the differences between eggs and egg substitutes.

Discuss

What are the differences between different grades of eggs? How might grades affect selection and use?

15-12

When buying eggs, check to make sure no shells are cracked.

amount of meat you need to buy depends on the cut and the number of people you plan to serve. Between two and three ounces of cooked lean meat is considered one serving. Boneless, fat-trimmed cuts yield more servings than cuts containing bones and fat. Ask in the meat department for advice on the amount to buy for the number of servings you need. When shopping for meats, use the following tips:

- *Look for government inspection and grading.* The "U.S. Inspected and Passed" stamp indicates that meat is wholesome and produced under sanitary conditions. Meat grades indicate quality characteristics such as flavor, juiciness, and tenderness. *Prime, Choice,* and *Select* are the grades most commonly found in retail stores for beef, veal, and lamb. All grades are comparable nutritionally. Prime, the top grade, is sold primarily to fine restaurants. Choice meats are the better-quality cuts available in supermarkets. Select meats are less-flavorful and tender.

- *Choose firm, moist, fine-grained, and well-marbled meat.* Marbling refers to the small flecks of fat throughout the lean that help make meat tender. Veal has little fat and little marbling. High-quality beef is bright red in color; veal is light pink; pork is grayish-pink; and lamb is pinkish-red.

- *Compare meat cuts and prices.* Although one pound of meat with bones may cost less than a pound of boneless meat, it yields fewer servings. Compare meat prices on the basis of cost per serving rather than cost per pound.

- *Consider variety meats, such as liver, kidney, heart, and tongue.* These are highly nutritious and are usually priced lower than other meats.

Poultry

Poultry includes chicken, turkey, duck, goose, and Rock Cornish hens. All of these, if sold across state lines, are federally inspected and marked for wholesomeness. Poultry may also be graded for quality. The highest grades go to the meatiest birds with the least pinfeathers and skin defects.

The age of a bird, not its grade, determines how tender it will be. Birds become less tender as they mature. Young chickens are labeled *broiler, fryer, capon, roaster,* or *Rock Cornish hens.* Young turkeys and ducks are labeled *young.* Mature chickens are stewed, steamed, or pressure-cooked. They are labeled *hen, fowl,* and *stewing chicken.*

When shopping for poultry, choose clean, moist, plump birds with meaty breasts, legs, and thighs. You can buy poultry whole, halved, or cut up. Larger birds usually cost less per pound than smaller birds. Whole chicken is less expensive than chicken cut into pieces. Chicken with the bone in is less expensive than boneless.

Fish

The two types of fish available are those with fins and backbones versus shellfish varieties with no backbones. Fresh fish is usually sold by the pound. Allow about two ounces of cooked boneless fish per serving. Check the labels on packaged, canned, and frozen seafood products for the amount to buy for the number of servings you need.

Inspection and grading of fish is not mandatory, but there is a voluntary inspection program for the fish industry. Since not all fish are inspected or graded, careful selection is especially important. Look for firm flesh; tight, shiny scales; and bright, bulging eyes. The fish should have no smell. Fresh fish and shellfish should always be refrigerated or kept on ice in the marketplace and transferred promptly to the refrigerator at home.

Whole fish is sold as it comes from the water. Dressed fish has head, fins, scales, and tail removed. Fish fillets are the sides of the fish cut lengthwise. Fillets have few or no bones and are ready to cook. Fish steaks are cross-sectional slices of a dressed fish with one large central bone. Steaks are also ready to cook.

Fruits and Vegetables

Fruits and vegetables are available in a variety of forms—fresh, canned, frozen, and dried. Fresh fruits and vegetables are called **produce**, 15-13. Price depends on the quality, time of year, growing conditions, and transportation costs.

The best time to buy various types of fresh fruits and vegetables is when they are "in season." Supplies are plentiful and lower in price then. When you shop for produce, consider size, weight, freshness, ripeness, and appearance. The way you use fruits and vegetables can influence your

Activity

Compare one variety of fish in three forms—fresh, canned, and frozen. What differences do you find?

Enrich

Compare one type of fruit or vegetable in its various forms—fresh, canned, frozen, and dried.

Activity

Make a chart showing which fresh fruits and vegetables are best at different times of the year in your area.

Enrich

Search for recipes in which lower-quality, less-expensive fruits and vegetables may be used without sacrificing taste or nutrition.

15-13

A supermarket usually has a large produce department with many choices.

choice. For example, there is no need to buy top-quality produce if you plan to mix it into a salad or casserole.

Compare prices of fresh, frozen, and canned fruits and vegetables. Usually frozen fruits and vegetables cost less than fresh produce. Canned foods cost less than frozen or fresh. You may also want to compare prices of different forms and brands of fruits and vegetables. Canned or frozen fruits and vegetables that are chopped, sliced, or cut cost less than whole pieces. Different brands of the same food also vary in cost, and the most expensive is not necessarily the best or more nutritious.

Grain Products

Grain products include breads, cereals, rice, and pastas. Whole-grain products provide fiber and more nutrients than products made from refined grains. For these reasons, half of your daily intake should be from whole-grain sources. Compared to many other foods, most grain products are inexpensive, well liked, and easy to include in meal plans.

Baked Goods

Wheat, barley, corn, oats, rice, and rye are the grains from which most baked goods are made. Flour is the basic grain product that is used to make breads and bakery products. Most flour is made from wheat, but you can also buy rye, potato, rice, and buckwheat flours.

Baked goods include rolls, cakes, and pastries. Ready-to-serve products generally cost more than home baked or those requiring some preparation. Fresh bakery goods usually cost more than refrigerated or frozen goods. Because of their sugar and fat content, you may want to limit your intake of these foods.

Breakfast Cereal

Cereals made from grains come in a variety of forms, flavors, and nutritive values. Many have added sugar plus other ingredients, such as nuts and dried fruit. Ready-to-eat and instant cereals are more convenient and more costly than cereals that require cooking. Small boxes and individual serving-size boxes of cereal cost more per serving than larger boxes. More breakfast cereals are including whole grains.

Pasta

Pasta comes in different shapes and sizes. Although pasta is a relatively inexpensive food, it is a favorite in a variety of recipes among consumers of all income levels. Look for whole-grain pastas for greater nutritive value.

Rice

Special rice products, such as wild rice, seasoned rice, and the instant rice varieties, tend to cost more than white rice that requires cooking.

Chinese fried rice and other seasoned and flavored rices are available canned or frozen, ready to heat and serve. These forms of rice cost more because of the additional processing required. Brown rice contains more nutrients than the more highly processed white rice products.

After You Shop

What you do with food at home is the key to enjoying all that you have carefully purchased. Proper storage is necessary to maintain food quality, flavor, and nutritive value. Proper handling is important to ensure food safety.

Food Safety

Guaranteeing food safety and avoiding foodborne illnesses begins in the grocery store and ends when you sit down to eat. The following guidelines can help you keep your food safe.

- Separate raw and cooked foods during shopping, storage, and preparation.

- Be sure hands and food-contact surfaces are clean.

- Wash fruits and vegetables, but do not rinse meats and poultry prior to cooking.

- Refrigerate perishables and leftovers promptly and defrost frozen items according to directions.

- Cook foods to high-enough temperatures to kill microorganisms. Use a food thermometer and follow temperature recommendations.

- Avoid unpasteurized milk, milk products, and juices.

- Do not eat raw sprouts or raw or partially cooked eggs, meats, or poultry.

For more detailed information, go to www.fsis.usda.gov, the USDA Food Safety and Inspection Service Web site.

Food Storage

There are three places to store foods—on a shelf, in the refrigerator, and in the freezer. Packaged foods usually have storage suggestions on their labels, 15-14. Bread and fruit that are used in a couple days usually stay fresh at room temperature. However, they keep for longer

15-14
Nonperishable food items can be stored in cabinets.

Discuss

What makes a meal attractive and appetizing?

Enrich

Investigate different ways of preparing foods that preserve nutritive values.

Reflect

How often do you try new and different foods?

Discuss

What do you consider to be an appealing atmosphere for eating?

periods of time in the refrigerator. Other items, such as meat or casserole dishes, keep one to three days in the refrigerator. They should be stored in the freezer for longer periods.

Food Preparation

Planning and preparing food in an attractive, appetizing way increases mealtime pleasure. Preparation also can affect the nutritive value, appearance, and taste of different foods. You can get more satisfaction from food dollars if you learn how to prepare foods that appeal to the people you are feeding.

Consider food contrasts. Try to combine foods that complement each other in flavor and appearance. Serve a colorful combination of hot and cold foods, sweet and tart flavors, and crisp and soft textures. Try to preserve natural colors and textures of food.

Include one or two known favorites in each meal, but try new foods and combinations. Fresh recipes and menus add interest and variety to mealtime.

Use recipes from a respected cookbook, magazine, or Internet site to guide you in planning meals. A pinch of this and a handful of that may work for experienced cooks. However, written, tested recipes are always more reliable.

Eating Out

Americans spend a considerable amount of money eating out. Whether eating away from home is a necessity or a pleasure, you will want to get a good food value for your money.

Choosing a Restaurant

When you eat out, you are paying for more than just the food. You are paying for someone to buy, prepare, cook, and serve the food. Even at inexpensive fast-food operations, meals usually cost more than similar foods you prepare at home. Consider how much and how often you are willing to pay someone else to shop and cook for you.

Before choosing a restaurant for a leisurely meal, find out about the types of foods served and the prices. A phone call before you leave home or a few questions before you are seated may save you time, money, and embarrassment. By calling ahead of time, you can find out if reservations are required or accepted; if a certain type of clothing is required or not allowed; and if credit cards are accepted. Much of this information can also be found on a restaurant's Web site. If you go to a restaurant and find it is not what you want, it is a good idea to leave quietly and find a place you can enjoy.

Case Study: Dining Out

Leroy and His Date

Leroy plans to take Patty to dinner and a movie on Saturday night. For this occasion, he wants to find a nice restaurant with a little atmosphere. He has heard commercials for a new place called Le Chateau.

Leroy doesn't realize they will need reservations. After waiting almost 45 minutes, Leroy and Patty are seated at a small table in a noisy, cramped spot. A waiter brings them a menu that is printed in French, which neither Leroy nor Patty understands. They both order the least expensive item on the menu. Even that is more than Leroy can easily afford.

The food they ordered is a baked egg dish with finely ground goose liver. It is not a dish either of them ever wants to try again. They both eat quickly with very little conversation and not much appetite.

When the check comes, it is twice the amount Leroy had planned to spend. Luckily, he has enough money with him to pay. All he has to do now is figure out what to do with the rest of the evening. He has no money left for a movie.

Case Review

1. How could Leroy have avoided this unforgettable evening at Le Chateau?
2. What might Leroy have done once they arrived at Le Chateau and he realized that it was not what he expected? How would you plan a dinner at a restaurant you have never tried before?

Restaurant reviews in local papers and magazines and online can be very helpful. They describe the types of food served, house specialties, atmosphere, and service. They tell the price range and the hours the restaurant is open. Sometimes you can find bargains as well as atmosphere at ethnic restaurants. In metropolitan areas you can find a wide variety of choices. Italian, Greek, Asian, Mexican, and German are among the popular ethnic restaurants. They usually serve foods and dishes you may not normally prepare at home. Prices are often reasonable, too.

If you are eating out with friends, decide ahead of time how you want to pay. Ask for separate checks when each person is paying his or her own way. Separate checks save figuring and hassling when the bill comes.

Reflect

What are your favorite restaurants? Why do you like them?

Activity

Role-play a person calling a restaurant about reservations, dress code, menu, and prices.

Case Study: Dining Out

An Even Split

Haajid has $10 to stretch over three more days until he gets paid again. He and four friends are eating at the Macho Taco. Haajid orders very carefully, trying to keep his tab under $5. He manages to get two tacos and a lemonade for $4.75. He is congratulating himself on his cheap meal while the other guys order big dinners.

The waitress puts all the orders on the same bill. When they are ready to leave, Haajid's friend Sam takes the check. He divides the total by five instead of trying to figure out who had what. He tells the guys that each share is $7.25. Haajid doesn't have the nerve to speak up and say his share is really only $4.75. He is afraid of looking cheap.

Case Review

1. How could Haajid have avoided this problem?
2. What would you have done if you were Haajid? How can you prevent similar experiences from happening to you?

Resource

Eating Out, Activity F, WB

Activity

Compare the cost of a meal prepared at home with the cost of the same meal served at a restaurant.

Enrich

Role-play an exchange between a customer and a waiter, including giving an order, asking questions about the menu, and asking for separate checks.

Selecting Healthful Choices

It can be a challenge to follow a healthful diet when eating out. Restaurants frequently offer large portions, high-calorie meals, and tempting dishes that are high in sugar, fat, and salt. Here are some suggestions to help you stay healthy even if you eat out frequently.

- Choose baked, broiled, or grilled foods over fried foods.
- Limit or stay away from foods that are high in sugar, fat, and salt. Look for "heart healthy" and low-calorie selections.
- Order whole-wheat breads, pastas, and cereals.
- Look for fresh fruits and vegetables.
- Take part of a super-size portion home for tomorrow's meal.
- Split orders or ask for a junior size where serving sizes tend to be too large.

Tipping

Include tips when you figure the cost of eating out. Fast-food, self-serve places do not usually call for tips. In most other restaurants, tipping is expected.

Be prepared to leave 15 to 20 percent of the bill for a tip. For a total food bill of $30.00, a 15 percent tip is $4.50 and a 20 percent tip is $6.00. A 20 percent or slightly higher tip is appropriate in expensive restaurants and for exceptionally good service.

Discuss

What specific types of service would lead you to tip more or less than the standard 15 to 20 percent?

Activity

Review and outline this chapter emphasizing the information you found most useful.

Resource

Chapter 15: Spending for Food, Teacher's PowerPoint Presentations CD

Chapter Summary

Food is an important item both in your budget and in your overall health and well-being. You will spend a sizable share of income in grocery stores and restaurants. The food you eat will affect the way you look, feel, and function.

Smart eating begins with nutritious meals and snacks. Two reliable guides to nutrition and good health are the Dietary Guidelines for Americans and MyPyramid. They offer suggestions for healthful eating.

To get the most for your dollars when shopping for food, you need to understand how supply and demand affect food prices. Establishing a food budget will help you control spending and get more for your money. Consider who eats in your household, any special dietary needs, and your family's food preferences. Your budget will also depend on how much you entertain and eat out, where you shop, and how skilled you are as a food shopper.

Planning purchases is one key to smart shopping. Food pages of local papers can give you ideas for menus. Using a list helps you remember all the items you need and gives direction to your shopping. Certain shopping aids in grocery stores can help you find the best buys. The labels on food products will be one of your most reliable guides.

Storing foods properly is a key factor in preserving flavor, freshness, and quality. The type of storage will depend on the food and how soon you intend to use it. Preparation of foods is a vital part to enjoying meals and snacks.

There are several factors to consider when eating in restaurants. Call ahead or check online when trying a new place to eat so you will know what to expect. Look for healthful choices on the menu. Be prepared to leave a tip in most restaurants.

Review

1. List the six types of nutrients.

2. List the five food groups represented in MyPyramid.

3. List five questions that can help you establish a food budget.

4. How can planning food purchases make consumers better food shoppers?

5. Name two reasons for shopping in the same one or two stores for groceries.

6. List three ways the UPC system can affect food shopping.

7. What information is required on nutrition facts panels?

8. How can you use unit pricing to save money?

9. What is the last day a product should be sold called?

10. What type of chicken should you select for frying, roasting, and broiling?

11. Why is it a good idea to call a restaurant ahead of time if you have never eaten there before?

Critical Thinking

12. Name three good food sources for each of the six types of nutrients the body needs.

13. How can MyPyramid help you plan meals and shop for foods?

14. How would you decide where to shop for food?

15. Why is proper food storage and food preparation important to successful food budgeting? For two weeks, keep track of the food that becomes waste in your home. Report to the class what foods were wasted, why, and how much money was lost.

16. Prepare a guide to healthful eating in restaurants.

Answers to *Review*

1. proteins, fats, carbohydrates, vitamins, minerals, water

2. grains, vegetables, fruits, milk, and meat and beans

3. (List five:) What are the ages and activity levels of household members? What special dietary needs must be met? What personal and family preferences will affect food choices? How much do you entertain and eat away from home? Where do you normally shop? How skilled are you at food shopping and preparation?

4. helps consumers get what they want while avoiding impulse buying

5. You will get to know the store well enough to find what you want quickly. You can compare prices of items from week to week to check which has the better buys.

6. (List three:) saves time and labor costs, shortens checkout lines, may reduce grocery prices since it cuts costs for retailers, reduces the chance of errors by checkout clerks, helps stores keep more accurate inventories, eliminates the need to mark the price on every item

Academic Connections

17. **Reading, research.** Bring to class news items from newspapers and magazines that describe events that could affect the supply and demand of food. In class, discuss how food prices could be affected.

18. **Social studies.** Evaluate three food stores in your community for prices, selection, and convenience. Report to the class which one of the three stores you prefer and why.

19. **Science.** Conduct an experiment to evaluate the effects of improper food storage by placing several foods in a variety of favorable and unfavorable storage situations. Discuss results in class.

20. **Research, writing.** Investigate a recent food recall and report the details to the class or write an article for the school paper.

21. **Research, math, speech.** Take responsibility for the food planning and marketing for your family for one week. Using MyPyramid, outline nutritious menus and snacks for the week and make up a shopping list of the foods you will need. Refer to newspaper food pages for ideas and specials. Then do the actual food shopping. (If this is not possible, go to the store and write down the prices of the items on your list.) Remember to look at unit pricing, open dating, and food labels. Prepare a three-minute oral report on your experience telling what foods you bought, how much money you spent, and how you would improve your plan if you were to do it again.

MATH CHALLENGE

22. The cereal you want to buy comes in two different sizes. What is the unit price of each one? Which is the better deal?
    - Box A: 10-ounce box for $5.00
    - Box B: 6-ounce box for $3.50

Tech Smart

23. Use an online calorie calculator, such as the one found on www.caloirescount.com. Figure out how many calories and grams of fat are in the following two lunches.

    Lunch A:
    - 1 regular cheeseburger
    - 1 large order of fries
    - 1 12-ounce milkshake

    Lunch B:
    - 1 tuna sandwich with 1 tablespoon light mayo, lettuce, tomato slice
    - 1 medium-size apple
    - 12 ounces of fat-free milk

    Make food substitutions in Lunch A to reduce the number of calories and fat grams.

7. serving size in both household and metric measures; servings per container; calories per serving and calories from fat; percent of Daily Values in grams or milligrams for total fat, saturated fat, trans fat, cholesterol, sodium, total carbohydrate including dietary fiber and sugars, and protein; percentages of Daily Values for vitamin A, vitamin C, calcium, and iron per serving

8. Unit pricing can help you compare like items in different quantities and sizes to determine the best buy.

9. pull date

10. young chickens

11. to find out what foods the restaurant serves, what prices it charges, if reservations are required or accepted, if a certain dress is required, if credit cards are honored

Answer to Math Challenge

22. A = $0.50 per ounce; B = $0.58 per ounce; A is the better buy

Reading for Meaning

If you wrote a paragraph about the link between clothing and personal finances, what subjects would you include and why? Look for these as you read this chapter. Note the subjects that you did not anticipate.

wardrobe

wardrobe inventory

accessories

fad

natural fibers

manufactured fibers

blend

woven fabrics

knit fabrics

nonwoven fabrics

fabric finish

CHAPTER OBJECTIVES

After studying this chapter, you will be able to

- **identify** wardrobe needs.
- **establish** a clothing budget.
- **evaluate** construction features, fabrics, fit, and appearance of garments when shopping.
- **describe** clothing that is appropriate for different occasions.
- **outline** guidelines to follow when buying footwear.
- **list** guidelines for proper care of clothing.

Central Ideas

- Having a wardrobe plan and understanding clothing construction and care will help you stretch your clothing dollars further.

- Choose appropriate clothing for specific places, activities, and events.

Resource

Clothes, Feelings, and Behavior, Activity A, WB

Reflect

What types of accessories do you own? What additional ones would you like to own?

Activity

Bring in photos from fashion magazines showing different types of accessories for a discussion of accessories and their uses.

Resource

My Wardrobe Inventory, Activity C, WB

The question of what to wear has occupied the minds of men and women around the world. "What will I wear?" "I have nothing to wear." "What is everyone else wearing?" These are familiar concerns in every household.

Most people want clothes that look nice and feel comfortable. Having the right clothes for all seasons, activities, and places calls for careful planning and buying. Learning how to analyze your wardrobe, shop for clothing, and care for clothes properly can help you achieve the look you want at a price you can afford.

Wardrobe Planning

At one time or another, you have probably said, "I have nothing to wear." You may have been staring at a closet full of clothes when you said it. At the time, you probably thought the clothes you had were not right for the occasion or your mood. Most teens need clothes for school, work, special occasions, active sports, and casual wear. Consider what clothing is appropriate for the way you live and the places you go, 16-1.

By developing a wardrobe plan, you can gradually add the clothes and accessories you need for different occasions. A **wardrobe** is the collection of clothes you own. A good wardrobe plan involves three major steps—taking inventory, clearing out clothes you never wear, and adding the clothes you need. The additions you make depend on your needs and the amount of money you can spend. Your shopping skills will determine how much you get for your money.

The Inventory

A **wardrobe inventory** is a list of all the clothes, shoes, and accessories you own. **Accessories** are items designed to go with an outfit. They include belts, ties, scarves, hats, gloves, handbags, and jewelry. An inventory can help you find gaps in your wardrobe so you can prioritize what you need to buy.

To make an inventory, list all the clothes you have according to their type (jackets, pants, shirts, and so forth). Consider where and how you wear different items. Include sleepwear, undergarments, shoes, and accessories in your inventory. Also list any special clothes or uniforms you wear for work, sports, and other activities.

The Clearance

One purpose of an inventory is to discard items you no longer wear, need, or want. When deciding which clothes to keep and what to give away, ask yourself three questions:

16-1

Casual clothes are right for leisure time and hanging out with friends.

- Does it fit?

- Do I like it?

- Will I wear it?

If clothes need laundering, mending, or altering, set aside a time to do the necessary work. It is frustrating to pull out a shirt you want to wear and discover it is missing a button or needs laundering.

Remove garments you do not or cannot wear. Perhaps you know someone who may want them. Clothes and shoes that are in good condition may be sold through a consignment store or at a garage sale. Consignment stores usually split the proceeds with you. You may want to donate wearable clothes to persons or organizations that can use them. If you follow IRS procedures about giving to nonprofit groups, the value of your giveaways may be deducted from your taxes.

The Additions

The final step in wardrobe planning is to complete your wardrobe. Using your inventory as a guide, list the clothes and accessories you need to fill the gaps. You can stretch your wardrobe by planning around one or two neutral colors that will go well with a variety of brighter colors. This lets you mix and match to create different outfits.

Before you buy anything, look through fashion magazines and walk through clothing stores. Check out colors and styles and the accessories used with different clothes. How would the colors look with your skin tone and hair coloring? Would the lines and textures be flattering on you? Will new fashions go well with clothes and accessories you already have?

Consider how long you are likely to wear the newest fashions. This is especially important for expensive items. **Fads** are styles that stay popular

Activity

Find an item in your wardrobe that you do not want to keep. Consider donating or selling the item. Describe your plans to the class.

Activity

Apply the wardrobe evaluation questions to the clothes in your closet.

Activity

Apply the wardrobe evaluation questions to items you see in a clothing store or catalog.

Vocabulary

Consider the meaning of the term *fad* in the fashion world.

Linking to... History

Denim Jeans

In the U.S., cotton denim jeans were first made by entrepreneurs Levi Strauss and Jacob Davis in the 1870s. The first jeans were created for miners working in California's gold fields. The popularity of denim jeans spread to others who sought durable and comfortable work pants.

Perhaps more than any other garment, jeans are associated with an attitude and a lifestyle. In the 1940s, they became synonymous with freedom and the Wild West because of their popularity among cowboys. During the 1950s, some parents and educators prohibited teenagers from wearing jeans because of their association with rebellion and delinquency.

During the 1970s, jeans became canvases of the wearer. Young people painted, embroidered, and beaded their jeans. Cutoff jeans were also popular. During the 1980s, designer jeans and stonewashed denim were popular. Jean styles became baggy and were worn below the hip.

Ripped, faded, decorated, and designer labeled, denim jeans have been the favorite wardrobe item for generations of Americans.

Reflect

Do you have most of the clothes you really need? What additions do you want?

Activity

Rank the items on your list of clothing needs in terms of purchase priority.

for only a short time. For example, this year's trendiest items will probably be "out" next year.

Other clothes can be worn for several seasons. If you buy a good pair of jeans, they will be "in style" for decades to come.

Generally it pays to go for quality over quantity, particularly for clothes you wear most. One good pair of dress pants is likely to serve you longer than three pairs that lose their shape with wear and laundering. Lower quality, less expensive items may be a fine choice for fads or for things you wear only occasionally.

Clothing Dollars

Once you decide what you want to add to your wardrobe, look seriously at your budget. What you buy will depend largely on how much money you have to spend.

Your inventory can help you organize the clothes you own and decide what to buy. You may want to set up your clothing budget on a seasonal basis. As you plan, consider the

- total amount you have to spend

- total amount of your essential nonclothing expenses

- importance of clothing and personal appearance to you

- amount you can allow for clothes after meeting other essential needs

Case Study: The Shopping Scene

Abby Is in a Hurry

Abby is always busy and rarely has time to shop. One day, during a rushed shopping trip, she buys an expensive coat at 30 percent off. She slips the coat on over her jeans. It seems to fit and the price is right, so she buys the coat.

A week later Abby is dressing for a special date. When she puts on her new coat, she realizes it is much shorter than her dress. The mismatched hem lengths look awful, but there is nothing Abby can do now. The dress is the right length, and the coat cannot be lengthened.

Case Review

1. How could Abby have avoided this problem?

2. What are some precautions to keep in mind when buying clothes on sale?

3. What are some practical shortcuts you can take when you don't have much time to shop for clothes?

If you can afford everything you want, you are ready to start shopping. If you cannot buy all you need, prioritize your needs and focus on your highest priorities. For example, if you have enough casual clothing, do not buy another casual shirt just because it is on sale. Look for the clothes that will fill the gaps in your wardrobe.

There are several ways to save money on your wardrobe purchases. Here are a few ideas:

- Compare the prices and quality of merchandise between different sellers. Comparison shopping can help you save money if you know how to judge quality and style.

- Try bargain-hunter sources such as clothing warehouses, factory outlets, surplus stores, resale shops, and discount stores.

- Watch store ads for specials and preseason sales. End-of-season sales offer some of the best savings. For example, in mid-July, swimwear and summer clothing is often reduced by 30 to 50 percent. By August, summer items will be marked down even more.

- If you or someone in your family sews, some of your clothes can be made at home. Sewing skills can cut wardrobe costs substantially.

Sometimes a low price signals a real bargain. Other times it signals poor quality or outdated fashions. It is important to know the difference.

Shopping for Clothes

You need to know how to judge quality and what quality level will best serve different purposes. You also need to know how much you can spend. It can be helpful to shop with a trusted friend who can help you make choices.

As you shop consider fit, style and color, fabrics, and construction features. Try garments on in front of a full-length mirror to check fit, appearance, and comfort. Hands-on inspection is the best way to check construction details and fabric characteristics. Labels and tags will give you the best care information. These tips apply to in-store shopping.

Catalog and online outlets often have values and variety that may be hard to find in local stores. Many clothing manufacturers sell clothing online or through catalogs. Once you know and like particular brands, you usually can trust their online and catalog offerings.

If you buy from these and other distance sellers, it is important to follow the suggestions in Chapter 14 under "dealing with distance sellers." Wherever you buy, be sure to

- check garment construction
- know what fibers, fabrics, and finishes have been used
- check fit, comfort, and appearance
- read labels and tags for use and care information

Clothing Construction

The way garments are put together can affect appearance, fit, and durability. Poorly made garments look worn and unattractive quickly.

Human Services

Buyers

Buyers determine which fashions their establishments will sell. They must have the ability to predict what will appeal to consumers. They must constantly stay informed of the latest trends, to maximize the profits and reputation of their company. They keep track of inventories and sales levels through computer software.

Better-quality clothes are usually more expensive, but they may be better buys. With proper care, they look attractive much longer.

To judge the quality of construction, check sewing and finishing details on the seams, linings, hems, collars, lapels, buttonholes, zippers, and pockets. Construction features to look for in well-made clothing include

- smooth seams, hems, zippers, and lapels
- reinforcement at points of strain
- firmly attached buttons, hooks and eyes, snaps, and trim
- generous allowances for seams, hems, pleats, slits, and lapels
- appropriate trim and decoration for the garment
- smooth and firmly stitched buttonholes

Fibers, Fabrics, and Finishes

Fiber content, construction methods, and finishes affect the way a fabric looks and feels, its performance and care, and its price. Knowing how fabrics are made can help you make informed clothing choices.

Fiber Content

Most fabrics are made from *natural* or *manufactured fibers*. **Natural fibers** come from plants and animals. They include cotton, linen, silk, wool, and

Arts, A/V Technology & Communications

Fashion Designers

Fashion designers study fashion trends and sketch designs of clothing and accessories. They then select colors and fabrics and oversee the final production of their designs.

Organic Fabrics

Interest in clothing labeled *organic* is growing. Items ranging from diapers to T-shirts to jeans, for example, are using organic cotton. Such items often cost more based on how much organic fiber is used.

Only raw natural fibers such as cotton and wool are eligible to be called *organic.* They come from crops and livestock, so are considered agricultural products. The U.S. Department of Agriculture (USDA) sets rules to assure consumers that agricultural products marketed as organic meet consistent, uniform standards. The rules are part of USDA's National Organic Program (NOP) regulations.

Only textiles that meet strict NOP production and processing standards are eligible for the

- **"100 Percent Organic" label**, which requires all fibers to be organic
- **"Organic" label**, which requires at least 95 percent of fibers to be organic

In both cases, the USDA Organic seal may be displayed. The claim "Made with Organic Fibers," however, has no use restrictions. This means consumers need to contact clothing manufacturers or retailers who use the claim to find out what percent of fibers are truly organic.

A USDA-licensed agent monitors production and processing steps to certify that producers and handlers comply with the standards. Organic crops are raised without most common pesticides, petroleum-based fertilizers, or sewage sludge-based fertilizers. Animals raised organically must have organic feed and access to the outdoors. They are given no antibiotics or growth hormones.

other hair fibers, such as camel's hair and cashmere. Following are some of the key characteristics of natural fibers commonly used for clothing.

- *Cotton* is absorbent, comfortable, easy to dye, and easy to combine with other fibers. If untreated it tends to wrinkle easily, shrink in hot water, and be highly flammable. It is reasonably durable and suited to many uses.

- *Linen* is absorbent, comfortable, durable, and lustrous in appearance. If untreated it wrinkles and creases easily and has poor resistance to mildew. It will be expensive if it is good quality.

- *Silk* looks and feels luxurious, combines well with other fibers, resists wrinkling, and is strong but lightweight. It also is expensive, requires dry cleaning unless labeled *washable*, and tends to water spot unless treated.

- *Wool* is the warmest of natural fibers. It is wrinkle resistant, easy to dye, durable, and absorbent. It also retains its shape and combines well with other fibers. Wool shrinks when moisture and heat are applied. It requires dry cleaning unless labeled *washable* and it burns easily. It is attractive to moths and carpet beetles.

Most **manufactured fibers** are made from chemicals. They include polyester, nylon, rayon, acrylic, acetate, and a host of others. Following are some of the key characteristics of manufactured fibers commonly used for clothing.

- *Polyester* is strong and durable, easy to dye, and colorfast. It retains its shape well and resists wrinkles, stretching, shrinking, moths, and mildew. It generally is easy to launder, but is subject to oily stains, soil, and pilling.

- *Nylon* is lightweight, stretchable, strong, and durable. It drapes well and dyes well. It dries quickly, cleans easily, and resists abrasion. It is nonabsorbent and can be uncomfortable in hot weather.

- *Rayon* is a soft, durable, comfortable, and absorbent fabric. It drapes and dyes well and is resistant to insect damage. If not treated, it wrinkles easily, is highly flammable, and shrinks in hot water.

- *Acrylic* is a soft luxurious fabric that resembles wool. It drapes well, dyes well, and gives warmth without weight. It is an absorbent, comfortable, easy care fabric that is resistant to wrinkles, moths, oil, and sunlight.

- *Acetate* is a soft, luxurious fabric that dyes and drapes well. It is resistant to shrinkage, moths, and mildew. It is nonabsorbent and usually requires dry cleaning.

A **blend** is made by combining two or more fibers. Blends usually have the best characteristics of the different fibers used. For example, cotton/polyester is a very common and popular blend. It combines the absorbency and comfort of cotton with the wrinkle-resistance and easy-care property of polyester.

Resource

The Smart Shopper Quiz,
Activity B, WB

Example

Bring in samples of fabrics made from each of the natural fibers listed. Discuss the advantages and disadvantages of each.

Example

Bring in samples of each of the manufactured fibers listed. Examine the samples and compare their similarities and differences.

Discuss

What are the advantages and disadvantages of woven fabrics and knit fabrics?

Example

Bring in samples of cloth made by the listed construction methods. Discuss the characteristics of each.

Enrich

Check out the construction features in clothing you own and items you want to buy. What do you learn by carefully inspecting construction features?

Knit sweaters and hats are comfortable because they stretch to fit the body.

Science, Technology, Engineering & Mathematics

Textile Engineers
Textile engineers specialize in the design of textile machinery, new textile production methods, or the study of fibers. They do research and development as well as initiate projects and plan and schedule production.

Fabric Construction

The way fibers are made into fabric affects appearance and performance. Weaving and knitting are the two most common methods of fabric construction.

Woven fabrics are made by interlacing two or more sets of yarns at right angles. A number of weaving variations are used to achieve special effects. Generally, weaving produces durable fabrics that hold their shape well. Fabrics that are tightly woven or knitted tend to hold their shape better than those loosely woven or knitted.

Knit fabrics are made by looping yarns together. Depending on the knitting methods and fibers used, fabrics can vary greatly in appearance and texture. Most knit fabrics offer natural stretch that makes them wrinkle-resistant and comfortable to wear, 16-2.

Some types of cloth are made from construction methods other than weaving or knitting. These include **nonwoven fabrics**, such as felt and artificial suede, bonded fabrics, quilted fabrics, lace, and net.

Finishes

A **fabric finish** is a treatment applied to a fabric to achieve certain characteristics. Finishes affect the appearance, comfort, feel, durability, performance, and care of fabrics.

Finishes can change the appearance of fabric by improving its color, luster, texture, and versatility. Certain finishes make clothing more comfortable to wear because they provide greater insulation, reduce static cling, resist water, or soften fabrics.

Before buying a garment, be sure you know how to care for the garment. Read labels and tags to know just what you are buying. Find out if it has a finish that requires special care when being cleaned. Also check the durability of the finish. Will it last for the life of the garment? Will it have to be renewed after laundering or dry cleaning? Following are some of the finishes commonly applied to fabrics along with their functions.

- *Antistatic* finish prevents the buildup of static electricity so garments will not cling.

- *Durable-press* or *permanent press* helps fabric retain its original shape and resist wrinkling after laundering.

- *Flame-resistance* makes fabrics resist flame. It is required on flammable fabrics used in children's sleepwear and other clothing and household items.

Case Study: Case Study: The Shopping Scene

Tina Buys a Mistake

Tina is going to a school party and wants to look her best. Nothing in her closet is right. Tina takes $95 she earned from babysitting and goes shopping for a new outfit.

Tina tries on several outfits at her favorite store, but none appeal to her. She goes into an unfamiliar store and sees some beautiful things. The clothes in this store cost more than she normally spends. A salesperson asks Tina what type of outfit she wants. Tina is not sure. The salesperson brings out several dresses, all of which cost more than Tina can afford. Since the salesperson is so persistent, Tina feels obliged to try on at least one or two of the dresses.

One dress looks great on Tina. The salesperson insists that she must have it. Not knowing how to say no, Tina buys the $125 dress, and must use a credit card instead of cash.

When Tina arrives home, she realizes her only coat is too casual to wear with the dress. None of her shoes look right either. To make matters worse, she learns that everyone else is wearing casual clothes to the party.

Case Review

1. Have you ever let a salesperson talk you into buying something you really did not want?
2. How might Tina have avoided her expensive mistake?
3. What information would you want to know about a store before buying something from that store?
4. Where could Tina have found information and ideas that might have helped her make a better choice?

- *Mercerization* increases luster and strength of cotton, linen, and rayon fabrics.
- *Mildew-resistance* helps prevent mildew from forming on fabrics.
- *Moth-resistance* is added to wool fibers to repel moths and carpet beetles.

Activity

Check out labels on different types of clothing in a store to learn what finishes are typically applied and what they achieve.

- *Sanforized*® guarantees that a fabric will not shrink more than one percent.

- *Scotchguard*® creates resistance to water and oil stains.

- *Soil-release* makes it possible to remove oily stains from durable-press fabrics. It makes water-resistant fibers more absorbent so detergents can release soil.

- *Waterproof* makes fabric completely resistant to water and air passage.

- *Water-repellent* makes fabric resist wetting, but does not make it waterproof or resistant to heavy rain. This finish must be renewed after several launderings.

Fit and Appearance

A dress or suit that is just right on one person may be all wrong for another. The only way to know which garments do the most for you is to try them on. As you evaluate the fit and appearance, ask yourself the following questions:

- Where will I wear these clothes? For what occasions are they suited?

- Can I use these clothes to look taller, thinner, shorter, or rounder?

- How can I combine these purchases with clothes in my wardrobe?

When possible, try on clothes with the shoes, accessories, and other garments you plan to wear with them. It is particularly important to check skirt lengths and pant cuffs with the shoes you will wear. You also may want to check skirt lengths with coats you will wear over them.

Stand, sit, move, and stretch to check comfort and fit of new garments. Inspect your overall appearance in a full-length mirror from the front, side, and back. If clothing fits well, it will not bind, wrinkle, or pucker. Select colors, lines, styles, and textures that flatter your figure type and coloring, 16-3. These elements can also call attention to your positive features and take attention away from negative features. You can use color, line, and texture to look thinner or heavier and shorter or taller. You can mix and match separates to stretch your wardrobe and create different looks.

Labels and Legislation

The labels and tags on clothes provide important information. Most labels will identify the manufacturer, designer, or seller; the name of the country where the garment was made; and the fiber content. If a special finish has been applied to the fabric, it is usually listed. Labels also give care instructions and size information.

Much of the data listed on clothing labels and other textile products is required by law. Four of the most important laws and regulations that govern the labeling, marketing, and safety of clothing and textile products are described in 16-4.

Create the Look You Want Through Color, Line, and Texture

Look thinner with

- cool colors (colors related to blue and green)
- dark, subtle colors
- vertical lines
- smooth, nonlustrous, medium weight textures
- subtle prints, checks, and plaids
- clothes that skim the body and are not tight
- simple, uncluttered styles
- thin shapes and narrow widths in coats, sleeves, collars, trousers, and belts

Look heavier with

- warm colors (colors related to red, orange, and yellow)
- bright, light colors
- horizontal lines
- nubby, bulky, or stiff textures with surface interest
- bold prints, checks, and plaids
- full sleeves, wide-leg trousers, large pleats, and gathers
- wide contrasting belts

Look taller with

- one color or related color tones head to foot
- vertical lines
- designs, lines, and trims that lead the eye up instead of down
- narrow, uncuffed trousers
- emphasis at or above the neckline

Look shorter with

- bright, contrasting colors
- horizontal lines
- designs, lines, or trims that lead the eye down instead of up
- wide-cuffed trousers
- emphasis below the waist or at the feet

Accentuate positive features with

- warm, bright, light colors
- lines and designs that lead the eye to your best features
- fabrics and textures that emphasize your best features

De-emphasize negative features with

- cool, dark, subtle colors
- lines that lead the eye away from poor features
- styles, fabrics, and textures that hide or cover poor features

16-3

Color, line, and texture in clothing can help you highlight attractive features and de-emphasize negative features.

Regulations Governing Clothing and Textile Products

Wool Products Labeling Act	Requires products containing wool to be labeled with the percentage and type of fibers used—new or virgin wool, reprocessed or reused wool. This act is enforced by the Federal Trade Commission.
Textiles Fiber Products Identification Act	Requires textile products to be labeled with the generic name, fibers used, and the percentage of each fiber present by weight. The name or identification of the manufacturer and the country of origin, if the item is imported, must also be listed. This is required for wearing apparel, accessories, and textile products used in the home such as draperies, upholstered furniture, linens, and bedding. This act is enforced by the Federal Trade Commission.
Permanent Care Labeling Rule	Requires manufacturers to attach permanent care labels to apparel explaining the best way to clean a garment including methods and temperatures for laundering, drying, ironing, and dry cleaning. Fabrics, draperies, curtains, slipcovers, upholstered furniture, carpets, and rugs must also be labeled with care instructions. This rule is enforced by the Federal Trade Commission.
Flammable Fabrics Act	Sets flammability standards for children's sleepwear, general wearing apparel, carpets, rugs, and mattresses to protect consumers from unreasonable fire risks. This act is enforced by the Consumer Product Safety Commission.

16-4

These laws regulate the labeling, marketing, and safety of clothing and textile products.

Discuss

Discuss what types of clothing are suitable and not suitable for different occasions.

Resource

Choosing Clothes for the Occasion, reproducible master 16-2, TR

Reflect

What is the dress code at your parents' or guardians' workplace?

Career and Work Clothes

Performance will be the most important factor in advancing on the job. However, your manner and appearance help you get from an interview to a job, and they contribute to your success at work.

When you are interviewed, you may want to ask what type of dress is expected in the workplace. A careful look at what other employees are wearing can guide you at a new job. If you already have a job, ask your employer if you are unsure about what is and is not acceptable.

There are some legal protections for employees whose dress or appearance relates to their religious practices. However, for the most part, employers have the right to set standards for dress and appearance in the workplace. These standards are important because they can lose business if employees' clothing offends customers.

It is a good idea to begin your career wardrobe with a few basic items and fill in as you become familiar with the dress codes and customs of your workplace. Workplace dress codes are often classified as *business* or *business casual*, 16-5.

Law firms, accounting firms, banks, insurance companies, and some government agencies often follow a business dress code. People in these fields usually work in office settings and frequently meet with clients. Employees are expected to present a professional image. This usually means suits and tailored clothing.

16-5

Follow the dress code established by your workplace.

Guide to Career Clothing		
	Women	**Men**
Business	• Suits with pants or skirt (stylish but not trendy) • Leather shoes, no sandals • Conservative, neutral colors • Hose in neutral colors • Simple jewelry and accessories • Smart handbag, not too bulky	• Suits of good quality • Dress shirt with tie • Dress shoes, polished • Dark or neutral colors • Socks in color to go with suit • Jewelry limited to watch and wedding band
Business Casual	• Khakis or other semitailored pants or skirts • Cotton shirts, polo or knit shirts with sleeves • Sweaters or turtlenecks • Blazers • Flats, loafers—no flip-flops, sandals, or sneakers • Neat, crisp, simple look	• Khakis or semitailored pants • Long sleeved cotton shirts, polo shirts with sleeves • Shirts tucked into trousers • Loafers—no sneakers or sandals • No T-shirts • No hats

Business casual varies from workplace to workplace. Even conservative offices may relax the dress code for "casual Fridays." Knowing what to wear in more casual settings can be tricky. Even if the dress code is relaxed, the following are not acceptable in the workplace:

Reflect

What is the dress code at your workplace?

- sloppy, baggy, soiled, tight, revealing, transparent, or simply inappropriate clothing

- clothing with a social message, particularly if the message is controversial

- workout clothes and flip-flops. Sneakers may be okay in a very casual workplace

Case Study: Clothing Speaks

The Scene Changes

Until Natesh graduated from high school, he never thought much about the clothes he wore. Everyone in school dressed pretty much alike. It was simple to wear the "right" clothes.

Now Natesh is more concerned about his appearance. He is wondering what clothes he will need for a summer office job and for college in the fall. He wants to make the right choices so he won't have to worry about the way he looks. He also has a limited budget so he wants to select useful and appropriate clothes.

Case Review

1. What do you think Natesh should wear for job interviews? How do you think the way he looks might influence possible employers?

2. What do you think Natesh should wear if he worked at the following jobs?
- stock clerk at a supermarket
- salesperson in a clothing store
- aide at a hospital
- Little League coach
- door-to-door salesperson
- file clerk in an office

3. What type of wardrobe do you think Natesh will need at college? How can he find out what he needs before buying?

For almost any job, clothes need to fit well and be clean, pressed, and in good condition. There should be no missing buttons, lint, or sagging hems.

Some jobs require uniforms that take the guesswork out of dressing. Simply make sure the uniform is clean, pressed, and properly fitted.

Shoes at work need to be suited to what you are doing. For example, if you are on your feet and moving around, shoes need to offer more comfort and support than if you sit at a desk. Keep shoes polished and in good condition.

Shopping for Footwear

As a rule, buy the best-quality footwear you can afford. In addition to comfort and quality, consider the style. Choose colors and designs that look well on your feet and fit into your wardrobe. The best-looking, well-made shoes are worthless if they do not fit.

Fit

The right fit adds to your comfort and helps you avoid aching feet and serious foot problems. Do not plan to "break in" a pair of shoes. If they do not fit in the store, they will not be comfortable later. Do not rely on size only when buying footwear. Sizes often vary with different styles or brands. Try on both shoes to check fit. Following are more tips to help you find a good fit:

- The entire shoe should fit snugly without being tight.
- Shoes should not slip or pinch your feet when you stand or walk.
- If you cannot move your toes freely, try a different size, width, or style.
- Check fit with the socks or hosiery you plan to wear with footwear.

Construction

Before buying shoes or boots, examine the construction.

- Are they stitched well and lined smoothly?
- Are the shoes made of soft, durable, flexible materials?
- Are they adequately cushioned for comfort?
- Do they provide adequate support?
- Are they easy to clean and maintain?

The materials used to make shoes can affect comfort. Feet need to "breathe" inside a shoe to stay dry and comfortable. Sandals and footwear made of leather allow air to circulate around the foot. Plastic, vinyl, and rubber materials do not allow feet to breathe well.

Athletic Shoes

Athletic shoes come in a variety of styles, materials, and weights. Specific types of athletic shoes provide support and protection against the strain and stress of different vigorous activities. If you practice a sport three to four times weekly, you may need one of the following sport-specific shoe types:

- walking

- court sports—tennis, basketball, volleyball, and badminton

- field sports—baseball, soccer, football

- track and field sports—running, jogging, jumping

- winter sports—figure skating, hockey, alpine skiing, cross-country skiing

- specialty sports—golf, cycling, aerobics

- outdoor sports—hunting, hiking, fishing, climbing

Depending on your sport, you need shoes that support and protect the foot and ankle. Look for the traction and flexibility your activities require. Evaluate durability and price, 16-6. The following general guidelines can help you find athletic shoes that are right for you:

- Buy shoes specifically designed for your sport. Your coach may have some pointers on what to buy.

- Shop after a workout or late in the day when feet tend to be larger.

- Measure both feet while standing and buy the size most comfortable on your larger foot.

- Try on both shoes with the socks you will wear with them.

- Walk around the store to check fit and comfort. You need room to wiggle your toes and a snug fit at the heel that does not slip when you walk.

- Check out special features such as gel-filled inserts, extra cushioning, and reflectors.

16-6

Comparison shopping for athletic shoes can help you select the right type for your sport at a reasonable price.

Discuss

What clothing care procedures do you follow?

Activity

Set aside at least one hour during the next week to care for any of your clothes that need attention.

Clothing Care

Proper clothing care helps clothes look better and last longer. Clean, pressed, and mended garments also enhance your appearance. By spending a few dollars on clothing care, you can get longer wear from your clothes.

Routine Care

Caring for clothes on a routine basis will keep clothes and accessories in good condition and ready to wear. Simple things, like dressing and undressing carefully, can help you avoid snagging, ripping, or stretching garments.

Before you put them away, check to see if they need cleaning, pressing, or mending. You may only need to brush garments to remove lint and dust. Air your clothes in an open room before returning them to the closet or drawer.

Remember to protect clothes with aprons or napkins when you are cooking or eating. Wear old clothes for tough, dirty jobs. Also avoid overstuffing pockets or handbags. This can stretch them out of shape.

Storing Clothes

Make it a habit to hang clothes straight on sturdy hangers. Close zippers and fasten buttons. Fold sweaters and knit garments neatly and store them in drawers. Avoid overcrowding closets and drawers so clothes will not be crushed or wrinkled.

Periodically, clean and organize closets and drawers. This will help you keep track of the clothes you own and make them easy to find. Make a clothing inventory at the beginning of each season. This is also a good time for sorting, repairing, and cleaning garments and footwear.

Before storing out-of-season clothes, make sure they are clean and pockets are empty. Store clothing in clean, dry places. Use airtight garment bags if your storage area is humid. Plastic bags and sturdy cardboard boxes are good for storing clothes in dry environments. Try to avoid crowding items to prevent wrinkling. You may want to spray woolens with moth repellents or store them with mothballs to prevent moth damage.

Laundering Clothing

Learning how to clean clothes properly is simply a matter of reading. If you follow the directions on clothing care labels, laundry products, and washers and dryers, clothes can continue to look nice after many launderings, 16-7.

Preparation

Preparing items to be washed is the first step in home laundering. Empty all pockets, fasten closures, make necessary repairs, and remove any nonwashable trims. Also remove stains and pretreat heavily soiled clothes before washing.

Sorting

The purpose of sorting is to separate items that could damage other clothes. Wash together those items that use the same water temperature, wash speed, and other treatment. For best results, wash similar colors and fabrics together. Avoid mixing "lint givers," such as towels, with other fabrics.

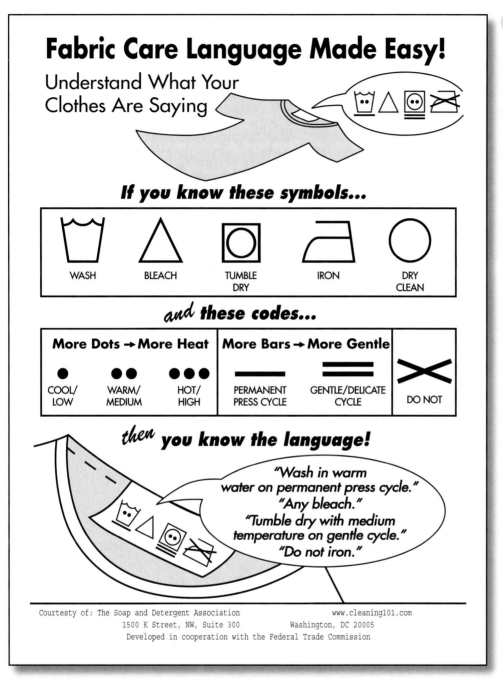

Courtesty of: The Soap and Detergent Association   www.cleaning101.com
1500 K Street, NW, Suite 300   Washington, DC 20005
Developed in cooperation with the Federal Trade Commission

16-7
Proper clothing care increases wear life and improves appearance of garments. These symbols are your guide to clothing care.

Choosing Cleaning Products

Of the many kinds of laundry products available, choose only the products you need. Follow the package directions carefully. Liquid or powder detergents are the basic laundry products.

Bleaches may be used to remove stains or to whiten clothes. Since chlorine bleaches are made of strong chemicals, they should not be used on all garments. The clothing label will tell you if an item cannot withstand bleaching.

Liquid fabric softeners may be added to the rinse cycle to make fabrics soft and to reduce wrinkles and static electricity. Sheet fabric softeners may be used in the dryer.

Enrich

Do the family laundry for a week and report on what you learned.

Activity

Bring garments with care labels to class and discuss care instructions.

Resource

Caring for Clothes, Activity E, WB

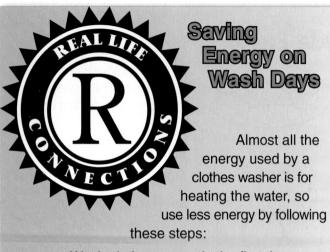

Saving Energy on Wash Days

Almost all the energy used by a clothes washer is for heating the water, so use less energy by following these steps:

- Wash clothes correctly the first time to avoid rewashing.

- Match the water level to the load size to avoid heating more water than needed.

- Use the right amount of detergent as indicated on the label. Avoid excess suds, which require extra rinses.

- Do not wash in hot water when warm or cold water will do the job.

- Always rinse with cold water.

You can save energy with an automatic dryer in the following ways:

- Use the air-dry instead of the heat-dry setting when possible.

- Remove dry clothes promptly. Overly long drying times causes wrinkling

Choosing Washer and Dryer Settings

Before washing clothes, make sure you select a wash cycle that is suitable for the load. Cycles on most washers include delicate or gentle, permanent press, and regular or normal. Select the water temperature recommended on the care labels.

If you do not know which automatic dryer cycle to use, read the appliance's directions and the clothing care labels. Whatever cycle you use, remove clothes as soon as they are dry to prevent wrinkling.

Dry Cleaning

Dry cleaning uses a chemical solution instead of water to remove stains, dirt, and soil. Clothes that require dry cleaning may be done in a coin-operated dry cleaning center or by a professional dry cleaner. Coin-operated machines are sometimes available at laundromats. Using these machines is less expensive than professional dry cleaning. However, dry cleaning clothes yourself takes more time and effort. It also does not include the advantages of professional spotting, pressing, and other services dry cleaning establishments may offer.

Professional dry cleaners can often remove spots and stains that you may have difficulty removing. They can add sizing to a garment to give it more body. They can also restore a water-repellent finish after cleaning. Dry cleaners may offer additional services, such as alterations, pickups, and deliveries.

Chapter Summary

Wardrobe planning usually begins with an inventory of clothes. It starts with taking a close look at what is wearable and clearing out what you no longer can use. Identifying the gaps in your wardrobe will serve as a guide to making new purchases.

Once you know what you want, it pays to do a little preshopping in magazines and stores to find current fashions that will work well for you. This will also give you a good idea of the prices of different items.

Setting up a clothing budget will help you avoid overspending. Bargain hunting, comparison shopping, and sales can help you stretch your clothing dollars. When it comes to shopping, learn how to judge clothing construction and develop a sense of fashion.

Fabric is a key factor in the look and feel of clothes. Fabric type will affect performance, price, and care. Reading labels will provide information on fabric finishes, fiber content, and care of fabrics.

Appropriate career and work clothes depend on the type of job you have. In office settings, business and business casual clothes tend to be the norm. Regardless of where you work, it is important to be neat and clean.

Buying footwear is a major part of dressing well. Comfort and support are particularly important. Mistakes can cause serious foot problems. Select appropriate shoes for appearance and for the way you will wear them. Choose athletic shoes for the specific sports activities you enjoy.

Proper clothing care is the secret to a ready-to-go wardrobe of clothes that look attractive and wear well. Laundering clothes requires reading labels and following directions. The user's manual that comes with washers and dryers provides important care information. Consider the environmental impact of different laundry products when you are buying them. Dry cleaning will be necessary for certain types of fabrics and clothing.

Review

1. What are the three major steps involved in wardrobe planning?

2. How can a clothing inventory guide shopping decisions?

3. What four things do you need to consider when establishing a clothing budget?

4. Where are some places to buy clothes and accessories at relatively low prices?

5. List two examples of nonwoven fabrics.

6. What is the difference between a waterproof finish and a water-repellent finish?

7. Why is it important to try on clothes before you buy them?

8. What is the purpose of care labels on clothes?

9. What are some differences between *business* and *business casual* dressing?

10. True or false. As a rule, buy the best quality footwear you can afford.

11. What are some additional considerations when buying athletic shoes?

12. List four routine clothing care tasks.

13. Describe three sources of clothing care information.

Critical Thinking

15. What clothes or outfits do you like most in your wardrobe? What is it you particularly like about each favorite item of clothing? How can you apply this knowledge to future purchases?

16. What colors, lines, and textures look best on you? What fashions and styles will flatter your body shape and accentuate your positive features?

17. How fashion-conscious are you? How much importance do you place on fashion when buying clothes?

18. If you owned a clothing store, what services would you offer to attract customers?

19. What problems have you had with clothing care? What did you do to solve these problems?

20. How would you interpret the following quotes about the clothes you wear:
    - "The fashion wears out more apparel than the man." Shakespeare
    - "Be not the first by whom the new are tried, nor yet the last to lay the old aside." Alexander Pope
    - "Every generation laughs at the old fashions, but follows religiously the new." Thoreau
    - "Fashion is made to become unfashionable." Coco Chanel

Answers to *Review*

1. taking a wardrobe inventory, clearing out clothes you never wear, and adding the clothes you need

2. It can help you find gaps in your wardrobe so you can prioritize what you need to buy.

3. the total amount you have to spend; the total amount of essential nonclothing expenses you have; the importance of clothing and personal appearance to you; the amount you can allow for your wardrobe after meeting other essential needs

4. clothing warehouses, factory outlets, surplus stores, resale shops, and discount stores

5. (List two:) felt, artificial suede, bonded fabrics, quilted fabrics, lace, and net

6. Waterproof fabrics completely resist water and air passage; water-repellent fabrics are resistant to wetting but are not resistant to heavy rain—they must be refinished periodically.

7. to make sure a garment fits and looks right

8. to identify the manufacturer, the country of origin, the fiber contents, and the size; to tell consumers the best way to clean a garment

9. business clothing is more formal, such as suits in neutral colors; business casual clothing is more relaxed, such as semitailored pants and cotton shirts

10. true

11. buy shoes for your specific sport; shop when your feet tend to be larger; buy the size most comfortable on your larger foot; try on the shoes with the socks you intend to wear with them; walk in the shoes to check fit and comfort; check for special features

12. (See pages 409–410.)

13. clothing care labels, laundry products, and washers and dryers

Academic Connections

21. **Financial literacy, speech.** Select five different items of clothing for comparison shopping. Shop for each of the five items in different outlets—clothing stores, factory stores, discount stores, department stores, and catalogs. Compare the price, quality, selection, and styles of like items. Also compare the services and policies of the places you shopped. In a short oral report, tell the class which places offered the best price, quality, selection, styles, services, and business policies.

22. **Math, research.** Compare the cost of buying a skirt at a store where you usually shop to the cost of making a similar skirt yourself. What is the cost difference? How much time would you spend shopping for the skirt compared to the time you would spend shopping for the fabric and making it?

23. **Research, speech.** At a time when stores are not too busy, interview an experienced salesperson in a clothing department of a store where you shop. Ask the following questions:
    - What clothing is selling best at the present time?
    - What is new in fabrics, styles, patterns, and colors?
    - What fashion changes do you notice from year to year?
    - What trends are expected for the upcoming season?
    - What type of customers do you most like to serve? Which do you find most disagreeable?

24. **Social studies.** Describe and find pictures to illustrate appropriate clothing for the following jobs:
    - receptionist in a doctor's office
    - waitress at a local upscale restaurant
    - salesperson in a department store
    - high school teacher
    - bank teller
    - accountant or lawyer in a large office

25. **Research, speech.** Research and give an oral report on developments in the fashion market that cause little or no harm to the environment. Include fabrics, finishes, and production techniques.

26. **Math.** Calculate the cost difference between taking three shirts to a professional dry cleaner and washing and ironing them at home.

MATH CHALLENGE

27. The price of a garment is broken down into these approximated categories:
    - 36 percent of the price is for the fabric
    - 11 percent of the price is for the labor of a garment maker
    - 33 percent of the price is for overhead, including the costs of rent, utilities, transportation of goods, marketing, and machines used to make the garment

    If the garment costs $40, calculate the fabric, labor, and overhead costs. How much profit does the manufacturer make?

Tech $mart

28. Plan a business wardrobe with a total budget of $350. Search Web sites to find appropriate shoes, clothing, and accessories for five outfits. Write down the wardrobe items and descriptions, retailer names, and prices. Repeat the exercise for a business casual dress code.

29. Use the Internet to research the availability of clothing advertised as environmentally friendly. Can you find such clothes in your community or must you shop online? What qualities about these clothes merit their consideration as environmentally friendly? Compare the prices of eco-friendly clothing and regular clothing. Which options are more affordable?

Answer to Math Challenge
27. fabric—$14.40; labor—$4.40; overhead—$13.20; profit—$8

Health and Wellness

Reading for Meaning

Think back over experiences you have had with weight-loss and fitness programs and products. What did you learn?

primary care physician

specialist

walk-in clinic

prescription drug

over-the-counter drug

generic drug

dietary supplement

physical fitness

body composition

hypoallergenic

CHAPTER OBJECTIVES

After studying this chapter, you will be able to

- **select** qualified health care professionals and evaluate the quality of care provided in health care facilities.
- **describe** services typically provided through walk-in clinics.
- **list** factors to consider when choosing a health or fitness club.
- **list** factors to consider when evaluating a weight-loss program.
- **compare and evaluate** personal grooming products and services.
- **manage** the money and time you spend pursuing fun and leisure-time activities.

Central Ideas

- The goals of feeling and looking your best require some expenditure of time and money.

- How you use your limited resources to achieve these goals will require good decision making.

Reflect

What self-care measures do you follow?

When you look and feel your best, you get more out of life. Developing health, fitness, and grooming routines are the first steps in improving the way you look and feel. Pursuing leisure activities improves your emotional health.

When you feel in top shape, you look better. Keys to looking and feeling your best at every stage of your life are listed in 17-1. It is nearly impossible to look and feel your best without a balanced approach in these areas. Still, thousands of people routinely ignore one or more of these basics. At the same time, they spend billions of dollars on products that promise effortless beauty and fitness.

Your lifestyle and the choices you make are the keys to staying healthy and preventing life-threatening diseases. Quality self-care involves developing healthful eating habits, which was covered in Chapter 15. It also involves avoiding illegal drugs, tobacco products, and limiting alcohol consumption. Getting adequate rest and physical activity and finding ways to deal with life's stressful situations are critical.

Medical attention when you need it is also important. Regular physical and dental check-ups may help you avoid serious illnesses or at least identify them in their early stages. Knowing how to select health care professionals and to evaluate hospitals and medical facilities can help you get adequate health care when you need it.

Keys to Looking and Feeling Your Best at Every Stage of Life

- Adequate sleep, rest, relaxation
- Regular exercise and physical activity
- A well-balanced, nutritious diet
- Maintaining a healthy weight
- Competent medical and dental care
- Attention to known safety precautions
- Attention to posture and grooming
- Challenge, achievement, involvement
- Positive mental attitude
- Family, friendship, and support
- Effective control of stress
- Avoidance of tobacco and drugs

17-1

This chart outlines the keys to good health and good looks.

Vocabulary

Differentiate between a *primary care physician* and a *specialist*. What is the role of each in treating patients?

Reflect

What personal experiences have you had with physicians and different types of specialists?

Selecting Health Care Providers

The best time to choose a physician, dentist, or specialist is when you are healthy. Most people go to a **primary care physician** for routine health care needs. This is a physician who is trained to diagnose and treat a variety of illnesses in all phases of medicine. This doctor oversees general treatment for most patients. When a specific health problem arises, your primary care physician may refer you to a specialist.

A **specialist** is a physician who has had further education and training in a specific branch of medicine. Chart 17-2 describes some of the many medical and dental specialists. These specialists are qualified and licensed to practice general medicine or dentistry, but they focus on care within their specialties.

A physician or specialist is a doctor of medicine, or MD. In your search for a physician, you may also come across a doctor of osteopathy, or DO. Both MDs and DOs are qualified to provide complete medical care. Both may decide to go beyond basic medical education into a chosen specialty. Both must pass comparable state licensing exams. Both practice in accredited, licensed hospitals and other care facilities.

Health Care Specialties

Medical	Area of Treatment
Cardiology	Diseases of the heart
Dermatology	Diseases of the skin, hair, and nails
Gynecology	Women's reproductive system
Internal medicine	Wide range of physical illnesses and health issues
Neurology	Disorders of the brain, spinal cord, and nervous system
Obstetrics	Medical care of pregnant women
Oncology	Diagnosis and treatment of tumors and cancer
Ophthalmology	Care of the eyes
Orthopedics	Fractures, deformities, and diseases of the skeletal system
Otolaryngology	Diseases and disorders of the ear, nose, and throat
Pediatrics	Development and care of children
Psychiatry	Mental and emotional issues and disorders
Surgery	Operations to diagnose or treat a variety of diseases or physical conditions
Urology	Urinary tract and male reproductive system
Dental	
Oral surgery	Operations to extract teeth or to treat injuries and defects of the jaw and mouth
Orthodontics	Irregularities and deformities of the teeth—often with braces

17-2
This chart lists some of the medical specialties in the health care field.

Chiropractors, optometrists, podiatrists, and psychologists provide limited medical services. (Coverage of these services varies with insurance and managed care plans.) A *chiropractor* treats problems of the musculo-skeletal system and their impact on the nervous system. Treatments may include manipulating parts of the body, particularly the spinal column.

An *optometrist* tests eyes for vision defects and prescribes corrective glasses and contact lenses. A *podiatrist* diagnoses and treats minor foot ailments. A *psychologist* diagnoses and treats mental and emotional problems and learning difficulties. Licensing requirements for these fields vary from state to state. Do not rely on these health care providers for medical advice beyond their limited fields.

If you do not have a primary care physician, use the following qualifications as a guide. When choosing health care professionals, select well-qualified persons who are

- graduates of approved medical or dental schools
- licensed to practice in your state
- board certified in their area of practice

17-3

Friends and family members can recommend health care providers they are happy with.

Activity

Access the caphis.mlanet.org site and review the health-related Web sites listed in the reference section. Go to one or two that particularly interest you to find out what information is provided. Discuss findings in class.

Enrich

Role-play a patient calling to ask about services available from a physician's office.

- members in one or more local, state, and national professional societies and associations

Look for doctors who are well established in their practice with a good reputation among both patients and fellow professionals. One way to find qualified health care providers is to ask friends, relatives, employers, and coworkers for advice, 17-3. The following are also sources of recommendations for medical professionals:

- If you move to a new area, your former doctor may be able to refer you to a new physician.

- If medical or dental schools are located in the area, administrators there can provide a list of faculty doctors and graduates who practice in the area.

- National and state medical associations operate referral services.

- Local hospitals can also be good sources of information.

- If you receive care through a managed care program, you may be required to choose a physician or hospital or other care provider that participates in the plan.

Before you make a final decision about a doctor, find out what services are performed in the office. Some doctors' offices are equipped to take X-rays and perform other tests that require special equipment. Tests performed in the office can save you a trip to the lab, hospital, or clinic. Ask in advance about charges and fees for routine office visits, a complete physical, and other services you may need.

You may also want to consider the location of the office, the office hours, and the backup staff available in the doctor's absence. If you have any special medical needs, make sure the doctor or group practice you choose can meet them.

Evaluating Hospitals and Medical Facilities

Doctors normally arrange for the hospitalization of their patients who need hospital care. The hospital or clinic where patients go for treatment may be determined by their choice of a primary care physician or their health care plan. Managed care plans often require that members use specific doctors or medical facilities.

Nevertheless, patients are wise to evaluate the facilities that provide care as well as the health care professionals who supervise their hospital stays. If the patient is unable to do this, a family member or a friend, acting as his or her advocate, may be able to help. The following questions are helpful in assessing health care facilities:

- *Is the hospital accredited?* A hospital should be accredited by the Joint Commission on Accreditation of Health Care Organizations or by the American Osteopathic Association. An accredited hospital must meet certain quality standards in providing health care.

- *Who owns or finances the hospital?* A nonprofit hospital is supported by patient fees, contributions, and endowments. A proprietary hospital is owned by individuals or stockholders and operated for profit. A government-supported hospital is operated with local, state, or federal funds. Ownership can make a difference in the eligibility for treatment, the services offered, and the charges.

- *Is it a teaching hospital?* Hospitals and clinics affiliated with a medical or nursing school generally provide a high level of training for students. As a result, they are likely to provide high-quality medical services.

- *Who staffs the hospital?* Does the hospital employ an adequate, qualified staff of physicians, specialists, nurses, therapists, and technicians? If a hospital is under staffed or if the staff is under qualified, patients may not receive the quality of medical care they need.

- *What types of facilities are located at the hospital or clinic?* Is there an intensive care unit? Is the emergency room well equipped and staffed? Look for the up-to-date equipment and facilities required to provide quality care.

Activity

Apply these questions to a local hospital or the health care facility you use.

Enrich

Conduct a study of local medical facilities to find out about the qualifications and certification of staff members, facilities offered, and services provided.

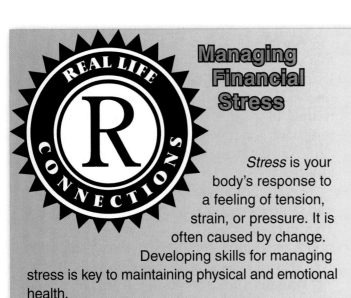

REAL LIFE CONNECTIONS

Managing Financial Stress

Stress is your body's response to a feeling of tension, strain, or pressure. It is often caused by change. Developing skills for managing stress is key to maintaining physical and emotional health.

Financial and health experts agree that finances are one of the leading causes of stress. Circumstances beyond consumer control can trigger stress, such as an economic downturn, rising health care costs, or layoffs. Poor financial habits, such as overspending or carrying large credit card debt, may also lead to stress.

Taking action to improve financial habits is the first step in reducing finance-related stress. The U.S. Department of Health and Human Services offers the following coping techniques for managing stress:

- ***Keep things in perspective.*** Recognize and focus on the positive aspects of life.

- ***Strengthen relationships with family and friends.*** They can provide emotional support through tough times.

- ***Engage in physical exercise, sports, hobbies, or other activities.*** Doing things you enjoy reduces stress and anxiety.

- ***Develop new skills.*** Learning new skills is a practical way to increase employment opportunities and earnings, leading to greater financial stability.

www.samhsa.gov/economy

- *What type of care and services are provided?* An acute care facility diagnoses and treats a broad range of illnesses and emergencies. A special disease facility diagnoses and treats a specific illness or group of diseases. A chronic disease facility provides continuing care for ongoing illnesses. People need to choose a hospital according to their specific medical needs.

- *Does the hospital enjoy a good reputation in the area?* If both medical professionals and patients speak highly of a hospital, that is a sign of quality health care.

- *How sensitive is the staff to patients' private and special needs?* Patients and their families are concerned with privacy. They want complete and honest information on diagnosis and treatment. They are also concerned with the attitude of nurses and others who deal directly with patients. Look for sensitivity to patients' comfort and special needs.

It pays to check out emergency room and ambulance services in the area before you are in an emergency situation. Knowing you are being treated in a facility that provides quality medical care can have a positive effect on your mental and physical health.

Walk-in Clinics

A **walk-in clinic** is a health care facility that provides certain routine medical attention. Usually these clinics are staffed by nurse practitioners or other health care providers who are trained to work in clinics. They can write prescriptions and give vaccinations as needed. The clinics also have a doctor on call if consultation is necessary.

These clinics generally offer quick, economical, same-day service with short waiting times. They may be located in pharmacies, workplaces, stores, or shopping malls. Often they are open evenings and weekends.

Walk-in clinics typically treat sinus and upper respiratory infections, bladder infections, strep throat, minor injuries, and other relatively minor illnesses. They may provide routine physicals and tests along with vaccinations, 17-4.

17-4

Staff at walk-in clinics provide routine care, such as conducting school physicals, and can diagnose and treat minor illness.

The costs of services at a walk-in clinic will normally be less than services of hospital emergency rooms. Generally you pay by cash, check, or credit card. Some clinics take insurance but not all insurance companies pay for treatments at a walk-in clinic.

Ideally these clinics cut down on emergency room visits and unnecessary trips to the doctor. However, under some conditions you need to go directly to an urgent care clinic or emergency room. Following is a partial list of these conditions:

- a fever over 103 degrees in connection with strep throat or other infections

- deep tissue damage or blistered burns

- stiff neck or severe pain along with ear or respiratory infections or strep throat

- life-threatening illness, such as a severe asthma attack, or injury

- heart attack symptoms, including chest discomfort, shortness of breath, and/or nausea, lightheadedness, and cold sweats

- complicated health problems

Discuss

Review the symptoms that signal the need to go directly to an urgent care clinic or emergency room.

Reflect

What experience have you or your family had with emergency health care?

Reflect

Have you used alternative health care treatments?

Emergency Health Care

You should go to a hospital emergency room or an emergency care center if you have an injury or sudden illness that requires immediate attention. When you go for emergency care, be ready to give

- your name, address, and phone number

- information on your injury or illness

- your managed care or insurance card or identifying data

- information on any current medication you take or allergies you have

If you call an ambulance, emergency medical technicians (EMTs) may provide preliminary health care. EMTs are trained to make an immediate, accurate diagnosis and give temporary treatment.

Alternative Medicine

Alternative medicine includes a group of health care practices and products that are not presently a part of conventional medicine. Alternative health care treatments include

- mind-body interventions such as patient education, cognitive-behavioral counseling, hypnosis, meditation, music and art therapy

- biological-based approaches such as herbal products, diet supplements and natural therapies

- manipulative and body-based methods such as manipulation and/or movement of the body as done by chiropractors, some osteopaths, and massage therapists

- energy therapies such as acupuncture, therapeutic touch, and magnetic field therapies

Some conventional health care providers combine alternative treatments with conventional methods. It is advisable to check with your health care provider before relying on alternative treatments.

Keeping Health and Medical Records

Activity

Create an organized file of family health care documents, records of claims, and medical records.

Activity

Check out your home record keeping to see which of the listed records you have available. To the extent possible, fill in the gaps.

Discuss

What types of health and medical records are important to keep on file? How might this information be used?

Up-to-date health and medical records are valuable for many reasons. If you switch doctors or health care plans, you will need to give your new care providers a thorough knowledge of your medical background.

Some medical background also will be required if you are admitted to a hospital. Health and medical records can help doctors with the diagnosis and treatment of illnesses as well as with the prevention of certain diseases. Having health facts readily available is very important for anyone with health conditions that would require special treatment in an emergency.

Data from health histories is also helpful when filling out school records and insurance forms. Organized receipts for paid medical bills and the purchase of medications are needed for filing insurance claims and tax forms.

Chart 17-5 lists types of information to keep in personal and family medical records. You may want to write some of this information on a card to carry with you. You may receive a medical identification card to carry with you as well. This card will identify the insurance company or managed care plan that covers your medical services and gives the necessary information to confirm your coverage.

17-5

Record this type of medical information for each family member.

Personal Medical Records
• Name, address, date and place of birth, height, weight, occupation, and blood type.
• Persons to notify in an emergency with addresses, phone numbers, and relationship.
• Personal physicians and health care providers with names, addresses, and phone numbers.
• Allergies.
• Medications with dosages, prescription numbers, prescribing physician, and pharmacies.
• Chronic illnesses with important details on history, medication, and treatment.
• Visual or hearing defects and other disabilities.
• Immunizations, screening tests and results, and dates for follow-up.
• Infections and childhood diseases with important details.
• Hospitalizations, injuries, and surgeries with dates and details.
• Physical checkups and laboratory tests with dates and details.
• Social security, Medicare, and Medicaid numbers.
• Details of employer-sponsored or individual health insurance or managed care plans including names, addresses, and phone numbers of plan managers or claims officers, medical services covered, policy and membership numbers, premium amounts and due dates, claims records, agent or contact person, and related membership data.
• Dental treatment records.
• A copy of advance directives, if any. This is a legal document describing what kind of care you want if unable to make medical decisions (such as going into a coma).

Drugs and Medicines

Vocabulary

Differentiate between *prescription* and *over-the-counter drugs*. Give five examples of each.

Example

Collect labels from over-the-counter drugs and look for the listed information.

Enrich

Interview a pharmacist about the differences between generic and brand-name drugs and about state laws governing prescriptions.

Drugs and medicines eat up a sizable portion of the health care dollar. Drugs fall into two major groups—prescription drugs and over-the-counter drugs. **Prescription drugs** are medications that can only be obtained with a physician's orders.

Insurance normally covers part of the cost of prescription drugs and medicines. Consumers pay a percentage or a set fee per prescription.

Over-the-counter drugs are nonprescription medications available on supermarket and drug store shelves. They are considered safe to use when label directions and warnings are followed. These include more than 300,000 different drugs. Painkillers, antacids, cough medicine, antihistamines, and vitamins are examples.

Brand Name and Generic Drugs

Most drugs are available either by generic names or by trade and brand names. A **generic drug** is sold by its common name, chemical composition, or class. Usually it costs considerably less than a similar brand-name drug. All prescription and over-the-counter drugs meet the same federal standards. Generic drugs are required to have the same active ingredients and effects as their brand-name equivalents.

When a physician prescribes a medication by brand name, a patient can ask if the generic equivalent may be substituted. If so, the patient can ask the doctor to write this on the prescription. Many health management and insurance plans call for the use of generic equivalents, but patients can get brand name medications with an increased co-payment.

Drug Labeling

With the ever-rising costs of drugs, consumers are asking more questions about what their doctors prescribe. They should also become better informed about the many over-the-counter drugs available without prescription. Labels on over-the-counter drugs serve as keys to choosing products and comparing generics with brand names. Information on these labels must include

- name and address of the manufacturer, packer, or distributor
- quantity of contents in weight, measure, or count
- purpose of the medication
- directions for use and storage
- recommended dosages for different purposes, ages, and conditions
- number of times and length of time the medication may be used
- conditions under which the drug should not be used
- adequate warnings and precautions related to use, possible side effects, and interactions with other drugs

Linking to... History

Food and Drug Safety

Before the early 1900s, government and industry regulations were weak or nonexistent. Consumers did not know what was in their foods and medicines, and producers did not have to tell them. Unethical businesspeople cut costs by adding inferior ingredients, some of which were harmful. They also made false "cure all" claims about their products.

It took public outrage and decades of effort by many groups to create laws that banned such practices. These groups included reformers in the food industry, politicians, government officials, food scientists, medical professionals, consumer groups, and journalists.

In 1906, after a 25-year debate, Congress passed the *Pure Food and Drug Act.* The law prohibited interstate commerce in foods and drugs that were mislabeled or that contained any foreign or impure ingredient.

At that time, the states were responsible for food and drugs made and distributed within their borders. Also at that time, science had advanced in its ability to detect unwanted ingredients. The job of checking food and drug complaints fell to a small federal agency of scientists, primarily chemists. Public health investigators and inspectors were added to handle its regulatory duties under the 1906 law.

The law was strengthened in 1938 with the passage of the *Food, Drug, and Cosmetic Act,* which gave new powers to the U.S. Food and Drug Administration. Today the agency has regulatory power over tobacco products, bottled water, medical devices, the nation's blood supply, and other items as well as food, drug, and cosmetics safety and labeling.

Resource

The Well-Stocked Medicine Cabinet, reproducible master 17-1, TR

Note

Research national spending on drugs and medicines. Obtain and compare past and current figures.

- list of active ingredients and the quantity of each per dosage
- list of all other ingredients including the name and quantity of any habit-forming drug contained in the product.
- the expiration date after which the product should not be used

Prescription drug labels dispensed by doctors or pharmacists are exempt from certain labeling requirements. These labels state

- pharmacist's name and address
- prescription number
- date of the prescription
- name of the prescribing physician
- patient's name
- directions for use
- any cautionary statements contained in the prescription
- number of refills, if any
- expiration date of the medication

Many pharmacies also provide leaflets with more complete information on prescription drugs.

Questions to Ask About Medicines

To be an informed partner in your own health care, ask the following questions when your doctor prescribes medicine for you:

- What is the brand name and the generic name of the drug?

- What is it intended to do? Is it really necessary for you to take it?

- How much of this drug should you take, at what time of day, and for how long?

- Is the medication habit-forming?

- What, if any, side effects should you expect?

- What activities, other drugs, foods, or beverages should you avoid while taking the drug? Be cautious with both over-the-counter and prescription drug interactions with other drugs, alcohol, herbal supplements, and various foods.

- Is this a generic drug? If not, is there a generic equivalent that is as effective at a lower cost?

Enrich

Role-play a patient posing the listed questions to a doctor.

Reflect

Do you take or have you taken dietary supplements?

Discuss

Name common reasons for taking dietary supplements.

Dietary Supplements

A **dietary supplement** is a product that is intended to enhance your diet. It contains ingredients such as vitamins, minerals, herbs, or amino acids and other substances. Normally supplements come in the form of a pill, capsule, tablet, or liquid. They must be labeled "dietary supplement" and carry a "Supplement Facts" label on the product.

Supplements can be helpful, harmless, risky, or dangerous. This depends on what substances they contain and the quantity you take. It also depends on the potential interaction with prescription medications or other supplements taken, and the body's reaction to the product.

People take supplements for a variety of reasons. Some look to vitamin and mineral supplements to provide nutrients they feel are not present in adequate quantities in their regular diet. Others look to supplements for weight loss, bodybuilding, a boost in energy and performance, extra brainpower, or other promised effects.

Weight-loss products are among the more common dietary supplements. You can find a number of weight-loss pills and supplements at your drug or food store and online. Most of these products have not been proved safe or effective. Some are dangerous and can produce unwanted side effects. To date there is no known way to lose weight without eating less and getting more physical activity.

Dietary supplements are not tested or approved by the Food and Drug Administration (FDA) or any other government agency. Proof of safety and effectiveness is up to the manufacturer/distributor of the products.

The FDA *Dietary Supplements Final Rule* requires that products are: produced under controlled conditions, free of contaminants or impurities, and accurately labeled. The rule also explains the requirements for testing ingredients and final products, and for recordkeeping and handling of consumer product complaints. The FDA can take action to ban or restrict the sale of any product that is shown to present risk of illness or injury.

For your own protection, thoroughly check any supplements you may be considering. Before using a dietary supplement,

- discuss the product with your health care provider or pharmacist. Be sure to let this person know what medications and other supplements you take.

- read the label carefully, particularly the "Supplement Facts" panel.

- take a hard look at the advertising claims for the product. Are they believable?

- determine whether you really need the supplement.

- decide whether the product is worth its cost.

You can find more detailed information on dietary supplements at the Web sites in 17-6.

Buying Drugs, Medicines, and Supplements Online

Many consumers buy both prescription and over-the-counter drugs and supplements online. Drugs and other health products are available through thousands of Web sites on the Internet. These include sites for familiar drugstore chains as well as legitimate independent pharmacies.

Online sites offer advantages such as shipping and delivery, easy comparison of products and prices, easy access to product information, and links to additional sources of information. Reliable sites also offer consultation with a pharmacist who is qualified to answer consumer questions concerning medications. In some cases, Internet drug shopping saves consumers money.

To use an Internet pharmacy, you usually open an account and submit your credit card and insurance information. Once your account is established, you submit a valid prescription that may be called or faxed in by your doctor. Medications are usually delivered within a few days, or for an extra fee, they may be shipped overnight.

17-6

Before using a dietary supplement, research it thoroughly and discuss the product with your health care provider.

Sources of Information on Supplements	
Food and Drug Administration	www.fda.gov/Food/DietarySupplements
National Institutes of Health	http://ods.od.nih.gov
Federal Trade Commission	www.ftc.gov
American Dietetic Association	www.eatright.org
American Pharmacists Association	www.pharmacyandyou.org
National Council on Patient Information and Education	www.talkaboutrx.org

Sites to Avoid

Although online shopping is convenient, there are many Web sites that sell unapproved products and do not follow the established procedures for filling prescriptions. For example, some of these sites distribute prescription drugs without requiring a lawful prescription, direct medical supervision, or a physical examination performed by a licensed health professional.

Consumers buying from such sites risk harmful drug interactions and may risk buying outdated, counterfeit, or contaminated medications. You can protect yourself if you buy medicines online by refusing to buy from sites that

- sell prescription drugs without a lawful prescription

- do not identify themselves or provide a U.S. address and phone number

- do not provide access to a registered pharmacist who is qualified to answer questions

- advertise new cures and quick cures for all types of illnesses and ailments

- make unsubstantiated and unbelievable claims

Activity

Check the licensing and standing of the several Web sites that sell drugs and medicines online with the National Association of Boards of Pharmacy at www.nabp.net.

Activity

Find out whether several Web sites that sell drugs and medicines are listed with the Verified Internet Pharmacy Practice Sites (VIPPS) at http://vipps.nabp.net.

Tobacco Products

Smoking is one of the most destructive habits a person can have. Smoking tobacco is linked to many diseases including heart disease, cancer, lung diseases, digestive problems, and infertility. It is also a cause of premature aging, yellow teeth, and bad breath. Chewing tobacco products can lead to cancers of the throat, lips, and gums.

You do not have to be a smoker to be affected by tobacco smoke. Just being around people who smoke and breathing in secondhand smoke can raise your risk of becoming ill.

Linking to... Science

The Effects of Alcohol on Health

Alcohol is a *depressant*, a drug that reduces body functions. It slows the central nervous system, delays reflexes, hinders coordination, and clouds judgment. When a person consumes alcohol, it enters the bloodstream rapidly. Within minutes, it reaches all parts of the body.

The liver breaks down alcohol at the rate of about one drink per hour. If a person consumes a lot of alcohol, it circulates in the bloodstream until the liver can handle it. Excessive amounts of alcohol can reduce body functions drastically and may lead to a coma or even death.

Clearly, consuming too much alcohol takes a serious toll on a person's health. Excessive drinking can even affect that person's health insurance policy. In some states, insurance companies can deny coverage if a policyholder sustains injuries caused by his or her intoxication.

Aside from the serious health risks, tobacco products can cost a lot of money over time. The cost of a pack or carton of cigarettes varies depending on brand name and taxes. A pack may cost as much as $7. At that price, if someone smokes a pack a day, he or she will spend $2,555 per year on cigarettes. Over five years, cigarettes will cost $12,775.

Buying insurance is also more costly for smokers than for nonsmokers. Health and life insurers charge higher premiums to smokers because they are more likely to get seriously ill than nonsmokers.

Smoking is a habit with a large price tag and many risks. If you smoke, quitting can lower your risk of disease. Plus you will save thousands of dollars each year. If you do not smoke, do not start and avoid secondhand smoke.

Health Science

Physical Therapy Assistants

Physical therapy assistants work on health teams with doctors, nurses, and physical therapists. They help physical therapists to provide treatment that improves patient mobility, relieves pain, and prevents or lessens patients' physical disabilities. They work in hospitals, rehabilitation centers, and schools.

Fitness and Weight-Loss Programs

Physical fitness is a state in which all body systems function efficiently. It includes heart health, muscle strength, power, endurance, flexibility, and body composition. **Body composition** is the proportion of muscle, bone, fat, and other tissue that make up body weight.

Inactivity puts you at unnecessary risk for developing serious life-threatening chronic diseases such as cancer, heart disease, diabetes, high blood pressure, and others.

You can improve your fitness through appropriate exercise and diet. Chapter 15 covered what you need to know about achieving a healthy diet. There are many benefits to following a sound fitness program tailored to your needs and abilities, 17-7.

There are many ways to begin your own fitness program. Start with a close look at your present fitness level. Decide what you want to improve

Rewards of a Sound Physical Fitness Routine		
Health	**Performance**	**Appearance and Well-Being**
• Improved heart and lung efficiency • Lowered cholesterol levels • Improved muscle strength • Lower blood pressure • Weight management • Stronger immune system • Stronger bones and bone density • Fewer injuries • Better resistance to minor and serious illnesses	• Mental alertness and agility • Stress management • Higher productivity • Better balance • More energy • Better sleep • Improved memory • Better focus and concentration • Quicker thinking and reactions	• Weight control • Improved muscle tone • Better posture • Improved self-image • Lower anxiety levels • Improved emotional stability • An alert, healthy look • Opportunity to meet new people and share activities • Positive mental outlook

17-7

These are some of the rewards for following a sound fitness program.

and what physical activities you would enjoy. Once you decide on the sports and exercises you want to pursue, plan your approach. It often is helpful to put your plan on paper and make adjustments as your needs and interests change. It will also be important to build fitness activities into your daily routine.

Organized Fitness Programs

Some people find it difficult to stay with a fitness plan on their own. Today many schools emphasize fitness and offer programs as part of the curriculum or as extracurricular activity. If your school has such offerings, it would be a good place to start your own routine.

Others turn to fitness centers, health clubs, or scheduled workout sessions. The following guidelines can help you find the best place for your needs and wallet:

- Look for a convenient location and hours that will work well for you. Find out whether classes and equipment you want will be available at times you want them.

- Ask about the classes and training offered and check out the equipment.

- Find out whether personal trainers and instructors are certified. The American Council on Exercise (ACE) operates a certification program. You can look it up on www.acefitness.org.

- Consider the overall atmosphere. Is the facility clean, well equipped, and well staffed? Is the environment friendly and inviting? Is equipment in working order? Will you feel comfortable working out there?

- Review the costs and payment arrangements. Is there a membership fee? What fees will you pay for extras such as personal training sessions or fitness classes? What are the payment options? Must you sign a contract? Are there refunds if you opt out? Is there a sign up special offered? Will payments fit into your budget? Carefully study any contract you are asked to sign.

- Investigate the reputation of the facilities you are considering. Talk with current members about their satisfaction. Check with the local Better Business Bureau as to whether there have been complaints registered against the facility. Find out whether the facility is a member of the International Health, Racquet, and Sportsclub Association. Members follow a code of ethics that protects the health and safety of club members. To find member clubs in your area go to www.healthclubs.com.

- Finally, find out whether you can sign up for a single session or a short trial membership before joining or signing on for a longer time frame.

Weight-Loss Programs

A weight-loss program is another "sign up" commitment that requires careful investigation. If you wish to lose weight, talk with your doctor first to determine your ideal weight and to learn how much you need to lose.

Reflect

When have you been aware of a connection between the way you look and the way you feel?

Reflect

Do you participate in an organized fitness program?

Activity

Create a spreadsheet of local fitness centers and health clubs. Record the costs and payment plans for each facility.

Human Services

Personal Trainers

Personal trainers work one-on-one with clients either in a gym or in the client's home. They help clients assess their level of physical fitness and set and reach fitness goals. Trainers also demonstrate various exercises and help clients improve their exercise techniques.

Most health care providers can help you find a weight-loss plan that will work for you. They also can advise you on the safety of any dietary supplements or special diets you may be considering.

If you do sign on for a weight-loss program be sure that it encourages healthy behaviors. These involve healthful eating and more physical activity to achieve gradual weight loss—usually at a rate of ½ to two pounds per week. The plan also should include access to medical care if you are following a program that requires monitoring by a physician. A few specifics to look for in a weight-loss program include

- counseling or group classes on diet and lifestyle changes
- diet recommendations and/or meal plans
- physical activity or exercise monitoring
- an ongoing plan for maintaining a desirable weight

Look into the qualifications of the staff and supervisors of the program. Find out whether there are any health risks connected with the program. It also is a good idea to inquire about the typical results of participating in the program.

Finally, take a close look at the costs. Are there sign-up fees, attendance fees, special foods or supplements to purchase, or printed material you must buy? Is there a contract or agreement you are expected to sign? Fully understand any weight-loss program you are considering before signing on to it.

Guarding Against False Claims

In the fitness and weight-loss field, you may come across exaggerated and false claims and promises made by the sellers and promoters of a variety of remedies and procedures. Be wary of

- quick and easy weight loss
- quirky diets and nutrition supplements that supposedly cure serious diseases
- effective "secret cures" your doctor does not know
- cure-alls to treat a wide range of unrelated diseases
- untried or unproven remedies for health problems your doctor calls "incurable"

Remember that eating wisely and exercising regularly are proven ways to achieve health and wellness.

Personal Care Products

Using personal care products such as cosmetics and grooming aids can help you look and feel your best. Cosmetics or grooming aids are used to cleanse, beautify, or alter the appearance of the body. They do not alter body structure or functions. They include lipstick, nail polish, hair gel, hair straighteners, face moisturizers, and teeth whiteners, among many others.

However, certain cosmetics also fit the definition of a drug. That is, they are intended to treat or prevent disease or to affect the functions of the body. These include fluoride in toothpaste, hormone creams, sunscreens, and antiperspirants.

Cosmetics and drug products must be labeled with the "active ingredients" and must meet Food and Drug Administration (FDA) standards for safety and effectiveness. The FDA is the government agency that regulates the safety and labeling of cosmetics.

Enrich

Collect cosmetic containers and study information on the labels. Discuss how this information can help consumers make wise purchases and use products safely.

Case Study: For Your Health

What's in a Face?

Gloria spends an hour and a half getting ready for school every day. She shampoos, blow-dries, and styles her hair every morning. Then she applies face moisturizer, foundation, blush, eyeliner, eye shadow, mascara, and lipstick. The top of her dresser is covered with bottles, jars, and tubes of cosmetics.

Gloria and several friends recently got ready for a school dance at Gloria's house. Some of the girls decided to try Gloria's cosmetics. They passed the jars and bottles from one to the other and experimented with different products.

Shortly after the dance, Gloria and three of her friends developed eye infections. Their doctors prescribed medicine and advised them not to wear makeup until the infections cleared.

Gloria was very disappointed that she could not wear makeup for several days. On top of that, she had to get rid of all her cosmetics, which were contaminated after the sharing session.

Case Review

1. How do you feel about Gloria's love of cosmetics and grooming?
2. How much do you think Gloria spends each month to maintain her storehouse of cosmetics?
3. How could Gloria and her friends have avoided the eye infection?
4. What are some guidelines for safe use of cosmetics?
5. How would you describe a balanced approach to buying and using cosmetics and grooming appliances?

Discuss

Give examples of excessive spending and necessary spending on grooming aids.

Resource

Looking Great: What Does It Cost? color lesson slide, TR

Enrich

Invite a representative from the FDA to speak to the class about labeling requirements for cosmetic products.

Enrich

Investigate a manufacturer's responsibilities for safety in regard to cosmetics and grooming products. Also investigate consumers' responsibilities. Report your findings.

When you buy a cosmetic or grooming aid, keep in mind these four questions:

- Is it safe to use?
- Will it work?
- Is it a good buy?
- Do I need it?

As you shop, read labels to compare the contents and prices of different products and brands. Often, salespersons can help you make the best choices. Read directions on how to use products before you buy and before you use them.

Look for special prices and sales on products you have tried and want to use again. Usually it is best to avoid buying sets of makeup, colognes, and other grooming aids unless you plan to use every product in the set. For products you have never used before, it is a good idea to buy a small, sample size to see if you will like it.

If you are dissatisfied with a product or it does not meet specific advertising claims, return it. Some products have a money-back guarantee and most retailers will allow reasonable returns.

Cosmetics, Safety, and the Law

Though law does not require it, reputable cosmetic manufacturers test products thoroughly before marketing. They test for safety, effectiveness, and customer appeal. Many manufacturers also voluntarily register their formulas with the FDA. They may make safety data available before marketing a product.

The FDA requires manufacturers who do not test a product for safety to place a warning on the label. The warning reads, "The safety of this product has not been determined." The FDA can also ban unsafe or misbranded cosmetics. However, the agency must first prove that the product is unsafe or misbranded.

Product labels can be helpful buying guides. The *Federal Food, Drug, and Cosmetic Act* requires labels on cosmetic products to state

- the name of the product
- a description of the nature or use of the product
- ingredients in descending order of predominance
- net quantity of contents by weight, measure, or count
- name and address of the firm marketing the product
- name of the manufacturer if different from the distributor
- country of origin if imported

Labels must also carry warnings and adequate directions for safe use on any products that may be hazardous to consumers if misused. In addition to labeling requirements, tamper-resistant packaging is required for certain cosmetic products. These include liquid oral hygiene products, eye drops, and contact lens preparations.

Keep in mind that cosmetics labeled *hypoallergenic* are not necessarily safe for persons with allergies. A product that is **hypoallergenic** does not contain ingredients likely to cause allergic reactions. There is no way of producing a cosmetic that is totally non-allergenic for all users. Learn what you can about the manufacturer as well as the product before you buy, 17-8.

For your own safety, keep a record of any harmful reactions you experience from cosmetic products. Avoid buying anything that irritates your skin. If you have a serious reaction to a specific product, contact both the manufacturer and the FDA. Manufacturers want to know of any adverse reactions caused by their products. They can then take steps to modify the product and address the problem. The FDA investigates products that cause unusual reactions and will take corrective action if necessary.

Selecting Grooming Appliances

In addition to cosmetics and grooming aids, consumers buy many personal care appliances. These include blow-dryers, curling irons, electric shavers, electric toothbrushes, and a host of other products. There are many brand names, models, features, and prices for each appliance. The money

Vocabulary

Find the term *hypoallergenic* on a product label and explain its meaning. What hypoallergenic products have you used?

Activity

Draft a letter to the FDA concerning an adverse reaction to a cosmetic product.

Activity

Find safety information on the labels of several cosmetic products.

Reflect

When have you been disappointed with a cosmetic or grooming product? What did you do?

Activity

Take an inventory of the grooming appliances in your home and rate them as to usefulness.

Use Cosmetics Safely

1. Read labels for information on ingredients and uses of product.
2. Follow directions exactly.
3. Stop using any cosmetic that causes irritation. If irritation continues or becomes serious, see a doctor and take the cosmetic with you. Report any serious reactions caused to the FDA and to the manufacturer.
4. Do not use eye cosmetics if you have an eye infection.
5. Avoid using cosmetics on irritated or infected areas unless it is a medicated product intended to aid healing.
6. Keep cosmetic products and containers clean. Wash your hands thoroughly before applying cosmetics.
7. Finish using one container of a cosmetic before opening a new container. Throw away cosmetics if they change color or an odor develops.
8. Do not share or borrow cosmetics. Another person's bacteria may be harmful to you.
9. Never add any liquid to a cosmetic product, especially saliva. Bacteria in saliva may contaminate the product and cause infection.
10. Be sure to do a "patch test" according to directions when products call for one. This is especially important for hair coloring products.
11. Tightly close cosmetic containers after each use to prevent contamination.
12. Keep cosmetics away from small children. Misuse of cosmetics may be hazardous.
13. Never apply cosmetics while driving.

17-8

These guidelines can help your choose and use cosmetic products safely.

Discuss

What are some of the features commonly available on different grooming appliances? Which do you find most important?

Activity

Read, compare, and discuss warranty coverage for several different grooming appliances.

Activity

Compare the price of the same brand and model of a grooming appliance sold in three different types of stores. Discuss findings.

Reflect

What types of grooming services have you purchased?

Enrich

Develop a questionnaire to guide consumers in shopping for grooming services.

you spend on these products will bring you greater satisfaction if you make the best choices for your wants and needs. Before buying an appliance

- make sure you really need it and will use it.

- look closely at the product features. Do not pay extra for features you will not use.

- make sure the appliance is made by a reputable company and sold by a reliable retailer.

- look for the Underwriters Laboratories symbol to learn which products meet industry safety standards.

Compare prices of similar appliances that have the same features. It also pays to compare prices at several stores. The cost of the same product can vary greatly from one retailer to another.

Once you buy a grooming appliance, read and carefully follow directions for its use, care, and storage, 17-9.

Buying Grooming Services

Beauty and grooming services include haircuts, hair coloring, hair removal, facials, massages, manicures, pedicures, and other procedures. Buying a service is different from buying a cosmetic product or grooming appliance. You cannot see the results of the service until after it is performed.

To avoid disappointments, check the qualifications and experience of persons performing services for you. Ask other customers if they were satisfied with the services they received.

When deciding where to get a haircut or any type of service, consider the location of the shop, its business hours, cleanliness, and any other factors important to you. Be sure to find out what the prices include ahead of time. For example, does the cost of a haircut include a shampoo and styling? If you are unsure how much to leave for a tip, ask what is appropriate. Find out all the details to avoid any surprises.

17-9

Follow these guidelines for safe use of grooming appliances.

Use Appliances Safely

1. Read the manufacturer's use and care instructions before using an appliance. Follow the directions carefully.

2. Use and store electrical appliances away from water.

3. Turn off appliances before connecting or disconnecting them. Disconnect by pulling the plug—not the cord.

4. Disconnect any appliance that gives a shock. Have it checked and repaired before using it again.

5. Keep electrical cords and plugs in good repair.

6. Avoid coiling cords tightly.

7. Check the wattage rating stamped on appliances. Avoid connecting more than 1600 watts on any single electrical circuit.

Planning for Leisure

Reflect

What are some of your favorite ways to have fun?

Planning time for leisure activities, such as pursing hobbies, playing a favorite sport, or traveling, contributes to your overall health and wellness. Recreation can help reduce stress and tension and improve the way you feel.

Case Study: For Your Health

Finding Time for Fun

Greg is feeling stressed out. He recently started high school and is finding the schoolwork a little tough. He is on the football and debate teams and plays in the band. He also likes to jog, read, and watch TV. Whether he is working or playing, he worries about everything else he should be doing. He is falling behind in his classes, and nothing is fun anymore.

Sixteen-year-old Eleni has lots of interests, but never seems to have time for any of them. She tends to sleep late in the morning and barely arrives at school on time. Eleni eats with friends and relaxes during her 45-minute lunch break. In study hall, she surfs the Internet or looks at fashion magazines. Eleni often stops for something to eat with friends on the way home from school.

Once at home, she usually watches TV even though the late afternoon programs are boring. Soon it's time for dinner. After dinner, she likes to watch her favorite TV shows and talk to friends on the phone or online. However, her parents won't let her do these things until her homework is done. Eleni feels like she doesn't have time in the evening to do the things she really likes.

Case Review

1. Have you ever signed up to do more than you could handle?
2. How might Greg deal with his problem? How might he have avoided it?
3. Do you know someone with a problem like Eleni's?
4. What time-wasters do you see in Eleni's day?
5. How do you think Eleni might solve her problem?
6. What time-wasters rob you of hours for fun?
7. Do you often feel like you have too much to do and not enough time? If so, what can you do about it?

To pursue the activities you like most, you will need time and probably money. Getting more out of your limited recreation hours and dollars calls for careful planning and decision making.

Selecting Sports and Hobby Equipment

The money you spend for pleasure will include equipment, supplies, and special clothes. It may also include lessons or coaching. Costs will depend on the activities you choose. Below is a list of guidelines to follow as you shop for leisure time necessities.

Anticipate Costs

Unless you already have the equipment, some sports and hobbies may be expensive. Golf, skiing, sailing, and photography require expensive equipment. Before becoming involved in a sport or hobby, find out how much it will cost. When money is limited, you may want to choose less costly activities such as hiking, chess, or dancing.

Do Your Homework

Before making any major purchases, check *Consumer Bulletin* and *Consumer Reports* product ratings. Also look for information in specialized sports and hobby magazines and from manufacturers and retailers. Talk with people who have experience in the sport or hobby that interests you. Coaches, pros, instructors, and experienced salespersons can offer good advice on the purchase or rental of hobby and sports equipment. You can also find information on individual sports and hobbies online. Find out what kinds of equipment are recommended and how much you are likely to pay.

Learn to Judge Quality and Performance

Find out the important quality and performance features of a piece of equipment before you spend your money. For example, suppose you want to buy a tennis racquet. You will need to decide whether to buy aluminum or graphite. You need to figure out the best head size and consider the weight and grip size you need. Do you want a top-of-the-line or beginner's racquet? Buy the equipment that best suits your ability, interests, and budget.

Rent Equipment

If you are not sure what equipment to buy or if you are not sure of your interest in a new sport or hobby, try renting equipment first. Sometimes rental fees can be applied toward the purchase of equipment if you later decide to buy. Ski equipment and musical instruments are often rented first and bought later.

Case Study: For Your Health

Having Fun with Hobbies

Bill loves watching hockey and decided to join a local team. His parents bought him new, expensive equipment. The following week, one of the area schools held a sports equipment exchange. Good, used gear was sold for a fraction of its original price. Unfortunately, Bill hadn't seen the notice posted at school. The next month, Bill dropped hockey. His ankles were weak, he didn't skate well, and the hockey schedule was too strenuous. Bill decided hockey was more fun to watch than to play.

Jada got a camera for her birthday several years ago and immediately started taking pictures. Last summer, she took a course on digital photography. After the class, she bought a good camera and now takes pictures for the school paper. She even won a few photo contests. Over the years, Jada is likely to invest money in new equipment as advancements are made in digital photography. She may even pursue a career in photography.

Manu has taken piano lessons for the last eight years and plays for the school chorus. He also organized a group of friends into a band. They play at parties and dances. Over the summer, they will each earn about $900. Except for the piano lessons, Manu and his family spent little money for Manu's music. Now, he can continue learning on his own and earn a little cash besides. Manu has a hobby that he can enjoy through the years.

Case Review

1. Do you think Bill would have done anything differently if he had been spending his own money? How might Bill have made a wiser choice?
2. What are some ways Jada might enjoy photography without spending as much money?
3. How could Manu's hobbies turn into a career?
4. What are your thoughts and feelings about expensive hobbies?
5. What are some ways to make a hobby pay for itself?
6. What are some relatively inexpensive hobbies?
7. What hobbies might be a source of income?

Look for Money Savers

When you need costly equipment, you may want to consider buying used equipment. Other ways to save are to check discount stores for good buys or to wait for end-of-season sales. Skis, for example, will sell for less in April than in November. Look for equipment exchanges in your area and check the classified ads in local papers. Online sites also may offer bargains.

Travel and Vacation Planning

Each year, consumers spend billions of dollars on travel within the United States and abroad. For most people, however, time and money for travel and vacation are limited. It takes careful planning to get the most fun and satisfaction out of these limited resources.

Smart travelers begin their vacation planning at the library or online. They check out articles, books, and Web sites on areas they want to visit and the special activities they like, such as biking, rafting, and skiing. Most airlines, hotels, resorts, restaurants, and cities operate their own Web sites you can use to plan your travel.

Questions for Travelers

Before you make travel or vacation plans, ask yourself the following questions.

- *How will you get there?* The transportation you choose will depend on where you are traveling and how much time and money you have to spend. Before buying airline or train tickets, check for any travel restrictions and penalties for changes or cancellations. Some tickets are nonrefundable.

- *Where will you stay?* Investigate choices of hotels, motels, resorts, youth hostels, and campgrounds. Find out about reservations and rates. Rooms will be easier to get and rates will be lower during off-season months.

- *What are the special things to see and do?* Are there seasonal festivals, sightseeing tours, athletic events, or historical sites? Check to see if you need tickets in advance for any special events.

- *How much will it all cost?* Make a list of estimated expenses for transportation, lodging, and meals. Also estimate costs for equipment rental, sports activities, or sightseeing. Check your estimates against your budget. Will you have enough money to cover your costs?

Package Tours and Trips

Throughout the year, travel agencies, airlines, and resorts offer many vacation packages and group tours at special rates. Before you sign up for a package trip, find out exactly what is included. For example, know the

- length of the trip and dates of departure and return
- type and quality of accommodations

- meals and other items that are included in the price

- total costs itemized

- available options

- penalties for cancellations

- size and makeup of the tour group

Deal only with a reliable travel agency or tour company. If possible, talk with other travelers who have dealt with the agency or company and find out if they were satisfied with their travel arrangements.

Activity

Consider your local area as a vacation spot and write a travel guide for visitors.

Resource

Chapter 17—Health and Wellness, Teacher's PowerPoint Presentations CD

Chapter Summary

Staying healthy starts with taking care of yourself. Routine checkups and appropriate health care are important. The key to getting the care you need is finding experienced and qualified health care providers. It is equally important to check out hospitals and health care facilities in your area. You may want to take a look at available walk-in clinics for minor routine health care needs. Alternative medicine offers a spectrum of health care services and therapies you may want to investigate.

When taking any type of medication, it is essential to read and follow the directions on the label. This is true for both prescription and over the counter drugs. Learn what to look for on the labels of medications you take. Usually you can save money buying generic rather than brand name drugs if your health care provider approves.

For many, fitness and weight-loss programs are a part of a health routine. When these involve signing on to formal programs it becomes important to study the details and any contract you are asked to sign. You will want to follow your own path to fitness and weight management.

You will undoubtedly use a number of grooming aids and appliances to enhance your appearance. To get the most from these products, choose them carefully and use them safely. Study the labels on cosmetics and follow the directions for use. Check out the qualifications of persons who offer grooming services. Find out about prices and what they include.

Having fun begins with knowing what you enjoy and then planning the use of time and money you spend on fun and recreation. Learning how to choose necessary sports and hobby equipment is an important consumer skill. Both used and rental equipment can save money for beginners in various sports and hobbies. Travel and vacation planning skills will also lead to good times and productive use of your time and money.

Review

1. What qualifications should you look for when choosing health care providers?

2. What are five questions to ask when evaluating health care facilities?

3. What services are typically offered at walk-in clinics?

4. Describe *alternative medicine*.

5. How do generic and brand name medications differ?

6. What are five questions you should ask your health care provider about medications prescribed for you?

7. What is a dietary supplement?

8. Who is responsible for testing the safety and effectiveness of dietary supplements?

9. Name five things to consider when evaluating a fitness center or health club.

10. Name five factors to consider before signing on to a weight-loss program.

11. What government agency regulates the safety of cosmetics?

12. What information must be listed on cosmetic products?

13. What symbol should you look for on electric appliances? What does this symbol mean?

14. List four guidelines that can help you shop for sports or hobby necessities.

15. List four details that you should know before signing up for a package tour.

Critical Thinking

16. What should you consider when selecting a physician or dentist?

17. Why is it important to check with a health care professional or pharmacist before taking dietary supplements?

18. What information appears on labels of supplements? Bring a supplement container to class and explain the information on the label.

19. What risks are connected with careless, unsanitary use of cosmetics?

20. How many grooming appliances do you and your family own? Do you use every appliance on a regular basis? What appliances could you do without? What more do you need?

21. What would you recommend to get inactive teens involved in a sports or fitness program?

22. Have you or your friends ever rented sports equipment? What are some advantages of renting equipment rather than buying it?

Answers to *Review*

1. (See pages 419–420.)

2. (See pages 421–422.)

3. Routine medical attention, such as treatment for sinus and upper respiratory infections, bladder infections, strep throat, and minor injuries. Prescriptions and vaccinations can be given.

4. Alternative medicine includes a group of health care practices and products that are presently not a part of conventional methods. Treatments include mind-body interventions, biological-based approaches, manipulative and body-based methods, and energy therapies.

5. Generic drugs cost less and are named with the drug's common name, chemical composition, or class.

6. (See page 427.)

7. a product that is intended to enhance your diet

8. The manufacturer/distributor of the product.

9. (Name five:) location and hours; classes and training; equipment; certification of trainers and instructors; condition of the facility; costs and fees; reputation; trial membership options

10. (Name five:) emphasis on healthy behaviors; access to medical care; counseling or group classes; meal plans; exercise component; maintenance plan; qualifications of staff; associated health risks; typical results; costs and fees

11. Food and Drug Administration

12. (See page 434.)

13. Look for the Underwriters Laboratories symbol. It indicates that the product meets standards for electrical safety.

Academic Connections

23. **Science.** Choose one of the medical specialties listed in 17-2 and investigate the areas of diagnosis and treatment within the field. What advanced training and education are required to practice the specialty?

24. **Research, writing.** Conduct a survey and develop a descriptive directory of health care services and facilities in your area.

25. **Science.** Investigate and report on one area of alternative medicine. Find out which health care facilities in your area offer alternative medical treatments.

26. **Speech.** Visit two reputable Web sites with information on dietary supplements. Give a five-minute report on what you learn. Identify your sources.

27. **Financial literacy, math.** Make a list of the cosmetics and grooming aids you own. Estimate the total amount you spend on these items monthly. Draw a line through items you do not use and determine how much you could have saved by not buying them.

28. **Writing.** Write a research report on the laboratory methods used to test cosmetics for safety. Cosmetic manufacturers and the FDA are good sources of information on this project.

29. **Math.** Make a list of five grooming aids or appliances you use regularly. Comparison shop and find the price of each item in three or four stores. If you were buying all five products from the same store, which store would charge you the least amount?

MATH CHALLENGE

30. Suppose the average consumer coinsurance is 23% for generic drugs and 36% for brand name drugs.
    - Drug A (generic): $49
    - Drug B (generic): $75
    - Drug C (brand name): $125
    A. What is the total amount a consumer owes when filling prescriptions for drugs A, B, and C?
    B. The generic version of drug C costs 40% less than the brand name. What is the total amount a consumer owes after switching to the generic drug C?

Tech Smart

31. Visit the Web sites of two fitness centers and health clubs in your area to learn what facilities and programs they offer, the cost of joining, the qualifications of staff members, and the benefits of membership. Which one would you join if you were looking for a place to work out? What impressed you both positively and negatively about the different centers?

---

14. (List four:) Anticipate costs. Do your homework. Learn to judge quality and performance. Try rental. Look for money savers

15. (List four:) length of the trip and dates of departure and return; type and quality of accommodations; meals and other items that are included in the prices; total costs itemized; available options; penalties for cancellations; size and makeup of the tour group

Answer to *Math Challenge*

26. A. Coinsurance drug A = $11.27, Drug B = $17.25, Drug C = $45; Total = $73.52
    B. Cost of generic drug C = $75; coinsurance = $17.25; Total consumer owes for generic drugs A, B, C = $45.77

Reading for Meaning

Where do you picture yourself living in five years? Write a paragraph describing your ideal living situation. Then list the steps you must take to get there.

condominium

cooperative

security deposit

lease

real estate broker

exclusive buyer
agent

purchase agreement

earnest money

contingency clause

mortgage

amortization

fixed rate mortgage

adjustable rate
mortgage (ARM)

graduated payment
mortgage

interest only
mortgage

subprime mortgage

FHA-insured loan

VA-guaranteed loan

closing costs

points

property survey

title

abstract of title

escrow account

private mortgage
insurance (PMI)

home equity loan

floor plan

CHAPTER OBJECTIVES

After studying this chapter,
you will be able to

- **list** key factors to consider when choosing a housing location.

- **evaluate** different types of housing.

- **describe** and compare the responsibilities and costs involved in renting versus buying a home.

- **compare** and shop for home financing.

- **decorate** and choose furnishings to fit your tastes, lifestyle, and budget.

- **evaluate** furniture and floor coverings in terms of quality, design, and price.

- **describe** key home care and maintenance responsibilities.

Central Ideas

- Finding a place to call home involves assessing your needs, wants, and budget.

- For home buyers, a home can be an investment. It is only a good investment if home owners fulfill their financial obligations, such as making regular mortgage payments.

- Housing costs also include the costs of moving, utilities, furnishing a home, and maintaining and repairing it.

The word *home* has different meanings for different people. To some people, a home is a base of operations—a headquarters. To others, a home is a secure shelter from an unfriendly world. It may be a place to relax and entertain, or simply a wise investment. A home may mean all of this and more. It is whatever people make it.

Over the years you will probably spend a large portion of your income on a place to live. Consider the choices very carefully. The home you choose will influence the way you live, the people you meet, and your overall sense of well-being.

When making housing decisions, location is one of your most important considerations. You also need to decide what type of housing you want and how much you can spend. Finally, you want to weigh the pros and cons of buying versus renting a home at different stages in your life. Once you have a home, you will need to furnish, decorate, and maintain your living space.

Housing Location

The location of your first home away from home may be determined largely by what you are doing. Will you be working, going to school, or getting married? Very often a job or school will dictate in part where you live. Even so, you will be able to make some choices within existing limitations.

Consider how you like to live. Would you prefer living in the country, a small town, a city, or a suburb? Some people like the pace and excitement of city living, 18-1. Others like rural areas with lots of open space. Still others try to have both by living in the suburbs. There is more to choosing a location than deciding between city and country, though. Here are some other factors to consider.

Employment Opportunities

What types of jobs are available in the areas that appeal to you? Will you be able to find the type of work you want? How much money can you expect to earn if you work in the area? Local or state employment offices and chambers of commerce are places to check out employment opportunities in different areas. You can also find job listings and career opportunities for different areas and in different fields online.

18-1

Some people like the excitement and fast pace of big city life while others prefer the peace and quiet of life in the country.

Cost of Living

What is the average cost of housing in different areas? The Bureau of Labor Statistics publishes cost of living figures for different cities and parts of the country. Business and world almanacs also give cost of living and other economic information on different places. Cost of living comparisons are available from a number of sites online.

It pays to find out the costs of food, housing, health care, transportation, and utilities for places where you would like to live. What are the rates for home and car insurance? What are the sales, income, and real estate tax rates? The cost of maintaining similar lifestyles in different areas can vary greatly.

Climate

What type of weather do you like—warm, dry, wet, cold, or mild? Is a change of seasons important to you? Would you rather live near the desert, the mountains, or the ocean? A world almanac or the National Climatic Center of the U.S. Department of Commerce can provide weather statistics for different cities. These statistics include average high and low temperatures, rainfall and snowfall, humidity, and wind speed.

Lifestyle

Will you be living alone or with a roommate or spouse? Do you expect to have children? Young, single persons or childless couples may prefer living in the heart of a city. Families with young children may want to live in a suburb or small town where there is more space and a stronger sense of community.

Try to decide what is most important to you. Do you want to live close to your family or friends? Do you want to live near a college or university to further your education? Do you want to be close to the mountains so you can ski in the winter? Would you rather be near water so you can enjoy water sports? Your answers to these and similar questions will help guide your choice of location.

Neighborhood

Once you have narrowed your choices to a specific region or city, you can begin evaluating different neighborhoods. Appearance is one of the most obvious factors to consider in a neighborhood. Are the buildings attractive? Do the architectural styles offer both variety and harmony? Are both private and public areas well kept? Are the yards attractively landscaped with trees, bushes, and flowers? Is the street layout attractive and functional?

What is the overall character of the neighborhood? Does it appear residential, commercial, industrial, or mixed? What zoning laws and building codes apply to the neighborhood? Is the area relatively free of heavy traffic, noise, and air pollution? How would you assess property values now and in the future? Does the neighborhood seem safe and crime-free? Local newspapers and law enforcement agencies may have information about crime rates.

You may want to consider the ages, interests, occupations, and educational backgrounds of the people in the area. Is the overall income level

Reflect

How do you feel about different climates?

Reflect

How would you answer these questions about lifestyle?

Activity

Write a short description of what you consider to be an ideal neighborhood.

Housing and Health

The place you live is as important to your health as what you eat and how much you exercise. Health hazards can result from poorly constructed and maintained housing. For example, residents in older homes and apartment buildings can be exposed to peeling paint containing lead. Water leaking in and around a home can trigger the growth of black mold that causes and aggravates health problems.

Neighborhoods near industrial areas, factories, and highways are more exposed to airborne pollutants. Breathing these pollutants has been linked to respiratory problems, such as asthma, and other illnesses.

Crime impacts health in some communities. In high crime areas, parents may not let their children outdoors to play. Even if parks and recreational facilities exist, people are afraid to use them. As a result, residents do not get the exercise they need.

Individuals and families can take action to improve their health. However, urban planners, health experts, law enforcement personnel, and others also play a role in creating healthful living environments.

18-2
Families with young children will probably prefer to live near a park or playground.

similar to your own? Are most people living in the area single or married? Are there children in the neighborhood? Are there enough similarities to make life comfortable and enough differences to make it interesting?

Community Facilities

Check out the community services and facilities. Are services convenient to use and reasonable in cost? Is fire and police protection adequate? What is the cost of utilities? Does the community provide trash pickup, recycling, and snow removal? Are streets and other public areas well maintained? Learn what you can about health care in the area. Is public transportation convenient and reliable?

Look for services and activities that are important to you, 18-2. For example, does the community sponsor athletic programs and cultural events? Are citizens actively involved in local government? Will you have access to a public library, churches, parks, and athletic facilities? Are there a variety of shops and stores?

Schools

The education system is important because its quality affects local property values. It is also important if you have children. Find out whether the schools in the area are noted for quality education. What are teacher qualifications and pay scales? What is the average class size? Are textbooks and lab equipment up-to-date? Are special education programs offered? What extracurricular activities are offered?

Sources of Information

Be sure to check out a location carefully before you settle. Moving into a place that does not suit you can be costly in terms of happiness, time, and money. The following sources can provide helpful information about specific regions and communities:

- chambers of commerce
- local newspapers and magazines
- classified ad pages and local government listings in phone books
- long-time and new residents of an area
- travel books and almanacs
- community organizations in the area
- real estate brokers
- the Internet

Activity

Investigate and describe the community services and facilities available in your area.

Reflect

What types of community services would be important to you?

Activity

Go online and check out your own community or a city in which you would like to live. How might the information provided help you choose a place to live? Discuss.

Enrich

Research your own community using these sources to see what you can learn.

Reflect

How do you see your housing needs and goals changing over time?

Types of Housing

At different times in your life, you will most likely choose different types and styles of housing. Your choices will be based on what you need and want, what you can afford, and what is available.

Apartments, Condominiums, and Cooperatives

Most rental apartments, condominiums, and cooperatives are multi-family dwellings. They are in buildings with more than one living unit. Each unit has private living quarters. Residents share common areas, such as lobby, grounds, laundry facilities, and other building facilities.

Apartment buildings vary in the types of services and facilities they offer. They may or may not have laundry equipment, parking space, recreational facilities, and other extras. If you are considering apartment living, the checklist in 18-3 can help you choose.

The main difference that separates rental apartments from condominiums and cooperatives is ownership. A person who lives in a rental apartment leases the apartment from the owner. A person who lives in a condominium or cooperative generally owns it. Condominium and cooperative ownership are somewhat similar. Buyers share common areas and have some voice in the management of the property. However, there are some distinct differences.

Checklist for Apartments, Condominiums, and Cooperatives

Building and Grounds

- ❑ Attractive, well-constructed building
- ❑ Good maintenance and upkeep
- ❑ Clean, well-lighted halls, entrances, stairs
- ❑ Reliable building management
- ❑ Locked entrances, protected from outsiders

Services and Facilities

- ❑ Laundry equipment
- ❑ Parking space (indoor or outdoor)
- ❑ Swimming pool or tennis courts
- ❑ Convenient trash disposal
- ❑ Adequate fire escapes
- ❑ Storage lockers
- ❑ Locked mailboxes
- ❑ Elevators
- ❑ Engineer on call for emergency repairs

Inside Living Space

- ❑ Adequate room sizes
- ❑ Windows located to provide enough air, light, and ventilation
- ❑ Windows have screens and storm windows
- ❑ Attractive, easy-to-clean floors
- ❑ Furnished appliances in good condition
- ❑ Clean, effective heating, thermostatically controlled
- ❑ Up-to-date wiring
- ❑ Conveniently placed electric outlets
- ❑ Well-fitted doors, casings, cabinets, and built-ins
- ❑ Extras—air conditioning, dishwasher, fireplace, patio

A **condominium** is a form of home ownership where a person owns the unit he or she occupies. The ownership of the surrounding building and grounds is shared. The owner pays a monthly *assessment* or maintenance fee to cover the costs of operating, maintaining, and repairing the shared property. The owners generally elect a board of managers to make policy and management decisions for the shared property.

In some ways, owning a condo is like owning a single-family house. Most people obtain a mortgage when buying a condo. They make mortgage payments and pay property taxes. Condo owners have the same tax and equity benefits as the house owner. Another similarity is both condo and house owners can make their own decisions about redecorating, refinancing, or selling their homes.

A **cooperative** is a form of home ownership in which a person buys shares in a corporation that owns the property. In return, the buyer lives in a designated unit and becomes a member of the cooperative. Owners pay a monthly fee that covers their share of maintenance and service costs. The fee also covers the building mortgage and taxes. Usually it is necessary to obtain approval from an elected board of directors before selling or remodeling a unit.

When buying a condominium or a cooperative, it is important to do some thorough homework. The soundness of this type of investment depends greatly on the management, restrictions, operating policies, and types of people involved in both ownership and management. Here are a few questions to answer before buying.

- How is the property managed, and by whom? What voice do owners have in management decisions?

- Are current residents generally satisfied with the management and the building?

- What is the financial status of the building? Is there a mortgage on the property? Are any major repairs or renovations anticipated? If so, are funds available to cover the cost? Does the appraised value compare favorably with the selling price?

- How much is the monthly maintenance fee or assessment? What does it cover? When and how can it be increased?

- What control do occupants have over their units? Are there restrictions on selling, remodeling, renting, or refinancing? Are pets permitted?

- How does the condominium or cooperative unit compare with similar units in other buildings and with other forms of available housing in the area?

Enrich

Interview a real estate or condo management company agent to discuss these questions.

Enrich

Interview a builder about the differences among the various types of single-family houses.

Discuss

What advantages and disadvantages can you name for each type of single-family house?

Vocabulary

Give a definition for each of the different types of single-family houses.

Single-Family Houses

The single-family house is still the most popular type of housing. If you decide to live in a house, you will face many decisions. A few people choose to build a house of their own. Most people rent or buy an existing house. If you decide to buy or build a home, there are many professionals who can help, 18-4. Become familiar with the various experts, what they do, and how they can help you make housing decisions.

If you are planning to move into a single-family house, there are a number of factors to consider, 18-5. If you are buying, solid construction is of great importance. Be sure to check both outside and inside construction features. It pays to carefully evaluate the outside of the house, the yard, and the neighborhood as well as the inside living space.

Choose a house that is conveniently designed for your lifestyle and housing needs. Looking at different types of houses can help you decide what you like best. If you are buying, it generally pays to hire an independent contractor to inspect the house and evaluate construction details you cannot judge.

If you decide to build a home you will have a host of decisions to make in the process. Single-family houses are built in a variety of ways.

- *Custom-built houses* are usually designed by architects to meet the specific needs and wishes of their clients. A contractor is hired to build the house according to an architect's plan. This can be a costly and lengthy project.

- *Tract houses* are neighborhoods of new homes built by developers who erect many houses at once within a given area. These houses are built from similar plans in order to keep costs down. Most tract

	The Experts	
Title	**Description of Services**	**When To Use Them**
Real Estate Agents	Bring buyer/tenant and seller/landlord together and negotiate a deal acceptable to both. Provide helpful information on community tax rates, schools, services, shopping, property values, etc. Recommend lenders and help arrange financing for home purchase. Represent the seller in a sale and receive a commission for services—usually a percentage of the price.	When you need help finding the housing you want in an area you like at a price you can pay. When you are unfamiliar with an area and need facts to decide exactly where and what to buy or rent. When you need help finding professional services and home financing. When you want to sell a home at a fair price in a reasonable length of time.
Lawyers	Represent either buyer or seller in transferring real estate. Protect client's interests when selling, buying, building, or leasing a home. Draw up agreements for client and check agreements drawn by others before the client signs. Represent client at the closing of a real estate transaction.	When you buy or sell a home. When you have questions about a housing contract or lease. When you become involved in a dispute with a landlord, seller, builder, or buyer in a real estate transaction. Before you sign any contract or agreement involving more money or time than you can afford to sacrifice.
Architects	Draw up plans for building or remodeling. Choose suitable building materials. Help find a lot suited to the house design, or design a house suited to the lot. Hire and work with the contractor and supervise building.	When you want to build a house or do extensive remodeling. When you want a custom-designed home.
Contractors	Accept responsibility for building or remodeling a home. Order building materials. Hire and supervise workers. See that work is done according to specifications and terms in the contract.	When you want to build a home or make home improvements.

18-4

These experts can help you buy, sell, lease, build, or remodel a home.

Reflect

What experiences has your family had with any of the listed experts?

houses look alike and lack the individuality of custom-built houses. They are less expensive, however, and builders often make minor alterations to meet individual buyers' needs.

- *Modular and kit houses* are partially built in factories. They are then moved in sections to the home site for completion. These houses are relatively inexpensive. Quality depends on the manufacturer as well as the builder who puts the house together.

Checklist for Single-Family Houses

Outside House and Yard

❏ Attractive, well-designed house

❏ Lot of the right size and shape for house and garage

❏ Good drainage of rain and moisture

❏ Mature, healthy trees—placed to give shade in summer

❏ Well-kept driveway, walks, patio, and porch

❏ Parking convenience—garage, carport, or street

❏ Well lighted and sheltered entry

Outside Construction

❏ Durable siding materials—in good condition

❏ Solid brick and masonry—free of cracks

❏ Solid foundation walls

❏ Weather-stripped windows and doors

❏ Noncorrosive gutters and downspouts, connected to storm sewer or splash block to carry water away from house

❏ Copper or aluminum flashing used over doors, windows, and joints on the roof

❏ Screens and storm windows

Inside Construction

❏ Sound, smooth walls with invisible nails and taping on dry wall surfaces

❏ Well-done carpentry work with properly fitted joints and moldings

❏ Properly fitted, easy-to-operate windows

❏ Level wood floors with smooth finish and no high edges, wide gaps, or squeaks

❏ Well-fitted tile floors—no cracked or damaged tiles—no visible adhesive

❏ Good possibilities for improvements, remodeling, expanding

❏ Dry basement floor with hard, smooth surface

❏ Adequate basement drain

❏ Sturdy stairways with railings, adequate head room—not too steep

❏ Leakproof roof—in good condition

❏ Adequate insulation for warmth and soundproofing

Living Space

❏ Convenient work areas (kitchen, laundry, workshop) with adequate drawers, cabinets, lighting, workspace, electric power

❏ Bedrooms located far enough from other parts of the house for privacy and quiet

❏ Social areas (living and dining room, play space, yard, porch, or patio) convenient, comfortable, large enough for family and guests

❏ Adequate storage—closets, cabinets, shelves, attic, basement, garage

❏ Windows located to provide enough air, light, and ventilation

❏ Usable attic and/or basement space

❏ Extras—fireplace, air conditioning, porches, new kitchen and baths

18-5

This checklist can help you evaluate the appearance, construction, and living space of single-family homes.

- *Town houses* are single-family units that share one or both sidewalls with other town houses. The units are usually built at the same time from similar blueprints.

Manufactured Homes

A manufactured home is a single-family house built in a factory and shipped to the home site where it is erected. These homes are constructed in compliance with the *Manufactured Housing Construction and Safety Standards Code,* called the *HUD Code.*

Manufactured homes generally cost considerably less than other types of housing with comparable living space and equipment. Maintenance

Building Code Officials

Building code officials examine buildings, highways and streets, sewer and water systems, bridges, and other structures. They ensure that their construction, alteration, or repair complies with building codes and ordinances, zoning regulations, and contract specifications.

Resource

Housing Choices, Activity A, WB

Reflect

How important is a home to you? What percent of your income would you be willing to spend for the home you want?

Reflect

How does your family decide what to spend on housing?

costs are usually low, too. However, over time they may decrease rather than increase in value.

They often are located in manufactured home communities but may be built on private lots. The home owner may purchase the lot that the manufactured home rests on. It may also be owned by a business that charges the home owner a monthly rent. Look to the following guidelines if you wish to consider a manufactured home:

- **Choose a dealer carefully.** Check dealer reputation with local banks, businesses, the Better Business Bureau, chamber of commerce, and previous customers. Also find out if the dealer is a member of the state manufactured housing association.

- **Figure and compare total costs.** Find out what the purchase price does and does not include. Compare the costs of finance charges and insurance. Check the prices of a home lot, delivery to the lot, and installation.

- **Check warranty terms.** Study the warranties on the manufactured home and on the appliances and equipment that come with it. Find out what is warranted, for how long, what the owner must do to receive warranty benefits, and who is responsible for carrying out warranty terms.

- **Check features and extras.** Find out how the home is heated, cooled, insulated, and furnished. Also check the capacity of the hot water heater. Make sure the model you choose will provide basic comfort, convenience, and safety.

- **Investigate the manufactured home community.** Look at the design and management. Find out what services and facilities are available free or for a fee. Ask about the rules and regulations. Talk to people who live there.

Monthly Housing Costs

Most financial advisers suggest that total monthly housing costs come to no more than one-third of monthly take-home pay. Take-home pay is the amount of money you receive after taxes and other deductions are subtracted from your paycheck.

Housing costs include not only rent or mortgage payments, but also utilities, maintenance, property taxes, and home owner's or renter's insurance. You can use the budgeting exercise in Chapter 6 to determine your monthly housing allowance. In summary, a budget takes you through the following steps.

1. Total the amount you have to spend each month. Include all income and earnings.

2. Total monthly non-housing expenses. Include food, clothing, transportation, recreation, loans, insurance, taxes, and any other ongoing obligations.

3. Subtract total monthly non-housing expenses from total monthly income to arrive at the amount you can afford for housing each month.

4. Adjust earnings, spending, and housing costs as needed.

If you do not have enough money for the home you want, you have three choices. You can try to increase your income, spend less on non-housing expenses, or choose a less expensive home. Before choosing a place to live, determine how much money you can spend on housing. The amount you can afford will depend on several factors. These include your income, other expenses and obligations, housing needs, and your expected future income.

Since housing is generally a monthly expenditure, begin by figuring a reasonable monthly housing allowance. If you plan to buy a home, you will need to determine a purchase price, a down payment, closing costs, and a mortgage you can handle over a long period of time. The cost of moving and furnishing your home should also be considered. Home buying expenses are covered later in this chapter.

Resource

How Much Can They Afford?
Activity B, WB

Discuss

What are some of the factors that would indicate you could spend more or less than recommended guidelines for housing?

Renting Versus Buying

The primary financial responsibility of renting a place to live is to pay the stated rent each month. The renter is also responsible for taking reasonable care of the rental unit and paying any utility bills that are not included in the rent.

Renting a home offers certain advantages. They include the following.

- *Fewer financial responsibilities.* You do not need a large sum of money for a down payment. Rents are generally lower than mortgage payments. You do not have to pay property taxes. Renters do not pay for major repairs and maintenance, such as a new roof or purchase of major appliances.

- *More free time.* Since renters are often not responsible for home maintenance, such as landscaping, and home repairs and improvements, they have more free time, 18-6.

- *Less financial risk.* Renters do not need to worry about property values or the inability to pay a mortgage.

- *Greater mobility.* Renters can usually move at the end of their lease if they give a month's notice.

18-6

Some people prefer to rent because they do not want to spend time on exterior maintenance tasks, such as landscaping and lawn care.

For many people, owning a home gives a sense of permanence and financial security. It is a source of pride and satisfaction. Buying a home is a smart move for the following reasons.

Discuss

What are the advantages of renting a home over buying?

Discuss

What are the advantages of buying a home over renting?

Reflect

Would you prefer to rent or buy a home? How might your preferences change throughout the life cycle?

- *Can increase wealth.* When you buy real estate, you build up equity or ownership in property. You are buying something you often can resell for a profit.

- *Tax benefits.* In addition, home mortgage interest and property taxes paid on a home are deductible expenses when figuring federal income tax. Renters do not enjoy these financial advantages.

- *Greater control.* When you buy a home, you generally have the freedom to make most of the decisions concerning your property: what color to paint it, where to hang pictures, whether or not to put in a swimming pool, etc. Condominiums and some housing subdivisions have rules that limit home owner freedoms.

The advantages of both buying and renting must be weighed against the disadvantages. The disadvantages of renting include

- *No buildup of equity.* Buying a home can be an investment and renting is not. Over time, homes generally increase in value. The mortgage payments that home owners make are payments on an asset that they eventually own. Rent payments do not benefit renters, but go into the pockets of landlords.

- *Little control.* Renters have less control over their living space. At the end of a lease period, landlords can raise their rent or ask them to mo ve out. They may not be allowed to own pets, hang pictures on the walls, or paint and decorate. Some renters have irresponsible landlords who do not maintain properties or make needed repairs. Inadequate heat, hot water, and pest control are just a few of the problems these renters endure.

- *No tax benefits.* There are no tax benefits from renting.

The disadvantages of buying a home include the following.

- *Greater costs and financial responsibilities.* When they purchase a home, most home owners make a down payment. This is often a large sum of money. Monthly costs include mortgage payments, home owners' insurance, and property taxes. Owners are also responsible for repair and maintenance costs, 18-7.

- *Less mobility.* Moving usually involves selling a home, which is often complicated and time consuming. In a slow real estate market, it can take many months to sell a house or condominium.

- *Complicated relationships.* When friends or roommates buy a home together, they usually plan on living together for a while. However, if they decide to go their separate ways, it can be difficult to agree on what to do with the home.

- *Greater financial risk.* Although property values generally rise over time, home owners risk losing money if property values drop or if they cannot keep up with mortgage payments. People who do not pay their mortgage can lose their home.

18-7

Home repairs and upkeep, such as maintaining a pool, are costly expenses for home owners.

Renting a Place to Live

Once you have narrowed your search to particular communities or areas, you can tour the area looking for "For Rent" or "Apartment Available" signs. A phone number for the management company, realtor, or owner will probably be written on the sign. Many apartment buildings have on-site managers who are usually available to show apartments and take applications. The manager's apartment may be flagged on the buzzer panel or mailboxes.

Other sources of information about available rentals include

- classified ads in newspapers and online

- real estate agencies

- college housing offices

- bulletin boards at local grocery stores, coffee shops, community centers, etc.

- friends, acquaintances, people who live in the area

Make a good impression on the landlord or manager by showing up looking clean and neat and by being polite. You should be given a tour of the rental unit. Make sure you ask questions about parking, laundry, pets, and other concerns.

If possible, find an opportunity to talk with several tenants. There are some questions that only those who live in a building can answer accurately. For example, are apartments warm enough in winter and cool enough in summer? Are other tenants agreeable? Is the noise level acceptable and is privacy adequate? Find out if current tenants are satisfied with

Discuss

Name sources of rental information in your community.

Enrich

Have students search on the Internet for rental apartments in the area. What is the average cost for a one bedroom apartment?

Discuss

List guidelines to follow when looking at rental properties.

Case Study: Housing Solutions

The Search Is On

Milt just finished an automotive technology training program and accepted a job in another city. He needs to move closer to his work.

Milt wants a one-bedroom apartment, not a studio. He does not want to live in a high-rise building. He needs a place for his car and wants to live near people his age.

Online apartment listings are not very helpful because Milt doesn't know the city. Here are some of his other options:

- contact the chamber of commerce for a map of the city and information on apartments
- make appointments to see some apartments listed online
- take a day or two to drive around the city and see the neighborhoods
- ask his employer about places to live
- use a real estate or apartment finder agency to help find an apartment
- check into a hotel for a few weeks until he is more familiar with the city

Case Review

1. If you were Milt, how would you search for a place to live?
2. Which ideas from Milt's list might you use in searching for a place to live?
3. What should Milt consider before he chooses an apartment?
4. If Milt wanted to share an apartment with a roommate, how could he go about finding someone?

maintenance and repairs, building services and security, and the overall atmosphere.

Rental Applications

You will probably have to fill out an application if you find a place you want to rent. Besides your name and contact information, you may be asked for the name, address, and phone number of your employer; financial information; names and contact information of references; and a list of previous addresses and landlords. Make sure you have this information with you.

You may also have to give your Social Security number, pay a fee, and give permission for your credit report or credit score to be checked.

Landlords are allowed to request a credit report on prospective tenants. Credit reporting agencies require them to provide your name, address, and Social Security number to get a report. Landlords usually will not rent to people with low credit scores. There may be other fees as well.

If you rent an apartment or house, you are expected to pay the first month's rent and sign a lease. Normally, renters must also pay a *security deposit*. A **security deposit** protects the landlord against financial losses in case the renter damages the dwelling or fails to pay rent. It usually must be paid before moving into a rental unit. The amount of the security deposit generally comes to one or two month's rent. The deposit should be returned, usually with interest when the lease expires, provided there is no damage to the property.

Rental Leases

Most renters are asked to sign a lease when they begin renting. A **lease** is a contract that specifies the conditions, terms, and rent for the use of an asset, 18-8.

The lease must be signed by the *lessee*, the renter, and the *lessor*, the person who owns the asset. An apartment lease explains the legal rights and responsibilities of both a tenant and a landlord.

Before signing a lease, read it carefully and know the answers to the following questions:

- *Rent.* How much is the rent and when must it be paid? What are the penalties for late payment?

- *Security deposit.* Is a security deposit required? If so, how much is it? Will it draw interest? How do you get the deposit back? Under what circumstances may the landlord keep part or all of it?

- *Utilities.* What utilities are included in the rent? How much should you expect to pay for utilities that are not included? (Ask to see a record of previous billings.)

- *Furnishings, appliances, services.* What furnishings and appliances are included? What building services and facilities are available? What is included in the rent and what costs extra?

- *Lease period.* What term or period of time does the lease cover? What are the beginning and ending dates of the lease? When do payments begin? When can you move in? When must you renew the lease or give notice that you will not renew? What happens if you leave before the lease expires? Can you sublet or assign the lease to someone else? What are the conditions for doing so? What are your responsibilities if the person taking over does not pay the rent?

- *Upkeep, maintenance, repairs.* Who is responsible for upkeep, maintenance, and repairs? What does the landlord maintain, and what must you maintain? What can either of you do if the other fails to carry out upkeep and maintenance responsibilities? Where and how do you contact the landlord or rental agent with questions, problems, or complaints?

WB-20 APARTMENT LEASE
Approved by Wisconsin Real Estate Examining Board

Nelco Forms
P.O. Box 10208
Green Bay, WI 54307-0208

APARTMENT LEASE

1　This lease of the apartment identified below is entered into by and between the Landlord and Tenant (referred to
2　in the singular whether one or more) on the following terms and conditions:

PARTIES

3　Tenant: _Raoul Doe_　　Landlord: _Sawdusky Realty_

Ilse Doe

Agent for maintenance, management:
name _Mike Manning_
address _1210 Fixit St._
Anytown, USA

APARTMENT ADDRESS

10　Building address:

street _1000 Collect St._

city, village/town _Anytown,_

county _Anycounty_　State _St_

Agent for collection of rents:
name _Lisa Brown_
address _1000 Collect St._
Anytown, USA

Agent for service of process:
name _Myra Lee_
address _508 Process St._
Anytown USA

24　Apartment number: _208_

TERM

25　Lease term: _8/1/xx_ to _8/1/xx_　　　　　Month to Month (strike if not applicable)
26　First day of lease term: _8/1/xx_　　Last day of lease term: _8/1/xx One Year Later_

RENTALS

27　Apartment: $ _950.00_ per _mo._　　Other: _Garage Sp._ $ _30_ per _mo_
28　Payable at _Apt. 101, 1000 Collect St._
29　before the _First_ day of each _Month_ during the
30　term of this lease.

UTILITIES

31　Utility charges, other than telephone, are included in the rent, except: _Heat And_
32　_Electricity_
33
34　shall pay promptly when due. If charges not included in the rent are not separately metered, they shall be allo-
35　cated on the basis of: _Separate meters are installed_
36

SPECIAL CONDITIONS

37　Special conditions: _No Pets_
38
39
40

RENEWAL OF LEASE TERM

41　(Strike clause 1 or 2; if neither is striken clause 2 controls.)
42　1. This lease shall be automatically renewed, without notice from either party, on identical terms for a like suc-
43　cessive lease term unless either party shall, at least 45 days before the expiration of the lease, notify the other
44　in writing of the termination of the lease. However, Landlord must, at least 15 days but not more than 30 days
45　prior to the time specified for giving the notice as herein set forth notify Tenant in writing of the above
46　provision for automatic renewal or extension.
47　2. This lease shall be automatically renewed, without notice from either party, on identical terms, except that it
48　shall be a month-to-month tenancy.

ASSIGNMENT SUBLETTING

49　Tenant shall not assign this lease nor sublet the premises or any part thereof without the prior written consent of
50　Landlord. If Landlord permits an assignment or a sublease, such permission shall in no way relieve Tenant of
51　Tenant's liability under this lease.

SECURITY DEPOSIT

52　Upon execution of this lease Tenant paid a security deposit in the amount of $ _950.00_ to be held by
53　_Sawdusky Realty_
54　If the person holding the security deposit is a licensed real estate broker, acting as agent, it shall be held in the
55　broker's trust account. The deposit, less any amounts withheld, will be returned in person or mailed to Tenant's last
56　known address within 21 days after Tenant vacates the premises. If any portion of the deposit is withheld, Landlord
57　will provide an accompanying itemized statement specifically describing any damages and accounting for any amount
58　withheld. Failure to return the deposit or provide a written accounting within 21 days will result in the waiver of
59　any claim against the deposit. The reasonable cost of repairing any damages caused by Tenant, normal wear and
60　tear excepted, will be deducted from the security deposit. Tenant has 7 days after the beginning of the lease term to
61　notify Landlord in writing of damages or defects in the premises; no deduction from Tenant's security deposit
62　shall be made for any damages or defects of which notification is given. Landlord will give Tenant a written
63　description of any physical damages charged to the previous tenant's security deposit as soon as such description is
64　available. (If none, so specify_____.) (Strike paragraph if no security deposit is paid.)

VACATION OF PREMISES

65　Tenant agrees to vacate the premises at the end of the lease term or the extended lease term, and promptly deliver
66　the keys to Landlord.

LANDLORD'S RIGHT TO ENTER

67　Landlord may enter the premises at reasonable times and with 12 hours advance notice, with or without Tenant's
68　permission to inspect the premises, make repairs, show the premises to prospective tenants or purchasers, or to com-
69　ply with any applicable law or regulation. Landlord may enter with less than 12 hours advance notice upon specific
70　consent of Tenant. No advance notice is required for entry in a health or safety emergency or where entry is neces-
71　sary to preserve and protect the premises from damage in Tenant's absence.

ABANDONMENT BY TENANT

72　If Tenant shall abandon the premises before the expiration of the lease term, Landlord shall make reasonable efforts
73　to re-lease premises and shall apply any rent received, less costs of re-leasing, to the rent due or to become due on this
74　lease, and Tenant shall remain liable for any deficiency. If Tenant is absent from the premises for three successive
75　weeks without notifying Landlord in writing of such absence, Landlord, at Landlord's sole option, may deem the
76　premises abandoned.

DISPOSAL OF TENANT'S PROPERTY

77　If Tenant shall leave any property on the premises after vacation or abandonment of the premises, Tenant shall be
78　deemed to have abandoned the property, and Landlord shall have the right to dispose of the property as provided
79　by law.

TENANT OBLIGATIONS

80　During the lease term, as a condition to Tenant's continuing right to use and occupy the premises, Tenant agrees
81　and promises:

USE

82　1. To use the premises for residential purposes only by Tenant and Tenant's immediate family.
83　2. Not to make or permit use of the premises for any unlawful purpose or any purpose that will injure the reputa-
84　tion of the premises or the building of which they are a part.
85　3. Not to use or keep in or about the premises anything which would adversely affect coverage of the premises or
86　the building of which they are a part under a standard fire and extended insurance policy.
87　4. Not to make excessive noise or engage in activities which unduly disturb neighbors or other tenants in the build-
88　ing which the premises are located.

PETS

89　5. Not to keep in or about the premises any pet unless specifically authorized as a special condition in this lease.

GOVT. REG.

90　6. To obey all lawful orders, rules and regulations of all governmental authorities.

MAINTENANCE IMPROVEMENTS

91　7. To keep the premises in clean and tenantable condition and in as good repair as at the beginning of the lease
92　term, normal wear and tear excepted.
93　8. If obligated to pay for heat for the premises, to maintain a reasonable amount of heat in cold weather to prevent
94　damage to the premises, and if damage results from Tenant's failure to maintain a reasonable amount of heat
95　Tenant shall be liable for this damage.

WB20　NTF 0074

18-8

The lease clearly states the rights and responsibilities of both landlord and tenant.

- *Legal remedies.* What legal remedies are available? What can you do if the landlord breaks the lease in some way, such as failing to make necessary repairs or to provide adequate heat? What can the landlord do if you break the lease by not paying the rent or failing to obey building rules? Does the lease outline ways, such as arbitration or legal action, to handle disagreements with the landlord? Who pays the legal costs of settling differences?

- *Other conditions of use.* Can you paint, wallpaper, and decorate? If you install shelving, carpet, or equipment, can you remove it later? Can you keep pets? Can you have a roommate?

Before signing, make sure all spaces in the lease are filled in accurately, including dates, dollar amounts, addresses, and names. All verbal agreements should be written into the lease. You should understand all clauses, obligations, and consequences. If you have serious questions or doubts about signing the lease, you may want to get a lawyer's advice. Make sure you receive a copy of the signed document and keep it in a safe place.

Discuss

How do you feel about the terms outlined in this lease? Would you be willing to sign it? Why?

Discuss

What are the most important terms of this lease from the renter's point of view? From the landlord's point of view?

Reflect

What difficulties have your family or friends had with lease agreements and with landlords?

Renter Protections

There are a variety of federal, state, and local laws and regulations that protect renters. For example, the *Title VIII of the Civil Rights Act of 1968*, also called the *Fair Housing Act*, prohibits discrimination against consumers who are looking to buy, rent, or get financing for a dwelling. Consumers cannot be discriminated against by race, color, national origin, religion, sex, familial status, or disability.

Other laws state that landlords cannot enter a renter's dwelling except in the case of an emergency. If a landlord needs to access the home to do maintenance, they are required to give tenants a certain amount of notice.

The lease protects renters as well as landlords. The rent that is stated in the current lease cannot be raised until the lease period is over. Some cities have laws that limit how much landlords can raise the rent on their tenants. If heat is included in the rent, it must be provided when temperatures are low. Landlords are required to install fire alarms. Tenant rights can be found on Web sites such as the www.hud.gov/renting.

When you gain access to your new home, the first thing you should do is conduct an inspection. You may be given a condition report to fill out when you move in. Make a note of problems on the form or the lease, such as a scratched floor, a dirty oven, and a dripping faucet, 18-9. The landlord should fix some of these right away. Other problems should be documented so you are not charged for them when

18-9

Carefully inspect a rental apartment when moving in and document any existing problems. Report problems promptly to the landlord.

Discuss

List the responsibilities of tenants.

Reflect

Would you like to live with a roommate in the future?

Activity

List characteristics of your ideal roommate. Do you display these qualities?

you move out. Take the time to fill out the form carefully and thoroughly and make a copy for yourself.

Renters should purchase renter's insurance to protect against losses due to theft, fire, or other damages. Renter's insurance was discussed in Chapter 10.

Being a Good Tenant

Tenants also have responsibilities to their neighbors and landlords. They are expected to do the following:

- Pay their rent on time. Failure to pay rent can result in eviction, or being forced to move out.

- Meet the terms of the lease.

- Keep their dwellings clean and free of pests.

- Prevent damage to the landlord's property.

- Report problems, such as leaks or broken windows, right away.

- Avoid noise and behaviors that could disturb neighbors.

- Give notice before they move out as required in the lease. Clean up before moving out.

Young Adults and Rental Housing

If you live with your parents or guardians, you may look forward to moving out on your own in the future. Like any other goal, this one takes planning and saving. Putting away a portion of your income in a savings account that earns interest can help you accumulate what you need to make this goal a reality.

Many young people, especially during difficult financial times, do not have the funds to move out on their own. They find that continuing to live with their families allows them to save money on rent, utilities, food, and other expenses. Parents may require working young adults to contribute to household expenses. However, these contributions are usually less than the cost of renting their own place.

Living with Roommates

Many college students and young adults make living expenses more affordable by sharing housing with roommates. However, prospective roommates should have a clear understanding about financial obligations and "house rules" before moving in together.

Prospective roommates should have a clear understanding about financial obligations before moving in together. The following questions should be discussed before signing the lease:

- When is rent due and what is each person's share of the rent?

- Is there a security deposit? How will that be divided if there are charges for damage to the residence?

- How long will each person live in the apartment? Who will pay the rent for the rest of the lease term if someone moves out early?

- How are utility bills to be divided?

- Will furniture, televisions, appliances be shared? If they are damaged, who will pay for repair or replacement?

- Will food and meals be shared? How will food costs be divided?

Other issues that need to be negotiated concern privacy. For example, which part of the apartment is public and which parts are private and off limits? Will guests be allowed? If so, how often? How will housework be divided? Discuss these issues honestly before moving in with someone or having someone move in with you.

Enrich

Ask these questions of someone you know who lives with a roommate.

Reflect

What do you see as the advantages of buying a home?

Enrich

Interview a real estate broker about services offered to home buyers.

Buying a Home

Buying a home involves many considerations and decisions. Begin by making a list of the home features you want and decide which ones are most important. This will help you narrow your options and stay within a budget. For example, do you want a house or a condominium? Do you want a house in a newly constructed subdivision or an older established neighborhood? Do you have a preference for a ranch-style home or a two-story?

Other factors to consider include the number of bedrooms and bathrooms you prefer, the size of the yard, and if you must have a garage. Evaluate whether you want a place in move-in condition or if you are willing to do some home renovation. Once you have an idea of what you are looking for, you can start your search.

Real Estate Brokers

Many consumers looking for a home work with real estate brokers. A **real estate broker** is a person licensed to arrange for the purchase and sale of real estate for a fee or commission. Some brokers specialize in commercial properties. Others work with residential properties. Many brokers can also assist in arranging rental housing.

Real estate brokers usually employ sales agents to work for them. When a home owner lists a home with a broker, the broker or a sales agent provides a variety of services. This person helps the home owner price the home, advertise it, show it, and negotiate the sale with a prospective buyer. Brokers and agents post their listings online on sites such as the Multiple Listing Service (MLS). Good brokers or agents know the territory in which they work. They have multiple contacts with people in the community and with other professionals in the business.

For their services, brokers and agents receive a commission, usually between 3 and 6 percent of the home's final sale price. The seller usually pays the commission.

Activity

On the Internet, research the services offered by exclusive buyer agents.

Enrich

Visit the Web site for the National Association of Exclusive Buyer agents at www.naeba.org. How many agents are available in your area?

Exclusive Buyer Agents

People searching for a home may also work with **exclusive buyer agents** who work for the buyer and not the seller. An experienced broker or agent can provide valuable information about the real estate market, including home prices, zoning laws, and property taxes. He or she can help buyers find neighborhoods that best meet their search criteria.

Since many people look at as many as 50 homes before they buy, brokers help them make the best use of their time. They set up appointments to tour houses, help find financing, and negotiate the sale, 18-10.

You can find an agent by asking friends and family for referrals. The National Association of Exclusive Buyer Agents at www.naeba.org can help you find an exclusive buyer agent in your area. Meet with the agent and ask questions about his or her experience. You should feel comfortable with the person and satisfied with the responses to your questions.

Your agent will interview you about the type of home you are looking for and ask how much you can spend. Then he or she will alert you to homes that meet your criteria and arrange showings.

18-10

Busy home buyers can save time by having a real estate agent review home listings, schedule tours, and gather information.

Your Offer

Buying a home is not like going to a department store to buy a jacket. Home buyers usually do not pay the asking price. There is some back-and-forth haggling involved. For example, if a home is selling for $300,000, you may offer 5 percent or $15,000 less. The buyer can accept or reject the offer. He or she may not accept your offer, but drop the price nevertheless. Now you must decide whether or not to accept the new reduced price.

Before making an offer, a buyer needs to research the sale price of comparable homes in the area. For example, if the home you are interested in is a 3-bedroom, 2-bath home with a 2-car garage, look for other homes of that description that have sold in the previous months in that neighborhood. What were the asking prices and the prices paid? A real estate broker can do this research for you. Use the prices paid as a guide to formulate your bid.

If the property is an exceptional value and others are also submitting offers, you will want to submit the asking price or near the asking price. However, there are many reasons to offer less than the asking price. A buyer may offer less if

- the property needs repairs
- the home has not sold despite being on the market a long time
- other comparable homes nearby sold for much less
- the seller is desperate to sell
- the buyer is flexible about the move-in date
- the market for selling homes is bad and there are many homes on the market

When you have an offer price, then an agent or real estate attorney can draw up a purchase agreement.

Purchase Agreements

When the buyer agrees to buy and the seller agrees to sell, they both sign a contract called a **purchase agreement**. Sometimes this contract is called a sales agreement. It should include a description of the real estate, its location, the purchase price, and the possession date.

The agreement should state all of the conditions and terms of the sale. For example, if the seller agrees to make any home repairs, these should be stated in the agreement. If the owner promises to leave the draperies, dishwasher, range, and refrigerator, these should also be listed and described.

When you sign a purchase agreement, you must also give the seller an **earnest money** check. This shows that your purchase offer is serious and prohibits the seller from selling the home to someone else. This is usually a percentage of the home price. It is applied toward the down payment at the closing of the sale. Buyers can lose the earnest money if they fail to go through with the agreement. A home purchase agreement may contain a **contingency clause** that calls for certain requirements to be met before

Discuss

What are the steps involved in negotiating an offer price?

Discuss

When might a buyer be able to offer less than the asking price?

Vocabulary

Look up and discuss the meanings of *earnest money* and *contingency clause*.

Discuss

What is a home inspection and why is it usually required?

Discuss

Name some of the problems that home inspectors examine.

Reflect

Why must most people get a mortgage to buy a home?

the contract is binding. For example, the validity of the agreement may depend upon obtaining a mortgage within a certain period of time or at a certain rate. It may be made contingent upon the sale of the buyer's current home.

Home Inspection

A common contingency is that the home must pass an inspection by a home inspector hired by the buyer. For a fee, home inspectors examine the home for problems that may affect the value of the home or require costly repair. These include cracks in the foundation, a leaky roof, and plumbing and electrical problems. Inspectors also check to make sure appliances work.

Buyers who live in areas where termites thrive or where mold is common may also have the home inspected for these problems by specialists. Specialized inspectors can also be hired to find problems with lead or asbestos exposure. If problems are found, buyers can ask sellers to fix them before they purchase the home. Buyers can use the inspection findings to negotiate a reduction in the sales price.

Obtaining a Home Mortgage

Most home buyers get loans to finance home purchases, 18-11. A home loan, called a **mortgage**, is a contract between a borrower and a lender. The lender is usually a bank or a mortgage company. The borrower promises to repay the lender the loan amount plus interest. The mortgage is paid in monthly installments over a set number of years. If the borrower fails to pay according to the terms of the mortgage contract, the lender can repossess the home.

18-11

Homes are one of the most expensive purchases people make. Most home buyers must secure a mortgage to finance their purchase.

Amortization is the process by which loan payments are applied to the principal, or amount borrowed, as well as to the interest on the loan according to a set schedule. Most home mortgages are amortized. In the beginning, payments are applied largely to interest. As the loan is repaid, an increasing amount of each payment is applied to the principal. This means the borrower builds up equity, or ownership, in the property as the loan is repaid.

Most mortgage lenders require that the buyer spend no more than 28% of gross monthly income on mortgage, property tax, and home insurance payments. The total amount you can spend on a home will depend on the purchase price, the amount you can pay for a down payment, and current interest rates. For example, monthly payments on a $150,000, 30-year mortgage would be

- $805 at 5 percent.
- $899 at 6 percent.
- $998 at 7 percent.

Interest rates can vary greatly from year to year. If you buy when interest rates are high, you may have to look at lower priced homes. If you buy when interest rates are low, you may be able to afford a more expensive home.

The amount you can afford will also depend on other factors. You may be able to spend more if living costs in the area are low; you can take care of most maintenance, repair, and decorating jobs yourself; interest rates are low; or you are able to make a large down payment.

You may want to find a relatively low-priced home if you buy an older house that needs many repairs; home mortgage rates are high and terms are unfavorable; you cannot make a large down payment; and you have other long-term obligations.

Types of Mortgages

Home financing alternatives vary from state to state and lender to lender. It pays to research all the options to find the method of financing that is best for you. Types of mortgages on the market today include the following:

- Conventional long-term, **fixed rate mortgages** guarantee a fixed or unchanging interest rate for the life of the loan. The loan rate does not go up or down as the economy changes. These loans are normally written with 20-, 25-, or 30-year repayment periods. However, shorter term, fixed rate loans are another alternative. Fifteen-year mortgages dramatically increase monthly payments, but bring an equally dramatic reduction in total interest charges.

- The **adjustable rate mortgage (ARM)** allows the interest rate to be adjusted up or down periodically. The adjustments are made according to a national rate index and other predetermined factors. These loans are often offered at lower interest rates than fixed rate mortgages. However, borrowers take the risk that interest rates and loan payments will increase when adjustments are made.

Vocabulary

Distinguish between a fixed rate and adjustable rate mortgage.

Resource

Financing a Home, Activity D, WB

Enrich

Develop a chart to show the advantages and disadvantages of each type of mortgage.

Linking to... History

Subprime Mortgage Crisis

From 1998 to 2006, the United States experienced a housing boom. Many consumers purchased homes because interest rates were low. The increase in demand caused housing prices to rise. Some homes doubled in value in just a few years.

Eager to reap the benefits of a good housing market, many lenders loosened mortgage requirements. They gave high-risk loans to borrowers with poor or no credit history. The lenders bundled the subprime mortgages together and sold them to investors and other financial institutions.

Many of the loans given during the housing boom were adjustable rate or interest only mortgages. When interest rates eventually rose, home owners faced higher monthly payments. Many consumers could no longer afford to pay and defaulted on their loans. Thousands of people had their homes repossessed.

Lenders and investors who purchased the bundled subprime mortgages experienced serious losses. Afraid of more losses, lenders stopped making loans to consumers, businesses, and other financial institutions. The freeze in the credit market affected the global financial system. Some banks failed and huge financial institutions went bankrupt. In 2008 the government had to step in to help ease the recession triggered largely by failures in the subprime mortgage market.

The crisis raised awareness to the risks associated with subprime lending and the need for mortgage reform.

Vocabulary

Distinguish between a graduated payment and interest only mortgage.

Note

For more information about the subprime mortgage crisis and recession, go to the Web site of the St. Louis Federal Reserve Bank at http://stlouisfed.org/education_resources.

Activity

Research first-time home buyer programs available in your area. What factors influence eligibility?

- The **graduated payment mortgage** allows the buyer to pay low monthly payments at first and higher payments in the future. It has the advantage of low monthly payments in the early years of the loan. Those who take this type of mortgage generally expect their earnings to increase.

- An **interest only mortgage** is a loan on which monthly payments are applied only to the interest, not to the principal, for a certain number of years. After the specified number of years, the borrower must begin making higher payments to cover both interest and principal, pay off the loan, or renegotiate a new mortgage at prevailing rates and terms. This type of mortgage is not recommended for most home buyers.

- **Subprime mortgages** are home loans made by lenders who charge substantially higher than prime rates to borrowers who have poor or no credit ratings and who often do not qualify for mortgages from other lenders. Subprime lenders often bundle these mortgages together and sell them to financial institutions that are willing to absorb the risks.

Financing Programs

Several government programs encourage home ownership. Some of these programs are described below.

- *First-time home buyer programs* provide buyers with assistance, including financial incentives, to buy a home. These include reduced down payments, tax breaks, and lowered requirements for obtaining credit.

- An **FHA-insured loan** is guaranteed by the Federal Housing Administration (FHA) and helps lower- and moderate-income people purchase homes. The FHA makes no loans, but it insures lenders against borrowers' defaults. The maximum loan amounts are determined by a formula based on average cost of homes in the area. Down payment for FHA-insured loans can be as low as 3 percent. Borrowers can take up to 30 years to repay. Interest rates may be lower than for conventional loans because the government insures the lender. The home being bought and certain loan terms must meet FHA standards.

- The **VA-guaranteed loan** is insured by the Veterans Administration. Only veterans of the U.S. Armed Forces are eligible for these loans. They are long-term, fixed rate mortgages. The Veterans Administration sets rates. There are no down payment requirements. Interest rates usually are lower than the current market rate. Borrowers can take up to 30 years to repay.

Consult a lawyer before signing any home financing agreement. Small mistakes can have big consequences.

Shopping for a Mortgage

Consumers can take steps to ensure that they are eligible for the best loan terms, including the lowest interest rates, when they are ready to buy. The key is maintaining the highest credit score possible. As discussed in Chapter 9, lenders look at credit reports and credit scores to evaluate the creditworthiness of loan applicants. Consumers with higher scores are offered the most favorable financing terms, including lower interest rates. Increasing your credit score can save you thousands of dollars in interest payments.

In the years leading up to buying a home, consumers can take steps to boost their credit scores. These include the following:

- Maintain steady employment.

- Establish a credit history by using credit wisely.

- Pay bills and taxes on time.

- Repay car loans, student loans, and other debt on schedule.

- Guard your financial information to avoid identity theft.

- Check your credit reports regularly. As discussed in Chapter 9, you are entitled to one free copy of your credit report from each of the three major credit-reporting agencies each year. If you find inaccuracies, have them corrected. Fixing problems on your credit report can be time consuming, but it can raise your credit score.

When you are ready to shop for a mortgage, shop carefully and ask questions. Sources of home loans include commercial banks, savings banks, mortgage companies, and credit unions. It pays to be thorough. Shop at least three sources to compare rates and terms.

Activity

Go to the Department of Housing and Urban Development Web site for information on FHA-insured loans.

Activity

Go to the Veterans Administration Web site for current information on VA-guaranteed loans.

Activity

Contact a local financial institution for information on mortgage loan rates and terms.

Enrich

Visit a local lender and ask for copies of forms and documents used in connection with home mortgages.

Items Lenders Require with an Application for a Mortgage Loan

- Income tax returns
- Paycheck stubs
- Employment information
- Property listing with a legal description
- Savings account records
- Real estate sales contract
- Debt history
- Application fee

18-12

This chart lists some of the information lenders will require to process a loan application.

Enrich

Interview a loan officer at a financial institution about applying for a mortgage loan.

Vocabulary

Define *mortgage lock-in.*

Nationwide mortgage search services report on mortgage terms and availability in different localities. Quotes are also available online. These services or a licensed mortgage broker might help you. Using a computerized program, they can help find the best mortgage package for your situation.

When you apply for a mortgage, the lender will ask detailed questions related to your financial circumstances. You should be prepared with facts and figures, 18-12. Here are some points to consider as you shop for and compare different types of mortgage financing:

- *Down Payment.* How much money can you put down to get a loan? The more you put down, the less your monthly payments and total interest charges will be.

- *Size of Mortgage.* How much do you need to borrow? What is the maximum size mortgage your income and resources will support?

- *Repayment Period.* How long can you take to repay? Are original terms in force for the life of the loan or must you renegotiate periodically?

- *Interest Rate.* What is the annual percentage rate (APR) for the loan? How does it compare with the current market rate? Will it remain fixed, or will it change?

- *Monthly Payments.* How much will you pay each month to cover mortgage interest and principle? How much will you pay for property insurance and taxes? Will you have enough left for maintenance, utilities, and other housing costs?

- *Special Features and Provisions.* What are the provisions and penalties for prepayment if you sell or refinance? Can the mortgage be assumed by a new buyer if you sell? What are the policies and penalties for late payments? How much and what type of insurance does the lender require?

When you shop for home financing, the terms you are quoted often apply only at the time you apply for the mortgage. These terms may change by the time your mortgage is approved. You may want to ask for a *mortgage lock-in*, sometimes called a rate lock or rate commitment. This is a promise from the lender to honor the quoted rates and terms while your application is being processed.

The Closing

After the seller accepts a buyer's offer, both parties set a deadline to finalize the sale of the home. This is called the *closing date*. On this day, the buyer, seller, lender's representative, real estate agents, and sometimes attorneys for the buyer or seller, meet to sign documents and to settle all outstanding matters. The buyer gives the seller a certified check for the down payment. Other fees must be paid.

Before the closing date, the buyer must obtain a mortgage, a process that can take weeks or sometimes months. The lender investigates the buyer's credit history and the property itself.

Closing costs are fees or settlement charges that must be paid before the sale of a home is final. As of January 1, 2010, the U.S. Department of Housing and Urban Development (HUD) requires lenders and brokers to give homebuyers a standard *Good Faith Estimate (GFE)* when they apply for a mortgage. This form clearly states important loan terms and closing costs. It makes it easy to compare from lender to lender the actual and estimated costs of obtaining a mortgage and closing on the purchase of a home. The Good Faith Estimate will include fees for many of the following services:

- **Points** are a one-time charge by lenders at closing. Most lenders charge one to four points. A point equals one percent of the mortgage amount. Four points on a $100,000 mortgage comes to $4,000. It may be possible to negotiate for a lower rate of interest if you are willing to pay more points at the time of purchase. Find out how many points different lenders charge.

- A **property survey** is a map of the property drawn by a surveyor to show size, boundaries, and characteristics of a property. Lenders usually require a survey to make sure the building is on the land according to its legal description. It is normally the seller's responsibility to hire a surveyor and pay for a survey.

- An *appraisal* is a written estimate of the value of the real estate. The buyer usually pays the appraisal fee. Before approving a mortgage loan, the lender will usually require an appraisal. It helps the lender decide if the home is worth its price and if the mortgage is a good investment.

- A **title** is a legal document that proves ownership of property. An **abstract of title** is a summary of the public records regarding the ownership of a property. The buyer should have an attorney or title insurance company review the abstract of title to be sure that the seller is the legal owner and that the property is free of debts or title problems. The buyer usually pays the title search fee.

- Recording fees must be paid to record the deed. This document transfers the ownership of the property from the seller to the buyer.

- Credit report fees are charged to the borrower. When someone applies for a mortgage, the lender orders the borrower's credit report and/or credit score.

- Loan application fees are charged by most lenders to process new loan applications.

Other expenses due at or after closing are commissions paid to real estate brokers and fees for attorneys' services. Some lenders require buyers to open *escrow accounts* to cover real estate taxes and property insurance.

Architecture & Construction

Surveyors
Surveyors measure and identify water, land, and airspace boundary lines. They record their results for legal documents such as deeds and leases. They also prepare maps and reports. Surveyors work outdoors and often use technology, such as global positioning devices, to gather preliminary data.

Activity

List and describe the items included in closing costs.

Reflect

What has been your family's experience with mortgage lenders and loans?

Reflect

What experience have you had with moving possessions?

Discuss

What steps would be important to take before a move?

Escrow accounts hold money until it can be paid to the party that is owed. Some home owners make these payments themselves when they are due.

Saving Money on Your Mortgage

You have already heard that you can save money you pay on mortgage by making a bigger down payment or by locking in a low interest rate. Other strategies include

- Avoid paying **private mortgage insurance (PMI)**. This insurance protects the lender from loss if the borrower defaults on the loan. If you make a down payment of 20 percent or more of the purchase price, however, you do not have to pay PMI. This can save you money.

- Make an additional mortgage payment each year. This can result in thousands of dollars of savings.

- Making extra payments on the principal to reduce the cost of the loan. Many loans are structured so that the bulk of the early loan payments go toward the finance charges.

- If you will move within a few years, it may be wise to look to the adjustable rate mortgage, which usually is available at lower rates than long-term, fixed rate mortgages. If you plan to live in a home for many years, the long-term, fixed rate mortgage may be a better choice if rates are low at the time of purchase.

- Refinance your mortgage. If interest rates drop below the rate you obtained for your mortgage, you may want to refinance. Refinancing at a lower rate can save you money on monthly payments. However, refinancing costs extra money for closing costs, points, and so forth. You only want to refinance if the savings is more than the costs.

Home Equity Loans

A **home equity loan**, also called a second mortgage, is a way that home owners can borrow money on their home equity. *Equity* is the difference between a home's market value and the amount the home owner still owes on the loan. These loans can be used by home owners to pay for home improvements, vacations, college costs, and to pay off other debt such as medical bills and credit cards.

In a home equity loan, the home serves as collateral. If the home owner cannot repay the debt, the lender can repossess the home. Therefore, home owners should use care in taking out these loans.

Moving Your Possessions

For some people, finding a place to live is easy compared with moving their belongings. People who do not own much furniture often move themselves, 18-13. A borrowed or rented truck and a few friends can accomplish a move in an afternoon. You can check advertisements for free boxes given away by people who recently moved. As you accumulate furniture and possessions, moving becomes more complicated and expensive. Moving a short distance away can also be handled by local movers. Moving to another state requires a national carrier. Consider and compare all the possibilities.

You will need to notify utilities, the cable company, newspaper, and other services of your move. Either terminate existing services or have them transferred to the new address. They need to know where to send a final bill. The utilities and businesses that service your new home will need to know when you will move in. They may also require that you fill out contracts and pay a refundable deposit.

18-13
For your first or second move, you may be able to move yourself. As you acquire more possessions, professional packers and movers may be needed.

Hiring a Mover

Many consumer complaints involve moves and moving companies. It pays to check out a moving company thoroughly. Contact the Better Business Bureau to check for complaints against the company. Talk to friends and acquaintances to get the names of movers they used with good results.

Following are some ways to make a move go smoothly.

- *Get rid of excess baggage.* The more items you move, the more you pay. Get rid of items you do not need or want before moving.

- *Get cost estimates from several movers.* Be sure estimators include everything that is to be moved. Find out what services are included in the estimates. Rates for interstate moves are regulated by laws and are based on weight and distance. Packing and other services add to the cost.

- *Time the move.* If you have a choice, move between mid-October and mid-April. You often get better service and lower rates than in the peak moving months of summer. The middle of a month is better than the first or last days of a month.

- *Collect information to help you move.* Most major carriers offer helpful publications for planning a move and settling in a new area. Interstate movers are required to give you a copy of the pamphlet, *When You Move: Your Rights and Responsibilities.* Carriers should also give you information about filing claims in case of loss or damage to your possessions.

- *Check insurance coverage.* A mover's liability for your possessions is limited to an amount per unit of weight. This often is less than replacement value for most items. Find out what additional protection is available if you need it. Make sure your possessions are adequately insured before you move.

Transportation, Distribution & Logistics

Residential Moving Coordinator

Residential moving coordinators help plan individual and family moves within the same city or to points throughout the world. They coordinate all aspects of relocating, such as completing an inventory of items, packing, delivery, and unpacking of items.

Enrich

Contact a major carrier for information on planning a move.

Activity

Contact a moving company to learn what services are offered in connection with moving. Discuss.

Discuss

What steps can you take while packing for a move that will make unpacking easier after the move?

Example

Obtain paperwork and insurance claim forms from a moving company for illustration and discussion.

Before your move take an inventory of your possessions. As you pack, label moving cartons with a list of contents and their location in your new home. Supervise both pickup and delivery to be sure everything is moved and delivered to your new address.

Read the shipping order and *bill of lading* carefully. A bill of lading is a receipt listing the goods shipped. Make sure these forms accurately state pickup and delivery dates, estimated charges, and services to be performed. They should also state any special agreements or arrangements between you and the mover.

You should be prepared to pay for your move on delivery with a certified check. Ask for an itemized receipt. In the event of loss or damage to your possessions, file reimbursement claims promptly.

Furnishing Your Home

What items will you need to buy? Start with items such as a bed, a comfortable chair, a light for reading, a clock, and anything else you cannot live without. Add other furnishings as you can afford them.

What furniture and decorative items do you already own? Make a list of usable items you own. Incorporate them into your plans. Many decorating and furnishing decisions involve adding to or working with what you have on hand.

Plan the best ways to use your money, time, and talents. If you are short on money, bargain hunting and do-it-yourself jobs may become important. Shop at house sales, secondhand stores, and warehouses. Can you paint, wallpaper, sew, or upholster? Put your talents to work.

Color is a great way to decorate without spending a lot of money. A simple coat of paint can transform a dark, dreary room into a cheerful space. Color choices can make a room seem larger or smaller, a ceiling seem higher, or a narrow space seem wider. It can make space seem warm or cool, cozy or sophisticated, restful or stimulating. Experiment with color and find ways to use it in decorating your living spaces.

Floor Plan

Your first home away from home probably will be temporary. Before spending any money, it is a good idea to make a **floor plan** for each room, 18-14. A floor plan is a diagram of a room drawn to a scale of ¼ inch to a foot. It shows the size, shape, and features of the room such as windows, doors, fireplaces, and built-ins.

Next, draw furniture patterns to represent the furniture you expect to place in the room. Follow the same scale as your floor plan. Arranging furniture patterns on the floor plan makes it easier to visualize furnishings in the room. It can also save you from buying furniture that will not fit the room.

When shopping for furniture and accessories, take your floor plan with you. Also take along any fabric and color samples you want to use.

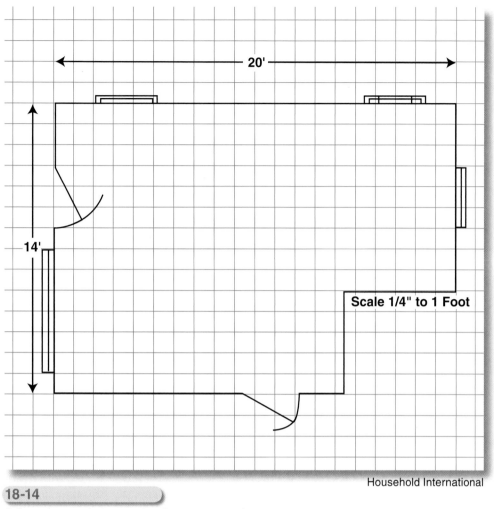

20'

14'

Scale 1/4" to 1 Foot

Household International

18-14

A floor plan can help you visualize space and furniture arrangements.

Let floor plan and samples guide your choices. Also carry a tape measure to check dimensions of furniture before buying.

Furniture Selection

Much of what you need to know about furniture selection will come from shopping experience. Even so, you stand to lose a lot if you enter the marketplace with no background information. It is helpful to learn a few basic facts about furniture before you shop.

Personal needs are a primary concern. Decide what pieces of furniture you most need and want. Then consider how and where you will use them. Look for new items that go well with furnishings you already have.

Quality and durability are important factors in furniture selection, too. The more use a piece of furniture receives, the more durable it needs to be. For example, a bed in a guest room does not need to be the same quality as the bed you use nightly.

Style and function also are key considerations. Choose sizes, shapes, styles, and colors that fit your space and decorating theme. You also want

Reflect

What experience have you had shopping for furniture?

Enrich

Debate the pros and cons of decorating one step at a time versus all at once.

Resource

Shopping for Furniture, Activity C, WB

Activity

Go to a furniture store and check out labels on wood furniture. Take note of the information provided and discuss in class.

Enrich

Shop for a piece of upholstered furniture and note the labels. What do they tell you and how do they help?

furniture to be functional. For example, your favorite chair needs to be comfortable.

Price is a key for most shoppers. Work out a spending plan before you shop. Compare prices at several stores. Find out about store policies on returns, exchanges, and warranties. Shopping in reliable furniture or department stores for brand-name furnishings is a safe but expensive way to furnish a home. With a little time, imagination, and legwork, you may be able to save money by shopping at furniture outlets and online furniture retailers. Secondhand furniture is often less expensive than new items. Sources of pre-owned furniture include online sellers, secondhand stores, house sales, thrift shops, and auctions.

Services such as credit and deliveries may be extra. Ask the price of each service you need. Get a commitment on delivery dates.

Case Goods

Case goods generally refer to furniture with no upholstered parts. It includes bookcases, desks, chests, cabinets, dining room and bedroom furniture. Case goods may be made from a variety of woods, plastics, metals, and glass.

When shopping for this type of furniture, pay attention to construction and finish as well as to size and style. Overall, try to select case goods that are attractive and sturdy in a style that fits your decorating plan.

Upholstered Furniture

Upholstered furniture includes primarily chairs and sofas. The durability of upholstery fabric is determined largely by fiber content and fabric construction. Protective finishes may be applied to provide resistance to soil, stains, and fading. Choose upholstery fabrics of colors and designs that fit your decorating plan.

Read labels and ask questions to learn about cushioning and filling materials and construction features you cannot see. Labels will also tell you fabric content and care instructions. Buy from reliable sellers. Be sure the furniture rests squarely on the floor and that it is sturdy and strong at points of strain. Reversible cushions keep furniture looking nice longer.

As a final test, sit on the chair or sofa. Does it feel comfortable in terms of size and firmness? Try it two or three times to test the height, depth, and shape for your comfort.

Sleep Furniture

Sleep furniture includes beds and dual-purpose sleeper chairs, sofas, or futons. When you buy a bed, comfort is the most important feature. Look for size and degree of firmness to suit your preferences. King- and queen-size beds are more expensive than the standard twin or double beds. A mattress and springs sold together as a set generally give the best wear and comfort.

Case Study: Housing Solutions

All at Once

Carmen is moving to Kansas City to begin her first full-time job. She decides to arrive a week early to decorate and furnish her new apartment.

Since she is new to the city, she goes to a department store instead of shopping around. The prices are high, but the store offers decorating advice and free delivery service.

Besides color and style, the most important thing on Carmen's mind is prompt delivery. She passes up several good buys because they aren't in stock. Here is a list of Carmen's major purchases:

- two chairs
- desk and chest
- sleeper sofa
- TV stand
- reading lamp
- two area rugs
- mirror
- draperies
- drop-leaf table

Carmen spends $1,000 of her savings and charges hundreds of dollars. In addition to rent and other monthly obligations, Carmen now faces credit card payments. It will take almost three years to pay the decorating bills. The finance charges on her credit card will reach a sizable amount, but Carmen doesn't mind. She is happily settled in her new place.

Case Review

1. What would be on your list of needs for a first home? How much do you think it would cost to buy all the items on your list?
2. If you were Carmen, how would you go about furnishing a place of your own?
3. How important would it be to you to decorate all at once?
4. How would you feel about making big charges on your credit cards and then having large debts to pay?
5. How would you feel about the extra money you would have to pay in finance charges if you used credit cards to buy your furnishings?

Sleeper sofas, chairs, and futons are designed for sitting and sleeping. When buying dual-purpose furniture, check both sitting and sleeping comfort and ease of converting from one use to the other.

Floor Coverings

Carpeting and rugs are the two basic types of soft floor covering. Both come in a variety of patterns, colors, and prices. Carpeting helps insulate floors, absorb sounds, and make rooms seem larger. Rugs help define activity centers in a room. They are easy to send out for professional cleaning and to move them from one location to another. Factors to consider when shopping for rugs and carpets are outlined below.

- *Fiber content.* Common carpet and rug fibers include nylon, wool, polypropylene (Olefin), acrylic, polyester, and blends of these fibers. Rugs made of sisal, coir, jute, or cotton rags are relatively inexpensive and may be suited to certain uses and decorating needs.

- *Pile.* The "pile" of carpeting refers to the surface yarns. Dense pile is a sign of quality.

- *Backing.* Another sign of quality is a carpet or rug backing that is sturdy enough to hold surface yarns in place.

- *Padding.* Padding improves durability, warmth, and resiliency or bounce. It also absorbs sound.

Be sure to read carpeting and rug labels carefully. They should list the fiber content, construction method, care instructions, backing materials, and style and color numbers. When you find carpeting or a rug you are seriously considering, ask to see it on the floor. If possible, take a sample home to try with your furnishings.

To compare prices accurately, be sure to ask for total prices that include the carpeting, padding, installation, and delivery. When investing in wall-to-wall carpeting, it may pay to have the seller come to your home to measure rooms, halls, and stairs to be carpeted. Make a point of being at home when carpet is delivered to verify that the carpet being installed matches what you ordered.

Furniture and Appliance Rentals

In most major cities and suburbs, you can rent furniture. If you move frequently or have not enough money to furnish a first home, this may be a reasonable option. Often it is possible to rent with an option to buy. This lets you apply the rent to the purchase price. Furniture rental companies may also be a source of used furniture at attractive prices.

Furniture rentals usually involve applying for credit, signing a lease agreement, and paying a security deposit and delivery charges. Read the contract carefully and be sure you understand all the terms of the agreement before signing.

Rent-to-Own Plans

Do not confuse furniture rental agreements with aggressive rent-to-own (RTO) plans. RTO plans are not regulated under the *Truth in Lending Act* or state credit laws. Fees typically add up to much more than rented items are worth and more than the cost of buying on credit. For example, a $500 television might be offered at $60 per month for 18 months. That comes to a total cost of $1,080.

Protect yourself if you consider renting furniture or appliances. Determine the total cost by multiplying the amount of each rental payment by the number of payments required in the contract. Compare this total with the cash price and the credit price of similar merchandise at reputable stores. Find out what will happen if you miss a payment. Check out provisions for servicing or repairs on rented appliances, insurance requirements and fees, and penalties for late payment or default. Read the fine print carefully.

Help with Problems and Complaints

The vast majority of manufacturers, retailers, and service people want to satisfy you, the consumer. Even so, there may be times when you have problems with appliances, furniture, electronics, and other home products. When you do, the first places to seek help include the manufacturer and the dealer or retailer where you bought the product.

Most manufacturers operate toll-free numbers and Web sites to deal promptly with consumer inquiries and problems. The operator's manual or other printed material that comes with products will usually list these consumer contacts along with troubleshooting information.

If you fail to obtain satisfaction from the retailer or the manufacturer, you may want to contact one of the following associations for assistance:

- National Home Furnishings Association, www.nhfa.org

- Association of Home Appliance Manufacturers (AHAM), www.aham.org

- Consumer Electronics Association (CEA), www.cnet.com and www.myceknowhow.com

- Carpet and Rug Institute, www.carpet-rug.com

These organizations also provide very helpful consumer information about the selection, use, and care of their products.

Home Care and Maintenance

When you move into your first home, whether it is a one-room apartment or a house, you will face home care and maintenance responsibilities. In a rental apartment this is largely a matter of keeping the space clean and caring for the appliances. If problems arise with the heating, air conditioning, plumbing, or major appliances, the landlord is usually responsible. When you buy a home, you become your own landlord and responsibilities increase dramatically.

Enrich

Contact the local Better Business Bureau or chamber of commerce to learn whether complaints have been filed on rent-to-own companies in your area.

Discuss

Why would consumers be willing to purchase items through rent-to-own plans if they are so costly?

Activity

Put together a checklist to use in evaluating a rental contract.

Enrich

Contact several of the resources listed to find out how complaints should be filed and how they are handled.

Discuss

Name three common responsibilities of homeowners.

Reflect

In your household, who is responsible for home maintenance? How are responsibilities divided?

Discuss

How can you find reputable workers for home maintenance and repair?

Home Owner Responsibilities

Maintaining a home is both costly and time-consuming. When you buy a home, housing experts recommend setting aside one to three percent of the purchase price each year to cover maintenance and repairs.

Maintenance involves routine chores you can often perform yourself. These include keeping drains running freely, faucets drip free, toilets flushing, floors and carpets clean and in good condition. You also need to periodically clean gutters, windows, garage, and basement.

Yards and plantings need seasonal attention, too. To maintain home appliances and equipment, follow instruction manuals and owners guides. Many manufactures operate interactive Web sites to address your questions and problems with their products.

Home repairs can become more involved. They include attention to roof leaks, broken windows, fallen trees, plumbing problems, and foundation damage. The electric and the heating and cooling systems also need routine maintenance as well as occasional repairs and replacement.

Regular inspection and maintenance is the best way to keep a home in good condition. It also helps you catch small problems before they become major and costly repair jobs. The checklist in 18-15 can help you identify areas that may need attention.

Hiring Workers for Your Home

Use care when selecting people to repair or work on your home. The bigger the job the more thoroughly you need to investigate them. Here are some tips:

- Contact your local government. Find out if permits must be obtained before the work is started. Ask about any guidelines you should follow in hiring people to work on your property.

Inspection Checklist	
Interior	**Exterior**
• Walls	• Foundation
• Ceilings	• Brick/siding
• Doors	• Windows/screens
• Windows	• Storm windows/doors
• Stairs	• Steps
• Plumbing	• Porch(es)
• Heating and cooling system	• Garage
• Hot water heater	• Roof
• Electrical	• Chimney
• Basement	• Gutters
• Attic	

18-15

This chart lists items to inspect for maintenance and repair both inside and outside the home.

Resource

Chapter 18—Housing, Teacher's
PowerPoint Presentations CD

- Find reputable workers by asking acquaintances for the names of people they have used with satisfaction. Check for memberships in trade or professional organizations and the local better business bureau. These offer some assurance of a worker's qualifications and reliability. Investigate carefully before hiring someone who comes to your door unsolicited.

- Interview the worker before you hire him or her. Ask for work experience and references from other customers. Follow up and check references. Ask workers about licensing and insurance. They should be insured and bonded. Ask to see the insurance certificate. Look for coverage that protects you from property damage workers may cause and any other financial risks associated with the work being done.

- Interview several candidates and get several written estimates for the work to be done. After you select someone, you will probably be asked to sign a contract. Read it carefully and ask any questions you might have before you sign. If a job is lengthy and expensive, you should refuse to pay the entire cost before work is begun. You will probably be asked to pay for a portion upfront, and the rest upon completion of the job.

Chapter Summary

Types of housing include apartments and houses. Multifamily buildings may be apartments, condominiums, or cooperatives. Single-family housing includes custom-built homes, tract houses, town houses, and manufactured houses. Choices will depend on the amount you can spend and on housing needs. These needs change with different stages of the life cycle.

Before making any decisions, set up a budget for housing costs. This involves determining how much you can spend on home and related costs, such as utilities, insurance, and taxes.

Renting a home usually involves signing a lease. It will state the rights and obligations of both landlord and tenant. Since this is a legal document that can be enforced in a court of law, it is important to fully understand all of the terms before signing.

When buying a home, a number of legal documents must be signed. To protect your interests, study these carefully. The mortgage is one of the most important commitments. Shop carefully for the best mortgage terms to fit your situation. Compare interest rates and other terms of different mortgages and compare the closing costs charged by different lenders.

When you begin to make furnishing and decorating decisions, consider your resources and your immediate needs. Floor plans can guide furniture choices. When buying furnishings consider quality, durability, style, and price.

Once you move into a place of your own, home care and maintenance become a new responsibility. Regular maintenance and inspection is the best way to keep a home in good condition.

Review

1. Name four factors to consider when deciding where to live.

2. What is the main difference that separates rental apartments from condominiums and cooperatives?

3. If you were considering a manufactured home, name five guidelines to follow in making a choice.

4. List three advantages and disadvantages of renting a home.

5. List three advantages and disadvantages of buying a home.

6. What are some of the questions renters should answer before signing a lease?

7. List three factors that might permit a buyer to offer less than the asking price on a home.

8. What percent of gross monthly income do most lenders allow for a mortgage commitment?

9. Name five factors to consider when shopping for a mortgage and comparing lenders.

10. Why do lenders require a survey of property?

11. Why is it important to take an inventory of your possessions before you move?

12. Name six factors to consider when shopping for furniture.

13. How much money can home owners expect to spend annually on home maintenance and repairs?

14. What is the best way to keep a home in good condition?

Critical Thinking

15. How does a person's lifestyle tend to influence housing location? Give examples.

16. What sources of information can help you find a place to live?

17. How would you prefer to finance a home if you were buying today? Why?

18. What are the advantages of an FHA-insured or a VA-guaranteed loan?

19. What are some ways to save money when decorating and furnishing a home?

Answers to *Review*

1. (Name four:) employment opportunities, cost of living, climate, lifestyle, neighborhood, community facilities, schools

2. ownership

3. Choose a dealer carefully; figure and compare total costs; check warranty terms; check features and extras; investigate the manufactured home community.

4. (List three of each:) advantages—fewer financial responsibilities, more free time, less financial risk, greater mobility; disadvantages—no equity, little control/freedom, no tax benefits

5. (List three of each:) advantages—increase wealth, tax benefits, greater control/freedom; disadvantages—greater costs and financial responsibilities, less mobility, relationship complications, greater financial risk

6. (See pages 459-461.)

7. (List three:) The property needs repairs; the home has been on the market a long time; comparable homes sold for less; the seller is desperate; the move-in date is flexible; the housing market is slow.

8. 28 percent

9. (Name five:) down payment, size of mortgage, repayment period, interest rate, monthly payments, special features and provisions

10. to make sure the building is actually on the land according to its legal description

11. so you can file reimbursement claims promptly in the event of loss or damage to your possessions caused by movers

12. personal needs; quality and durability; style and function; price; reputations of furniture manufacturers and sellers; and services offered, such as delivery and credit

13. one to three percent of the purchase price of the home

14. with regular inspection and maintenance

Academic Connections

20. **Social studies, research.** Investigate housing issues in your area to learn what is being done about housing for low- and middle-income families, problems of the homeless, and zoning for different types of housing. Check out the role of the local and state government, federal government, community organizations, and private business interests in each area.

21. **Research, speech.** Find information on the Internet about apartments for rent and homes for sale in your area. Describe to the class what type of information you find.

22. **Financial literacy.** Survey several realtors and home mortgage lenders. Find out the range of current interest rates, what is required to qualify for a mortgage, and what forms of financing most buyers are using to purchase homes.

23. **Financial literacy, math.** Develop a plan for furnishing a one-bedroom apartment. Draw up a floor plan and furniture patterns to show space and furniture arrangements. In planning, consider the resources you have available and the color, style, and design of furnishings you like. Visit furniture stores and retail outlets to determine how much money you would need to complete your furnishing plans. Itemize the expenses and discuss possible ways to reduce costs.

MATH CHALLENGE

24. What is the maximum amount each of the following people should spend on housing given their monthly take-home pay? Experts say that monthly housing costs should be no more than one-third of take-home pay.
Consumer 1 earns $1,000 a month.
Consumer 2 earns $4,000 a month.
Consumer 3 earns $400 a month.
Consumer 4 earns $2,250 a month.

Tech Smart

25. How much would it cost per month to pay for your dream home? Make a list of the features you want in a home. Using online resources, complete the following steps:
    1. Using a real estate listing Web site, find a home in your area that meets your criteria. What is the asking price?
    2. Assume you qualify for financing, have excellent credit, and make a 10 percent down payment on a 30-year fixed rate mortgage. Go to the Web site of a bank or credit union that makes mortgage loans. What is today's interest rate on a 30-year fixed mortgage?
    3. Use an online mortgage calculator to calculate your monthly payment.
    4. Find a mortgage calculator that allows you to calculate additional payments toward the loan each month. How many years would it take you to pay off your mortgage if you paid an additional $250 per month? How much money would you save?

Answer to Math Challenge

24. consumer 1—$333; consumer 2—$1,333; consumer 3—$133; consumer 4—$750

Reading for Meaning

Before you read this chapter, write a page about all the forms of transportation you have used. Describe the pros and cons of each.

certified used car

options

vehicle identification
number (VIN)

moped

motor scooter

CHAPTER OBJECTIVES

After studying this chapter, you will be able to

- **explain** the advantages and disadvantages of different forms of transportation.

- **evaluate** types of car sellers.

- **evaluate** car makes and models, options, fuel efficiency, and warranties.

- **identify** the pros and cons of buying a used car versus a new car.

- **compare** finance charges and other credit terms of auto loans.

- **identify** the pros and cons of buying versus leasing a car.

- **describe** the responsibilities of car ownership.

- **list** factors to consider in the choice of a bicycle, moped, or motorcycle.

Central Ideas

- The average consumer has many transportation alternatives.
- Using each transportation method involves costs and benefits that must be carefully weighed.

Whether you drive the family car, buy or lease your own car, or ride a bus, you will do a lot of traveling over the years. Americans spend billions of dollars each year on transportation. You personally will spend thousands of dollars transporting yourself in your lifetime.

In the United States, the car is the most widely used form of transportation. If you plan to own a car, you will face many decisions. This chapter presents information on choosing, paying for, insuring, and maintaining a car. Since cars are not the answer to everyone's transportation needs, public transit, bicycles, mopeds, and motorcycles will also be covered.

Transportation Choices

The transportation choices open to you depend partly on where you live. In most urban and suburban communities, you will be able to choose from several forms of public and private transportation. You may have access to buses, trains, subways, and taxis. In rural areas, riding a bike or taking the school bus may be the only alternatives to driving a car. Whatever way you choose to get from here to there, it pays to look carefully at the advantages and disadvantages of each option.

Mass Transit

In major cities, mass transit is widely used, 19-1. It usually costs less than owning a car and for many it is the only choice. People who use public

19-1

In many urban areas, buses, subways, and trains offer a fast and economical way to go from here to there.

transit frequently can save money by purchasing transit fare cards, if they are available.

The quality, cost, safety, and reliability of mass transit systems vary from city to city. One of the major advantages of traveling by bus, subway, or train is freedom from car owner responsibilities. In the city, a car can be a nuisance as well as an expense because of traffic and parking.

On the downside, it may be difficult to match your travel schedule with the transit schedule. Unless you plan carefully, you may waste a lot of time waiting for the bus or train. If public transit is not within walking distance, you may have to drive or be driven to it. You may also have to pay to park at the stop or station.

If you use mass transit during rush hours, it can be difficult to find a seat. If you travel during off hours or late into the night, there may be safety concerns connected with using public transit.

Taxicabs

Taxicabs offer door-to-door service with no parking problems and no car owner responsibilities. However, using taxis on a regular basis is very costly. It can also be difficult to find a taxi during rush hours or in bad weather. For most consumers taxis are not a reliable, affordable form of transportation.

Cars

Automobiles are the preferred answer to transportation needs for many Americans. Many people take pride and pleasure in owning a car. When you drive your own car, you can come and go as you please. If your work involves time on the road, having your own car may be a necessity.

Although a car is a convenient and comfortable form of transportation, it is a major responsibility and expense. The purchase price of a car is only the beginning. Other expenses include insurance, licensing, maintenance, fuel, and parking. In some urban areas, parking and traffic problems are serious enough to make owning a car more trouble than it is worth.

A carpool is economical for people who come from and go to the same places at the same times. Carpooling can save energy, minimize parking problems, and reduce traffic congestion. Some may find carpooling inconvenient. Since the needs of other riders must always be considered, carpooling offers only limited flexibility. Also, it does not provide an answer to transportation needs outside the pooling situation.

Two-Wheelers

Two-wheelers may offer adequate transportation in some situations. Riding a bicycle, moped, or motorcycle can be a convenient and economical way to get around. Two-wheelers conserve energy, require little parking space, and are easy to maneuver in traffic, 19-2.

A major disadvantage of two-wheelers is the high accident rate, particularly on highways and in heavy traffic. Riding a bike, moped, or motorcycle

Reflect

To what extent have you used taxicabs to get around?

Discuss

Why do you think bicycles are such a popular form of transportation in many other countries?

Discuss

Do the advantages of two-wheelers outweigh the disadvantages?

Transportation, Distribution & Logistics

Dispatchers
Dispatchers schedule and dispatch workers, equipment, or service vehicles to carry materials or passengers. Some dispatchers take calls for taxi companies, for example, or for police or ambulance assistance. They keep records, logs, and schedules of the calls that they receive and of the transportation vehicles that they monitor and control.

safely requires special skill, constant attention, and appropriate safety equipment. This type of transportation is also uncomfortable in bad weather and inconvenient if you need to carry passengers, baggage, or supplies.

Evaluating the Choices

One person's ideal means of transportation may not work for the next person. As you consider your transportation alternatives, follow these guidelines.

- *Determine transportation needs.* Where do you live? Where must you go? When and how often do you need to travel?

19-2

Commuters in bike-friendly cities may choose to ride a bike to work.

- *Identify available choices.* Do you have access to mass transit? Could you join or form a carpool? Do you own a bicycle, moped, or motorcycle you can use to get around? Can you walk to most of the places you need to go? Is a family car available to you? Would buying or leasing a car be a practical and affordable alternative?

Case Study: You Decide

Good News and Bad News

Luis is in college and has a part-time job at a law firm. His apartment is close to campus, so he walks or bikes to classes. To get to work, Luis rides the bus for an hour and transfers twice. During rush hour, he often waits a long time for the bus. Luis would like to find an easier way to get to work.

He wants a car, but he can't afford to pay for maintenance, gas, and parking. Plus, he doesn't need a car except for work.

He's interested in carpooling, but he doesn't know anyone who drives near his work.

Case Review

1. If you were Luis, what factors would you consider in making a transportation choice?

2. For Luis, what would be the advantages and disadvantages of public transportation? a bicycle? car ownership? a carpool?

3. How could Luis find out if there is a carpool he could join?

- *Compare costs.* What are the daily, weekly, and monthly fares for public transportation? How much would it cost to drive and maintain a car? How much would it cost to carpool?

- *Consider comfort and convenience.* Is public transportation close to your home? Will it take you where you want to go? Is it reliable and safe? Does it run at convenient times? If you drive your own car, would there be a problem with traffic and parking? Would the weather permit you to ride a bicycle, moped, or motorcycle?

- *Consider safety.* What is the safety record of the mass transit system? Would you feel safe getting on and off or waiting at the transit stop during the hours you travel? If driving, would you have to travel on congested highways during rush hours? Is your car, bicycle, moped, or motorcycle equipped with important safety features?

- *Consider personal preferences.* Do you want a car of your own? Would you rather not have the responsibilities and expenses of car ownership? Do you prefer public transportation to driving your own car?

- *Consider values.* Are you an environmentalist who bases consumer choices on environmental impact? Can you avoid driving? Can you take public transit, bike, or walk, instead of using cars?

The Automobile Marketplace

The way people acquire autos has changed dramatically the past few years. Traditional auto dealerships have become more "user friendly" as a result of competition from auto superstores and the Internet. The result is a competitive market and a confusing array of ways and places to look for the car of your choice. All of this can work to your advantage.

Traditional Dealerships

Traditional dealerships usually represent one or two manufacturers and sell new and some used cars. Many dealerships, as well as auto manufacturers and superstores, sell *certified used cars* with full warranties. **Certified used cars** provide some buyer protection. Certification means that a car has received a thorough mechanical and appearance inspection along with necessary repairs and replacements.

Most certified vehicles meet age and mileage restrictions, pass inspections that include checks for damage, top-off of fluids, and repair or replacement of damaged parts. Once a vehicle passes this process, the dealer or manufacturer often extends the existing warranty or issues a new 12-month or 12,000-mile warranty.

Dealerships will offer financing and take your car as a trade-in if you have one. As you shop, check out the service department. Is it well-equipped and staffed with skilled, certified automotive technicians?

You can usually earn top dollar for a used car by selling it to another individual. However, if you plan to trade-in a car, take time to research its resale value beforehand. Sources of information on used cars are given

Enrich

Research what percentage of the world's cars people use in highly populated countries, such as India and China.

Enrich

Investigate and report on the use of cars compared with other types of transportation in other nations.

Reflect

How do you feel about owning a car versus using other means of transportation?

Discuss

What personal circumstances make different types of transportation desirable?

Activity

Before reading further, list cost estimates of all the car ownership expenses that come to mind. Compare your estimates with actual costs figured later in the chapter.

Vocabulary

Differentiate between the different types of car sellers.

Activity

Make a list of the points of information included in this bill of sale.

later in this chapter. Also, dealers will usually offer trade-in customers one price that includes the new car with the trade-in value subtracted. You will usually get a better deal if you negotiate separately on the price of your trade-in and the price of the car you wish to buy.

The Internet

On the Internet, you can find up-to-the-minute information on new and used vehicles, financing, insurance, and compare different makes and models. Most manufacturers and many dealerships have online services. If you do not want to do your own shopping and bargaining, car-buying services such as Auto-by-Tel and Autoweb will find and price the car you want and put you in touch with a dealer near you. A few helpful Web sites include

- http://auto.howstuffworks.com
- www.autobytel.com
- www.car-buying-strategies.com
- www.carbuyingtips.com
- www.edmunds.com
- www.kbb.com

Auto Superstores

Auto superstores sell both new and used vehicles that are inspected, serviced, and warranted. They typically carry huge used car inventories. Most superstores are computerized. You can enter into the system the type of vehicle you want, price you are willing to pay, and other details, and the computer will locate cars in stock that meet your requirements. Prices are normally fixed. Financing, insurance, and auto servicing can be arranged as well as trade-ins if you own a car to trade.

Private Sellers or Auctions

Private sellers or auctions are other options if you are buying a used car. Normally, you receive no warranty coverage from private sellers unless the original warranty is still in force, 19-3. Cars sold at auction are usually sold "as is" which offers no protection either, if you later have problems with the vehicle. In these cases, you want to make very careful inspections and have the vehicle checked by an independent, certified automotive technician.

BILL OF SALE

I, Mark Smith ("Seller"), do hereby convey title and possession of my 20XX Ford Mustang, Vehicle Identification Number 1VWBA 0123GV012345, to _John G. Canap_ ("Purchaser"), in exchange for consideration of $ _7500 —_ .

FURTHERMORE, it is understood by the parties that the above vehicle is a used vehicle, has approximately 42,500 original miles on it, and is sold AS IS. It is further understood that SELLER MAKES NO WARRANTIES, EXPRESS OR IMPLIED, AS TO THE CONDITION OR FITNESS OF SAID VEHICLE.

FURTHERMORE, it is understood by the parties that the expense of transferring and registering the title and license of said vehicle shall be borne by the Purchaser.

WE THE PARTIES HEREBY ACKNOWLEDGE THAT WE HAVE READ THIS BILL OF SALE AND FULLY UNDERSTAND ITS CONTENTS.

Mark Smith
SELLER

John G. Canap
PURCHASER

Dated this _20th_ day of _August_ , _XXXX_

19-3

This bill of sale shows the information you should receive if buying a used car from a private seller.

Assessing Car Needs

It helps to enter the marketplace knowing what you want and how much you can afford. You will need to shop carefully to determine your preferences and match your car choice to your transportation needs and budget. Think about why you want a car and how you will use it. Is a car primarily a necessity, a convenience, or a pleasure? Will you drive mostly on city streets, in heavy traffic, on highways, or on rugged country roads? Will you travel short or long distances? Will you drive frequently or only occasionally?

You may want to rank certain car characteristics from most to least important in meeting your needs. For example, consider the importance of the following items in evaluating a car for your own use:

- size
- appearance and styling
- performance and handling
- safety record and features
- model or body type
- features and options
- fuel efficiency
- hybrid or standard
- domestic or imported
- warranty coverage

Plan to research online and make several shopping trips before you buy. This will let you become familiar with different makes and models, compare prices, and check out options without falling prey to high-pressure salespersons. As you research different cars, you may want to consult the following resources online and at local bookstores or libraries:

- *Kelley Blue Book* and *Edmunds* list the estimated resale value of new and used cars.

- *Official Used Car Guide,* from the National Automobile Dealers Association, lists general information on cars by the make, model, and year.

- Auto Safety Hot Line, a toll-free number that gives safety data on various car models from the National Highway Traffic Safety Administration. It should be listed in your local phone directory.

- Web sites as Autobytel, Edmunds, Intellichoice, SmartMoney Auto Guide, and individual car manufacturers provide new and used car information, such as pricing, safety, and more.

- Magazines, such as *Automobile Magazine, Car and Driver, Motor Trend,* and the auto issues of *Consumer Reports, Consumer Research,* and *Kiplinger's Magazine* provide useful information on car buying and ownership.

Activity

Describe needs you or your family would want to meet if buying a car.

Discuss

What differences do you see in transportation needs in the city versus a rural area?

Activity

Rank these items in terms of how they would impact your decision about buying a car.

Enrich

Use the Internet to compare features and prices of various makes and models of new and used cars.

Enrich

Go to the library and check out the latest car buying guides to learn about the styling and features of new models. What would be your choice if you were buying?

Activity

From newspaper ads or old auto magazines, find pictures of different auto body styles and bring them to class for illustration and discussion.

Reflect

Which options and features do you find most and least important?

Size, Style, and Make

Cars come in a variety of standard sizes and styles. You can find compact, small, mid-size, and large cars in almost all styles and makes. Common styles or body types include 2- and 4-door sedans, station wagons, hatchbacks, convertibles, sport cars, pickups or light trucks, sport-utility vehicles (SUVs), mini-vans, and full-size vans. Consider how much space you will need for carrying passengers or cargo.

Options

Options are the features available with a particular car. Some options contribute to safety, performance, and economy. Others are primarily for appearance and convenience. The chart in 19-4 outlines common features and categorizes them according to purpose.

Standard options come at no additional cost. Different makes and models come with different sets of standard options or features. *Extra options* can add significantly to the price of a car.

Every year, manufacturers add to the available options or features on new cars. Very often, you will find option packages offered at special prices. Try not to pay for any options you do not really want and be sure you know the cost of each extra.

Common Options or Features			
Safety options or features	• Air bags • Antilock brakes • Child restraint seats • Automatic restraint system • Alarm system • Rear wiper and defrost • Fog lights • Daytime running lights	**Convenience and preference options or features**	• Air conditioning • Sound system • Sunroof • Electronic instrument panel • Power seats • Intermittent windshield wipers • Rear wiper and defroster • Leather seats • Plush interior • Power mirror adjustment • Trip computer • Adjustable steering column • Adjustable ride control • Electronic vehicle monitor • GPS (global positioning system)
Performance options or features	• Automatic transmission • Power steering • Front-wheel or four-wheel drive • Large engine • Cruise control		
Security options or features	• Antitheft alarm system • Single switch lock • Cellular phone • Remote keyless entry		

19-4

These options or features are usually available at additional cost, although a few of these may be standard equipment for certain cars.

Warranty

Normally, new cars carry full warranty protection on some parts and limited protection on others. Items such as the air conditioner, radio, and tires carry separate warranties. When shopping for a car, study the warranties to learn just what they cover and what you must do to receive warranty coverage.

Auto warranties usually run for three years or for the first 36,000 miles. Most warranties set forth specific maintenance requirements the owner must meet during the warranty period. If the car needs any repairs during that time, they must be made by a factory-authorized service department to keep the warranty valid. However, routine maintenance may be done by an independent service center as long as the work and the parts meet specifications in the owner's manual.

Shopping for a Pre-Owned Car

If you buy a new car, your car loses 15 to 20 percent of its value when you drive it off the lot. This is not so with used or pre-owned cars. Used cars can be great bargains. However, buyers who do not do some research first can end up with a *lemon*, a car with serious problems that are costly to repair. Unscrupulous dealers and private sellers may hide these problems so they can charge more money for a car. The tips in this section can help you get a good deal.

Buyers Guide Sticker

One source of information is the Buyers Guide sticker. The Federal Trade Commission's Used Car Rule requires a Buyers Guide sticker on the window of any used car sold by a dealer. This guide describes warranty coverage or lack of it. It directs the buyer to ask that all promises from the dealer be in writing.

The sticker suggests the buyer ask to have the vehicle inspected by an independent automotive technician. It also lists some major defects that may occur in used cars. Look up performance, safety, and service records for the make and model you are considering.

VIN Check

You can check the history of a used car online using its **vehicle identification number (VIN)**. Every auto has a unique VIN assigned by the automobile industry. An auto VIN will be found on the car dashboard, on a sticker on the driver's side doorjamb, and in the title documents of the car. The history report will include information on accidents, flood damage, theft, recalls, liens on the vehicle, odometer records, and manufacturing details.

To access the VIN history online, enter "VIN" in the search engine of your choice. You will find a number of Web sites that perform VIN

Environmental Engineers

Environmental engineers use the principles of science and chemistry to solve environmental problems. In the automotive industry, environmental engineers work to minimize the effects of automobile emissions on the environment by developing hybrid or alternative fuel vehicles.

Example

Bring several auto warranty booklets to class for study and discussion.

Activity

Make a list of what to look for when shopping for a used car.

Activity

Visit a dealership that sells used cars to check warranty coverages, choices, and prices. Discuss advantages and disadvantages of buying a used car.

Resource

Buyer's Guide, transparency master 19-1, TR

Case Study: You Decide

David Needs a Car

David needs a car to carry supplies and equipment for his job as a painter. He has $2,000 cash to make a down payment. David makes the following list of his car needs:

- used, but in good condition
- large enough to carry paint, supplies, and equipment
- useful for personal driving
- fuel-efficient
- sold by a reliable dealer or private seller
- equipped with good tires, air conditioning, a radio, and a luggage rack

David reads the classified ads in the local paper and online. He also visits several used car dealers. After test-driving several vehicles, he narrows his choices. One is a five-year-old van in good condition but missing some of the features he wants. It would be perfect for his job needs, but awkward for personal use. It comes with a warranty.

Another choice is a four-year-old station wagon. It is not in the best condition, but costs only $1,500. This would leave him $500 to make improvements. It is adequate for both job and personal use, and includes all the features he wants. However, an individual is selling it, so it has no warranty.

The third choice is a small wagon, priced at $1,400. A reliable dealer is selling the car with a used-car warranty. The car has the features he wants and gets good gas mileage. The only drawback is its size. It is fine for personal driving but a little small for business. However, David can carry his extension ladder on the car's luggage rack, and he can squeeze everything else inside.

After much debating, David decides to buy the small wagon. It comes closest to meeting all his work and personal transportation needs.

Case Review

1. How do you think systematic decision-making helped David make a good choice?
2. How did David's list of goals help him make a decision?
3. What goals would you have if you were in the market for a car?
4. How can a list of goals help someone shop for cars and talk with car dealers?

searches. Fees range from about $15 to $30 for one report to $40 or more to check several cars. Generally this is a good investment if you are spending the money for a car.

Previous Owner

If you buy the car from the owner, ask a lot of questions. Normally you receive no warranty coverage so it is important to learn all you can about the reliability of the car. Is the seller the original owner? Try to find out how the car was driven and maintained. Ask for service and other records on the car. If you buy from a car dealer, you can also ask for these records.

Estimating Car Costs

Before you make any commitments, it is important to be sure you can pay all the expenses associated with owning a car. The chart in 19-5 outlines some of those expenses. The figures will vary from car to car, owner to owner, and area to area. You will need to estimate how the figures are likely to play out for you and how much money you can spend on car ownership expenses.

When buying a car, you need to consider both the purchase price and the ongoing costs of car ownership. This initial cost of a car is only the beginning. Most car buyers do not pay the full purchase price at once.

Activity

Use a copy of the *NADA Official Used Car Guide* to look up two or three specific cars. Discuss what you learn.

Enrich

Visit a used car lot and discuss pros and cons of used versus new with a salesperson.

Activity

Read classified ads for used cars. What can you learn from the ads? Discuss the pros and cons of buying from an individual rather than from a dealer.

Activity

Using a chart similar to 19-5, estimate ownership costs of your family's car, if your family owns one.

Car Ownership Costs		
Ownership costs		
• Depreciation	$_____	
• Insurance	$_____	
• Sales tax	$_____	
• License & registration	$_____	
• Finance charges	$_____	
Total ownership costs	$_____	$_____
Operating costs		
• Fuel & oil	$_____	
• Maintenance & repairs	$_____	
• Tires	$_____	
• Parking	$_____	
• City permits	$_____	
Total operating costs	$_____	$_____
Total annual car costs		$_____
Costs per mile (Divide total annual costs by number of miles driven.)		$_____

19-5
This worksheet can help you figure annual costs of owning and operating a car. You may want to check *Consumer Reports* "Ownership Costs Ratings" for different makes and models of cars.

They pay a portion of the purchase price, or a down payment and take out a loan to pay for the balance. These buyers will make monthly payments on the auto loan and interest charges until the loan is paid off. Taxes and fees are also paid when a car is purchased. This will be discussed later in the chapter.

Auto costs will also include many of the following:

- insurance premiums, usually paid monthly or semi-annually
- licensing and registration usually paid annually
- operating costs such as gasoline, 19-6
- maintenance, such as oil changes, new battery, new tires and tire rotation, car wash, and interior cleaning
- car repair costs such as repairs to brakes, transmissions, etc.
- possibly parking

Depreciation

Depreciation is a major cost of car ownership. Depreciation is a decrease in the value of property as a result of use and age. It represents the difference between the amount you pay for the car and the amount you get for it when you sell or trade it in for another car.

Although it is not an expense you actually pay, depreciation can represent a sizable amount of money, particularly if you buy a new car. For example, you buy a new car this year and plan to sell or trade it in three years. Its value is likely to drop by close to 50 percent. You lose less to depreciation if you buy a used car.

Calculating Gas Costs

Starting with a full tank of fuel, record the mileage on the odometer. From that point on, record how many gallons of gasoline you buy, the price, and the odometer reading.

Example:

Full tank		Odometer 8,500
10 gallons	Cost $25.00	Odometer 8,725
13 gallons	Cost $34.75	Odometer 8,970
9 gallons	Cost $21.60	Odometer 9,243
Total gallons = 32	Total cost = $81.35	Total miles = 743 (9,243 − 8,500)

Miles per gallon: 743 miles ÷ 32 gallons = 23.22

Cost of gas per mile: $81.35 ÷ 743 miles = 11 cents

19-6

Calculating the cost of gasoline can help you estimate the expenses associated with owning a car.

For first-time buyers, the used car market can be the best place to satisfy both budget and transportation needs. Used cars cost less to buy and to insure. They also depreciate more slowly. You can choose from a wide selection of makes, models, and sizes. Generally, it is a good idea to look for a two- to three-year-old car with low mileage and in good condition. It is a plus if the manufacturer's warranty is still in force.

What You Can Afford

Buying a car is not a spontaneous purchase. Many people save money for months and even years before they accumulate enough to buy a car. Following the advice about budgeting in Chapter 6 can help you meet the goal of having your own car.

To determine how much you can afford to spend on a car, start with the amount of cash you have on hand for a down payment and initial costs. If you own a car you can sell or trade, add its value to the amount you can spend. You will also need cash up front for licensing, registration, taxes, and insurance.

Next, determine how much you can spend each month to cover ongoing costs of car ownership. These will include fuel, maintenance, payments, insurance, parking, and an allowance for miscellaneous expenses.

Take a look at your overall income and expense picture. Total your monthly income after deductions and subtract your total monthly expenses. You will need to cover monthly car costs out of the amount left. To buy the car you want, it may be necessary to increase your income or cut your spending in other areas.

Reflect

How much do you think you could afford to spend on a car?

Reflect

Based on your current financial situation, is used or new a better car choice?

Enrich

Investigate recent changes in the design of cars to increase fuel efficiency.

Linking to... Science

Fuel Efficiency

Fuel economy is a topic on everyone's mind. Gasoline prices continue to rise while resources decrease. Auto manufacturers continue to experiment with other sources of power to reduce dependence on fuel and to reduce carbon dioxide emissions.

Hybrid vehicles are autos that use two or more sources of power. Hybrids frequently combine a gasoline or diesel engine with an electric motor. The cars have a gas tank and small gasoline or diesel engine along with an electric motor powered by battery. An onboard computer balances power between the gasoline engine and the electric motor, using both for high speeds and for heavy acceleration.

Neighborhood electric vehicles (NEVs) are powered by electricity and used for short distances at speeds not exceeding 25 to 30 miles per hour. These vehicles are particularly useful in small communities.

The U.S. government is also helping to promote fuel efficiency. For vehicles manufactured in the 2011 model year, fuel efficiency standards were raised for the first time in over 20 years. In the past, passenger cars were required to meet a standard of 24.1 mpg (miles per gallon). Vehicles in the 2011 model year will need to meet 30.2 mpg. By 2020, passenger cars will be required to meet at least 35 mpg.

The Final Four-Point Check

After answering the many questions about car buying, you may be ready to zero in on the car of your choice. However, before you part with your money, take time to check the car over carefully—in the driver's seat, on the road, under the hood, and on paper.

In the Driver's Seat

Sit in the driver's seat and see if you are within comfortable reach of the steering wheel, foot pedals, and controls. Also check for good visibility. Make sure you can see well out the front, side, and rear windows. Check seat position and adjustments for comfort.

On the Road

Test-drive the car to see how well it handles in traffic, on the open road, and when starting, stopping, turning, and parking. Is it comfortable and easy to drive? Also test all the equipment and controls, such as the emergency brake, turn signals, horn, radio, windshield wipers, and headlights.

Under the Hood

A careful check of the engine and working parts of a car is particularly important when buying a used car. Unless you know all about cars, ask an independent, certified automotive technician to look under the hood with you.

Take an overall look at the engine. Check the levels of all the fluids—oil, water, brake, transmission, and power steering. If fluid levels are low, it could be a sign of leakage or of poor maintenance.

Also check the condition of the tires. Then start the engine. If you hear any strange noises, find out the cause. The car should idle smoothly and should not emit any burning odors.

On Paper

The checklist in 19-7 should help you evaluate the items that are important to you when buying a car. When the car you are considering passes the four-point check, you are ready to buy with confidence.

Wherever you shop, whether you buy or lease, start the process with a low offer. Negotiate the cash price of the car first, then negotiate the trade-in allowance, if any. Do not be afraid to walk away if you are not getting what you want. You always can come back.

If you are looking at a used vehicle, ask to see the service record, which will tell you how the vehicle has been maintained. Check out the VIN history as well.

Car Review Checklist		
Cost Factors	**O.K.**	**Not O.K.**
Total price including:	____	____
base price	____	____
options	____	____
delivery, preparation, and other charges	____	____
Down payment requirement or capitalized cost reduction	____	____
Amount and number of monthly payments	____	____
Finance charge or money factor in a lease	____	____
Estimated cost of maintenance and service	____	____
Projected fuel economy	____	____
Warranty Coverage		
Number of miles and period of time	____	____
Parts covered	____	____
Labor covered	____	____
Owner responsibilities	____	____
Safety Features and Considerations		
Visibility	____	____
Acceleration speed	____	____
Braking speed	____	____
Ease of handling	____	____
Antilock brakes	____	____
Air bags	____	____
Automatic restraint system	____	____
Other features	____	____
Comfort and Convenience		
Smooth riding	____	____
Sound insulation	____	____
Passenger space and seating comfort	____	____
Ease of getting in and out	____	____
Luggage space	____	____
Air conditioning	____	____
Sound system	____	____
Other features	____	____
Seller		
Reputation of the dealership, superstore, or Web site	____	____
Service facilities and competence	____	____
Convenient location	____	____
Appearance of the Car		
Design	____	____
Model	____	____
Color	____	____
Interior	____	____

19-7

This checklist can help you run a final check on what is important to you in a car before buying or leasing.

Resource

The "On Paper" Car Review, Activity C, WB

Activity

Review this checklist to become familiar with important items to check before signing a car deal.

Enrich

Discuss this chart with your parents or someone else with car buying experience to learn what they found most important in buying a car.

Be sure the title is in order and get all of the figures and quotes in writing when you are shopping. Take a day or two to think over the deal you are offered before committing.

Financing

Most purchases of new and used cars are financed. This means the buyer takes out a loan and pays for the car with monthly payments. Financing a car costs more than paying cash because you pay interest on the amount borrowed. By understanding the ins and outs of financing a car, you will be able to shop more intelligently for auto loans.

Sources of Financing

Common sources of car loans include auto dealers, banks, credit unions, and finance companies. It is a good idea to shop around for loans before you go to the car dealer.

In general, the minimum age for obtaining a car loan is 18. When you apply for a car loan, the lender will want proof that you have a job and earn income. The lender will also look at your credit report and/or credit score to determine whether or not you are creditworthy.

Dealer financing is a convenient, on-the-spot source of financing. Rates may also be attractive when dealers are overstocked and need to sell cars to reduce their inventories. When asking a dealer about auto financing, be sure to insist on separate quotes for the car and the financing. This is the only way you can accurately compare finance charges and terms with other loan sources. Be wary of a dealer who tries to package the car and the financing together. This can be a costly package.

After looking at the dealer's credit terms, check financing terms from other sources. You can always come back to the dealer. You can also investigate financing sources online and compare rates and terms.

To obtain an auto loan, the borrower pledges the car as security or collateral. This means the creditor will hold the title to the car until the loan is paid in full. If the borrower fails to repay the loan, the lender may legally take back or repossess the car and sell it.

The installment loan is the most common form of auto financing. It is repaid in monthly payments over a period of time. The size of the monthly payments and the length of the repayment period for installment loans vary greatly. Loan periods are usually between 3 and 7 years for new cars and 2 to 5 years for used cars. This makes it relatively easy for car buyers to obtain loans they can afford to repay comfortably.

Cost of Financing

The overall cost of auto financing varies with the principal, or the original amount borrowed; the annual percentage rate (APR); and the length of the repayment period. These concepts were covered in Chapter 9. Consider them carefully if you shop for a loan.

The more money you borrow, or the greater the principal, the more interest you pay, 19-8. You want to make the biggest down payment you can and pay for taxes, title, and other fees up-front to lower the amount you need to borrow.

The higher the APR, the more money you will pay in interest. The longer the repayment period, the more interest is paid. A low monthly payment with a long repayment period is often no bargain.

You can use the principal, the APR, and the repayment period length to compare the cost of credit between different loans, 19-9. Using the figures in Chart 19-9 as a starting point, you can calculate the finance charges on different amounts of principal. For example, if you borrow $4,000, multiply the finance charge in the chart by four.

In summary, save money on car loans by

- shopping for the lowest rates available

- increasing the down payment and decreasing the size of the loan

- increasing the size of monthly payments

- shortening the repayment period

Loan Amount (Principal)	Finance Charges
$1,500	$150.30
$2,000	$200.04
$3,000	$300.60

19-8

This chart shows how much interest is paid on loans from $1,500 to $3,000. Each loan has an APR of 18 percent and is repaid in 12 monthly payments.

Repayment Period	Annual Percentage Rate		
	6%	8%	10%
12 Months	$32	$43	$54
24 Months	$63	$85	$107
36 Months	$95	$128	$161

19-9

This chart depicts the estimated finance charges for a $1,000 loan given different rates and repayment periods.

Truth in Lending Law

The *Truth in Lending Law* requires creditors to provide borrowers with a complete written account of credit terms and costs. According to this law, a loan contract must state

- amount borrowed or financed.

- total amount to be repaid.

- dollar cost of finance charges, which is the total amount paid for the use of credit, including interest charges and any other fees.

- annual percentage rate or APR.

- date charges begin to apply.

- number, amount, and due dates of installment payments.

- list and explanation of any penalties for late payment, default, or prepayment. A loan with a *prepayment penalty* does not allow the borrower to pay off the loan early and save on interest charges. Avoid these types of loans.

- description of the security pledged, which is usually the car.

  If the agreement is with the dealer, the contract must also state

- full description of the car

- retail or cash price of the car

- deferred payment price (price with credit charges)

- amount of the down payment

Discuss

How does the length of the repayment period affect the cost of an auto loan?

Discuss

What items must be stated on a loan contract?

For your own protection, before signing any car loan agreement, be sure to read it carefully. Ask questions if any part of the contract is unclear. Make sure there are no blank spaces or lines to be filled in later.

Also, pay special attention to the creditor's legal rights in case of late payment, default, or prepayment. You should be aware of any possible consequences. More information on buying a new or used car is available on the Federal Trade Commission (FTC) Web site at www.ftc.gov.

Finally, review your financial situation one more time. Be sure you can carry out your responsibilities and make payments according to the terms set forth in the contract.

Leasing

Today, over 50 percent of consumers lease their cars, 19-10. An auto lease is similar to an auto loan in that the lessee makes an initial payment and makes monthly payments for a set period of time. Generally, the lessee's initial costs and monthly payments are less than those of the buyer. However, the lessee does not own the car at the end of the lease term. Like buyers, lessees must also pay fees for registration, licensing, and other charges.

If you lease a car, your initial payment usually includes the first monthly payment, a security deposit, and a *capitalized cost reduction*. Familiarize yourself with the following terms before negotiating a car lease:

- *capitalized cost* of a leased car is the price or value of the vehicle on which the lease is based. The lower the figure, the lower monthly payments will be.

- *capitalized cost reduction* may include a cash down payment, trade-in allowance on a car you are trading, rebates, and other buying incentives. These reduce the capitalized cost, and thus, lower your monthly payments.

- *residual value* is the worth of a car at the end of the lease. The higher the residual value, the lower monthly payments will be. The residual value is based on depreciation estimates. Consult the *Automotive Lease Guide* at your local library or bookstore for a list of the residual values of leased cars.

- *lease term* is the length of the lease—usually 24, 36, or 48 months. Try to limit the lease term to the length of the car warranty.

19-10

Auto leasing isn't right for everyone. Consider the pros and cons of leasing versus buying before signing a lease.

- *mileage limitations* are stated in the lease. You will usually be limited to 12,000 or 15,000 miles annually. Check out extra charges for excess mileage and wear and tear.

- *money factor* is the interest you pay, usually stated as a small decimal such as .00265. To convert this to an annual interest rate, multiply by 24 (for example, .00265 × 24 = 6 percent). The money factor should be similar to or lower than new car loan rates. Compare lesser offers with your own sources.

Negotiate all of the terms of the lease including the capitalized cost of the car. Be prepared to negotiate the trade-in allowance or capitalized cost reduction if you are trading a car or making a down payment. It also is important to be aware of the penalties if you terminate the lease early. Try not to do this. It can be very costly.

Check the lease for turn-back condition requirements and car care packages you may be required to purchase. Review the warranty and be sure it is good for the entire term of the lease. Consider "gap insurance" which covers you if the car should be stolen or totaled in an accident. It pays the difference between what you owe on the lease and what the car is worth.

Finally, look for a fixed residual price option to buy at the end of the lease if you think you may want to own the vehicle rather than lease a new car.

Get answers to any questions you have and be sure you understand all the terms of the agreement before you sign a lease contract. Review all of the charges you must pay up front and at the termination of the lease. Get all of the figures and promises in writing.

Discuss

Can you think of any other items that might be negotiated on a car lease?

Discuss

What responsibilities go with owning and driving a car?

Reflect

With what auto operation and maintenance responsibilities are you familiar?

Activity

Read and discuss the owner's manual that came with your family's car. What helpful information did you find?

Car Owner Responsibilities

Once you become a car owner, you assume two major responsibilities. You are expected to carry adequate auto insurance and to operate and

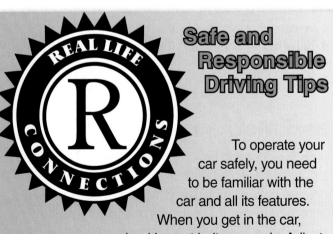

Safe and Responsible Driving Tips

To operate your car safely, you need to be familiar with the car and all its features. When you get in the car, buckle seat belts securely. Adjust the rearview mirror and side mirrors so you can see traffic behind and to the side of you.

Reckless drivers who speed and drive aggressively cause many accidents. Follow posted speed limits, be alert, and try to anticipate the unexpected. Keep a safe distance between your car and the car ahead of you. Signal well in advance your intentions to turn, stop, or change lanes.

Give driving your full attention. Avoid reading maps, eating, drinking, applying makeup, or talking on the phone when you are behind the wheel. It is illegal to talk on a handheld cell phone in many areas. If you do not have a hands-free phone system, pull over into a safe area to make and receive calls.

Never send text messages while driving. Your full concentration should be on the road, not trying to enter or read a message. Many accidents occur while teens are texting. Even a short distraction can cause you to be unaware of another driver's actions.

Finally, do not drive under the influence of drugs or alcohol. Stay out of cars driven by someone who used alcohol or drugs.

19-11
Responsible car owners prolong the life of their vehicles by driving safely and scheduling regular maintenance.

Transportation, Distribution & Logistics

Automotive Technicians

Automotive technicians inspect, maintain, and repair automobiles and light trucks. They perform simple mechanical repairs as well as high-level technology-related work. They use computerized shop equipment and work with electronic components while also using their skills with traditional handtools.

maintain your car properly and safely. Failing to carry out these responsibilities can endanger lives and financial resources of the car owner as well as passengers, other drivers, and pedestrians. Auto insurance was covered in Chapter 10.

You have much to gain by operating and maintaining your car properly. 19-11. Rewards include better car performance, driving safety, and car reliability. You will also have fewer breakdowns and repairs, better fuel economy, less pollution, and greater trade-in value.

Maintaining Your Car

Keeping your car in good driving condition is necessary for safety, economy, and performance. Study and follow the owner's manual for routine maintenance and service schedules. Manufacturer's instructions offer guidelines for lubrications, tune-ups, and other routine servicing. However, if you drive a car hard or under severe conditions, your car may need more frequent attention than indicated in the owner's manual.

One key to long car life is anticipating and avoiding potential problems. Listen to your car and investigate strange noises and sluggish performance. Pay attention to warning lights, gauge readings, and any leaks, drips, or unusual odors. Check out irregularities promptly. If you ignore little sounds and changes in performance, a small problem may become major and costly. Your car may have to be towed or you may have to take the car to the nearest service station or repair shop. Then you may not get the best service at the best price.

For safer driving and better fuel economy, keep the tire pressure at the recommended level. Replace worn tires with the proper size as recommended in the owner's manual. Tires also need to be rotated periodically.

Service Shops and Mechanics

It pays to investigate service centers before you need one. Look for a service shop or mechanic you can trust and go to the same place whenever your car needs service or repairs. Basically, you have three choices: a dealer, a chain auto service center, or an independent, certified automotive technician. For warranty servicing, it may be necessary to go to the dealership. For routine repairs and maintenance, it pays to shop around. Evaluate service and repair centers according to the following guidelines.

Reputation

Look for membership in such organizations as the local chamber of commerce or Better Business Bureau. Also ask several customers of the shop about their satisfaction with services and prices.

Competence

Look for experienced, well-trained automotive technicians. Certification is one indication of competence. ASE certified technicians have completed the training and passed the tests of the National Institute for Automotive Service Excellence, 19-12.

Certified technicians receive credentials listing their areas of competence. They usually wear the blue and white ASE insignia. Where these technicians are employed, an ASE sign usually appears on the premises. The sign may also appear in Yellow Page listings of auto repair shops.

An endorsement by the American Automobile Association is another indicator of reliable servicing. Endorsed repair centers must meet the high standards of the Association.

Facilities, Equipment, and Parts Inventory

Look for auto service shops and centers that are adequately equipped to care for your car and to perform the specific services required. Also ask about the availability of necessary parts.

Convenience

It pays to find servicing in convenient locations when you need to leave your car for service. Business hours that work well for you may also be important when dropping off or picking up your car. Before taking your car in for service, it is a good idea to call for an appointment and to ask how long you can expect to be without your car.

Charges

Compare fees and charges for routine maintenance jobs, such as a lubrication, wheel alignment, and oil change. You can often make these comparisons on the telephone. Though it is not certain, it is likely that shops with reasonable charges for routine maintenance will be reasonable on bigger jobs as well.

Paperwork

It pays to get certain things in writing when you buy costly services. Be sure you receive written estimates, itemized bills, and written guarantees on the work performed. When you leave your car to be serviced, make it clear you want to be contacted before any unexpected major repairs or services are performed. Keep your own file of auto records or purchase, maintenance, repairs, and insurance claims.

We employ technicians certified by the National Institute for

AUTOMOTIVE SERVICE EXCELLENCE

Let us show you their credentials.

19-12
Look for the blue and white symbol, as worn on the technician's arm, when shopping for auto servicing.

Activity

Visit several auto service centers to look for the ASE certification symbol. Interview ASE certified technicians to learn about their training.

Resource

Car Operation and Maintenance, Activity D, WB

Enrich

Conduct a survey of local auto servicing facilities to check reputation, competence, and charges.

Enrich

Interview the owner of an auto service facility to learn about the business, its challenges, and its relationship with customers and with auto manufacturers.

Discuss

What do you see as the primary advantages and disadvantages of traveling by two-wheeler?

Enrich

Visit a local bike shop to check out models, features, and safety equipment.

Enrich

Invite the owner or a salesperson from a local bike shop to discuss bike styles and features.

Reflect

If you have a bike, how did you choose it? If you were buying one today, how would you choose?

Two-Wheelers

Whether you ride a bicycle, motor scooter, moped, or motorcycle, two-wheelers are economical to drive, easy to maneuver, and easy to park. They offer environmental advantages, too. Bicycles are pollution-free, and powered cycles use less fuel and pollute less than cars.

If you can satisfy part or all of your transportation needs with a two-wheeler, there are many choices to consider. Bicycles, scooters, mopeds, and motorcycles come in many styles and sizes. Choose your two-wheeler according to how you will use it, what size and style you prefer, and how much money you have to spend.

Bicycles

Bicycles are the most energy efficient means of transportation and cost less than most motorized two wheelers. People who bike rather than drive, just for trips of three miles or less, save sizable amounts each year in fuel costs.

It cuts down on pollution as well. With worldwide environmental concerns, many countries and some major cities in the U.S. are working to make cycling a convenient and safe alternative to the automobile. It also offers pleasure and fitness advantages.

If you can use a bicycle for some or most of your transportation needs, finding the right bike is the first step. The many types and styles from which to choose can be overwhelming unless you know exactly what you want.

If you plan to invest a sizable amount in a bicycle you hope to ride often and for many years, buy from a reliable bike or sports shop. If you are already knowledgeable about bikes, you may want to shop for one at a superstore, a discount store, or online. You can find used bikes for sale in classified listings, auctions, house sales, and bike shops.

Bike prices range from under $200 to $5,000, depending on a bike's type, style, and performance. Special features can be expensive, so weigh the benefits against their costs. The chart in 19-13 outlines some of the types and styles of bikes and their suitability for different types of riding. Expect to pay a considerable amount for a top-of-the-line bike in any category. You might find a good used bike for much less if you shop carefully. Remember to include the cost of accessories in your budget. These extras can add up and prices vary from dealer to dealer.

Mopeds and Motor Scooters

These low-powered vehicles can be an efficient, economical means of transportation. Generally they are suited to local riding and short distances. For either a moped or motor scooter, check state and local laws on insurance, permits, licensing, and rules of the road. The technical definition of low-powered cycles varies from state to state. Generally these vehicles are characterized as follows:

Bicycle Choices		
Type and Style	**Designed for:**	**Characteristics**
Mountain bikes	• Off road, rough terrain riding	• Rugged construction • Strong brakes • Tough wheels • At least 21 gears • Upright handlebars • 22 to 28 pound weight
Road bikes	• Riding on hard, flat surfaces • Good for touring and commuting	• Relatively light frame • Dropped handlebars • Narrow high pressure tires • At least 14 speeds • 20 to 25 pound weight
Hybrid bikes	• Casual road riding • Good for commuting and some off road terrains	• Combined features of road & mountain bikes • Upright handlebars • Multiple gears • Narrow tires suited to street & paved surfaces
Comfort bikes	• Comfortable riding on and off road surfaces	• Mountain bike style frame • Upright padded seating • Shock absorbers • Upright handlebars • At least 21 gears • 24 to 29 pound weight
Cruisers	• Casual riding on flat surfaces, good for short trips and commutes	• Usually single speed but some models have multiple speeds • Balloon tires • Coaster brakes but some have hand brakes • Padded seats

19-13

This chart describes in general terms a few of the more common types of bicycles on the market. A tour through a good bike shop or bike department in a sports store is the best way to compare different bikes before you make a choice.

Enrich

Look in current biking magazines to research new developments in bicycle design. Discuss findings in class.

Activity

Investigate opportunities in your area for buying quality used bikes. Put together a listing of sources.

Enrich

Contact the National Highway Traffic Safety Administration for information on bicycle injuries, accidents, and safety equipment.

• The **moped** is a low-powered motorized two-wheeler. It has a small engine of less than 50cc capacity that rests at the rear of the bike. The vehicle may or may not have pedals in addition to the motor. Top speed is about 25 miles per hour. It is suitable only for off-highway riding.

• The **motor scooter** is a two-wheeled motor vehicle with a step through frame and an engine located beneath and to the rear of the rider. Wheels are less than 16 inches in diameter and the engine capacity ranges from 50cc to 250cc. It is larger than a moped and typically reaches speeds of 30 to 40 miles per hour or more with the larger engine. It is designed primarily for off-highway riding though higher-powered models may be suited to highway travel.

Mopeds and motor scooters may be either gas powered or electric. The gas vehicles are faster and more powerful. They go further and some are suited to both highway and local riding. Electric scooters use battery-powered motors and can travel between 10 and 20 miles per hour. They go from eight to 16 miles per charge. Speed and distance between charges depend on the size of the battery. Electric models are not suited to highway driving and are limited to short distances.

Motorcycles

Over six million Americans choose a motorcycle for transportation and riding pleasure. There are several basic models, each designed for a different type of cycling. The best choice for you will depend on how you plan to use the bike. For on-road and highway cycling and commuting, you may want to consider a traditional cycle, a cruiser, or a touring cycle.

Visit a dealership or go online to see the differences and to compare models. The Internet offers volumes of information on selection, maintenance, insurance, safety, and related topics. *Cycle World, Motorcycle Consumer News,* and *Motorcyclist* magazines are among the most popular publications providing information on buying, owning, and enjoying a motorcycle.

Financing and Other Expenses

The cost of a motorcycle can be substantial, ranging from $5,000 to $25,000. You may want to look for a good used motorcycle for your first buy. Check the "Financing" section of this chapter if you plan to finance a bike. The process will be the same.

A motorcycle averages 35 to 60 highway miles per gallon and costs relatively little to drive. However, insurance is essential and will be expensive. Since motorcycles are considered a greater risk than cars, insurance companies charge higher premiums. The types of insurance coverage offered is similar to that provided by auto insurance. Talk to a reliable insurance agent about coverage and cost before you buy a motorcycle.

Motorcycle licensing, registration, and traffic laws vary from state to state. For example, some states require cycle drivers to wear helmets and other states do not. Check your state laws before driving or buying a motorcycle. A good helmet is a safety necessity whether required by law or not.

Buying

When shopping for a motorcycle, check out the dealers as you would car dealers. The Internet also is a good place to shop for a motorcycle and to find volumes of information on selection, maintenance, insurance, and related topics. Buy from a reputable dealer that has a reliable service department.

If you are considering a used motorcycle, check it out with great care. Very often, mechanical problems occur two or three years after buying a motorcycle.

Visit several dealers and test drive different makes and models. You should feel comfortable and confident riding the bike you buy. You also should be able to put both feet on the ground when the bike is upright. Check noise, vibration, cruising speed, comfort, and ease of handling. Excessive noise and vibration can be very tiring on long trips.

Reflect

If you were in the market for a motorcycle, how would you choose the cycle and dealer?

Resource

Chapter 19—Transportation, Teacher's PowerPoint Presentations CD

Chapter Summary

Most consumers can choose from a variety of transportation possibilities. These include mass transit, a car, or traveling on two wheels. The best choices will depend on personal needs, available options in the area, and the costs of different ways of getting around. Comfort, convenience, safety, and personal preferences are also important.

Buying an automobile calls for careful analysis of your transportation needs and finances. For many first-time buyers, a used car is a good choice to satisfy both budget and transportation needs.

The cost of owning a car includes the purchase price and any finance charges. Insurance, licensing, registration, taxes, operating costs, maintenance, and parking are other expenses connected with a car of your own. Auto financing costs will depend largely on the interest rate charged, the amount borrowed, and the length of the repayment period.

Proper operation and maintenance are also important for car owners. This means safe and sensible driving and timely car care and servicing. Finding a reliable service center is a key factor in auto maintenance and repairs.

Two-wheelers are a transportation choice for many consumers. There are a wide variety of bicycles, low-powered two-wheelers, and motorcycles to meet different needs and preferences.

Review

1. Name two advantages and two disadvantages of mass transit.

2. What is a disadvantage of buying a car from a private seller or at an auction?

3. Describe three ways to evaluate if a used car is a good deal.

4. List eight expenses associated with having a car.

5. How does depreciation affect the price of a car?

6. What three factors influence the cost of financing a car?

7. True or false. Long-term loans cost more than short-terms loans.

8. Describe similarities and differences of buying and leasing a car.

9. How can early attention to car problems save hundreds of dollars?

10. What are some advantages and disadvantages of two-wheeler transportation?

Critical Thinking

11. If you were to organize a carpool of four to six people to go to and from work or school, what rules or policies would you want to make clear to each rider?

12. How can you decide if you have enough money to buy, operate, and maintain a car?

13. Why do finance charges vary with different sources of credit?

14. What steps can car owners take to operate cars safely and smoothly?

15. What are some things a car owner can do to get reliable auto servicing?

16. What are some factors to consider when buying a motorcycle?

Academic Connections

17. **Reading, speech.** Obtain copies of two or three new and used car warranties from dealers or from car owners in your family. Study the warranties and compare the
    A. parts and labor covered
    B. length of time or number of miles under warranty
    C. buyer responsibilities
    D. conditions for receiving warranty servicing and keeping the warranty in effect
    How do used car warranties differ from new car warranties? Discuss your findings with the class.

Answers to *Review*

1. (See pages 486–487.)

2. You usually get no guarantee or warranty and the car is sold "as is."

3. (List three:) read the Buyers Guide sticker; check the history of the car online using its VIN; talk to the previous owner; ask for service records

4. (Name eight:) purchase price, interest on a car loan, taxes, registration, license plate, insurance, operating costs, maintenance and repair costs, parking

5. (See pages 496–497.)

6. the principal, the annual percentage rate, the repayment period

7. true

8. similarities—both buyers and lessees make initial and monthly payments, and pay for registration and licensing fees; differences—at the end of the term, buyers own the car but lessees do not.

9. Early attention lets you get your car to a service center of your choice, tend to problems before they become serious, avoid towing charges, and shop for the best servicing.

10. (See pages 506–509.)

18. **Math, writing.** Check at least four sources of auto financing in your area and compare credit costs and terms for
    A. a two-year, $5,000 loan for a used car
    B. a two-year, $15,000 loan for a new car
    In a short written report, explain how the annual percentage rate, the amount of the loan, and the repayment period affect credit costs. Also explain why credit costs differ for used and new cars.

19. **Financial literacy, research.** Arrange, as a class or individually, to visit at least three auto service and repair facilities. Take note of the
    A. experience and qualifications of technicians
    B. equipment and facilities for servicing different cars
    C. guarantees on parts and servicing
    D. charges for routine jobs such as a tune-up or an oil change
    E. attitude of service people toward answering questions and complaints and satisfying customers
    As a class, discuss how the three service facilities compare. Does one seem preferable to another? If so, why?

20. **Research.** Take a trip to a car dealership and to an auto superstore if there is one in your area. Compare the two. What type of selection did you find? Were salespeople helpful? Were prices competitive? How did the service center look? What guarantees and warranties were offered? Were there both new and used cars? Could you lease a car? Which place would you prefer if you wanted to buy? Why?

21. **Science, speech.** Research and report on the latest developments in one of the following areas:
    - electric cars
    - alternate fuels
    - disposal of car batteries
    - hybrid cars

MATH CHALLENGE

22. You find the car of your dreams at a used car lot. You negotiate the price down to $5,000. You put $2,000 down and borrow the rest. The dealer offers you a car loan with an APR of 8 percent for 36 months. How much interest will you pay for the loan? (Refer to Figure 19-9.)

23. A hybrid car costs $30,000 and gets 55 miles per gallon. A comparable car that is not a hybrid costs $22,000 and gets 25 miles per gallon. Consumer A drives 125 miles a week. Consumer B drives 500 miles a week.
    Assuming each customer pays cash for the sticker price of the cars and fuel stays at $3 a gallon, how many years would each consumer need to drive the hybrid before fuel savings justify the higher price?

Tech Smart

24. Imagine you are working at the mayor's office in a nearby city. You are asked to deliver a package to the city's main library. Using online resources for the nearest large city, research the following:
    - How would you get from the mayor's office to the library? Can you walk there? Describe your route.
    - Is there a form of public transportation you could take? If so, describe the route you would take. How much would it cost in fares to go to and from the library? How long would it take?

25. Pick three new cars you would consider buying. Specify make, size, style, and features. Shop for these cars online. Use the Internet to locate the best buys on the cars you want in your area. Report your findings to the class.

Answers to *Math Challenge*

22. Approx. $384 ($128 × 3)

23. It would take Consumer A 18.78 years. It would take Consumer B 4.7 years.

Electronics and Appliances

Reading for Meaning

Before you read the chapter, make a list of the appliances and consumer electronics products and services you use. How does each device or service enhance or complicate your life?

obsolescence

consumer electronic product

home appliance

telecommunication

mass communication

convergence

wired carriers

dial-up

digital subscriber line (DSL)

broadband

bandwidth

fiber optics

Direct Broadcast Satellite (DBS)

Wireless Fidelity (Wi-Fi)

software applications

prepaid phone

high-definition TV (HDTV)

firewall

EnergyGuide label

ENERGY STAR label

CHAPTER OBJECTIVES

After studying this chapter, you will be able to

- **explain** convergence and its impact on consumer electronic products and services.
- **define** broadband and describe the pros and cons of several broadband delivery technologies.
- **evaluate** telecommunications service providers.
- **compare** similar electronic products and home appliances.
- **identify** reliable sources of information about consumer electronic products and appliances.
- **outline** steps consumers can take to ensure online security and safety.
- **compare** energy efficiency ratings of different home appliances and electronics.
- **describe** some key causes of product obsolescence.

Central Ideas

- Technological advances have created a steady stream of new consumer electronics and appliances.

- These goods and services can improve the ways people communicate, learn, spend their leisure time, and do business. However, consumers need to examine their needs and budgets before they spend their money.

20-1

GPS navigation systems have become more common and affordable in the last few years.

Discuss

What electronic devices and home appliances does your family own?

Major Appliance Technicians

Major appliance technicians fix appliances such as refrigerators, dishwashers, washers, and dryers. They replace or repair defective belts, motors, heating elements, switches, gears, and electronic components. They tighten, align, clean, and lubricate parts as necessary.

Many of today's most popular electronic devices and services were unheard of just a few decades ago. These include phones that receive e-mail, matchbox-sized music players holding thousands of tunes, and satellite-based navigation systems to guide drivers, 20-1. Home dishwashers were uncommon. Microwave ovens were rare, generally unaffordable, and looked upon with suspicion.

New technology has revolutionized how people communicate with one another. It has led to the creation of new products, as well as new ways to buy and sell them. Entertainment and education can be delivered in stimulating ways.

Technology has also led to the need for new service industries, such as providers of cell phone service and satellite radio. The fast pace of technological change will soon make many of today's popular products and services obsolete. The term **obsolescence** refers to the state of being no longer useful or in use.

With so many current and soon-to-be-released products and services to choose from, shopping becomes especially challenging. Besides the volume of products and services, consumers are bombarded with claims from businesses. They promise that a product or service is the fastest, sharpest, lightest, or most technologically advanced. You do not need to be a technological genius to be able to separate the facts from the hype.

Faced with constant upgrades and new products and services, consumers need to examine their needs carefully before falling for the latest sales pitch. Some basic knowledge and careful planning will go far in helping you select the products and services you really need and can afford.

A Flood of New Products and Services

Consumer electronic products run on electric current or batteries. They are devices used for communication, entertainment, education, or information gathering. Many of them are portable. They can be used in homes or cars. Even children's toys contain computer parts that make them almost lifelike.

Home appliances are devices that run on gas or electric current. They include major home appliances such as stoves, refrigerator/freezers, dishwashers, and clothes washers and dryers. Small home appliances are coffeemakers, toasters, blenders, and personal care products such as hair dryers.

In 1975, American homes contained an average of 1.3 consumer electronic devices because most homes had a TV. In 2008, that number grew to

25 electronic devices. Examples of popular consumer electronic products are computers, televisions, gaming systems, digital cameras, personal media players, DVD players, and phones.

Purchasing a consumer electronics product is often just a first step. You may also need to purchase a service in order to use the product. The most popular services are cell phone, Internet access, and pay television. Pay television includes cable, satellite, video on demand, and other services for which consumers must pay.

Industries providing these services and products are lumped together under the label *telecommunications* or *telecom*. **Telecommunication** is communication at a distance. Telecom industries transmit voice, data, graphics (images), and Internet access. When you talk on the phone or send e-mails and text messages, you are using telecommunications services. You also use these services when you download photos, music, and videos.

Telecommunication is closely tied to mass communication. **Mass communication** refers to device-dependent communications that reach large and dispersed audiences. It includes books, newspapers, magazines, radio, television, the Internet, movies, musical recordings, and video games. Mass communication industries, or *mass media*, provide the content that telecom companies deliver.

New telecommunications technologies are changing the way people communicate with one another. They are changing workplaces, including where and how people work. They are changing the education system and entertainment.

Convergence

Convergence is sometimes described as cramming several products into one. However, it has a broader definition. **Convergence** is the merging of separate devices, technologies, or industries into one.

A *smart phone* is a good example of product convergence, 20-2. A smart phone lets users make phone calls and send text messages like regular cell phones do. It also performs the scheduling and organizing functions of a *personal digital assistant (PDA)*. By using a smart phone with Internet access, a person can talk to friends, transmit photos, download music, play electronic games, locate the nearest pizza parlor, and more.

Another example is the refrigerator with a flat-screen television built into the door. This is an example of the convergence of a home appliance with a consumer electronic product.

20-2
This smart phone includes functions such as a calendar, media player, and Internet access.

The 1996 Telecommunications Act

Convergence has occurred and continues to occur between industries. For example, consumers used to use cell phone companies for cell phone service. The phone company could not also offer cable television services. Consumers had to contact cable television companies for those services. Government regulations kept these industries separate by regulating the services telecommunications companies could provide.

However, the 1996 Telecommunications Act changed that. This law greatly relaxed ownership regulations. It also forced phone companies to share their wire lines with other companies. Today, the boundaries between these industries are blurring or nonexistent. You can now go to one company—a phone or cable company, for example—and obtain TV, phone, and Internet services.

Supporters of the law believed it would increase competition among telecommunications industries and companies. This would lead to more choices for consumers, as well as lower prices and better service. However, critics of the law say it did the opposite. It allowed companies to merge and large companies to absorb smaller ones. As a result, critics say, just a few large and powerful companies dominate the telecom and mass communication industries.

The distinction between goods and services is blurring as more and more products come bundled with services. A growing number of businesses that once sold products are now also selling services to go along with their products. For example, many cell phone companies provide free phones to customers who purchase service contracts. The monthly service charges create more revenue for the companies.

Pros and Cons of Converged Products

Some converged devices can be good buys. Purchasing and carrying one product instead of two or three can save you money and space in your backpack or purse. For example, you may be able to leave your laptop at home if you have an Internet-enabled cell phone. Having to recharge one product is also easier than recharging two or three. However, before you buy a converged device, ask yourself the following questions:

- *Do I need all the functions this device provides?* If not, you may pay a premium for something you do not use. The more complex a device, the more expensive it usually is.

- *How user-friendly is this product?* Merging multiple devices and functions sometimes results in a complicated, difficult-to-use product. For example, small screens and keyboards can make a device hard to use, 20-3.

- *Does the device require more energy to run because of the added functions?* If a converged device requires more batteries or more frequent recharging, then it may not be worth the cost and bother.

- *Will this device be harder to service?* Some combination devices are more difficult to service if they break down.

Telecommunication Services

There are different methods of transmitting information, from the use of copper wires to bouncing signals off satellites in outer space. A telecommunication company often uses several different technologies to deliver a service. For example, cable television uses both wired and wireless technologies. Many phone companies provide both wired and wireless services.

In some areas the companies offer options including cable TV, telephone service, and Internet access for reduced fees. Each company claims to offer more services at faster speeds and for lower costs. You may be limited to one or two choices depending on where you live.

Wired Carriers

For many decades, the only telecommunication service consumers and businesses required was the telephone. Homes and offices were connected to one another through a network of copper wires, cables, and phone company switching centers. These **wired carriers** transmit signals primarily over wire or cables.

According to the Bureau of Labor Statistics of the U.S. Department of Labor, wired carriers still make up the largest segment of the telecom industry. Many homes and offices continue to rely on landline phone services. However, besides voice, they also transmit data and video.

20-3
Make sure you are comfortable operating a converged product before you buy it.

Dial-Up and DSL

The earliest Internet Service Providers (ISPs) used phone lines to transmit information. **Dial-up** refers to Internet access through a telephone line using a modem in the computer. The modem directs the computer to dial a phone number that connects it to the Internet. This is the least expensive Internet access and the slowest. It also ties up your phone line when you are online.

Digital subscriber line, or **DSL**, also comes through copper telephone wires. It uses a digital frequency that does not interfere with your telephone service. You can talk on the phone and use the Internet at the same time. The speed depends on how close you are to the telephone switching station. DSL is not an option for people who live far away from switching stations.

Broadband

DSL is a type of Internet access called *broadband*. **Broadband** is high-speed Internet access. What constitutes broadband service varies. Many broadband Internet service providers transmit data at far greater speeds than 200 kilobits per second. A *bit* is the smallest unit of data a computer uses. Speed is measured in bits per second.

An important factor in transmission speed is **bandwidth**. It is the maximum amount of information that can be carried over an electronic cable or device at one time. The larger the bandwidth, the greater the amount of information transmitted.

Telecommunications companies are constantly updating their communication networks to carry more information at faster speeds. This means increasing bandwidth. Types of information that require large bandwidths to transmit over the Internet include the following:

- *Streaming video and audio.* These are video or sound files transmitted in real time over an Internet connection. (*Real time* refers to what is happening right now.)

- *Interactive television.* In the past, the networks and cable channels chose what to broadcast and when. Now viewers can control when and where they watch their favorite shows. *Interactive Television (ITV)* enables viewers to make their own choices. For example, people used to go to stores to rent a movie on a DVD. Now movies can be downloaded or streamed from the Internet onto television screens.

- *Two-way communication services.* If you like a jacket worn by an actor during a TV show, you can access the Internet and order it in minutes. If you enjoy a show's theme song, you can immediately download that tune. Businesses will use (ITV) to reach shoppers in their homes.

For many Americans, the Internet is ever present. Consumer electronic manufacturers are finding many new ways, apart from computers, to connect consumers to the Internet. People already use handheld devices, such as cell phones and PDAs, to surf the Internet when they are away from home.

Cable and Satellite Program Distribution

Another sector of the telecom industry provides cable and other types of program distribution. These services—mostly television programs and movies—are provided for a fee or on a subscription basis. *Pay-per-view* and *Video-on-demand* are offered. Today, the services offered also include phone service and Internet access.

Cable providers download information broadcast through the air and from satellites orbiting the Earth. The information is routed through cables into customers' homes. These cables carry more information than telephone lines. However, both cable and telephone companies are replacing their old lines with newer *fiber optic cables*.

Bandwidth Bottlenecks

Super-fast Internet service is called "big broadband." The technology necessary to bring big broadband to consumers and businesses in the U.S. exists. The problems are bandwidth bottlenecks, which slow down broadband transmissions before they reach homes and offices.

To fix these bottlenecks, the copper wire lines carrying data, video, and voice into most American homes and offices must be replaced with fiber optic cable. The American Recovery and Reinvestment Act of 2009 required the Federal Communications Commission to create a national broadband plan by 2010.

Fiber Optic Cables

Fiber optics technology carries data along glass strands at the speed of a laser light beam. These strands are as narrow as a human hair, 20-4. Many of them can be bundled together, increasing bandwidth. With increased bandwidth, there is increased speed of transmission. Telephone and cable companies are replacing copper wire and cables with fiber optic cable.

Data, especially streaming video, is transmitted much faster through fiber optic wires than through DSL or cable. Fiber optic customers register high satisfaction with speed, reliability, and tech support. Fiber optic cables at the bottom of the oceans carry data information between North America and the other continents. This data may include phone calls, e-mails, and audio and video files. However, once the data reaches the U.S., most of it is routed over slower copper-wire networks. Most U.S. households are not connected to a fiber-to-the-home network, and paying to get connected is costly.

20-4
Fiber optic cables allow information to travel at faster speeds than copper wires do.

Note

The FCC's 2010 national broadband plan addresses the "digital divide" in the U.S. Have students research and examine how it threatens the overall health of the U.S. economy.

Enrich

High speed Internet service is slower and more expensive in the U.S. than it is in other countries. Have students research commonly available broadband speeds and costs for consumers in other countries.

Direct Broadcast Satellite

Dozens of satellites orbit the Earth. Signals can be beamed to a satellite from the Earth's surface, 20-5. **Direct Broadcast Satellite (DBS)** works by bouncing transmissions off orbiting satellites directly to receivers on customers' homes. To receive the transmissions, customers must attach a mini-dish, or small satellite dish, to the outside of their home. Global Positioning Systems (GPS) locator devices also utilize these satellites. The satellites determine the user's location.

In the past, satellite customers had to buy expensive hardware. However, these costs have decreased. In rural and remote areas, DBS may be the only Internet and television service available. Also, satellite

20-5

A satellite reflects transmissions beamed from earth to satellite dishes on individual homes.

Note

The Federal Communications Commission (FCC) is the main government agency that oversees the nation's telecommunications capabilities

customers may receive more television channels than many cable customers. However, it is often slower and more expensive than the other options.

Wireless Carriers

Wireless telecommunication carriers make up another part of the telecommunications industry. They include companies providing cell phone service, as well as those selling pager and beeper services.

Internet data and graphics can also be transmitted wirelessly. Internet broadband access is referred to as **Wireless Fidelity**, or **Wi-Fi,** technology. Wi-Fi works by transmitting information using electromagnetic waves from radio towers. Using Wi-Fi, a laptop user can connect to the Internet without cables or wires. Wireless Internet access is now available on laptops, cell phones, PDAs, and other mobile devices.

Wi-Fi makes it possible to use your computer in *hotspots*, or public areas where a wireless network connection is available. These hotspots are usually located in places such as coffee shops and airports. You can also purchase devices allowing you to create your own Wi-Fi hotspot wherever you are. Advances in wireless technology have boosted the speed of Internet access through Wi-Fi.

Linking to... Science

What Is the Electromagnetic Spectrum?

How do television programs travel from the television station to your TV? How does your e-mail get from a Wi-Fi-enabled laptop to your friend's computer?

Data, video, and voice travel through air mostly over radio waves. Radio waves are part of the electromagnetic spectrum. The spectrum consists of different types of electromagnetic radiation. It also includes the waves that cook food in microwave ovens, visible light rays, infrared

waves, X-rays, and gamma rays. Except for visible light, these waves are invisible to the naked eye.

Radio waves are the longest and weakest waves. Electronic devices such as computers, radios, televisions, phones, and handheld devices send and receive information over radio waves. Some devices use infrared waves.

The electromagnetic spectrum is a national resource controlled by the federal government. It is also a limited resource because the waves can interfere with one another. This interference is the static you hear when you move from one radio channel to another.

Questions for Service Providers

Whichever system you are considering, here are some questions to pose in your search for an ISP or other service provider that will best meet your needs.

The Provider

Is the provider local, regional, or national? What reputation does the provider have for prompt, responsive customer service and tech support? Is this support available both online and by phone? How long is the typical wait for over-the-phone tech support?

Services

What functions will the company provide? Also ask about any emerging technology. Will the provider be offering these services, and when? Make sure the company offers what you are looking for.

Cost

How much will service cost—both initially and in ongoing monthly costs? Compare service plans and costs for different service packages. Most carriers offer a variety of plans based on usage, geographic area covered, functions used beyond basic service, and contract terms.

For cell phone service, for example, look at both monthly and per minute charges. Also check other charges such as those for roaming, texting, Internet browsing, and other functions your phone may perform. Finally, note how much you are paying for taxes. If you sign a contract for the service, check the penalty for early termination.

Equipment

What are the equipment requirements? Does the provider supply necessary equipment, or must you buy or rent it? Who pays repair costs? Make sure you receive and understand the answers to these questions before choosing equipment.

Reliability

How reliable is performance and connectivity? You want to avoid frequent interruptions in service. For instance, if you are choosing a cell phone carrier, is reception clear without static and dropped calls?

Software and Product Information

Does software come with the service? For Internet service, this may include a firewall and anti-virus, anti-spam, and anti-spyware packages. Is the software user-friendly? Are you given adequate and clear information

Resource

Visit the Web site of the National Aeronautics and Space Administration (NASA) for more information about the electromagnetic spectrum and radio waves.

Enrich

Ask students to research the role and activities of the Federal Communications Commission. When and why was it created? How have technological advances resulted in changes in the FCC's activities?

Discuss

Give examples of devices that use wireless technology to communicate with other devices.

Discuss

Ask students to speak with their families about their experiences with Internet service providers. What types of problems, if any, occurred? How were those problems resolved or not resolved?

Activity

Ask students to research a consumer electronics product or appliance that they wish to buy. They should collect information from a variety of sources. Have them make a list of sources of information to discuss in class.

about the service it provides and the installation and operating packages available to you?

Buying Consumer Electronics

Some of the most popular consumer electronics products are discussed in this section. However, in a few years' time, these products may be obsolete and replaced with upgrades. Many of the tips you will find here will also apply to upgrades. For new products, you will want to do careful research. Find out as much about the product as possible using consumer Web sites and magazines. Make careful comparisons of different brands and features. Speak to friends who have purchased the product. Above all, never make an impulse decision about an expensive electronic product. Become informed before you shop.

Computers

As you shop for a computer, you will find a dizzying selection of features and functions to consider. Knowing how you intend to use the computer can help you make intelligent choices and avoid paying for extras you do not need.

Desktop or Laptop

If you have no need for portability, a desktop computer generally will offer more capabilities for less money than a laptop. It is likely to provide more hard-drive capacity and better sound quality. There will also be more options for expanding and adding functions you may decide you want later. *Upgrade potential* refers to the ease and expense of adding new memory and other features that make the computer faster and more useful. Desktop computers are usually easier to upgrade than laptops.

If portability is important to you, or if space is limited, a laptop or notebook may be a better choice. A laptop can do almost anything a desktop computer can do, but it will generally cost more for comparable capabilities. The key advantage to a laptop is its portability, which permits you to take your computer wherever you wish to use it, 20-6. *Notebooks* are similar to laptops, but with smaller screens and keyboards and less upgrading capabilities. The newer *netbooks* generally offer Internet access and few other features. Notebooks and netbooks are less expensive than laptops because of their more limited functions.

20-6

Laptops make it easy to do computer tasks no matter where you are.

Keep in mind that portability can be a disadvantage because these devices can be lost or stolen. You will need to guard against theft. You will also have to be more cautious with online security if you use wireless connections.

If you are considering a laptop, think about the weight and size that best suits your needs. Powerful laptops that are both thin and lightweight are available, but they are higher priced. A smaller, less expensive notebook or netbook may work for you. However, neither has all the features of the larger and heavier laptops.

A large battery capacity is also a plus. The laptop manufacturer should tell you how many hours you can use the laptop between charges and how long it takes to charge.

Basic Features

Computers are often sold as a system that includes a monitor, printer, keyboard, speakers, and either a mouse or touchpad. Knowing exactly what you are looking for will help you decipher computer advertisements and find the best deal.

The computer's speed depends on the power of the microprocessor and the amount of working memory. However, the faster a computer works, the more it costs. You will want to buy a computer with as much processor power as you can afford. People who play high-end computer games or edit videos and photos usually buy the most powerful CPUs.

Random Access Memory (RAM) is also called working memory. The higher the RAM, the faster the computer runs. RAM is measured in gigabytes (GB). If you need more RAM, it can usually be added fairly easily. More RAM means a higher price.

Software programs are instructions that tell a computer what to do. A computer's *operating system* controls the basic functions of a computer. Adding **software applications**, or programs that perform specific tasks, enable consumers to customize their computers.

Some of the most popular applications software allow users to do word processing, prepare spreadsheets, and create presentations. Other applications include those for gaming, computer security, and education. The number and types of applications are endless. Many programs are tailored to the needs of a particular business or profession.

Software is constantly updated. Software companies usually offer updates to their programs. However, eventually they come out with new versions and stop selling or supporting older versions. People usually buy the most recently released software programs.

Peripheral devices include printers, keyboards, and digital cameras. When a new peripheral device is added to a computer, it often comes with a program called a *driver*. The driver tells the computer how to use the device. Many computer companies have the latest drivers available for download from the Internet.

Choosing Other Features

What do you need your computer to do? Do you intend to use your computer for routine e-mail, Web surfing, and word processing? Will you

Arts, A/V Technology & Communications

Video Graphics Designers

Video graphics designers plan, create, and analyze video communications. They also develop material for Web sites, interactive media, and multimedia projects. They must be able to use color, illustration, photography, and animation techniques to enhance communications.

use it for more complicated tasks such as downloading video files and editing photos? Do you need a connection to cell phones or other computers?

Assess your needs realistically before making choices. It is important to investigate thoroughly before you invest in a computer. This way, you will be sure you end up with what you need at a reasonable price. Additional features you may want on your computer include the following:

- *DVD and BD burners.* People use their computers to store and access data, video, and audio. DVDs and the newer Blue-ray Discs (BDs) are storage mediums. A burner is a device that can write to a DVD or a BD.

- *Universal serial bus (USB) ports.* Peripheral devices such as digital cameras and personal media players are plugged into USB ports. There are often multiple ports located on both the fronts and backs of computers.

- *Webcams.* A webcam is a type of camera that allows users to stream live video over the Internet. If two computer users have webcams on their computers, they can go online and see each other in real time. Some webcams are built into the computer. Others can be purchased separately.

New developments in computer hardware and software surface almost daily. You can review what is available and keep up-to-date by reading computer publications, manufacturers' literature online, and online articles. The more capabilities a computer offers, the more you will pay.

Cell Phones

Choosing a cell phone can be a complicated process. As electronic devices continue to converge, cell phones come packaged with other devices such as PDAs and personal media players. The variety of phones on the market can be confusing. Deciding on the best carrier or service provider and service plan are major decisions as well. Start with a careful look at how, when, and where you will use your cell phone, 20-7.

- Is it primarily for emergency calling, routine calling, or business?

- Will you use your phone frequently and during peak hours? Approximately how many minutes per month do you think you will use?

- Will you make long distance as well as local calls?

- What geographical areas do you want to cover—local, regional, and national? If international calling will be important for you, be sure to ask about it.

- Will you use a landline too, or depend only on your cell phone?

20-7

If text messaging is a feature you desire, make sure the phone you choose has that capability.

Look at the phone design. Each type has pros and cons. When shopping, consider the appearance and handling of the phone.

- Do you like the style of the phone?
- Is it comfortable to hold and easy to use?
- Is the size right for you?
- Is the display screen easy to see and to read?

Cell Phone Features

Review cell phone features to identify the ones you need. Today's cell phones take you far beyond chatting. The more your phone can do, the more you will pay for the phone and the carrier services. Expanded features include

- text and multimedia messaging
- e-mail and Web browsing with a search engine
- instant messaging
- music, video, and podcast downloads
- cameras
- hands-free systems
- GPS navigation
- PDAs

Thousands of applications, also called *apps*, are available online. These specialized computer programs can be downloaded from a Web site commonly called an app store. By adding apps, consumers can customize their cell phones and other electronic devices. Apps are available to do the following:

- record notes for later playback
- download books
- learn a foreign language
- keep track of spending
- calculate tips
- convert currency
- count calories

In some U.S. cities, bus and train riders are using their cell phones instead of tickets and fare cards. By swiping their phones by a special electronic device, the cost of their ride is deducted from an online account.

Prepaid Phones

If you have credit problems or do not make many calls, a basic prepaid or pay-as-you-go phone may be right for you. With a **prepaid phone**, you

Discuss

What are additional charges that can add to the cost of having a cell phone?

pay for phone service before you use it. You do not sign a long-term service contract, pay a monthly bill, or have to pass a credit check.

The costs include the purchase of a phone and a set number of minutes of phone service. The cost per minute charged by these phones is often higher than what other phones charge. However, you save money on monthly service fees. You only pay for the time you use.

Airtime is sold as a total number of minutes or by days used. For example, you may buy 200 minutes of service over 90 days. Once you reach either 90 days or 200 minutes, you will need to buy more minutes. Therefore, it is much easier to control costs with prepaid phones.

Case Study: Consumer Electronics

Confusion in the Marketplace

Laticia saved $250 she received for her birthday to buy a cellular phone. At a local cell phone store, a salesperson demonstrates several phones. There are many different features and options for each phone.

Laticia wants text messaging, e-mail, and Internet access. A camera phone wasn't one of her original wishes, but it would be handy. She has a personal media player, but it would be nice to have music on her phone. The only phone offering all the features she wants is over $300.

The service plan is $99 per month, plus a $35 sign-up fee. If she signs a two-year contract, the cost of the phone is reduced by 50%. There is a $175 release fee for breaking a contract.

Laticia cannot afford $99 per month. Feeling discouraged, she leaves the store to think it over. The salesperson cautions that the prices will not last forever and urges her to make a decision soon.

Case Review

1. How might Laticia have prepared for her trip to the cell phone store?
2. What are some ways Laticia can lower the costs of buying a phone and monthly service charges?
3. What experience have you had with cell phones and service plans?
4. What do you think are the basic cell phone features needed?
5. What advice would you give Laticia?
6. What should you find out before signing a cell phone contract?

The phones and airtime cards can be purchased at retail outlets, online, or by phone. Many of the services available in monthly calling plans, including voicemail, caller ID, and call waiting, are available in prepaid plans. Other services can be purchased at an additional cost.

Phone Billing Problems

Phone bills can be especially difficult to decipher. However, since billing errors are common, you need to read your bill carefully. If you do not understand a particular charge, contact your carrier to ask for an explanation. A monthly $5 mistake adds up to $60 in one year.

Billing errors may be simple mistakes or even fraud. There are several common scams you can catch if you are alert. *Cramming* is the practice of adding charges that were unauthorized or misunderstood by the consumer. Scan your phone bills for extra charges. Some may have vague labels such as "service charges" or "minimum monthly usage fees." Whenever you authorize a deduction from your phone bill, make sure the correct amount is deducted.

Slamming occurs when a phone service provider switches you to their service without your permission. Both slamming and cramming are illegal. If you think you are a victim of either of these practices, contact your service provider or carrier for an explanation. If you cannot resolve the problem with your carrier, contact the Federal Communications Commission and the Federal Trade Commission for assistance.

Personal Media Players

Personal media players perform a variety of tasks. The first devices allowed users to play audio music files, 20-8. Other functions were added, and users were soon using these products to display digital photos and view online video content.

Before you begin to shop, ask yourself two questions. How would you use the player? How much can you spend? The available personal media player choices—brands, models, and features—are staggering, and the technology is constantly changing. If you are shopping for one of these devices, research the options first.

Once you know what you want and how much you are willing to spend, you can begin shopping. A good source of information is an informed salesperson in a retail outlet handling personal media players. The following are a few items to consider as you shop:

20-8

Personal media players are a convenient way to enjoy music and video files.

- *Memory.* Storage capacity for personal media players range from 4 GB, or about 1,000 songs, to over 160 GB, or 40,000 songs. The capacity you need depends on the content you want on your player.

- *Compatibility.* Look for a player that works with the sources of music and other content you wish to use.

- *Style, size, and ease of use.* You will find some tiny units and other palm-sized units with LCD screens. Some are simple to use. Others with more functions can be complicated.

- *Features.* Personal media players offer a variety of features. These include wireless Internet connectivity, personal organizers, LCD screens for viewing videos and TV shows, and more.

- *Accessories.* Extras to go with your player include quality headphones, carrying cases, memory cards, and speakers. Consider these items carefully. These can add a lot to your initial investment.

Personal Digital Assistants

A personal digital assistant, or PDA, is a portable handheld device. Early PDAs were electronic organizers and planners. They helped users keep track of appointments and scheduling. They stored the names, addresses, and phone numbers of friends, relatives, and business contacts.

PDAs became much more powerful once they could connect users to the Internet. PDAs are now used to send e-mail and access Web sites. Downloaded computer software or applications allow users to customize their PDAs.

Convergence has created devices combining PDAs with cell phones and personal media players. Some are even loaded with features of GPS devices and electronic book readers.

When buying a PDA, you can use many of the tips given for personal media players. Following are a few additional considerations:

- Is your PDA compatible with your computer? Will you be able to move information, music, photos, and other material back and forth between the two devices?

- Can you use the keyboard comfortably? If you will do a lot of texting and e-mailing, the keyboard should be easy to use. Make sure you try it before you buy the device.

Televisions

In the past decade, television sets have advanced from chunky boxes to large, thin screens that can be hung on walls, 20-9. In addition, images and sound quality have improved significantly. There are several reasons for this. First, after June 2009, the federal government required all-digital TV broadcasts. Digital signals replaced analog signals in over-the-air broadcasts. Digital signals create sharper images.

20-9

Modern televisions have larger screens, yet take up less space.

Older televisions containing cathode-ray tubes are being replaced by **high-definition TV (HDTV)** sets. The newer sets receive the digital signals and display them as crisp images. The quality of DVDs has also risen. Blue-ray discs deliver the clearest images.

TVs with better resolution cost more than non-HDTV sets. When the first HDTVs reached stores, they were expensive. Now prices on HDTVs have fallen, making them a better buy.

TVs have become home entertainment centers. A growing number of devices attach to televisions. In addition to cable and satellite TV boxes, there are digital video recorders, video game consoles, and streaming video devices. A television should have jacks to plug in the devices you plan to use.

Consumers can access Internet content, including streaming video, on their televisions. However, they need a device, such as a video game console or a DVR. TVs will soon include built-in Internet access.

Be aware of the power consumed by your entertainment system. HDTVs and the devices plugged into them can use a lot of electricity. Generally, the larger the screen, the more electricity is used.

Protecting Against Online Threats

Online security is a serious problem. The U.S. government wants to protect itself from people who use the Internet to access sensitive government information. This information could be used to steal government secrets or plot terrorist attacks. U.S. businesses have reported thefts of online information about their research and products.

Online security is also a major concern for individuals. According to the FBI, instances of cybercrime are continuing to grow rapidly. See 20-10 for a list of cybercrimes and online annoyances.

Activity

Ask students to log for one week how much time they spend watching television, playing video games, talking on cell phones, and using the Internet. Discuss the results in class.

Enrich

Challenge students to go a day without consumer electronic devices including cell phones, television, computers, cameras, and personal media players. They should choose a day when they are not working or in school. Ask them what is most difficult to give up and how they spend their time when electronic devices are not available.

Discuss

What can you do to protect your computer and data from electronic threats?

Types of Online Attacks
• **Viruses**—malicious programs or codes inserted into your computer without your knowledge or permission. *E-mail viruses* come as attachments to e-mail messages. After infecting your computer, they can automatically transmit themselves to everyone in your address book.
• **Worms**—programs that can duplicate themselves over consumer networks and cause serious damage to your computer.
• **Spyware infections**—software programs installed on your computer hard drive without your knowledge. They collect information about you and your online habits and pass it to third parties.
• **Phishing and smishing**—official-looking messages that ask for immediate action to update your financial and identity information. *Smishing* is phishing via a text message. Identity theft often is the main goal of these attacks.
• **Spam**—junk e-mail designed to sell you something.
• **Trojan Horses**—destructive software programs that look to be legitimate, but can disable a computer and cause serious damage.
• **Cyberbullying, cyberstalking, and predatory messages**—online threats that may be disturbing and dangerous. They should be reported to authorities.

20-10
Take precautions to protect yourself and your computer from these online threats.

Reflect

Most of the information you find on the Internet is not filtered or edited for accuracy. How can you evaluate the content of a Web site? What are some indications that the information may be from a bad source?

Discuss

What types of information should you not reveal, especially on the Internet?

Reflect

What steps do you currently take to ensure your online safety? What additional steps might you take?

What You Can Do

The people and groups perpetrating these crimes and making these threats access computers through e-mail messages and downloads. Cell phones and other electronic devices are vulnerable to some of the same threats. Following are steps you can take to protect yourself and your information online.

Set Up Defenses

One of the most effective ways to thwart electronic threats is to create protective electronic walls around your devices. To create the strongest defense, take the following actions.

- Install anti-virus software and anti-spyware software to protect against damaging virus and spy attacks. Effective and free antivirus software can be downloaded from some Web sites. Consult computer publications for the names and reviews of free software.

- Set up a spam filter to prevent annoying pop-ups and advertising.

- Use a **firewall**, which is a protection system to block unwanted e-mail, offensive Web sites, and potential hackers.

- Update your protection regularly. It is very important to keep current on all updates provided by your operating system and protective software.

- Use adequate passwords and authentication methods to keep online accounts secure—and do not share these with anyone.

- Back up your files regularly in case you need to restore them.

Safeguard Personal Information

Internet users often let their guard down with people they meet or hope to meet online. Since the Internet allows users to remain anonymous, it is easy to forget that people may not be who or what they claim to be. The people you meet online may be criminals. Avoid sharing personal information that may enable a stranger to find or harass you or steal your identity. Sensitive information includes your name, birth date, mother's maiden name, account passwords, and Social Security number. Other information you should hold back includes your age, address, phone number, parents' names, school and workplace names and addresses, and photos of you and your family.

To protect yourself, take the following steps:

- Check for security features on commercial Web sites when you shop online. Read each site's privacy policy statements.

- Do not open e-mail if you do not recognize the sender. Delete messages from unknown sources without delay. Do not download files unless you know who sent them and why.

- Do not disclose personal information unless you initiated the contact and there is a legitimate reason for providing this information.

- Report requests for sensitive financial information to the authorities. Government agencies and financial institutions do not e-mail consumers asking for this information.

- Avoid posting information on social networking and other public sites that enables someone to locate or harass you.

- Deal immediately with such cybercrime as cyberbullying, cyberstalking, identity theft, and predatory threats. Report them to your Internet service provider, Web site host, and law enforcement agencies.

For more information on Internet safety, see the Web sites listed in Figure 20-11. These sites are designed to inform and protect you and your online activities.

Wi-Fi Security Issues

Wi-Fi networks may not be secured. Security risks arise when these sites are accessed by hackers. You can do the following to protect yourself:

- Check the safety of your browser and its security record.

- Make sure your computer security and firewall software are adequate, operating, and up-to-date.

- Use strong passwords with a combination of capital letters and numbers. Change them periodically.

- Avoid conducting financial transactions over unsecured connections. Do not submit sensitive information such as Social Security numbers, bank account numbers, credit card numbers, or passwords.

Reliable Web Sites Related to Cyber Security	
www.wiredsafety.org	Wired Safety
www.snopes.com	Snopes
www.usdohs.gov	U.S. Dept. of Homeland Security
www.bsacybersafety.com	Business Software Alliance
www.cybercrime.gov	U.S. Dept. of Justice
www.cyberangels.org	CyberAngels
www.ikeepsafe.org	Internet Safety Coalition
www.staysafeonline.org	National Cyber Security Alliance
www.cisecurity.org	Center for Internet Security
www.onguardonline.gov	Partnership of Government Agencies

Enrich

Invite someone from a local law enforcement agency to class to discuss online crime and scams. Ask students to prepare a list of questions before the visit.

Discuss

What steps can you take to make sure that your wireless network is secure?

Activity

Visit a local outlet for computers, software, and accessories. Interview a longtime employee about growth, changes, and product development over the years.

20-11

These Web sites provide information and assistance related to your safety online.

- Turn off your computer's Wi-Fi capabilities when not in use.

- Disable file sharing on your mobile computer.

- Limit e-mail and instant messaging on hotspots to casual communications. Do not send or receive anything you would not want to be made public.

Buying Guidelines for Appliances and Consumer Electronics

Most consumers buy home appliances and consumer electronics from one of three sources: large retail stores, electronic outlets online, or local independent sellers. Shop around before you buy. Identical appliances vary in price from store to store. When making decisions on where to buy, consider

- product selection and quality

- after-purchase customer support and service

- price

- warranty provisions

- return policies

- delivery and installation charges, 20-12

- whether the seller will take away or recycle an old appliance or electronic device you are replacing, or if portable items can be swapped at the store

As you shop, consider safety, ease of use, performance features, energy efficiency, warranties, and servicing. Be sure to check and recheck the size and dimensions of a new purchase against the size and shape of the space where you will put it. Read the labels, seals, and instruction booklets accompanying products. They provide facts and directions on use and care, performance, safety, energy efficiency, and proper disposal or recycling.

The more durable a product is, the longer it will last. Begin with a careful check of construction features. Appliances should be sturdy, well built, and evenly balanced. Look for hard, durable finishes that do not scratch or dent easily. Ovens and refrigerators should have sturdy shelves with shelf supports. Supports prevent shelves from falling and from being pulled out accidentally. Handles and control knobs on appliances should be firmly attached.

20-12

If you want your appliance to be delivered, check ahead of time to see how much this will cost.

Assessing Your Needs

Before buying an appliance or electronic device, determine your needs. The following questions can help:

- What jobs do you need the product to perform for you?

- What size (physical dimensions, power level) do you need?

- What special features are important to you?

- Do you have the space required to use all the product's features?

- What special safety features do you want?

- Is the appropriate power source available and convenient to the product's location?

Calculating Costs

After determining your needs, figure out how much money you can spend. Look at your savings to see how much cash you have on hand. Study your budget to determine how much money you have to spend for monthly operating costs, service charges, or loan payments.

If you need more than one product, set priorities. For example, having a working refrigerator is a need. Without one, you must eat most of your meals out, which is expensive and inconvenient. However, a new gaming system is a want and is used for entertainment only. Purchasing a refrigerator will be higher on your to-do list than buying a gaming system. Based on your savings and budget, decide how much you can spend for the appliance or electronic device you want to purchase.

- Will you buy on credit or can you pay cash?

- How much more is the credit price than the cash price? Is it worth the difference?

- If you choose to use credit, how much can you afford to pay in monthly installments? What are the total finance charges?

- How much money will you need for installation, servicing, and operating costs?

Researching the Market

The time to obtain information on appliances and electronic devices is before you buy. It pays to find out what is new before you shop. This is particularly true when you buy costly products you expect to enjoy for a long time.

Most manufacturers' Web sites provide promotional materials about their products that usually focus on sizes, functions, and features. You may need to dig deeper to learn about installation requirements, warranties, use, and care. Collecting and comparing this information on different brands can help you make a wise choice.

Discuss

What are some sources of information about the features, prices, and performance of appliances?

Reflect

What is the most expensive or valued product you own? Do you know and follow the manufacturer's recommendations regarding care for that product? If not, how does disregarding these instructions affect the performance and your enjoyment of the product?

Discuss

How can EnergyGuide labels help consumers make decisions when buying home appliances?

Activity

Ask students to guess how much their families spend on electricity and gas per month and per year. Then ask them to check several months of bills and calculate an average per month and an estimated total for a year. How close were their estimates to these figures?

Reflect

What steps can your family take to cut back on energy expenditures?

Sources of information also include consumer publications and materials from retailers, government, trade associations, utility companies, and consumer groups. Look especially for articles that compare similar products or different brands. The Internet is an excellent, comprehensive source of information on products, features, energy efficiency, and prices. Accessories can be expensive, but also vital. Almost every type of product offers a variety of performance features. Of course, the more features an appliance or device has, the higher its purchase price and operating costs usually are. Features that extend the product's life or make it safer, more efficient, and easier to use may be worth the extra cost.

Ease of Installation, Use, and Care

The easier it is for you to keep a product well maintained, the more you will use and enjoy it. Be sure you understand what you need to know about its installation, use, and care. Choose products with controls that are easy to read, understand, and operate. Look for the operating cycles and functions you need.

Easy care and cleaning features are especially important on kitchen and laundry appliances. These products handle messy jobs and, therefore, need more frequent cleaning. Features such as self-cleaning ovens and frost-free refrigerators eliminate some cleaning jobs.

Ask salespersons for demonstrations before you buy. When installing major appliances, insist on qualified and reliable service persons to make the required gas, electrical, and plumbing connections. For some products, installation may be included in the purchase price. Do-it-yourself installations and servicing are risky unless you are trained to do these jobs. Non-authorized service people may also jeopardize warranty coverage.

Energy Efficiency

When you buy appliances and electronic products, it pays to consider energy efficiency and operating costs. This is especially true for major home appliances and products you expect to use for a number of years.

Energy efficient equipment and appliances cost less to own and operate. Over time, even if the purchase price of an energy efficient product is high, it may still be a bargain. Energy efficiency saves you money in lower utility bills. It reduces air pollution and helps conserve natural resources at the same time.

You can also save energy by unplugging electronic devices when they are not in use. Even though they are turned off, televisions, computers, and even device chargers draw electricity.

EnergyGuide Label

As you shop, look for the EnergyGuide labels that appear on these appliances: refrigerators, freezers, dishwashers, clothes washers, water heaters, air conditioners, and furnaces. The **EnergyGuide label** shows the estimated annual cost of operating an appliance, 20-13. By comparing the average cost estimates for similar appliances, you can determine which would be the most energy-efficient and least costly to own and operate.

These labels tell you the estimated yearly energy used in operating an appliance based on national average utility rates. The lower part of the label gives an estimate of the electricity or gas the appliance uses in one year based on typical use. You can multiply this figure by your local electric or gas rate to estimate costs for your area.

Energy efficiency rating labels appear on climate-control equipment such as air conditioning and furnaces. These labels show the range of efficiency ratings for competing equipment of the same cooling or heating capacity.

ENERGY STAR Label

The ENERGY STAR program is a voluntary partnership of the U.S. Department of Energy and the Environmental Protection Agency, product manufacturers, local utilities, and retailers. Its purpose is to encourage the purchase of the most energy-efficient consumer electronics and appliances. The **ENERGY STAR label** appears on appliances and home electronics that meet strict energy- and water-saving criteria. The label on a clothes washer, for example, means the model cuts energy costs by one-third and water costs by one-half.

By choosing products labeled with the ENERGY STAR, you can conserve energy and water and keep your utility bills down. You will also help to protect the environment. The ENERGY STAR label appears on the EnergyGuide label when the product has one. This mark may also appear directly on the product or its packaging.

Warranties and Service Contracts

When you shop, compare warranty coverage just as you compare other features. A product may carry a full or a limited warranty. Service contracts are often available for both electronic products and home appliances. If you use appliances carefully and buy from reputable manufacturers and dealers, warranty servicing usually is adequate. A service contract may be worth considering if you move frequently and need installations and follow-up services with each move. Someone who expects to give an appliance maximum use may also consider purchasing a service contract. For example, a clothes washer in a household of five or more members may need more servicing than a similar machine in a couple's home.

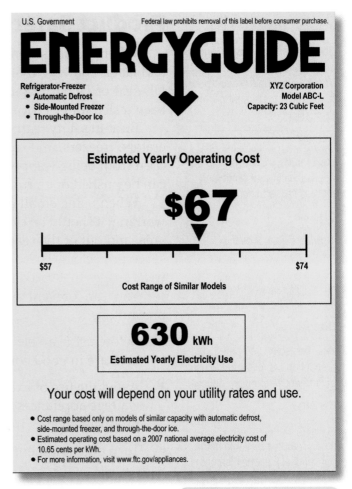

20-13
The EnergyGuide label can help you determine which appliance is the least costly to operate.

Resource

Calculate Energy Waste in Your Home, reproducible master 20-2, TR

Discuss

How is the EnergyGuide label different from the ENERGY STAR label? For what is each used?

Enrich

Visit an appliance department. Use the EnergyGuide labels to identify the most efficient appliances.

Resource

Calculating Energy Use, Activity D, WB

Product Safety

When purchasing electronics and home appliances, check for seals and labels showing that products meet safety standards. For example, the UL seal of Underwriters Laboratories, Inc., indicates that products have been tested for electrical, thermal, and fire hazards.

Built-in safety features are a plus in home appliances. Doors on refrigerators, freezers, and dryers should have safety latches that prevent children from being trapped inside these appliances accidentally. Such doors can be pushed open from inside.

When using small electric appliances, select a space large enough for working. It should be close enough to electrical outlets, away from the sink area, and out of the reach of small children. Plug electronic products into surge protectors. These inexpensive devices provide protection from electrical surges that can damage delicate electronic components.

You can prevent many home accidents by following these simple precautions.

- Before using an electric appliance, make sure the appliance and the cord are in good condition.

- Avoid the use of extension cords. If needed, use them only for low-wattage appliances. Extension cords are not safe for high-wattage products, such as irons, toasters, and coffeemakers.

- Turn off equipment before connecting or disconnecting at outlets.

- Be sure to avoid using several electric appliances on a single circuit. Overloading circuits can blow a fuse and create a fire hazard.

- If you have gas appliances, promptly call the gas company if you ever smell gas or suspect a leak. Since gas leaks are very dangerous, most gas utility companies will check your home for suspected gas leaks for little or no charge.

Product Servicing

Most appliances and electronic products require service or repair at some point. You can reduce the need for repairs by buying well-built products and carefully following use-and-care directions. If the product is under warranty or you purchased a service contract, take advantage of the services to which you are entitled.

If the product is not under warranty, service or repair can be expensive. The first question you need to ask is whether repair costs are as much or more than the price of a new model. If the answer is yes, buying the new product is the better choice.

Keep important paperwork filed and ready for reference as you need it. Paperwork includes receipts of appliance purchases, copies of warranties, and records of servicing with dates and charges. Have your file in hand when you call for service. Service providers will want to know the make, model, and serial number of the product. They will also need the date of purchase and details of the problem you are experiencing.

Activity

Bring to class a warranty and an appliance instruction booklet from an electronic product your family owns for illustration and discussion.

Activity

Look for the UL seal on appliances in your home and discuss its meaning.

Discuss

To what extent does the responsibility for safety in using appliances rest with the consumer? To what extent does it rest with the manufacturer?

Discuss

What are some safety precautions to follow in the use of different electronic products?

Enrich

Investigate and report on the safety features built into home appliances. For which safety and convenience features are you willing to pay extra?

Enrich

Develop an appliance safety checklist to use at home.

Finding Reliable Service

Finding a reliable service facility is the key to getting the most for your service dollars. It is a good idea to do this before you have problems. This way, you know where to call for prompt, reliable service when you need it.

Check your warranty for a list of service centers. You can also ask friends, neighbors, and appliance dealers for recommendations. Once you have the names of several service centers, check with your local Better Business Bureau or consumer protection agency. If complaints have been filed against a facility and not resolved to the customer's satisfaction, it may be best to look for servicing elsewhere. Finding the answers to the following questions can help you choose a service center:

- Is it authorized to work on the specific products you own?

- What are the qualifications of service technicians? Ask about years of experience, special training, certification, or licensing.

- How much does the center charge for basic repair services, house calls, pickups, and deliveries? Compare fees of several service centers.

- Does the center provide emergency service?

- Do the technicians guarantee their work?

- How long will it take to have your appliance or electronic product serviced?

Activity

Role-play a consumer calling an appliance service center to ask about fees for various services.

Resource

Shopping for Major Home Appliances, Activity E, WB

Activity

Apply the checklist in 20-14 to three major appliances in your home. Discuss what you learn.

Avoiding Unnecessary Service Calls

One sure way to trim costs for appliance repairs is to avoid unnecessary service calls. In most cases, when a service person comes to your home, you pay even if there is nothing wrong with the product. An estimated 30 percent of all calls for service are unnecessary. Often the product is unplugged, not set properly for operation, or not running because of a blown fuse.

To avoid unnecessary calls, read the checklist in 20-14 before you call for service. Also look to the owner's manual for items to check before calling for service. Most manuals provide a troubleshooting section that can help you identify problems and fix those you can take care of yourself. When servicing is necessary, make sure you understand what caused the problem and what was done to correct it.

The "Before You Request Service" Checklist

- Is the appliance plugged in and turned on?
- Did you check fuses and circuit breakers?
- Are water, gas, or electric connections turned on and operating properly?
- Are the controls set properly for the job you are doing?
- Did you follow all operating instructions?
- Did you check the owner's manual for a possible explanation of the difficulty?
- Did you check the warranty to see if it covers service or parts that may be required?
- Do you have all the data handy to give the service facility—the appliance make, model number, date purchased, and a brief description of the problem?

20-14

You may be able to avoid unnecessary service calls if you run through this checklist before calling for service.

Obsolescence

Most products eventually break or outlive their usefulness. They become obsolete. Obsolescence gives manufacturers the opportunity to introduce new products and increase sales. Consumers benefit when obsolete products are replaced by something better. *Better* can mean something cheaper, more powerful, more efficient, or with more features.

Obsolescence also benefits producers because it stimulates demand. The more often consumers replace an outdated product with a new one, the more they buy overall. Consumer electronics products are especially susceptible to obsolescence because of the constant new developments in technology. Companies also strive to outdo each other in competitive markets. Every company wants to introduce something new. For example, consider the ways that functions and applications for cell phones have changed in the past 10 years.

Planned obsolescence, or built-in obsolescence, occurs when a business designs its products to become obsolete or broken after a certain time or after a certain amount of use. Some ways businesses create obsolescence include the following:

- **Discontinued parts or service.** If consumers cannot have a product fixed, they are forced to buy a new one.

Case Study: Consumer Electronics

Recycling Electronic Products

Fredrick and Omar are seniors in high school. A speaker from the Environmental Protection Agency recently gave a presentation at their school. She talked about the hazards of electronic waste and encouraged the community to dispose of the items safely.

Fredrick and Omar discussed starting an electronics recycling service. They could collect discarded electronics and deliver them to the recycling center 25 miles from town. They could make deliveries twice a month and charge $5 to $15 for a pickup. First, though, they needed to discus expenses, demand, potential profit, and how to publicize their service.

Case Review

1. What do you think of Frederick and Omar's idea?
2. How would you address some of the items Fredrick and Omar discussed as they pursued the possibilities?
3. What services and facilities are available in your area for recycling electronics?
4. Why do you think it is important to recycle electronics? What are the consequences of carelessly disposing electronic waste?

- *Discontinued upgrades.* Consumers must buy a new product when the older one cannot use the latest upgrades and applications. For example, newer computer software programs often require more memory than older computers possess.

- *Unavailable parts or refills.* For example, when printer ink cartridges ran out of ink, the entire cartridge had to be replaced at a high cost. Today, most cartridges are refillable.

- *Use of parts that wear out or break.* Use of cheap, breakable parts during manufacturing can cause a product to wear out sooner.

- *Superficial design changes.* This occurs when consumers are convinced they need to buy new products because they are better looking, more fashionable, or trendy. In the clothing and shoes market, for example, new trends quickly make current fashions obsolete.

As a business strategy, planned obsolescence is risky. Businesses that create products with built-in obsolescence often develop a reputation for poor-quality goods. Consumers will buy from other businesses that offer more durable products.

As a consumer, you can protect your wallet by continuing to use products you own as long as they meet your needs. Buy new products only when improvements offer significant advantages.

Enrich

Ask students to research local solutions to the problem of e-waste. Where can electronic products be safely recycled or discarded? Have students design a poster or brochure listing these resources.

Note

Both mercury and cadmium used in batteries are toxic substances that require proper handling and disposal. Learn and follow any guidelines your community or state has established for disposal of batteries.

Resource

Chapter 20: Electronics and Appliances, Teacher's PowerPoint Presentations CD

Chapter Summary

Buying consumer electronics and appliances was much easier when choices were limited. Today there are dozens of ways to receive phone service, Internet service, and mass communication. New telecommunications industries have been formed. Many industries and the devices they produce are converging.

Consumer electronics and home appliances represent a major investment for most consumers. You should start with a clear idea of your needs and your budget. Learn all you can before investing in electronics and appliances. To make the best choices, consider product performance, operating and safety features, energy efficiency, warranties, and servicing.

Because there are new product developments each year, you will want to find out what is new on the market before buying. Over time, electronic products and appliances will become obsolete. Carefully consider the benefits versus the cost before upgrading to a new model or product.

Review

1. How is telecommunication related to mass communication?

2. Explain what is meant by *convergence* and give one example.

3. What law allowed companies to offer cable, phone, and Internet service?

4. What is the difference between dial-up Internet service and DSL?

5. List three questions to ask before choosing a service provider.

6. List two advantages and two disadvantages of a laptop computer.

7. Why might a person who makes few mobile calls choose a prepaid phone?

8. List five items to consider when choosing a personal media player.

9. What are four ways to prevent online threats?

10. List two types of information you can find on an EnergyGuide label.

11. What information does the ENERGY STAR label give you about an appliance?

12. What are some ways businesses create obsolescence in a product?

Critical Thinking

13. Approximately how many appliances and consumer electronics does your family own? How many do you use daily? Which ones would you consider necessary for your first home?

Answers to *Review*

1. Mass communication is the content delivered through telecommunication.

2. Convergence is the merging of separate devices, technologies, or industries into one. (Examples are student response but may include smart phones and refrigerators with flat screen TVs built in.)

3. the 1996 Telecommunications Act

4. Dial-up uses the telephone line to connect the computer to the Internet and ties up the phone line. DSL uses a digital frequency that does not interfere with telephone service.

5. (List three. Student response. See pages 521–522.)

6. (List two for each:) advantages—portability, takes up limited space; disadvantages—harder to upgrade, costs more for same features on a desktop, can be easily lost

or stolen, wireless connections require more security (Students may justify other responses.)

7. You pay only for the time you use and do not pay monthly service fees.

8. (List five:) memory, compatibility, style, size, ease of use, features, accessories

9. (List four:) Install anti-virus and anti-spy software. Set up a spam filter. Use a firewall. Update protection regularly. Use adequate passwords and authenticiation methods. Back up files regularly.

14. Explore the features in two electronic devices and two major appliances. Characterize each feature as *necessary*, *desirable*, or *unimportant*. How much does each feature add to the cost of the product?

15. What electronic product or home appliance do you or your family plan to replace or buy in the near future? Make a list of the qualities and features you would want in this product and determine a price range. Investigate the product and develop a buying guide that includes a product description, features, warranty terms, energy efficiency data, and price.

16. Investigate telecommunications service providers in your area. Develop a chart outlining the pros and cons of each server. Criteria you might use include the type of access provided, reliability of service, speed, tech support, service packages offered, costs, and contract terms.

17. Investigate at least three forms of cybercrime and the consequences of each. Outline the steps consumers can take to protect themselves.

Academic Connections

18. **Writing, research.** Research and write a report on significant developments in the consumer electronics industry since 1980.

19. **Speech.** In teams, debate the advantages and disadvantages of cell phones in American society.

20. **Social studies.** Research government departments and consumer organizations to contact if you become a victim of cybercrime. Compile a booklet to distribute throughout the school.

21. **Research, speech.** Conduct a survey on safety hazards created by the misuse or abuse of a specific appliance or electronic product. Report your findings to the class. Discuss how the hazards could be avoided through proper use and care of the product.

MATH CHALLENGE

22. You find an MP3 file you want to buy on the Internet. The song is 3 minutes long and was recorded at a bit rate of 128 kilobits (thousands of bits) per second.
    A. Calculate the size of the music file in kilobits.
    B. Digital information is often expressed in *bytes*. One byte equals 8 bits. What is the file size expressed in kilobytes?

Tech $mart

23. The price that utilities charge for electricity changes from hour to hour and month to month. Check your electricity provider's Web site for information about energy pricing and saving tips. See if the Web page shows real-time pricing (the price the utility charges for electricity hour by hour). The price is given in cents per kilowatt-hour (kWh). Use a graphic organizer to display the price of electricity in your area on an hourly basis, including a.m., and p.m., hours. If your provider's Web site does not show this information, use the prices provided at www.thewattspot.com. Find out if your utility offers a real-time pricing program. It could save you money on electric bills.

help you conserve energy and water, keep utility bills down, and protect the environment.

12. by discontinuing parts or service; designing upgrades that require new equipment; making parts or refills unavailable; using parts that wear out or break; and making superficial design changes

Answer to *Math Challenge*

22. A. 3 minutes = 180 seconds; 180 seconds x 128 kilobits/ sec = 23,040 kilobits
    B. 3,040 kilobits ÷ 8 = 2,880 kilobytes

10. estimated yearly energy used and operating costs of the appliance based on national average utility rates, an estimate of the electricity or gas the appliance uses in one year based on typical use

11. The appliance meets strict energy- and water-saving criteria. Using a product with the ENERGY STAR label will

Unit 4
Planning Your Future

In This Unit

Now is the time to begin planning for the training and education you will need to open doors to future opportunities. The career choices you make should fit the way you want to live. Planning for the future also includes considering the impact of your choices. Your activities will have an effect on the planet and the quality of life experienced by future generations.

CHAPTER 21

Planning for Your Career

Reading for Meaning

List the main sections in the chapter, leaving blank lines between each one. As you read each section, write down three to five main ideas that were presented.

career plan

interests

aptitudes

abilities

career clusters

career ladder

e-learning

distance learning

occupational
   training

community college

internship

apprenticeship

Reserve Officers'
   Training Corps
   (ROTC)

continuing
   education

CHAPTER OBJECTIVES

After studying this chapter, you will be able to

- **identify** personal interests, aptitudes, abilities, and personality traits that influence career decisions.
- **prepare** a career plan.
- **list** sources of career information.
- **identify** employment trends.
- **describe** the education and training you will need.
- **outline** the steps you can take to pay for the education and training you will need.

Central Ideas

- Evaluating your personal interests, aptitudes, abilities, values, and goals can help you form a career plan.

- The career clusters can help guide you to choose a career area of interest.

- Once you choose a career path, you can determine the education and training you will need to meet your career goals.

Reflect

How do you picture yourself in the future world of work?

Resource

Worker Profile, reproducible master 21-1, TR

Note

Investigate the median income last year for college graduates and high school graduates by gender. What were the differences? Discuss.

Most Americans enter the workforce at some point in their lives. People work primarily to earn money for life's necessities and a few extras. Most people begin working during their teens or early 20s and continue to retirement age. Because you will likely be working for many years, it pays to get the training and education that will lead to good jobs and good pay.

If you are like most young people, entering the world of work will be a major step. It calls for thoughtful choices. You will spend about one-third of your waking hours at the occupation you choose. Therefore, you will want to find work you can do well *and* enjoy. This can be a challenge.

Some people seem to know from an early age what they want to do with their lives. Most have to search out the jobs that will bring adequate income and job satisfaction. For high school students who plan to go on to college or enter a training program after graduation, the world of work may seem far away. However, it is not too early to begin thinking about your future and the career choices that will bring you satisfaction.

Case Study: Career Choices

Lee Goes from School to His Favorite Hobby

Lee loves computers. He works part-time at Compumart doing sales and service. Compumart offered him a full-time position when he graduates from high school. The money will be good and Lee already knows a lot about the business. The best part is the opportunity to develop new programs and work with the latest equipment.

Eventually, Lee might become a computer programmer or a systems analyst. Both careers require more schooling, so for the moment he just plans to enjoy his job.

Case Review

1. What are the advantages of being able to move right into the job you want from high school? Do you see any disadvantages for Lee?
2. Under what circumstances would Lee be smart to delay his computer job and go to college or enroll in an advanced training program?
3. What are some of the occupations that are open to high school graduates?
4. What other hobbies or activities can you think of that could lead to satisfying full-time employment?

Making a Career Plan

Even if college and training stand between you and the work world, you can begin a career plan once you decide which career fields interest you the most. A **career plan** is an outline of steps or action you can take to reach a career goal. It will include required courses and training, job-related experiences, and extracurricular activities and projects that will help prepare you for the career of your choice. Very often career plans are set up over a number of years from junior high school through college and beyond.

It may be too soon to choose a lifetime career path, but it is not too early to begin thinking about what you would like to do in the world of work. Career planning begins with a careful look at yourself—at what is important to you, what you like to do, what you do well, how you see yourself both now and as an adult. Your interests, aptitudes, skills, and abilities will determine, to a large degree, what type of career will be right for you. Your values and goals will also be important indicators of the type of work that will bring you satisfaction.

Career Counselor

Career counselors help people with career decisions. They explore and evaluate the client's education, training, work history, interests, skills, and personality traits. They may arrange for aptitude and achievement tests to help the client make career decisions. They also work with individuals to develop their job-search skills and assist clients in locating and applying for jobs.

Identify Your Interests

Your **interests** include activities you enjoy, subjects you like, ideas that fascinate you, sports you play, or hobbies you follow. Some of your interests may be key factors in choosing work you will enjoy. Very often, identifying your interests can start with a look at your life. What are your favorite hobbies, subjects, and extracurricular activities?

Projecting yourself into the work world can include a look at you in the present school setting. Consider subjects you have taken. List those you like most. List also the hobbies, activities, and part-time jobs you have pursued outside of school. Which of these interested you the most?

Consider the ways school and nonschool interests could carry over into a job or career, 21-1. For example, if you are a member of a school athletic team, what skills and learning might you develop that would make you a better employee? Maybe you write for the school newspaper, are great with numbers, or are really at home in the science lab. How might these experiences and talents help you find a job? You may be president of the student council, act in the school play, or play in the band. What might you learn that will help you in the work world? What part-time jobs have you held? Has part-time work given you any insight into what you do or do not want to do with your future?

21-1
These teens are learning valuable lessons in cooperation and teamwork. Athletic experience can often help prepare a person for future job situations.

Identify Your Aptitudes and Abilities

A look at your strengths and weaknesses, talents, and skills can lead to deeper self-knowledge. **Aptitudes** refer to natural physical and mental talents. For example, if you score high in verbal aptitude, you may find it relatively easy to learn language arts. You may be well suited for work in written or oral communications. If you do well in math, you may find work with numbers satisfying. It may be possible to take aptitude tests through your school guidance department.

Abilities refer to physical and mental skills developed through learning, training, and practice. You are born with certain aptitudes, but your abilities are learned.

When aptitude and ability go together, you are likely to learn quickly and well. For example, if you are highly coordinated and athletic, you could learn a sport quickly and play relatively well. If you are interested in playing tennis but do not have athletic aptitude, you might overcome a lack of coordination with hard work and practice. When you can put interests, aptitudes, and abilities together into a job choice, you are likely to be successful on the job.

Try to picture yourself at work. If you have a burning desire to paint, act, dance, protect the environment, teach, or practice medicine or law, find out what jobs will let you follow your dream. Take the path that leads to your ultimate goal.

If you enjoy a number of activities but are not clear on a career path, you will need to keep your options open. It might help to consider job categories in terms of what you do well and what you like doing. For example, try completing this sentence: "I like working with _____." Possible answers might be words, numbers, people, animals, plants, machinery, computers, books, ideas, cars, or whatever else you really enjoy. List your options and try to rank them in order of importance. Start with what you like the most and work down to what you like least.

Assess your strengths by completing another sentence: "I am particularly good at _____." Possible answers might include communication, selling, research, acting, design, sports, problem solving, science, helping people, or teamwork. Again, list your strengths, then rank them starting with your greatest strength.

Look at Your Personality

Personality traits also provide a clue to the type of work you can do well and enjoy doing. Seeing yourself as others see you is not always easy, but it is a useful exercise when trying to match yourself to a job. Think about the type of person you are. For example, would others describe you as quiet or talkative, shy or outgoing, tense or easygoing? Are you an energetic self-starter or do you often need a push to get going? Are you quick to try new things, or are you more comfortable with the familiar? Are you cautious, or are you willing to take risks?

Try to write a paragraph describing your personality. Pretend you are writing to a prospective employer for a job you really want. Which of the adjectives in 21-2 would you use?

Assess Your Values and Goals

Consider what you want to do with your life. This will be closely connected with your personal values and goals. *Personal values* are the ideals and principles that are important to you. *Goals* are the specific achievements or objectives you want to reach. The two are usually related. For example, you may place importance on a clean and safe environment. A related work goal may be a job that involves environmental research and protection, waste management, or conservation.

Analyzing personal values and goals can help you make the most appropriate career and job choices. What is really important to you? What contribution do you want to make? Most people need to feel that the work they do has importance and meaning. What job or career will make you feel you are making a difference?

Which of the following adjectives would you apply to yourself?
organized   responsible
persistent
enthusiastic   honest
thorough   cautious
intellectual   helpful
friendly   trustworthy
creative
imaginative   willing
determined   loyal
sensitive   hardworking

21-2

These are just a few of the many terms you might use to describe your personality.

Case Study: Career Choices

Brandy Is a Mass of Indecision

Brandy is a senior in high school and doesn't know what to do after graduation. She was accepted at the state university, but she is sick of school. There is nothing she wants to study or pursue. She thinks the parties and social life at the university sound fun.

Brandy wishes graduation wasn't approaching so fast. High school is fun and not too demanding. Now she has to make hard choices. Should she go to college like many of her friends? Should she look for a job and try living on her own? Should she wait and see what the future brings?

Case Review

1. How would you advise Brandy?
2. If you were undecided and unfocused, what would you do?
3. Do you think it is a good idea to go to college if you aren't interested in going? Why?
4. Where might Brandy go for advice on planning her future?
5. What choices do you see for Brandy? for yourself?

Reflect

What type of work or job would make you feel like you were doing something worthwhile and satisfying?

Activity

Contact two or three major corporations to learn what types of career opportunities they offer in finance.

Reflect

What types of careers in finance appeal to you?

Many people find satisfaction in jobs that serve others. It is possible to serve others in almost any career. However, there are more opportunities in such fields as social work, health care, education, the ministry, and other services to the public.

The Career Clusters

The **career clusters** are 16 general groupings of occupational and career areas, 21-3. The clusters were developed by a partnership among the states, educators, and employers. The object of the career clusters concept is to link material learned in school to a career path. Within each cluster are subgroups called *career pathways*. The pathways reflect associations among occupations that require similar knowledge and skills. These associations help guide students to the course of study they will need to achieve their career goals.

Students may be drawn to one or two of the clusters based on their interests, aptitudes, and abilities. If students focus on one career cluster and pathway, they will learn knowledge and skills related to different occupations in that pathway. This will allow students to be somewhat flexible in choosing an occupation. They can more easily explore different occupations within their areas of interest.

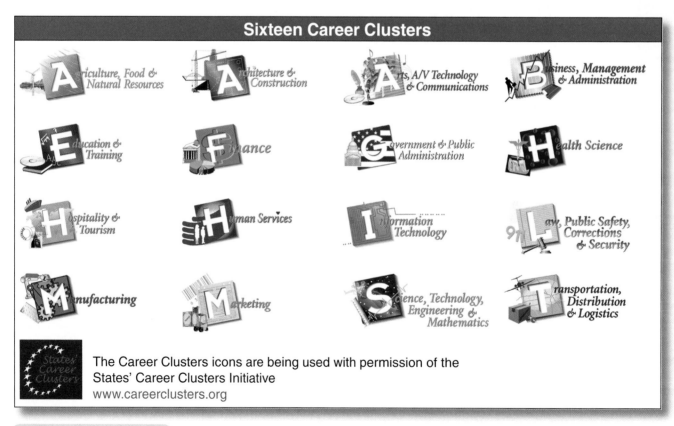

Sixteen Career Clusters

Agriculture, Food & Natural Resources

Architecture & Construction

Arts, A/V Technology & Communications

Business, Management & Administration

Education & Training

Finance

Government & Public Administration

Health Science

Hospitality & Tourism

Human Services

Information Technology

Law, Public Safety, Corrections & Security

Manufacturing

Marketing

Science, Technology, Engineering & Mathematics

Transportation, Distribution & Logistics

The Career Clusters icons are being used with permission of the States' Career Clusters Initiative
www.careerclusters.org

21-3

The career cluster icons represent different career areas. Further information identifies specific careers and the knowledge and skills needed for employment in each one.

The career pathways include jobs from entry-level to management positions. With this information, students can establish a career ladder in a chosen pathway. A **career ladder** is an outline of jobs in a given career field that are available at different levels of education and training and experience, 21-4. This gives you some idea of work opportunities in your chosen field as you progress from one level of learning to the next. The career plan in 21-5 shows how one person planned ahead for a career in the consumer and resource management field.

Career Ladder for Work in Consumer and Resource Management

Advanced Degree	• family counselor • family and consumer sciences educator or extension agent • consumer advocate • consumer affairs director for a corporation or financial institution • executive director of a consumer interest organization
College Degree	• financial planner • consumer journalist • product researcher • consumer information specialist • consumer advocate • consumer education director
Advanced Technical Training	• consumer product tester • consumer product representative • credit counselor • family debt counselor • financial services salesperson • consumer consultant • consumer representative for a utility company • public relations officer for a business
High School Diploma	• consumer hotline operator for the state consumer services office • personal shopper • customer service representative for department store • consumer complaint handler • product demonstrator • research assistant
Pre-High School Graduation	• food planner and shopper for the family • part-time checkout clerk at the supermarket • reporter on consumer issues for the school paper

21-4
This career ladder outlines some of the job opportunities in the consumer and resource management field at different levels of education and training.

Resource
Making a Career Plan, Activity B, WB

Enrich
Select a career that appeals to you and put together a career plan and a career ladder for your chosen field.

Activity
Select a local government agency serving the consumer and interview one of the administrators about services offered and job opportunities.

Discuss
Can you name any columnists, newscasters, and TV personalities who cover consumer and economic issues?

Discuss
What type of training and education would be required for careers in finance?

Career Plan for College Professor in Consumer and Resource Management			
	Education and Training	**Work Experience**	**Personal Projects and Activities**
Junior High School	• family and consumer sciences courses • extra credit projects related to consumer issues	• operate an errand service for neighborhood families	• family meal planner and food shopper • comparison shopper for family purchases
Senior High School	• take college prep issues courses with emphasis on consumer economics	• part-time checkout clerk at the supermarket	• start a consumer study group at school • research consumer product purchases
College	• take B.S. degree program in family and consumer sciences	• part-time consumer product tester	• volunteer in student financial aid department • consumer issues editor for student newspaper
After College	• enroll in graduate consumer sciences program • complete graduate degree	• part-time consumer research assistant • assistant professorship in family and consumer sciences • full professor and department head	• continue involvement in consumer issues

21-5

This career plan shows the planned steps toward a career goal beginning in junior high school and going through college.

Business, Management & Administration

Human Resources Specialists

Human resource specialists focus on the recruitment and management of the people who work for an organization. They deal with hiring, firing, performance management, structuring of employee positions, safety, wellness, benefits, employee motivation, communication, and training.

Study the Job Market

Knowing a few basic facts about different jobs and careers can help you make the right choices in the work world. Study the job market as you make career decisions. What careers and occupations do you think will be in the greatest demand over the next ten to twenty years? Take a look at the help-wanted sections in the newspapers and online to learn what fields offer the most job opportunities in the present.

Job and Career Information

It is important to learn what you can about the occupations and careers that interest you. You will want to look for job areas that offer the most and best opportunities for the future. Early planning can help you find the courses and experiences that will open career doors for you later. Following is a list of some of the many sources of career and job information that are readily available.

Career Guides

The U. S. Department of Labor sponsors a variety of career information resources including the following:

- O*NET is the principal source of information about occupations in the United States. Its Web site is http://online.onetcenter.org. You can use the site to search for specific occupations or search for occupations that match skills you possess. You can also search for jobs that are currently in high demand.

- The *Occupational Outlook Handbook*, updated every two years, profiles over 250 jobs. For each, it describes work activities, earnings, education and training requirements, personal qualifications, and outlook for employment. The *Handbook* is available in most public libraries and online at www.bls.gov/oco.

- *CareerOneStop* provides information about education and training, salary and benefits, and résumés and interviews. Its address is www.careeronestop.org. This site provides links to other helpful sites, including *America's Career Infonet, America's Service Locator,* and *Career Voyages.*

- *Occupational Outlook Quarterly* includes practical, up-to-date information about job choices and preparation for the careers of your choice in the job markets of today and tomorrow. It can be found online at www.bls.gov/opub/ooq.

Internet

The Internet is an incredible tool for researching colleges, jobs, career information, and employment opportunities. Most colleges and universities have Web sites that provide information on the school, courses of study, tuition, financial aid, scholarships, and other details. You may even be able to take certain courses online.

You can conduct a widespread job/career search on the Internet, 21-6. It allows you to post your résumé, locate job listings and related information, research individual companies, and explore career opportunities and employment trends. You can also apply for some jobs online. If you do not have Internet access at home, you may be able to go online at school or at your public library. Ask for any assistance you need.

Career and Job Search Web Sites	
dol.gov	careers.org
bls.gov	quintcareers.com
usajobs.gov	hotjobs.yahoo.com
careers.msn.com	jobweb.com
jobbankusa.com	wetfeet.com
monster.com	jobfox.com

School Guidance Counselors

In many schools, guidance counselors offer a wealth of job information. They can help you determine the areas best suited to your aptitudes and abilities. The guidance department at your school may provide files of information on education, training, and careers. Counselors may also help you evaluate your options, direct you to more information, and guide

21-6

These are useful Web sites for job searches and career information.

Discuss

In what ways has the Internet made job searching easier? Would you be comfortable posting the personal information contained in a resume on the Internet?

Enrich

Visit the Web to learn more about job opportunities in the fields that interest you. Try the Web sites listed in 21-6.

Enrich

Invite a school guidance counselor to speak to the class about job opportunities, training, and education.

you in the choice of a college or training program. Check out the guidance department in your school to find out what services it offers.

Libraries

School and community libraries also offer a host of information. Some libraries may have an education and employment section containing a variety of books and publications. When searching online or in card catalogs, look under headings such as *careers, colleges and universities, jobs,* and *occupations.* Also check headings related to specific career fields that interest you.

Career Events

Special career days at school and career fairs in the community can provide up-to-date information on jobs, education, and training. In addition, college or business representatives often visit high schools to speak with interested students. It is a good idea to take advantage of both. You can learn firsthand about opportunities in the work world. It is also helpful to talk to people who work in fields that interest you. Ask about job training, experience and qualifications needed, and opportunities in the field.

Employment Trends

In job markets, it is very possible that today's opportunity will become tomorrow's dead end. It is important to stay abreast of new technology and to follow the trends in industry, 21-7. Consider where the best jobs are likely to surface given current trends and developments. The *Occupational Outlook Handbook* can help you keep up with these changes. Following the news and relating it to the work world will also give you timely clues to upcoming opportunities.

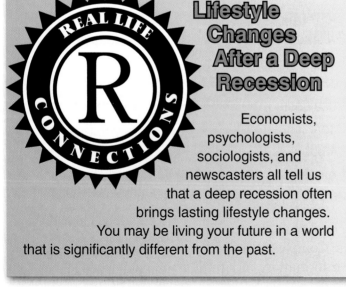

Lifestyle Changes After a Deep Recession

Economists, psychologists, sociologists, and newscasters all tell us that a deep recession often brings lasting lifestyle changes. You may be living your future in a world that is significantly different from the past.

After a serious recession, people are likely to drive less and walk, bike, and take public transit more frequently. Many buy smaller, more fuel-efficient cars. Consumers may travel less and experience more close-to-home vacations. They likely spend less on entertainment, eating out, expensive clothing, and unnecessary items. The overall trend is to spend less and save more.

Consumers become more judicious in their use of credit and credit cards. Many begin to save for major purchases instead of charging them. Many people defer retirement plans, and others seek meaningful later-life careers.

New technology requires highly trained and skilled workers in a variety of fields. Untrained workers will either be unemployed or remain at bottom-level, low-paying jobs. Not only is initial training important, the willingness to retrain over the years is equally important. Technology makes dramatic and sometimes sudden changes. These changes often lead to a demand for workers with different types of skills and training. You need to learn and relearn work skills over a lifetime.

Economic factors, both at home and around the world, can seriously affect employment in different fields. Recession, inflation, tax policies, and international trade all have an impact on what and how many jobs are available. These factors also affect the qualifications workers will need to find employment. For example, when unemployment is high and jobs are hard to find, training, education, and competence become even more important in finding and keeping a job. When taxes and interest rates are high, there may be fewer jobs because businesses are less likely to expand and are more likely to cut back on hiring.

Economic conditions can vary around the world and from one part of the country to another. It pays to look at opportunities in different areas when you are searching for employment. Supply and demand in the job market varies greatly from one field of employment to another and from one area to another.

Think long and hard about your career goals. The work you choose will affect the way you live, the people you meet, the money you earn, and the satisfaction you get out of work and life. Try to decide what will be the best preparation for the work you want. Will you need a college degree or occupational training? Will the job require an internship, an apprenticeship, or previous work experience? Will you need a combination of these to achieve your career goals? This is a good time to start planning for your future.

21-7
New jobs are being created in renewable energy industries. Wind farms are one source of renewable energy.

Plan the Training and Education You Need

In the years ahead, a college education or occupational training will be required for many jobs. It will be an advantage in almost all occupations. Preparation for the work you want will normally pay off in the form of higher earning power, better job opportunities, greater job satisfaction, and security. It can enrich your life in other ways as well.

Following high school, you will find many opportunities for further education and training. Your choices will depend largely on the career

Discuss

How do current economic conditions affect the job market?

Reflect

What are your career goals and how do they relate to the way you want to live your life?

Reflect

What are your plans for the future in terms of school and job training?

Activity

Write a paragraph answering the questions about your personal educational goals.

Activity

Write a description of the type of college or future training you would like to attend.

Activity

Write a description of your qualifications for college including academic, athletic, and other extracurricular achievements.

path you want to pursue. The following pages describe several after-high school options that may work for you.

College or University Education

Higher education will be the first choice for many high school students. It can be the most costly single investment of a lifetime. It can also bring the best return in higher earnings, better job opportunities, and a fuller life. If college is in your plans for the future, start planning now. There are many factors to consider in choosing a school and field of study.

Personal Goals

Take a look at your reasons for going to college. Are you interested in a specific field of study? Do you want to learn more in broad areas to help you decide what you want to pursue in greater depth? Is your primary goal to learn and broaden your horizons or to qualify for a particular career? Answers to these questions can help you choose the path to your future education and career choices.

Personal Preferences

Consider whether a small or large school appeals more to you. Do you want to be near home or far away? What part of the country attracts you

ECONOMICS in ACTION

Financing Education

In an extended economic downturn, many families find it difficult to save enough money for college or job training. Normal sources of cash for college become scarce. Grants and loans become harder to get. Investments in savings programs lose value. Colleges and universities experience declining values in their endowments and dwindling contributions. State governments are often forced to cut funding for state schools, which means increases in tuitions and fees.

Demand for financial aid becomes stronger, which makes it difficult to qualify for available assistance. While financial aid becomes more limited, college costs are rising. In 2009 the average annual cost for in-state students at four-year universities came close to $7,000. At some private schools, the cost was over $25,000. At the same time, the importance of education has never been more important for individual students and for the country.

In order to finance an education, families need to start planning and saving as early as possible. As a student, you should work toward a high school record of achievement that will appeal to college admissions boards. Explore every possible source of money for college—scholarships, grants, loans, savings, work/study programs, and part-time work. Also remember to complete and submit a Free Application for Federal Student Aid through www.fafsa.gov.

Case Study: Career Choices

Monique Wants to Change the World

Monique is a junior in high school. She gets good grades and is active in student government. She participates in student organizations for animal rights, community service, conservation, and adult literacy.

Monique won the "Teen Volunteer of the Year" award for organizing a food and clothing drive. Last summer, Monique worked as an intern at a local campaign office.

Monique intends to go to a top college and then law school. After she finishes her education, Monique wants to find a job in Washington. Finally, she wants to run for office—the Congress, the Senate, or even the White House.

Case Review

1. What do you think of Monique's plan of action?
2. How might Monique's activities and accomplishments to this point help her reach her ultimate goals?
3. In what ways do you think Monique is unusual?
4. What future goals and objectives are important enough to you that you would work and sacrifice now in order to achieve them?
5. How do you see yourself immediately after high school and beyond?

most? Weigh the pros and cons of an urban versus a rural setting, and private versus state schools.

Your Record and Performance

Colleges look at grades, test scores, class rank, activities, special talents, and other achievements of prospective students. Some schools are more competitive than others. However, if you have a reasonably good record and really want to go to college, there will be a school for you. Prepare a résumé and outline your strongest points to present to the admissions office of the schools that interest you.

College Choices Open to You

Schools differ greatly. No doubt several will meet your needs and accept you as a student. When looking at colleges, check out and compare the following:

Reflect

What can you do now, other than study, to help you prepare for the future world of work?

Discuss

Emphasize that there is more than one "right" school. Each student will choose at least three schools that would meet his or her needs.

21-8

In choosing a college, you will consider many factors, including a college's library system.

Enrich

Obtain copies of financial aid applications to study and explain in class.

Enrich

Collect college brochures and pamphlets and use them to create a bulletin board or display.

Resource

Choosing a College, Activity C, WB

- *Programs of study.* Look at the courses offered in different fields, foreign study opportunities, work-study, student-designed majors, and exchange programs with other schools.

- *Faculty.* Consider the number of doctorates, faculty/student ratio, and the academic reputation of the school—particularly in the field you want to pursue.

- *Facilities.* Check out the library, science labs, computer labs, athletic facilities, fitness programs, and other items of special interest to you, 21-8.

- *Environment.* Find out about dormitories and living quarters, the makeup of the student body, extracurricular activities, campus size and setting, existence and importance of fraternities and sororities, safety on campus, and other factors that are important to you.

- *Geographic location and campus setting.* Think about whether you wish or need to be close to home. Do you wish to go to school in a different part of the country? What advantages do you see in one part of the country versus another? Do you prefer an urban or more rural setting?

- *Cost.* Determine the total amount of tuition, room and board, fees, books, and overall cost of living.

- *Financial aid.* Investigate loans, scholarships, grants, part-time job opportunities, and work-study programs.

You also may want to compare private versus public schools, coed versus single sex, religious versus non-denominational, and small versus large schools. Visit the colleges you are considering if possible to get a sense of life on campus and the academic focus. Most colleges operate Web sites that provide detailed information on all aspects of college life. You can find almost unlimited sources of information online. Other sources include

- catalogs and printed material from schools that interest you

- college and career orientation programs and fairs

- college representatives who visit your school or community

- students and graduates of schools that interest you

College and Job Training Online

Online education and training offerings include college and university courses, training for specific occupations, certification programs, and company-sponsored employee training. You may be able to earn a college degree online or complete certification requirements in a variety of fields. This also is an excellent way to continue your education, enhance career advancement, and enjoy lifetime learning.

Internet education and training programs are called **e-learning**. These are forms of **distance learning** in which education or training is delivered to the student online, by mail, or on television. Distance learning offers many choices in both individual courses and total program options. Before signing up for any form of distance learning, do some homework on course selection and on the schools and institutions offering courses. The U.S. Distance Learning Association (USDLA) is an excellent source of information. The following are some questions to guide your decisions:

- What prerequisites must you meet to enroll? Find out whether you need a high school diploma, a college degree, or specific skills to take the course or program you want. Ask what computer skills you need to complete course work.

- What equipment and supplies will you need? You will probably need an up-to-date Internet browser and multimedia applications. You may need cable or digital access to the Internet. Find out what you need and the cost of required equipment you do not already own, 21-9.

- What computer skills might you need? Be sure you can manage the computer tasks the course demands.

- What is the offering institution's reputation and reliability? Find out if it is accredited by an agency that is recognized by the U. S. Department of Education. It should also be licensed in the state where it is headquartered. Look for accredited programs that promise qualified instructors, complete and up-to-date instructional materials and methods, and adequate reference materials. Check to see whether any credits you earn are transferable. It also is a good idea to check out the institution's standing among employers in the field you are studying.

- What qualifications, degrees, and experience do faculty members bring to the class? Find out what you can about instructors and about the way they relate to students. Reputable institutions will be proud of their faculties and ready to answer your questions about their qualifications.

- What teaching and instruction methods are used? Formats for online learning include video, e-mail, discussion boards, chat rooms, books, interactive communication with instructors and other students, and combinations of these. Look for the format and methods that best fit your learning style.

- What is the cost of the course or program? Find out the cost of tuition, fees, supplies, books and software, and any equipment you will need. Total all expenses and find out what payment arrangements you can make through the institution or elsewhere.

21-9

If you choose a distance learning program, make sure you have or can purchase the necessary equipment.

Discuss

Are there any types of e-learning offered at your high school now? Are there any components of your classes that are offered electronically? How do these options affect the classes to which they apply?

Reflect

Would you ever be interested in participating in distance learning? Why or why not?

Activity

Have students research the cost of e-learning classes. How do these compare with the cost of comparable classes at a university or local community college?

- How does the institution's Web site look to you? When you learn online it is important to be able to navigate the Web site where instructions and materials will be made available to you. Take a careful look at this site and see if you can find information you want with ease. Does it include toll-free phone numbers and tech support in case you have trouble accessing the site?

- How are students and assignments evaluated? Find out whether you will be preparing papers, participating in online discussions, or completing projects for your grade. Are there midterm or final exams? Will you receive constructive comments and suggestions on papers and projects you complete?

- What do you receive when you complete the course or program? Find out whether you will receive a degree or a certificate in a specific field. Ask what assistance you can expect in finding suitable employment as a result of work you complete. Ask about the institution's success in placing graduates in desirable jobs and careers.

Note that TV stations may also offer both academic and occupational courses for credit or certification. This form of distance learning can be an effective and relatively inexpensive way to get the education and training you need. Check program listings in your area for courses offered.

Keep in mind that there are both pros and cons to distance learning. There is no face-to-face teacher or classroom contact to assist and motivate students to complete the work. It is easy to procrastinate. You may need advanced computer skills, and you will have to find whatever support you need online. Distance learning offers no social interaction with other students and no campus atmosphere. Even so, for students with the ability to work independently, distance learning can be an excellent path to the education you need.

Occupational Training

Preparing for employment in a specific field may be a smart move for many students. This type of education generally costs less and takes less time than a college degree. **Occupational training**, which prepares you for a specific type of work, is available through a variety of schools and programs in addition to online offerings. You may want to consider one of the following options:

21-10
Occupational training can often be the fastest way into the field of your choice if you know what you want to do. This student is training to be a medical technician.

- Occupational schools are usually privately owned and depend on satisfying students for their continued success. Training, equipment, facilities, and qualifications of instructors vary greatly, 21-10. Check thoroughly before enrolling.

Case Study: Career Choices

Omar Knows What He Wants

After graduating high school, Omar plans to enter an emergency medical technician (EMT) program. He wants to become a paramedic.

Omar may also train to be a firefighter. The job outlook and pay is better for combination paramedics and firefighters. In addition to job security, Omar likes the idea of knowing what to do in several types of emergencies.

Case Review

1. What do you think of Omar's plan for the future?
2. With his interest in medicine, what advantages or disadvantages might there be in considering nursing or medical school rather than paramedics?
3. What advantages and disadvantages do you see in Omar's plan?

- **Community colleges** are usually two-year schools offering both academic and occupational courses. It may be possible to transfer credits from a community college to a four-year college degree program.

- Adult education programs include academic and occupational courses offered in a "night school" setting. They may be an extension of a nearby college or university or offered through the local board of education. Course offerings vary in different areas.

- Online and home-study programs are offered by public and private schools and colleges. Today most of these will be at least partly online presentations. Students fulfill the course requirements at home and mail or e-mail their work to the school for evaluation and credit.

- Employer-sponsored training is often offered to new employees to teach them how to operate equipment or perform certain job skills. Many companies provide this type of training online.

Since the quality and content of occupational education varies greatly, investigate carefully before enrolling. Be sure you understand all the terms of any agreement or enrollment contract before you sign it. In making your choices, look for

- qualified, experienced instructors

- adequate, up-to-date equipment and facilities

Vocabulary

Define and describe each of the listed sources of occupational training.

Activity

Prepare a directory of occupational training opportunities in your area.

Enrich

Ask representatives of reputable local occupational training schools or programs to visit the class and describe their programs.

Resource

Choosing an Occupational Training Program, Activity D, WB

Reflect

What interests and talents do you possess that you could develop through an internship program?

- state licensing or accreditation from industry or educational agencies
- recommendations from prospective employers and former students
- reasonable costs for tuition, equipment, supplies, and fees
- fair policies on transferring credits and refunds for non-completed courses
- degrees or certifications you need for the employment you seek

Internships

An **internship** is a short-term position with a sponsoring organization that gives the intern an opportunity to gain on-the-job experience in a certain field of study or occupation. Internships are available in a variety of career areas. You can find listings online at www.internweb.com or www.usinterns.com.

Case Study: Career Choices

Raul Looks to Internships

Raul is a junior in high school and is known for his artistic talent. His paintings often win awards in local art exhibits. He recently led a community mural painting project, and his technique earned recognition from several established artists.

Raul wants to pursue art after high school, but he can't afford college. His school counselor suggested an art-related internship. An internship might not pay well, but it would open doors in the future.

On the Internet, Raul searched for internships where he could paint and learn about creative arts careers. With the help of his counselor, Raul applied for five internships that met his requirements.

Case Review

1. What advantages does an internship offer someone like Raul?
2. What disadvantages do you see in internship programs?
3. What are some factors to consider when applying for and choosing an internship program?
4. What might internships offer for the college graduate?

Apprenticeships

An **apprenticeship** is a combination of on-the-job training, work experience, and classroom instruction. About 350 apprenticeships are registered with the Bureau of Apprenticeship and Training, a division of the U.S. Department of Labor. Over 800 occupations fall into the apprentice category. The jobs involve manual, mechanical, or technical skills, 21-11. An apprenticeship requires on-the-job work experience along with classroom or other types of learning. These programs offer pay and job benefits, training by experienced tradespeople, certification, and improved employment opportunities. The regulations governing apprenticeships were updated in 2008. For more information contact the nearest regional or state office of the Bureau of Apprenticeships and Training or look online at www.doleta.gov/oa/regulations.cfm.

The Armed Forces

The military offers a wide range of education and training programs at little or no cost both through recruitment services and the **Reserve Officers' Training Corps (ROTC)**. Some high schools offer Junior Reserve Officers' Training Corps (JROTC) to prepare high school students for leadership roles. If your school has this program, you may want to investigate its benefits. Each branch of the service also offers a service academy where students can earn tuition-free college degrees.

Vocational Rehabilitation Counselors

Vocational rehabilitation counselors counsel people coping with personal, social, and vocational difficulties that result from birth defects, illness, disease, accidents, or the stress of daily life. They help to maximize each client's independence and employability, assess client needs, and design and implement rehabilitation programs that may include personal and vocational counseling, training, and job placement.

Vocabulary

Differentiate between *internship* and *apprenticeship*.

Activity

Contact the Bureau of Apprenticeship and Training for more information on apprenticeship programs.

Enrich

Contact the nearest ROTC office for information on educational offerings and opportunities. Discuss in class.

21-11

Valuable on-the-job work experience can be acquired from an apprenticeship. This construction foreman is training a new worker.

In colleges, ROTC involves taking ROTC courses and training along with college courses. Participants enter the service as officers upon graduation. ROTC graduates make up approximately 39 percent of all active duty officers in the Department of Defense. The service commitment varies, but usually calls for several years of active duty followed by a period of time in the reserves. The ROTC program is slightly different in each branch of the service.

In addition to education and training opportunities, those who enter the military through the ROTC program generally receive good salaries and generous benefits such as health care, housing, travel opportunities, and use of social and athletic facilities. However, once in the service, there is always the possibility of being called to active duty during times of war. Participants are also required to serve out the entire term of their contracts—two, four, or six years. In most cases, it is not possible to resign or quit early.

Continuing Education

Continuing education is learning you pursue after you complete your formal education and training. It can take many forms, from individual courses to complete programs. You may choose to continue your education in order to advance on a current job, to qualify for employment in a new field, or simply for personal satisfaction. Many of the education and training opportunities already discussed offer continuing education possibilities. Some careers require a specific program of continuing education. Keeping up-to-date in your field is an advantage in almost all occupations.

Paying for Training and Education

When you invest, you are using money to make money. Education is an investment in yourself. Higher education and job training programs can cost thousands of dollars. Deciding how much you can afford to invest and how you will pay for it requires careful thought. The following are a few steps to guide you in financing your education:

- Estimate the cost of attending the colleges or occupational schools you are seriously considering.

- Estimate the resources available to you, including savings, investments, student earnings, and family income.

- Measure estimated costs against estimated resources to determine how much additional money you need.

- Consider ways to cut costs without sacrificing important goals and objectives for your future.

- Search for additional resources—scholarships, grants, loans, and earnings—to help pay for your education.

Financial aid for students comes in many forms. An online search of the sites listed in 21-12 is a good place to start looking for the help you may need. The federal government offers a variety of financial aid programs including scholarships, grants, and student loans. A number of nongovernment agencies also sponsor student financial aid programs, as do many colleges and universities. If you have a reasonable high school record, search for options diligently. You will likely find the help you need to complete the education or training for the career of your choice.

Education and Financial Aid Web Sites

Financialaidfinder.com	Studentaid.ed.gov
IEFA.org	Ed.gov/finaid
Students.gov	Mymoney.gov/ education
Nasfaa.org	

21-12
These Web sites can help you zero in on sources of financial aid for higher education.

Activity

Make a directory of sources to contact for financial aid.

Enrich

Summarize your career goals and outline steps you plan to follow in reaching them.

Resource

Chapter 21: Planning for Your Career, Teacher's PowerPoint Presentations CD

Chapter Summary

You will spend almost one-third of your waking hours at whatever job you choose. Finding work you can do well and enjoy is important. It requires an objective assessment of your interests, aptitudes, and abilities. It calls for insight into your personality, values, goals, and expectations for the future. It will pay to work out a career plan that can lead you to work choices and opportunities that suit your interests and fit the way you wish to live.

Knowledge about the career clusters will help you make intelligent career choices. Once you narrow down your interests, you need to learn what qualifications, training, and education are required for the areas you want to pursue. As you search out employment opportunities, look to reliable sources of career information. These include government publications, the Internet, school guidance counselors, and public libraries. Career days and exhibits can also offer reliable information and guidance.

Now is the time to begin planning for the training and education you will need. Explore the opportunities open to you, including four-year colleges and universities, community colleges, and occupational training. Take time to learn about education and training opportunities offered online. Internships and apprenticeships may open doors in certain fields. The Armed Forces also offer job training and college courses.

Paying for training and education after high school requires advance planning for most families. It begins with estimates of costs and of resources with plans to cover the difference. Financial aid may be available to some. Scholarships and other forms of assistance exist as well.

Review

1. How do interests, aptitudes, and abilities apply to education and career choices?

2. Give an example of how values and goals affect career choices.

3. List three reliable sources of information on job and career opportunities.

4. Give two ways that employment trends in industry and technology affect job markets.

5. What are four factors to consider when choosing a college?

6. What are five questions to consider in choosing online learning opportunities?

7. Name three sources of occupational training.

8. Where can you find detailed information about internships and apprenticeships?

9. What are two advantages and two disadvantages of receiving training and education through the Armed Forces?

Critical Thinking

10. Discuss the key advantages and disadvantages of going from high school to each of the following:
    - college
    - occupational training
    - an internship
    - an apprenticeship
    - the Armed Forces

CareerOneStop, *Occupational Outlook Quarterly*, school guidance counselors, Web sites, libraries, career fairs and events, potential employers, employment classified sections in newspapers

Answers to *Review*

1. They are keys to helping individuals make appropriate career choices.
2. (Student response.)
3. (List three:) O*NET, *Occupational Outlook Handbook*,

11. What are the pros and cons of going to college when you do not really want to go and have no special field you wish to study?

12. What types of experiences and activities in high school do you feel would be helpful in getting full-time employment? Explain.

13. What career fields or job areas are of particular interest to you? How might you begin to pursue these interests while still in high school?

14. What types of training and education do you think would be required to obtain the type of employment and position you want to achieve?

15. Discuss advantages, disadvantages, and cautions to consider in e-learning or other forms of distance learning.

Academic Connections

16. **Writing.** Obtain and study college application forms. These may be available from the guidance office at your school, at the public library, or online. Complete forms as practice for filling out forms correctly. Write essays as required for the college applications of your choice.

17. **Reading, writing.** Review the help-wanted section of the local paper or go online to find at least three jobs you would like. Discuss the reasons these jobs appeal to you. Write a letter that you could use to request an interview for one of the positions.

4. (List two:) types and numbers of jobs available, training and qualifications required for different types of employment, creation of new jobs, competition in job markets

5. (List four:) personal goals, personal preferences, record and performance, college choices open to you, faculty, facilities, environment, cost, financial aid possibilities

6. (List five:) What are the prerequisites? What equipment and supplies are needed? What computer skills are needed? What is the institution's reputation and reliability? What qualifications, degrees, and experience do faculty members have? What teaching and instruction methods are used? What is the cost? Is the Web site easy to navigate? How are students evaluated? Do you receive a degree or certificate upon completion?

7. (Name three:) occupational or vocational schools, community colleges, adult education programs, correspondence courses, employer-sponsored training

18. **Research.** Research and outline your findings in one of the following areas:
- finding a college
- apprenticeship and internship opportunities
- conducting a job search
- occupational outlook for the next decade and beyond

Math Challenge

19. Obtain college financial aid forms. These may be available from the guidance office at your school or online. Complete forms as practice for filling out forms correctly. Identify what types and amounts of financial aid you might be eligible to receive from three different schools.

Tech Smart

20. Using a word processing program or spreadsheet software, develop charts to use in assessing yourself and assessing job or career choices.

21. Using a word processing program, develop an annotated bibliography of informative sources on college choices, occupational training programs, internship opportunities, and apprenticeships. Use the footnote features of the program to create the annotations.

22. Investigate distance learning opportunities available to you via Internet and television. Pick one program that appeals to you and obtain detailed information you would need before enrolling in the program.

8. regional or state office of the Bureau of Apprenticeship and Training and online

9. (Name two each:) advantages—wide range of training and educational opportunities at little or no cost, good salaries, generous benefits (paid health care, free housing, and travel), veteran's benefits after leaving the military; disadvantages—commitment of several years in the service, possibility of being called to active duty during times of war or crisis, requirement of taking orders and sacrificing personal control over your life

22

Entering the Work World

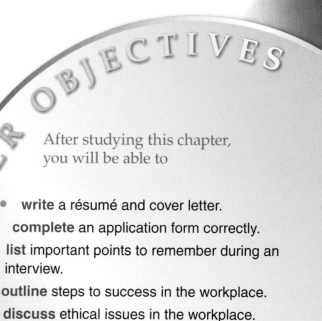

Reading for Meaning

With a friend or a classmate, role-play a job interview. Switch roles so each of you play both the employer and the employee. After you read the chapter, perform the role-plays a second time using what you learned.

résumé

reference

interview

entrepreneur

sole proprietorship

partnership

corporation

franchise

dual-career family

social responsibility

CHAPTER OBJECTIVES

After studying this chapter, you will be able to

- **write** a résumé and cover letter.
- **complete** an application form correctly.
- **list** important points to remember during an interview.
- **outline** steps to success in the workplace.
- **discuss** ethical issues in the workplace.
- **list** advantages and disadvantages of becoming an entrepreneur.
- **distinguish** between multiple roles of adults.

Central Ideas

- Learning to properly prepare résumés, cover letters, and applications will help you get hired.

- Following workplace ethics can help you succeed on the job.

- Workers must learn to balance their work life with family time and social responsibility.

Getting a Job

Whether you are going from school to a training program, a college, or a job, there are several skills you will want to master. These include writing a résumé and cover letter, filling out an application form, and interviewing. These are likely to turn up more than once in your lifetime. It will benefit you to learn how to be successful in each situation.

The Résumé

A **résumé** is an outline of what you have to offer a prospective employer, school, or organization, 22-1. You may need to tailor your résumé for different purposes, but the basic information and general format will be the same. It should be typed and include the following:

- Identifying information—your name, address, and phone number.

- Goals and objectives—a specific statement of what you expect to bring to and learn from the school, program, or job you want.

- Education—schools attended, dates, degrees earned, class rank, major and minor areas of study, and courses completed.

- Work experience—a listing of jobs held with names and addresses of employers, dates, and brief descriptions of responsibilities. Be sure to include both paid and volunteer positions that give a true picture of your previous experience.

- Activities and honors—names of school or community activities and organizations in which you have participated, offices held, honors received, and any specific skills and talents you possess if they would be assets on the job.

- References—on your résumé, state "References available upon request." A **reference** is a person who is qualified and willing to speak on your behalf. References may include former teachers, employers, counselors, or others with knowledge of your character and qualifications. Always ask permission from anyone you wish to use as a reference. Provide the name, title, address, and phone number of each reference.

Some potential employers may ask for an electronic résumé. In these cases, save your prepared résumé in a separate file without formatting, such as text only format. Then you can attach this file in an e-mail to the employer contact. (Be sure not to save over your original résumé, with its spacing, special font use, and other formatting.)

The Cover Letter

This letter introduces you and your résumé. It also gives you an opportunity to expand on material in the résumé, 22-2. Print out your letter on

Kim R. Garcia

1036 Spring Street
Vallejo, California 94590
(707) 555-3214
kgarcia@provider.com

Objective	Mature and responsible high school senior seeks an entry-level job as an office assistant.
Work Experience	• Watkins Sportswear, Vallejo, CA 9/20XX–present Retail Sales Person Assisted customers with clothing and athletic shoe selections; scanned purchases and collected payment from customers; inventoried stock monthly; returned merchandise to racks and shelves. • Ojay's Restaurant, Vallejo, CA 6/20XX–9/20XX Grill Crewperson Prepared and cooked food; cleaned work area.
Volunteer Experience	• Solano County Food Bank 12/20XX–present Solicited food donations from grocery store and restaurant managers; prepared bags of food for clients; designed and distributed informational flyers to community groups. • Vallejo Recreation Department 6/20XX–9/20XX Coached elementary school students in playing soccer.
Education	Vallejo High School, Vallejo, CA 20XX to present; Graduation date: 6/12/20XX Emphasis on business education and accounting.
Honors and Activities	National Honor Society, 20XX–20XX Business Professionals of America, member, 20XX–20XX. Treasurer during junior year. Vallejo High School Student Council during sophomore year. 4-H member for eight years.
Skills	Proficient with Microsoft Word, Excel, PowerPoint, and Internet. Fluent in Spanish. *References available upon request.*

22-1

Your résumé is one of the first things that introduces you to a prospective employer. It pays to give it careful, detailed attention.

Discuss

How do you expect your résumé to change with future education, training, and experience?

Activity

Go online to find sample résumés and pointers for writing a good résumé. Write your own résumé for a job of your choice.

Kim R. Garcia
1036 Spring St.
Vallejo, CA 94590

April 25, 20XX

Mr. Robert Drake
Personnel Manager
Whitaker Publishing Company
1822 W. Meridian St.
Vallejo, CA 94590

Dear Mr. Drake:

Through Mr. James Mitchell, vocational counselor at Hogan High School in Vallejo, I learned your company plans to hire a full-time office assistant in June. I know your company is a worldwide leader in outdoor publications and I would like to apply for this position.

To prepare for office work, I have taken a number of business courses in high school. As mentioned in my résumé, I am skilled in Microsoft Word, Excel, PowerPoint, and navigating the Internet. I am also fluent in Spanish. I am presently gaining on-the-job experience as a retail salesperson with Watkins Sportswear. With my education and work experience, I feel confident I can perform well as an office assistant for your company.

May I have an interview to discuss the job and my qualifications in greater detail? I can be reached at 707-555-3214 or at kgarcia@provider.com. I will appreciate the opportunity to talk with you. Thank you for taking time to consider my application.

Sincerely,

Kim R. Garcia

Kim R. Garcia

22-2

A cover letter gives you another opportunity to make a positive impression.

good-quality paper, taking care to use correct spelling and punctuation. Include the following:

- your name, address, and phone number
- the date
- name, title, and address of the person receiving the letter
- the purpose of the letter—to go with your résumé, ask for an interview, or inquire about a position

- a brief statement of your interest in the school, job, or program for which you are applying

- highlights from your résumé along with other pertinent information on your experience or qualifications

- mention of follow-up steps you plan to take, such as calling to arrange an interview; include how and where you can be reached for an interview or more information

- a thank you

The Application Form

It pays to master application forms, because they will come up in one way or another throughout your life. You complete application forms for jobs, schools, credit, apartments, mortgages, and insurance, 22-3. Following are some pointers to help you complete a typical application form:

- Copy the form so you can work on it before completing the final form to submit.

- Read the entire form before filling in any spaces. Be sure you understand each question before trying to answer it.

- Follow directions with care, making sure to write clearly and spell correctly.

- Complete all the questions that apply to you on the front and back of the form. For those that do not apply, write "Not applicable" or "NA."

- Give factual, accurate, and positive answers to questions about your education, work history, and past experience.

- Include names, titles, addresses, and phone numbers of former employers and references.

The Interview

An **interview** is a talk between you and the admissions officer of a school or a prospective employer. This is an important talk and calls for careful preparation. Following are some tips for interviewing.

Learn Important Background Information

Find out as much as you can about the school, company, or program for which you are applying. Be informed about your field of interest, if it is established at this point.

Anticipate What Questions Might Be Asked of You

These may include: Why do you want to go to school here, work for our company, or apply for this position? What can you contribute to our school or organization? What are your strengths and weaknesses? What

Resource

Apply Here, Activity A, WB

Activity

Check the job market online and download applications for different jobs. Fill out three or four applications for practice. If you are actually looking for a job, submit your application online.

Enrich

Role-play interviews between employers and job applicants.

APPLICATION FOR EMPLOYMENT

Whitaker Publishing Company
1822 W. Meridian Street
Vallejo, CA 94590

PERSONAL INFORMATION

Date _April 25, 20XX_   Social Security Number _Will provide if hired_

Name _____ Garcia _____ Kim _____ R. _____
                  Last   First   Middle

Present Address _____ 1036 Spring Street _____ Vallejo _____ CA _____ 94590
                         Street   City   State   Zip

Permanent Address _____ 1036 Spring Street _____ Vallejo _____ CA _____ 94590
                           Street   City   State   Zip

Phone No. _____ (707) 555-3214 _____

If related to anyone in our employ, state name and department

_____ N/A _____

Referred by

_____ Mr. James Mitchell, Vocational Counselor _____

EMPLOYMENT DESIRED

Position _Office Assistant_   Date you can start _June 10, 20XX_   Salary desired _Open_

Are you employed now? _Yes_   If so, may we inquire of your present employer? _Yes_

Ever applied to this company before? _No_   Where _N/A_   When _N/A_

EDUCATION

	Name and Location of School	Years Completed	Subjects Studied
Grammar School	Spring Grove School Vallejo, CA	6	General Education
Middle School	Vallejo Middle School Vallejo, CA	3	General Education
High School	Vallejo High School Vallejo, CA	4	Business Education
College	N/A		

Trade, Business or
Correspondence School _N/A_

22-3

Most job application forms will call for the information that appears in this form.

Languages
(besides English)   Speak   _Spanish_   Read/Write   _Spanish_

U.S. Military or   Present membership in
Naval Service   N/A   Rank   N/A   National Guard or Reserves   N/A

Activities other than religious
(civic, athletic, fraternal, etc.)_   National Honor Society, Business Professionals of America,_

Vallejo High School Student Council, 4-H

Exclude organizations the name or character of which indicates the race, creed, color, or national origin of its members.

FORMER EMPLOYERS   List below last two employers starting with last one first.

Date Month and Year	Name, Address, and Phone Number of Employer	Salary	Position	Reason for Leaving
From _9/20XX_ To _Present_	Watkins Sportswear 1122 Market Street Vallejo, CA 94590 (707) 555-1234	$8.50/hr	Salesperson	Seeking full-time job after graduation
From _7/20XX_ To _9/20XX_	Ojay's Restaurant 1301 Main Street Vallejo, CA 94590 (707) 555-5678	$8.00/hr	Grill Crewperson	Summer job
From _____ To _____				

REFERENCES   Give below the names of two persons not related to you, whom you have known at least one year.

	Name	Address/Phone	Job Title	Years Acquainted
1	Mr. James Mitchell	Vallejo High School 3300 W. Glendale Ave. Vallejo, CA 94590 (707) 555-4321	Vocational Counselor	3
2	Ms. Angelica Ortiz	Watkins Sportswear 1122 Market St. Vallejo, CA 94590 (707) 555-9876	Store Manager	1

PHYSICAL RECORD

In case of   1036 Spring St.
emergency notify _Mrs. Louise Garcia_   _Vallejo, CA 94590_   _(707) 555-3214_
                        Name   Address   Phone No.

I authorize investigation of all statements contained in this application. I understand that misrepresentation or omission of facts called for is cause for dismissal.

Date _April 25, 20XX_ Signature   _Kim R. Garcia_

22-3

(Continued.)

Enrich

Check with the Department of Labor to learn what questions may and may not be asked on application forms and in interviews.

Case Study: Career Choices

Mimi's Interview

Mimi was all set for her interview at the library. She was applying for a job as a page, restacking returned books. She was so confident that she hadn't practiced answering interview questions or preparing questions of her own, even though her guidance counselor had suggested it. She was feeling pretty self-assured in her trendy jeans, colorful T-shirt, and favorite high-heeled sandals.

At the interview, Mimi shook the hand of Mrs. Webber, the head librarian, and smiled in a friendly way. She sat down in the chair Mrs. Webber offered, remembering not to blow bubbles with her chewing gum. When Mrs. Webber asked why Mimi was interested in the job, Mimi explained that she needed money for new clothes. She was disappointed that she hadn't been hired at a boutique at the mall, but she figured stacking books was almost as good. Mrs. Webber asked Mimi about her career goals. Mimi said she wasn't sure what she wanted to do. She was sure she had plenty of time to decide later. When Mrs. Webber asked if Mimi had any questions, Mimi said no. She was positive she could figure out how to do such an easy job.

Case Review

1. Do you think Mimi was hired for the job? Why or why not?
2. What did Mimi do right on her interview?
3. How could Mimi improve her interviewing skills?

Resource

Bright Ideas for Interviewing, transparency master 22-2, TR

Activity

Draft an appropriate thank-you letter to send as a follow-up after a job interview.

are your educational and professional goals? What type of work do you most enjoy? least enjoy?

Prepare a List of Questions to Ask During the Interview

Ask specific questions about job responsibilities, opportunities for advancement, courses of study, and other items that fit the situation. Practice answering these questions with someone before the interview.

Collect and Bring with You Any Material You May Need

Materials to bring include copies of your résumé, application form, correspondence, references, and transcripts. Be ready with your Social Security number, class rank or grade point average, and other facts that may be requested.

Consider Your Appearance and the Impression You Make

Pluses here include appropriate clothing, prompt arrival, and a firm handshake, 22-4. Also keep the following in mind: eye contact, direct answers to questions, intelligent questions of your own, and a confident manner.

Thank the Interviewer and Clarify the Follow-Up You Can Expect

Will you be contacted, or should you call to learn the results of the interview? Should you send additional information or materials? Where and when can the interviewer contact you?

Follow Up Each Interview with a Thank-You Letter

Be sure you note the interviewer's name and title so you can use it in the letter. Also include your name, address and phone number, the date of the interview, and the job you applied for. If you do not receive a response from your interview within two or three weeks, call to inquire about the results.

Success in the Workplace

Landing the job you want is just a beginning. You want to do all you can to succeed and advance in your chosen field. Some work habits will be important for success in almost any job, from stock clerk to top executive. These include promptness, reliable attendance, dependability, a positive attitude, and eagerness to do the work as best you can. Meeting the dress standards of your work environment will help you fit in and move ahead. If there is no dress code to guide you, take your cue from reliable coworkers or ask superiors what is appropriate. This applies to "casual Fridays," too.

You will need to master basic communication skills such as meeting and greeting clients and customers, interacting with other employees and your superiors, and handling business telephone calls and e-mails. Most jobs call for written communication skills. Face-to-face communications call for eye contact, a firm handshake, and an easy conversational manner. Listening to what other people say is important as well. Concentrate on names, dates, and information and instructions you will need to remember. Take notes when you are receiving detailed instructions or information you will need later.

A businesslike approach to your job will take you a long way. This means taking job responsibilities seriously. Stick to the work you have to

22-4
By using a firm handshake and direct eye contact, you present a positive image.

Business, Management & Administration

Employment Interviewers

Employment interviewers help job seekers find suitable job openings and employers find qualified staff. They may work for private employment agencies, state government employment services, or private companies. They interview applicants to explore their interests and abilities. They then attempt to match the applicants with jobs that are on file.

Activity

Interview at least five employers in different types of businesses to find out what types of clothing employees are expected to wear. Discuss appropriate clothing and behavior for different work environments.

Activity

Carry out role-playing of these communication exchanges A) an employee greeting a customer, B) an employee making a suggestion to a boss, C) an employee answering a workplace telephone inquiry, and D) a superior correcting an employee oversight.

Discuss

What are correct ways to leave a job? Give some examples of actions to avoid when leaving a job.

do and try not to be idle during working hours. If you find yourself with time on your hands, ask for more work to do. If you end up with more than you can complete, discuss the situation with your superior before falling hopelessly behind. Behavior to avoid on the job includes sending and receiving personal e-mail and phone calls on company time. Do not let friends drop by to see you at your workplace.

In many workplaces, it is important that you be able to work as a team member. You will be working with others toward common goals. To do this successfully you will need to cooperate with coworkers, give others credit for their ideas and contributions, do your fair share of the work, and be a reliable part of the group effort. Very often experience on an athletic team or group project in school provides a helpful background in coopera-tion with others to achieve a common goal.

As you learn to work with a team, you may find that you have leadership qualities as well. Being a leader means more than giving directions to others. Qualities of leaders include the ability to motivate others to participate in tasks. Encouraging open communication among team members is another important aspect of this role. Leaders make sure that each team member feels valued and that each voice is heard. They identify the individual strengths of each team member and make sure team members are recognized for accomplishments. They encourage team diversity and promote all cultures.

Leaving a Job

Leaving a job, whether by resignation or termination, is something most workers experience at some point in their work life. Knowing how to leave can help you make a positive transition into a new job. If you leave by choice, it is a good idea to have a new job before you leave your present position. Keep in mind that it is almost always easier to find a job when you have one. It is important to give appropriate notice—usually two weeks. Put your resignation in writing. The letter, addressed to the appropriate person in the human resources department, should be a simple statement of your intent to leave and the date on which you will be leaving. Include the date of your letter and your signature, address, and phone number. It pays to leave with as much goodwill as possible. You may need references or cooperation of coworkers and superiors in future positions.

If you are fired or terminated, you need to know your rights and benefits under the law. In most states you can be fired for incompetence, breaking company rules, excessive absence or tardiness, and many other reasons. You also may be laid off because business is not good and your employer is downsizing or merging with another company. However, you cannot legally be fired for any form of discrimination, such as age, race, religion, sex, marital status, sexual orientation, or disability.

If you feel your rights have been violated, it is important to contact the appropriate government office. This will usually be the nearest Equal Employment Opportunity Commission (EEOC) or the State Department of Human Rights. Find out whether you are eligible for unemployment benefits and employer-sponsored health insurance. See 22-5 for a listing and brief summary of laws that protect the rights of workers.

Worker Protection Laws	
Law	**Key Provisions**
FLSA—Fair Labor Standards Act	Establishes fair minimum wage, overtime pay, child labor standards and other workplace conditions that affect workers
Family and Medical Leave Act	Requires employers to allow employees up to 12 weeks of unpaid job protected leave annually for birth or adoption and care of a child, care of a seriously ill family member, or a serious personal health condition
COBRA—Consolidated Omnibus Budget Reconciliation Act	Gives eligible workers who leave their place of employment the right to continue their employer-sponsored group health insurance, including coverage for preexisting conditions, for up to 18 months at their own expense
OSHA—Occupational Safety and Health Act	Promotes and enforces safety and health standards in the workplace
EEOC—Equal Employment Opportunity Act	Protects employees against discrimination based on race, color, disability, religion, sex, age, and national origin in hiring, promoting, firing, wages, testing, training, and all other terms and conditions of employment
ERISA—Employee Retirement Income Security Act	Outlines employees' rights as participants in an employer's pension and/or profit-sharing plans

22-5

These federal laws protect the rights of workers.

Workplace Ethics

Ethics in the workplace have become a significant issue in the business world. *Ethics* are a set of moral values that guide a person's behavior. They help a person determine what is right and wrong in given situations. Ethics are based on traits such as trustworthiness, honesty, loyalty, respect, responsibility, and fairness. Over 90 percent of business schools now require ethics courses as part of their curriculum.

Companies differ in their approach to workplace behavior. Some simply assume that employees bring their own standards to the job, and management offers very little guidance. Some companies rely on an informal corporate culture that guides job-related decisions and actions. Other businesses follow a carefully developed program. This may include a statement of corporate values and a code of ethics to guide employees.

Today, more and more businesses are adopting clearly formulated ethics programs to guide behavior and decisions in the workplace. In companies that take ethics seriously, top management will project the value system that drives behavior. A company may convey its expectations for ethics on the job in different ways. These include employee handbooks, training sessions or seminars, or printed formal statements of company values and ethics.

Government & Public Administration

Equal Employment Opportunity Specialists

Equal employment opportunity specialists provide advice to management concerning how to prevent discriminatory practices in recruiting, hiring, promotions, pay, and benefits. They analyze workforce characteristics and organizational structure and make recommendations to ensure compliance with laws and requirements.

Case Study: Career Choices

Desiree Makes a Hard Choice

Desiree works at a local clothing store and gets a 20% employee discount. She spends a good share of her income on new outfits. Her best friend Lillea admires Desiree's clothes and wishes she could add to her wardrobe.

One Saturday, Lillea stops by the store to see the new fall clothes. The owner is at the bank and Desiree is in charge. Lillea tries on several outfits but can't afford everything she wants. Lillea asks Desiree to buy the outfits using her discount, and then Lillea will pay Desiree for the clothes.

Desiree is troubled by this suggestion. The owner of the shop made it clear the discount was for employees only—not family members or friends. It would be dishonest to use her discount this way and she could lose her job. On the other hand, Desiree doesn't want to lose Lillea's friendship.

Case Review

1. How do you think Desiree should resolve this dilemma?
2. How would you react if your best friend asked you to do something that compromised your values?
3. How do you think the store owner would react to this situation?
4. Why do you think Desiree should or should not let Lillea use her discount in this way?
5. How does this situation relate to ethics issues in the workplace?

Resource

Code of Workplace Ethics,
Activity B, WB

The standards only have meaning when the message comes from management and is enforced by example. Stated codes of ethics generally address relationships of the business with employees, customers, suppliers, investors, creditors, competitors, and community. Business codes of ethics frequently relate to such issues as fair treatment of employees, teamwork, competition, and conflicts of interest. Other issues include use of business resources and assets, confidentiality, and environmental concerns.

When you apply for jobs, inquire about an employer's policies regarding employee decisions and behavior on the job. If ever in doubt about what is and is not acceptable, ask before you act.

Linking to... History

Entrepreneurs Forge Ahead

Research shows that bad times are often good for entrepreneurs. During a recession, start-up costs on everything from space to supplies are lower. When unemployment is high, talent is often available and willing to work for less. In addition, the competition is not as active. Entrepreneurs tend to be optimistic, so they may not be as discouraged by the economic climate as others are.

A recession is also a good time to begin a business because entrepreneurs can help restart the economy by creating new jobs. New innovative companies are the keys to bolstering a faltering economy. Many of the successful businesses you know were started during a recession. Among them are Twitter, E-Bay, Burger King, and Hyatt Hotels.

Entrepreneurship

Becoming an **entrepreneur**, owning and operating your own business, is another way to become employed. It involves investing your money and talents for profit and income. Creating a business of your own can take three basic forms: a **sole proprietorship**, meaning a single owner; a **partnership**, meaning two or more owners; and a **corporation**, meaning a separate entity created and owned by the founder and shareholders.

Another way to go into business is through a franchise. A **franchise** is an agreement that permits the franchisee to market and sell goods and services in a given area that the franchiser provides. Fast-food outlets, car rentals, and cleaning services are among the many franchise businesses.

Entrepreneurs have always played a key role in the growth and success of the American economy. A few of the most successful entrepreneurs have names you will recognize. Bill Gates, Walt Disney, and Oprah Winfrey are all well-known entrepreneurs. Most major corporations were started by one person who stepped up with an idea and a plan. These individuals started with a dream and a willingness to work hard and take risks. Figure 22-6 lists a few of the Web sites that offer both practical and inspirational information for starting your own business.

You may think "big business" dominates the marketplace, but small businesses are the backbone of the U. S. economy. Since the mid-1970s, over two-thirds of the new jobs in the nation were created by small businesses. Small firms employ approximately 60 percent of the non-government workforce. Approximately 21 million small businesses exist in America today. Most of these employ fewer than 20 workers. For those who like to be their own boss, becoming an entrepreneur may be the answer, 22-7.

Activity

Look in the local Yellow Pages to find examples of franchises; big firms; and small, independent businesses.

Resource

Entrepreneurship, Activity C, WB

Resources for Entrepreneurs

www.entrepreneurship.org

www.business.gov

www.sba.gov

www.kauffman.org

www.entrepreneur.com

www.startupnation.com

22-6

These Web sites contain useful information for people who are interested in starting a business.

22-7
Small businesses create the majority of non-government jobs in the U.S.

Resource

Making the Most of Your Resources, Activity D, WB

Enrich

Interview two local entrepreneurs about what they consider to be their greatest satisfactions and problems.

Discuss

Why do you think the executive summary is written last in a business plan?

However, starting a business can be risky. Thousands of small businesses fail each year. To succeed in a business of your own, it is a good idea to have previous work experience with the service or product you plan to sell or produce. You need to know how to manage a business, sell your goods and services, and deal with customers and suppliers. You need to keep accurate financial records and know the legalities involved in running a business. You will require enough money to get started and operate until the business begins to pay for itself.

To establish your own business, you will need to work long and hard. Unfortunately, there is no sure income, no guarantee of success, and very little financial security when you begin. However, for those who do succeed, the rewards are great. They include not only income and profits, but also independence and personal satisfaction.

Writing a Business Plan

Writing a business plan is the first step to creating a business. This document serves several purposes. It helps an entrepreneur think through his or her ideas and set goals and objectives. A well-thought-out business plan can help convince investors and bank loan officers to put money into a new or already existing company. A business plan should be updated as a business grows.

The U.S. Small Business Administration (SBA) provides a wealth of information and resources for business people and entrepreneurs. These include an online training course in business planning and business plan samples. According to the SBA, a business plan consists of the following parts.

1. Executive Summary

This is a succinct one- to two-page description of the business. It should grab the reader's attention and make him or her want to learn more. Although it comes first in the plan, it is written last.

2. Company Description

This section gives details about the business and who will run it. It should include the following:

- mission and vision statements, or brief descriptions of the business's purpose and its plan for future growth

- company goals and objectives

- company history

- list of company principals, or key employees

Case Study: Career Choices

Born Technician

Martin got his first computer at age three. His computer knowledge and expertise grew with each passing year. After high school graduation, Martin took computer technician and business courses at the Institute of Electronics. With certification in the field in which he excelled, Martin decided to open his own business.

Martin contacted the local office of the U.S. Small Business Administration for information and guidance. He got a $10,000 loan and rented a small storefront. He also used the money to purchase parts, tools, and software.

Martin then created a Web site advertising computer repairs, installations, consultations, and tech support by a certified computer technician. He distributed fliers to small businesses and homes in the area.

Most customers want on-site service, so Martin only opens the store for three hours a day. Since most business is from repeat customers, Martin now offers services on a contract basis. This provides a more predictable monthly income.

Case Review

1. What do you think of Martin's dream of having his own business?
2. What do you see as the advantages and disadvantages of going into computer technology as your own boss versus working for an established computer tech company?
3. Under what circumstances would you be willing to take the risks and devote the time and effort required to start and run a business?
4. How would you evaluate Martin's approach to reaching his goal?
5. What factors do you think will contribute to the success or failure of Martin's business over time?

3. Market Definition

An overview of the industry and market are given here. This includes the current and projected size of the entire market and who competitors are. The plan provides an estimate of how much of that market the entrepreneur hopes to capture. Characteristics of target customers are given, as well as the customer needs the business will satisfy.

Activity

Have students investigate the SBA Web site at www.sba.gov.

Discuss

Why do you think it's important to know how a company will be organized before the company is even started?

Activity

Have students find examples of business plans online and bring them to class to discuss. Do they follow the format presented here?

Note

In the marketing area, *positioning, pricing, promotion,* and *place* are known as "the four Ps."

4. Products and Services

The goods and/or services the business creates, as well as prices charged, are described here. Business plan writers must address the issue of competitiveness, or why the products and services they produce will be successful despite competition from other companies.

5. Organization and Management

This section details how the company is organized, including its legal structure (proprietorship, partnership, corporation). It may include an organizational chart that shows the interrelationships among various departments and employees. Biographies of company leaders and any special licenses and permits held by the business are given.

6. Marketing and Sales Strategy

The target market was defined in step 3. How the business will reach this market is outlined in this section. It includes the following:

- *Positioning* describes the niche this product or service will fill relative to products and services already available.

- *Pricing* describes what competitors charge and what customers are willing to pay. It gives a rationale for pricing.

- *Promotion* outlines advertising, sales events, and other strategies to get product or service information out to consumers.

- *Place* gives information about how the product will be distributed or put into the hands of consumers.

7. Financials

These financial statements should include the following:

- A balance sheet measures the net worth or value of a business at a particular time. Net worth is computed by subtracting liabilities from assets.

- An income statement shows whether or not a business is profitable. Revenues and expenses are given.

- A cash flow statement lists income and expenses during a month or other period of time.
  Financial statements for a proposed business should contain estimates of these costs over one year, as well as a summary of start-up costs.

8. Appendices

These may include company brochures, résumés of those in leadership roles, copies of published articles about the business, photographs of products, and contracts.

Sample business plans can be found online at the U.S. Small Business Association's Web site (www.bplans.com/samples/sba.cfm) or at the Small Business Administration's Web site (www.sba.gov/smallbusinessplanner.)

Managing Multiple Roles

The career goals you set for yourself may one day overlap marriage, parenting, and other life goals. As you consider your future in the world of work, it may be a good time to think about your personal life as well. How will you manage the different roles you will play? Your work may well determine where you live, how much you earn, and how much free time you have. You may have to travel for your job, relocate frequently, or be involved in work-related organizations. Consider how all these factors will relate to your life goals and your family life if you marry.

Since many young people plan to marry and have a family, discussing marriage and career goals together makes sense. If you and your spouse both plan to have careers outside the home, you will be part of a **dual-career family**. You will have to work together to manage the demands of a career as well as family and community responsibilities.

Success in managing multiple roles depends on the attitudes of both marriage partners. Friction may arise when couples disagree on the way they will share family responsibilities. It is important for engaged couples to talk through their career and parenting goals before marriage. They need to measure the risks and rewards of dual careers against the quality of family life they desire.

The way families manage their multiple roles varies from one household to the next. In some families, the wife takes more responsibility for child care and household management. However, some men also assume the major role in raising children and running the household. In other families, husbands and wives share these responsibilities on an equal basis.

Child care is often the most critical issue for working parents to resolve. Some couples can arrange for child care in their own home. Others may have relatives, friends, or neighbors that provide child care in their homes. Many people use child care centers where children are cared for in small groups by qualified child care providers.

Some employers offer assistance to employees with children. They may offer *flextime*, an arrangement that allows employees to set their own work schedules within certain limits. Flexible work schedules permit parents to spend more time at home with their children, 22-8. For example, parents with school-age children could benefit by starting work early and arriving home by the end of the school day.

Reflect

How do you feel about both parents working when children are young? Discuss pros and cons.

Reflect

What do you see as advantages and disadvantages of having a dual-career family?

Discuss

What are some compromises and adjustments couples may need to make in order to manage careers and family?

22-8

Flexible work arrangements, including telecommuting, enable parents to spend more time with their children.

Some companies provide on-site child care facilities to help parents arrange for the care and supervision of their children. This makes it convenient for parents to drop off and pick up the children. Parents may also check on the children during breaks and lunch.

Some parents may choose part-time jobs so one parent can spend more time at home when the children are there. This may also help with child care costs. In other cases, one spouse may set up a business that he or she can operate out of the home.

The Family and Medical Leave Act requires employers with more than 50 workers to provide employees up to 12 weeks unpaid leave per year for care of a new baby, a sick relative, or personal medical needs. Under the law, employees who take this leave are assured that their jobs will be available when they return.

In addition to child care concerns, dual-career couples must find ways to manage household responsibilities. They need to set priorities and schedule their time. By doing this, they can complete household tasks and have time left over to enjoy one another. Outside help can make an important contribution in completing some tasks. If all family members support the dual-career arrangement, they will find ways to manage child care and household responsibilities while still spending quality time together.

Social Responsibility

In addition to the roles of family member and employee, adults also fill the role of citizen. The call to citizenship requires more than just political knowledge and voter turnout. Good citizens participate, volunteer, and accept responsibility for themselves. They respect the environment, behave ethically, and often accept responsibility for helping others as well. Citizens play these expanded roles in the community, organizations,

Businesses Give Back

Businesses and community groups are beginning to place greater emphasis on social responsibility. They are working to identify and meet the needs of individuals, groups, and society as a whole. For instance, businesses may sponsor literacy programs, adopt schools, and create corporate volunteer programs.

The Committee Encouraging Corporate Philanthropy is an international forum of top business executives. This group looks for ways their businesses can give back to the community and encourages other companies to do so as well. See www.corporatephilanthropy.org to learn what these companies are doing. You will see many familiar corporate names.

Most small local businesses also make significant contributions in their communities. Look for examples in your area.

places of worship, and many other places where they can make a positive difference.

Another part of good citizenship is **social responsibility**, a general sense of concern for the needs of others in the community, country, and world. Social responsibility is about people's duty to take care of one another and the world they share, 22-9. It also involves finding constructive approaches to current social issues and needs.

Social responsibility can include a duty to help control crime and violence. It can mean providing relief for disaster victims, working at shelters, and creating jobs for the unemployed. Protecting the environment and conserving natural resources are other aspects of social responsibility. All these tasks require going above and beyond taking responsibility for yourself and your family. The impact you can make is limited only by your imagination and willingness to follow through on your ideas.

Resource

The Roles You Play,
reproducible master 22-3, TR

Resource

Chapter 22: Entering the Work World, Teacher's PowerPoint Presentations CD

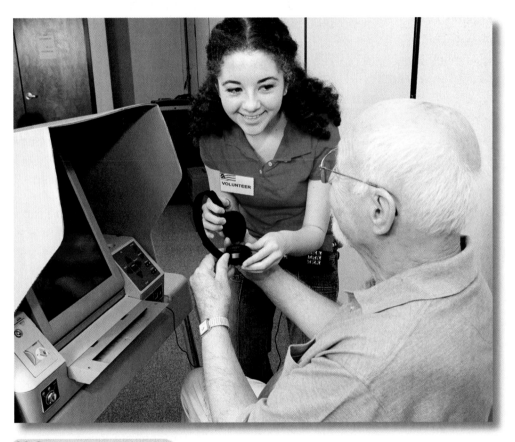

22-9

You can contribute to your community in many ways. This volunteer assists a voter on Election Day.

Chapter Summary

Certain tools help open doors to future opportunities. These include résumés, application forms, interviews, and correspondence with possible employers. You will want to learn to use each of these to your advantage. Once you land the job you want, follow the necessary steps to success on the job.

Ethics in the workplace has become an important issue in the business world. While employers set the standards in their own businesses, you might take a careful look at the personal ethics you bring to the job. Some companies follow detailed codes of ethics, but others are more relaxed.

At some point, you may want to consider a business of your own. Writing a business plan is an important step. However, starting a business can be risky. Take a careful look at the advantages and disadvantages. Success involves time, effort, and hard work.

For most working adults, career goals overlap with marriage, parenting, and other life goals. Success in managing the goals of career and family depends on careful planning and cooperation of all family members. Another role adults fill is that of citizen. Social responsibility is part of fulfilling this role.

Review

1. List the six types of information you need on a résumé.

2. List four tips for a successful job interview.

3. Why is teamwork in the workplace important?

4. In what ways may companies convey expectations for ethical standards?

5. List and explain the three forms of business ownership.

6. Name two advantages and two disadvantages of being an entrepreneur.

7. What are two major challenges of managing a dual-career family?

8. Give three examples of how a person can accept social responsibility.

Critical Thinking

9. Discuss pointers for using a résumé, an interview, and an application form to make yourself look like a suitable job candidate.

10. What personal characteristics do you think an employer would look for when filling a job opening? Role-play a job interview, making sure to demonstrate these characteristics.

Answers to *Review*

1. identifying information, goals and objectives, education, work experience, activities and honors, references

2. (List four:) Learn important background information. Anticipate questions that might be asked of you. Prepare a list of questions to ask during the interview. Collect and bring with you any material you may need. Consider your appearance and the impression you make. Thank the interviewer and clarify the follow-up you can expect. Follow up each interview with a thank-you letter.

3. Coworkers must be able to work together to meet a common goal.

4. employee handbooks, training and seminars, printed formal statements of company values and ethics, behavior of managers

5. In a sole proprietorship, the business has a single owner. A partnership has two or more owners. A corporation is a separate entity created and owned by the founder and shareholders.

11. If you owned a business, what characteristics would you look for in people you hire to work for you? Working in small groups, make a checklist of personal qualities a successful entrepreneur needs.

12. Develop a general "code of ethics" for the workplace. Give examples of ethical and unethical behavior on the job.

13. What steps might couples take to resolve conflicts that arise over multiple roles?

Academic Connections

14. **Speech, writing.** Write a guide to success in the workplace for three different types of jobs, such as waiter, teacher, health care provider, police officer, and retail store manager. Interview several employers for comments and suggestions. Discuss how the keys for success may differ for various jobs and find those keys that are common to almost all work.

15. **Speech, writing.** Interview an entrepreneur in your community to learn about the challenges and rewards of being in business for yourself. Also interview an employee of a large company to learn about the challenges and rewards of working for an employer. Write a report comparing the advantages and disadvantages of being an entrepreneur versus working for an employer.

16. **Social studies, research.** Research some of the laws that protect the rights of workers. Discuss the situations in which each applies to workers' rights.

MATH CHALLENGE

17. A family consists of two parents and two children, ages 3 and 7. The father works full-time outside the home. The mother takes care of the children at home. She is considering finding a job, which would require her to pay for child care. Her monthly expenses would be the following:
    - child care for the younger child: $800
    - after-school care for the older child: $350
    - transportation to and from work: approximately $300
    - clothing, dry cleaning costs, and other work-related expenses: $200

    How much must the woman's annual net pay be in order for her to earn $2,000 a month more than her expenses?

Tech Smart

18. Use the Internet to collect general career information on résumés, interviews, career opportunities, and success on the job. Share findings with the class. Use word processing or desktop publishing software to create a booklet of helpful Web sites.

19. Use a job search Web site to find at least three jobs you would like. Discuss the reasons these jobs appeal to you. Write a letter that you could use to request an interview for one of the positions.

20. Use résumé software to create a résumé. Exchange résumés with a partner and offer constructive criticism.

---

6. (List two of each:) advantages—being your own boss, controlling whatever profits the business generates, creating a business of your own, independence, personal satisfaction; disadvantages—financial risk, the need to know all aspects of business operations, hard work with no assurance of success, no sure income

7. child care, household responsibilities

8. (List three. Student response may include the following:) help control crime and violence, provide relief for disaster victims, work at shelters, create jobs for the unemployed, protect environment, conserve natural resources

---

Answer to *Math Challenge*

17. Work expenses total $1,650. Her net pay would have to be at least $3,650 a month or $43,800 annually.

23

Your Role in the Environment

Reading for Meaning

Choose an environmental issue and read several articles about it. After reading the chapter, write a page summarizing the problem and solutions using information from the text and from your research.

sustainable

conservation

ecology

environmentalist

climate change

global warming

landfill

hazardous waste

fossil fuels

renewable energy

biofuels

nonrenewable
  energy

biodegradable

recycle

composting

CHAPTER OBJECTIVES

After studying this chapter,
you will be able to

- **outline** today's major environmental challenges.
- **explain** steps individuals and citizen groups can take to conserve natural resources and protect the environment.
- **identify** the role of government in protecting the environment.
- **explain** steps businesses can take to reduce their impact on the environment.

Central Ideas

- Depletion and destruction of natural resources are some of the most serious environmental threats today.

- Many everyday choices that people make can directly affect the health of the environment.

- Consumers, businesses, and governments need to work together to protect and preserve the environment.

Reflect

What steps have you taken to protect the environment?

Example

Collect articles from current newspapers and magazines on environmental issues and make a display of them for review and discussion.

Reflect

What do you see as the top environmental priorities?

Example

Name some well-known environmentalists.

Resource

Protecting the Environment, color lesson slide, TR

Protecting the world around you is one of your most critical roles as a consumer, citizen, and taxpayer. Individuals, governments, and businesses share responsibility for preserving the environment and being good *stewards*, or managers, of the earth's natural resources.

Scientists predict a future in which shortages of natural resources—water, food, and fuel—will affect a growing number of people. By 2040, the world's population is expected to reach over 9 billion people. Sustainable practices and conservation preserves natural resources. **Sustainable** refers to responsibly using resources to prevent depletion or permanent damage. **Conservation** is the protection and management of the environment and valuable natural resources.

You will pay the costs of protecting the planet and solving environmental problems far into the future. Your tax dollars pay for research to find earth-friendly ways to meet basic human needs. Your votes for policymakers will decide how the country manages natural resources. Learning how your money is spent and what environmental choices you have is in your own best interest.

Environmental Challenges

Ecology is the study of the relationship between living things and their environment. Scientists who study ecology have found that life on earth exists in a delicate balance. When that balance is disrupted, the consequences can be serious, unpredictable, and irreversible.

Environmentalists are people who are concerned with the quality of the environment and how to maintain it. Current environmental issues include climate change, water and air pollution, depletion of natural resources, and land use. All of these issues can disrupt the balance needed to preserve the environment.

Climate Change

Climate change refers to shifts in measurements of climate—such as temperature, precipitation, or wind—that last decades or longer. It is linked to **global warming**, the steady rise in average temperatures near the earth's surface. Warming temperatures are causing climate changes throughout the world.

Both natural processes and human activity contribute to climate change. In recent decades, however, human activity has been an increasingly dominant cause of global warming. Activities such as driving cars and generating electricity by burning coal release carbon dioxide, one of the *greenhouse gases (GHG)*. Like a greenhouse roof, these gases form a layer in the atmosphere that prevents heat from escaping.

Adding to global warming is the problem of *deforestation*, which is the clearing of forests. Large tracts of trees are cut down by loggers and removed by farmers. The trees are sold as timber, and the land is used for grazing animals, growing crops, and building towns. Trees and other

Linking to... Science

Greenhouse Gases

Greenhouse gases include the following:
- **Carbon dioxide.** Mainly from the burning of substances: wood, solid waste, fossil fuels, etc.
- **Methane.** A by-product of fossil fuel production and the decay of organic material.

Common sources are landfills and agriculture. Animals also release methane gas.
- **Nitrous oxide.** The burning of fossil fuels and solid waste releases this gas.
- **Fluorinated gases.** Powerful gases released during industrial activities.

plants filter carbon dioxide from the air, using it and sunlight to grow. With fewer plants to absorb carbon dioxide, more remains in the atmosphere.

If carbon dioxide and other greenhouse gases continue to collect in the atmosphere, experts predict serious consequences, 23-1.

Waste Disposal

The average U.S. citizen generates about 4 pounds of garbage each day. All that waste must be disposed somehow. Some solid waste is disposed through burning, but most household waste is buried in a landfill. A **landfill** is a permanent waste disposal site for most solid, non-hazardous waste.

Special sites are devoted to the disposal of *hazardous waste*. **Hazardous waste** includes substances—liquids, solids, and gases—that are dangerous or potentially harmful to health or the environment. They are discarded by-products of agricultural, manufacturing, medical, national defense, and

Enrich

Research developments in climate change and assess the threat.

Discuss

What has your community done to dispose of solid waste?

Example

Bring pesticide and chemical product labels to class and study label information and cautions.

Possible Results of Climate Change

Rising sea levels and flooding. Ice in artic regions and high altitudes would melt faster if temperatures rise. This would release large volumes of water, possibly flooding many coastal areas.

Weather pattern changes. Some regions would suffer water shortages and drought. Warmer oceans would trigger more hurricanes that could cause flooding.

Famine. Extreme weather changes would threaten crop production in many regions, causing food shortages.

Animal and plant extinction. Weather would probably change faster than many plants and animals could adjust. In the short term, animals would probably try to migrate to more comfortable climates that supported familiar food supplies. Plants, however, would likely die off.

Human migrations. Flooded coastal areas plus shortages of food and safe water could force millions of people from their homes. This might lead to regional conflicts.

23-1
Climate change could permanently alter weather and other conditions.

other sources. Households discard hazardous waste, too. Some examples are paint, cleaners, auto products, pesticides, and flame-retardants. Also hazardous are fluorescent lamps, batteries, consumer electronics, and anything with mercury, such as fever thermometers.

Existing landfills are filling up, and building new landfills is costly. Few communities are willing to permit landfills in their area, so new sites are located further from the areas they serve. This requires transporting waste for long distances at considerable cost.

Improper disposal of waste poses serious threats to human health and the environment. If hazardous waste ends up in landfills, it can contaminate groundwater and cropland. Without proper controls, burning waste can release greenhouse gases that contribute to climate change.

Dwindling Resources

Natural resources—land, water, forests, fuel, and wildlife—are valuable economic assets. Everyone shares the challenge of making sure these resources continue to be available to future generations.

Fossil Fuels

Fossil fuels—coal, petroleum, and natural gas—are derived from the decomposed remains of animals and plants that lived in prehistoric times. Burning fossil fuels is the major source of greenhouse gases. Fossil fuels provide more than 85 percent of all energy consumed in the United States. This includes gas that powers cars and heats homes and coal that produces electricity.

Energy sources can be classified as renewable or nonrenewable. **Renewable energy** sources are those that are continually available or can be replenished. They include wind, water, solar (sun), and biofuels. **Biofuels** are fuels composed of or produced from biological raw material. An example is ethanol made from corn or sugar beets.

Nonrenewable energy sources are those that can be used up or cannot be used again, 23-2. Once they are gone, they cannot be replaced. Fossil fuels are nonrenewable energy sources. Nuclear energy is also a nonrenewable resource because it is created from uranium, a substance available in limited amounts.

At present, the United States depends on foreign sources for over 50 percent of its petroleum. This dependence is a big concern because the U.S. has little or no control over the supply or price of fuel imports. Achieving energy independence will require greater fuel efficiency and conservation. It will also require development of new energy sources that are renewable, affordable, and environmentally safe.

Clean Water

Most people in the United States take fresh, pure water for granted. In many parts of the country, water is plentiful and relatively cheap. This natural resource, which is vital to all forms of life, is becoming more precious. Many of the common items you buy require huge amounts of water to manufacture. For example, hundreds of gallons of water are used in the production of one pair of denim jeans.

Both the availability and quality of water are important environmental issues. Water scarcity creates severe problems. Demands for fresh water increase dramatically with population growth. In the years ahead, conserving water and keeping the water supply clean, will become vitally important.

Renewable Energy Source	Description	Disadvantages
Solar	The sun's radiation that reaches the earth. It can be converted to electricity and heat. Produces almost no undesirable side effects. Used most often and most effectively in warm climates. In cloudy areas, solar energy systems usually must be used with other forms of power.	• Cannot be concentrated into high-grade, usable fuel in large enough quantities. • Limited use at night and on cloudy days unless new storage systems are installed to absorb, store, and release energy as needed.
Wind	Large windmill-like turbines turn wind energy into electricity. A wind farm is a business that generates power from multiple turbines at one location.	• Many areas lack sufficient wind or space to set up wind turbines. • Not a constant or dependable source of energy. • Getting wind energy to places that need it requires creating a system of power lines across many miles. • The equipment to harness wind energy requires an investment. • People who live near wind farms complain about disturbances such as light deflection off turbine blades.
Hydro	Captures the power of ocean waves or water flowing over a dam to create electricity.	• Depends on the presence of enough water.
Geothermal	Uses hot water and steam produced deep inside the earth to create energy.	• Sources of geothermal energy are very limited.
Biofuels	Made of biological matter from plants and animals that can be converted to energy. Ethanol is made from grains—corn, sorghum, wheat, sugar cane, etc. It is usually mixed with gasoline. Biodiesel is made from plant and animal oils and fats.	• Not yet possible to produce adequate quantities of usable energy from any of these sources. • Depends on availability of farmland and forests. When land is used to grow sources of biofuels, it cannot be used to grow food.

(Continued.)

23-2

Dependence on nonrenewable energy sources will eventually use up remaining supplies.

Nonrenewable Energy Source	Description	Disadvantages
Petroleum, Natural Gas	Fossil fuels. Main forms of energy used in the United States today.	• Their use contributes to air pollution and climate change. • Oil spills foul water and kill wildlife. • U.S. is dependent on imports to meet demand. • Supplies (and prices) are controlled by other governments, including those hostile to the U.S.
Coal	Also a fossil fuel. A plentiful U.S. source of energy and a major export. Coal is likely to be a major source of energy well into the future.	• Difficult to transport. • Burning coal adds to climate change. • Strip-mining causes long-lasting damage to the land. • Converting coal to a gaseous or liquid form is a costly process.
Nuclear	Energy is produced from nuclear fission, or splitting apart, of uranium in nuclear power plants. Produces 20 percent of our electric power and 8 percent of our total energy production. Releases little greenhouse gas. Is used as the main source of energy in some countries, including France and Japan.	• Questions persist about plant safety and safe waste disposal. • Nonrenewable because uranium is scarce. • Nuclear waste, improperly handled, could cause catastrophic environmental damage.

23-2

(Continued.)

Resource

Identifying Environmental Concerns, reproducible master 23-1, TR

Discuss

What are the pros and cons of using coal?

Discuss

What are the pros and cons of using nuclear energy?

Discuss

What is the chief drawback of relying on solar energy?

Urban Sprawl

Before the invention of cars, most people worked and went to school within walking distance of their homes. Everything a person needed was concentrated in a compact town center. If public transportation was available, most people used it.

Cars gave people more mobility. Homes and businesses were built along highways that led to and from city centers. Open land was converted into housing developments, roads, malls, and business parks. This dispersed development is described as *urban sprawl*. Many environmental groups oppose urban sprawl, especially when it replaces forests or prime farmland. They argue that sprawling areas require more roads, more driving, and more services than well-planned, concentrated business and residential developments.

While some areas of the country allow unchecked growth, others areas carefully plan new developments. Many towns and communities focus on smart growth policies that protect ecologically sensitive regions, yet address future population needs.

What You Can Do

"Think globally, act locally" is a guideline often used to address environmental challenges. There are many steps you can take in your home and community to improve and protect your world. Making a few small changes in your shopping habits, reducing your water and energy use at home, reducing waste, and conserving fuel all make an impact on sustaining the environment.

Shop Wisely

Green has become the symbolic color of earth-friendly products, policies, and lifestyles. Many products now carry "green" labels identifying them as *earth-friendly*, *eco-friendly*, or *environmentally-friendly*. These terms have no official definition. A careful examination of the manufacturer's goals and accomplishments can help you judge if the company's practices benefit the environment.

The following tips can help you address environmental issues when shopping for goods and services:

- Look for energy-saving features when buying products such as autos, appliances, furnaces, air conditioners, and electronic equipment. See Chapter 20 for more details. Look for water-saving features when buying dishwashers, clothes washers, toilets, and bathroom showerheads.

- Buy pre-owned consumer goods when they address your needs. You can buy used items at resale shops, garage sales, and online auction and sales sites.

- Buy products with packaging that is biodegradable. **Biodegradable** materials, such as cardboard, can be broken down naturally by microorganisms into harmless elements. Also, bring your own reusable bags when you shop.

- Support businesses and manufacturers that operate recycling and take-back programs, such as permitting consumers to return old electronics for disposal when they purchase a new model.

- Shop locally. Transporting food and other products uses fuel. Look for locally grown foods at farmer's markets and grocery stores, 23-3.

Reflect

Find out if urban sprawl is an environmental challenge in your area.

Resource

Reality Check, Activity A, WB

23-3

Many foods are transported long distances to reach grocery stores. Buying locally grown produce at farmer's markets is one way consumers can conserve fuel.

Resource

It's on the Meter, Activity B, WB

Enrich

Decide on three specific energy conservation habits to adopt in your own life.

Activity

Find out how much your family spends each month for gas and electricity in the home.

Reflect

What energy-saving habits does your family practice?

Resource

Energy Conservation, Activity C, WB

Conserve Energy

Most people can conserve a considerable amount of energy without major inconvenience. Often it simply involves a new mindset to get into the habit of using less, economizing, and saving. Some ways to reduce personal and family energy use follow.

Conduct a Home Energy Audit

A *home energy audit* is an assessment of how much energy your home uses. It also identifies ways to reduce consumption.

Your electric and gas meters measure the amounts of electricity and gas you use each month. Look at your bills or visit utility company Web sites to learn how to read your electric and gas meters. Your utility company may provide free or low-cost energy auditing services. You can also hire a company that provides this service.

The government's Home Energy Saver™ calculator, available at http://hes.lbl.gov, is an easy way to get a quick assessment of the energy used at a residential address. The calculator also computes greenhouse gas emissions.

You can visit the government's Energy Star Web site at www.energystar.gov. The Home Energy Yardstick can help you see how your home's energy use compares with similar homes across the country.

Heating and Cooling

Home heating and cooling consumes the greatest share of energy in the home. You can use the thermostat in your home to conserve energy. Consider saving energy by setting the thermostat no higher than 68° F in winter and no lower than 78° F in summer.

You also conserve energy by keeping equipment clean and in good working order. Be sure to change or clean filters regularly.

When heating or cooling equipment is in use, you can save energy by closing off unused rooms and keeping all outside doors and windows tightly closed. Also, keep heating and cooling vents clear of furniture, rugs, and other obstacles.

Insulate Your Home

Well-fitted storm doors and windows prevent winter heat loss and the escape of cool air in the summer. You can buy inexpensive weather-stripping kits and materials that can be used to stop drafts through loose-fitting windows and doors.

Insulation is necessary in all homes, especially older homes. *Insulation* is a material used to slow the movement of hot or cool air. It is installed in ceilings, walls, and floors to help maintain the desired indoor air temperature. Although insulating a home can be costly, over time, it more than pays for itself in lower fuel costs.

Conserve Hot Water

The gas or electric water heater is a major energy user in the home, but insulating the hot water tank cuts energy use. Less energy will be needed to keep the water hot. If you buy a new water heater, look for one with high energy-efficiency ratings.

Water heaters have an adjustable thermostat. Set the temperature no higher than 140°F to avoid scalding.

Use Appliances and Electrical Devices Wisely

Electrical appliances and equipment account for about 23 percent of energy used at home. Some energy-use strategies were discussed in Chapter 20. Following are more tips.

- Replace incandescent bulbs with compact fluorescent lightbulbs (CFLs), 23-4. They use about 75 percent less electricity and last up to 10 times longer. Look for "dimmable" bulbs if you have dimmer controls.

- Turn off the television, computer, lights, and other electrical equipment when not in use.

- Keep appliances and equipment in good working condition. Periodically check and clean refrigerator and freezer door seals to make sure they fit tightly. Open doors for only as long as necessary.

- Use the appliance that takes the least amount of energy for the job. For example, use your microwave if you have one. It uses approximately one-third of the energy of a conventional oven.

- Use dishwashers, clothes washers, and clothes dryers in the early morning or late evening to ease energy demand during peak usage times. Use dishwashers only for full loads and select the shortest cycle able to do the job well. For greater energy efficiency from clothes dryers, clean the filters after each use.

Buy Green Energy

Many homes are heated by *conventional power*—coal, natural gas, oil, and power created by nuclear power plants. In some parts of the country, homes and businesses can choose to purchase electricity from companies that supply green power. *Green power* includes forms of renewable energy, such as wind and solar power.

Some major energy suppliers also offer green energy sources as an alternative or as a supplement to conventional energy. You may be charged

23-4
Using compact fluorescent lightbulbs is an easy way for consumers to lower electricity use.

Recyclers

Recyclers turn old products, used appliances, and automobiles into useful, environmentally safe raw materials. They may analyze waste reduction and recycling opportunities and design and implement reduce, reuse, and recycle programs. They may operate machines that compress materials into easy-to-transport bundles.

more for green power than for conventional power. However, as green power becomes more widely available, the costs should come down.

For information about green power sources in your area, go to the Web site of the Office of Energy Efficiency and Renewable Energy of the U.S. Department of Energy. Look under "Green Power Network."

Conserve Water

There are many ways you can cut down on water usage. The following tips will help you save on your water bill as well as conserve a valuable resource.

In the bathroom, take shorter showers and install a low-flow shower-head. Turn off water while brushing your teeth or shaving. When installing a new toilet, buy a water-saving model. For new installations, this is required by law in most communities.

In the kitchen, do not let water run while washing or rinsing dishes or cleaning vegetables and fruits. Repair leaky faucets promptly. When using the dishwasher and clothes washer, wash only full loads.

Outdoors, water gardens and lawns in the early evening to prevent evaporation by the sunlight. Use a soaker hose—they water more efficiently than sprinklers. During dry spells, water trees and plantings rather than the grass. Lawns will normally recover after a drought, while big trees and delicate plantings can suffer permanent damage.

Reduce Waste

Reducing trash involves an overall sense of economizing—buying less, using less, reusing, and recycling. To **recycle** means to reprocess resources so they can be used again, 23-5. Recycling reduces waste in landfills, conserves resources, and saves energy. Almost every community provides some type of recycling and waste disposal programs. Many areas offer pick-up services for recyclables and others have drop-off centers.

Reducing paper trash is a good place to start. You can reduce the junk mail you receive by contacting the Direct Marketing Association. By signing up with their Mail Preference Service, you will stop getting unsolicited mail from direct-mail marketers. You can have your bills and bank statements sent to you electronically instead of on paper. Many utilities and financial institutions provide this service.

Some communities encourage composting as a method of reducing and recycling yard and other organic waste. **Composting** is a natural process that transforms materials like food waste, leaves, and grass clippings into useful soil-like particles. Find out whether

23-5

Most communities have recycling programs for plastic, glass, paper, and some metals.

Case Study: Town Meeting

When the Landfill Is Full

Devon is president of the town council. He inherited a number of community problems, including a landfill almost filled to capacity. A sanitation report calls for closing the landfill in three years.

To extend the use of the landfill, Devon and the town council want to find another place to dispose of solid waste. Transporting waste to a distant landfill will be very costly. Increases may run as much as $200 to $300 annually per household.

Devon suggests the following approaches to the problem:

- Promote voluntary recycling with curbside pickup of recyclable materials.
- Establish mandatory recycling with curbside pickup and fines for failure to recycle.
- Charge a fee-per-pound of waste over a specified minimum to encourage recycling and composting of yard wastes. Establish a community-based compost program for yard wastes.
- Assist households with composting of both yard and food waste.
- Designate convenient drop-off centers for all recyclable waste.
- Levy a special tax per household to pay for solid waste disposal.
- Require local merchants to recycle packing materials and other recyclable waste.
- Organize an awareness campaign to encourage residents and merchants to reduce, reuse, and recycle solid waste materials.

Case Review

1. Which three ideas would you favor most? Explain.
2. Which three ideas would you favor least? Explain.
3. What other actions can you think of for reducing, recycling, and disposing of solid waste?
4. Which of the above would be the most and least costly for individuals, businesses, and local government? the most and least convenient?
5. Choose one of the alternatives and prepare a report describing the environmental pros and cons of the action and the costs for individuals, merchants, and the local government.
6. Which of the described actions have been carried out in your area and how well do they work?

Resource

The Four R's, transparency master 23-2, TR

Discuss

Give examples of the three ways to reduce waste—reducing, reusing, and recycling.

Reflect

What materials do you routinely recycle?

Resource

What's in America's Trash? transparency master 23-3, TR

Discuss

How would you weigh world food needs against the use of pesticides to increase production? How can we decide what is a reasonable and safe use of pesticides?

Discuss

What are the nonenergy-related benefits of walking or biking when possible?

Reflect

How often do you or your family drive unnecessarily?

your local government sponsors a composting project or offers information on home compost measures.

Disposing of Hazardous Waste

Most areas also provide specified pick-up days or drop-off sites for disposal of hazardous waste and electronic products. Find out how your community handles household waste and direct your waste to the appropriate place. You can also locate sites for various types of waste disposal and treatment online at www.epa.gov.

The mercury in compact fluorescent lightbulbs makes them more efficient. They release no mercury when in use. However, because of the mercury content, you must use extra care when disposing of used or broken bulbs. Many retailers who sell CFLs will accept used bulbs for recycling. You also can check in your community for recycling programs. Go to www.epa.gov for information on recycling CFLs and on the procedures to follow if a bulb breaks.

In caring for your yard and garden, limit or eliminate the use of pesticides. In household cleaning, look for biodegradable, nontoxic products with low or no phosphate and chlorine content.

Web sites provide helpful information on recycling and responsible disposal of home appliances and electronic products. Check the government listings in your phone book or look for the Environmental Protection Agency's E-Cycling page online.

Make Each Mile Count

Transportation accounts for almost two-thirds of the petroleum used in the United States. There are many opportunities for energy conservation and pollution control in this area. The greatest difference you can make is switching from driving to biking, walking, or taking public transportation. Limiting airplane travel can also help reduce petroleum use.

Drivers can conserve fuel and cut down costs by following these tips:

- Consider buying a small car to reduce fuel needs.

- Plan trips carefully, combining errands when possible.

- Carpool when possible.

- Lower your driving speed. Most cars get about 20 percent better fuel economy on the highway at 55 miles per hour than they do at 70 miles per hour.

- Maintain your car to improve engine life and performance.

What Citizen Groups Can Do

At the local level, citizen action is often the driving force that protects a community's environment. The grassroots efforts of citizens working together have led to investigations of polluting industries and the establishment of local air and water quality standards. Citizen groups also help launch recycling and composting centers. In some communities, they promote programs for recycling electronic products and safe disposal of hazardous waste. These groups frequently organize clean-up days for local public areas such as beaches, parks, and playgrounds.

Some communities have managed to turn solid waste into an asset by producing energy from gas built up in landfills. Other landfills are turned into golf courses and recreational areas.

Many communities sponsor a variety of programs to protect and enhance the environment. These include restrictions on land use, emissions controls, and environmental education and awareness programs. To reduce air pollution from cars, some communities restrict downtown parking, ban auto traffic in certain parts of the city, and improve public transportation. Other areas encourage carpooling by establishing express highway lanes for cars with two or more passengers.

Enrich

Investigate and report on environmental activities of citizen groups in your area.

Reflect

What types of recycling programs exist in your community?

Enrich

Investigate environmental programs in your community and report to class.

Case Study: Town Meeting

One Can Make a Difference

Maxine recently attended a community presentation titled "Survival on Planet Earth." The speaker outlined five critical environmental issues:

- solid waste disposal
- energy conservation
- climate change
- water purity and conservation
- hazardous waste disposal

The speaker also shared powerful "what you can do" directives. After the presentation, Maxine started forming a "Mother Earth" action group at her high school. Within a week's time, Maxine had 25 enthusiastic members. The group wants to take steps in each of the five areas. They hope to gain both individual and community participation.

Case Review

1. Choose two environmental issues and outline at least three actions the Mother Earth group could take in each area. Include individual and community projects.

2. Discuss environmental protection and conservation projects that might work in your home, school, and community.

Local action is the speediest, most direct way to deal with problems in and near your community. Watch for activities in your community. Take whatever steps you can to protect the air you breathe, water you drink, and parks and open spaces you enjoy. Environmental information Web sites are good places to find examples of actions individuals and communities can take to protect and enhance the environment, 23-6.

Activity
Participate in a beautification or clean-up project in your area.

23-6
The Internet offers a wealth of information related to environmental concerns. Consult Web sites from reliable sources such as the government or reputable organizations and groups.

Enrich
Find an area in your community in need of cleanup or beautification and develop a plan for it.

Activity
Make a list of environmental groups and publications for reference.

Activity
Visit each of the Web sites listed for information on environmental issues.

Environmental Information Web Sites

Government

National Aeronautics and Space Administration (NASA) on Global Climate Change	http://climate.jpl.nasa.gov
U.S. Department of Energy and U.S. Environmental Protection Agency ENERGY STAR Program	www.energystar.gov
U.S. Department of Energy Office of Energy Efficiency and Renewable Energy	www.eere.energy.gov
U.S. Environmental Protection Agency	www.epa.gov
U.S. Fish & Wildlife Service Endangered Species Program	www.fws.gov/endangered
United Nations Environment Programme	www.unep.org

Consumer Groups and Nonprofits

Basel Action Network	www.ban.org
Center for Resource Solutions	www.green-e.org
Consumers Union	www.greenerchoices.org
National Resources Defense Council	www.nrdc.org
The Nature Conservancy	www.nature.org
Ocean Conservancy	www.oceanconservancy.org
World Wildlife Federation	www.wwf.org

Business/Industry Groups

American Council for an Energy-Efficient Economy	www.aceee.org
Association of Home Appliance Manufacturers	www.aham.org
Consumer Electronics Association	www.ce.org
E-Cycling Central, Telecommunications Industry Association	www.eiae.org
U.S. Chamber of Commerce Institute for 21st Century Energy	www.energyxxi.org

What Government Can Do

In Chapter 2, you learned about the role of government in the U.S. economic system. Another important function of government is to ensure a safe and healthy environment for its citizens. Because both the environment and the economy are critical issues, the methods used to protect and conserve the environment and its resources need to be cost-effective.

Many environmental problems—climate change, deforestation, and water pollution, among others—are global. The government frequently pursues environmental interests at the international level.

Regulation and Legislation

In 1970, the federal government passed legislation creating the Environmental Protection Agency (EPA). The agency serves as the national watchdog and coordinating bureau for matters affecting the environment. The EPA focuses on air and water quality, noise, solid waste, hazardous waste, toxic substances, and other ecological issues.

Under a 1975 law, the Department of Energy (DOE) was required to set efficiency standards for major home appliances and several commercial products. The goal of the standards was to reduce the nation's energy use. Since then, the list of products under the DOE's review has grown. Besides setting minimum efficiency standards, it also sets maximum water-use standards for certain products. The DOE is charged with periodically reviewing opportunities for more energy- and water-savings from the items under its authority. These reviews involve input from manufacturers and consumers.

In addition, many state and local regulations govern environmental activities. To find out how your state is involved, go to your state Web site and look for the department or agency that deals with environmental issues.

Taxation

The use of taxes as a tool in fighting pollution is a recent concept. The so-called "green tax" offers a way to charge the cost of pollution to the polluter, whether producer or consumer. Examples of possible items subject to a green tax include excess household waste and auto emissions.

Green taxes could take the form of direct tax, fines, or user fees. They would provide greater incentive and pressure to find cost-effective ways of reducing and controlling pollution. Green taxes would also produce revenues that could be used to help clean up waste and pay for government pollution control services.

In some cases, government can use tax incentives to reward and encourage good environmental stewardship by both consumers and business. Examples include tax benefits for insulating homes, using solar energy, or purchasing fuel-efficient cars and appliances.

Transportation, Distribution & Logistics

Environmental Compliance Inspectors

Environmental compliance inspectors examine, evaluate, and investigate eligibility for or conformity with laws and regulations governing contract compliance of licenses and permits, and other compliance and enforcement inspection activities. They work to control and reduce the pollution of water, air, and land.

Enrich

Find out where policymakers in your community and your congressional district stand on environmental issues.

Activity

Write a description of an environmental law you would propose if you were a local official.

Enrich

Study and report on the cost/benefit relationship of various environmental regulations.

Enrich

Debate the pros and cons of using taxation as a tool for environmental purposes.

ECONOMICS in ACTION

Can Pollution Credits Work?

The U.S. government uses market incentives to tackle environmental problems. New programs create markets where "pollution credits" are bought and sold like stocks and bonds. The laws of supply and demand set credit prices.

For example, conservation banking programs reward landowners and local governments for preserving open space, endangered species, and habitats. They earn credits that can be sold. Other people or businesses must buy credits to offset environmental damage they cause. Having to buy credits is costly and discourages practices that are harmful to the environment.

Another example is a cap-and-trade program for greenhouse gas emissions. The government sets a cap, or maximum allowable amount, for GHG emissions. Businesses get an initial allowance of credits from the government.

They are awarded additional credits for good environmental stewardship, such as planting trees.

If a business exceeds the emissions cap, it must pay the government with credits. If a business doesn't have enough credits, it can buy them from other lower-polluting businesses. Having to purchase credits is like paying a fine.

These programs, especially the cap-and-trade program, are controversial. Program promoters say they minimize the cost of government regulation. Business owners, not government regulators, decide how to keep their emissions under the cap. However, some environmentalists say the programs don't do enough to curtail fossil fuel burning and other environmental damage. Other critics say they create undue hardship for businesses and will boost energy prices for consumers.

Resource

Where Has All the Gasoline Gone? Activity E, WB

Discuss

Which conservation methods do you think should be voluntary and which should be required by law?

Enrich

Debate the pros and cons of increasing fuel prices to encourage conservation and exploration for new sources.

Clean Energy Development

Energy policies and choices affect jobs, prices, industries, the environment, and lifestyles here and around the world. It is clear that dependence on nonrenewable and polluting sources of energy must be severely curtailed. Harnessing the energy of the sun, wind, and water may provide a large share of the energy used in the future. Scientists and entrepreneurs are also developing other sources of energy. Government is heavily involved in these efforts both through its own laboratories and through funding of research in leading universities.

Other actions government could take on energy issues include the following:

- Tax fossil fuels to encourage greater efficiency and discourage excessive energy consumption.

- Provide incentives for industries to conduct comprehensive clean energy research.

- Work out a cooperative policy with other nations for the development, allocation, and efficient safe use of world energy resources.

Water Conservation

Areas experiencing water shortages can lower the system-wide operating pressure to reduce the flow of water. Government can also enact bans, restrictions, and rationing for different types of water usage. These normally are temporary measures taken during periods of severe shortages. More permanent conservation measures include

- local building codes that require water-efficient faucets, toilets, showerheads, and appliances in new construction

- utility billing that imposes higher rates for excess water usage

- increased recycling of industrial water

Enrich

Find out where there have been water shortages in the U.S. in recent years and how the communities dealt with the problem.

Discuss

What are some of the consequences of water shortages?

Enrich

Find out whether your community restricts water usage in any way and report to the class.

Case Study: Town Meeting

The Well Runs Dry

Two summers after Devon became town council president, a drought hit the area and the water table dropped substantially. The town needed to reduce its water usage.

Devon suggested raising water rates by 20 percent. A town council member recommended a ban on watering lawns, trees, shrubs, and gardens. Other council members advised limiting watering to evening and early morning hours.

Council members also suggested educating residents about taking shorter showers and finding ways to reduce water use. Another idea mandated low-flow toilets, showerheads, and appliances in new and remodeled bathrooms and kitchens. Members also discussed installing a water-rationing system to limit water usage in each household.

Case Review

1. What other steps can you think of for conserving water?
2. How would each of the council's suggestions affect you and your family?
3. Which idea do you think would be most effective? Why?
4. How would you be willing to change your own habits to help conserve water and other resources in a crisis situation?
5. What are some important considerations for government bodies to think about when passing laws and policies to deal with resource shortages?

Enrich

Research an environmental issue you read about in this chapter. Write a report summarizing current information.

Resource

In Your Hands, color lesson slide, TR

Resource

Chapter 23—Your Role in the Environment, Teacher's PowerPoint Presentations CD

- public education programs to encourage voluntary reductions in water usage

- water meter accuracy and leak detection

What Businesses Can Do

Manufacturers and retailers share responsibility for the environmental impact of the production, use, and disposal of their products. *Product stewardship* is an environmental concept that calls on businesses to take a leadership role in reducing the health and environmental impacts of consumer products. For example, producers should try to:

- design products to be upgraded instead of discarded

- incorporate energy-saving features

- use recycled materials in the product or its packaging, if feasible

- avoid excess packaging

- use renewable energy and recycled water in the manufacturing process

- upgrade machinery and vehicles to energy-saving models

- minimize the discharge of pollutants into the environment

Manufacturers and retailers can encourage recycling by providing free pickup of unused goods, such as old appliances. They can sponsor education programs to identify the efforts being made to preserve natural resources.

Some businesses are taking back products that reach end-of-life and offering free recycling to customers. Others are refurbishing used products for resale or donation. By planning for disposal during product design, producers can also minimize disposal problems.

Chapter Summary

Protecting the environment is one of the most pressing challenges of our day. It calls for the attention, participation, and best efforts of all of us—individuals, local communities, government, and businesses. Climate change, waste disposal, dwindling resources, and urban sprawl are some of the environmental challenges that need attention and action.

You can take an active role in protecting the earth. Stay informed about current environmental issues. Learn to conserve resources in your own life and participate in community environmental protection programs.

Government protects the environment with regulation, legislation, and tax policies that encourage and enforce conservation and sustainable practices. The government also supports research to find solutions for environmental challenges.

Manufacturers and retailers also play an important role in solving environmental challenges. Businesses can reduce the toll of manufacturing on the environment by minimizing waste, conserving resources, and recycling materials.

Review

1. Name three key environmental issues facing the United States and the world today.

2. What factors contribute to climate change?

3. Explain the difference between fossil fuels and biofuels and give an example of each.

4. Name three renewable energy sources.

5. What are the two main forms of energy used in the United States?

6. What are three drawbacks of using coal as an energy source?

7. List five ways to conserve energy in the home.

8. Name three ways to conserve water in the home.

9. List three ways to reduce waste.

10. What are three ways to use less gasoline in your car?

11. Which government agency was created to serve as the national watchdog and coordinating bureau for the environment?

12. What are green taxes?

13. Name three actions government can take regarding water conservation.

14. What steps can businesses take during the design process to reduce a product's environmental impact?

Critical Thinking

15. What are some of the problems that concern environmentalists today? What environmental problems concern you the most?

16. Investigate to find out where water shortages have been a serious problem in the United States. Find out how affected communities coped with the problem.

17. Why is it important for consumers to be informed about threats to the environment?

18. Name several steps you as an individual can take to preserve and protect our planet.

19. How can consumer spending habits and decisions serve as an environmental protection tool?

20. What are some environmental problems that exist in your community? How might they be solved? What are some things you personally can do to address environmental issues?

Answers to *Review*

1. (Name three:) climate change, waste disposal, dwindling resources, urban sprawl
2. global warming; natural processes; human activities that release greenhouse gases; deforestation
3. (See page 594.)
4. wind, water, and sun
5. petroleum and natural gas
6. Coal is difficult to transport. Mining and burning coal damage the environment. Converting coal to a gaseous or liquid form is costly.
7. (See pages 598–600.)
8. (See page 600.)
9. (List three:) buy less, use less, reuse, recycle, compost
10. buy a smaller car; plan trips; carpool; lower your driving speed; maintain your car
11. Environmental Protection Agency
12. Taxes that charge the cost of pollution to the polluter (either the producer or consumer).
13. (See pages 607–608.)
14. (See page 608.)

Academic Connections

21. **Research, writing, speech.** Visit the Web sites of the Environmental Protection Agency, the Department of Energy, or another government agency for facts and data you need to prepare a written or an oral report on one of the following:
    - climate change
    - ecosystems
    - urban sprawl versus smart growth
    - air quality
    - conservation
    - The Kyoto Accord
    - water shortages
    - Earth Day
    - recycling
    - pollution control regulations and costs
    Make an effort to present a balanced view covering both sides of controversial issues. Cite authorities, events, dates, figures, pros, and cons.

22. **Research, science.** Divide into research teams to investigate one of the following sources or types of energy: nuclear, natural gas, coal, solar, geothermal, petroleum, wind, water, or underwater technology. Prepare a report on its use, cost, safety, effectiveness, availability, and impact on the environment.

23. **Reading, speech, writing.** Select one of the current local, state, or federal laws or pending bills designed to protect the environment. Study it carefully to find out:
    A. Its main objectives and key provisions.
    B. Its costs and benefits.
    C. Its impact on different segments of society.
    D. Its effectiveness in achieving its purpose.
    E. The ease of enforcing it.
    Present your findings to the class in an oral report or a written report.

24. **Speech.** Debate the pros and cons of an energy tax to reduce pollution, conserve energy, and generate government revenues.

25. **Science.** Conduct an experiment to explore biodegradable materials. Bury the following items in soil in milk cartons (cut off the tops). Add a cup of water to each carton.
    - plastic utensil
    - apple slices
    - piece of trash bag marketed as biodegradable
    - piece of plastic trash bag
    - piece of newspaper
    - wood chip
    After three weeks, remove and examine the items. Rate each item high or low in terms of biodegradability.

26. **Writing.** Write a letter to an appropriate government agency, representative, or official at the federal, state, or local level regarding an environmental issue of concern to you. Define the issue, suggest possible solutions, and express your opinion with supporting arguments. Cite authorities and relevant publications or studies, if available.

MATH CHALLENGE

27. Suppose a car gets 20 miles per gallon (mpg) going 70 miles per hour (mph). If the car gets 20 percent better fuel economy going 55 mph, how much farther does it travel per gallon of fuel at the lower speed?

Tech Smart

28. Go to www.epa.gov/climatechange. Use the greenhouse gas household emissions calculator to estimate the amount of GHGs you create. You may need recent gas and electric bills to estimate utility use for your family's home. What are your total emissions?environmental issues.

Answer to *Math Challenge*
27. An extra 4 mpg. (20 mpg x 20% = 4 mpg)

GLOSSARY

A

abilities. Physical and mental skills developed through learning, training, and practice. (21)

abstract of title. A summary of the public records or history of the ownership of a particular piece of property. (18)

accessories. Items designed to go with an outfit. (16)

adjustable rate mortgage (ARM). A mortgage in which the interest rate is adjusted up or down periodically. (18)

advertising. A paid message touting the attributes of something in order to convince consumers to buy it. (13)

amortization. The process by which loan payments are applied to the principal, or amount borrowed, as well as to the interest on a loan according to a set schedule. (18)

annual percentage rate (APR). The annual cost of credit a lender charges. (9)

annual percentage yield (APY). The rate of yearly earnings from an account, including compound interest. (11)

annuity. A contract with an insurance company that provides income for a set period of time or for life. (12)

appraisal. An estimate of the current value of property. (10)

appreciation. An increase in the value of an investment. (12)

apprenticeship. A type of education that combines on-the-job training, work experience, and classroom-type instruction. (21)

aptitudes. Natural physical and mental talents. (21)

asset. An item of value that a person owns, such as cash, stocks, bonds, real estate, and personal possessions. (3)

ATM card. A card that allows customers to withdraw cash from and make deposits to their accounts using an ATM. (8)

automated teller machine (ATM). A computer terminal used to transact business with a financial institution. (8)

B

bait and switch. A fraudulent sales technique that involves advertising an attractive offer to bring the customer into the store. The item is either sold out or is undesirable. The seller then presents a more expensive substitute. (14)

balance of payments. An account of the flow of goods, services, and money coming into and going out of the country. (4)

bandwidth. The maximum amount of information that can be carried over an electronic cable or device at one time. (20)

bankruptcy. A legal state in which the courts excuse a debtor from repaying some or all debt. In return, the debtor must give up certain assets and possessions. (9)

bank statement. A record of checks, deposits, and charges on a checking account. (8)

bear market. Term for the market when investors feel insecure and stock prices fall. (12)

beneficiary. Person named by the policyholder to receive the death benefit of an insurance policy. (10)

binding arbitration. A method of settling disputes outside of court in which the parties involved agree to accept the decision of a third party. (14)

biodegradable. Describes a material that can be broken down naturally by microorganisms into harmless elements. (23)

biofuel. A fuel composed of or produced from biological raw material. (23)

blend. A yarn made by combining two or more fibers. (16)

bodily injury liability. Coverage that protects insured persons when they are liable for an auto accident that injured or killed others. (10)

body composition. The proportion of muscle, bone, fat, and other tissue that make up body weight. (17)

bond. A certificate of debt issued by a corporation or government that entitles the bondholder to a set rate of interest on the face value of the bond until it matures. (12)

bonus. Money added to an employee's base pay. It is usually a reward for performance or a share of business profits. (7)

brand name products. Products that have distinctive packaging and are identified with one manufacturer. (15)

broadband. High-speed Internet access that transmits data at speeds greater than 200 kilobits per second. (20)

budget. A spending plan for the use of money over time based on goals and expected income. (6)

bull market. Term for the market when investors are confident in the economy and stock prices are rising. (12)

business cycle. A cycle of economic activity with periods called *contraction, trough, recovery,* and *peak.* (2)

buying incentives. Trading stamps, coupons, store games, and prizes offered by sellers to help sell goods and services. (14)

C

capital. Money used to generate income or to invest in a business or asset. (4)

capital gain. Income earned from selling an asset for more than the purchase price. (12)

career clusters. Sixteen general groupings of occupational and career developed by a partnership among the states, educators, and employers. (21)

career ladder. An outline of jobs in a given career field that are available at different levels of education and training experience. (21)

career plan. An outline of steps or action you can take to reach a career goal, including required courses and training, job-related experiences, and extracurricular activities or projects. (21)

cartel. A group of countries or firms that control the production and pricing of a product or service. (4)

cash flow statement. A summary of the amount of money received as well as the amount paid out for goods and services during a specific period. (6)

cashier's check. A check drawn by a bank on its own funds and signed by an authorized officer of the bank. (8)

caveat emptor. A principle meaning the risk in the transaction is on the buyer's side; literally, *let the buyer beware.* (14)

certificate of deposit (CD). Money deposited for a set period of time that earns a set annual rate of interest. (11)

certified check. A personal check with a bank's guarantee the check will be paid. (8)

certified used car. A previously owned car that received a thorough mechanical and appearance inspection along with necessary repairs and replacements. (19)

chain letters. Letters or e-mails that generally promise big returns for sending something, such as a postcard or a dollar, to the first person on the list. (14)

class action lawsuits. Legal actions in courts of law brought by a group of individuals who have been similarly wronged. (14)

climate change. Shifts in measurements of climate—such as temperature, precipitation, or wind—that last decades or longer. (23)

closed-end credit. A loan that must be repaid with finance charges by a certain date. (9)

closing costs. Fees that must be paid before the sale of a home can be made final. (18)

coinsurance. A percentage the policyholder must pay for certain services. (10)

collateral. Property that a borrower promises to give up in case of default. (9)

collusion. When companies make illegal secret agreements, usually to engage in price fixing or to shut out smaller competitors. (2)

command economy. An economy in which a central authority, usually the government, controls economic activities. (1)

commercial bank. A bank owned by stockholders and organized to receive, transfer, and lend money to individuals, businesses, and governments. (8)

commission. Income paid as a percentage of sales made by a salesperson. (7)

common stock. Stock that pays dividends declared by the company and gives stockholders certain voting rights. (12)

community colleges. Two-year school offering both academic and occupational courses. (21)

comparative advantage. The benefit to the party that has the lower opportunity cost in pursuing a given course of action. (4)

comparison shopping. The process of gathering information about products and services to get the best quality or usefulness at the best price. (13)

compensation. Payment and benefits received for work. (7)

composting. A natural process that transforms materials like food waste, leaves, and grass into useful soil-like particles. (23)

compound interest. Interest figured on money deposited plus interest. (11)

condominium. A form of home ownership in which an individual owns his or her own unit and shares ownership and expenses of maintaining common areas such as halls, stairs, lobby, and grounds. (18)

conservation. The protection and management of the environment and valuable natural resources. (23)

consumer. The buyer or user of goods and services. Also, a person who provides the demand for goods and services at prices he or she can afford to pay. (1)

consumer advocates. Individuals or groups who promote consumer interests in areas such as health and safety, education, redress, truthful advertising, fairness in the marketplace, and environmental protection. (14)

consumer cooperative. A nonretail association owned and operated by a group of members for their own benefit rather than for profit. (13)

consumer electronic product. Devices that run on electric current or batteries and are used for communication, entertainment, education, or information gathering. (20)

consumer price index (CPI). A measurement of changes in the prices of selected consumer goods and services. (2)

contingency clause. An agreement that calls for certain requirements to be met before the contract is binding. (18)

continuing education. Learning pursued after a person completes formal education and training. (21)

contract. A legally binding agreement between a borrower and a creditor. (9)

convenience foods. Foods that are partially prepared or ready-to-eat. (15)

convergence. The merging of separate devices, technologies, or industries into one. (20)

cooperative. A form of home ownership in which an individual buys shares in a corporation that owns the property. In return, the buyer becomes a resident in a designated unit and a member of the cooperative. (18)

co-payment. A flat fee the policyholder must pay for certain services. (10)

corporation. A business that is a separate entity created and owned by the founder and shareholders. (22)

cosigner. A responsible person who signs a loan along with a borrower thereby agreeing to pay the obligation if the borrower fails to do so. (9)

cost-benefit principle. The idea that an action should be taken or a purchase made only if the benefits are at least as great as the costs. (5)

credit. An arrangement that allows consumers to buy goods or services and pay for them later. (9)

credit card. Allows consumers to make purchases or borrow money on a time-payment plan. (9)

creditor. The party that supplies money, goods, or services in a credit agreement. (9)

credit report. A record of a person's credit history and financial behavior. (9)

credit union. A nonprofit financial cooperative owned by and operated for the benefit of its members. It accepts deposits, makes loans, and provides other services. (8)

creditworthy. A credit applicant judged to have the assets, income, and tendency to repay debt. (9)

D

decision-making process. A method of choosing a course of action after evaluating information and weighing the costs and benefits of alternative actions and their consequences. (5)

deductible. The amount you will be required to pay before insurance pays for any services. (10)

default. When a borrower fails to pay the debt owed. (9)

deficit spending. When government spends more than it collects in tax revenues and must borrow money. (2)

demand. The amount of a product or service consumers are willing to buy. (1)

demographics. The statistical characteristics of the population. (6)

dependent. An individual who relies on someone else for financial support. (10)

depreciation. A decrease in the value of property as a result of age or wear and tear. (10)

depression. An extended period of economic recession. (2)

dial-up. Internet access through a telephone line using a modem in the computer. (20)

Dietary Guidelines for Americans. Suggestions for choosing nutritious foods and maintaining a healthful lifestyle developed by the U.S. Departments of Agriculture and Health and Human Services. (14)

dietary supplement. A product that is intended to enhance a person's diet. It contains ingredients such as vitamins, minerals, herbs, or amino acids and other substances. (17)

digital subscriber line (DSL). Internet access that uses a digital frequency that does not interfere with telephone service. (20)

direct broadcast satellite (DBS). A type of television and Internet service that works by bouncing transmissions off orbiting satellites directly to receivers on customers' homes. (20)

direct mail advertising. Advertising circulars, catalogs, coupons, and other unsolicited offers that arrive through mail or another delivery service. (14)

disability. A limitation that affects a person's ability to function in major life activities. (7)

distance learning. Education or training delivered to the student online, by mail, or on television, offering many choices in both individual courses and total program options. (21)

diversification. Spreading risk by putting money in a variety of investments. (12)

dividend. A portion of a company's earnings paid to stockholders. (12)

dollar-cost averaging. A strategy of investing a fixed dollar amount at regular intervals. (12)

dual-career family. A family where both spouses have careers outside the home. (22)

durable goods. Products that have lasting value, such as furniture, appliances, and cars. (3)

E

earned income. Income from employment. (7)

earnest money. The deposit you make when you sign a purchase agreement to show that your offer is serious. (18)

easy-access credit. A short-term, high-interest loan granted to borrowers regardless of credit history. (9)

ecology. The study of the relationship between living things and their environment. (23)

e-commerce. Buying and selling goods and services online. (13)

economic globalization. The flow of goods, services, labor, money, innovative ideas, and technology across borders. (4)

economic system. The structure in which resources are turned into goods and services to address unlimited needs and wants. (1)

economies of scale. The concept that cost of producing one unit of something declines as the number of units produced rises. (4)

e-learning. Internet education and training programs. (21)

electronic funds transfer (EFT). The movement of money electronically from one financial institution to another. (8)

employee benefit. A form of nonmonetary compensation received in addition to a wage or salary. (7)

endorse. To sign one's name on the back of a check in order to cash or deposit the check. (8)

endowment insurance. Insurance that pays the face value of the policy to beneficiaries if the insured dies before the endowment period ends. It also pays the face amount to the insured if he or she lives beyond the endowment period. (10)

EnergyGuide label. A label that lists the estimated annual cost of operating an appliance. (20)

ENERGY STAR label. A program that is a voluntary partnership of the U.S. Department of Energy and the Environmental Protection Agency, product manufacturers, local utilities, and retailers. Its purpose is to encourage the purchase of energy-efficient consumer electronics and appliances. (20)

entitlement. A government payment or benefit promised by law to eligible citizens, such as Social Security and Medicare benefits, unemployment benefits, veterans' services, food stamps, and housing assistance. (7)

entrepreneur. A person who owns, operates, and assumes the risk for a business. (22)

environmentalist. A person concerned with the quality of the environment and how to maintain it. (23)

escrow account. An account used to hold money until it can be paid to the party that is owed. (18)

estate. The possessions, such as property, savings, investments, and insurance benefits, a person leaves when he or she dies. (12)

ethic. A moral principle or belief that directs a person's actions. (5)

euro. A common currency used in Europe among the nations participating in the European Union (EU). (4)

European Union (EU). A group of nations joined together to form a trade sector, most of which use a common currency called the euro. (4)

exchange rate. The value of one currency compared to another. (4)

exclusions. The services that are not covered in an insurance plan. (10)

exclusive buyer agent. A real estate agent who works for the buyer, not the seller. (18)

executor. A person appointed to carry out the terms outlined in a will. (12)

exemption. A tax benefit that reduces the amount of income a person is taxed on. (7)

expense. The cost of a good or service a person buys. (6)

expiration date. The last day a product should be used. (15)

exports. The goods and services grown or made in a particular country and then sold in world markets. (4)

extended warranty. A contract that provides for the servicing of a product, if needed, during the term of the contract. (13)

F

fabric finish. A treatment applied to a fabric to achieve certain characteristics. (16)

fad. A fashion style that stays popular for only a short time. (16)

family crisis. A major problem that impacts the future of the family and its lifestyle. (6)

family life cycle. The stages of change a family passes through from formation to aging. (6)

Federal Deposit Insurance Corporation (FDIC). A U.S. government agency that protects bank customers by insuring deposits as well as examining and supervising financial institutions. (8)

Federal Reserve System. The U.S. government system that regulates the nation's money supply and banking system. It is comprised of the Federal Reserve Board, 12 Federal Reserve Banks, and the Federal Open Market Committee. (2)

fee-for-service. A health insurance plan that pays for covered medical services after treatment is provided. (10)

FHA-insured loan. A loan in which the Federal Housing Administration insures the lender against the borrowers' possible default or failure to pay. (18)

fiber. The indigestible or partially indigestible part of foods that helps move food and digestive byproducts through the large intestine for healthy digestion. (15)

fiber optics. Glass strands as narrow as a human hair that carry data at the speed of a laser light beam. (20)

FICA (Federal Insurance Contributions Act). The law that requires the collection of social security payroll taxes. (7)

financial literacy. The understanding of the basic knowledge and skills needed to manage financial resources. (6)

firewall. A protection system to block unwanted e-mail, offensive Web sites, and potential hackers. (20)

fiscal policy. The government's taxing and spending decisions. (2)

fixed expense. A set cost that must be paid each budgeted period. (6)

fixed rate mortgage. A mortgage that guarantees a fixed or unchanging interest rate for the life of the loan. (18)

floor plan. A drawing that shows the size and shape of a room on a scale of ¼ inch to a foot. (18)

food grades. An indication of how well a food meets quality standards. (15)

foreclosure. The forced sale of a property. (9)

Form W-2. A Wage and Tax Statement that states the amount an employee was paid in the previous year. It also gives the amounts of income, Social Security, and Medicare taxes withheld from an employee's income during the year. (7)

Form W-4. The Employee's Withholding Allowance Certificate that tells the employer how much tax to withhold from an employee's paycheck. (7)

fossil fuel. A fuel derived from the decomposed remains of animals and plants that lived in prehistoric times. (23)

franchise. An agreement that permits the franchisee to market and sell goods and services in a given area that the franchiser provides. (22)

free enterprise system. An economy in which privately owned businesses operate and compete for profits with limited government regulation. Also called *market economy* or *capitalism* (1)

free trade. A policy of limited government trade restrictions. (4)

freshness date. The last day a product should be expected to have peak quality. (15)

full warranty. Provides for free repair or replacement of the warranted item or part if any defect occurs while the warranty is in effect. (13)

G

garnishment. A legal procedure requiring a portion of a debtor's pay to be set aside by the person's employer to pay creditors. (9)

GDP per capita. The market value of final goods and services produced per person. (3)

generic drug. A drug sold by its common name, chemical composition, or class. Generally costs less than a similar brand-name drug. (17)

generic products. Plain-labeled, no-brand grocery products. (15)

global warming. The steady rise in average temperatures near the earth's surface. (23)

goal. An objective a person wants to attain. (5)

good. A physical item that is produced, such as food or clothing. (1)

grace period. The time between the billing date and the start of interest charges. (9)

graduated payment mortgage. A mortgage that allows the buyer to pay low monthly payments at first and higher payments in the future. (18)

gross domestic product (GDP). The value of all goods and services produced by a nation during a specified period. (2)

gross income. A worker's earnings before deductions. (7)

H

hazardous waste. Substances—liquids, solids, and gases—that are dangerous or potentially harmful to health or the environment. (23)

health savings account (HSA). A tax-advantaged savings account available to people enrolled in qualified High Deductible Health Plans (HDHPs). (10)

high-definition TV (HDTV). Televisions that receive digital signals and display them as crisp images. (20)

home appliances. Major or small devices that run on gas or electric current and perform a specific function in the home. (20)

home equity loan. A loan in which home owners borrow the money they paid on a mortgage. (18)

human resource. A quality or characteristic a person has within himself or herself. (1)

hypoallergenic. A type of product that does not contain ingredients likely to cause allergic reactions. (17)

I

identity theft. The crime of stealing someone's credit cards, bank and investment account numbers, or social security number and using the information to commit theft or fraud. (14)

implied fitness. An unwritten warranty that guarantees a product is fit for any performance or purpose promised by the seller. (13)

implied merchantability. An unwritten warranty that guarantees a product is what it is called and does what its name implies. (13)

imports. Goods and services that come into a country from foreign countries. (4)

impulse spending. Unplanned or "spur of the moment" purchases. (15)

income. Any form of money a person receives from various sources. (6)

income tax. A tax on the earnings of individuals and corporations levied by the federal government and most state governments. (3)

inflation. An overall increase in the price of goods and services. (2)

infomercial. A program-length form of paid television programming designed to sell a service, product, or idea. (14)

innovation. The process of creating something, such as new or improved products and new ways to do things and solve problems. (1)

inpatient. A person whose care requires a stay in the hospital. (10)

inspection stamps. Stamps indicating foods are wholesome and safe to eat. (15)

interest. Payments from financial institutions, businesses, and government to use customers' money. (7)

interest only mortgage. A mortgage in which monthly payments are applied only to the interest, not the principal, for a certain number of years. (18)

interests. Activities, subjects, ideas, sports, or hobbies a person enjoys. (21)

international trade. The buying and selling of goods and services across national borders and among the people of different nations. (4)

internship. A short-term position with a sponsoring organization to gain experience in a certain field of study. (21)

interview. A meeting in which a prospective employer or an admissions officer of a school talks with an applicant. (22)

investment. An asset bought to increase wealth over time, but that carries the risk of loss. (3)

investment portfolio. The collection of securities and other assets a person owns. (12)

K

knit fabrics. Fabrics made by looping yarns together. (16)

L

labor force. Composed of people, age 16 and over, who are employed or looking for and able to work. (2)

labor productivity. The value of the goods and services a worker creates in a given time. (3)

labor union. A group of workers who unite to negotiate with employers over issues such as pay, health care benefits, and working conditions. (2)

landfill. A permanent waste disposal site for most solid and nonhazardous wastes. (23)

lawsuit. Civil action brought by a person who claims to be damaged, or negatively impacted, by another person. (14)

lease. A contract that specifies the conditions, terms, and rent for the use of an asset. (18)

liability. A financial obligation that a person currently owes or will owe in the future. (6)

lien. A legal claim on a borrower's property by a creditor who is owed money. (9)

limited warranty. Provides service, repairs, and replacements only under certain conditions. (13)

living will. A statement of instructions for specific medical treatment if a person becomes unable to make medical decisions. Also called a *healthcare directive*. (12)

loan shark. Someone who loans money at excessive rates of interest. (9)

loss leader. An item that is priced at below cost to attract buyers who will then purchase other merchandise. (14)

lottery. A form of advertising in which prizes are awarded to participants by chance in exchange for some form of payment. (14)

M

managed care plan. A health care plan that contracts with specific doctors and other health care providers, hospitals, and clinics to provide a range of medical services and preventive care to members of the plan at reduced cost. (10)

management. The process of organizing and utilizing resources to accomplish predetermined objectives. (5)

manufactured fibers. Fibers, such as polyester, nylon, and rayon, that are produced artificially from chemicals. (16)

marginal benefit. The change in total benefit of using one additional unit. (5)

marginal cost. The change in total cost of using one more unit. (5)

market economy. An economy in which privately owned businesses operate and compete for profits with limited government regulation. Also called *free enterprise system* and *capitalism*. (1)

marketplace. An arena in which consumers and producers meet to exchange goods, services, and money. (1)

mass communication. Device-dependent communications that reach large and dispersed audiences, including books, newspapers, magazines, radio, television, the Internet, movies, musical recordings, and video games. (20)

Medicaid. A government program administered by the states that pays certain health care costs for eligible low-income individuals and families. (7)

Medicare. A federal government program that helps pay the medical expenses of people 65 and older and others with certain disabilities. (7)

migrants. People who move from one place or country to another. (4)

minimum wage. The lowest hourly wage employers can pay most workers by law. (7)

mixed economy. An economic system that combines elements of the market and command systems. (1)

monetary policy. Government actions that change the amount of money in circulation by controlling interest rates and credit terms. (2)

money market fund. A type of mutual fund that deals only in high interest, short-term investments such as U.S. Treasury Bills, certificates of deposit, and commercial paper. (12)

money order. An order for a specific amount of money payable to a specific payee. (8)

monopoly. A market situation in which one seller produces the entire output of a given product or service. (2)

moped. A low-powered motorized two-wheeler with an engine capacity less than 50cc. (19)

mortgage. A home loan. (18)

motor scooter. A two-wheeled motor vehicle with an engine capacity of 50cc to 250cc. (19)

multinational corporation. A business that operates in more than one country. (4)

mutual fund. An investment created by pooling the money of many people and investing it in a collection of several securities. (12)

mutual savings bank. A saving depository owned by the depositors that divides the profits among depositors in the form of dividends. (8)

MyPyramid. A tool developed by the U.S. Department of Agriculture for developing a personal eating plan, including nutritious foods and plenty of physical activity to maintain a healthful weight. (15)

N

National Credit Union Association (NCUA). An agency that grants federal charters to qualified groups, supervises credit unions, and insures accounts in all federally chartered and many state chartered credit unions. (8)

national debt. The total amount the government owes at a given time. (2)

natural fibers. Fibers made from natural sources, such as cotton, linen, silk, and wool. (16)

needs. Items a person must have in order to survive. (1)

net asset value. A mutual fund's assets minus its liabilities. Also called *current market value*. (12)

net income. Gross income (plus bonuses) minus payroll deductions. (7)

net worth. The difference between what a person owns and owes. (6)

net worth statement. A written record of a person's current financial situation. (6)

no-fault auto insurance. Coverage that eliminates the faultfinding process in settling claims by having each policyholder make a claim after an accident. (10)

nonhuman resource. A resource external to people, such as money, time, and equipment. (1)

nonrenewable energy. A source of energy that can be used up or that cannot be used again, such as petroleum, natural gas, and coal. (23)

nonstore sellers. Also called direct marketers, they sell goods and services in different ways and from different locations. They include door-to-door salespersons, catalogs, telemarketers, electronic sales via television or Internet, consumer cooperatives, and vending machines. (13)

nonwoven fabric. Cloth, such as felt, artificial suede, lace, and net, made from construction methods other than weaving or knitting. (16)

North American Free Trade Agreement (NAFTA). An agreement that lowered trade barriers and opened markets among the United States, Canada, and Mexico. (4)

nutrient. A chemical substance found in foods that furnishes energy, builds and maintains body tissues, and regulates body processes. (15)

nutrition facts panel. A label for food products that must include certain information listed in a certain order. (15)

O

obesity. The condition of having an excess amount of body fat. (15)

obsolescence. The state of no longer being useful. (20)

occupational training. Program that prepares students for a specific type of work, available through schools and online. (21)

offshore outsourcing. The procedure of moving sections of a business to another country. (4)

oligopoly. A market situation in which a few large companies dominate an industry. (2)

open dates. Date on food that indicates when it should be used for best quality, flavor, and nutritive value. (15)

open-end credit. Allows the borrower to use a certain amount of money for an indefinite period of time. (9)

opportunity cost. The value of the best option or alternative given up in a trade-off. (1)

options. Features available with a particular car. (19)

organic foods. Foods that are produced without most modern-day farming methods and do not use manufactured fertilizers, pesticides, growth stimulants, generic engineering, and other banned processes. (15)

outsourcing. The procedure of a company moving sections of its business to other companies or to its own subsidiaries. (4)

over-the-counter drugs. A nonprescription medication available on supermarket and drug store shelves. (17)

P

pack date. The day the product was processed or packaged. (15)

partnership. A business consisting of two or more owners. (22)

pawnshop. A business that gives customers high-interest loans with personal property, such as jewelry, held as collateral. (9)

payday loan. A short-term, high interest loan that must usually be repaid on the borrower's next payday. (9)

payroll deduction. An amount subtracted from gross income. (7)

peer pressure. The power a social group has over someone who seeks the group's approval and acceptance. (13)

perfect competition. A market structure in which competition between producers results in greater innovation, better service, lower prices, and efficient allocation of resources. (2)

philanthropy. The act of giving money, goods, or services for the good of others. (6)

phishing. A crime committed online with messages that seek personal information. (14)

physical fitness. A state in which all body systems function efficiently. (17)

piecework income. A wage that is based on a rate per unit or item completed. (7)

point-of-sale. In-store shopping aids that save the consumer time and money and help him or her make appropriate selections. (15)

points. A one-time charge by lenders at closing. A point is one percent of the amount of the loan. (18)

policyholder. A person who owns an insurance policy. (10)

preexisting condition. An illness or injury a person has before signing up for a health care plan. (10)

preferred stock. Stock that pays regular dividends at a set rate. Preferred stockholders have priority in receiving dividends and assets, but do not have voting privileges. (12)

premium. Amount of money paid to an insurance company for a policy on a regular basis. (10)

prepaid phone. A type of phone service that you pay for before using instead of signing a contract and paying a monthly bill. (20)

prescription drug. A medication that can only be obtained with a physician's order. (17)

primary care physician. A doctor trained to diagnose and treat a variety of illnesses in all phases of medicine. (17)

principal. The amount borrowed on a loan. (9)

priority. A goal or value that is given more importance than other goals or values. (5)

private mortgage insurance (PMI). Insurance that protects the lender from loss if the borrower defaults on the loan. (18)

probate court. The government institution that processes a deceased individual's will and estate. (12)

produce. Fresh fruits and vegetables. (15)

producer. A person who provides the supply of goods and services to meet consumer demands. (1)

product placement. A type of advertising in which a brand name product or its trademark is shown in movies and television programs. (14)

profit. The total amount of money earned after expenses are subtracted from income. (1)

property damage liability. Coverage that protects insured persons when they are liable for an auto accident where the property of others is damaged. (10)

property survey. A map of the property drawn by a surveyor to show size, boundaries, and characteristics of a property. (18)

property tax. Tax paid on real estate owned by individuals and corporations. (3)

prospectus. A legal document that gives a detailed description of a security. (12)

prosperity. A time period of growth and financial well-being. (3)

pull date. The last day a product should be sold. (15)

purchase agreement. A contract between a home buyer and a seller that includes a description of the real estate, its location, the purchase price, the possession date, and any other conditions and terms of the sale. (18)

pyramid schemes. Scams calling for each participant to buy into the plan for a given amount of money and to sign up a certain number of additional participants to do the same. The only way you can move up the pyramid and collect the promised profits is to recruit new participants who in return will recruit other participants. The many participants at the bottom of the pyramid end up paying money to the few at the top. (14)

R

real estate broker. A person licensed to arrange for the purchase and sale of real estate for a fee or commission. (18)

rebate. A deduction in price that is returned after a product has been purchased. (14)

recession. An extended period of slow or no economic growth. (2)

recordkeeping. The process of setting up and maintaining an organized system for your financial affairs. (6)

recycle. To reprocess resources so they can be used again. (23)

reference. A person who has direct knowledge of a person and his or her past work record. (22)

renewable energy. A source of energy that is continually available or can be replenished, such as wind, water, and the sun. (23)

rent-to-own. A credit arrangement in which a consumer pays rent for the use of a product and eventually owns it. (9)

repossession. A lender takes back collateral when a borrower fails to repay a loan. (9)

Reserve Officers' Training Corps (ROTC). Program offered by the military that offers education and training for low cost. Participants enter the service as officers upon graduation. (21)

resources. Any input used to generate other goods or services. (1)

résumé. A summary of a person's skills, training and education, and past work experiences. (22)

retail stores. Stores that sell goods or services directly at their place of business. (13)

risk. A measure of the likelihood that something will be lost. (10)

risk management. The process of measuring risk and finding ways to minimize or manage loss. (10)

Rule of 72. A method used to estimate the amount of time or interest it will take for savings to double in value. (11)

S

salary. Payment for work that is expressed as an annual figure. (7)

sales tax. Tax added to the price of goods and services you buy. (3)

savings and loan association (S&L). A for-profit financial institution that receives and pays dividends on depositors' savings, makes mortgage loans, and offers most of the services commercial banks offer. (8)

scarcity. The challenge of stretching resources to cover needs and wants. (1)

secured loan. A loan that requires collateral. (9)

securities exchange. A formal market where securities are bought and sold by stockbrokers. (12)

security deposit. Amount of money a renter pays a landlord to insure against financial losses if the renter damages the dwelling or fails to pay rent. (18)

services. Work performed, such as dentistry, food preparation, and hair styling. (1)

simple interest. Interest computed only on the principal. (11)

skill contest. An opportunity to win prizes in which contestants pay an entry fee or make a purchase to enter, and the winners are determined by skill. (14)

small claims court. A simple, inexpensive way to settle minor differences involving small amounts of money without the aid of lawyers. (14)

social responsibility. A general sense of concern for the needs of others in the community, country, and world. (22)

Social Security. The federal government's program for providing income when earnings are reduced or stopped because of retirement, disability, or death. (7)

software applications. Instructions written to direct a computer's operations in performing specific tasks. (20)

sole proprietorship. A business consisting of one owner. (22)

spam e-mails. Unrequested e-mails usually sent by a company to a variety of e-mail addresses as a form of advertising, but may also be sent by criminals. (14)

specialist. A physician who has had further education and training in a specific branch of medicine. (17)

specialization. The range of products and services a country can produce and then trade for whatever it cannot produce. (4)

stagflation. A period of slow growth and high inflation. (2)

standard. An established measure of quantity, value, quality, or excellence. (5)

standard of identity. Common foods that contain ingredients in preset amounts and have standard names, such as ice cream, catsup, and mayonnaise. (15)

standard of living. The overall level of comfort of a person, household, or population as measured by the amount of goods and services consumed. (3)

stock. A share in ownership of a corporation. (12)

stockbroker. An agent who buys and sells securities for clients. (12)

subprime mortgage. A mortgage made by lenders who charge higher than prime rates to borrowers who have poor or no credit ratings. (18)

supply. The amount of a product or service producers are willing to provide. (1)

sustainable. Responsibly using environmental resources to prevent depletion or permanent damage. (23)

sweepstakes. A form of advertising in which the chance to win items of value or prizes is offered to consumers with no purchase or entry fee required to participate. (14)

T

tax. A fee imposed by a government on income, products, or activities, and paid by citizens and businesses. (2)

tax credit. An amount that can be subtracted from the taxes a worker owes, if eligible. (7)

tax deduction. An expense that can be subtracted from a worker's taxable income. (7)

tax deferred. Savings or earnings that are not taxed until the funds are withdrawn. (11)

tax exempt. Earnings that are free of certain taxes. (11)

t-commerce. Shopping done on the television. (13)

technology. The application of scientific knowledge to practical uses and product development. (1)

telecommunication. Communication at a distance, including phone and Internet. (20)

telemarketing. A form of selling that generally involves the seller calling you on the telephone to sell goods or services. (13)

term life insurance. Insurance that covers the policyholder for a specific period of time—5, 10, or 20 years or until a specified age. (10)

tip. Money paid for service beyond what is required. (7)

title. A legal document that proves ownership of property. (18)

title loan. A loan made using the borrower's car as collateral. (9)

trade barrier. Any action taken to control or limit imports. (4)

trade deficit. The loss of economic power due to a country importing more than it is exporting over a period of time. (4)

trade-off. An item given up in order to gain something else. (1)

trade surplus. A gain of economic power due to a country exporting more than it is exporting over a period of time. (4)

traditional economy. A type of economic system in which economic decisions are based on a society's values, culture, and customs. (1)

traveler's checks. Checks that can be cashed in most places around the world. They are often used by people who travel and do not want to carry large amounts of cash. (8)

trust. A legal agreement where assets and property are managed by a trustee on behalf of the beneficiaries. (12)

trustee. A person or institution named to manage an estate on behalf of the beneficiaries. (12)

U

underemployment. Workers who are employed only part time or who are "over qualified" for their jobs. (2)

unearned income. Earnings from sources other than work. (7)

unemployment rate. The percentage of the labor force that is out of work and seeking employment. (2)

unit price. The price of an item based on the cost per unit, weight, or measure. (15)

universal product code (UPC). A series of black lines, bars, and numbers that appear on products to facilitate computerized check-out and inventory control in stores. (15)

U.S. savings bond. A savings tool that loans money to the U.S. government for a specified period of time. The bondholder is repaid with interest at the time of maturity. (11)

V

VA-guaranteed loan. A long-term, fixed rate mortgage insured by the Veterans Administration for veterans of the U.S. Armed Forces. (18)

values. Beliefs and principles about what is important or desirable. (5)

value system. A system that guides a person's behavior and provides a sense of direction in his or her life. (5)

variable expense. A cost that changes both in the amount and time it must be paid. (6)

vehicle identification number (VIN). A unique number assigned by the automobile industry and used to identify an individual auto. (19)

W

wage. A payment in exchange for an employee's labor or services. The payment, which is usually in money, is paid by the hour, day, or by the piece. (7)

walk-in clinic. A health care facility that provides certain routine medical attention. (17)

wants. Items a person would like to have that are not essential for life. (1)

wardrobe. The collection of clothing a person owns. (16)

wardrobe inventory. A list of all the clothes, shoes, and accessories a person owns. (16)

warranty. A guarantee that a product will meet certain performance and quality standards. (13)

wealth. An abundance of assets that are accumulated over time. (6)

whole life insurance. Insurance that provides the policyholder with basic lifetime protection so long as premiums are paid. (10)

will. A legal document stating a person's wishes for his or her estate after death. (12)

wired carriers. A network of copper wires, cables, and phone company switching centers that transmit signals. (20)

Wireless Fidelity (Wi-Fi). Wireless Internet broadband access that works by transmitting information using electromagnetic waves from radio towers. (20)

work order. A request for service; also includes a description of work to be done. (13)

World Trade Organization (WTO). An international organization that mediates trade disputes among 151 member nations and establishes trade practices that are acceptable and fair to all nations. (4)

woven fabrics. Cloth made by interlacing two or more sets of yarn at right angles. (16)

INDEX